Worlds of Music

Worlds of Music

An Introduction
to the Music of the World's Peoples

THIRD EDITION

Jeff Todd Titon, *General Editor*

Linda Fujie
David Locke
David P. McAllester
David B. Reck
John M. Schechter
Mark Slobin
R. Anderson Sutton

SCHIRMER BOOKS
An Imprint of Simon & Schuster Macmillan
NEW YORK

Prentice Hall International
LONDON   MEXICO CITY   NEW DELHI   SINGAPORE   SYDNEY   TORONTO

Schirmer Books
An Imprint of Simon & Schuster Macmillan
1633 Broadway
New York, NY 10019

Library of Congress Catalog Number: 96–13309

Printed in the United States of America

Printing number:
    3 4 5 6 7 8 9 10

Library of Congress Cataloging-in-Publication Data
Worlds of music : an introduction to the music of the world's peoples.
  —3rd ed.
    p. cm.
  Includes bibliographical references and index.
  ISBN 0–02–872612–X (alk. paper)
    1. Folk music—History and criticism.   2. Music—History and criticism.   3. Ethnomusicology. I. Titon, Jeff Todd, 1943– .
  ML3545.W67   1996
780′.9—dc20   96–13309
                                                  CIP
                                                  MN
This paper meets the requirements of ANIS/NISO Z39.48–1992 (Permanence of Paper).

Contents

3. *Africa/Ewe, Mande, Dagbamba, Shona, BaAka*   **71**

David Locke

7. Asia/Indonesia   316
R. Anderson Sutton

10. *Discovering and Documenting a World of Music* *495*
David B. Reck, Mark Slobin, and Jeff Todd Titon

Recorded Selections

1. "Sioux Grass Dance song" (1'47"). Source: Canyon Records Productions 12" LP, ARP 6059. Phoenix, Ariz., n.d. Recording by Ray Boley. Used by permission.
2. "Zuni lullaby" (0'55"). Lanaiditsa. Source: Field recording by David P. McAllester, White Water, New Mex., 1950.
3. "Iroquois Quiver Dance song" (0'45"). Joshua Buck and Simeon Gibbon. Source: Library of Congress Archive of Folk Culture 12" LP, AFS L6. Washington, D.C., c. 1942. Recording by William Fenton. Used by permission.
4. "Navajo Yeibichai song" (2'07"). Sandoval Begay, leader. Source: Library of Congress Archive of Folk Culture 12" LP, AFS L41. Washington, D.C., n.d. Recording by Willard Rhodes. Used by permission.
5. "Folsom Prison Blues" (2'48"). Words and music by Johnny Cash; published by The Harry Fox Agency, Inc. The Fenders. Source: *The Fenders, Second Time Roun'*, 12" LP. Thoreau, New Mex., 1966. Used by permission.
6. "Shizhané'é (Navajo Circle Dance song)" (1'16"). Albert G. Sandoval, Jr., and Ray Winnie. Source: Field recording by David P. McAllester. Sedona, Ariz., 1957. Used by permission from Albert G. Sandoval and Ray Winnie.
7. "Navajo Shootingway Song" (0'51"). Dinet Tsosie, leader. Source: Field recording by David P. McAllester. Lukachukai, Ariz., 1958.
8. "Navajo peyote song" (1'11"). George Mitchell and Kaya David. Source: Library of Congress Archive of Folk Culture 12" LP, AFS 14. Washington, D.C., n.d. Collected by Willard Rhodes. Used by permission.
9. "Clinging to a Saving Hand" (3'36"). The Chinle Galileans. Source: *Navajo Country Gospel*, 12" LP, LPS 909. Chinle, Ariz., n.d. Used by permission.
10. "Mother Earth" (2'59"). Sharon Burch. Source: Canyon Records Productions 534. Phoenix, Ariz., 1989. Used by permission.
11. "Proud Earth" (3'27"). Arlienne N. Williams and Chief Dan George. Source: *Proud Earth*, Salt City Records 12" LP, SC-80. Provo, Utah, n.d. © Arlienne N. Williams. Used by permission.
12. "Origins" (3'43"). R. Carlos Nakai. Source: *Cycles: Native American Flute Music*, Canyon Records Productions 614. Phoenix, Ariz., 1985. Used by permission.

13. "Postal workers canceling stamps at the University of Ghana post office" (2'57"). Source: Field recording by James Koetting. Legon, Ghana, 1975.

14. "Agbekor" ([a] 2'45"; [b] 1'16"; [c] 1'05"). Ewe. Source: Field recording by David Locke. Anlo-Afiadenyigba, Ghana, 1976. (Three slow-paced songs, one song in free rhythm, and one fast-paced song.)

15. "Lambango" (2'59"). Mariatu Kuyateh, Kekuta Suso, and Seni Jobateh. Mande. Source: Field recording by Roderic Knight. The Gambia, 1970.

16. "Nag Biegu" (2'06"). Dagbamba. Source: Field recording by David Locke. Ghana, 1984.

17. "Nhemamusasa" (2'37"). Shona. Source: Field recording by Paul Berliner. Zimbabwe, 1971.

18. "Nyarai" (2'28"). Thomas Mapfuno and Blacks Unlimited. Source: *Thomas Mapfuno: The Chimurenga Singles*, Shanachie CD 43066. Used by permission.

19. "Makala" (2'18"). BaAka. Source: Field recording by Michelle Kisliuk. Central African Republic, 1988.

20. "Amazing Grace" (2'38"). New Bethel Baptist Church. Source: Field recording by Jeff Titon. Detroit, Mich., 1977.

21. "Amazing Grace" (2'51"). Fellowship Independent Baptist Church. Source: Field recording by Jeff Titon. Stanley, Va., 1977.

22. "Field holler" (solo worksong) (0'43"). Leonard "Baby Doo" Caston. Source: Field recording by Jeff Titon. Minneapolis, Minn., 1971.

23. "Rosie" (2'48"). Prisoners at Mississippi State Penitentiary. Source: Field recording by Alan Lomax. Parchman, Miss., 1947. © Alan Lomax. Used by permission of Alan Lomax.

24. "Poor Boy Blues" (3'14"). Lazy Bill Lucas Trio. Source: Field recording by Jeff Titon. Minneapolis, Minn., 1970. Background noise from the apartment is audible.

25. "I Need $100" (2'58"). One-string Sam. Source: *Detroit Blues: The Early 1950s*, Blues Classics 12" LP, BC-12. Detroit, Mich., c. 1956.

26. "Sweet Home Chicago" (3'09"). The Fieldstones. Source: *The Fieldstones*, High Water Records 12" LP, LP-1001. Memphis, Tenn., 1981.℗ 1983, Memphis State University. Used by permission.

27. "You Don't Love Me" (3'34"). Magic Sam. Source: Field recording by Jeff Titon. Ann Arbor, Mich., August 1969.

28. "Ain't Enough Comin' In" (5'58"). Otis Rush. Source: *Otis Rush: Ain't Enough Comin' In*, Mercury 314518769–2, 1994. "Ain't Enough Comin' In" by Otis Rush, © 1994 OTIS RUSH MUSIC, administered by BUG. Used by permission.

29. "Paparuda" (0'25"). Gypsy children. Source: *Folk Music of Rumania*, Columbia Records 12" LP, KL 5799. Gistetsi village, Romania.

30. "Highlander women's *ganga* song" (0'39"). Šecira Kadrić, Aiša Kadrić, Enisa

Trešnjo. Source: Field recording by Mirjana Laušević. Umoljani village, Bosnia, 1990.

31. "Highlander men's *ganga* song" (1'22"). Safet Elezović, Muhamed Elezović, Zejnil Masleša. Source: Field recording by Mirjana Laušević. Gornji Lukomir village, Bosnia, 1990.

32. "Lowlands song with *šargija* lute" (1'05"). Škiba and friends. Source: Field recording by Mirjana Laušević. Bosnia, 1989.

33. "Lowlands *sevdalinka* song with *tamburitza* orchestra" (1'17"). Hinzo Polovina. Source: Field recording by Ankica Petrović. Bosnia, 1986.

34. "Newly composed folksong" (1'53"). Lepa Brena. Source: *Lepa Brena i Slatki Greh*, Bosnia, 1984. Used by permission of RTB PGP.

35. "Da zna zora" (2'40"). Zeljko Bebek and Bregić. Source: *Bebek: Niko vise ne sanja*, Croatia Records. Bosnia, 1989. Used by permission of Croatia Records.

36. "Train piece" (3'33"). Mensur Hatić. Source: Field recording by Mark Slobin. Detroit, Mich., 1994.

37. "Klaro del dija" (1'24"). Flory Jagoda. Source: *Kantikas diminona,* Global Village CD C139. Used by permission of Global Village Records, 1989.

38. "Hristianova kopanitsa" (3'28"). Ivo Papazov and Trakiya. Source: *Balkanology,* Rykodisc CD HNBC 1363, Bulgaria, 1991. Used by permission of Rykodisc Records.

39. "Bujdosodal" (3'14"). Marta Sebestyen and Muzsikas. Source: *Soldier's Song,* Rykodisc CD HNCD 1341, Hungary, 1988. Used by permission of Rykodisc Records.

40. "Engal kalyanam" ("Our Wedding"), cinema song (3'23"). P. Susheela, T. M. Soundararajan, P. B. Sreenivos, and L. R. Eswari. Music by M. S. Viswanathan, lyrics by Vali. Source: *Hits from Tamil Films,* vol. 6, EMI Odeon (India) 12" LP, 3AECS 5519. Dum Dum, India, 1969. © Gramophone Company of India, Ltd. Used by permission.

41. "Nagapattu" (song to the snake deities), folk song (3'27"). G. P. Saraswathi, voice and *kudam.* Source: Field recording by Carol S. Reck. Cheruthurthy, Kerala, 1970. Used by permission of Carol S. Reck.

42. "Panchavadyam" (3'57"). Percussion and wind orchestra. Source: Field recording by David B. Reck. Trichur, Kerala, 1970.

43. *Karnataka sangeeta:* performance segment built upon Tyagaraja's composition "Ivaraku jucinadi." *Raga sankarabharanam, adi tala* (11'13"). T. Viswanathan, flute; Ramnad V. Raghavan, *mridangam.* Source: Field recording by David B. Reck, USA, 1995.

44. "Bubaran Kembang Pacar," *pélog pathet nem* (2'58"). Central Javanese *gamelan* music in "loud-playing" style, performed by musicians affiliated with the royal palace in Yogyakarta. Source: Field recording by R. Anderson Sutton.

45. "Ladrang Wilujeng," *pélog pathet barang* (8'45"). Central Javanese *gamelan* music in "soft-playing" style, performed by musicians of Ngudya Wirama

gamelan group, Yogyakarta, under the direction of Ki Suhardi. Source: Field recording by René Lysloff. Used by permission.

46. "Playon Lasem," *sléndro pathet nem* (1'18"). Central Javanese *gamelan* music for shadow puppetry performed by *gamelan* group of Ki Suparman. (Rendition 1.) Source: Field recording by R. Anderson Sutton.

47. "Playon Lasem," *sléndro pathet nem* (0'30"). Central Javanese *gamelan* music for shadow puppetry, performed by *gamelan* group of Ki Suparman. (Rendition 2.) Source: Field recording by R. Anderson Sutton.

48. "Tabuh Gari" (6'18"). *Gamelan semar pegulingan* music from Pliatan, Bali. Source: Nonesuch Explorer H–72046. Recorded by Robert E. Brown. Used courtesy of Nonesuch Recordings by arrangement with Warner special products.

49. Excerpts from a performance of *gendang keteng-keteng* (1'54"), from the Karo Batak highlands of North Sumatra, performed by Tukang Ginting and his group. Source: Field recording by R. Anderson Sutton.

50. "Begadang II" (3'30"), popular *dang-dut* music performed by Rhoma Irama and his Soneta Group. Source: *Begadang II,* Yukawi Indomusic. Used by permission.

51. Excerpts from "Indonesia Maharddhika" (3'19"), performed by "heavy pop" group Guruh Gipsy, under the direction of Guruh Sukarnoputra. Source: *Guruh Gipsy.* Used by permission.

52. "Tsuru no sugomori" (3'40"). Kawase Junsuke, *shakuhachi,* and Kawase Hakuse, *shamisen.* Field recording by Linda Fujie, Tokyo, Japan, 1989.

53. "Hakusen no" (3'22"). Shitaya Kotsuru. Source: Nippon Columbia WK-170. Used by permission.

54. "Nikata-bushi" (5'07"). Asano Umewaka and Asano Sanae. Field recording by Karl Signell, Washington, D.C., 1986. Used by permission of the collector.

55. "Yatai," excerpt from "Kiri-bayashi" (1'30"). Ueno Shachū. Field recording by Linda Fujie, Tokyo, Japan, 1981.

56. "Nonki-bushi" (2'35"). Ishida Ishimatsu. Source: Nippon Columbia SP-ban fukugen. Used by permission.

57. "Naite Nagasaki" (3'34"). Kanda Fukumaru. Source: Nippon Columbia AH-210. Used by permission.

58. "Pajarillo" (2'27"). *Joropo* of Venezuela. Source: Disques Ocora 12" LP, OCR 78, Música Folklórica de Venezuela. Recorded in 1968 in Barinas state by Isabel Aretz, Luis Felipe Ramón y Rivera and Alvaro Fernaud. Song 5 "Golpe (Joropo)" / Ocora Radio France OCR 78 / Distribution Harmonia Mundi. Used by permission.

59. "El lazo" (3'55"). Víctor Jara (Chile). Source: *Víctor Jara: Desde Lonquén hasta siempre.* Monitor Music of the World, vol. 4. Monitor Records, MFS 810. 12" LP, n.d.

60. "Kutirimunapaq" (3'52"). *K'antu* of Bolivia. Source: Ruphay, Discos Heriba 12" LP, SLP 2212. Bolivia. Jach'a Marka. 1982. Eduardo Ibáñez W., Gerente General, Heriba Ltda., P.O. Box 3120, La Paz, Bolivia. Used by permission.

61. "Cascarón" (3'26"). *Sanjuán* of Ecuador, played by Quichua harpist Efraín. Source: Field recording by John Schechter. Outside Cotacachi, Ecuador, April 1980.

62. "Rusa María wasi rupajmi" (2'30"). *Sanjuán* of Ecuador, played by three Quichua musicians. Source: Field recording by John Schechter. Outside Cotacachi, Ecuador, January 1980. [Note: microphone noises in original recording.]

63. "Ilumán tiyu" (3'20"). *Sanjuán* of Ecuador, played by the Quichua ensemble Conjunto Ilumán. Source: Field recording by John Schechter. Ilumán, Ecuador, October 1990.

64. "Vacación" (1'30"). Quichua harpist Sergio, at a child's wake. Source: Field recording by John Schechter. Outside Cotacachi, Ecuador, February 1980.

65. Ecuadorian Quichua mother's lament to her deceased two-year-old girl, the morning after the child's wake (preceded by fifteen seconds of Sergio's "Vacación") (3'11"). Source: Field recording by John Schechter. Outside Cotacachi, Ecuador, January 1980.

66. "Toro barroso" (3'32"). *Albazo* of Ecuador, played by Don César Muquinche. Source: Field recording by John Schechter. Outside Ambato, Ecuador, 1980.

67. Lowland Quichua [Ecuador] shaman curing song (1'40"). Source: *Soul Vine Shaman.* 12" LP, in situ recording made in 1976 by Dan Weaks and Neelon Crawford; LP was recorded and produced and is distributed by Neelon Crawford. This song [#1 on the recording] is excerpted from *Soul Vine Shaman,* a recording made by Neelon Crawford in Ecuador in 1976. This recording is copyright © 1976. All rights are reserved by Neelon Crawford. No portion of this recording may be reproduced and/or transmitted through any medium without specific written permission from Neelon Crawford. Further information about this recording may be obtained by writing Neelon Crawford, 10 East 23rd Street, Suite 600, New York, NY 10010. Used by permission.

68. "Vamos pa' Manabí" (3'00"). *Bomba* of Ecuador, played by Fabián and Eleuterio Congo. Source: Field recording by John Schechter. Chota Valley, Ecuador, March 1980.

The Authors

LINDA K. FUJIE received the Ph.D. in ethnomusicology from Columbia University, where she was a student of Dieter Christensen and Adelaida Reyes Schramm. She has conducted field research in Japan under grants from the National Endowment for the Humanities, Columbia University, and Colby College. Her interest in overseas Japanese culture has also resulted in research on Japanese-American and Japanese-Brazilian communities, the latter funded by the German Music Council. Her research has been published in articles in the *Yearbook for Traditional Music*, publications on popular music, and in Japanese journals. She has taught at Colby College as assistant professor and currently resides in Berlin.

DAVID LOCKE received the Ph.D. in ethnomusicology from Wesleyan University in 1978 where he studied with David McAllester, Mark Slobin, and Gen'ichi Tsuge. At Wesleyan his teachers of traditional African music included Abraham Adzinyah and Freeman Donkor. He conducted doctoral dissertation fieldwork in Ghana from 1975 to 1977 under the supervision of Prof. J. H. K. Nketia. In Ghana his teachers and research associates included Godwin Agbeli, Midawo Gideon Foli Alorwoyie, and Abubakari Lunna. He has published numerous books and articles on African music and regularly performs the repertories of music and dance about which he writes. He teaches at Tufts University, where he currently serves as chair of the music department, director of the masters degree program in ethnomusicology, and faculty advisor to the Tufts-in-Ghana Foreign Study Program. His current projects include an ethnomusicological study of the music-culture of Dagbon, the documentation and analysis of repertories of African music, and the preparation of multimedia materials on music and culture. He is active in the Society for Ethnomusicology and has served as president of its Northeast Chapter.

DAVID P. MCALLESTER received the Ph.D. in anthropology from Columbia University, where he studied with George Herzog. He has been a student of American Indian music since 1938. He has undertaken field work among the Comanches, Hopis, Apaches, Navajos, Penobscots, and Passamaquoddies. He is the author of such classic works in ethnomusicology as *Peyote Music, Enemy Way Music, Myth of the Great Star Chant,* and *Navajo Blessingway Singer* (coedited with Charlotte J. Frisbie). He is one of the founders of the Society for Ethnomusicology, and he has served as its president and editor of its journal, *Ethnomusicology*. He is professor emeritus of anthropology and music at Wesleyan University.

DAVID B. RECK received the Ph.D. in ethnomusicology from Wesleyan University where he was a student of Mark Slobin and David P. McAllester. He has studied and traveled in India, Southeast Asia, and the Far East under grants from the American Institute of Indian Studies, the Rockefeller Foundation, the John Simon Guggenheim Memorial Foundation, and the JDR IIIrd Fund. An accomplished musician on the south Indian *veena,* he has performed extensively in the United States, Europe, and India both as a soloist and accompanist and as a member of the group *Kirtana.* As a composer, he has received commissions from the Library of Congress, the Koussevitsky Foundation, and the Fromm Music Foundation, and had performances at Tanglewood and Carnegie Hall. The author of *Music of the Whole Earth,* his research and publications include work on India's music, American popular styles, the music of J. S. Bach, Bartók, and Stravinsky, and cross-influences between the West and the Orient. Currently he is professor of music and of Asian languages and civilizations at Amherst College.

JOHN M. SCHECHTER received the Ph.D. in ethnomusicology from The University of Texas at Austin, where he studied ethnomusicology with Gérard Béhague, Andean anthropology with Richard Schaedel, and Quichua with Louisa Stark and Guillermo Delgado. He pursued fieldwork in the Andes of Ecuador in 1979–1980, and in 1990, and he is the author of *The Indispensable Harp: Historical Development, Modern Roles, Configurations, and Performance Practices in Ecuador and Latin America.* His recent publications have explored the conceptual issues behind the Andean Corpus Christi celebration, the issues of ensemble self-image and construction of symbolic value with respect to the *bomba,* a focal African-Ecuadorian musical genre, and the ethnography, visual semiotics, culture history, and religious philosophy of the Latin American/Iberian child's wake music-ritual. His articles on Quichua and Incaic music-culture, on the Latin American/Iberian child's wake, and on Latin American musical instruments have appeared in sundry periodical journals, anthologies, and encyclopedia articles. Since 1985 he has taught ethnomusicology and music theory, and has directed the Latin American Ensembles, at the University of California, Santa Cruz, where he is now associate professor of music.

MARK SLOBIN received the Ph.D. in musicology at the University of Michigan. He is the author, editor, or translator of many books, some on the music of Afghanistan and Central Asia and others on Jewish music in Europe and the United States, East European music, and the theory and method of studying subcultural musics in Euro-America. *Tenement Songs: The Popular Music of the Jewish Immigrants* won the ASCAP-Deems Taylor Award. He is a Past President of the Society for Ethnomusicology and of the Society for Asian Music, having edited the latter's journal, *Asian Music,* from 1971–1987. He has taught at Wesleyan University, where he is professor and chair of the music department, and has visited at Harvard, Berkeley, and NYU.

R. ANDERSON SUTTON received the Ph.D. in musicology from the University of Michigan, where he studied with Judith Becker and William Malm. He was introduced to Javanese music while an undergraduate at Wesleyan University, and made it the focus of his master's study at the University of Hawaii, where he studied gamelan with Hardja Susilo. On numerous occasions since 1973 he has conducted field research in Indonesia, with grants from the East-West Center, Fulbright-Hays, Social Science Research Council, National Endowment for the Humanities, Wenner-Gren Foundation, and the American Philosophical Society. He is author of *Traditions of Gamelan Music in Java, Variation in Central Javanese Gamelan Music,* and numerous articles on Javanese music. Active as a gamelan musician since 1971, he has performed with several professional groups in Indonesia and directed numerous performances in the United States. He has served as first vice president and book review editor for the Society for Ethnomusicology, and as a member of the Working Committee on Performing Arts for the Festival of Indonesia (1990–92). He has taught at the University of Hawaii and at the University of Wisconsin-Madison, where he is professor of music and past director of the Center for Southeast Asian Studies.

JEFF TODD TITON received the Ph.D in American studies from the University of Minnesota, where he studied ethnomusicology with Alan Kagan. He has done fieldwork on religious folk music, blues music, and old-time fiddling, with support from the National Endowment for the Arts and the National Endowment for the Humanities. For two years he was the guitarist in the Lazy Bill Lucas Blues band, a group that appeared in the 1970 Ann Arbor Blues Festival. The author or editor of five books, including *Early Downhome Blues*, which won the ASCAP-Deems Taylor Award, he is also a documentary photographer and filmmaker. In 1991 he wrote a hypertext-multimedia computer program on old-time fiddler Clyde Davenport that is now regarded as a model for weblike interactive computer representations of people making music. His current projects include fieldwork with Old Regular Baptists in eastern Kentucky, an anthology of Kentucky old-time fiddle tunes, and a continuation of the theoretical writings on the field of ethnomusicology that have occupied him since he completed the *Powerhouse for God* book, recording, and documentary film in 1989. He developed the ethnomusicology program at Tufts University, where he taught from 1971 to 1986. From 1990 to 1995 he served as editor of *Ethnomusicology*, the Journal of the Society for Ethnomusicology. Since 1986 he has been professor of music and director of the Ph.D. program in ethnomusicology at Brown University.

Preface

WHY STUDY MUSIC? There are many reasons, but perhaps the most important are pleasure and understanding. We have designed this book and its accompanying CDs and cassettes to introduce undergraduates to the study of music the world over. Although *Worlds of Music* contains musical notation, it may be used by students who do not read music. The only prerequisite is curiosity.

University courses in world music have increased dramatically since World War II, and the reasons are easy to comprehend. Most music departments now recognize that confining the study of music to the Western classics is ethnocentric. Students who love music are alive to *all* music. So are composers, and many use the world's musical resources in their newest works. This is an important feature of today's music, and the people who listen to it—now and in the future—will want to keep their musical horizons broad. Another reason for the interest in world music is the upsurge in ethnic awareness. As modern people try to locate themselves in a world that is changing with bewildering speed, they find music especially rewarding, for music is among the most tenacious cultural elements. Music symbolizes a people's way of life; it represents a distillation of cultural style. For many, music *is* a way of life.

Interest in and appreciation of world music has grown enormously just in the past five years. World music has become a significant part of the surrounding concert world; more recordings and videos are available than ever before; world music is now a part of the MTV mix; New Age music is strongly influenced by various kinds of world music; and musicians from all over the globe now appear on college and university campuses. Not only is world music now important in the mass media, but multiculturalism—the celebration of America's multi-ethnic heritage—has brought a flood of ethnic festivals, always featuring music. Many younger people, searching for musical roots, have looked into their ethnic pasts and chosen to learn the music of their foreparents, while others view the variety of musics in the world as a vast resource to be drawn upon in creating their own sounds.

The authors of this book are ethnomusicologists; and our field, *ethnomusicology*, is usually defined as the study of music in culture. Some ethnomusicologists define the field as the study of music as culture, underlining the fact that music is a way of organizing human activity. By the term *culture* we do *not* mean "the elite arts," as it is sometimes used. Rather, we use the term as anthropologists do: culture is a people's way of life, learned and transmitted through the centuries of adapting to the natural and human world. *Ethnomusicology is the study of music in the context of human life.*

I like to think of ethnomusicology as the study of people making music. People "make" music in two ways: they make or construct the *idea* of music, what it is (and is not) and what it does; and they make or produce the *sounds* that they call music. Although we experience music as something "out there" in the world, our response to music depends on the ideas we associate with that music, and those ideas come from the people (ourselves included) who carry our culture. In other words, people "make" music into a cultural domain, with associated sets of ideas and activities. We could not even pick out musical form and structure, how the parts of a piece of music work together to form a whole, if we did not depend on the idea that music must be organized rather than random, and if we did not learn to make music that way. Analyzing form and structure is characteristic of some cultures, including Western ones, but in other areas of the world people do not habitually break a thing down into parts for analytical purposes.

As students of music in culture, ethnomusicologists have every reason to investigate Western art music; that is, the tradition of Palestrina, Bach, Beethoven, Verdi, Stravinsky, and the like. But with some recent and notable exceptions, ethnomusicologists in North America have specialized in music outside this tradition. They know the Western classics well, but their interest embraces all music. Indeed, many have devoted years to performing music outside the Western mainstream. Further, because ethnomusicologists study more than the music itself (and some even deny that there is such a thing), they are not satisfied merely to analyze and compare musical forms, structures, melodies, rhythms, compositions, and genres. Instead, they borrow insights and methods from anthropology, sociology, literary criticism, linguistics, and history to understand music as human expression. In fact, until the 1950s, ethnomusicology courses in the United States were more likely to be found in anthropology departments than music departments, and some nineteenth-century founders of ethnomusicology were psychologists. Ethnomusicology is therefore interdisciplinary, combining elements of the arts, humanities, and social sciences. Because of its eclectic methods and worldwide scope, ethnomusicology is well suited to students seeking a liberal arts education.

The number of world music textbooks in print is very small, and most are theory and method books aimed at graduate students. The rest are world music surveys, but we think there are good reasons to avoid a survey course at the beginning level in particular. In its broad sweep a survey offers only a passing acquaintance with the music of many peoples. Too often a survey turns into a musical Cook's tour: if today is Tuesday, this must be India. The inevitable result is musical overkill; by the term's end students are so overloaded they can barely recognize different musics of the world, let alone understand any one.

Instead of surveying the world of music, the best introduction, we think, explores in depth the music of a small number of representative human groups. This approach is not new; it adapts to ethnomusicology the case method in anthropology, the touchstone approach in literature, and the problems approach in history. Its object is not to pile up factual knowledge about various musical worlds, though certainly many facts will be learned. Rather, the point is to experience what it is like to be an ethnomusicologist puzzling out his or her way toward understanding an unfamiliar music. This process, we believe, is the best foundation for either future coursework (including surveys and seminars) or self-directed study and enjoyment of world music after college.

We decided on a small number of case studies because that is how we teach the introductory-level world music course at our universities. We thought also that by writing about music in societies we know firsthand, we could write an authoritative book. Ethnomusicologists are a notoriously independent bunch, and the idea of adopting a textbook may strike some as a trifle confining. That is why we have tried to leave plenty of room for instructors to add examples and case studies of their own.

Each chapter, then, reflects our own choice of subject. It also reflects our different ways of approaching music, for we agree that music cannot be "caught" by one method only. Still, we organized the chapters on six guiding principles. First, we think a textbook in world music should go beyond merely avoiding elitism and ethnocentrism. As much as possible, an unfamiliar music should be understood at the outset in its own terms; that is, as the people who make the music understand it. Second, asking what the life of a musician is like in different societies, and answering in life histories and autobiographies, is essential if we are to know music as a human activity, not just a sequence of organized sound. Third, we single out the words of songs for special attention because they often convey the meaning and purpose of musical performances as the music-makers comprehend them. Fourth, we regard the musical examples not just as illustrations but as points of departure; therefore most of them can be heard on the recordings accompanying this book. Fifth, student music-making projects—singing, building, and playing instruments—can, if property directed and seriously approached, greatly increase appreciation of a musical style. Sixth, and most important, an introduction to world music should provide pleasure as well as knowledge.

The major changes in this third edition are two completely new chapters. David Locke has written an entirely new chapter on African musics, replacing the late Jim Koetting's chapter. But David has retained Jim's popular musical example in which postal workers are heard whistling to their own percussive stamp canceling. The other new chapter is Mark Slobin's, recast in response to the revolutionary changes in Eastern Europe resulting from the breakup of the Soviet Union and the war in the Balkans. Its focus on music in Bosnia is particularly poignant at this time. David McAllester added some new recordings and a discussion of recent developments in Native American musics, which have become popular in the New Age music culture. David Reck has given us a different extended example of *karnataka sangeeta,* a lovely performance by T. Viswanathan and Ramnad V. Raghavan. John Schechter has expanded his section on Latin American *nueva canción.* I have expanded the discussion of the contemporary blues revival and included a blues recording by Magic Sam and another by Otis Rush that was chosen best of the year 1994 by the readers of *Living Blues* magazine.

We suggest that students begin with chapter 1, which introduces fundamental concepts about music in any culture. Chapter 10 guides the student through a fieldwork project. Because the project should begin well before the end of the term, we suggest that chapter 10 be read just after the first case study, and that students begin fieldwork immediately afterward. Many students say the field projects are the most valuable experiences they take away from this or any course, particularly when they must make sense of what they document in the field. The case studies, chapters 2 through 9, make be taken in any order.

Many colleges and universities have a one-term introductory world music course, often called something like "Music of the World's Peoples." We have found that two weeks per case study is about right, so in a one-term course the teacher should choose four or five that best suit the course's pace and purpose. Some universities offer a full year's introductory course in world music, usually divided on the basis of broad geographical areas. The third edition of *Worlds of Music* is appropriate as a core textbook for this kind of course as well, because it offers in-depth case studies of eight music-cultures. If the first term focuses on Europe and the Americas, for example, the teacher will choose the case studies in chapters 2, 4, 5, and 9; if the second term focuses on Africa and Asia, the teacher will choose chapters 3, 6, 7, and 8. Each term should then have enough time for a case study in the teacher's research area or elsewhere and for a student field project.

We are grateful to Bonnie C. Wade and James W. Kimball, who read the book in its final stages and offered constructive suggestions. We have appreciated the assistance over the years of Maribeth Anderson Payne, Robert Axelrod, Ken Stuart, Richard Carlin, Jill Lectka, James Hatch, and Jonathan Wiener, editors at Schirmer Books, in seeing this project through production. We would be pleased to hear from our readers, and we may be reached by writing the publisher or any of us at our respective universities.

Jeff Todd Titon
General Editor

CHAPTER ONE

The Music-Culture as a World of Music

JEFF TODD TITON AND MARK SLOBIN

THE MUSIC-CULTURE

So far as we know, every human society has music. Music is universal, but its meaning is not. A famous musician from Asia was brought to a European symphony concert approximately one hundred fifty years ago. Although he was a virtuoso musician in his own country, he had never heard a performance of Western music. The story goes that after the concert he was asked how he liked it. "Very well," he replied. Not satisfied with this answer, his hosts asked (through an interpreter) what part he liked best. "The first part" he said. "Oh you enjoyed the first movement?" "No, before that!"

To the stranger, the best part of the performance was the tuning-up period. It was music to him, and who was to say otherwise? His hosts. Music, then, though a universal phenomenon (scientists even send out music in space capsules, hoping to communicate with intelligent beings in distant solar systems), gets its meaning from culture. Recall from the preface that by *culture* we mean the way of life of a people, learned and transmitted from one generation to the next. We stress "learned" because we differentiate a people's cultural inheritance from what is passed along in their genes. From birth a person absorbs the cultural inheritance of family, community, schoolmates, and increasingly, the mass-mediated culture of magazines, movies, television, and computers. This cultural inheritance tells you how to understand the situations you are in (what the situations mean) and how you might behave in those situations. It works so automatically that you are aware of it only when it breaks down, as it does on occasion; for cultures are not perfectly functioning systems. Musical situations, and also the concept "music," mean different things and involve different activities among people in various societies. Because music and all the beliefs and activities associated with it are a part of culture, we use the term *music-culture* to mean a group of people's total involvement with music: ideas, actions, institutions, artifacts—everything that has to

1

do with music. Accordingly, the European music-culture prescribes that the sound made by symphony musicians tuning up is not music.

We call music *music,* but not all music-cultures have a word for it. Writing about Rosa, the Macedonian village she lived in, Nahoma Sachs points out that "traditional Rosans have no general equivalent to the English 'music.' They divide the range of sound which might be termed music by Americans into two categories: *pesni,* songs, and *muzika,* instrumental music" (Sachs 1975:27). Of course, this distinction between songs and music is found in many parts of the world, even in the United States. Old-time Baptists in the South sometimes say, "We don't have music in our service," meaning they do not have instrumental music accompanying their singing. Other music-cultures have words for song types (lullaby, epic, historical song, etc.) but no overall word for music. Partly because we have so broad a term as *music* in English, we can write a book like this.

Sound exists with or without people. Sound is a phenomenon of the world of nature. You probably remember the old puzzle, "If a tree falls in the forest and nobody hears it, does it make a sound?" We take the position that it does. In the West we would call that tree-falling sound noise, not music. Music and noise are ideas or concepts, something that people make out of sound. Our scientists tell us bird calls are for mating and marking territory and give them no significance outside the bird world. But for the Kaluli or Papua New Guinea, bird sounds are part of a song pattern that connects directly to the human world and involves feelings of sadness (Feld 1990). In sum, while sound exists as an independent phenomenon in the world, music is not an object "out there" and separate from us. Rather, music, like all other aspects of culture, is humanly constructed. That does not mean music is necessarily organized like anything else; it may have unusual, even unique, patterns. The ethnomusicologist John Blacking has defined music as "humanly organized sound" (Blacking 1973).

All of us are born into a world of sound, and we learn from other people what sound is music and what sound is not. We may, of course, decide for ourselves; but the point is that people do decide what music is. Many years ago the avant-garde composer John Cage wrote a piece for typewriters. At its first concert performance the typists took their seats and started typing. The only sounds were the clicks of the keys, the tapping of the type, the movement of the carriages, and the bells signaling the end of each line. Many in the audience were perplexed: Was this music? a joke? or what? Would you consider it humanly organized sound? If nothing else, Cage's composition makes us realize that music is not something "given" but that it rests on an agreement among composer, performer, and listener.

AFFECT, PERFORMANCE, COMMUNITY, AND HISTORY: A MUSIC-CULTURE MODEL

We assume that all the readers of this book are curious about the music of the world's peoples and want to understand more about it. But confronting a new music can be daunting. Our first impulse might be simply to listen to it, to absorb it, to see whether we like it, whether it moves us. Our next impulse may be to let our bodies respond, to move to the music ourselves. But soon we ask questions about it: What is that instrument that sounds so lovely? How does one play it? Why are the people dancing? (Or are they dancing?) Why is someone crying? Why are the musicians in costume? What do the words mean? What kind of a life does the head musician lead? To formulate and begin to answer these questions in a comprehensive way we need to have some kind of systematic outline, or model, or any music-culture, or subculture, that tells us how it might work and what are likely to be its component parts.

We propose a music-culture model that is grounded or centered in music through performance (Titon 1988:7–10). To see how this model works out, take a familiar music-culture and recall a music event such as a concert, for example, that has moved you. At the center of the event is your experience of the music, sung and played by performers (perhaps you are one of them). The performers are surrounded by their audience (in some instances performers and audience are one and the same), and the whole event takes place in its setting in time and space. We can represent this by a diagram of concentric circles (fig. 1–1). Now we transpose this diagram into four circles representing a music-culture model (fig. 1–2). At the center of the music (as you experience it) is its radiating power, its emotional impact, whatever makes you give assent, smile, nod your head, sway your shoulders, dance. We call that music's *affect,* its power to move, and place affective experience in the central circle of the model.

Performance brings music's power to move into being, and so we move from performers in figure 1–1 to *performance* in figure 1–2. Performance involves a great many things. In the first place, people mark performances, whether musical or otherwise, off from the flow of ordinary life: "Have you heard the story about . . ."; or "Now we're going to do a new song that one of the members of the

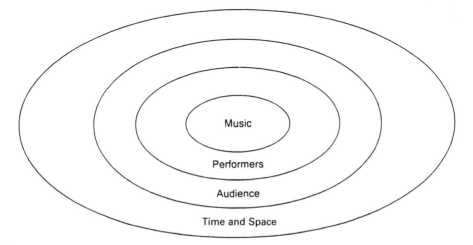

Fig. 1–1.   Elements of a musical performance.

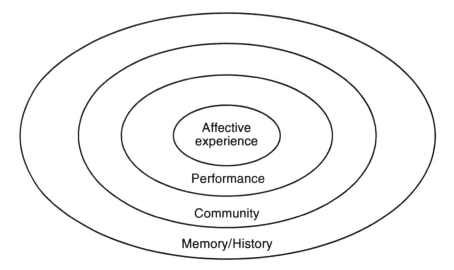

Fig. 1–2.   A music-culture model. (After Titon 1988:11.)

band wrote while thinking about. . . ." When performance takes place, people know the difference. Sammy Davis, Jr., told an interviewer, "Once I get outside my house in the morning, I'm *on.*" We often mark endings of performances with applause. Second, performance has purpose. The performers intend to move (or not move) the audience, to sing and play well (or not well), to make money, to have fun, to learn, to advance a certain rite or ceremony; performance is evaluated partly on how well those intentions are fulfilled. Third, a performance is interpreted as it goes along, by the audience (who may cry out or applaud, or hiss a bad pun) and by the performers, who may smile when things are going well or wince when they make a mistake.

The most important thing to understand about performance is that it moves along on the basis of agreed-on rules and procedures. These rules enable the musicians to play together and make sense to each other and to the audience. The performers do not discuss most of the rules; they have absorbed them and silently agreed to them. Starting at the same time, playing in the same key, playing in the same rhythmic framework, repeating the melody at the proper point—these are a few of the many rules that govern most of the musical performances that you have experienced. Even improvisation is governed by rules. In a rock concert, for example, guitarists improvise melodic "breaks," but they usually do not use all twelve tones of the chromatic scale; instead they almost always choose from the smaller number of tones represented by the blues scale (see chapter 4). Rules or accepted procedures govern the audience, too. Shouting is not only permitted but in some situations it is expected, along with other kinds of abandonment. What to wear, what to say—these, too, are patterned at any musical performance. Sometimes musicians try to break these rules or expectations, as in a ritual destruction of their instruments at the close of the concert. (And then that becomes an expectation.)

In our music-culture model, music in performance is understood as meaningfully organized sound that proceeds by rules. Finding out those rules or principles becomes the task of analysis. These rules include (but are not limited to) what is usually covered under musical analysis: mode, motif, melody, rhythm, meter, section, and so forth. Beyond that, we try to discover the rules covering ideas about music and behavior in relation to music, and the links between these rules or principles and the sound that a group of people calls music. You may resist the notion that music, which you think should be free to express emotion, is best thought of as governed by rules. We do not want to claim that musical performance is predetermined by rules, only that it proceeds by them. Music, in this view, is like a game or a conversation: without rules you could not have a game, and without agreement about what words are, what they mean, and how they are used, you could not hold a meaningful conversation. Nonetheless, just as meaningful conversations can express emotion, so can meaningful music, though not, of course, in exactly the same way. We claim, further, that if a listener does not understand the rules, he or she cannot understand the composer's or musician's intention, or the music's structure.

Audience occupied the third circle in figure 1–1; in our music-culture model we turn audience into the *community*, the group (including the performers) that carries the traditions and norms of performance. Performance is situated in community and is part and parcel of culture, for people bear the traditions that make up the culture. The community pays for and supports the music, whether directly with money or indirectly by allowing the performers to live as musicians. Community support usually influences the future direction of the music. In a complex society such as that of the United States, various communities support different kinds of music—classical, rock, jazz, gospel—and they do so in different ways. Classical music, for example, gets its strongest boost from middle-class people climbing the social and economic ladder. When music becomes a mass-media commodity, then packaging, marketing, and advertising are as crucial to the success of musicians as to perfume. How the community relates to the music-makers has a profound effect on the music. Among the folk music-cultures of nonindustrial village societies, the performers are drawn from the community; everyone knows them well, and communication is face-to-face. At the other end of the spectrum is the postindustrial music-culture celebrity who guards his or her private life, performs from a raised platform, is a disembodied voice coming through a machine, and remains enigmatic to the audience. How the community relates to itself is another important aspect of performance. For example, do men, women, old people, and young people experience music differently? We will consider this issue later under Social Organization of Music.

Time and space, the fourth circle in figure 1–1, becomes *memory and history* in our music-culture model (fig. 1–2). The community is situated in history and borne by memory, official and unofficial, whether remembered or recorded or written down. Musical experiences, performances, and communities change over time and space; they have a history, and that history reflects changes in the rules governing music as well as the effect of music on human relationships. The development of radio, recordings, and television meant that music need not be heard in the performer's presence. This took the performer out of the community's face-to-face relationships and allowed people to listen to music without making it themselves. Today music is an almost constant background to many people's lives, but the musicians are largely absent. The music historian, too, alters the effect of music, for the historian's writing enters the stock of ideas about music. When white America became interested in blues music in the 1960s and began presenting blues concerts and festivals (see chapter 4), magazine and newspaper writers began asking blues singers questions about their music and its history. Knowing they would be asked these questions, the blues singers prepared their answers, sometimes reading and then repeating what writers had already said about blues, sometimes having fun with their interlocutors and deliberately misleading them.

Many times the subject of music is history itself. The Homeric poets sang about Odysseus; Serbian *guslars* sang about the deeds of their heroes; European ballads tell stories of nobles and commoners; African griots (see chapter 3) sing tribal genealogies and history. Today, cassette tape recorders and, increasingly, computers and multimedia are revolutionizing community music history in the West, for they empower musicians and audience alike to record what they want to hear, represent it as they wish, and listen to it again and again; in this way they gain partial control over their history. When we study the history of a music-culture, or some aspect of it, we want to know not only what that history is, but who tells or writes that history and what is the historian's stake in it.

As you read through each of the case studies in the following chapters, you will want to bear this underlying music-culture model in mind. Because each of the case studies is centered in music and grounded in performance, you can use this model to understand how each chapter moves back and forth from experience to performance to community to memory and history. Musical analysis—that is, finding patterns in the sound by breaking the music into parts and determining how the parts function in the whole—is an important part of our procedure. Unlike the analyst who investigates Western classical music by looking at the composer's written score, we must usually deal with music that exists only in performance, without a notated set of instructions from a composer. The ethnomusicologist usually transcribes the music—that is, notates it—and then analyzes its structure. But it is impossible to understand structure fully without knowing the cultural "why" as well as the musical "what." A music-culture ultimately rests in the people themselves—their ideas, their actions, and the sound they produce (Merriam 1964:32–33).

If we think about the elements of a music-culture that our grounded model isolated (fig. 1–2), we can see that they represent four interlocking components (table 1–1), and that we can transform them into a set of useful questions that you can ask of any unfamiliar music-culture (or even a familiar one). As you read this book, and as you prepare for your field research project (chapter 10), see how each music-culture you encounter can be viewed through your particular answers to these broad, very abstract questions. Even now, while you read through the

Table 1–1.   The four components of a music-culture.

   I. Ideas about music

      A. Music and the belief system

      B. Aesthetics of music

      C. Contexts of music

      D. History of music

  II. Social organization of music

III. Repertories of music

      A. Style

      B. Genres

      C. Texts

      D. Composition

      E. Transmission

      F. Movement

 IV. Material culture of music

---

rest of this chapter, choose a music-culture you are familiar with (classical, jazz, alternative rock, etc.) and see how it measures up to these questions.

COMPONENTS OF A MUSIC-CULTURE

I. IDEAS ABOUT MUSIC

A. Music and the Belief System

What is music (and what is not)? Is music human or divine (or both)? Is music good and useful for humankind? Is it potentially harmful? These questions reach into the music-culture's basic ideas of the nature of human society, art, and the universe. Cultures vary enormously in their answers to these questions, and the answers often are very subtle, even paradoxical; they are embodied in rituals that try to reconcile love and hate, life and death, the natural and the civilized. Even within one music-culture the answers may change with time: a medieval Christian would have trouble understanding one of today's folk masses.

B. Aesthetics of Music

When is a song beautiful? When is it beautifully sung? What voice quality is pleasing, and what grates on the ear? How should a musician dress? How long should a performance last? Again, not all cultures agree on these aesthetic questions involving judgments of what is proper and what is beautiful. Some Americans find Chinese opera-singing strained and artificial, but likewise some Chinese think the European *bel canto* opera style is imprecise and unpleasant. Music cultures can be characterized by preferences in sound quality and performance practice, all of which are aesthetic discriminations.

C. *Contexts for Music*

When should music be performed? How often? On what occasions? Again, every music-culture answers these questions about musical surroundings differently (see ill. 1–1). In the modern world, where context can depend on just the flip of an on-off switch and a portable cassette or CD player, it is hard to imagine the old days when all music came from face-to-face performance. Our great-grandparents had to sing or play, overhear music, or ask for it from someone near; they could not produce it on demand from the disembodied voice of a radio, television set, CD player, tape recorder, or computer. How attentively you would have listened to a singer or a band a hundred years ago if you thought that this might be the only time in your life you would hear that music!

D. *History of Music*

Why is music so different among the world's peoples? What happens to music over time and space? Does it stay the same or change, and why? What did the music of the past sound like? Should it be preserved? What will the music of the future be? Some cultures institutionalize the past in museums and the future in world's fairs; they support specialists who (like the authors of this book) earn their living by talking and writing about music. Other cultures pass along knowledge of music history mainly by word of mouth down through the generations. Recordings, films, videotapes and CD-ROM now allow us to keep and re-hear musical performances much more exactly than our ancestors could—but only if we want to. One ethnomusicologist was making tapes as he learned to sing Native Ameri-

Jeff Todd Titon

Ill. 1–1.   Gospel singers at a pentecostal revival in the Southeastern United States. Guitars, banjos, and camp-meeting songs that would be out of place in some U.S. churches are appropriate in this context.

can music. His teacher advised him to erase the tapes and re-use them, but he decided to preserve his lessons.

Questions about music history may be asked inside or outside a particular music-culture. Most music-cultures have "historians" or music authorities, formally trained or not, whose curiosity about music leads them to think and talk about music in their own culture, ask questions, and remember answers. In some music-cultures, authority goes along with being a good musician; in other music-cultures, one need not be a good musician to be a respected historian. Historians usually are curious about music outside their own cultures as well, and they often develop theories to account for musical differences.

Of course, these four categories of ideas about music that we have just discussed—music and the belief system, aesthetics, contexts, and history—overlap. In most music-cultures, "good" music is tied to "beautiful" music and takes place in the right context. We separate them for convenience.

The individuals in a music-culture usually differ to some extent in their ideas about music. Ragtime, jazz, rock 'n' roll and rap were revolutionary when they were introduced. They met (and still meet) opposition from some Americans. This opposition is based on aesthetics (the music is thought to be loud, awful noise) and contexts (the music's associated lifestyles are thought to involve narcotics, violence, free love, radical politics, and so forth). When smaller divisions exist within a music-culture, we recognize music-subcultures, worlds within worlds of music. In fact, most music-cultures can be divided into several subcultures, some opposed to each other; classical versus rock 'n' roll, for example, or (from an earlier era) sacred hymns versus dance music and drinking songs. Sometimes the subcultures overlap: the performance of a hymn in a Minnesota church may involve region (the upper Midwest), ethnicity (German), and religion (Lutheranism)—all bases for musical subcultures. What musical subcultures do you identify with most strongly? What do you dislike? Are your preferences based on contexts, aesthetics, or the belief system?

II. SOCIAL ORGANIZATION OF MUSIC

Social organization refers to how a group of people divides, arranges, or ranks itself. The sum of musical ideas and performances is unevenly divided among the people in any music-culture. Some perform often, others hardly at all. Some make music for a living, while others are paid little or nothing. Because of age and gender, children, women, men, and old people sing different songs and experience music differently. Racial, ethnic, and work groups also sing their own special songs, and each group may be assigned its own musical role. All of these matters have to do with the social organization of the music-culture, and they are based on the music-culture's ideas about music, as described in section I above. We may ask, "What is it like [in such-and-such music-culture] to experience music as a teenage girl, a young male urban professional, a rural grandmother of German ethnic heritage living on a farm?" In each of the following chapters we follow the biography or autobiography of a musician partly because we are interested in how different individuals experience music and what part it plays in their lives.

Sometimes the division of musical behavior resembles the social divisions within the group and reinforces the usual activities of the culture. For example, when African pygmies sing as a group, they weave in their parts to build a complex, well-integrated whole (see chapter 3). Researcher Alan Lomax points out that cooperative performances like these symbolize the pygmies' emphasis on cooperative coordination in other spheres of life, such as daily work (Lomax 1976:41; see Turnbull 1962 for a vivid description of pygmy life and music).

On the other hand, music sometimes goes against the broad cultural grain, especially at festival time, or at important moments in the life cycle (initiations, weddings, funerals, etc.). Then people on the cultural fringe become important when they play music for these occasions. In fact, many music-cultures assign a low social status to musicians, yet also acknowledge their power and sometimes even see magic in their work. The two most important features of music's social organization are status and role: the prestige of the music-makers, and the different roles assigned people in the music-culture. Many of the musical situations in this book depend on these basic aspects of social organization.

III. REPERTORIES OF MUSIC

A repertory is a stock of ready performances, and a music-culture's repertory is what most of us think of as the "music itself." It consists of six basic parts: style, genres, texts, composition, transmission, and movement.

A. Style

Style includes everything related to the organization of musical sound itself: pitch elements (scale, mode, melody, harmony, tuning systems), time elements (rhythms, meter), timbre elements (voice quality, instrumental tone color), and sound intensity (loudness and softness). All depend on the music-culture's aesthetics.

Together, style and aesthetics create a recognizable sound that a group understands as its own. Old Regular Baptists in southeastern Kentucky prefer their own hymns to those of their other Baptist neighbors. They say the other Baptist songs are "none of theirs." Yet to many people outside southeastern Kentucky these songs all sound pretty much alike. Are they alike? Not if each group can distinguish its own music. Outsiders studying Baptist music know that they are getting somewhere when they are able to recognize the differences among Baptist musics of different denominations and put those differences into words—or music.

B. Genres

Genres are the named, standard units of the repertory, such as "song" and its various subdivisions (e.g., lullaby, Christmas carol, wedding song) or the many types of instrumental music and dances (jig, reel, waltz, etc.) Most music-cultures have a great many genres, but their terms do not always correspond to terms in other music-cultures. Among the Yoruba in the African nation of Nigeria, for example, powerful kings, chiefs, and nobles retain praise singers to sing praises to them (Olajubu 1978:685). The praise songs are called *oriki*. Although we can approximate an English name to describe them (praise songs), no equivalent genre exists today in Europe or America.

C. Texts

The words to a song are known as its text. Any song with words is an intersection of two very different and profound human communication systems: language and music. A song with words is a temporary weld of these two systems, and for convenience we can look at each by itself. Every text has its own history; sometimes a single text has several different associated melodies. On the other hand, a single melody can suffice for several texts. In blues music, for example, texts and melodies lead independent lives, coupling as the singer desires. The song (language and music together) is a recognizable, emotionally powerful unit in its own right. Anyone who has been abroad and suddenly hears a familiar homeland song knows just how powerful this impact can be.

D. Composition

How does music enter the repertory of a music-culture? Is music composed individually or by a group? Is it fixed, varied within certain preset limits, or improvised spontaneously in performance? Improvisation fascinates most ethnomusicologists, and we are no exceptions; chapters 3, 4, and 6 consider improvisation in African, African-American, and South Indian music. Perhaps at some deep level we prize improvisation not just because of the skills involved but because we think it exemplifies human freedom. Composition is also bound up with social organization: Does the music-culture have a special class of composers, or can anyone compose music? Composition is related to ideas about music: some music-cultures divide music into songs composed by humans and songs "given" to humans from deities, animals, and other nonhuman composers.

E. Transmission

How is music learned and transmitted from one person to the next, from one generation to the next? Does the music-culture rely on formal instruction, as in South India (chapter 6)? Is there a system of musical notation? Does a body of music theory underlie the process of formal instruction? How much is learned informally, by imitation? Does music change over time? If so, why and how?

Some music-cultures transmit music through a master-apprentice relationship that lasts for a lifetime (chapter 6). The master becomes a parent, teaching values and ethics as well as music. In these situations music truly becomes "a way of life," and the apprentices "devoted" to the music his master represents. In other music-cultures (chapter 4, for example) there usually is no formal instruction, and the aspiring musician must glean from watching and listening, usually over a period of years. In these circumstances it is helpful to grow up in a musical family. When a repertory is transmitted chiefly by example and imitation and performed from memory, we say the music exists "in oral tradition." Music in oral tradition shows greater variation over time and space than music that is tied to a definitive, written musical score.

F. Movement

A whole range of physical activity accompanies music. Playing a musical instrument, alone or in a group, involves physical activity in producing the sound, but it also produces culturally specified movement inseparable from the music sound. That is, music quite literally moves people (dance), and the movement is an essential part of the performance. How odd it would be for a rock band to perform without moving in response to their music, in ways that let the audience know they were feeling it, was demonstrated some years ago by new-wave rock bands. Groups like Devo projected the image of automatons. In one way or another, music connects with movement in the repertory of every culture.

IV. Material Culture of Music

Material culture refers to the tangible, material "things"—physical objects that can be seen, held, felt, used—that a culture produces. Examining a culture's tools and technology can tell us about the group's history and way of life. Similarly, research into the material culture of music can help us to understand the music-culture. The most vivid body of "things" in it, of course, are musical instruments. We cannot hear for ourselves the actual sound of any musical performance before the 1870s, when the phonograph was invented, so we rely on instruments for important information about music-cultures in the remove past and their development. Here we have two kinds of evidence: instruments preserved more or less intact, such as Sumerian harps over 4,500 years old, and instruments pictured in art. Through the study of instruments, as well as paintings, written documents, and other sources, we can explore the movement of music from the Near East to China over a thousand years ago, or we can outline the spread of Near Eastern influence to Europe that resulted in the development of most of the instruments in the symphony orchestra.

We ask questions of today's music-cultures: Who makes instruments and how are they distributed? What is the relation between instrument makers and musicians? How are this generation's musical taste and style, rather than those of the old generation, reflected in the instruments it plays? Sometimes musical instruments become patriotic symbols of the culture's musical heritage. Examples are the Highland bagpipe of Scotland or the rebuilt ancient Celtic instruments of the peoples of Brittany and Ireland.

Sheet music, too, is material culture. Scholars once defined folk music-cultures as those in which people learn and sing music by ear rather than from print, but research shows mutual influence among oral and written sources during the past few centuries in Europe, Britain, and America. Printed versions limit variety because they tend to standardize any song, yet paradoxically they stimulate people to create new and different songs. Bertrand Bronson observed that printed ballad texts tend to fix people's memory of the words, but fail to curb their interest in melodic variation (Bronson 1969:61–62). Also, the ability to read music notation has a far-reaching effect on musicians and, when it becomes widespread, on the music-culture as a whole.

One more important part of music's material culture should be singled out: the impact of the electronic media—radio, record player, tape recorder, compact disc, television, and videocassette, with interactive computers that themselves can be programmed to represent music-cultures, talk, and sing at our command. This is all part of the "information revolution," a twentieth-century phenomenon as important as the industrial revolution was in the nineteenth. These electronic media are not just limited to modern nations; they have affected music-cultures all over the globe.

WORLDS OF MUSIC

In the eighteenth century, when Europeans began collecting music from the countryside and from exotic, faraway places outside their homelands, they thought the "real" traditional music was dying out. From then on, each time a new music-culture was discovered, the European and American collectors took the music of its oldest generation to be the most authentic, giving it a timeless quality and usually deploring anything new. But this outsider's opinion never reflected the way music-cultures actually work, or gave people enough credit for creative choice. At any given moment three kinds of music circulate within most communities: (1) music so old and accepted as "ours" that no one questions (or sometimes even knows) where it comes from; (2) music of an earlier generation understood to be old-fashioned or perhaps classic; and (3) the most recent or current musics, marketed and recognized as the latest development. These recent musics may be local or imported or, most likely, a combination of both, because today the world is so linked electronically that musics zip back and forth much more quickly than a hundred years ago.

Music-cultures, in other words, are dynamic rather than static. They constantly change in response to inside and outside pressures. It is wrong to think of a music-culture as something isolated, stable, smoothly functioning, impenetrable, and uninfluenced by the outside world. Indeed, as we shall see in chapter 4, the people in a music-culture need not share the same language, nationality, or ethnic origin. In the 1990s blues is a popular music with performers worldwide. People in a music-culture need not even share all of the same ideas about music—in fact, they do not. As music-cultures change (and they always are changing) they undergo friction; and the "rules" of musical performance, aesthetics, interpretation and meaning are negotiated, not fixed. Music history is reconceived by each generation.

Music is a fluid, dynamic element of culture, and it changes to suit the expressive and emotional desires of humankind, the most changeable of the animals. Like all of our expressive culture, music is a peculiarly human adaptation to life on planet Earth. Each music-culture is a particular adaptation to particular circumstances. Ideas about music, social organization, repertoires, and music's material culture vary from one music-culture to the next. It would be unwise to call one music-culture's music "primitive" because doing so imposes one's own standards on a group that does not recognize them. Such ethnocentrism has no place in the study of world music.

In this book we have tended to describe first the older musical layers of a given region, then the increasingly more contemporary musical styles, forms, and attitudes. We would not like to leave you with the impression of the world as a set of untouched, authentic musical villages, but rather as a very fluid, interactive, interlocking, overlapping soundscape in which people listen to their ancestors, their parents, their neighbors, and their personal cassette machines all in the same day. Ultimately, what is really important is to think of people as musical activists, choosing what they like best, remembering what resonates best, forgetting what seems irrelevant, and keeping their ears open for exciting new musical opportunities. This happens everywhere, and it unites the farthest settlement and the largest city.

In the chapters that follow we explore several worlds, and worlds within worlds, of music. Although each world may seem strange at first, all are organized and purposeful. Each world can be regarded as an ecological system, with the forces that combine to make up the music-culture in a dynamic equilibrium. A change in any part of the ecosystem affects the whole of it. Viewing music this way leads to the conclusion that music represents a great human force that transcends narrow political, social, and time boundaries. Music offers an arena where people can talk and sing and play and reach each other in ways not allowed by barriers of status, wealth, location, and difference. This book can present only a tiny sample of the richness of world musical experience; the authors hope you will continue your exploration after you put this book on the shelf.

REFERENCES CITED

Blacking, John
   1973   *How Musical Is Man?* Seattle: Univ. of Washington Press.

Bronson, Bertrand
   1969   "The Interdependence of Ballad Tunes and Texts," In *the Ballad as Song.* Berkeley: Univ. of California Press.

Feld, Steven
   1990   *Sound and Sentiment: Birds, Weeping, Poetics, and Song in Kaluili Expression.* 2nd ed. Philadelphia: Univ. of Pennsylvania Press.

Kodály, Zoltán
   1960   *Folk Music of Hungary.* London: Barrie and Rockliff.

Lomax, Alan
   1976   *Cantometrics: A Method in Musical Anthropology.* Berkeley: Univ. of California Extension Media Center.

Merriam, Alan P.
   1964   *The Anthropology of Music.* Evanston, Ill.: Northwestern Univ. Press.

Olajubu, Chief Oludare
   1978   "Yoruba Verbal Artists and Their Work." *Journal of American Folklore* 91: 675–90

Sachs, Nahoma
    1975   "Music and Meaning: Musical Symbolism in a Macedonian Village." Ph.D. diss., Princeton Univ.

Titon, Jeff Todd
    1988   *Powerhouse for God: Speech, Chant, and Song in an Appalachian Baptist Church.* Austin: Univ. of Texas Press.

Turnbull, Colin
    1962   *The Forest People.* New York: Clarion Books.

ADDITIONAL READING

Berliner, Paul
    1994   *Thinking in Jazz.* Chicago: Univ. of Chicago Press.

Crafts, Susan D., Daniel Cavicchi, Charles Keil, and the Music in Daily Life Project
    1993   *My Music.* Hanover, N.H.: Univ. Press of New England.

Hamm, Charles, Bruno Nettl, and Ronald Byrnside
    1975   *Contemporary Music and Music Cultures.* Englewood Cliffs, N.J.: Prentice-Hall.

Herndon, Marcia, and Norma McLeod
    1981   *Music as Culture.* 2nd ed. Darby, Pa.: Norwood Editions.

Hood, Mantle
    1982   *The Ethnomusicologist.* 2nd ed. Kent, Ohio: Kent State Univ. Press.

Ives, Edward D.
    1978   *Joe Scott: The Woodsman-Songmaker.* Urbana: Univ. of Illinois Press.

Keil, Charles
    1979   *Tiv Song: The Sociology of Art in a Classless Society.* Chicago: Univ. of Chicago Press

Kingsbury, Henry
    1988   *Music, Talent, and Performance.* Philadelphia: Temple Univ. Press.

Lomax, Alan
    1968   *Folk Song Style and Culture.* Washington, D.C.: American Association for the Advancement of Science.

May, Elizabeth, ed.
    1981   *Musics of Many Cultures.* Berkeley: Univ. of California Press.

McAllester, David P.
    1949   *Peyote Music.* New York: Viking Fund Publications in Anthropology no. 13.
———, ed.
    1971   *Readings in Ethnomusicology.* New York: Johnson Reprint Corp.

Merriam, Alan
    1967   *Ethnomusicology of the Flathead Indians.* Chicago: Aldine.

Myers, Helen
    1992   *Ethnomusicology: An Introduction.* New York: Norton.
———.
    1993   *Ethnomusicology: Historical and Regional Studies.* New York: Norton.

Nettl, Bruno
    1964   *Theory and Method in Ethnomusicology.* New York: Free Press.

————.
    1983   *The Study of Ethnomusicology: Twenty-Nine Issues and Concepts.* Urbana: Univ. of Illinois Press.

————.
    1985   *The Western Impact on World Music: Change, Adaptation, and Survival.* New York: Schirmer Books.

————.
    1995   *Heartland Excursions: Ethnomusicological Reflections on Schools of Music.* Urbana: Univ. of Illinois Press.

Pantaleoni, Hewitt
    1985   *On the Nature of Music.* Oneonta, N.Y.: Welkin Books.

Reck, David
    1977   *Music of the Whole Earth.* New York: Scribner's.

Rice, Timothy
    1994   *May it Fill Your Soul: Experiencing Bulgarian Music.* Chicago: Univ. of Chicago Press.

Seeger, Charles
    1977   *Studies in Musicology, 1935–1975.* Berkeley: Univ. of California Press.

Slobin, Mark
    1976   *Music in the Culture of Northern Afghanistan.* Tucson: Univ. of Arizona Press.

CHAPTER TWO

North America/Native America

DAVID P. McALLESTER

American Indian music is unfamiliar to most non-Indian Americans. Accordingly, the plan of this chapter is to present, first, a bit of overall perspective by contrasting three of the many different Native American musical styles. Then we will look in detail at some of the many types of music being performed today in just one tribe, the Navajos. Here the musical life of the people will be studied in relation to their traditional culture and their present history. When we learn the cultural setting we add an important level to our understanding of the music.

THREE DIFFERENT STYLES

SIOUX GRASS DANCE

The essence of music is participation, either by listening or, better still, by performing. We will start with the most "Indian" sound the non-Indian American imagination can conceive of, a Sioux War Dance (ill. 2–1). This is also called a Grass Dance, from the braids of grass the dancing warriors used to wear at their waists to symbolize slain enemies. It is also called the Omaha Dance, after the Omaha Indians of the western plains who originated it.

Listen for a moment to the first recording (recorded selection 1; ex. 2–1) on the sound recordings that accompany this book. When European scholars first heard this kind of sound on wax cylinder field recordings brought back to Berlin in the early 1900s, they exclaimed, "Now, at last, we can hear the music of the true savages!" For four hundred years European social philosophers had thought

I am grateful to vigilant student-colleagues for several corrections and improvements in this chapter; I would especially like to thank John Kelsey and Patrick Hutchinson. Mr. Hutchinson made a careful study of "Folsom Prison Blues," noting interesting textual and rhythmic elisions and complications not found in the original Johnny Cash recording. These are similar to alterations noted by Robert Witmer in popular music performed by Blood Indians in Canada (1973:79–83).

17

Douglas Fulton. Courtesy of Gertrude Kurath

Ill. 2–1.   War dancers at a Michigan powwow.

of American Indians as noble wild men unspoiled by civilization, and here was music that fitted the image.

Nothing known to Europeans sounded like this piercing falsetto, swooping down for more than an octave in a "tumbling strain" that seems to come straight from the emotions. The pulsating voices with their sharp emphases, the driving drumbeat with its complex relation to the vocal part, the heavy slides at the ends of phrases—what could better portray the warlike horsemen of the limitless American plains? Another feature that intrigued Europeans was the use of vocables (nonlexical or "meaningless" syllables) for the entire texts of the song, as in this Grass Dance. Curt Sachs found this another reason for labeling this music *pathogenic* (arising from the emotions), as contrasted with *logogenic* music, in

Ex. 2–1. Sioux Grass Dance song. With the permission of Robert Doyle.

which translatable words are the basis of the song (Sachs 1962:51–58). Sachs theorized that pathogenic music was what one would find in the early stages of cultural evolution. Did his own Paleolithic ancestors sing like this when they were hunting wild horses across the plains of Europe and had not yet discovered agriculture?

Another supposed proof that American Indians belonged to an early stage of musical evolution was the surprising limitation in kinds of musical instruments they used. From north of Mexico to the Arctic the music was almost entirely vocal and the instruments were chiefly rattles and drums used to accompany the voice. It should be pointed out, though, that the varieties of rattles and drums invented by North American Indians are legion. There are rattles made from gourds, tree bark, carved wood, deer hooves, turtle shells, spider nests, and, recently, tin cans, just to name a few. There are frame drums and barrel drums of many sizes and shapes, and the water drum (described in detail on pp. 56–58), with its wet membrane, is unique in the world. There are a few flutes and flageolets, and one-stringed fiddles played without the voice, but these are rare. Instrumental ensembles like our orchestras are unknown in traditional North American Indian music.

In Central and South America, on the other hand, the native high civilizations did have orchestras before the Europeans came. They readily added European instruments to their ensembles and blended their music with new ideas from Portugal and Spain. But only in the last forty or fifty years has this mingling of musics begun to happen on any large scale in native North American music. The vast majority of traditional songs are still accompanied only by the drum or rattle or sometimes both together.

To go back to evolutionary ideas for a moment, few scholars today find that a notion of "delayed evolution" explains the so-called simpler cultures of the world. In fact, they turn out not to be simple at all. Survival, whatever the climate, requires encyclopedic knowledge. A language, though it may never have been written down, may contain the most complex grammatical structures known to linguists. Folk music with no harmonies may contain melodic, modal, and rhythmic sophistication unattainable in harmonic music.

Now for participation: listen again to the Sioux Grass Dance song and see if you can sing along with it. You may think it is impossible, especially if you are a man and have never tried to sing in the falsetto register before. Until you get your courage up you might find it easier to try singing the song an octave lower than the Sioux singers. The transcription (ex. 2–1) will help you with the words and melody.°

If you cannot read notes, think of the transcription as a kind of graph tracing the line of the melody. Even with no musical training you can see patterns of movement from high to low and back up again. I have labeled the sections of the song that sound alike with the same letter of the alphabet to help the reader see where similar musical ideas are repeated. The overall structure of phrases in this song may be represented as shown in figure 2–1.

The song starts with an A phrase, sung by a leader, but before he can finish it the other male singers break in with the same phrase, repeated, and he joins them to sing it all the way through. I have indicated the leader's first, uncompleted phrase as ½A. Most of the melodic movement takes place in the B phrase. Here is where the melody drops a full octave below the tonal center established in the A phrase. In fact, the lower part of B is almost an exact repeat, twice, of A, an octave lower. I have indicated this pattern by writing A with a subscript 8 (A_8) at the points where this transposition begins and repeats. After three repeats of the whole melody, there is a pause; then B is repeated one last time to end the song. Indian singers often call that last brief section of the "tail" of the song, which is also what the European musical term *coda* means.

°All musical transcriptions in this chapter are by David P. McAllester.

½ A A B B
½ A A B B
½ A A B B B

Fig. 2–1.   Phase structure, Sioux Grass Dance song.

This song may be easy to understand in its overall structure, but it is not easy to sing. It goes fast, and it does not have a regular meter. Most of it is in triple, or three-beat, patterns, but every now and then the singers introduce a four-beat phrase. I have drawn brackets ⌐ over those spots so that the reader-listener-performer can see where they are. Notice that the melody makes the same downward dip at each of these spots where the meter breaks into four. Another difficulty is that the song meter does not seem to coincide with that of the drum: to give some idea of the difference I have written the approximate metronome readings of each. "C = B♭" means that I have transposed the melody level up a whole step so that it will be easier to read.

The best way to sing this is to "hang loose" and not try to count it out mechanically. Concentrate on the excitement that has made this kind of music the most popular Native American style all over the country where there are Indian fairs, rodeos, and powwows. Like the Plains Indians' eagle-feather warbonnet and their stately, beautifully decorated tipis, the War Dance is a symbol for "Indian," everywhere. Though Indian singing styles differ from region to region, many non-Plains Indians, especially young people, have learned this style so well that they have been able to compete with Plains singers in song contests. There are non-Indians, also, who have risen to the challenge of this music and have won prizes for their singing, costumes, and dancing at powwows. In singing this song, pay particular attention to the sharp emphases, the pulsations, and the glides. These are not mere "ornamentation" but an important part of the special art of Plains singing.

The dancing that goes with this song style is based on a toe-heel movement first on one foot and then on the other. An elaboration is shown below:

Foot:	left	right	right	left	left	right	
Movement:	step	toe-heel,	change	toe-heel,	change	toe-heel,	etc.

Each male dancer creates many personal variations and makes a solo display of his virtuosity. His body dips and bends, but his head is very erect, sometimes nodding in time to the drumbeat and turning this way and that. His eyes are fixed on space and the expression is rapt and remote. Often he carries a decorated stick or other object in one hand; during the dance he may manipulate it with all the subtlety a Japanese dancer uses with a fan. Every dancer must stop precisely on the last beat at the rhythmic break before the "tail." Then the dancing resumes with all its intensity for the last few moments and must stop exactly on the last beat of the song. One extra step disqualifies a dancer from the competition.

The movement and sound of the costume is an essential part of the Grass Dance and its music. Bells are often tied around the legs; today they are sleigh bells, often quite large, mounted on a leather strap. These resound with every step. Ribbons sway, feathers and porcupine-hair roaches (see the heads of the dancers in ill. 2–1) quiver, beads and small mirrors gleam and flash. The costume is as elaborate as the vocal style.

Women participate in the dance by moving around the periphery of the dance area using a subdued version of the dance step, or just walking. They wear shawls with very long fringes that sway in time to their movements. In recent years women's "jingle dancing" has become a competitive event. Wearing a dress decorated with scores of cone-shaped metal jingles, younger women leap and step, filling the air with glitter and tintinnabulation. Some women stand behind the male singers, who are seated around a bass drum, and enter the song an octave higher than the men, often on the B phrase when it starts down. In the song we are hearing their voices do not come in until the first point marked A_8 in the transcription.

ZUNI LULLABY

The next song (recorded selection 2, ex. 2–2) is chosen to provide a contrast with Plains singing and help demonstrate that there is no single "Indian" musical style. It is a lullaby recorded in 1950 by an old grandmother, Lanaiditsa, on the Zuni Reservation in western New Mexico (ill. 2–2). You will have little difficulty in following her and joining in with the song. The meter is rather free, and the whole gentle song is on only two pitches. In this case the text is in translatable words instead of vocables (fig. 2–2), and you can see that the singer's feeling for the child is expressed in the repetition of diminutives. The pet names seem to be interchangeable in the first half of the song but then settle into the same sequence.

Hm atseki	*my boy*
okshits'ana	*cottontail little*
pokets'ana	*jackrabbit little*
kochits'ana	*rat little*

1. *My boy, little cottontail,*
     Little jackrabbit, little jackrabbit;
2. *My boy, little cottontail,*
     Little rat, little boy, little boy;
3. *My boy, little jackrabbit,*
     Little cottontail, little cottontail;
4. *My boy, little jackrabbit,*
     Little cottontail, little rat, little rat.
5. *My boy, little jackrabbit,*
     Little cottontail, little rat, little rat (3 times)

Fig. 2–2. Lyrics, Zuni lullaby.

Ex. 2–2. Zuni lullaby. Lanaiditsa, Zuni, 1950.

Repetition is a prominent feature in most North American Indian music: in the vocables, in the lexical texts (where they occur), and in the melodic and rhythmic patterns. This is not because Indians are unable to create text and music with a "fuller" content, in our sense, but because their aesthetic taste delights in repetitions with slight variations that are sometimes too subtle for the ears of outsiders to detect. In Lanaiditsa's song each textual phrase can be used with either of the two musical phrases except for "my boy," which is always on an A. She settles on "my little rat" for the ending of verse 4 and the three repeats of verse 5, which suggests that she finds it the most endearing of the diminutives.

The love of repetition that we have just been studying is present in Indian folk tales and other narratives and is very much a part of the way the Navajo singer or "medicine man," Frank Mitchell, tells the story of his life (see pp. 47–54).

Ill. 2–2.   Zuni mother and child, showing costume and hair style of the
early twentieth century. Neg. No. 121630, photo: Coles/Bierwert.
Courtesy Department of Library Services, American Museum of
Natural History.

IROQUOIS QUIVER DANCE

This Quiver Dance song illustrates still another of the many different musical styles in North American Indians singing (recorded selection 3, ex. 2–3). Another name for it is Warrior's Stomp Dance song. This was recorded in 1941 by Joshua Buck and Simeon Gibson at the Six Nations Reserve in Ohsweken, Ontario, but the song was made up years before that by Twenty Jacobs of Quaker Bridge, on the Allegheny Reservation in western New York.

The first thing to strike the ear in example 2–3 is the "call and response" form. One singer utters a phrase of lexical text (the "call") and the other answers him with a vocable pattern: "yowe hi ye ye!" This alternation continues through the song. It is a pattern quite common in the Eastern Woodlands but rare elsewhere in North American traditional Indian singing. (Call-and-response singing can be heard in many world music cultures, as we shall see in later chapters.) William Fenton's translation of the text (fig. 2–3) shows the jocular content often found in Stomp Dance songs.

Ex. 2–3. Iroquois Quiver Dance song (note difference between the lyrics in fig. 2–3, as they would be spoken, and those here, as they appear in the song). With the permission of William N. Fenton.

'Tga na hóna' 'Ohswégen	*yowe hi ye ye!*
Filled is Ohsweken	
Dedjo dinyaakon' on	*yowe hi ye ye!*
With divorced women	
Wegah hano hiiyo	*yowe hi ye ye!*
With good looking ones	
We hoonon hiiyo	*yowe hi ye ye!*
Fine looking ones!	

Fig. 2–3.   Lyrics, Iroquois Quiver Dance song. With the permission of William N. Fenton.

The voices in this Iroquois song are relatively relaxed compared with Plains singing. A characteristic Iroquois feature in singing style is a pulsation of the voice at the ends of phrases, indicated in the transcription by ♫ and ♩ ♩ (in Plains singing, by contrast, pulsations occur all through the song).

The Stomp Dance is a favorite recreational dance among Woodland Indians in the eastern United States and Canada. Among the Iroquois it usually takes place in the longhouse, a meetinghouse with a stove at each end of the hall and benches along the sides. The participants form a line behind the leader. They imitate his "short jog step" (Fenton 1942:31) and any other turns and gyrations he may invent as they sing the responses to his calls. More and more of the audience joins the dance until the line is winding exuberantly all over the longhouse floor. Woodland tribes other than the Iroquois may not have longhouses and often do the Stomp Dance outdoors. The singers accompany themselves with a cowhorn rattle.

MAKING A "COWHORN" RATTLE

The adventure of Native American music involves not only singing but also making instruments to accompany the voice. Following are steps for creating a serviceable imitation of a cowhorn rattle (fig. 2–4). A section of cow's horn is not easy for most of us to obtain; a small fruit juice can, open at one end, will make a good substitute.

1. Any small metal can, two or three inches tall and two to two and one-half inches in diameter, will do. Make a plug for the open end of the can out of a disc of soft wood slightly wider than the diameter of the can. With a sharp knife or a file, bevel one edge of the disc just enough that it can be tightly wedged into the can.

2. Find a stick of hard wood, such as a straight tree branch, about three-fourths of an inch in diameter; cut a one-foot length. A piece of birch dowel will do. Whittle away one end of the stick to make a tapering spindle about an inch longer than the height of the can. At the base of the spindle leave a shelf as shown in the drawing.

3. Drill a hole in the wooden plug so that it will fit snugly over the spindle and seat itself, beveled side up, on the shelf. Punch a smaller hole in the bottom of the can

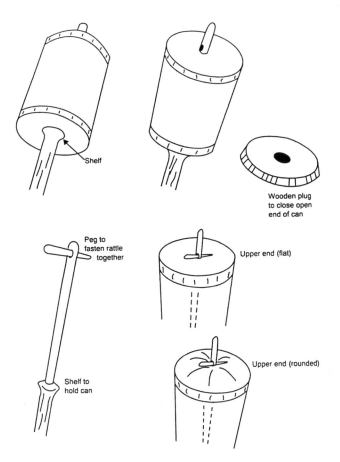

Shelf

Wooden plug
to close open
end of can

Peg to
fasten rattle
together

Upper end (flat)

Upper end (rounded)

Shelf to
hold can

Fig. 2–4. Steps in making a cowhorn rattle.

and slide it, open end down, over the spindle until the rim of the can fits over the beveled edge of the plug. The end of the spindle should project an inch beyond the bottom of the can. Mark the spindle at the point where it emerges from the hole in the can. The mark should be as close to the bottom of the can as possible.

4. Remove the can and plug and fasten the plug in the open end of the can with furniture tacks with shiny brass heads. Drop fifteen or twenty BB shot or small pebbles into the can to produce the rattling sound.

5. Drill a small hole in the spindle at the marked place and obtain a nail or peg that will fit tightly in the hole and project on both sides of the spindle. Fit the can back into place, plug-end down, and wedge the nail or peg through the hole in the spindle. This should hold the can firmly, supported by the shelf at the bottom end.

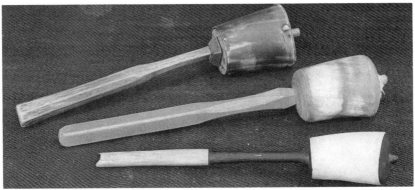

Susan W. McAllester

**Ill. 2–3 Iroquois cowhorn rattles, showing a variety of shapes
and handles.**

Extra Niceties

You could remove both ends of the can and have a wooden plug in each end. This
would give you two rows of ornamental tacks, holding in the plugs. If you are
good at woodworking you could turn the plug for the upper end on a lathe so that
it is rounded instead of being merely flat.

To make the can look like a cowhorn you could paint it dark brown with
cream-colored streaks or cream-colored with brown streaks. See illustration 2–3
for how a cowhorn looks.

Notice in the illustration the different ways the handle can be carved to break
the monotony of a straight stick. You can express your own creativity in how you
do it.

How to Play the Rattle

This kind of rattle may be struck against the user's thigh or palm to produce a
sharp impact. At the beginning of a song a tremolo effect is often produced by
rapidly shaking the rattle, held high in the air.

MUSIC OF THE NAVAJO INDIANS

In the brief survey above, three of the many different North American Indian
musical styles were sketched to give an idea of their variety. Now we will take a
deeper look into the musical life of still another Indian group, the Navajos of the
Southwestern desert. By studying their music in some detail we can see how
many different kinds of music there are in even one Indian community. When we
consider the cultural context of the music we will see how closely music is integrated with Indian life. The autobiographical sketch of Frank Mitchell is included
to give the reader a firsthand account, by a professional Navajo singer, of how he
learned his music and what it meant to him.

A Yeibichai Song from the Nightway Ceremony

To begin again with sound, we will go first to one of the most exciting kinds of Navajo music, their Yeibichai songs. *Yé'ii-bi-chái* (gods-their-grandfathers) refers to ancestor deities who come to dance at one of the major ceremonials, known as Nightway. The masked dancers who impersonate the gods bring supernatural power and blessing to help cure a sick person.

With its shouts, ornamentations, and falsetto voices, this song (recorded selection 4, ex. 2–4) makes one think of the Plains Indians. Also similar to the Plains style is the tense energy of the singing. But the long introduction (phrases X, Y, and Z), sung almost entirely on the base note (the "tonic") of the song, is strikingly different from the Indian songs we have heard before. Then the melody leaps *up* an octave. In the first phrase, A, after the introduction, the song comes swooping briskly down to the tonic again to an ending which I have labeled "e^1." This ending appears again later on in the song in two variations, "e^2" and "e^3." (I am using capital letters to denote main phrases and small letters for motifs within the phrases.) The same descent is repeated (the second A and e') and then another acrobatic plunge takes place in B after two "false starts" that are each very close to the first half of A. I call these ½a and ½a. The song then hovers on the tonic e^2 and e^3 and the phrase *hi ye, hi ye,* which also appears in Y and Z. I call it "z" since it has the weighty function of ending the introduction, and, eventually, the song itself, in the Z phrase. After B, another interesting variation in the use of previous motifs occurs: the *second* half of A is sung twice, a½ and a½, followed by the first half of A, also repeated, ½a and ½a.

The Navajos are noted for their bold experiments in artistic form. This is true in their silversmithing, their weaving, their sandpainting, and their contemporary commercial painting. Here is an example from their music of the play of melodic and rhythmic motifs. Listen again, following the pattern of this complex and intriguing song, and try to sing it yourself along with Sandoval Begay and his group of Yeibichai singers.

The text is entirely in vocables, but this song gives a good illustration of how far from "meaningless" vocables can be. From the first calls it is clear to almost any Navajo that this is a Yeibichai song: these and the other vocables all serve to identify the kind of song. Moreover, in this song there is the call of the gods themselves:

Hi ye, hi ye, ho-ho ho ho!

Though there are hundreds of different Yeibichai songs, they usually contain some variation of this call of the Yei.

Yeibichai singers are organized in teams, often made up of men from one particular region or another. They create new songs or sing old favorites, each team singing a number of songs before the nightlong singing and dancing are over. The

Ex. 2–4.   Navajo Yeibichai song. With the permission of Willard Rhodes.

* Repeat from A twice. High yell replaces 1st 2 notes of A on the first repeat; second repeat ends at "Fine".

teams prepare costumes and masks and practice a dance of the gods that proceeds in two parallel lines with reel-like figures. They also have a clown, who follows the dancers and makes everyone laugh with his antics: getting lost, bumbling into the audience, imitating the other dancers. The teams compete, and the best combination of costumes, clowns, singing, and dancing receives a gift from the family giving the ceremony. The representation of the presence of the gods at the Nightway brings god power to the ceremony and helps the sick person get well.

This dance takes place on the last night of a nine-night ritual that includes such ceremonial practices as purification by sweating and vomiting, making prayer offerings for deities whose presence is thus invoked, and sand-painting rituals in which the one-sung-over sits on elaborate designs in colored sands and other dry pigments. The designs depict the deities; contact with these figures identifies the one-sung-over with the forces of nature they represent and provides their protective power (see ill. 2–4). In the course of the ceremony hundreds of people may

Neg. no. 2A 3634. Courtesy American Museum of Natural History (Photo: Boltin)

Ill. 2–4.   Ceremonial practitioner making a sandpainting of a Lightning Deity in flint armor.

attend as spectators, whose presence lends support to the reenactment of the myth upon which the ceremony is based. The one-sung-over takes the role of the mythic hero, and the songs, sand paintings, prayers, and other ritual acts recount the story of how this protagonist's trials and adventures brought the Nightway ceremony from the supernatural world for the use of humankind (Faris 1990). Besides the Yeibichai songs there are hundreds of long chanted songs with elaborate texts of translatable ritual poetry (see pp. 43–47 below).

Such a ritual drama as Nightway is as complex as "the whole of a Wagnerian opera" (Kluckhohn and Leighton 1938: 163). The organization and performance of the whole event is directed by the singer or ceremonial practitioner, who must memorize every detail. Such men and women are among the intellectual leaders of the Navajo communities. The life story on pages 47–54 is a rare glimpse into the mind of such a person.

Most readers find the Yeibichai song difficult to learn. The shifts in emphasis, the many variations, and the difficult vocal style demand hours of training before one can do it well. But there are many other kinds of Navajo music.

"FOLSOM PRISON BLUES"

Of course you can join in this song (recorded selection 5) right away, especially if you are familiar with country and western music. This version of Johnny Cash's "Folsom Prison Blues," is played and sung by the Fenders, an all-Navajo country band from Thoreau, New Mexico, who were popular in the 1960s and 1970s (ill. 2–5). This song is here to make sure the reader knows that country music has long been a great favorite with Indian people, especially in the West, just as it is with a large part of the general American public. There are several country and western bands on the Navajo reservation, and some, like the Sundowners and Borderline, have issued records that sell well in Indian country. Even more popular are non-Indian country singers such as Garth Brooks and Tim McGraw. The cowboy and trucker image is appealing to most Westerners, including Indians, who identify with the open life and the excitement of the roundup and the rodeo. The Fenders' liner notes begin:

> The five Fenders are genuine cowboys . . . as much at home on the back of a bucking rodeo bronc as behind the wild guitar at a good old rodeo dance. These boys believe that to be a No. 1, all-around cowboy, you must be able to play the guitar and sing just as well as you ride, rope and bull-dog.

THE NAVAJO WAY OF LIFE

Who are these Navajos we are listening to, and where and how do they live? At more than 200,000, they are our largest Indian tribe. Descended from Athabascan-speaking nomadic hunters who came into the Southwest as recently as six or seven hundred years ago, they now live in scattered communities ranging from extended family groups to small towns on a reservation of some 25,000 square miles (larger than West Virginia) spread over parts of New Mexico, Arizona, and Utah (see fig. 2–5). The exact census of the Navajos is uncertain, since there are

**Ill. 2–5.   Album cover of the Fenders, an early Navajo country and
western group.**

thousands living off the reservation in border towns such as Farmington, Gallup,
and Flagstaff and such cities as Chicago, Los Angeles, and San Diego. The reason
for their move is largely economic: their population has outgrown the support af-
forded by the reservation.

On the reservation the Navajos' livelihood is based to a small but culturally significant degree on farming, stock raising, weaving, and silversmithing (see ill.
2–6). But the major part of their $110 million annual income comes from coal,
uranium, oil, natural gas, and lumber. Much of their educational and health care
funds derive from the Department of the Interior, some of it in fulfilment of the
1868 treaty that marked the end of hostilities between the Navajos and the
United States Army. Personal incomes range from the comfortable salaries of
tribal administrative and service jobs to the precarious subsistence of marginal
farmers. Many Navajos are supported on various kinds of tribal or government
relief.

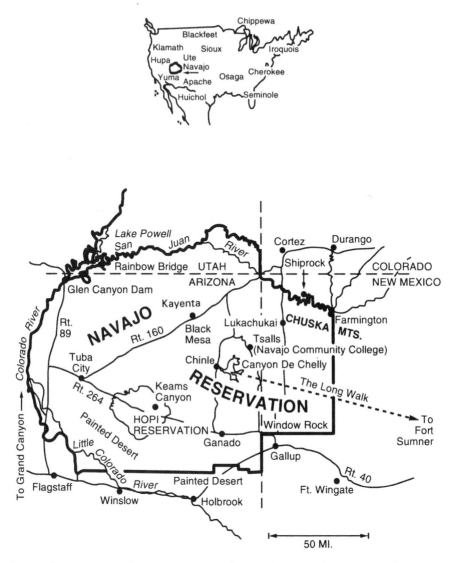

Fig. 2–5. Location of some American tribes, and points of interest on the Navajo Reservation.

Neg. no. 335258. Courtesy American Museum of Natural History (Photo: M. Raney)

Ill. 2–6.   Navajos still travel on horseback in many parts of the reservation.

Though much of traditional Navajo culture remains intact, the People (*Diné*), as the Navajos call themselves, also welcome new ideas and change. Their scholarship funds enable hundreds of young people to attend colleges and universities around the country, including their own Navajo Community College on the reservation. A battery of attorneys and a Natural Resources Committee keep watch on the mining leases and lumber operations. The Navajos also operate motels, restaurants, banks, and shopping centers, and they encourage small industries to establish themselves on the reservation. Some Navajos jet to administrative and development conferences in Washington, D.C.; others speak no English and herd sheep on horseback or on foot miles from the nearest paved road.

The men dress in western style, and some of the women still wear skirts and blouses copied from the dresses worn by United States Army officers' wives in the 1860s, during the imprisonment of the Navajos at Fort Sumner, New Mexico. The skirts have shortened in recent years, and Navajo taste has always demanded the addition of buttons, rings, bracelets, necklaces, and heavy belts of silver set with turquoise. The men wear this jewelry, too, sometimes with the added panache of silver hatbands on big cowboy hats. Young people, male and female, are now usually seen in the blue jeans attire of other young people anywhere in the country. Bright blankets from the Pendleton mills in Oregon used to be worn as an overcoat in cold weather. This garment is now so identified with traditional Navajo costume that it is often worn by the protagonist in ceremonials. The Navajos' own famous rugs are woven for cash income; most of them go to the local store, sometimes still called a trading post, to pay for food and other supplies. Some of these rugs are so finely designed and woven that they have brought $20,000 apiece and more in the world market for fine arts (see ill. 2–7).

Navajo houses range from the modern stucco ranch houses and large trailer homes of tribal officials, administrative staff, and school personnel to smaller one-room houses of every description. Some of the old-style circular log hogans

Neg. no. 14471. Courtesy American Museum of Natural History (Photo: P. E. Goddard)

Ill. 2–7.   Hand-weaving is a source of income for many Navajo women. This scene, from the 1920s, is still common today.

(Navajo *hooghan,* place home) can still be seen. Navajo ceremony requires a circular floor plan, and many adaptations of this well-loved and ceremonially important shape are designed into new kinds of structures. The Tribal Council Building in Window Rock, Arizona, is a round sandstone structure with Indian murals inside. It is large enough to accommodate the seventy-four council members from all parts of the reservation. The Cultural Center at the Navajo Community College at Tsaile, Arizona, is six stories of concrete, steel, and glass, but it is octagonal, with a domed roof. Inside, at the heart of the building, is a replica of a traditional log hogan with a dirt floor and a smoke hole that goes up four stories through a shaft to the open sky. It is there as a religious symbol and a meditation room. School buildings, chapter houses, information centers, and arts and crafts outlets exhibit other variations in size and design on the circular shape, which is symbolic of the earth, and on the domed roof, which is symbolic of both mountaintops and the vault of the sky.

TRADITIONAL POPULAR MUSIC

Until the 1940s the most popular musics on the reservation were the different kinds of dance songs from the ceremonials. We have already studied a Yeibichai dance song from Nightway. Corral dance songs from several ceremonies were also popular, but the several different kinds of Squaw Dance songs from Enemyway made up the largest body of traditional popular music. These include Circle Dance, Sway songs, Two-step, Skip Dance, and Gift songs. After being eclipsed by country and western in the 1960s and 1970s, the traditional songs are once again very popular on the reservation.

A new recreational pastime called "song and dance" has emerged in the 1990s that makes use of Skip Dance and Two-step songs. These can take place in any large hall; couples of all ages, in traditional costumes, participate. Singers or tapes provide the music, and the dancers, identified by large numbered tags, circle the hall while judges note their costumes and dancing skill. Winners receive trophies, and entry fees and donations solicited during the dancing go toward the expenses of the Song and Dance Association hosting the event, or for specified benefits such as school programs.

Some traditionalists have objected to Squaw Dance songs being used in this new, secular context, but this is only the latest in a number of new uses. Radio broadcasts have featured Squaw Dance songs since the 1930s, and they are having a new wave of radio popularity in the 1990s.

THE CIRCLE DANCE SONG "SHIZHANÉ'É"

Squaw Dance songs are the hit tunes of traditional Navajo life. Compared with the Yeibichai songs, Squaw Dance songs are easy to sing, though to an outsider they can contain some surprises. Many of them are sung entirely on vocables, but the Circle Dance song "Shizhané'é" (recorded selection 6; ex. 2–5) contains words that can be translated as well. If you play this song a few times and follow the words and music provided here, you should be able to get into the swing of this

Ex. 2–5. "Shizhané'é." Navajo Circle Dance song. With the permission of
Albert Sandoval Jr. and Ray Winnie.

lively melody. Since you do not have to worry about producing the high falsetto
sounds of the Yeibichai songs, you can concentrate on other fine points.

Pay attention to the sharp little emphases marked with >. See if you can reproduce the nasal tone the Navajos like in their singing. Every phrase ends with

This, and the triple meter are characteristic of Circle Dance songs (McAllester
1954:52). Notice how the A phrases introduce the melodic elements that are
more fully developed in B and then even more so in C. The whole structure is too
long to include on the sound recording.

The translatable portion of the text, in the C phrases, is like a nugget in the
middle of the song, framed by a vocable chorus before and after it. This is a favorite principle of design in other Navajo arts as well as music. It is the dynamic
symmetry discussed by Witherspoon (1977:170–74) and illustrated in weaving
and silver jewelry designs. The brief, humorous text (figs. 2–6, 2–7) is, like many

The text as it is sung:
Shizhané'é, shizhané'é, kiya sizini shika nootaał,
'aweya he nai ya.

Free translation: I'm in luck, I'm in luck!
She's leaning up against the store front,
Looking everywhere for me!

As the Navajo is spoken, with literal translation:

shizhané	me-good luck
kíyah	house-under/against
sizíní	standing-the one who
shíká	me-for/after (as in running after one)
nóotááł	searching for (3rd person)

Fig. 2–6. Lyrics, "Shizhané'é." With the permission of Albert Sandoval Jr. and Ray Winnie.

another in Navajo song, intended to make the girls laugh and pay attention to the (male) singers. Though the dance is part of a ceremony, it is also a courtship situation and a social dance as well.

It helps in the enjoyment of the song to linger for a moment on the choices of expression that make the words so witty. The song begins with fatuous self-congratulation. But then we learn both from the form "yah" after "house" and from the neuter static form of sizí, "the one who is standing", that the girl is really propped against the house. The suggestion is that she has had too much to drink and therefore is unable to be actively searching for ("running after") the singer at all, even though he claims she is. The irony of the situation is combined with a jesting implication that women drink too much and chase after young men. Since it is actually the men who do most of the drinking and chasing after the opposite sex, the song is all the funnier. *Kiyah sizíní* also carries the meaning "prostitute." As in all clever poetry, the zest is in the subtle shades of meaning.

The ' indicates a glottal stop, as in "oh-oh!" (6-6).

ł	is like the Welsh ll in Flloyd, unvoiced with the breath coming out on either side of the tongue.	
aa	indicates a long "a"	likewise: oo and other vowels
ą	indicates a nasal "a"	likewise: o and other vowels
é	indicates a high "e:"	Navajo has speech tones like Chinese.
ée	indicates a long "e" falling from high to low in tone	

Vowels have "Continental values."

Fig. 2–7. Note on pronunciation in Navajo.

THE ENEMYWAY CEREMONY

Religion is one of the keys to understanding culture. We will know the Navajos better if we take a closer look at the Enemyway ceremony in which "Shizhané'é" is used. Enemyway is one of the most frequently performed rites in traditional Navajo religion. Like Nightway, discussed above, it is a curing ritual. In this case the sickness is brought on by the ghosts of outsiders who have died. Enemyway is often performed for a returned Navajo member of the United States Armed Forces or for others who have been away from home among strangers for a long time. A Navajo who has been in a hospital and returns home cured, in our sense, may have an Enemyway performed because of the inevitable exposure to the spirits of the many non-Navajos who have died in such a place (see ill. 2–8).

The ceremony involves two groups of participants, the "home camp" and the "stick receiver's camp." Members of the latter represent the enemy and are custodians of a stick decorated with symbols of the warrior deity, Enemy Slayer, and of his mother, Changing Woman, who is the principal Navajo deity. The decorated stick is brought from the home camp along with gifts of many yards of brightly colored yarn. The first night of the ceremony consists of singing and dancing at the stick receiver's camp. This kind of dancing is the only time in traditional Navajo life that men and women dance together. It was, and is, a time for fun and courtship. Before the dancing starts there is a concert of "Sway songs," in which the courtship theme may be expressed (fig. 2–8). A majority of the Sway songs, however, have texts entirely of vocables.

Courtesy Andy Tsihnahjinnie

Ill. 2–8.   Scene by Navaho painter Andy Tsihnahjinnie shows drumming, singing, and dancing at the public part of an Enemyway ceremony.

Heye yeye ya,
 Lonesome as I am,
 Lonesome as I am, ha-i na,
 Lonesome as I am,
 Lonesome as I am, ha,
 Lonesome as I am, na'a- ne hana. . . .

Fig. 2–8. Lyrics, Navajo Sway song. David P. McAllester, *Enemy Way* Music, pp. 29, 37. Papers of the Peabody Museum of Archaeology and Ethnology, vol. 41, no. 3. Copyright © 1954 by the President and Fellows of Harvard College.

After an hour or so, the singing shifts to dance songs and the women appear, looking for partners. It is always "ladies' choice," a reflection, perhaps, of the powerful position women have in Navajo society. They own the household; the children belong to the mother's clan, not the father's; and when a couple marry it is traditional for the husband to move in with his wife's family.

In the dance the women are likely to act bashful, but they find partners and the couples dance along together following other couples in a large circle. The step is simply a light stepping along with a bounce on each step. When a woman is ready to change partners she lets the man know by demanding a token payment. Even some Navajos do not know that this is a symbol of the war booty brought back by Enemy Slayer from a mythical war and given away to Navajo women in the story in celebration of the victory. The song texts of the dance songs often poke fun at the women and sometimes refer to these payments (fig. 2–9). After a few hours of dancing, a Signal song (McAllester 1954:27) indicates that the singing is to go back to Sway songs. The dancing stops, and the Sway songs may go on for the rest of the night. Again, the symbolism is of war; the group of singers is divided into two halves, representing the home camp and the enemy, and the singers compete in vigor, repertory, and highness of pitch.

He-ne, yane, yana-,
 Yala'e-le- yado'eya 'ana he,
 Yala'e-le- yado'eya ne. . . .

Your daughter, at night,
 Walking around, yado'eya yana hana,
 Tomorrow, money,
 Lots of it, there will be, yana hana,

Yala'e-le- yado'eya na'ana,
 Yala'e-le- yado'eya na'ana he. . . .

Fig. 2–9. Lyrics, Navajo Enemyway Dance song. David P. McAllester, *Enemy Way Music*, p. 45. Papers of the Peabody Museum of Archaeology and Ethnology, vol. 41, no. 3. Copyright © 1954 by the President and Fellows of Harvard College.

They stop at dawn, but after a rest and breakfast a new kind of singing, a serenade of Gift songs, takes place. The home camp people sing outside the main hogan in the stick receiver's camp, and in exchange small gifts like oranges and boxes of Cracker Jack are thrown to the singers through the smoke hole. Larger gifts such as expensive blankets are brought out and handed to responsible members of the singing group; these presents will be reciprocated later in the ceremony. Most of the Gift songs are old and have text entirely in vocables, but a few of the newer ones have words concerning the hoped-for gifts (fig. 2–10).

The gifts, like the payments during the dancing, represent war booty. The trip of the home party can be seen as a raid into enemy country and the gifts as the booty they take home with them. But reconciliation is symbolized at the same time, since the stick receiver's camp provides supper and camping facilities, and since the meal and gifts will be returned in a similar exchange on the third morning.

After the breakfast and gift singing on the second day, the stick receiver's party prepares to move toward the home camp. Most of the home camp people leave early, but one of their number remains as an official guide to lead the stick receiver to a good camping place a few miles from the home camp. They time their arrival to take place at about sundown, and another night of singing and dancing follows at this new camp.

Early the next morning the war symbolism of the ceremony is sharply emphasized with a sham battle. The stick receiver's people ride into the home camp with yells and rifle shots, raising a lot of dust and committing small depredations such as pulling down clotheslines. After four such charges they retire to a new campsite a few hundred yards away and a procession from the home camp brings them a sumptuous breakfast. After the meal, the return gift singing takes place at the hogan of the one-sung-over.

Now comes further, heavy war drama. In a secret indoor ritual the afflicted person is given power and protection by sacred chanting and is dressed for battle. At the climax of the ceremony he goes forth and shoots at a trophy of the enemy, thus ritually killing the ghost. The songs used in the preparation of the warrior in-

> *Heye yeye yana,*
> *Your skirts, how many? yi-na,*
> *To the store I'm going, 'e hyana heye yeye ya,*
> *To Los Nores I'm going, 'e hya 'ena hya na. . . .*
>
> *'e-ye yeye yana,*
> *Goats, I came for them, yo'o'o 'ene hanena,*
> *Goats, I came for them yo'o'o 'ene hahe,*
> *Yo'o'o 'ena heye yeye yana. . . .*

Fig. 2–10.   Navajo Enemyway Gift song. David P. McAllester, *Enemy Way Music*, p. 48, songs 52, 53. *Papers of the Peabody Museum of Archaeology and Ethnology*, vol. 41, no. 3. Copyright © 1954 by the President and Fellows of Harvard College.

clude long derisive descriptions of the enemy and praise of Navajo warriors (Haile 1938:276–284). If the person being sung over is a woman, a male proxy takes her place when it comes to shooting the enemy ghost.

In the late afternoon a Circle Dance is performed at the stick receiver's new camp. Men join hands in a circle, the two halves of which represent the two camps. It is now that songs like "Shizhané'é" (ex. 2–5) are sung. The two sides of the circle take turns singing in a competition to see who can sing the best songs most beautifully. As the songs alternate, so does the direction in which the Circle Dance moves. Most of the songs have no translatable words, and those that do are not overtly about war; but the presence of the two competing sides is a reminder of conflict, and it is thought that every drumbeat accompanying the songs drives the enemy ghosts farther into the ground. After a while a girl carrying the stick and several other women may enter the circle and walk around following the direction of the dancing men. The symbols of Changing Woman and her warrior son incised on the sacred stick are further reminders of the meaning of the dance.

After the Circle Dance, another dramatic event takes place: the secret war name of the afflicted person is revealed. Members of the stick receiver's camp walk over to the home camp, singing as they go. Four times on the way, they stop and shout out the identity of the enemy. Then the stick receiver sits down in front of the ceremonial hogan and sings four songs that mention the name of the enemy and that of the one-sung-over. In traditional Navajo life it is impolite to address anyone by name and, in particular, by his or her war name. Polite address is by a kinship term, real or fictitious. Examples of war names are She Went Among War Parties, or He Ran Through Warriors (Reichard 1928:98–99).

The songs describe battle with the enemy and refer to the anguish of the enemy survivors. The death of the enemy ghost is mentioned. Then, after a serenade of Sway songs, the stick receiver's party move back to the dance ground at their camp, and the last night of the ceremony begins with a further selection of Sway songs. After an hour or so the singing changes to dance songs and dancing, which, as on the previous two nights, may go on for several hours. Again the Signal song indicates the end of dancing, and the rest of the night is spent in Sway song competition between the two camps.

At dawn the ceremony ends with a brief blessing ritual conducted while facing the rising sun. The stick receiver's party departs, and the afflicted person, now protected by the many symbolic ways in which the ghost has been eliminated, spends a period of four days in rest and quiet while the effect of the ceremony becomes established over the entire household.

THE "CLASSICAL" MUSIC OF THE NAVAJOS

We have listened, so far, to examples of the public or popular music in two Navajo ceremonials, and a new kind of popular music, Navajo country and western. But we have not considered the music at the core of Navajo traditional religious philosophy, the great ceremonial chants. These are the long series of songs that accompany the ritual procedures such as we have described for the Nightway (the purifications, prayer offerings, and sand-painting procedures) and for Enemyway (preparation of the drum and decorated stick, dressing the one-sung-over, and giving him or her power and protection). Illustration 2–9 shows yet another ceremonial chant, the Mountainway.

These chants are "classic" in that they have a tradition going back for generations (no one knows how many); they have enormous scope—one chant may contain over five hundred songs, and the texts comprise many thousands of lines of religious poetry; they contain in their prayers and songs, and in the related myths, the meaning the Navajos find in the natural and supernatural worlds.

The performance of the chants may be brief or extended depending on the needs of the one-sung-over, the person to be cured. Excerpts of a few hours may be sufficient, or an extended version of as much as nine nights may be needed. To understand why, we need to consider the Navajo concept of illness.

The disease theory of the Euro-American world is recognized by the Navajos, and they gladly take advantage of hospitals, surgery, and antibiotics. But, in addition, they see bad dreams, poor appetite, depression, and injuries from accidents as resulting from disharmony with the world of nature. This view is somewhat like our own in the realm of psychiatry and psychosomatic medicine, but the Navajos go still further. They see the power of animals, birds, and insects, and also of earth, water, wind, and sky, not just in a sentimental way but as active potencies that have a direct influence on human life. All of these forces may speak directly to human beings and may teach them the songs, prayers, and ritual acts that make up the ceremonials. At the center of this relationship with the natural world is the concept of *hózhǫ́ǫ́* (beauty, blessedness, harmony), which must be maintained,

Neg. no. 127657. Courtesy American Museum of Natural History.

Ill. 2–9. Navajo fire dance from the Mountainway ceremony. The dancers represent fire deities who have come to help a sick person recover.

and which, if lost, can be restored by means of ritual. The prayers invoke this state over and over at their conclusions (fig. 2–11).

The ceremonial chants, some fifty of them, dramatize the Navajo creation story, an interlocking network of myths as long and complex as Greek mythology or the Vedas of India. No one person knows the entire story, but the tradition lives in the remarkable memories of several hundred ceremonial practitioners, men and women called "singers" (hatááłí) in Navajo. They direct the dance, art, and theater, chant the music, and recite the prayers that constitute these extraordinary achievements of the human spirit. They learn in the oral tradition, as apprentices, over many years. Some of these practitioners are now teaching religion at such culturally oriented schools as the Rough Rock Demonstration School, near Chinle, Arizona, and the Navajo Community College at Tsaile, Arizona. One practitioner has dictated his life story, a narrative of over three hundred pages. Excerpts from this remarkable account are presented here (pp. 47–54).

No complete recording of a ceremonial is available on commercial discs or tapes, and there are very few commercial recordings of even one of the thousands of songs that make up this great literature of religious music. The main reason is that most singers feel these matters are too sacred to be made public. Often the concern is expressed that an uninitiated person might use one of these songs improperly, through ignorance, and cause great harm to the community, or worse yet, rob the song of its potency. Though the singers who recorded the next song (recorded selection 7) did not share this belief, we respect the feelings of those who do and therefore present only a fragment of the song and give the text only in translation here.

The song form is characteristic of ceremonial music (see fig. 2–12). There is an introduction on the tonic, after which a chorus in vocables begins. The melody may be restricted, as in this case, to only three or four notes, or it may move about with a range of an octave or more. In any case, the interest of the music is in the many subtle variations of a highly repetitive form. A section of the chorus is usually repeated at the end of each verse in a kind of refrain; adding still further to the feeling of repetition.

'Shootingway is a ceremonial that reenacts that part of the creation myth in which a hero, Holy Young Man, goes in search of supernatural power. Before his

Hózhǫ́ǫ́ nahasdlį́į́',
Hózhǫ́ǫ́ nahasdlį́į́',
Hózhǫ́ǫ́ nahasdlį́į́',
Hózhǫ́ǫ́ nahasdlį́į́'!

Conditions of harmony have been restored,
Conditions of harmony have been restored,
Conditions of harmony have been restored,
Conditions of harmony have been restored!

Fig. 2–11.   Concluding phrase of Navajo prayer.

'Eye neye yaŋa,
'Eya wane yaneye ne-ya
'Eya wane yane yene yaŋa 'eyo weneya. . . .

I have been searching everywhere,
  Over the earth,
  That is what I was told to do,
I have been searching everywhere,
  Over the earth.

I have been searching everywhere,
  Over the mountains,
  That is what I was told to do,
I have been searching everywhere,
  Over the mountains.

I have been searching everywhere,
  Under the sun,
  That is what I was told to do,
I have been searching everywhere,
  Under the sun.

I have been searching everywhere,
  For the fire,
  That is what I was told to do,
I have been searching everywhere,
  For the fire.

I have been searching everywhere,
  With water,
  That is what I was told to do,
I have been searching everywhere,
  With water.

'Eya wane yaneye ne-ya,
'Eya wane yaneye na-yaŋa 'eyo weneya. . . .

Fig. 2–12.   Lyrics, Navajo Shootingway song.

adventures are over he has lived among snake people, fish people, and buffalo people, and has been carried up into the sky by thunder people. In the sky he was taught the Shootingway ceremonial by the Sun so that this knowledge might be brought back to earth for the protection of humankind. The ceremony has many purposes, among them being the restoration of harmony between people and snakes, water and lightning. A person suffering from snakebite might be taken to the hospital for treatment and then, later, might undergo Shootingway in order to end the bad relations with the snake people that led to the snakebite in the first place.

The Shootingway song tells about Holy Young Man's journey to the snake country. He is singing to the Sun, whom he met when he was in the mountains, and he tells about a fire that he has seen glimmering in the distance at night when he was camping. Each day he tried to find the fire and this is what led him at last into the snake country. He married four beautiful snake wives and thus became related to these powerful creatures. During his stay among them he was given their power to take back to earth. Today, when someone is having trouble with the snake people the restoration of harmony can be achieved by the ceremonial reenactment of this episode in Shootingway.

Before the song begins, a fire has been kindled in the ceremonial hogan and a symbolic representation of the snake country prepared. To the east, south, west, and north of the fire images of snakes are laid out in colored pigments on the ground. A black, zigzag snake about three feet long faces the fire from the east, and a blue one of the same shape faces the fire from the south. On the west is a straight white snake and on the north a pink one, also straight, and sprinkled with bits of glittering mica. As the song goes on, the one-sung-over, in the role of Holy Young Man, walks around the fire stepping over the snakes, thus acting out the journey into the snake country. The heat of the fire causes all the participants in the ceremony to sweat profusely in a rite of purification, and a series of other acts also drive out evil and further identify the one-sung-over with the protagonist in the myth. To conclude this part of the ritual the singer cools off the people in the hogan by sprinkling them liberally with water shaken from a bundle of eagle feathers. This is the water mentioned in the last verse of the song.

Even this brief account of a fraction of one of the great ceremonials is enough to give the reader an idea of how the music functions in support of an impressive drama. Shootingway is one of the ways the Navajos remind themselves of the sources of their means of dealing with the supernatural. The ceremony depicts the Navajo view of themselves in relation to the natural world about them.

The beauty of the music, the poetry, the sand paintings, and the myths that lie behind all of these has attracted the attention of scholars worldwide since the 1890s. Some representative examples of the many books written about Navajo myths and ceremonies are listed in the bibliography: Matthews 1894, Kluckhohn and Wyman 1940, Haile 1947, Reichard 1950, Witherspoon 1977, McNeley, 1981, Wyman 1983, Farella 1984, and Griffin–Pierce, 1992.

THE LIFE STORY OF A NAVAJO CEREMONIAL PRACTITIONER

Frank Mitchell (Oltai Tsoh: "Big Schoolboy") was born near Wheatfields, Arizona, in 1881 (see ill. 2–10). In the course of his eventful life he was a sheepherder, railroad worker, cook, handyman-interpreter, wagon freighter, headman, tribal council member, and tribal judge. In his early maturity he learned Blessingway, one of the most important of the Navajo ceremonies, from his father-in-law. How this affected his whole life is told in his autobiography.

There is no other full autobiography of a Navajo singer. In the excerpts presented here, a number of aspects of Navajo life and music are illustrated:

Mable Bosch

Ill. 2–10.   Frank Mitchell, Navajo Blessingway singer, Chinle, Arizona, 1957.

Repetitive, narrative style: Repetition has been mentioned above as a significant element in the form of Navajo music, narrative, and the other arts.

Importance of women: In the opening we are given a glimpse of a matrilocal, matrilineal family. Traditional Navajo families live in the mother's household and the children belong to the mother's clan. Women own their own property. It is not surprising that the principal deity is Changing Woman.

Traveling about: The old nomadic lifestyle of the Navajos has not entirely disappeared. Frank's childhood memories show how it was to follow the livestock a hundred years ago.

Navajo practicality: Frank became a singer for practical as well as spiritual reasons. The spiritual dimension of his calling can be seen only between the lines.

The value of Navajo songs: This is stated not in aesthetic terms but in terms of healing the sick, bringing prosperity, and enabling the possessor of certain songs to become a leader in the community.

Speech and leadership: "Chief" in Navajo means "one who speaks." The voices of humans and all other creatures are the culminating point of sacred descriptions in prayers and songs. In Navajo thought, wind is the ultimate power and the voice is the wind made articulate.

Navajo humor: It is important to remember that Indians, too, have their witty songs and funny stories. Frank was the beloved jokester of his large family. He was known for his ability to keep up the spirits of the participants in a long ceremonial with his ready supply of jokes and funny comments.

Frank Mitchell died in the hospital at Ganado, Arizona, in 1968, a few weeks after he dictated his last paragraphs of the life story that he wanted to leave as a legacy to his children and grandchildren. (All excerpts reprinted with permission from Frisbie and McAllester 1978.)

I was just a small boy when I began to remember things. We happened to be living at a place called Tsaile; that is where I first began to remember things. I remember that I had a grandmother and my mother had some sisters besides herself. In those days a family like that used to stay close together. We moved around together; when we moved from one place to another, we always went in groups.

In those days the men who were singers and performed ceremonies were the only ones who went around and treated the sick. That is what they were occupied with. I had an uncle on my father's side who was very harsh. He would scold us all of the time. One time there was someone sick in the family and they were performing a ceremony. While that was going on we were told not to sleep. Whenever we fell asleep, they would wake us and make us stay awake. Finally I got so sleepy that I could not stay awake any more. I was sitting next to this uncle of mine who was pretty harsh, and I guess that I fell asleep and just rolled over right beside him. My uncle jumped up, grabbed me by the hair on the side of my head, and yanked me up, putting me back down in a sitting position. I could see he was pretty angry. Of course I did not look straight at him; I just glanced sideways over there every now and then to watch him. After that I did not go to sleep again; I just stayed awake for the rest of the ceremony until it was over. Then we were told, "Now you can go to sleep." That was something I remember very plainly because of course I was old enough to remember things then. . . .

The People traveled mostly on horseback; when we moved with the sheep we used horses to carry our belongings. We, being children, of course had to go along. Whenever the family started moving like that we children would sit in back of the rider. We were small and fell asleep sometimes, so they used to take anything they could find and tie us around the waist to the rider so we would not fall off. That is the way we moved around, tied to the riders so we could sleep sitting on those horses. The main reason for moving around like that was to look for new grazing ground and water for the sheep and horses. [29–30]

The leaders who went around recruiting children for school talked to the People about what the advantages would be in the future if they would put their children in school. The People would get angry and say, "No, absolutely not! I'm not going to give up my child; while I'm still alive I'm not going to turn my child over to those foreigners. Outsiders are not going to take my child away while I am still living." That's what they used to say. They would sometimes get out a butcher knife and toss it in front of those doing the recruiting and say, "Well, go ahead, cut my throat first; you'll have to do that before you can take my child." [57]

At school we just went by the bell. It was a big bell like the one they have there by the cattleguard at the Franciscan church here in Chinle. At a certain hour we would go to bed. Every time that bell rang, it meant that we had to get in line, or go to bed, or get up and get ready for breakfast, or dinner, or supper. . . . [63]

After awhile I thought I had had enough of school life so I took the first chance I got when I heard of some work that was available down on the railroad. The reason that I did not stay at school was because another boy, a schoolmate of mine, and I planned together to work on the railroad in the west somewhere. We planned this secretly, skipped out from school and went down on the railroad. The Navajos were already working on the railroad then, the railroad that was coming out of California, around Needles, and all down this way. So without telling my folks or his where we were going, we sneaked off. . . . [68–69]

Everybody at home started to get suspicious about where we were and my late uncle, my mother's brother whom we called Old Man Short Hair, inquired around and learned that it was likely we were with the railroad crew somewhere in the west. So he went in to Gallup and asked to work on the railroad. Of course he really did not want a job; he just wanted to look for us. . . . After my uncle overtook us and worked with us for a while, the railroad moved our crew back toward Flagstaff to a place called Seligman, Arizona, at the other side of Ash Fork. They had a railroad camp there where we all worked for a while. Then we were told, "You'll have to move now, go back to your country. There is no more work here. . . ." [80–81]

[Editor's note: Because Frank knows a little English he finds various jobs at trading posts, a mission, and a sawmill. He marries, obtains a wagon from the government, and becomes a freighter, hauling supplies from Gallup, New Mexico, to Chinle.]

Later on I came back over here because my wife's parents were getting pretty old and sick. I gave up hauling freight and started tending their farm and livestock. My father-in-law was a well-to-do man: he had cattle and sheep and horses and I just started taking care of them for him. Also, I knew that he was a Blessingway singer and I went out with him whenever he performed this ceremony. I noticed that the songs I learned from He Who Seeks War were the same as the ones my father-in-law was singing.

Before I began to learn these things, way back before that, I did not even think about life as being an important thing. I did not try to remember things or keep track of what happened at certain times. Nothing seemed to matter to me, I just didn't care about anything, so long as I kept on living. But then when I began to learn the Blessingway it changed my whole life. I began really thinking about ceremonies. I had heard singing before that but now I began to take it more seriously because I began to realize what life was and the kind of hardships we have to go through. Before I started learning Blessingway, the older people used to tell me that I should think about life more seriously. "If you don't know any songs you have nothing to go by. If a child grows up in a family like that he doesn't know where he is going or what he is doing." That is what the older people told me, that I should have something to live by. . . . I used to go out with my father-in-law, Man Who Shouts, whenever he was asked to perform the Blessingway. I went wherever he did. At first I just watched and then finally I had learned practically everything he was doing and before I knew it I was helping him with the ceremony. Finally I reached the point where I had learned it well enough so that I had a ceremony of my own. . . . [192–93]

[My father-in-law said to me,] "If you are a singer, if you remember your ceremonies really well even if you get old, even if you get blind and deaf, you'll still remember everything by heart, how each part of the ceremony is performed." He said to me, "Even though you are so old you can't ride a horse or you can't even see anymore, people will still have a use for you until old age finally finishes you off."

So that is why I chose that way of life. And I believe it now: it is true that even as old as I am now, unable to get around too much, people still come to have my ceremony done over them. I have it inside my head so well that I remember everything and even though I can't get around they come in a wagon or a car for me and take me over to where the ceremony is needed and then bring me back. So I think my father-in-law was right. If I had decided to be a farmer at that time I probably wouldn't have lasted very long. [193–94]

It is a custom with the People that, for instance, some family, even though everything may be going all right and nothing is wrong, still may say, "Well, let's have a Blessingway to freshen things up, to renew ourselves again." So they do. Or sometimes they might have acquired some valuable goods, if they have been off trading or something, and have brought them home. Then the things that they brought in from other places, well, it is on their minds that, "That's what we're blessed with in this family." They might feel they need the Blessingway because you do not wait until some misfortune happens before you have it. That is the reason it is called the peaceful way, the healing way, the blessing way. There is no specific time . . . it depends on the family. If they feel they should have it, then they do it, just an ordinary Blessingway.

Of course if you are able to have that ceremony, if you have the means to put it on, well, then you should do it. But if you have not, then in that case you just keep putting it off until you are able to bear the cost. . . .

Blessingway is used for everything that is good for a person, or for the people. It has no use other than that. For instance, when a woman is pregnant she has the Blessingway in order to have a good delivery with no trouble. It is also done so that she and her child may have a happy life. In case of bad dreams it is a kind of warning that there are some misfortunes ahead of you; in order to avoid that you have Blessingway so that you will have happiness instead. Or if you are worried about something, your family will want to get you back, to get that out of your mind, out of your system, so that you may have a good life. It is the same for any other things that could cause you to worry, to feel uneasy about yourself. That is the sort of thing it is used for. As for the prayers, you say, "Beauty shall be in front of me, beauty shall be in the back, beauty shall be below me, above me, all around me." On top of that you say about yourself, "I am everlasting, I may have an everlasting life with beauty." You end your prayers that way. . . .
[218–19]

I remember all that I know about the Blessingway because I had those years of study to get it all in my head. And from my experience of learning I understand that it is not just my ability that makes it possible. I believe that there is a spirit that really is answering my prayers, because all these years I would not have been able to learn so much if I did not have such help. I could not do it by myself, so there must be something beyond human power helping me. . . . [237–38]

In Navajo religion there are prayers for certain purposes. I found out from my own father that in Blessingway there was a song for headman, and I learned that from him. I think that this is another reason why things came easily for me when I was talking to the People. It may be one reason that I was recognized for being a talker and a leader among the People, why I became well known as a headman and even eventually ended up in the Tribal Council. . . . [241]

There are lots of songs that go with being a headman or leader. They start out from the beginning, way back with the first people. The story starts with how it was planned at first and how the first people decided who were to be the chiefs. After these chiefs were elected, the songs go along describing how they were dressed. They tell about all of the things they were wearing, their shoes, leggings, sash and skirts, belts, wristlets and beads, their head plumes and everything up to the last thing, that which is put in their mouths from which their speeches are known. That last thing is like the power to speak; it was put into their mouths so they could have the wisdom to say wise things and so the People could understand them. There are enough of those songs to sing them all night without sleeping. The songs are used in a series, but they are not just to be sung any place. You can only use them when someone is going to be a chief, a good leader; they can have the songs done for them. There are so many songs in that series that you could almost have a Blessingway done with them; there are just about as many songs involved in that as there are in the Blessingway itself. From the start to the end of that, the whole thing is like a Blessingway. The story of the songs are just like Blessingway right from the beginning: how the earth was first formed, how the mountains came up. The songs go on like that. It would probably take a little longer to do than the regular Blessingway; it is just like Blessingway when you do that except that the ceremony is mostly just singing. Almost all of what takes place is the singing of the Chief songs. . . . [244]

Once I was placed there as one of the councilmen, I began to be asked to do different things. One of the things that there was a lot of talk about during this time was education and the need for building schools on the reservation. We also talked about hospitals and preventing outsiders from moving in with different things like industrial plants. We did a lot of work and I concerned myself with all those things. . . . [256] We talked about that a lot on the Council, and we decided to ask for the schools and also hospitals and all of those things from Washington.

Several of us were then appointed to go to Washington to ask that these things be granted. I went over there with several other men. We went before those people and asked for a school and a hospital and other things. Henry Taliman, the tribal chairman, Howard Gorman, the vice-chairman, and Red Moustache's brother were some of the others who went over there, too. We were asked to fly there but most of the delegates were afraid of going in an airplane, so we went on the train. While we were there we were given sight-seeing tours around Washington. I got to see the White House, Arlington Cemetery, the Unknown Soldier's Tomb, and other places. One of the delegates got tired when we were near the Washington Monument. He wanted to rest but he could not find a place to sit down. So he took off his moccasins and laid down on the grass in front of the Monument. He was wearing half-socks like the ones I used to knit for myself. This man went to sleep and while he was sleeping a crowd gathered around looking at him. When he woke up he asked me, "What are all of these people standing around here looking at me for?" I said, "My younger brother, they are waiting for you to get up to see what kind of a creature you are. They are wondering whether or not when you get up you will crawl on all fours, like a bear." He replied, "You bear, you would say that." [257–58]

While I, myself, stand for the good of the People, right now I am just watching these things. I cannot step in there and try to do some of the things I used to do because I am getting pretty well along in years. So I just sit by and watch. I think about the future; of course I may never get to see it, but I just wonder how things will be in so many years, what improvements there will be for the benefit of the People. I wish I were young again, so I could see more of these things as time goes on. But those are just wishes and of course I do not expect to see those things. . . . [310–11]

In the early days, the old people were our teachers. They said that as long as we observed the rules laid down for us by the Holy People, everything was going to go along smoothly. But they said it would not last forever. Sooner or later we were going to start breaking the rules. Then that would lead us to ruin. It is like a seed of any kind, like corn, or beans, or anything that you put in the ground. You plant it, and it sprouts and bears fruit and grows to a certain extent. When it matures you harvest what it has produced; the stalks and leaves wither because their use is past. But you still have the seeds to continue planting and arriving at a new life. That is what the older people taught us. If you did not observe these things you are bound to ruin yourself. . . . [311]

When you get put into a position of leadership, that teaches you to have some respect. Even if you have been irresponsible in the past, you now have to behave and lead a good life as an example to your people. [315]

There are still lots of people coming around here wanting me to do Blessingway for them, but sometimes now because of my physical condition I have to refuse. When they come to ask, it just depends on how I feel. If I think that I can stand it, then I accept. . . . But a lot of the time now I'm not able to sing Blessingway. I can't stand the strain of being in a sitting position for that long, and my voice also gets tired. I especially feel the strain in the wintertime. The nights are long then, and performing that Blessingway is very strenuous even though we wait to start the all-night singing until pretty well on into the night. Of course in the summertime the nights are short. I will do Blessingway again when I get well and when I think that I am able to do it.

As you know, last fall I had my sacred bundle renewed and, of course, a Blessingway was used for that. But even though I had that and all of the other ceremonials I've been telling you about, right now my ailments are still hanging on. I still think we have not done the complete cure. The doctors do not seem to be able to tell me what the matter is, either. I went over to the Ganado hospital and they thoroughly examined my body. They could not find anything anywhere that could be causing my troubles. Finally they decided to take some tissue out of my stomach, just a small piece. I was not really operated on then. The doctor just said that there was no equipment there at Ganado to analyze what they had taken out of me, and that he would send it to Denver to find out what it was. They gave me some medicine and told me to go home. . . . [321–22]

While I was over at the Ganado hospital, and even before I went there, I had a lot of dreams and most of them were about dead people, those who had already passed away, even women. Those things were beginning to bother me; I was worrying about them. So I decided to have another ceremony. I also wanted to see if I could get some relief from the pains that I was feeling a lot of time. So I went and asked Black Sheep from Black Mountain to come over here and perform some of his small ceremonies for me to see if those could straighten out my dreams and give me some relief from those pains. He came down here and did some Ghostway rituals for me. He said prayers, cut prayersticks, bathed me and painted me with the blackening and reddening cere- monies. You can do those things to find out what effect they will have. If you feel a bit better after those, then you can go ahead and have the big ceremonial. After he did that I don't remember having any more dreams. I just forgot all about them. Before those things were done, as soon as I woke up, I would begin to think about what I had been dreaming about, but since then I do not do that any more. I still dream, but I do not remember what those dreams are about. I have felt a little better since Black Sheep performed all of those things for me, and right now I am thinking about calling him back again for a big, regular five-night Ghostway. Then, maybe I will go back to the hospital again. . . . [323]

THE NATIVE AMERICAN CHURCH

In their comparatively recent history the Navajos have felt the call of two highly organized religious movements from outside their traditional culture. One is evangelical Christianity. The other is the Native American Church, an Indian movement with roots in ancient Mexico and recent development in Oklahoma. This religion established itself firmly in the United States in the nineteenth cen- tury and thereafter developed different perspectives and music from that which can still be seen among the Tarahumare and Huichol Indians of Mexico. It found its way into the Navajo country in the 1930s. By the 1950s it had grown in this one tribe to a membership estimated at twenty thousand.

This music is strikingly different from traditional Navajo music. Let us listen to a hymn from the Native American Church and then consider the role of this music in contemporary Navajo life (recorded selection 8, ex. 2–6).

What first arrests the attention is the quiet, introspective quality of the singing in this simple melody. Members of the Native American Church speak of their music as prayer. Although the text has no translatable words, the repetitive sim- plicity of vocables and music expresses a rapt, inward feeling. According to one theory, Native American Church hymns are derived from Christian hymnody. The quiet, slow movement and the unadorned voice, so unlike the usual boister- ous, emphatic, out-of-doors delivery in Indian singing, seem to suggest this inter- pretation. On the other hand, there are many more features that are all Indian: the rhythmic limitation to only two note values, ♪ ♩ (a specialty of Navajo and Apache music), the descending melodic direction, the rattle and drum accompa- niment, the pure melody without harmony, the use of vocables. These features are present in Native American Church music in many different tribes all across the continent to such a marked extent that a distinct, pantribal "Peyote style" can be identified (McAllester 1949:12, 80-82). In the present song, every phrase ends on "he ne yo," anticipating the "he ne yo we" of the last phrase. This ending, al- ways sung entirely on the tonic, is as characteristic of Native American Church music as "amen" is to Christian hymns and prayers.

Ex. 2–6.   Navajo Peyote song. With permission of Willard Rhodes.

True to its Oklahoma origin, the Native American Church ideally holds its meetings in a large Plains Indian tipi. This is often erected on Saturday evening for the all-night meeting and then taken away to be stored until the next weekend. Such mobility enables the meeting to move to wherever members want a service. Meetings are sometimes held in hogans since they, too, are circular and have an earth floor where the sacred fire and altar can be built.

The Indians of the Native American Church use a water drum and a rattle to accompany their singing. The drum is made of a small, old-fashioned, three-legged iron pot with a wet, almost rubbery, buckskin drumhead stretched over the opening. The pot is half full of water, which is splashed over the inside of the drumhead from time to time by giving the drum a tossing motion. This act serves to keep the drumhead moist and flexible while in use. The player kneels, holding the drum on the ground tipped toward his drumming hand. He controls the tone with pressure on the drumhead from the thumb of his holding hand. He strikes the membrane rapidly and rather heavily with a smooth, hard, slightly decorated drumstick. It is supposed that the water inside the pot has something to do with the strong resonance of this and other kinds of water drums, but no physical studies have yet been made to test the theory.

The peyote rattle is made with a small gourd mounted on a handle stick in much the same way as the cowhorn rattle of the Iroquois (see pp. 26–28). There is no carved shelf on the handle, however: the stick merely fits very snugly into the gourd plug so that it is wedged tight. The distal (far) end of the stick protrudes two or three inches beyond the gourd, and a tuft of dyed horsehair is attached. This is often red to symbolize the red flower of the peyote cactus. Many Native American Church members hold a beautifully decorated feather fan during the service and use it to waft toward themselves the fragrant incense of cedar needles when these are put into the fire. The feathers of the fan are mounted in separate moveable leather sleeves, like the feathers of the Plains warbonnet. This allows the user to manipulate the fan in such a way that each feather seems to have a quivering life of its own.

The ritual consists of long prayers, many groups of four songs each (sung in turn by members of the meetings), a special water break at midnight, and a fellowship breakfast in the morning. At intervals, under the direction of the leader of the meetings, a Cedar Chief builds up the fire, puts cedar incense on the coals, and passes the cigarettes to make the sacred smoke that accompanies the prayers. He also passes small pieces of a cactus called *peyote* (from the Aztec *peyotl* "wooly," describing the fine white hairs that grow in tufts on the cactus). When eaten, peyote produces a sense of well-being and, sometimes, visions in vivid color. The peyote is eaten as a sacrament, since Father Peyote is one of the deities of the religion. The Native American Church is sometimes called the Peyote Church.

A crescent-shaped earthen altar six or seven feet long lies west of the fire, and a large peyote cactus, symbolic of Father Peyote, is placed at the midpoint of the crescent. Prayers may be directed to Father Peyote, and some members can hear him responding to their pleas for help in meeting the difficulties of life. The intense feeling of dedication and piety at Peyote Meetings is expressed through prayers and testimonies, often with tears running down the cheeks of the speaker. Prayers include appeals to Jesus and God, as well as to Father Peyote. Peyotists consider that the Native American Church is hospitable to all other religions and includes their ideas in its philosophy and beliefs. Prayers are made for friends and family members who are ill or otherwise in need of help. Leaders of the church, of the Navajo tribe, and of the country at large are also included in the prayers.

The Native American Church was bitterly opposed by the more tradition-minded Navajos; in the late 1940s meetings were raided by the police and church leaders were jailed. But the church constituency grew so large that the new religion had to be accepted, and today the tipis for peyote meetings can be seen in many Navajo communities. One of these tipis stands near the Cultural Center of the Navajo Community College, where participation in the Native American Church's meetings is a recognized student activity.

THE WATER DRUM

The water drum is widespread in North and South America. It is the only drum used in traditional Navajo and Apache music. The Navajos make theirs on a clay pot eight or ten inches high and use an unusual drumstick made of a twig bent around and tied in a loop at the distal end. The Apaches use the same kind of drumstick but make the drum of a large iron pot. The buckskin drumhead is stretched over an opening two or two-and-a-half feet across, and several of the singers beat the drum at the same time. A deep booming sound is produced, in contrast to the softer thump of the Navajo drum (see ill. 2-11).

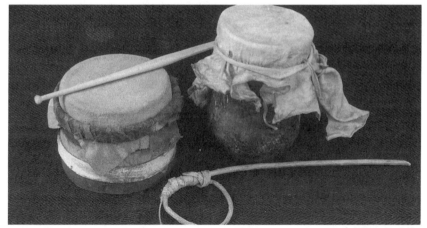

Susan W. McAllester

**Ill. 2–11.   Two kinds of water drum. On the left is an Iroquois drum
made from a short section of hollowed-out log. On the right is a
Navajo pottery water drum, used only in the Enemyway ceremony.**

The Iroquois and the Chippewas in the Eastern Woodlands make water drums using a hollowed-out log or a wooden keg. They do not have the looped drumstick but use a straight stick somewhat carved or, as in the case of the medicine drum of the Menomini, a somewhat elaborate curved stick. Eastern Woodland water drums range from five or six inches to two feet or more in height and from five or six inches across the drumhead to as much as fourteen inches or more.

The peyote drum seems to be an elaboration on the pot drum of the Navajos and Apaches. Nowadays the old-fashioned pot is hard to find, and members of the Native American Church can buy a specially manufactured aluminum replica that is much lighter to handle and gives the same sound. The church has also developed its own kinds of jewelry and costume and a genre of Indian painting depicting peyote meetings and peyote visions.

Since the water drum is so widespread in North and South America, it would be an interesting project for students of Native American music to make one. The peyote drum is difficult to assemble. It is also so intensely symbolic to members of the Native American Church that it might be in questionable taste for a non-member to attempt to make this particular kind of water drum. However, the traditional Iroquois, Navajo, and Apache water drums are used for social dancing and so do not have the same religious feelings associated with them.

Figure 2–13 contains the instructions for making a simple water drum. Iron pots or wooden kegs are hard to find, but a number ten tin can makes a good substitute. Buckskin is also difficult to obtain, but a chamois skin from an auto supply store or a piece of rubber from an inner tube can be used instead. Indians sometimes make such an alternative drum themselves if they cannot obtain the traditional materials.

#10 can with one end / open

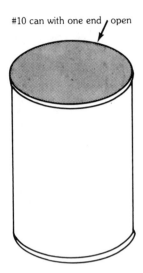

Inner tubing or chamois skin cut to size

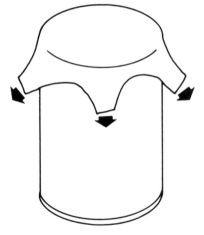

Water added and drumhead stretched in place. This takes two people to give the four pulling points needed (indicated by arrows).

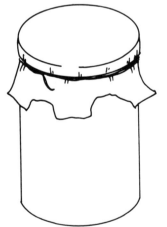

Drumhead tied in place with cord, or better yet with something stretchy like wet rawhide or a long, thin rubber strip cut from an inner tube.

hard, smooth wooden drumstick, slightly carved or incised.

Fig. 2–13.   Steps in making a water drum.

THE SUN DANCE

Another importation of a Native American religion, the Plains Sun Dance, has occurred as recently as the 1980s on the Navajo reservation. This world renewal ceremony has undergone a revival on the Plains, and Sun Dance priests have been invited to Navajo communities to perform the ceremony and teach it to Navajo participants.

NAVAJO HYMN MUSIC

Sharing the popularity of peyote hymns among the requests that come in at the rate of several hundred a week at such radio stations as WGLF in Gallup, New Mexico, are Christian hymns. The many Christian missions on the reservation are appreciated for their ministry by the Navajos who have joined them. The hospitals, schools, and other services associated with the missions are a boon not only to church members but also to the hundreds of other Navajos who take advantage of them.

Navajo listeners make requests for particular hymns on the occasion of a birthday in the family, the anniversary of a death, or some other signal family event. When the request and the hymn are broadcast, the occasion is made known to hundreds of listeners. The hymns may be performed by nationally known gospel singers, but Navajo gospel singers as well have made records, and requests are likely to focus on these. One such group is the Chinle Galileans, a Navajo country gospel group. Their lyrics are in English, and their music is the familiar country combination of electric guitar and percussion (recorded selection 9, ex. 2-7).

Ex. 2–7. "Clinging to a Saving Hand." With the permission of Roland Dixon.

The interesting thing about this music is that it has so few features that could be called traditionally Indian. Like the Fenders (p. 32), the Galileans have adopted a new style of music wholeheartedly. The clues that the performers are Navajos are in the singers' Navajo accent and, in the case of the Fenders, in certain melodic and rhythmic short-cuts, compared with the Anglo original. This is what appeals to Navajo listeners and makes them feel that the performing groups are some of "their own."

NEW COMPOSERS IN TRADITIONAL MODES

Among the new kinds of Navajo music is a genre of recently composed songs based, musically, on Enemyway style (usually Sway songs or Dance songs) but not intended for use in that ceremony. The texts are in Navajo, since the songs are intended for Navajo listeners, but they contain social commentary in a different vein from that in the popular songs of Enemyway. The new message is one of protest. A good illustration would be the treatment of the use of alcohol in the old songs and the new. The first example in this contrast is a Skip Dance song from Enemyway (fig. 2–14), probably dating from the 1920s.

"Navajo Inn" is a recent song by Lena Tsoisdia, a social service worker at Window Rock, the headquarters of the Navajo tribal government. The title takes its name from a drive-in liquor store that used to do a thriving business a few miles from Window Rock. The store was just across the reservation boundary and was thus outside the jurisdiction of the tribal prohibition laws. The lyrics refer to the Inn and speak despairingly of women finding their husbands, unconscious, behind "the tall fence."

Ruth Roessel, a prominent Navajo educator, has composed a song about the "Long Walk," when the Navajos were rounded up by Kit Carson and his troops in 1864 and forcibly removed to a large concentration camp at Ft. Sumner, New Mexico. The hardships of the march, which preceded four years of captivity, and the Navajo love for their land are recounted here (fig. 2–15).

The two examples here have not been recorded on commercial discs, but several Navajo composers of new songs in styles based on Enemyway popular songs have published their work on popular discs. Kay Bennett (Kaibah) has produced three records on her own label. Danny Whitefeather Begay, Cindy Yazzie, and Roger McCabe have released *My Beautiful Land* on the Canyon Records label with fifteen popular songs in this new genre. "Los Angeles Sweetheart" by Danny Whitefeather Begay gives an idea of how those songs go (fig. 2–16). It is in the Skip Dance style as indicated by the formula

he   ye,   ya - na

'E- ne- ya,

My younger brother,
My whiskey, have some! Naṇa, he, ne-ye,

My younger brother,
My whiskey, have some! Naṇa, he, ne-ye,

Your whiskey is all gone, ne,
My whiskey, there's still some, wo,

He yo-o-wo-wo, he yo-o-wo-wo,
Heya, we, heyana, he, nai-ya.

Fig. 2–14.   Lyrics, Navajo Enemyway Skip Dance song.

In this record many of the songs are nostalgic, about Navajos who have left the reservation to find work and wish they could go home again. Others are "flirting songs" referring to the courtship situation at a Squaw Dance. The mingling of the new experience in big cities and the traditional dance scene at an Enemyway ceremonial is reflected in the record's cover design, which combines the four sacred mountains, automobiles, hogans, and skyscrapers.

Long, long ago, our people,
Our grandfathers, our grandmothers,
Walking that long distance,
There was no food, there was no water,
But they were walking a long distance,
But they were walking a long distance!

At Fort Sumner, it was when they got there
They were treated badly,
They were treated badly.

"I wish I were still back in my own home,
I wish I were still back in my own home!
We shall never forget this,
The walk that we are taking now.
We shall never forget this,
The walk that we are taking now.
Even then, we still like our own land,
Even then, we still like our own land!"

Fig. 2–15.   Lyrics, "The Long Walk." With the permission of Ruth Roessel.

Heye, yaŋa, heye, yaŋa,

Awe 'a-no 'aweya'a heye, yaŋa,
Awe 'a-no 'aweya'a heye, yaŋa,

Hene ya'o wowo 'awe ya'a heye, yaŋa,
Hene ya'o wowo 'awe ya'a heye, yaŋa,

Oh, that girl, oh, that girl,
To a place called "L.A.," that's where she went,
She went, aweya'a heye, yaŋa,
To a place called "L.A.," that's where she went,
She went, aweya'a heye, yaŋa,
"All kinds of jobs for you," she wrote,
But she had another man, 'ano 'aweya'a heye, yaŋa,

Hene ya'o wowo 'awe ya'a heye, yaŋa,
Hene ya'o wowo 'awe ya'a heye, yaŋa.

Fig. 2–16. Lyrics, "Los Angeles Sweetheart." With the permission of Robert Doyle.

MUSIC WITH NEWLY CREATED NAVAJO TEXTS AND MELODIES

This recent genre is well-represented by Sharon Burch's "Mother Earth" (recorded selection 10, fig. 2–17) from her tape *Yazzie Girl* (1989). She accompanies herself on a guitar in a chantlike melody of her own composition. "She credits her inspiration as a songwriter to the songs, prayers and chants she recalls from her childhood" (Burch 1989).

Chorus:
Heiyee' t' áá al tso baa hózhóogo.   Heiyee' everything brings happiness.
Heiyee' t' áá al tso baa hózhóogo.   Heiyee' everything brings happiness.
Heineiyaa.   Heineiyaa.

Nahasdzáán bii' sézį,   I am part of Mother Earth.
Nahasdzáán bikee' shikee'.   Mother Earth's feet are my feet.
Nahasdzáán bijáád shijáád.   Mother Earth's legs are my legs.
Nahasdzáán bidziil shidziil.   Mother Earth's strength is my strength.
Nahasdzáán bigaan shigaan.   Mother Earth's arms are my arms.

Nahasdzáán bináá' hóló, shináá' hóló   Mother Earth has a vision, I have a vision.

(Chorus)
(first five lines of second verse, as in first verse)

Nahasdzáán binitsékees shinitsékees.   Mother Earth's consciousness is my consciousness.

(Chorus)

Fig. 2–17. Lyrics of "Mother Earth," in Navajo with English translation. With permission of Robert Doyle.

Ill. 2–12.   Sharon Burch. Photo © John Running. Courtesy of Robert Doyle.

NEW NAVAJO MUSIC WITH ENGLISH TEXTS AND ORCHESTRAL ACCOMPANIMENT

Arliene Nofchissey Williams has been called "the Navajo nightingale." Her compositions stem from the Mormon sect of Christianity and express, musically and in words, both her religious perceptions and her Indian-ness. She wrote one of her songs, "Proud Earth" (recorded selection), when she was a student at Brigham Young University. The words (fig. 12–18) reflect the Mormon respect for Native American culture and the Indian closeness to nature. At the same time, the song conveys the aspiration of the Latter Day Saints to unite the Indian people under one God. Musically, there are such Indian elements as the use of a steady, repetitive drumbeat and vocables, as well as European-American elements such as a string orchestra, harmonies, interpretive dynamics, and a text in English. The use of the voice of the late Chief Dan George, an Indian film star, as narrator adds to the richness of the production. The song has been a "hit" on the Navajo reservation and elsewhere among Indian people. It was produced in Nashville with all the musical technology that the name implies, and at the same time it is an Indian message song, telling the world what the Native Americans feel they have to contribute to world culture from their mythopoeic philosophy of nature. A more recent rendition of "Proud Earth" can be heard on Williams 1989.

Proud Earth (The Song of the People)

The beat of my heart is kept alive in my drum,
And my plight echoes in the canyons, the meadows, the plains,
And my laughter runs free with the deer,
And my tears fall with the rain,
But my soul knows no pain.

I am one with nature,
Mother Earth is at my feet,
And my God is up above me,
And I'll sing the song of my People.

Come with me, take my hand, come alive with my chant (heya, heya)
For my life already knows wisdom, balance and beauty.
Let your heart be free from fear (heya, heya)
And your joy meet with mine,
For the peace we can find.

We are one with nature,
Mother Earth is at our feet,
And our God is up above us,
And we'll sing the song, the song of the people (heya, heya),
And we'll sing the song, the song of the people.

Fig. 2–18.   Lyrics, "Proud Earth." With permission of Arliene Nofchissey Williams.

THE NATIVE AMERICAN FLUTE REVIVAL

The Native American flute revival probably began in the 1970s in Oklahoma when "Doc Tate" Nevaquaya made the first commercial recording consisting entirely of music of the Plains courting flute (Smythe 1989:68). But it was a Navajo, R. Carlos Nakai, whose moving, improvisatory compositions, often with synthesizer or orchestral accompaniments, carried the instrument to worldwide popularity and created a large following of imitators, both Indian and non-Indian (McAllester 1994). Nakai's first album appeared in 1982; since then he has made nineteen others to date, one of them in Germany and another in Japan. *Cycles* (1985) was chosen by the Martha Graham Dance Company to provide the music for their ballet *Nightchant.* Nakai has performed with several symphony orchestras and was awarded the Arizona Governor's Arts Award in 1992 and an honorary doctorate by Northern Arizona University in 1994. In that same year, *Ancestral Voices,* his third collaboration with guitarist William Eaton, was a Grammy Awards finalist in Best Traditional Folk Music. An example of his improvisation with synthesizer (recorded selection 12) is taken from *Cycles.* It is entitled "Origins"; Nakai comments in the liner notes: "My clan, Naashteezhi dine-e Taachiinii, allows me to be one of the People" (Nakai 1985). Throughout his work the commentary accompanying the music stresses respect for the environment and a very Navajo celebration of tribal connections and harmony with nature.

We have ranged over the music of several generations and several religions in an effort to find clues to the thought of just one Indian tribe. Even so we have barely touched on the complexities of this rich and rapidly changing culture. One of the most powerful messages that reaches the outsider is that Indian traditional culture is still vital and growing in its own ways even while Native American people are adopting new ideas and technology from the Euro-American culture around them. This fact is clearly reflected in the many different kinds of music that coexist on the Navajo reservation and in thousands of Navajo homes in Chicago, Los Angeles, San Francisco, and innumerable other locations away from the reservation.

To varying degrees this picture of Navajo music exemplifies what is happening to other Indian communities around the country. The different Indian cultures are embarked on an adventure in which the larger populace around them must inevitably share. Many Indian elements have already become part of the culture that is called "American." Some of these have been superficial: an Indian word such as "squash" or "moose," or a bit of local legend. Other contributions have had enormous economic import, such as the corn and potatoes that feed much of the world. There is now evidence that some of the music and the other Indian arts, and the religious and philosophical ideas that lie beneath them, are becoming accessible to an increasingly sympathetic American public. No culture remains static, and the Indians will continue to contribute to other world cultures, which are themselves in the process of change.

John Running

Ill. 2–13.   R. Carlos Nakai. Navajo flutist and educator.

REFERENCES CITED

Burch, Sharon
  1989   *Yazzie Girl.* Canyon Records CR534 (Phoenix, Ariz.). Cassette.

Densmore, Frances
  1910   *Chippewa Music.* Washington, D.C.: Bureau of American Ethnology Bulletin 45.

Farella, John R.
  1984   *The Main Stalk: A Synthesis of Navajo Philosophy.* Tucson: Univ. of Arizona
          Press.

Faris, James C.
  1990   *The Nightway: A History and a History of Documentation of a Navajo Ceremo-
          nial.* Albuquerque: Univ. of New Mexico Press.

The Fenders
  1966   *Second Time 'Round.* Thoreau, N. Mex. 12″ LP recording.

Fenton, William
  1942   *Songs from the Iroquois Longhouse.* Washington, D.C.: Smithsonian Institution
          Publication 369.

———.
  N.d.   *Songs from the Iroquois Longhouse.* Library of Congress AFS L6.

Frisbie, Charlotte J., and David P. McAllester.
  1978   *Navajo Blessingway Singer: Frank Mitchell, 1881-1967.* Tucson: Univ. of Ari-
          zona Press.

Gill, Sam D.
  1981   *Sacred Words: A Study of Navajo Religion and Prayer.* Westport, Conn.:
          Greenwood Press.

Haile, Fr. Berard
  1938   *Origin Legend of the Navajo Enemy Way.* New Haven, Conn.: Yale Univ. Press.

———.
  1947   *Prayerstick Cutting in a Five Night Ceremonial of the Male Branch of Shoot-
          ingway.* Chicago: Univ. of Chicago Press.

Kluckhohn, Clyde, and Dorothea Leighton
  1938   *The Navajo.* Cambridge: Harvard Univ. Press.

Kluckhohn, Clyde, and Leland C. Wyman
  1940   *An Introduction to Navajo Chant Practice.* Menasha, Wis.: Memoirs of the
          American Anthropological Association, no. 53.

Kurath, Gertrude P.
  1966   *Michigan Indian Festivals.* Ann Arbor, Mich.: Ann Arbor Publishers.

Matthews, Washington
  1894   "Songs of Sequence of the Navajos," *Journal of American Folk-Lore* 7:185–94.

McAllester, David P.
  1949   *Peyote Music.* New York: Viking Fund Publications in Antropology, no. 13.

———.
  1954   *Enemy Way Music.* Papers of the Peabody Museum of Archaeology and Eth-
          nology, vol. 41, no. 5. Cambridge, Mass.: Harvard Univ. Press.

————.

1994 "The Music of R. Carlos Nakai." In *To the Four Corners: A Festschrift in Honor of Rose Brandel,* ed. Ellen C. Leichtman. Warren, Mich.: Harmonie Park Press.

My Beautiful Land and Other Navajo Songs

N.d. Canyon Records Productions ARP 6078 (Phoenix, Ariz.). Danny Whitefeather Begay, Cindy Yazzi, and Roger McCabe. LP.

Nakai, Carlos

1985 *Cycles: Native American Flute Music.* Canyon Records Productions CR614-C (Phoenix, Ariz.). Cassette.

Navajo Country Gospel

N.d. The Chinle Galileans. LPS 9039 (Chinle, Ariz.) Larry Emerson, Jerry Tom, Roland Dixon, Donnie Tsosie, Lee Begaye, Emerson Luther. LP.

Proud Earth

N.d. Salt City Records SC-60 (Provo, Utah). Chief Dan George, Arliene Nofchissey Williams, Rick Brosseau. LP.

Reichard, Gladys A.

1928 *Social Life of the Navajo Indians.* New York: Columbia Univ. Press.

————.

1950 *Navajo Religion.* New York: Bollingen Foundation.

Rhodes, Willard, ed.

N.d. *Navajo: Folk Music of the United States.* Washington, D.C.: Library of Congress, Division of Music, Archive of American Folk Song AFS L41.

————.

N.d. *Puget Sound: Folk Music of the United States.* Washington, D.C.: Library of Congress, Division of Music, Archive of American Folk Song AAFS L34. With 36-page booklet on Northwest Coast culture (Erna Gunther) and music (Willard Rhodes).

Sachs, Curt

1962 *The Wellsprings of Music.* The Hague: Martinus Nijhof.

Sioux Favorites

N.d. Canyon Records Productions ARP 6059 (Phoenix, Ariz.). Cassette.

Smythe, Willie

1989 "Songs of Indian Territory." In *Songs of Indian Territory: Native American Music Traditions of Oklahoma.* Oklahoma City: Center for the American Indian.

Songs from the Navajo Nation

N.d. Recorded by Kay Bennet (Kaibah). Produced by K. C. Bennet. (Gallup, N. Mex.). LP.

Witherspoon, Gary

1977 *Language and Art in the Navajo Universe.* Ann Arbor: Univ. of Michigan Press.

Witmer, Robert

1973 "Recent Change in the Musical Culture of the Blood Indians of Alberta, Canada." *Yearbook for Inter-American Musical Research* 9:64–94.

Wyman, Leland C.

1983 *Southwest Indian Drypainting.* Albuquerque: Univ. of New Mexico Press.

ADDITIONAL READING

Bailey, Garrick, and Roberta Glenn Bailey
1986   *A History of the Navajos: The Reservation Years.* Santa Fe, N. Mex.: School of American Research Press.

Deloria, Vine, Jr.
1969   *Custer Died for Your Sins: An Indian Manifesto.* London: Collier-Macmillan.

Dyk, Walter
1966   *Son of Old Man Hat.* Lincoln: Univ. of Nebraska Press.

Goodman, James B.
1986   *The Navajo Atlas: Environments, Resources, People, and the History of the Diné Bikeyah.* Norman: Univ. of Oklahoma Press.

Griffin-Pierce, Trudy
1992   *Earth Is My Mother, Sky Is My Father: Space, Time, and Astronomy in Navajo Sandpainting.* Albuquerque: Univ. of New Mexico Press.

Hadley, Linda
1986   *Hózhǫ́ǫ́jí Hané' (Blessingway).* Rough Rock, Ariz.: Rough Rock Demonstration School. (In English and Navajo.)

McNeley, James K.
1981   *Holy Wind in Navajo Philosophy.* Tucson: Univ. of Arizona Press.

Neihardt, John G.
1961   *Black Elk Speaks.* Lincoln: Univ. of Nebraska Press.

Underhill, Ruth M.
1953   *Red Man's America.* Chicago: Univ. of Chicago Press.

ADDITIONAL LISTENING

Anilth, Wilson, and Hanson Ashley
1981   *Navajo Peyote Ceremonial Songs, vol. 1.* Indian House 1541 (Taos, N. Mex.). LP.

Boniface Bonnie Singers
1968   *Navajo Sway Songs.* Indian House 1581 (Taos, N. Mex.). LP.

Boulton, Laura
1957   *Indian Music of the Southwest.* Smithsonian/Folkways 8850 (Washington, D.C.). With 11-page booklet. LP.

———.
1992   *Navajo Songs.* Recorded by Laura Boulton in 1933 and 1940. Annotated by Charlotte Frisbie and David McAllester. Washington, D.C.: Smithsonian/Folkways, SF 40403. CD, cassette.

Burton, Bryan
1993   *Moving Within the Circle: Contemporary Native American Music and Dance.* Danbury, Conn.: World Music Press. WMP 012. Cassette.

DeMars, James
1991   *Spirit Horses, Concerto for Native American Flute and Chamber Orchestra.* Composed for and performed by R. Carlos Nakai. Phoenix, Ariz.: Canyon Records Productions, CR-7014. CD, cassette.

Four Corner Yeibichai
    1988   Canyon Records Productions 7152 (Phoenix, Ariz.). LP, cassette.

Iroquois Social Dance Songs
    1969   Iroqrafts QC 727 (Ohsweken, Ontario, Canada). 3 vols. LP.

Isaacs, Tony
    1968   *Night and Daylight Yeibichai.* Indian House IH 1502 (Taos, N. Mex.). LP.

Rhodes, Willard
    1949   *Music of the Sioux and the Navajo.* Smithsonian/Folkways 4401 (Washington, D.C.). LP. With 6-page pamphlet.

Smith Family Gospel Singers
    1987   *Touching Jesus, vol. 2.* Canyon Records, 620 (Phoenix, Ariz.). Cassette.

Williams, Arliene Nofchissey
    1989   *Encircle . . . in the arms of His love.* Composed and performed by Arliene Nofchissey Williams, featuring flutist John Rainer, Jr. Blanding, Utah: Proud Earth Productions, PE-90. Cassette.

XIT
    1972   *Plight of the Red Man.* Motown Record Corp. R536L (Detroit). LP. Protest songs in rock style; XIT is an acronym for "Crossing of Indian Tribes," in reference to the pantribal makeup of the group.

MAJOR SOURCES FOR RECORDINGS

Canyon Records Productions,   4143 North Sixteenth Street, Phoenix, Ariz. 85016, phone: (602) 266-7835. This is the major distributor of native American recordings. It not only stocks the large inventory under its own label but keeps in print many of the recordings of smaller distributors, some of which might otherwise have gone out of business. It carries recordings of traditional music and also newer genres such as Indian rock, gospel, and country and western.

Indian House,   Box 472, Taos, N. Mex. 87571, phone: (505) 776-2953. This company specializes in traditional Indian music and typically devotes an entire recording to one genre such as Taos Round Dance songs, or Navajo Yeibichai songs. The abundant examples and the excellent notes make these recordings valuable for scholars as well as other interested listeners.

Library of Congress.   Archive of Folk Culture, Motion Picture, Broadcast, and Recorded Sound Division, Library of Congress, Washington, D.C. 20540, phone: (202) 707-7833. This collection includes the Willard Rhodes recordings of Native American music: excellent recordings and notes from all across the country.

Smithsonian/Folkways.   The Folkways Collection, Smithsonian Institution, Washington, D.C. 20560, phone: (202) 287-3262. The inventory of the Ethnic Folkways Records and Service Corp., formerly of New York City, has been preserved at the Smithsonian Institution and new recordings on a joint label are being produced. Their holdings include many early recordings of native American music.

CHAPTER THREE

Africa/Ewe, Mande, Dagbamba, Shona, BaAka

DAVID LOCKE

QUESTIONS

Consider a misleadingly simple question: Where is Africa's beginning and end? At first you might say, At the borders that mark the continent. But musically, Africa spills over its geographic boundaries. Calling to mind the narrow Strait of Gibraltar, the recently dug Suez Canal, the oft-crossed Red and Mediterranean Seas, and the vast Atlantic Ocean, we realize that people from Africa always have shaped world history. If we invoke images—Egypt, Ethiopia, the Moors, Swahili civilization, commerce in humans and precious metals—we know that Africa is not separate from Europe, Asia, and America. As pointed out in chapter 1, music is humanly made sound; it moves with humankind on our explorations, conquests, migrations, and enslavements. This chapter, therefore, refers us not only to the African continent but wherever African music-culture is found.

Another question: What music is African music? We could be poetic and say, "Where its people are, there is Africa's music—on the continent and in its diaspora": but truth is messier. Music never is pure. A music-culture always is a process shaped by many outside influences. From Benin and Luanda to Bahia, Havana, London, and Harlem, music-cultures blend on a subtle continuum. African-influenced music now circulates the planet by means of electronic media. After you learn new things about music, your own personal music-culture adjusts.

The African continent has two broad zones: (1) the Maghrib, north of the Sahara Desert, and (2) sub-Saharan Africa. North Africa and the Horn of Africa have much in common with the Mediterranean and West Asia; Africa south of the Sahara in many ways is a unique cultural area. But history records significant contacts up and down the Nile, across the Sahara, and along the African coasts. Just as civilizations from the north (Greece, Rome) and east (Arabia, Turkey) have had indelible impact on northern Africa, the Maghrib has been influenced from the south, as well. Similarly, Africa south of the Sahara never has been isolated from the Old World civilizations of Europe and Asia. As I will show later in this chapter, the history and cultural geography of sub-Saharan Africa peoples vary tremendously (see Bohannan and Curtin).

Permit an ungrammatical question: When is an African? In everyday circumstances, persons do not usually think of themselves as "African" (Mphahlele 1962). Identity arises from local connections of gender, age, kinship, place, language, religion, and work. Ethnicity comes into play only in the presence of people from a different group. One "becomes" a Serer, so to speak, in the presence of a Wolof, an African when among the French, a White in the company of a Black, a Yellow, a Red (Senghor 1967). These terms suggest relationships among people more than they mark essential characteristics of individuals. Physical appearance and genetic inheritance do not determine culture, but the bogus concept of "race" is crucial to the ignorance that spawns prejudice and the bigotry that fosters injustice (Appiah 1992). Although they pervade our global village, such labels should be marked: USE WITH CARE.

In an intercultural context, "Africa" is a resonant symbol. People of African descent, wherever they are in the world, may regard Africa as the ancestral homeland, the place of empowerment and belonging (Asante 1987). Industrialized citizens of "information societies" may envision Africa either as a pastoral Eden or the impoverished Third World. Land of "heathens" to the Muslim and Christian, Africa is a fount of ancient wisdom for those who practice religions such as *santería* or *vodun*. Famine relief and foreign aid, wilderness safari and Tarzan, savage or sage—Africa is a psychic space, not just a physical place.

The sections below introduce six African music-cultures (see fig. 3–1). They show Africa's diversity and some of its widely shared characteristics. Information for two of the sections comes from my own field research; other sections are based on the ethnomusicological scholarship of colleagues—the late James Koetting, Roderic Knight, Paul Berliner, and Michelle Kisliuk. The cooperative effort that underlies this chapter seems fitting, since one vital function of African music is to mold separate individuals into a group.

POSTAL WORKERS CANCELING STAMPS

Jim Koetting, the author of the Africa/Ghana chapter in the two previous editions of this text, recorded selection 13 in the 1970s. It has been one of the best-loved sound recordings in *Worlds of Music*. Organizing my remarks with ideas from chapter 1 (see table 1–1), I shall use this sound recording as the basis for generalizations about African music-culture.

Koetting described the recorded example:

The men making the sounds you hear are workers canceling letters at the University of Ghana post office. . . . This is what you are hearing: the two men seated at the table

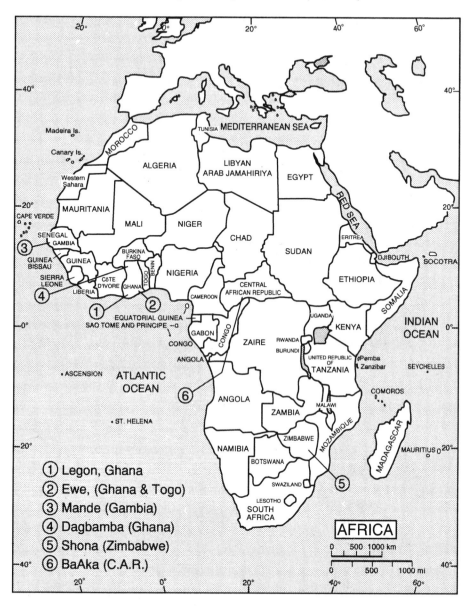

Fig. 3–1.   African continent, showing location of six music-cultures.

slap a letter rhythmically several times to bring it from the file to the position on the table where it is to be canceled (this act makes a light-sounding thud). The marker is inked one or more times (the lowest, most resonant sound you hear) and then stamped on the letter (the high-pitched mechanized sound you hear). As you can hear, the rhythm produced is not a simple one-two-three (bring forward the letter—ink the marker—stamp the letter). Rather, musical sensitivities take over. Several slaps on the

letter to bring it down, repeated thuds of the marker in the ink pad and multiple can-
cellations are done for rhythmic interest. . . . The other sounds you hear have nothing
to do with the work itself. A third man has a pair of scissors that he clicks—not cutting
anything, but adding to the rhythm. . . . The fourth worker simply whistles along. He
and any of the other three workers who care to join him whistle popular tunes or
church music that fits the rhythm. (Koetting 1992:98–99)

In what ways does this musical event exemplify widely shared characteristics of
African music-culture?

GENERALIZATIONS ABOUT AFRICAN MUSIC-CULTURE

Music-Making Events

A compelling feature of this recording is its setting. Canceling stamps can sound
like this? How marvelous! Obviously, the event was not a concert, and this most
definitely is not art for art's sake. Like work music everywhere, this performance
undoubtedly lifted the workers' spirits and enabled them to coordinate their efforts. The music probably helped the workers change their attitude toward the
job. Music often helps workers control the mood of the work place (Jackson
1972). (See Music of Work in chapter 4.)

African music often happens in social situations where people's primary goals
are not artistic. Instead, music is for ceremonies (life cycle rituals, festivals), work
(subsistence, child care, domestic chores, wage labor), or play (games, parties,
lovemaking). Music-making contributes to an event's success by focusing attention, communicating information, encouraging social solidarity, and transforming
consciousness.

Multimedia Expression

Just as Africans set music in a social context, they associate it with other expressive
media (drama, dance, poetry, costuming, sculpture). Indeed, this example is unusual because it is a wordless instrumental. Although music-making usually is not
the exclusive purpose of an event, people do value its aesthetic qualities. Music
closely associated with a life event still is enjoyed at other times for its own sake.

Musical Style

The whistled tune probably seems familiar to many listeners. The melody has European musical qualities such as duple meter, a major scale, and harmony (ex.
3–1). On the other hand, the percussion exhibits widespread African stylistic features such as polyrhythm, repetition, and improvisation (ex. 3–2).

History

These observations about genre and style lead to an important point about the
history of music in Africa: The music-cultures of Europe, Asia, and the Americas
have had strong impact in Africa. Foreigners—Christians and Muslims, sailors
and soldiers, traders and travelers—have brought to Africa their instruments, musical repertories, and ideas. Modern media technologies like radio and audiotape
only have increased the intensity of a very old pattern of border crossing. Like

Ex. 3–1. Postal workers' melody.

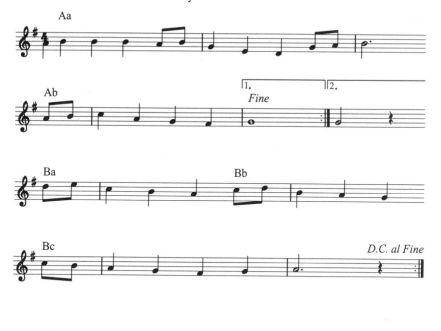

Note: $\frac{4}{\downarrow}$ means four quarter notes per measure without implication of stress patterns.

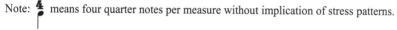

people everywhere, Africans have imitated, rejected, transformed, and adapted external influences in a complex process of culture change.

The concert music repertory of Europe has held little attraction for most Africans, but many other musical traditions have affected African music-making. Throughout Africa, Christian hymns and Muslim cantillation have exerted a profound influence on musical style. West Asian civilization has had an effect on African musical instruments such as the plucked lutes, double reeds, and goblet-shaped drums of the Sahel area. Euro-American influence shows up in the elec-

Ex. 3–2. Postal workers' percussion "voices."

tric guitar and drum set, although East Asians manufacture many of these instruments. We hear the American influence of Cuban rumba on pop music from central Africa and African-American spirituals on southern African religious music. From praise singers to pop bands, musical professionalism is an idea about music that developed in Africa by means of the intercultural exchange of ideas.

Participation

The postal workers join simple musical parts together to make remarkably sophisticated and satisfying music. This kind of musical design welcomes social engagement. Others could participate by adding a new phrase to the polyrhythm or cutting a few dance moves. Undoubtedly, Jim Koetting "got down" while picking up his mail! Much African music shares this generous, open-hearted quality that welcomes participation.

Training

We admire the postal workers because their music seems effortlessly beautiful. The genius we sense in this recording lies in the way the workers are musical together, in their sensitivity to a culturally conditioned musical style. Here, a musical education depends on a society-wide process of enculturation, that is, the process of learning one's culture gradually during childhood. Babies move on the backs of their dancing mothers, youngsters play children's games and then join adults in worship and mourning, teenagers groove to pop tunes. Raised in this manner, Africans learn a way-of-being in response to music; intuitively, they know how to participate effectively. Genetic and sacred forces may shape musicality, but culture is the indispensable element in musical training.

Beliefs and Values

Often, Africans conceive of music as a necessary and normal part of life. Neither exalted nor denigrated as Art, music fuses with other life processes. Traditional songs and musical instruments are not commodities separable from the flux of life. In his book *African Music: A People's Art*, Francis Bebey quotes a musician who was asked to sell his instrument: "He replied rather dryly that he had come to town to play his drum for the dancing and not to deliver a slave into bondage. He looked upon his instrument as a person, a colleague who spoke the same language and helped him create his music" (Bebey 1975:120).

Intercultural Misunderstanding

These beliefs and attitudes about music make intercultural understanding a challenge, especially for scientifically minded persons from what might be called concert-music-cultures. What a non-African listener assumes is an item of music may be the voice of an ancestor to an African. When he recorded this example, Jim Koetting found himself in this type of cross-cultural conundrum. He wrote, "It sounds like music and, of course, it is; but the men performing do not quite think of it that way. The men are working, not putting on a musical show; people pass by the work place paying little attention to the 'music' (I used to go often to watch and listen to them, and they gave the impression that they thought I was somewhat odd for doing so)" (Koetting 1992:98).

Musical Analysis: Toward Participation

I too think this recording "sounds like music," but I hesitate to say "it is" because that would imply that the postal workers share my ideas about music. Even though they do not "quite" regard this as music, their musicking sounds great to me. I want to participate. In my music-culture, analysis can be an effective path toward active involvement, a bridge into the musical style of another culture. I use tools of musical analysis with caution, however, because I know that music can never be pinned to cardboard like a lifeless butterfly. For many Africans, music is "a living thing ensouled by the spiritual energy that travels through it" (Amoaku 1985:37).

Melody: Tonality, Texture, Form, Rhythm

The postal workers' melody (ex. 3–1) uses a seven-note scale in a major mode (transcribed for convenience with the tonal center on pitch G). The tune contains two melodic ideas: phrase A, which can be segmented into two shorter motives (Aa, Ab), and phrase B, which has a sequence of three shorter motives (Ba, Bb, Bc). If there were no improvisation, we could mark the musical form as AABA, but because the performers never repeat phrase A in exactly the same way, a more careful marking is $A^1A^2BA^3$. The recording fades in at the end of phrase A^3; then we hear four complete choruses of the tune before it fades out at the beginning of phrase A^2. As the recording ends, the homophonic texture fractures into a polyphonic interplay of independent melodies. I have set the rhythm within a meter of four quarter-note beats. The melody accentuates beats 1 and 3. Beats 2 and 4 play off beats 1 and 3, giving the music a sense of lift.

Percussion

It is hard to reconstruct exactly who played what on the recording; only by slowing the tape speed could I "get inside" the percussion texture (ex. 3–2). Guided by timbre and rhythm, I hear three percussive "voices":[*]

• A high-pitched, loud, dry sound (A) plays an ostinato (repeated phrase) on the upbeat of counts 2, 3, and 4. This part (the scissors) shapes musical time, giving a distinctive rhythmic character to the tune and other percussive voices.

• The lowest-pitched, resonant bass sound (C) plays occasional fills. This must be inking the stamp. Often it responds to the tune like an accompaniment, but at other times its interjections seem disconnected to the tune's progress. The prominent rhythmic figure shown in example 3–2 answers the scissors' part in a question-answer oscillation.

• The middle voice in the ensemble (B) may be the sound of moving the letters into position, augmented with tapping on the table just for fun. This part proba-

[*]In this chapter, I refer to musical "parts" I hear on sound recordings as "voices."

bly is a composite of separate actions by several people. With much less silence than the other two, this part increases the music's textural density. The workers occasionally break the bubbling flow, allowing brief moments of silence that greatly enhance the music's rhythmic design.

Each layer in the texture has a different rhythmic character. Through a clever balance of action and silence, the players generate forward motion in musical time while remaining within a repeating circle of percussion.

This example gives us a feeling for African music in general. The next example affords a more detailed look at a type of music with profound connections to the history of a specific African ethnic group, the Ewe people.

AGBEKOR: MUSIC AND DANCE OF THE EWE PEOPLE

Drawing on my field research in West Africa during the 1970s, we will now consider a type of singing and drumming called *Agbekor* (pronounced "ah-*gbeh-*kaw"). As you hear on recorded selection 14, Agbekor's music features a percussion ensemble and a chorus of singers. A complex lead drumming part rides on a rich polyrhythmic texture established by an ensemble of bells, rattles, and drums of different sizes. Songs are clear examples of call-and-response. *Agbekor* is a creation of Ewe-speaking people (pronounced *"eh*-way") who live on the Atlantic coast of western Africa in the nation-states of Ghana and Togo.

THE EWE PEOPLE

History

Triumph over adversity is an important theme in Ewe oral history. Until they came to their present territory, the Ewe people had lived precariously as a minority within kingdoms of more populous and powerful peoples such as the Yoruba and the Fon. Prominent in their oral traditions is the story of their exodus in the late 1600s from Agokoli, the tyrannical king of Notsie, a walled city-state located in what is now southern Togo. Intimidating Agokoli's warriors with fierce drumming, the Ewes escaped under cover of darkness. Moving southwestward, they founded many settlements along a large lagoon near the mouth of the Volta River. At last Wenya, their elderly leader, declared that he was too tired to continue. Thus, this Ewe group became known as the *Anlo* (pronounced *"ahng-*law"), a word that means "cramped." Other families of Ewe-speakers settled nearby along the coast and in the upland hills.

In these new lands, the Ewe communities grew and multiplied. Eventually, the small Ewe settlements expanded into territorial divisions whose inhabitants all could trace male ancestors to the original villages. Family heads or distinguished war leaders became chiefs. Despite bonds of common culture and history, each division zealously cherished its independence. The Ewe people have never supported a hierarchical concentration of power within a large state (compare them with the Mande and Dagbamba kingdoms, discussed later in this chapter).

Ever since those early days, the important units of Ewe social life have been extended families. Members of a lineage—that is, persons who can trace their genealogy to a common ancestor—share rights and obligations. Lineage elders hold positions of secular and sacred authority. The ever-present spirits of lineage ancestors help their offspring, especially if the living perform the necessary customary rituals.

The eighteenth and nineteenth centuries saw the Ewes in frequent military conflict with neighboring ethnic groups, European traders, and even among themselves. The Anlo-Ewe gained a fearsome reputation as warriors. Decades of frequent battle took a toll, however. Just before imposition of British administration (1874), civil order was in tatters. "The bitterness bred by slave-raiding alienated village from village and community from community. . . . For a time people of the same stock became bitter enemies" (Chapman 1946:1, in Locke 1978:22).

Religious Philosophy

An Ewe scholar has commented on the sacred worldview of his people: "A traveler in Anlo is struck by the predominating, all-pervasive influence of religion in the intimate life of the family and community. . . . The sea, the lagoon, the river, streams, animals, birds and reptiles as well as the earth with its natural and artificial protuberances are worshipped as divine or as the abode of divinities" (Fiawo 1959:35, in Locke 1978:32). The Ewe supreme being, Mawu, is remote from the affairs of humanity. Other divinities, such as Se (pronounced "seh"), interact with things in this world. Se embodies God's attributes of law, order, and harmony; Se is the maker and keeper of human souls; Se is destiny. Many Ewes believe that before a spirit enters the fetus, it tells Se how its life on earth will be and how its body will die. If you ask Ewe musicians the source of their talent, most likely they will identify the ancestor whose spirit they have inherited. Ask why they are so involved in music-making, they will say it is their destiny.

According to the worldview of many Ewes, God has endowed certain natural substances with extraordinary force. By combining these special substances in appropriate ways, knowledgeable persons can influence what happens in the world. Medicine can heal, protect, or enhance human capability. Performers often use charms to enhance their ability or to defend themselves against jealous rivals. Hunters are among the most learned herbalists.

Ancestral spirits are another crucial spiritual force in the lives of Ewe people.

> The Ewe believe that part of a [person's] soul lives on in the spirit world after his [or her] death and must be cared for by the living. This care is essential, for the ancestors can either provide for and guard the living or punish them. . . . The doctrine of reincarnation, whereby some ancestors are reborn into their earthly kin-groups, is also given credence. The dead are believed to live somewhere in the world of spirits, *Tsiefe*, from where they watch their living descendants in the earthly world, *Kodzogbe*. They are be-

lieved to possess supernatural powers of one sort or another, coupled with a kindly interest in their descendants as well as the ability to do harm if the latter neglect them. (Nukunya 1969:27, in Locke 1978:35)

Funerals are significant social institutions because without ritual action by the living, a soul cannot become an ancestral spirit. A funeral is an affirmation of life, a cause for celebration because another ancestor now is there to watch over the living. Because spirits of ancestors love music and dance, funeral memorial services feature drumming, singing, and dancing. Full of the passions aroused by death, funerals have replaced war as an appropriate occasion for war drumming such as *Agbekor*.

Knowledge of Ewe history and culture helps explain the great energy found in performance pieces like *Agbekor*. Vital energy, life force, strength—these are at the heart of the Ewe outlook: "In the traditional . . . Anlo society where the natural resources are relatively meager, where the inexplicable natural environment poses a threat to life and where the people are flanked by warlike tribes and neighbors, we find the clue to their philosophy of life: it is aimed at life" (Fiawo 1959:41, in Locke 1978:36).

AGBEKOR: HISTORY AND CONTEMPORARY PERFORMANCE

Legends of Origin

During my field research, I interviewed elders about how *Agbekor* began.° Many people said it was inspired by hunters' observations of monkeys in the forest. According to some elders, the monkeys changed into human form, played drums, and danced; others say that the monkeys kept their animal form as they beat with sticks and danced. Significantly, hunters, like warriors, had access to esoteric power.

> In the olden days hunters were the repository of knowledge given to men by God. Hunters had special herbs. . . . Having used such herbs, the hunter could meet and talk with leopards and other animals which eat human beings. . . . As for Agbekor, it was in such a way that they saw it and brought it home. But having seen such a thing, they could not reveal it to others just like that. Hunters have certain customs during which they drum, beat the double bell, and perform such activities that are connected with the worship of things we believe. It was during such a traditional hunting custom that they exhibited the monkey's dance. Spectators who went to the performance decided to found it as a proper dance. There were hunters among them because once they had revealed the dance in the hunting customary performance they could later repeat it again publicly. But if a hunter saw something and came home to reveal it, he would surely become insane. That was how Agbekor became known as a dance of the monkeys. (Kwaku Denu, quoted in Locke 1978:38–39)

°I conducted these interviews with the assistance of a language specialist, Bernard Akpeleasi, who subsequently translated the spoken Ewe into written English.

Although many Ewes consider them legend rather than history, stories like this signify the high respect accorded to *Agbekor*. Hunters were spiritually forceful leaders, and the forest was the zone of dangerously potent supernatural forces. We feel this power in a performance of *Agbekor*.

Agbekor *As War Drumming*

The original occasion for a performance of *Agbekor* was war. Elders explained that their ancestors performed it before combat as a means to attain the required frame of mind, or after battle as a means of communicating what had happened.

> They would play the introductory part before they were about to go to war. When the warriors heard the rhythms, they would be completely filled with bravery. They would not think that they might be going, never to return, for their minds were filled only with thoughts of fighting. (Elders of the Agbogbome Agbekor Society, quoted in Locke 1978:44)

> Yes, it is a war dance. It is a dance that was played when they returned from an expedition. They would exhibit the things that happened during the war, especially the death of an elder or a chief. (Alfred Awunyo, quoted in Locke 1978:43)

> If they were fighting, brave acts were done. When they were relaxing after the battle, they would play the drums and during the dance a warrior could display what he had done during the battle for the others to see. (Kpogo Ladzekpo, quoted in Locke 1978:43)

The Meaning of the Name Agbekor

I asked whether the name *agbekor* has meaning. "I can say it signifies enjoying life: we make ourselves happy in life. The suffering that our elders underwent was brought out in the dance, and it could be that when they became settled, they gave the dance this name, which shows that the dance expresses the enjoyment of life" (Kwaku Denu, quoted in Locke 1978:47). Another elder told me that when people played *Agbekor* during times of war, they called it *atamuga* (pronounced "ah-*tam*-gah"), which means "the great oath." Before going to battle, warriors would gather with their war leaders at shrines that housed spiritually powerful objects. They would swear on a sacred sword an oath to their ancestors to obey their leaders' commands and fight bravely for their community. When the Anlo no longer went to war, the name changed to *Agbekor* (Kpogo Ladzekpo, quoted in Locke 1978:45–46).

The word *Agbekor* is a compound of two short words: *agbe* means "life" and *kor* means "clear." The professional performer Midawo Gideon Foli Alorwoyie translates *Agbekor* as "clear life": the battle is over, the danger is past, and our lives are now in the clear (Locke 1978:47). Many people add the prefix *atsia* (plural *atsiawo*), calling the piece *atsiagbekor* (pronounced "ah-chah-*gbeh*-kaw"). The word *atsia* has two meanings: (1) stylish self-display, looking good, or bluffing, and (2) a preset figure of music and dance. As presented below, the form of the lead drumming and the dance consists of a sequence of *atsiawo*.

Learning

In Ewe music-culture, most music and dance is learned through enculturation. *Agbekor,* on the other hand, requires special training. The eminent African ethnomusicologist J. H. K. Nketia describes learning through slow absorption without formal teaching:

> The very organization of traditional music in social life enables the individual to acquire his musical knowledge in slow stages, to widen his experience of the music of his culture through the social groups into which he is progressively incorporated and the activities in which he takes part. . . . The young have to rely largely on their imitative ability and on correction by others when this is volunteered. They must rely on their own eyes, ears and memory. They must acquire their own technique of learning. (Nketia 1964:4)

Midawo Alorwoyie explains how one learns from the performance of an expert:

> All you have to do is know when he is going to play. . . . You have to go and pay attention to what you hear . . . to how the drums are coordinated and to the drum language, to what the responses are to the calls, and so on. You have to use your common sense right there to make sure that you get the patterns clear. Up to today, if you want to be a drummer, you go to the place where people are playing and then pay attention and listen. That's it. (Davis 1994:27)

Because of its complexity *Agbekor* is hard to learn in this informal way. Members of an *Agbekor* group practice in a secluded area for up to a year before they appear in public. Of course, all the novices are familiar with the general style of Ewe music and dance. Instruction entails demonstration and emulation. With adept dancers in front, the whole group performs together. No one breaks it down and analyzes it. Rather than mastering elements arranged as exercises, people learn long sequences of movement and music in a simulated performance context (compare this with the teaching of *karnataka sangeeta,* described in chapter 6).

This style of learning depends on gifted students who can master long rhythmic compositions merely by listening to them several times. For certain people, drumming comes as easily and naturally as spoken language. Ewes know that drumming talent often comes from one's ancestors. A precocious youngster may be the reincarnation of an ancestor who was a renowned musician. One village drummer told me of a special drummer's ritual: "My father was a drummer and he taught me. It was when he was old and could no longer play that he gave me the curved sticks. A ceremony has to be performed before the curved sticks are handed over to you. . . . If the custom is not done the drum language will escape your mind" (Dogbevi Abaglo, quoted in Locke 1978:53). Midawo Alorwoyie explains the effects of this ritual: "Once the custom has been made, you can't sleep soundly. The rhythms you want to learn will come into your head while you sleep. . . . The ceremony protects the person in many ways. It protects your hands when you play and protects you from the evil intentions of other people who may envy you. . . . Whenever you see a master drummer in Africa, I'm telling you, he has got to have some sort of backbone" (Locke 1978:54–55).

Performing Organizations

Times have changed since Ewe hunters created *Agbekor*. Britain, Germany, and France administered Ewe territory during a brief colonial period (1880s to 1950s); now the Ewe people live in the nation-states of Ghana and Togo. Today, relatively few villages have preserved their heritage of *Agbekor*. But the tradition vigorously continues within drum and dance societies of several types: mutual aid organizations, school and civic youth groups, and theatrical performing companies. Throughout Africa, voluntary mutual aid societies are an important type of performing group (Ladzekpo 1971). *Agbekor* groups of this kind are formal organizations with a group identity, institutionalized procedures, recognized leaders, and so forth. Many group members are poor and cannot afford funeral expenses by themselves. People solve this financial problem by pooling resources. When a member dies, individuals contribute a small amount so the group can give a lump sum of cash to the family. The society's performance of music and dance makes the funeral grand.

In the mid-1970s I studied *agbekor* with members of this type of cooperative society, the Anya Agbekor Society of Accra (see ill. 3–1). One of their leaders re-

Ill. 3–1. The Anya Agbekor Society (with the author) in performance. Photo by Godwin Agbeli.

counted how the group came into existence: "The first Anya Agbekor group in Accra was formed by our elder brothers and uncles. They all scattered in the mid-sixties and that group died away. We, the younger ones, decided to revive it in 1970. Three or four people sat down and said, 'How can we let this thing just go away? Agbekor originated in our place, among our family, so it is not good to let it go.' We felt that it was something we had to do to remember the old family members. We formed the group to help ourselves" (Evans Amenumey, quoted in Locke 1978:63). I also studied with school groups trained by my teacher Godwin Agbeli. In colonial times, missionaries whipped students for attending traditional performance events. These days, most Ewes value their traditional repertory or music and dance as a cultural resource. Since Ghana achieved statehood in 1957, the national government has held competitions for amateur cultural groups from the country's many ethnic regions. Young people often join groups because rehearsals and performances provide social opportunities. Like many African nations, Ghana sponsors professional performing arts troupes. With its spectacular, crowd-pleasing music and dance, *Agbekor* is a staple of their repertory.

A PERFORMANCE

On Sunday, March 6, 1977, in a crowded, working-class section of Accra, the Anya Society performed in honor of the late chief patron of the group. His son may have been thinking of his father when he described a patron's role in a drum society: "A patron is somebody who you can trust, somebody who is sympathetic and has love and interest in the thing the group is doing. He should be someone who can organize and knows how to talk to people. The patron solves many of our problems, quarrels and money matters" (Evans Amenumey, quoted in Locke 1978:61).

The evening before, the group held a wake during which they drummed *Kpegisu,* another prestigious war drumming of the Ewe (Locke 1992). Early Sunday morning, they played *Agbekor* briefly to announce the afternoon's performance. Had the event occurred in Anyako, the group would have made a procession through the ward. People went home to rest and returned to the open lot near the patron's family house by 3:30 in the afternoon for the main event.

The performance area was arranged like a rectangle within a circle. Ten drummers were at one end; fifteen dancers formed three columns facing the drummers; ten singers were in a semicircle behind the dancers; about three hundred onlookers encircled the entire performance area. All drummers and most dancers were male. Most singers were female; several younger females danced with the men. Group elders, bereaved family members, and invited dignitaries sat behind the drummers. With the account book laid out on a table, the group's secretary accepted the members' contributions.

The action began with an introductory section called *adzo* (pronounced "ah-dzo"), that is, short sections. Dancers sang songs in free rhythm. After the *adzo,* the main section, *vutsotsoe* (pronounced "voo-*tsaw*-tso-eh"), that is, fast drumming, started. The first sequence of figures had ritual significance: after dancing vigorously forward toward the drums, dancers bent toward the ground and three times intoned, "Aa-oo." The dance leader called out "Kutowo" (pronounced "koo-

taw-woh"), that is, the dead ones, and the group responded, "Yaa," a vocable indicating strong emphasis. After that, in time to a specific lead drum rhythm, the dancers did an especially strenuous yet graceful movement. The prolonged "Aa-oo" summons the spirits of departed ancestors, especially those slain in battle; the call-and-response "Kutowo-Yaa" honors the dead, reminding everyone of the sacrifices made by the ancestors; the dance figure shows their readiness to act in the manner of the ancestors.

Following this ritually charged passage, the dancers performed approximately ten more *atsiawo*. The lead drummer spontaneously selected these "styles" from the many drum and dance sequences known to the group.° The singers also were busy. Their song leader raised up each song; the chorus received it and answered. One song was repeated five to ten times before another was begun.

After about twenty minutes the *adzokpi* (pronounced "ah-dzoh-*kpee*") section of the performance began. Group members came forward in pairs or small groups to dance in front of the lead drummer. The dance movement differed for males and females. As in genres of Ewe social dancing, friends invited each other to move into the center of the dance space. When everyone had their fill of this more individualistic display, the lead drummer returned to the group styles. Soon, he signalled for a break in the action by playing the special ending figure.

During the break, the group's leaders went to the center of the dance area to pour a libation. Calling on the ancestors to drink, elders ceremonially poured water and liquor onto the earth. An elder explains: "We pour libation to call upon the deceased members of the dance [group] to send us their blessings [so we can] play the dance the same way we did when they were alive. How the Christians call Jesus, call God, though Jesus is dead—they do not see him and yet they call him—it is in the same manner that we call upon the members of the dance [group] who are no more so that their blessings come down upon us during the dancing" (Kpogo Ladzekpo, quoted in Locke 1978:82–83).

The performance resumed with *vulolo* (pronounced "voo-*law*-law"), that is, slow drumming, the processional section of *Agbekor*. After about fifteen minutes, they went straight to *vutsotsoe*, the up-tempo section, and then *adzokpi*, the "solos" section. After a brief rest, they did another sequence of group figures at slow and fast pace, followed by individual display.

At the peak of the final *adzokpi* section, elders, patrons, and invited guests came out onto the dance area. These dignitaries danced the stately women's movement rather than the more acrobatic male figure. While they danced, singers and dancers knelt on one knee as a mark of respect. After dancing back and forth in front of the drummers, they returned to their position on the benches in back of the drummers.

By six o'clock, with the equatorial sun falling quickly, the performance was over. As the group members contentedly carried the equipment back to the Anya house, the audience dispersed, talking excitedly about the performance.

°Perhaps because the word *atsia* means "stylishness," many English speaking Ewe musicians refer to the preformed drum and dance compositions as "styles."

Although a performance follows a definite pattern, *Agbekor* is not rigidly formalized. A. M. Jones, a pioneering scholar of African music, has commented on the elasticity of African musical performance: "Within the prescribed limits of custom, no one quite knows what is going to happen: it depends quite a lot on the inspiration of the leading performers. These men [and women] are not making music which is crystallized on a music score. They are moved by the spirit of the occasion" (Jones 1959:108).

MUSIC OF THE PERCUSSION ENSEMBLE

We now turn to music of the percussion ensemble for the slow-paced section of *Agbekor* (ex. 3–3).° Instruments in the ensemble include a double bell, a gourd rattle, and four single-headed drums (see fig. 3–2). One by one the phrases are not too difficult, but playing them in an ensemble is surprisingly hard. The challenge is to hear them within a polyphonic texture that seems to change depending on one's point of musical reference. The reward in learning to play these parts is an experience of African musical time.

The Bell

"Listen to the bell"—that is the continual advice of Ewe teachers. Every act of drumming, singing, and dancing is timed in accordance with the recurring musical phrase played on an iron bell or gong called *gankogui* (pronounced "gahng-*koh*-gu-ee"). On first impression, the part may seem simple, but when set in the rhythmic context of Ewe drumming, it becomes a musical force of great potency. Repetition is key. As the phrase repeats over and over, participants join together in a circling, spiraling world of time.

Seven strokes with a wooden stick on the bell make one pass through the phrase. Example 3–4 represents the bell part in equivalent linear and circular images. As the part repeats in polyrhythmic context, the musical ear groups the bell tones into a variety of patterns. Although the sonic phenomena are unchanging, the part appears different. We experience an aural illusion.

Despite the chameleon-like nature of the bell part, two phrase shapes are more important than others (ex. 3–5). The note marked with the asterisk may be struck on the lower pitched of the *gankogui's* two bells, a helpful landmark if one becomes rhythmically disoriented. For analytic clarity, I number the bell tones as shown in example 3–5.

Tempo, Pulsation, and Time-Feels

Although many contrasting rhythmic phrases occur simultaneously in the percussion ensemble, competent Ewe musicians unerringly maintain a steady tempo. Rather than confusing players, musical relations among parts help them maintain a consistent time flow.

°I have decided not to present the music of the lead drum here. Not only is the material quite complicated, but I believe it best if students approach lead drumming only after a significant period of study, preferably with an Ewe teacher.

Ex. 3–3.   Polyrhythm of Agbekor percussion ensemble.

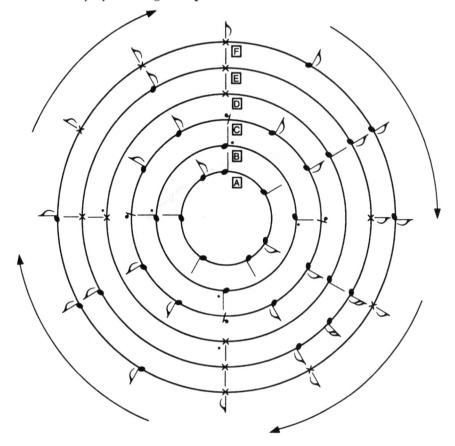

Note: read in clockwise direction

F Kidi
E Kloboto
D Totodzi
C Kaganu
B Axatse
A Gankogui

For those of us not bred in Ewe music-culture, a set of timing units provides a useful tool for understanding the musical rhythm of *Agbekor*. In example 3–6, I have put these timing units (beats and pulses) on concentric circles, each circle representing the duration of one bell phrase. Moving outward from the center circle, we see the bell's time span in terms of one, two, three, four, six, eight,

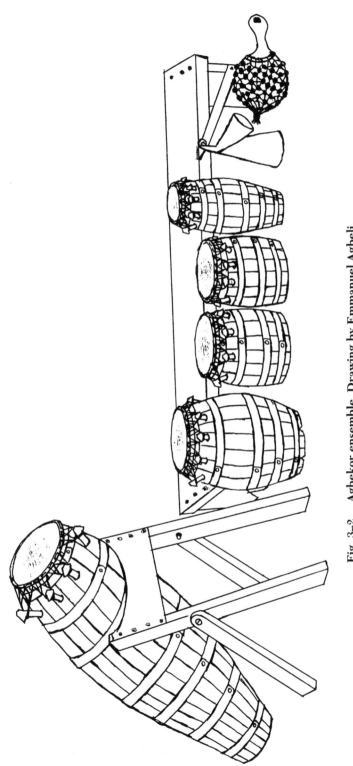

Fig. 3–2. Agbekor ensemble. Drawing by Emmanuel Agbeli.

Ex. 3–4. Bell phrase.

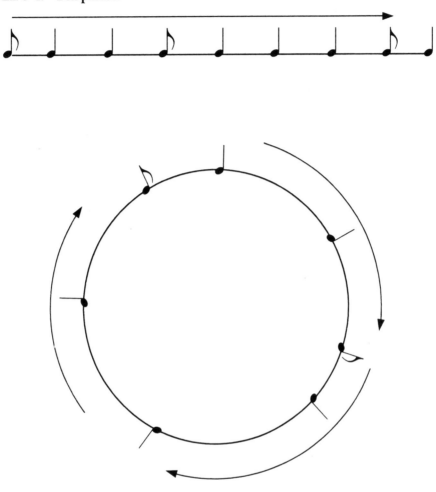

Ex. 3–5. Two shapes of the bell phrase.

Ex. 3–6.   Timing units for Agbekor: 24, 12, 8, 6, 3, 2, 1.

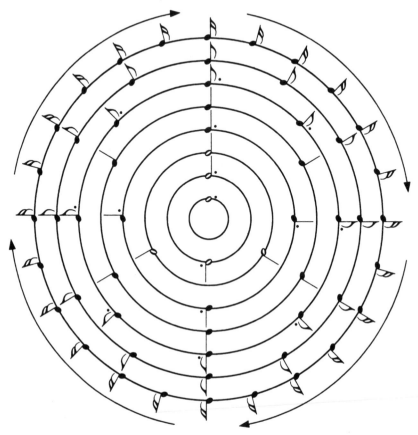

twelve, and twenty-four units. We can observe 3:2 and 3:4 relationships among pulses at several rates of speed. Each circle of pulsations stands for a musical groove, a feeling of marked moments in time.

In my experience, the time-feel (meter) most significant to Ewe performers is what I call the "four-feel." Together with the explicit bell phrase, these four ternary beats (each beat has three quicker units within it) are a constant, implicit foundation for musical perception. When my students first learn a dance step, a drum part, or a song melody, I advise them to lock into the bell phrase and the four-feel beats. Interestingly, this type of groove (often marked by a $\frac{12}{8}$ time signature)° is widespread in African-American music (see chapter 4).

Godwin Agbeli uses an Ewe children's game to teach the polyrhythm of bell and the four-feel beats (ex. 3–7). The chant "Matikpo matikpo kple ku dza" means

---

°In this chapter, I use an unconventional "fraction" as the time signature: the numerator shows the number of beats per measure; the note in the denominator shows the type of beat, that is, its internal pulse structure (ternary or binary). All beats in the measure have equal "weight" or metric stress.

Ex. 3–7.   Composite: bell and four-feel beats.

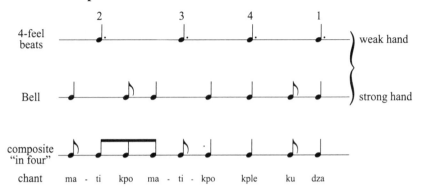

"I will jump, I will jump [to the sound of] 'kple ku dza'"; children leap upward as they say "kple" and land with a hand clap on "dza." I suggest that readers begin to practice the bell and four-beat combination by striking their thighs with open palms. When this is flowing easily, bring out the contrast between the parts by changing one hand to a fist.

To an Ewe musician, these four-feel beats automatically imply a "six-feel" (six quarter notes, or $\frac{6}{4}$ meter). The four- and six-feels are inseparable; they construct musical reality in two ways at once. Using both hands as shown in example 3–8, try playing the bell phrase and the six-feel. The bell part feels different. This is the power of 3:2. After mastering the bell and four-feel hand pattern, add a foot tap on the six-feel. Now you have more fully entered the rhythmic world of Ewe music.

Perhaps some readers are wondering, How does this analytic perspective relate to an Ewe point of view? How do they hear it? These are hard questions to answer. First, we cannot assume that there is just one pervasive Ewe perspective. Second, until recently Ewe musicians had no reason to think about musical structure in terms suited to intercultural education of the kind attempted in *Worlds of Music.* Based on my many years of research, performance, and teaching, I believe

Ex. 3–8.   Composite: bell and six-feel beats.

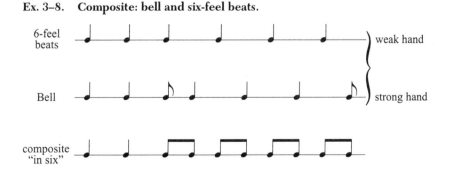

Ex. 3–9.   *Axatse* phrase.

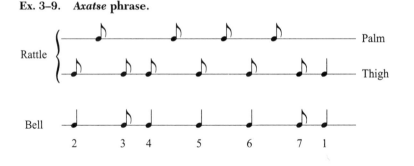

that my approach here is co-cultural with the perspective of my Ewe teachers. However, the discovery of ethnographic truth is not my only intent. I also ask practical questions: Does this approach help one hear the music with insight? Does it help people play? Students must answer this question for themselves. I hope the answer is yes!

Music of the Drum Ensemble

The *axatse* (pronounced "ah-*ha*-tseh") is a dried gourd about the size of a cantaloupe covered with a net strung with seeds. In some *Agbekor* groups its role is to sound out the four-feel beats. In another frequently heard phrase, downward strokes on the player's thigh match the *gankogui* while upward strokes against the palm fill in between bell tones. The longer duration of the tone that matches bell stroke 1 gives definition to the shape of the bell phrase; it suggests to the musical ear that the bell phrase begins on stroke 2 and ends on stroke 1 (ex. 3–9). As the only instrument played by many persons at once, the *axatse* "section" provides a loud, indefinite-pitched sound that is vital to the ensemble's energy.

The high pitch and dry timbre of the slender *kaganu* (pronounced "kah-gahng") drum cuts through the more mellow, midrange sounds of the other drugs. The *kaganu* part articulates offbeats, that is, moments between the four-feel beats (ex. 3–10). Although not every *Agbekor* group uses the same phrase

Ex. 3–10.   *Kagan* phrase.

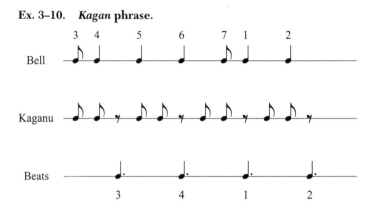

(Locke 1983:23–27), a good one for newcomers to learn marks the second and third pulses within each four-feel beat. Many Ewe teachers advise students to focus on the synchrony between *kaganu* and bell tones 3 and 4; remember— listen to the bell! The late Freeman Donkor, one of my first teachers of Ewe music, said that the rhythm of *kaganu* brings out the flavor of the other parts, like salt in a stew.

The *gankogui, axatse,* and *kaganu* parts create a distinctive quality of musical temporal experience (Locke 1988). The long and short tones in the bell phrase sculpt time into asymmetrical proportions. Symmetrical units also are important: the duration of the bell phrase literally is a measure of time; the tones of *axatse* and *kaganu* mark that measure into four equal ternary units. All four beats are strong, but the moments when bell and beat fall together—beats 4 and 1, bell tones 6 and 1—are specially marked in musical awareness; beat 3 is distinctive because it marks the midpoint in the bell phrase. These stable qualities of musical time provide the solid rhythmic foundation for the shifting offbeats found in the songs and lead drumming.

In descending order of relative pitch, the three other drums in the ensemble are *kidi, kloboto,* and *totodzi* (pronounced "*kee*-dee," "*kloh*-boh-toh," and "toh-toh-*dzee*"). Each drum adds its own phrase to *Agbekor's* unique polyphony. There are two ways of striking a drumskin. Bounce strokes (the stick bounces off the drumskin) have an open ringing sound, whereas press strokes (the stick presses into the drumskin) have a closed muted sound. Bounces make the significant contribution to the group's music; presses keep each player in a groove. The parts discussed below are widespread, but some *Agbekor* groups use slightly different versions.

• In the *kidi* part, three bounces and three presses move at the twelve-unit pulsation rate; the phrase occurs twice within the span of one bell phrase (ex. 3–11). Polyrhythmic relationships to the time parts help in learning the *kidi*: (a) in each group of bounces and presses the third stroke is on a beat; (b) bell tones 5 and 6 match open *kidi* tones, and (c) *kidi* closely coincides with *kaganu*.

Ex. 3–11. *Kidi* **phrase.**

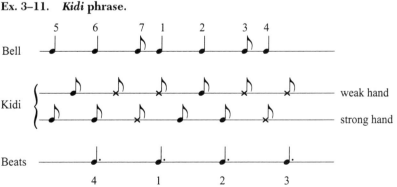

Ex. 3–12. *Kloboto* phrase.

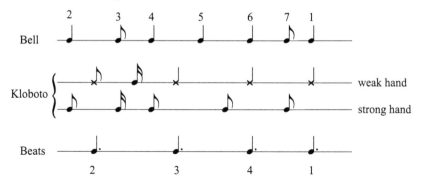

• The *kloboto* phrase has the same duration as the bell phrase (ex. 3–12). As if inspired by bell tones 7–1, the part's main idea is a brief bounce-press, offbeat-onbeat figure. *Kloboto's* insistent accentuation of offbeat moments can reorient a listener into perceiving them as onbeats. This type of implied beat shift (displacement) adds to the multi-dimensional quality of the music. For example, a person concentrating on *kloboto* may hear the second stroke in each pair of *kaganu* tones to be on the beat. Competent Ewe musicians, however, never lose orientation—they always know the *kloboto* presses are right on the four-feel time.

• The *totodzi* part begins and ends with the *kloboto* (ex. 3–13). Its two bounce strokes match bell tones 2 and 3, its three press strokes match four-feel beats 3, 4, and 1. Notice the impact of sound quality and body movement on rhythmic shape: the phrase is felt as two strong-hand bounces followed by three weak-hand presses, not according to a three-then-two timing structure.

Let me offer advice for getting into the drumming. Begin by hearing each phrase "in four" and in duet with the bell. Then, stay "in four" but hear ever-larger combinations with other parts. Next, switch to the six-feel. For added fun, try hearing the music "in three" and "in eight" (Locke 1982). The point is to explore the potency of these phrases, not to create new ones. Stretch your way of hearing, rather than what you are playing. Strive for a cool focus on ensemble relationships, not a hot individual display (Thompson 1973).

Ex. 3–13. *Totodzi* phrase.

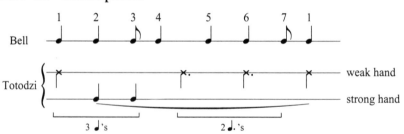

Drum Language

As happens in the instrumental music of many African peoples, Ewe drum phrases often have vernacular texts. Usually, only drummers know the texts. Even Ewe speakers cannot understand drum language just by hearing the music—they must be told. Secrecy makes restricted information valuable and powerful. In many parts of Africa "speech must be controlled and contained if silence is to exercise its powers of truth, authenticity, seriousness and healing" (Miller 1990:95).

During my field research, I asked many experts whether they knew drum language for *Agbekor*. Saying he learned them from elders in his hometown of Afiadenyigba, Midawo Alorwoyie shared the following texts with me (ex. 3–14). His word-for-word and free translations appear beneath the Ewe texts. *Agbekor's* themes of courage and service are apparent.

Totodzi	*Dzogbe dzi dzi dzi.* battlefield/on/on/on We will be on the battlefield.
Kloboto	*'Gbe dzi ko mado mado mado.* Battlefield/on/only/I will sleep/I will sleep/I will sleep I will die on the battlefield.
Kidi	*Kpo afe godzi. Kpo afe godzi.* Look/home/side-on. Look/home/side-on. Look back at home. Look back at home.
Kaganu	*Miava yi afia.* We will come/go/will show We are going to show our bravery.

Ex. 3–14. *Agbekor* **drum language.**

SONGS

Texts

Agbekor songs engage the subject of war. Many songs celebrate the invincibility of Ewe warriors; others urge courage and loyalty; some reflect on death and express grief. Songs memorialize heroes but do not provide detailed historical information. Unlike the freshly composed songs found in contemporary idioms of Ewe traditional music, *Agbekor* songs are inherited from the past. A song's affective power derives, in part, from its association with the ancestors.

Structural Features

In performance, a song leader and a singing group share the text and melody. As illustrated in the songs presented below, this call-and-response idea supports a variety of subtly different musical forms. The tonal system of *Agbekor* songs has evolved entirely in response to the human singing voice, without being influenced by musical instruments. An ethnomusicologist can identify scales, but in comparison to tuning in South Indian music-culture, for example, an Ewe singers' intonation seems aimed at pitch areas rather than precise pitch points. Melodic motion usually conforms to the rise and fall of speech tones, but Ewe speakers easily understand song lyrics even if the melodic contour contradicts the tonal pattern of the spoken language. Songs add another layer to the rhythm of *Agbekor*. Not surprisingly, a song's polyrhythmic duet with the bell phrase is all-important.

On recorded selection 14 we hear excerpts from my recording of a performance by an *Agbekor* group from the town of Anlo-Afiadenyigba on August 14, 1976. We hear three slow-paced songs, one song in free rhythm, and one fast-paced song. I discuss their texts and musical features below.

Slow-Paced Songs

Song #1

Leader:	‖:	*Emiawo miegbona afeawo me.*	A^1
		Afegametowo/viwo, midzra nuawo do.	
Group:		repeat lines 1 and 2 :‖	A^2
Leader:	‖:	*Oo!*	B
Group:		*Midzra nuawo do.* :‖	
All:		repeat lines 1 and 2	A^2
Leader:		We are coming into the homesteads.	
		People/Children of the noble homes, get the things ready.	
Group:		Repeat lines 1 and 2	
Leader:		Oh!	
Group:		Get the things ready.	

Song #1 announces that people should prepare for the arrival of the *Agbekor* procession (ex. 3–15). It has a rounded ABA musical form: ‖:A^1A^2:‖BBA^2. In the A section, the group repeats the leader's text but with a different tune; in the B sec-

Ex. 3–15. *Agbekor* **song no. 1.**

tion, the melodic phrases are shorter, the rhythm of call-and-response more percussive; the song ends with leader and group joining to sing the group's first response. The song's rhythm moves in the three-then-two groove. I hear the song's final pitch as its tonal center (here set on E). The intonation of the second scale degree is variable—sometimes natural, sometimes flat, often somewhere in between. When the song's transcribed pitches are ordered into a scale, we see five pitches with two half steps—1 ♭2 or ♮2 ♭3 5 ♭6. (Compare to the *pélog* scale in chapter 7.)

Song #2

Leader:	*Agbekoviawo, midze aye ee.*	A^1
Group:	*Ada do ee,*	B^1
	Kpo nedze ga nu.	
	Ada do!	
Leader:	*Manyo hawo, midze aye ee*	A^2
Group:	Repeat lines 2–4	B^2
Leader:	*Agbekor* group, be cunning.	
Group:	The day has come.	

> Beat the double bell.
> The day has come.

Leader: Manyo's group, be cunning.

Group: Repeat lines 2–4.

Set at sunrise on the day of battle, song #2 urges Manyo and his warriors to "be cunning." Leader and group divide the text: the leader identifies the actors and the action, the group evokes the scene. Unlike the rounded form of song #1, this song has a linear AB musical form: $A^1B^1A^2B^2$. This song has five pitches with no half steps (ex. 3–16). As I hear it, the melody moves between two tonal centers: the phrases in A^1B^1 strongly cadence on A; A^2 shifts the tonal center to G; B^2 begins there, but then ends back on A. Form, melody, and tonality combine in creating a circular musical effect.

Song #3

Leader:	‖:	*Avu matodzo,* *Dewoe lawuma?*	A^1
Group:		Repeat lines 1 and 2 :‖	A^2
Leader:	‖:	*Dewoe?*	B^1
Group:		*Dewoe lawuma?* :‖	B^2
All:		*Avu matodzo* *Dewoe lawuma?*	A^2

Leader:	A hornless dog. Are there any greater than we?
Group:	Repeat lines 1 and 2.

Ex. 3–16.   *Agbekor* song no. 2.

Leader: Any?

Group: Greater than we

All: Repeat lines 1 and 2

Song #3 expresses an important sentiment in *Agbekor* songs: celebrating the singers' power and denigrating the opponent (ex. 3–17). Here, the enemy is a "hornless dog," that is, an impotent person, and "we" are incomparably great. Ewe composers often make this point by means of rhetorical questions: "Who can trace the footprints of an ant?" that is, Who can defeat us? "Can the pigeon scratch where the fowl scratches?" that is, Can the enemy fight as strongly as we can? "Can a bird cry like the sea?" that is, How can the enemy compare to us? In these playful self-assertions and witty put-downs, we see a parallel with the genres of African-American expressive culture called "signifying" (Gates 1988; see chapter 4 for examples).

Adzo *Songs*

Rhythmically free songs from the *adzo* section have longer texts than songs from the slow- and fast-paced portions of an *Agbekor* performance. Like songs #1 and #3, song #4 begins with two sections of leader-group alternation, but has a noticeably longer third section sung by the whole group. The issues raised in song #4 are not new to us; this song, however, does make a factual historical reference to Avusu Kpo, an enemy war leader.

Ex. 3–17.   *Agbekor* song no. 3.

Song #4

Leader:	‖:	*'Gbekoviwo, xe de ado ahoyo gbe,* *Be tsawoyo?*	A
Group:		*Xe ke lado gbe,* *Gavi tsawoyo?* :‖	B
Leader:		*Tu nedi!*	C^1
Group:		*Miahee de alada me.*	D
Leader:		*Hewo nu,*	C^2
Group:		*Miahee de alada me.*	D
All:		*Be la bada fo soshi* *Ko de alada me.* *Tu la kaka,* *Mietsoe da de agboawo dzi* *Xe de mado ahoyo gbe ee?* *Avusu Kpowoe mado lo na xe* *Be xe nedo dika na alado me.* *Tsawoyo* Repeat lines 3 and 4	E B
Leader:	‖:	Members of the *Agbekor* group, can a bird cry like the sea, "Tsawoyo?"	
Group:		Which bird can cry like the sea, "Gavi Tsawoyo?" :‖	
Leader:		Fire the gun!	
Group:		We will turn it aside!	
Leader:		The tips of knives,	
Group:		We will brush them aside!	
All:		A wild animal has found a horsetail switch And put it at his side. The gun broke, We put it on the barricade. Can a bird cry like the sea? Avusu Kpo and his people cannot talk in proverbs to the bird. [unknown] "Tsawoyo." Repeat lines 3 and 4	

Fast-Paced Songs

Song #5, like many songs from the fast-paced section, celebrates heroic passion. For example, another song says simply, "Sweet, to put on the war belt is very sweet." Song #5 opens with the vivid image of a confrontation between two war gods (*So*). The Fon from Dahomey and the Anlo are about to fight; the beautiful warriors are preparing; will they have the courage to enter the fray?

Song #5

Leader:	‖:	*So kpli So, ne ava va gbedzia*	A
		Tsyo miado.	
Group:		*Woyawoya*	B
		Ava va gbedzia,	
		Tsyo miado. :‖	
Leader:		*Oo,*	C
Group:		*Fowo do gbea,*	C
		Miayia?	
		Anlowo do gbe.	
Leader:		*Oo,*	D
Group:		*Anawo do gbea*	
		Tsyo miado.	
All:		Repeat lines 3–5	B
Leader:	‖:	So and So—if war breaks out on the battlefield	
		We will have to dress gorgeously.	
Group:		"Woyowoya"	
		War breaks out on the battlefield.	
		We have to dress gorgeously. :‖	
Leader:		Oh,	
Group:		The Fon are out on the battlefield,	
		Should we go?	
		The Anlo are out on the battlefield.	
Leader:		Oh,	
Group:		The cowards are out on the battlefield.	
		Should we go?	
		The Anlo are out on the battlefield.	
		Repeat lines 3–5.	

Agbekor, as we have seen, is a group effort. Music and dance are a force in cementing social feeling among members of an *Agbekor* society. Others types of African music depend more on the virtuosity and special knowledge of individuals. We turn now to an example of such a solo tradition. Information for the next section of the chapter draws primarily on the research of the ethnomusicologist Roderic Knight.

MANDE *JALIYA*: "LAMBANGO"*

In recorded selection 15 we hear the artistry of Mariatu Kuyateh (vocal), her husband, Kekuta Suso (stringed instrument), and Seni Jobateh (speech and percussion) as they preform the piece "Lambango." My ear is drawn toward Ms.

---

*Roderic Knight and Eric Charry reviewed drafts of this section. I would like to acknowledge their invaluable assistance.

Kuyateh's wordy solo song and Mr. Suso's virtuosity on the *kora* (a twenty-one-string bridge-harp). These experts in speech, song, and the playing of instruments are often called *griots* (pronounced "*gree*-oh"). Not only musicians, they are counselors to royalty, entertainers for the public, and guardians of history (see ill. 3–2).

The performers, who call themselves *jalolu* (singular *jali*), are professional "sound artisans" of the Mande ethnic tradition (Charry 1992: 74–75). *Jaliya*, that is, what *jalolu* do, has had important functions in Mande civilization since the thirteenth century, when Sunjata Keita founded the empire of Mali. At its apogee (fourteenth to sixteenth centuries), Mali exerted authority over a vast territory of river and grassland stretching west from the Upper Niger to the Atlantic coast. Age-old patterns of Mande culture remain influential today.

Historical and Social Background

Cultural Crossroads

Distinct civilizations meet in the West African savannah lands south of the desert and north of the forest—Sudanic African, Tuareg, Berber, Arab, European. The routes of intercultural communication run both north-south and east-west. For Arabic-speakers on trading caravans between the Mediterranean and the Sudan

Ill. 3–2.   **Mariatu Kuyateh and Kekuta Suso (with *kora*), Boraba, Gambia, 1970. Photo by Roderic Knight.**

(*Bilad es Sudan,* "land of the Blacks"), the Sahara was a sand sea. The semiarid Sahel literally was its southern "coast." East-west travel followed rivers such as the Gambia and the Senegal, but most importantly the Niger, whose seasonal floods fostered an agricultural base for empire.

Mali

A succession of great states arose in this broad cultural crossroads: first Ghana, then Mali, Songhai, Kanem-Bornu, Hausa, Mossi, and others. Mali was fabulously wealthy. It was a centralized, hierarchically organized empire with distinct social classes. Islamic libraries and universities of world renown flourished in great cosmopolitan cities. A class of literati (writing in Arabic) operated the empire's systems of commerce and law.

The duty of Mande *jalolu* was to serve this array of wealthy patrons. "The jali held the only records of genealogy and history and was the only one who knew and could perform the music called for on important occasions. The people who most often employed the services of these people were in a position to provide ample recompense in the form of lodging, cattle, clothing and other manifestations of wealth. For the jali . . . this meant that he was virtually assured of permanent patronage. . . . As one jali has put it, 'The jali was king'" (Knight 1984:62).

Learning helped determine one's place in the status hierarchy of such cities as Timbuktu. Some intellectuals became praise singers (*muddah*) who received alms for lauding the Prophet Muhammad (Saad 1983:86). Erudite *jalolu* were among such refined professionals. In the Islamic Sudan, the formal exchange of praise for wealth remains a respected institution. In this music-culture, gifts to a *jali* are not commercial payments for products sold but rather are respectful offerings that mark the interdependence of praiser and praised (Charry 1992:80).

Although the political leaders were nominally Muslim, the bulk of the population kept faith with pre-Islamic religion. Some Mande peoples still retain a mythic consciousness that links natural landmarks to the primordial, creative feats of superhuman ancestors (Dieterlen 1957, in Skinner 1973). In addition to serving their elite patrons, the *jalolu* transmit these ancient, secret mysteries to every member of society (Laye 1983).

After 1600, the history of these Sudanic empires is a story of fracture and gradual decline. Forces of change included internal rebellion, invasion by a Moroccan expeditionary force (1591), the Atlantic slave trade (1700s), Islamic jihads (1800s), and finally British and French colonialism (1800s and 1900s). All the while, in songs like "Lambango," the Mande bards told legends of the empire's founder, Sunjata Keita, and news of more recent heroes.

Kingdoms Along the Gambia

At the western edge of the Mande heartland, many small kingdoms formed along the Gambia River. Modeled on the much larger empires of the Upper Niger, each state had its hierarchy of royals, courtiers, warriors, state officials, merchants, clerics, and so on. Prospering through trade with Europe—notably, slaves for manufactured goods—the elite were remarkably cosmopolitan.

French traders in the eighteenth century reported that the mansas of Niumi [kings of a state on the north bank of the Gambia] lived in European-style houses and dressed in elaborate costumes. . . . [One] mansa's daughter, who was said to read and write French, Portuguese and English, had established herself as the chief intermediary between the traders and her father. At one time married to a Portuguese, she lived in a large square European house and held soirees for the commercial community in a style that boasted fine table linen and other imported luxuries. (Quinn 1972:41)

A distinctive music-culture of *jali* with *kora* developed in these kingdoms along the Gambia.

MUSIC-CULTURE

Social Organization

Where do the *jalolu* fit within the Mande system of social rank and its associated roles? Slavery existed in this African society; even today, descendants of the freeborn (*horon*) are distinguished from persons of slave descent (*jong*), especially in the matter of marriage. Among the freeborn, *nyamalo*—craft specialists including *jalolu*—occupy a separate niche from *sula* who are a *jali*'s prospective patrons—nonspecialists, including royals, Islamic literates, merchants, and farmers. Among *nyamalo*, boys inherit their fathers' craft as a lifelong profession; young women marry within their fathers' occupational group (see Knight 1984:60–66).

Duties to Patrons

In former times when kings were rich, *jali* and patron shared a mutually beneficial relationship. Playmates as children, they retained their intimacy as adults.

Griots woke the king each morning by singing his praises outside his quarters, they accompanied him wherever he traveled, singing and playing behind him and especially when he met another king, they were in attendance singing their patron's praises. From time to time a court griot would entertain the king and members of his court by reciting accounts of the careers of some of the king's forebears, perhaps of some deeds of the king himself. . . . The whole narration glorified the king, often bathing him in the reflected glory of his mighty ancestors. . . . [The griot] would take real pride in [this] history and would want to present it in the best possible light, for he would surely feel able to share in the glory of his patron's family. (Innes 1976:5)

Before our era, the *jali* received the wholehearted respect merited by a learned artist with significant duties in the affairs of state. A *jali*'s performance bridged time and space, bringing the historical and mythic past into the lives of the living. "When the jali sings the name of a past hero, he views what he is doing as waking him up, bringing him back to life (*Mb'a wulindila*). . . . If in the end the listener can say of the music, *Wo le dunta n na* (It has entered me), then the desired effect will have been achieved" (Knight 1984:73). This music-culture changed after The Gambia became a British protectorate in 1894. Since the wealth of the royals was much reduced, their patronage alone could not sustain a *jali*. Thus today, *jalolu* must serve a broader clientele by freelancing at social occasions such as weddings and naming ceremonies where people value their knowledge and artistry. Yet even in our cash-oriented, dislocated world, where an African royal may hold a menial job in Europe, the *jalolu* retain warm relations with their patrons and provide a vital link to profound dimensions of Mande culture (Knight 1991:56).

Transmission

A *jali* learns the craft of playing a musical instrument in an apprentice-master relationship. During adolescence and young adulthood, fathers send their sons to a relative who enforces a strict training regimen. Some *jalolu* specialize in the *kora,* others play xylophone (*balo*) or a plucked, long-neck lute (*konting, ngoni,* or guitar). Young women, whose primary duty is to sing, participate in a more informal apprenticeship. At the same time they serve their elders, young *jalolu* gradually learn an impressive body of knowledge. *Jalolu* keep elaborate genealogies and stories of their patrons' forebears. More than dry objective historical accounts, their performances entail rousing artistry designed to elicit the respect and gratitude of an audience (Innes 1976:27).

The Jali's Knowledge

A key element in *jaliya* is speech (*kuma*) (Charry 1992:76). Narratives in the Gambian tradition refer to two historical periods: (a) the times of Sunjata and the formation of Mali (1200s), and (b) the times of the last *mansas* (1800s). The stories are told in the vernacular with few poetic devices; the *jali* enlivens the characters by recreating their words (Innes 1976:17). Songs contain wise sayings about people and situations that are always relevant to the living. Some examples (Knight 1984:78–80):

Islamic fatalism:	"Before God created life, he created death."
Moral judgments:	"The talkative kings are plentiful, but men of great deeds are few."
	"Misery is hard on a woman, shame is hard on a man."
Advice:	"The world is ever-changing. If someone doesn't know your past, don't tell him your present affairs."
Observations:	"Life is nothing without conversation."
On wealth:	"Wealth is not a tonic for life; wealth is to save you from disgrace."
	"The wealthy inherit the wealth."
On *jaliya:*	"For the person who puts one hundred in my hand, I will give him a hundred-worth praise with my mouth."
	"The great carrier of loads has put me on his back—the elephant never tires of carrying his trunk."

ELEMENTS OF PERFORMANCE

Kora

The *kora* is an indigenous African instrument with a unique array of parts (fig. 3–3). Scholars of musical instruments (organologists) classify the instrument as a spiked bridge harp: "spiked" because its straight neck passes entirely through the large, skin-covered, half-calabash resonator, "bridge" because the strings pass

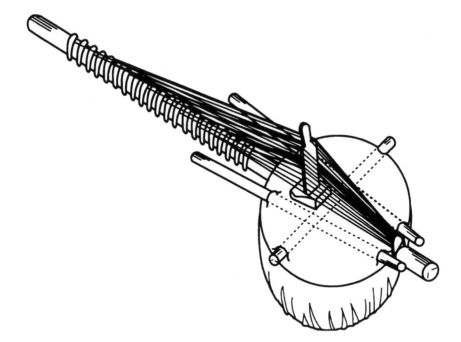

Fig. 3–3.   The *kora*.

through notches on the sides of a high bridge, and "harp" because the plane of the strings is perpendicular to the soundboard (see DeVale 1989, Charry 1992 and 1994, and Knight 1971 and 1972).

The *kora* has left and right sides, just like the human body. Plucking in left-right alternation, the player takes full advantage of this bilateral symmetry. Sometimes a flat metal rattle attached to the bridge enhances rhythmic and timbral flavor. As we hear in "Lambango," pieces may call for *konkon*, an ostinato (repeated phrase) rapped on the resonator. By adjusting the tuning rings along its neck, the *jali* tunes his *kora*'s twenty-one strings in patterns of seven pitches per octave. Just as the tonality of each Javanese *gamelan* is a unique variant of a general standard, the intervals between pitches on a *kora* are not precisely reckoned against an invariant abstract standard. "Lambango" is in the *sauta* tuning (ex. 3–18).

As in most music-cultures, Mande musicians metaphorically link musical pitch to physical space through the words like "high-low" and "ascend-descend" (Charry 1992:208–9). The terminology of English-speakers and Mande-speakers is opposite. When a *jali* holds the instrument, the longer, thicker strings are physically above the shorter, thinner strings. This is why *kora* players call the bass strings "high," the treble strings "low." An ascending passage in western terms "goes down" for the *kora* player.

Ex. 3–18.   Bridge of *kora*, with strings shown as pitches in *sauta* tuning. Drawing by Roderic Knight.

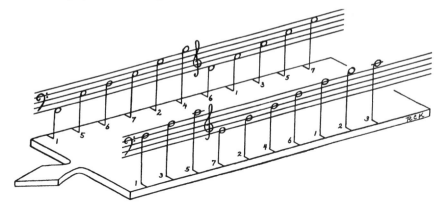

During performance, when the emphasis is on text, the kora player accompanies the singer with *kumbengo,* an instrumental ostinato. Played over and over with subtle variation, the *kumbengo* establishes the tonal and metric framework of a piece. Virtuosic instrumental passages *(birimintingo)* provide interludes between vocal sections. In recorded selection 15, Mr. Suso accompanies Ms. Kuyateh by playing *kumbengo* with occasional *birimintingo*-like passages. Unlike full-fledged *birimintingo* that forcefully suspend the *kumbengo*'s framework, these fills always remain within its time span.

During apprenticeship, lessons focus on the *kumbengo.* Talented youngsters pick up *birimintingo* riffs as they listen to their master's playing. Interestingly, a master does not teach tuning until an apprentice is ready to leave. "Giving him an actual lesson on how to tune the instrument is regarded as the final key to his independence. This lesson is therefore withheld from him until his master feels he is fully qualified to embark on his own career" (Knight 1984:77).

Verbal Art

Recorded selection 15 shows that singers can mix several styles of verbal presentation in one performance. At different points in a performance *jalolu* may tell stories in everyday speech, chant narrative songs associated with specific heroes, sing tunefully, or declaim highly formulaic praises and proverbs. The preferred timbral quality, a forceful chest resonance sung with a tensed throat, evokes the strength of the Mande heroes in sound itself.

The vocalist works with two building blocks of form: *donkilo,* a tune with several phrases of text, and *sataro,* an open-ended, extemporaneous passage of spoken or chanted text (Knight 1972:9). After a section of *sataro,* a singer may return to the *donkilo,* or give way for an instrumental break. In the performance of "Lambango," Ms. Kuyateh begins by ever so briefly singing the tuneful *donkilo;*

the rest of the performance is *sataro*. As Mr. Jobateh taps the *konkon* part, he interjects comments and praises with stylized speech.

Women (*jali musolu*) set the standard for all singers. As one *jali* told Roderic Knight:

> A *ngara* [superior singer] is a woman who is not afraid of crowds, not afraid of anything, except God. She can stand before a crowd with all eyes upon her and not become confused (*kijo fara*). She can shout (*feten*), literally "split" the air with her voice, but do it with feeling (*wasu*) and sentiment (*balafa*), so that people will sympathize with her. She sticks to her forte (*taburango*) in performing, never jumbling the words together (*faranfansandi*) so that they are unintelligible, but choosing words which contain the essences of her message (*sigirango*), words which all listeners will agree are true (*sahata*). (Nyulo Jebateh, quoted in Knight 1984:74)

A HEARING OF "LAMBANGO"

I have never studied *jaliya* with experts. The following section is an interpretation of "Lambango" based on my careful listening to the sound recording. I urge readers to apply this type of creative hearing to all the sound recordings in *Worlds of Music*.

Musical Instruments

In recorded selection 15 the repeating phrases of the *kora* and *konkon* establish the tonal and rhythmic context for the song. (There is plenty of variation in Mr. Suso's playing, but I will discuss only the frequently repeated basic phrases of the *kumbengo*.) I hear the *kumbengo* part within a metric setting of eight quickly moving ternary beats (dotted quarters). The slowly moving knocks in the konkon part mark three moments within a cycle of eight beats: **5** 6 **7 8 1** 2 3 4 (see ex. 3–19). In the *kora* part, I hear three "voices." Voices 1 and 2, which range from g' to a, work together to create one melodic phrase whose steady, dronelike melody

Ex. 3–19.   *Kumbengo* of "Lambango."

Konkon

"Voice" 1

"Voice" 2

"Voice" 3

occurs twice over the span of one *konkon* phrase. Voice 3, which ranges from C to F, has a lively melody set within the time span of the three *konkon* knocks.

As I hear this recording of "Lambango," three features of the *kumbengo* stand out. First, during beats 5–1 the texture sounds multilayered and polyrhythmic; during beats 1–5, however, we hear only the *kora*'s treble voice. Second, the sequence of pitches sets up the following tonal cycle:

Voices 1 & 2	*f'*	*f'*	*a*	*g'*	*f'*	*a*	*f'*	*f'*	*a*	*g'*	*f'*	*a*
Voice 3	C	.	.	.		C	A	F	A			

Third, two important cross rhythms are at play: 3:2 (quarter notes:dotted quarter notes) between voice 1 and the implicit ternary beats and 3:4 (quarter notes:dotted eighth notes) between voices 1 and 3.

Song

Ms. Kuyateh works within the restrained melodic range of a fifth or sixth. Her pitches conform to the tuning system of the *kora*. Because her phrases cadence on f, the song helps establish that pitch as the tonal center of the piece. A Western analyst could describe the contour of her melodies as terraced descent with some undulating motion. She phrases the rhythms freely, giving the impression that her voice floats elusively over the tightly interlocked instrumental parts. The text comes in a rapid explosion of syllables; occasionally, however, she sings several pitches to one syllable of text (melisma). Like members of an African-American church (see chapter 4), Mr. Jobateh responds to Mrs. Kuyateh's "sermon" with affirmation and elaboration.

Text

This rendition of "Lambango" celebrates three twentieth-century Gambian leaders: Musa Molo (lines 1–10), Dembo Dansa (lines 11–21) and Jewuru Kurubali (lines 22–29). The text cites places where significant events in their lives occurred, praises their generosity, and honors them through recitation of stylized praise lyrics (*jamundiro*). The text is not a continuous narrative, but rather a series of praises and a commemoration of events. The *kora* player Alhaji Papa Susso and the ethnomusicologist Roderic Knight have provided the following transcription and translation.

(1) [spoken] *Nte Kekuta Suso, ning Seni Jobate, ning Mariatu Kuyate. Ntelu be rekotola jang bi.*

> I am Kekuta Suso, with Seni Jobateh and Mariatu Kuyateh. We are recording here today.

(2) [sung] *Ye, mba jaja, Jaba Sirimang ning Jaba Tarawari. Fulo ning kelo be mang kanyang.*

> [*Jamundiro* for Musa Molo.][1] The Fulas and war are not one and the same.

---

1. Stylized praise lyrics for Musa Molo, a king of the Fula people, neighbors to the Mande.

(3) [spoken] *Bande banna. Fulo Sirimang jang.*
Wealthy Fula. Sirimang, the Fula here.

(4) [sung] *Wo Bala. Jigi-o Bala banta, Nya-naani Musa.*
Oh, Bala. Bala is gone, Four-eyed Musa.[1]

(5) [sung] *Aniya na Bala. Parumba kumbengo diyata Bala la, Nya-naani Musa.*
Aniya's Bala. The events at Parumba went in Bala's favor,[2] Four-eyed Musa.

(6) [spoken] *Bala Mafaro. Surabali janjungo diyata a la.*
Bala the Great. The campaign at Surabali was successful for him.[3]

(7) [sung] *Aniya la Bala. Surabali kumbengo diyata Bala la, Nya-naani Musa.*
Aniya's Bala. The events at Surabali were sweet for Bala, Four-eyed Musa.

(8) [sung] *Bala mfa Musa me do go jameng to (?) Bala mfa Musa aning bulu si simba (?) Bala mfa Musa aning ke domoda (?). Jigo-o Bala, Bala sumayata.*
[*Jamundiro.*][4] Bala has grown cold [is dead].

(9) [spoken] *A fele laring Keserekunda. A ning malo mang ta Yomali Kiyama.*
He is buried in Keserekunda. He went without shame to the next world.

(10) [sung] *Wo ka mansaya ke, duniya; wolu bee, i jamano banta.*
Those people made kingship in this world; all of them, their days are gone.

(11) [sung] *Wo ka mansaya di, Kibili-o Demba; E, Yasin Baro la Demba sumayata.*
Those people gave us kingship, Kibili-o Demba; Eh, Yasin Barrow's Demba has grown cold.

(12) [spoken] *Salimata Bunja Fara. Demba Damudu aning Demba Tegelema (?). Wo fanang be Kanjelebeti.*
[*Jamundiro* for Demba Danso.] He too lies at Kanjelebeti.

(13) [sung] *Kibili-o Demba. Bu Majila na Demba sumayata (?). Demba . . . Kanjelebeti. Kibili-o Demba. Yasin Baro la Demba sumayata.*
[*Jamundiro* for Demba.] Demba has died and lies at Kanjelebeti. Yasin Barrow's Demba has grown cold.

(14) [spoken] *Wo fanang mu ninsi dimba le ti. A ka a dingolu balundi, aning wandi dingolu balundi. Salimata Bunja Fara. Wo le mu Dembo Danso ti.*
He was like a mother cow. He could feed his own young and those of others too. Salimata Bunja Fara. That was Dembo Danso.

---

1. Bala is a nickname for Musa. "Four-eyed" means "all-seeing."
2. Literally, "were sweet for Bala."
3. Parumba and Surabali were strongholds of the Soninke people, a Mande subgroup; the text alludes to battle between Fula and Soninke.
4. Praise to the effect that Bala was a man who did not enter a battle if he knew he might die in it.

(15) [sung] *Wo lungolu bee mang di. Lungolu bee mang di mogo fanang na lungolu bee mang di (?).*

> Every day is not a holiday (?).

(16) [sung] *Nte Musa fele lota Dembo da la lung do la. A ko, "Mansa jong si kemo di n na?" Dembo kamfata.*

> I saw Musa standing at Dembo's door one day. He said, "What king can give me a hundred?" This made Dembo angry.[1]

(17) [sung] *Nying ne mang na keme di . . . Musa Fili. Konte la Demba mang tumbung ke (?).*

> Did he not give a hundred to Musa Fili? Konte's Demba did not make ruins of the village (?).

(18) [sung] *Keme ni mansolu banta; jali mara mansolu dogoyata.*

> The hundred-giving kings are gone; the jali-patron kings are few.

(19) [sung] *Ntelu keta konoba ti. M be yaarana; sita yoro te n na. I salam aleka.*

> We [*jalis*] have become like vultures. We are soaring; we have no place to sit down.[2] My peace be upon you.

(20) [spoken] *Salimata Bunja Fara, Dembo Damudu aning Dembo Tegelema (?). A ye Kosemari ke, a ye Jakaling ke.*

> [*Jamundiro* for Dembo Danso]. He did well for the villages of Kosemari and Jakaling.

(21) [sung] *Siba-o, wolu bee tambirinna ko (?). Sarakata Bunja Fara, Bunja Mamadi.*

> Siba-o, those are all in the past. [*Jamundiro* for Bunja, an associate of Dembo and son of Mamadi.]

(22) [sung] *Ko, ni i be na 'waye' folo la, i sa folo Ma Biraima Konate. Yamaru jang, siba-o.*

> Say, when you begin your "waye" [singing], you should begin with praise for Ma Biraima Konateh.[3]

(23) [sung] *Sibo banta. I salam aleka.*

> The great one is gone. Peace be upon you.

A DRUMMER OF DAGBON

Musicians have had important functions in the political affairs of many African traditional states. We turn now to a life story of one such person.

On recorded selection 16 we hear singing and drumming of the Dagbamba people (also known as Dagomba) from the southern savannah of western Africa

---

1. To be asked for only a hundred was demeaning to Dembo, famous for his largesse in giving cows or slaves.
2. That is, searching for patrons.
3. *Jamundiro* for Sunjata Keita.

(Ghana). I recorded the music in 1984. The performers are *lunsi* (pronounced "*loon*-see," sing. *luna,* pronounced "*loong*-ah"), members of a hereditary clan of drummers. Like a Mande *jali,* a *luna* fulfills many vital duties in the life of the Dagbamba—verbal artist, genealogist, counselor to royalty, cultural expert, entertainer. The *lunsi* tradition developed in Dagbon, the hierarchical, centralized kingdom of the Dagbamba (Chernoff 1979, DjeDje 1978, and Locke 1990).

THE DRUMS

Lunsi play two kinds of drums—*gungon* (pronounced "goong-*gawng*") and *luna* (ill. 3–3). For both types, a shoulder strap holds the drum in position to receive strokes from a curved wooden stick. The *gungon* is a cylindrical, carved drum with a snare on each of its two heads. The cedar wood of a *luna* is carved into an hourglass shape. By squeezing the leather cords strung between its two drumheads, a player can change the tension of the drumskins and, consequently, the pitch of the drum tones. In the hands of an expert, the drum's sound closely imitates Dagbanli, the spoken language of the Dagbamba. *Lunsi* "talk" and "sing" on their instruments. These musicians are storytellers, chroniclers of the history of their people and their nation.

A PRAISE NAME DANCE

The music we hear on recorded selection 16, called "Nag Biegu" (pronounced "*nah*-oh bee-*ah*-oo"), is one of the many Praise Name Dances (*salima*) of Dagbon. Its title means "ferocious wild bull." This *salima* praises Naa Abdulai, a king of

Ill. 3–3. *Lunsi* **in performance. Photo by Patsy Marshall.**

Ex. 3–20.   "Nag Biegu" chorus phrases and verse answer.

Dagbon in the late 1800s who is remembered for his courage and firm leadership. The "wild bull" refers to a marauding enemy who was killed in combat by Naa Abdulai. As they dance to the drumming, people recall the bravery of the king.

The music has a two-part or verse-chorus form. In the verse, the vocalist and leading *luna* drummers, praise Naa Abdulai and allude to events of his chieftaincy; the answering *lunsi* and two *gungon* drummers punctuate the verses with booming, single strokes. The drummed chorus phrase works like a "hook" in a pop song, that is, a catchy, memorable phrase (ex. 3–20).° The Dagbanli text and an English translation are as follows:

Nag Biegu la to to to,	It is Nag Biegu
Nag Biegu la to to to,	It is Nag Biegu
Nag Biegu la to—n nyeo!	It is Nag Biegu—that's him
Nag Biegu la to,	It is Nag Biegu
Nag Biegu la to,	It is Nag Biegu
Nag Biegu la to—kumo!	It is Nag Biegu—kill him!

LIFE STORY: ABUBAKARI LUNNA

I have tape-recorded many interviews with my teacher from Dagbon, Abubakari Lunna. When I met Mr. Lunna in 1975, he was working as a professional with the Ghana Folkloric Company, a government-sponsored performing arts company based in Accra, the capital of Ghana. In 1988 he retired from government service and returned to northern Ghana, where he served his father, Lun-Naa Wombie, until Mr. Wombie's death. Presently, Mr. Lunna supports his large family as a drummer, farmer, and teacher. The following excerpt of his life story focuses on his teachers.

°The rhythm in measures 5–7 is a standard, if simpler, version of the more exciting phrases heard in example 3–20.

"My Education in Drumming"

My father's grandfather's name is Abubakari. It is Abubakari who gave birth to Azima and Alidu; Azima was the father of [my teacher] Ngolba and Alidu was father of Wombie, my father. Their old grandfather's name is the one I am carrying, Abubakari. My father never called me "son" until he died; he always called me "grandfather." I acted like their grandfather; we always played like grandson and grandfather.

When I was a young child, my father was not in Dagbon. My father was working as a security guard in the South at Bibiani, the gold town.° I was living with one of my father's teachers, his uncle Lun-Naa Neindoo, the drum chief at Woriboggo, a village near Tolon. When I was six or seven, my mother's father, Tali-Naa Alhassan [a chief of Tolon], took me to his senior brother, a chief of Woriboggo at that time. I was going to be his "shared child." In my drumming tradition, when you give your daughter in marriage and luckily she brings forth children, the husband has to give one to the mother's family. So, I was living in the chief's house.†

I was with my mother's uncle for four or five years when he enrolled me in school. They took four of us to Tolon, my mother's home. I lived with my mother's father. We started going to the school. Luckily, in several weeks' time my father came from the South. He called my name, but his uncle told him, "Sorry. The boy's grandfather came and took him to be with the chiefs. Now he is in school." My father said, "What?! Is there any teacher above me? I am also a teacher. How can a teacher give his child to another teacher for training in a different language?" Early in the morning, he walked to Tolon. He held my hand. I was happy because my father had come to take me [ill. 3–4].

My father spent one month. When he went to the South, he took me with him. Unfortunately, at Bibiani my father didn't have time to teach me. One year when my father came back to Dagbon for the Damba Festival [an annual celebration of the birth of The Holy Prophet Muhammed], he told my grandfather, Lun-Naa Neindoo, "If I keep Abubakari at Bibiani, it will be bad. I want to leave him at home. I don't want him to be a southern boy."

I began learning our drumming talks and the singing. Lun-Naa Neindoo started me with *Dakoli Nye Bii Ba,* the beginning of drumming [i.e., the first repertory learned by young *lunsi*]: "God is the Creator. He can create a tree, He can create grass, He can create a person." You drum all before you say, "A Creator, God, created our grandfather, Bizum [the first *luna*]." The elders have given *Dakoli Nye Bii Ba* to the young ones so that they can practice in the markets. When they know that you are improving, they start you with drumming stories and singing stories. On every market day we, the young drummers, came together and drummed by ourselves.

When the Woriboggo chief made my father *Sampahi-Naa,* the drum chief second to the *Lun-Naa* [the highest rank of drum chief], he could not go back to Bibiani.‡ My father said, "Now, I am going to work with you on our drumming history talks." He began with the story of Yendi [seat of the paramount chieftaincy of Dagbon]: how Dagbon started, how we traveled from Nigeria and came to Dagbon, how we became drummers, how it happened that our grandfather Bizum made himself a drummer. If he gave me a story today, tomorrow I did it correctly.

°There are very significant differences of ecology, history, and culture between what Abubakari calls "the North" and "the South."

†While his father comes from a long line of drummers, Abubakari's mother comes from a royal family.

‡Just as the royals of Dagbon have an elaborate hierarchy of chieftaincies, so the *lunsi* have a pyramid-like system of titled positions of authority.

Ill. 3–4a.   Lun-Naa Wombie, Abubakari's father. Photographer unknown.

Ill. 3–4b.   **Abubakari as a young man. Photographer unknown.**

Ill. 3–4c.   Abubakari holding the frame of Mba Ngolba's *luna*. Photo by David Locke.

I was with my father for a long time, more than five years. My father was hard. I faced difficulty with my father because of his way of teaching. My father would not beat the drum for you. He would sing and you had to do the same thing on *luna*. If you couldn't do it, he would continue until you got it before adding another.

[Later] . . . my father sent me to my teaching-father, Ngolba. He had a good voice, a good hand—every part of drumming, he had it. He had the knowledge, too, and people liked him. When he was drumming, he would make people laugh. People would hire him: "We are having a funeral on this day. Come and help us." I traveled with him, carrying his *luna*. Because of his drumming, Ngolba never sat at home: every day we went for drumming. That was how people got to know me. Any time I was walking, people started calling, "Ngolba, small Ngolba." And with my sweet hand and my quick memory, everyone liked me.

Already I knew something in drumming, so for him to continue with me was not hard. I only had to listen to his story and follow him. When we went to a place and he told stories, I tried to keep it in my mind. When we were resting that night, I asked him, "Oh, my uncle, I heard your talk today. Can you tell me more about it?" There, he would start telling me something. That is how I continued by education with Mba Ngolba.° I was very young to be drumming the deep history rhythms with a sweet hand.

My father called Ngolba and advised him, "I am not feeling happy about all the traveling you and Abubakari are doing. Drummers are bad. Somebody might try to spoil your lives. Find something to protect yourself. And protect Abubakari too." Father Ngolba—I can never forget him. Sometimes, when I was sitting at home, he would call me to get something to drink. I couldn't ask him, "Father, what is this?" In Dagbon, you can't ask him—you have to drink it.† My Mba Ngolba did it for me several times.

Another reason why I liked my teacher, my Father Ngolba, is that despite his quick temper, he didn't get angry with me. He loved me. He didn't take even one of his ideas and hide it from me. Even if I asked him about something common that many drummers know, the thing left—he didn't hide it. He would tell me, "I have reserved something. If you bring all your knowledge out in public, some people with quick learning can just collect it."

I respected Ngolba like my father. During farming time I got up early in the morning and went straight to the farm. When he came, he met me there already. If it was not farming time, I would go to his door, kneel down, and say good morning to him. I would stay there, not saying anything until at last he would ask me, "Do you want to go some place?" Only then could I go. Teachers can give you laws like your own father. That is our Dagbamba respect to teachers.

Father Ngolba died in the South. When an old drummer dies, we put a *luna* and a drumstick in the grave. The man who was with Ngolba when he died told me, "Your father said, 'Only bury me with this drumstick—don't add my *luna* to bury me. Give my *luna* to Abubakari.'" I said thank you for that. We finished the funeral back in Dagbon. The second brother to Ngolba spoke to all their family, "Ngolba told me that if it happens he dies, Abubakari should carry on with his duties. He should take his whole inheritance. And Ngolba had nothing other than his *luna*." I have his *luna*; it is in my room now.

SHONA MBIRA MUSIC

The next musical example features another uniquely African type of musical instrument. It is known outside Africa as "thumb piano"; speakers of the Shona language call it *mbira* (pronounced "mmm-*bee*-rah"). The "kaleidophonic" sound of

°"Mba" means "father"; for a *luna* drummer, your teacher becomes your teaching-father.
†According to Dagbamba etiquette children never question the orders of their father.

its music (Tracey 1970:12) provides us with another insight into the musical potential of 3:2 rhythmic structures. The mbira tradition shows another way African music can transform a group of separate individuals into a participatory polyphonic community. Information for this section draws primarily on the research of the ethnomusicologist Paul Berliner (Berliner 1993).

CULTURAL CONTEXT

History

The Shona, who live in high plateau country between the Zambezi and Limpopo rivers, are among the sixty million Bantu-speaking people who predominate in central and southern Africa. Since ca. 800 C.E., kingdoms of the Shona and neighboring peoples have ruled large territories; stone fortresses like the Great Zimbabwe are among Africa's most impressive architectural achievements. These kingdoms participated in a lively Indian Ocean commerce with seafaring powers such as the Arabs, Persians, and Indians (Mallows 1984:97–115). The Portuguese arrived about 1500. Eventually, the large-scale Shona states faded under pressure from other African groups, notably the more militaristic Ndebele in the 1800s. The Shona became a more decentralized, agricultural people.

At the turn of the twentieth century, English-speaking settlers took over the land and imposed their culture and economy on the local Africans. The colonial period in what was then called Rhodesia was brief, but it had a radical impact on most local institutions. As in neighboring South Africa, a systematic policy of land grabbing left Africans materially impoverished. Racist settlers scorned African culture; many local people came to doubt the ways of their ancestors. For two decades after the independence of other contemporary African nation-states in the 1950s and 1960s, white Rhodesians maintained their dominance. Finally, a war of liberation (1966–79) culminated in majority rule and the birth of the nation-state Zimbabwe in 1980.

Music played a part in the struggle. Popular and traditional songs with hidden meanings helped galvanize mass opinion; spirit mediums were leaders in the war against white privilege (Frye 1976 and Lan 1985). After decades of denigration by some Africans who had lost faith in traditional culture, the *mbira* became a positive symbol of cultural identity.

Shona Spirits

From the perspective inherited from the Shona ancestors, four classes of spirits (literally *mweya* or breath) affect the world: spirits of chiefs (*mhondoro*), family members (*mudzimu*), nonrelatives or animals (*mashave*), and witches (*muroyi*) (Lan 1985:31–43). Although they are invisible, ancestral spirits nonetheless have sensory experience, feel emotions, and take action to help and advise their beloved descendants. *Mbira* music helps connect the living with their ancestors.

Humans and spirits communicate by means of possession trance. In possession, a spirit enters the body of a living person, temporarily supplanting his or her spirit. Once embodied in its medium, an ancestral spirit can advise his or her living relatives, telling them things they have done wrong and how to protect themselves and ensure good fortune. Similarly, a *mhondoro* spirit may advise a gathering of several family groups regarding matters that affect the entire community, such as the coming of rain. Possessions occur at *mapira* (sing. *bira*), all-night, family-based, communal rituals. *Mbira* music and dancing are significant elements in these events (Berliner 1993:186–206; Zantzinger n.d.).

THE MBIRA

Construction

Mbiras of many different styles of construction occur throughout Africa and its diaspora. Most *mbiras* have four features of construction: (1) a set of long, thin keys made of metal or plant material, (2) a soundboard with a bridge that holds the keys, (3) a resonator to shape and amplify the sound of the plucked keys, and

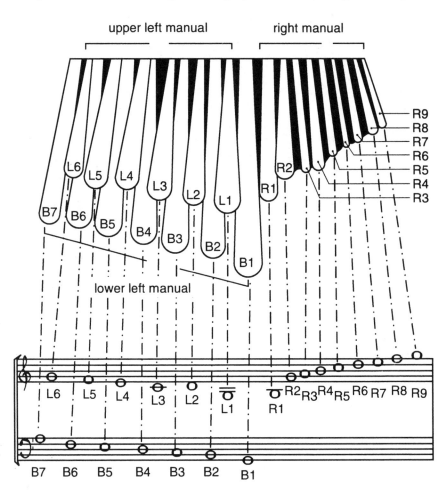

Fig. 3–4. **A tuning plan of *mbira dzavadzimu*.**

Ill. 3–5.   *Mbira* **players. Photo by Paul Berliner.**

(4) jingles that buzz rhythmically when the keys are plucked. Like the *kora,* the instrument matches the bilateral symmetry of the human body; that is, left-side keys are for the left thumb, right-side keys are for the right thumb and index finger. The longer, bass keys lie toward the center of the soundboard, the shorter, treble keys toward its edges (Berliner 1993:8–18).

On recorded selection 17 ("Nhemamusasa") we hear an instrument that is frequently used at spirit possession ceremonies: the *mbira dzavadzimu,* literally "*mbira* of the ancestors" (pronounced "mmm-*bee*-rah dzah-vah-*dzee*-moo"). Figure 3–4 shows a characteristic layout of its keys and one tuning arrangement. In performance, musicians place the *mbira* within a large gourd resonator (*deze*) that brings out the instrument's full tone; when playing for personal pleasure or during learning-teaching sessions, the resonator may not be needed (ill. 3–5). Bottle cap rattles or snail shells attached to the soundboard and resonator provide the important buzzing ingredient to the music. Performances usually include hand clapping, singing, and a driving rhythm played on a pair of gourd rattles called *hosho.*

Tuning (Chuning)

Shona musicians refer to the tonal qualities of an *mbira*'s sound with the English word *tuning* or the modified term *chuning.* Artists use *chuning* to refer not only to interval configurations but also to qualities of tone, sound projection, pitch level, and overtones (Berliner 1993:54–72). The *mbira dzavadzimu* is tuned to a seven-pitch scale over a range of three octaves; interval size varies among different chunings. Musicians debate the affective quality of different chunings and symbolically link the *mbira* keys with features of culture such as family relationships, emotional or physical responses to music, and animal imagery.

The Player and the Instrument

In performance, the instrument faces toward the player. Repeatedly plucking the keys in prescribed patterns, musicians establish cycles of harmony, melody, rhythm, and counterpoint. Each key on the *mbira* emits a fundamental pitch and a cluster of overtones; the resonator shapes, reinforces, prolongs, and amplifies this complex tone. The buzzing bottle caps not only provide rhythm to the music's texture but also add to the instrument's array of tuned and untuned sounds. Tones overlap. The *mbira*'s sound surrounds the player. In this music, the whole is far more than the sum of the parts (Berliner 1993:127–35).

Creative, participatory listening is an essential aspect of this music-culture. Performer and audience must hear coherent melodies in the *mbira*'s many tones. Many pieces exploit the creative potential of 3:2 relationships; often one hand is "in three or six" while the other is "in two or four." Hand-clapping phrases provide a good way to join in the performance and experience this polymetric feeling (ex. 3–21). For players immersed in the process, the *mbira* takes on a life of its own. Here is how Dumisani Maraire, one of the first teachers of Shona music to non-Africans, explains it: "When a mbira player plays his instrument . . . he is . . . conversing with a friend. He teaches his friend what to do, and his friend teaches him what to do. To begin with, the mbira player gives the basic pattern to the mbira; he plays it, and the mbira helps him produce the sound. He goes over and over playing the same pattern, happy now that his fingers and the mbira keys are together. So he stops thinking about what to play, and starts to listen to the mbira very carefully" (Maraire 1971:5–6).

Ex. 3–21.   Hand-clapping phrases for *mbira* music.

"Nhemamusasa"

According to the Shona, ancestral spirits love to hear their favorite *mbira* pieces. Musical performance is an offering that calls them near, thus making possession more likely. Because of its important social use, this repertoire is stable over many generations. Pieces for *mbira dzavadzimu*, most of which have been played for centuries, are substantial musical works with many fundamental patterns, variations, styles of improvisation, and so forth. These pieces have two interlocking parts: *kushaura*, the main part, and *kutsinhira*, the interwoven second part (Berliner 1993:73). Since each part is polyphonic in its own right, their interaction creates a wonderfully multilayered sound. The vocal music, which has three distinct styles—*mahonyera* (vocables), *kudeketera* (poetry), and *huro* (yodeling)—adds depth to the musical texture and richness to the meanings expressed in performance (Berliner 1993:115). Below, we only scratch the surface of the *kushaura* part of one piece.

On recorded selection 17 we hear "Nhemamusasa" (pronounced "*neh*-mah-moo-*sah*-sah"), revered by the Shona as one of their oldest and most important pieces (Berliner 1993:74). It was played for Chaminuka, a powerful spirit who protects the entire Shona nation. The song title literally means "cutting branches for shelter." One of Berliner's teachers reports: "'Nhemamusasa' is a song for war. When we [the Shona] were marching to war to stop soldiers coming to kill us, we would cut branches and make a place [tent shelter] called a *musasa*" (John Kunaka, quoted in Berliner 1993:42). In 1991 Erica Kundizora Azim, an experienced American student of *mbira*, heard a contemporary interpretation of the song's meaning from a female Shona friend:

Homeless people sit in their shantytowns with nothing to do.
No work.
Trouble is coming.

Evidently, the piece evokes profound feelings. For the Shona, sentiments evoked by pieces like "Nhemamusasa" make them effective for use in rituals of spirit possession. Even for those of us without inside knowledge of Shona cultural history, the musical surface of "Nhemamusasa" sparks a powerful affective response.

Rhythm

Tapping out a four-stroke plucking pattern—right index, left thumb, right thumb, left thumb—provides insight into a Shona *mbira* player's experience of the *kushaura* part of "Nhemamusasa" (ex. 3–22). When the pattern repeats over and over, any of the four actions may be taken as the first one. Within this circular structure that has no beginning or end, melodies arise from the *mbira* as players apply the plucking pattern to the appropriate keys.

Each melodic phrase requires three repetitions of the four-pulse pattern; four of these twelve-pulse phrases make one pass through "Nhemamusa's" principal musical unit. From the perspective of playing technique, the pulse structure can be expressed in the equation $(3 \times 4) \times 4 = 48$. Given the right-left alternation in

Ex. 3–22. **Plucking pattern of *kushaura* part of "Nhemamusasa."**

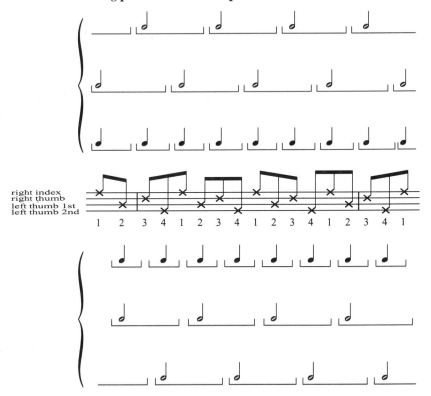

the plucking pattern, we can also interpret the pulse structure as $(6 \times 2) \times 4 = 48$. The music's most fundamental time-feel does not derive from playing technique, however. Instead, players feel a steady flow of ternary beats, that is, three pulses per beat. Within each twelve-pulse melodic phrase, the three explicit four-pulse plucking units are felt in terms of four implicit three-pulse beats. From the perspective of the player's inner feeling, the pulse structure is $(4 \times 3) \times 4 = 48$. Example 3–22 shows the several ways one twelve-pulse phrase can be felt: *x*-shaped note heads are beamed together in groups of three to show the player's basic four-feel; different placements of crossing time-feels "in three" and "in six" are suggested by brackets above and beneath the staff.

The flow of ternary beats is emphasized audibly by the *hosho* and the *kutsin-hira mbira* parts. In recorded selection 17 the coexistence of the two different pulse structures generates a powerful musical effect. The example highlights the interaction of *kushaura* and *kutsinhira*: it begins with the *kushaura* part by itself, then the *kutsinhira* joins and the whole ensemble swings into action. I hear the music "in three" at the start and then find myself reoriented to the four-feel when the other parts enter.

Table 3–1. Pitch sequences in "Nhemamusasa."

		1 2 3 4	1 2 3 4	1 2 3 4	1 2 3 4	1 2 3 4	1 2 3 4	1 2 3 4	1 2 3 4	1 2 3 4	1 2 3 4	1 2 3 4	1 2 3 4
1)	c'		c'		b		c'		c'		c'		d'		d'		c'
2)	c		e		d		c		e		e		c		f		e		d		f		e
3)	g		g		g		g		g		a		g		a		a		a		a		a
4)	C		e		d		C		e		e		C		f		e		d		f		e
5)	c' g	c' g	b g	c' g	c' g	b a	c' g	c' a	c' a	d' a	d' a	c' a

Melody

Let's see and hear how a polyphonic texture is generated within this rhythmic and tonal environment. First, we will consider melodies closely connected to the movements of a player's fingers. Over the course of a forty-eight-pulse cycle, the plucking pattern generates five pitch rows, one each from keys plucked by (1) right index, (2) first left thumb stroke, (3) right thumb, (4) second left thumb stroke, and (5) right index-right thumb as a pair. Read table 3–1 from left to right to get the pitch sequence of each row; read rows 1–4 from top to bottom, left to right to get the pitches in the sequence of four-unit plucking patterns.

Without rhythm these pitch rows are musically incomplete. When set in polymetric context, many melodies emerge. The plucking pattern suggests melodies "in three" and "in six," but the inner feeling guides the ear to melodies "in four." By creatively combining these time-feels in their musical imaginations, experienced Shona listeners hear many interweaving melodies. In example 3–23, eighth

Ex. 3–23. *Kushaura* part of "Nhemamusasa."

Ex. 3–24.   An inherent melody in "Nhemamusasa."

x = left thumb y = left thumb z = right thumb

notes are flagged to the four-feel; three-feel and six-feel conceptions emerge by following each finger's row by itself.

Many melodies emerge from the crossover between hands. Example 3–24 shows one such "inherent" melody (see Kubik 1962). The right thumb "voice" functions like a drone (first on g, then on a) in relation to the steady movement of the two left-thumb "voices." Because of their proximity in pitch, the ear hears the tones sounded by the first left thumb and the right thumb as cohesive rhythmic figures that articulate the upbeats of a three-feel unit ($\frac{3}{2}$ time) marked off by the second left thumb stroke—3 4 **1** 3 4 **2** 3 4 **3**. The multiple possibilities of beginnings and endings are evident in the pattern of octave leaps in the left thumb: Does the lower pitch anticipate the higher? Does the higher note echo the bass?

THOMAS MAPFUMO AND *CHIMURENGA* MUSIC

We close this section on Shona music-culture with an example of what might be termed modern traditional music: "Nyarai" by Thomas Mapfumo and Blacks Unlimited (recorded selection 18). Mapfumo has dubbed this style *chimurenga* music. With its pop band instrumentation and studio production, the music sounds new, but Mapfumo and his audience hear its links to *mbira* music (Eyre 1991:51; Bender 1991:163). Mapfumo and his guitarist, Jonah Sithole, intentionally model their arrangements on traditional music (Eyre 1988:87–88). Like some types of *mbira* music, "Nyarai" is recreational music for dance parties that also comments on topical issues.

Chimurenga music helps us realize that centuries-old traditions need not be obsolete or nostalgic (Waterman 1990). The word *chimurenga* ("struggle") refers both to the war against the white regime in Rhodesia and to a style of music that rallied popular support for the cause (Bender 1991:160–65; Manuel 1988:104–6; Eyre 1991). In the 1970s the music became popular among Africans despite white censorship of song lyrics and an outright ban on artists and recordings. Just as African slaves in the Americas encoded their own meanings in the texts of African-American spirituals, African freedom-fighting songwriters used allusion to make their points. The baffled censors knew a song was subversive only when it was on everyone's lips, but by then the word was out.

Thomas Mapfumo remembers the development of the *chimurenga* music in the following interview with the music journalist Banning Eyre (square brackets mark Eyre's comments, curly braces mark my comments):

I grew up in the communal lands, which used to be called reserves, for the African people. . . . I grew up with my grandparents who were very much into traditional music. Each time there was an mbira gathering, there were elder people singing, some drumming, some clapping. I used to join them. In the country, there were no radios, no TVs. . . . {Later Mapfumo lived with his parents in the city.} I was into a lot of things . . . even heavy metal.

{He joined bands doing rock 'n' roll covers.} There were rock band contests held in Salisbury {now Harare}. . . . Some South African bands would cross the Limpopo [River] into Rhodesia to compete. There were a lot of black bands playing rock 'n' roll music, and we were one of them. But not even one black band ever won a contest. And I asked myself: "What are we supposed to be if this isn't our music? If they [the whites] claim it to be their music, then we have to look for our own music." As a people who had actually lost our culture, it was very difficult to get it back. . . .

{After several years of singing with different bands that toured the beer halls of Rhodesia in the early 1970s, Mapfumo began writing more serious lyrics.} One afternoon, we came up with a nice tune opposing Mr. Ian Smith [the final prime minister of white-minority-ruled Rhodesia]. . . . This tune was called "Pa Muromo Chete," which means "It Is Just Mere Talk." Mr. Smith had said he would not want to see a black government in his lifetime, even in a thousand years. So we said it was just talk. We were going to fight for our freedom. This record sold like hot cakes because the people had got the message. Straight away, I composed another instant hit called "Pfumvu Pa Ruzheva," which means "Trouble in the Communal Lands." People were being killed by soldiers. They were running away from their homes, going to Mozambique and coming to live in town like squatters. Some people used to cry when they listened to the lyrics of this record. The message was very strong. . . .

The papers were writing about us. . . . Everyone wanted to talk to us about our music, and the government was very surprised, because they had never heard of a black band being so popular among their own people. They started asking questions. . . . {In 1979 Mapfumo was detained by the police. After liberation, the popularity of the *chimurenga* style declined, but in the late 1980s he regained local popularity with songs that criticized corruption.} We were not for any particular party. . . . We were for the people. And we still do that in our music. If you are a president and you mistreat your people, we will still sing bad about you. Never mind if you are black or white or yellow. . . .

{His lyrics still make social comment.} Today, Zimbabwe is free. . . . So we are focusing our music worldwide. . . . We have been in a lot of world cities. We have seen people sleeping in the streets and governments don't look after these people. That is what our music is there for today. We will never stop singing about the struggle. (Eyre 1991)

"Nyarai" ("Be Ashamed") dates from after the government headed by Robert Mugabe came to power in Zimbabwe. Recorded selection 18 contains an excerpt from the longer recorded version. Its traditional stylistic features include musical form based on an eight-beat melodic/harmonic cycle (I-IV-I-V), polyphonic interplay of melodies on two guitars and bass, collective improvisation, occasional climaxes using higher register, and insistent articulation by percussionists of the on-beats and selected offbeats. The lyrics celebrate victory and chide people who are unreconciled to change. The song is a praise poem for the warriors, their leaders, their families, and their supporters.

We are celebrating the birth of Zimbabwe
Mothers are proud of Zimbabwe
Fathers are proud of Zimbabwe
We boys are proud of Zimbabwe
Girls are proud of Zimbabwe

Congratulations comrades
And congratulations to all the others
Who fought the *Chimurenga* war
To liberate Zimbabwe
All our ancestral spirits give thanks
The whole nation gives thanks
Congratulations to Mr. Mugabe
And many others
Who fought the liberation war
They liberated Zimbabwe
All ancestral spirits adore the liberators
Congratulations Mr. Machel
And many others who fought the *Chimurenga* war
They liberated Zimbabwe
But there are some reactionaries
Who don't like to be ruled by others
What sort of people are you?
Why are you not ashamed, when you have been defeated
Be ashamed
Be ashamed
Be ashamed
When you have been defeated
Get out
When you have been defeated

Who do you want fight with?
Isn't the war over?
What is left to be done in Zimbabwe?
Mr. Mugabe has won
He has brought peace
Congratulations to the *povo* [black liberation soldiers]
You fought in the *Chimurenga* war
You liberated Zimbabwe
(Translation courtesy of the Information Office, Zimbabwe High Commission,
    London)

BAAKA SINGING: "MAKALA"

Our final example of African music-culture differs dramatically from the tradi-tions of the Ewe, Mande, Dagbamba and Shona. It brings us full circle back to the communal, inclusive spirit of African music so clearly present in the music of the Ghanaian postal workers. (Information for this section relies upon the field research of Michelle Kisliuk.)

On recorded selection 19 we hear singing, hand clapping, and drumming of the BaAka people (pronounced "*Bah*-ka"). An immense, ancient, thickly canopied tropical forest exerts a powerful influence on life in central Africa. The BaAka are one of several distinct yet similar ethnic groups who share features of physique, history, culture, social system, and adaptation to the natural world (Turnbull 1983). No one name refers to all these groups; I will refer to them as "Forest Peo-ple." Because of their physical size, non-Africans have called the Forest People "Pygmies." It is an ethnocentric label; their size is a benefit in the forest and plays a minor role in the way they are viewed by their larger African neighbors.

For millennia, the Forest People existed in ecological balance with their forest environment. Sheltered in dome-shaped huts of saplings and leaves, people lived with kin and friends in small, loose-knit groups. Needing only portable material possessions, a hunting band easily shifted its encampment every few months ac-cording to the availability of food. They obtained a healthy diet through coopera-tive hunting and gathering, allowing them ample time for expressive, affectively satisfying activities such as all-night sings. The social system was informal and flexible: males and females had roughly equal power and obligations, consensus decisions were negotiated by argument, children were gently treated. Individuals were not coerced by formal laws, distant leaders, or threatening deities. The for-est was God, and people were children of the forest (Turnbull 1961:74).

Why is the preceding paragraph written in the past tense? During the colonial and postcolonial eras, external forces have confronted the Forest People to a de-gree unprecedented in their history. They now live within nation-states forged in violent anticolonial wars; multinational timber and mining companies are at work in the forest; scholars and adventurers visit some of them regularly. How are the Forest People received in the imaginations of the non-African outside world?

THREE IMAGES OF THE FOREST PEOPLE

Primal Eden

For thousands of years, members of the world's imperial civilizations have found renewal in the music of the Forest People. In 2300 B.C.E. an Egyptian pharaoh wrote to a nobleman of Aswan who had journeyed south to the Upper Nile, "Come northward to the court immediately; thou shalt bring this dwarf with thee, which thou bringest living, prosperous and healthy from the land of the spirits, for the dances of the god, to rejoice and (gladden) the heart of the king of Upper and Lower Egypt, Neferkere, who lives forever" (Breasted in Davidson 1991:55).

Aided by books and recordings, the Forest People continue to exert a pull on the world's imagination. In particular, the beautiful life of the BaMbuti recounted in Colin Turnbull's *The Forest People* has entranced many of us. Recordings by Simha Arom have opened many ears to the intricacy of BaAka vocal polyphony (Arom 1987). For many people, this music-culture evokes cherished values—peace, naturalness, humor, community. In the music of the Forest People we want to hear an innocence lost to our complex, polluted, violent world.

Primitive Savage

Paired to this image of primal utopia is the notion of primitive savagery. According to this view, Pygmies are of the Stone Age epoch, their way of life an early stage of cultural evolution. Primitives do not know the achievements of "high" civilization—science, mathematics, engineering, philosophy. They have no electricity, no industry, no nations, no armies, no books. If this is the stuff of civilization, then like other native peoples in remote locations on earth, the Forest People must be "primitive."

But calling a human group "primitive" establishes a dangerous inequality. It can justify genocide; enslavement; servitude; colonialism; underdevelopment; land grabbing for lumbering, mining, agriculture, and tourism; and reculturization through evangelism, schooling, wage labor, and military service. From this imperialist perspective, cultures that differ from the "modern" way must change or be eradicated.

Coexistence

Instead, we can characterize the Forest People with concepts that are less emotionally charged. They are nonliterate and nonindustrial, with a relatively unspecialized division of labor and a cashless barter/subsistence economy; theirs is a homogeneous society with small-scale, decentralized social institutions, egalitarian interpersonal social relations, and relative gender equality. Their God is everywhere in this world, and they exist within the web of nature.

Forest life is not an idyllic paradise, however. Hunters sometimes share meat from the day's hunt only after other members of their group complain about its unfair distribution. People suffer with disease, hunger, violence, and anxiety. For the past four hundred years they have shared the forest with Bantu and Sudanic agriculturalist villagers; more recently, they have adjusted to international forces. Compared to one's own culture, the Forest People may seem better in some ways, worse in others. Undoubtedly, their culture is unique.

In hopes readers will feel the music's power, I begin with a detailed presentation of one song. Then I suggest ways their music-culture functions as a resource in their adaptation to change.

"MAKALA," A *MABO* SONG

Setting

The performance studies scholar Michelle Kisliuk recorded "Makala" (pronounced "*mah*-kah-lah") in December 1988 in the Central African Republic (recorded selection 19). The setting was a performance event, or *eboka*, of *Mabo* (pronounced "*mah*-boh"), a type of music and dance associated with net hunting (ill. 3–6). Hunting not only provides food but is a key cultural institution as well. At this performance, novices (*babemou*) and their entourage from one group had walked to a neighboring camp to receive hunting medicine and related dance instruction from more fully initiated experts (*ginda*). Over the course of two days, *Mabo* was performed for this ritual purpose and also for the pleasure of learning new songs and dance flourishes. At times a small-scale affair involving only the *Mabo* specialists and their students, the *eboka* sometimes swelled into a much larger social dance attended by a crowd of BaAka and villagers. Kisliuk recorded this song on the evening of the first day (Kisliuk 1991:211–56).

Form and Texture

An *eboka* of *Mabo* consists of sections of singing, drumming, and dancing. Each song has a theme, that is, a text and tune. By simultaneously improvising melodic variations, singers create a rich polyphony. After five to fifteen minutes of play with one song, they begin another. From time to time, the *eboka* is "spiced up" with an *esime*, a section of rhythmically intensified drumming, dancing, and percussive shouts (Kisliuk 1991:352).

Timbre

Men and women of all ages sing "Makala." Using both chest and head voices, they obtain a great variety of tone colors that range from tense/raspy to relaxed/breathy. A strikingly noticeable feature is yodel, that is, quick shifts between head

Ill. 3–6.   BaAka in performance. Photo by Michelle Kisliuk.

and chest voices. Musical instruments include drums and hand claps. Two different drum parts are played on the drumskins that cover the ends of carved, cone-shaped logs. Often, Forest People enrich the percussion by rapping with wooden sticks on the drum's body and striking together metal cutlass blades; example 3–25 visualizes some of their favorite polyrhythmic combinations. Although not used in *Mabo,* Forest People also make music with melodic instruments such as flutes, trumpets, and harps.

Ex. 3–25.   BaAka polyrhythms (source Arom 1991:305, used with permission).

"Ngbòlù"

	1	2	3	4	5	6	7	8	9	10	11	12	13	14	15	16	17	18	19	20	21	22	23	24
Wooden Sticks			I			I			I			I			I			I			I			I
Drum 2	▲		▲		▲			▲	▲	▲	▲	▲									▲		▲	
Bell	*		*		*		*	*		*		*		*		*		*	*		*		*	

"Mò.kóndi"

	1	2	3	4	5	6	7	8	9	10	11	12	13	14	15	16	17	18	19	20	21	22	23	24
Drum 2	●			●		●	●		●	●			●			●		●	●			●	●	
Sticks	I		I			I		I			I			I			I		I			I		
Drum 1	▲			▲	▲				▲	▲	▲		▲			▲	▲				▲	▲	▲	
Bell	*			*	*		*		*		*		*			*	*		*		*		*	

"Yómbè"

	1	2	3	4	5	6	7	8	9	10	11	12	13	14	15	16	17	18	19	20	21	22	23	24
Drum 2		●			●			●			●			●			●			●			●	
Sticks			I			I			I			I			I			I			I			I
Drum 1		▲			▲	▲	▲	▲			▲			▲			▲	▲	▲	▲			▲	
Bell	*		*		*		*		*	*		*		*		*		*		*		*	*	

"Mò.nzòli"

	1	2	3	4	5	6	7	8	9	10	11	12	13	14	15	16	17	18	19	20	21	22	23	24
Drum 2	●	●			●	●			●	●			●	●			●	●			●	●		
Sticks			I			I			I			I			I			I			I			I
Drum 1	▲				▲		▲				▲		▲				▲		▲				▲	
Bell	*	*		*		*			*		*		*	*		*		*		*		*		

"Mò.mbénzélé"

	1	2	3	4	5	6	7	8	9	10	11	12	13	14	15	16	17	18	19	20	21	22	23	24
Drum 2	●	●			●	●			●	●			●	●			●	●			●	●		
Sticks			I			I			I			I			I			I			I			I
Drum 1	▲	▲	▲	▲	▲			▲			▲			▲			▲			▲			▲	
Bell	*		*		*		*		*		*		*	*		*		*		*		*		*

Theme

Example 3–26 shows the main melody of "Makala" (adapted from Kisliuk 1991:219). Because many different parts occur simultaneously, it is hard to know a song's melodic theme by listening to a recording. Kisliuk learned the theme when hearing it sung in isolation from other parts by a young woman walking along a path. Singers often do not raise the theme until they have established a richly interwoven polyphony; even then, they are free to improvise on its melodic features. Example 3–26B is a transcription from recorded selection 19 of a version of the theme and an immediately following variation.

As is true in Native American songs, singers mostly use vocables (see chapter 2). The sparse text of "Makala" is typically cryptic (Kisliuk 1991:190–91).

moto monyongo	beautiful person
Makala	name of an unknown deceased person from the Congo, where *Mabo* originated
na lele, oh	I cry [implying a funeral setting in this song]

Turnbull reports that songs of the BaMbuti often mean "We are children of the Forest" or "The Forest is good." In troubled times they sing a longer text: "There is darkness all around us; but if darkness *is,* and the darkness is of the forest, then the darkness must be good" (Turnbull 1962:93).

Makala's theme in example 3–26 establishes important musical features of "Makala." The song's musical form relies upon the continuous reiteration of the eight-beat phrase. The melody's intervals may be written with four pitches, given here as D, C, B flat, G. Shaped into two four-beat motives, the tune oscillates between qualities of movement and repose: I hear the B flat on beat four moving toward a cadence at beat eight on C. The tune's rhythm moves toward the cadences on beats four and eight. A beat-by-beat analysis of the rhythm of the theme as

Ex. 3–26.   Theme of "Makala."

Ex. 3–27.   Rhythmic analysis of "Makala."

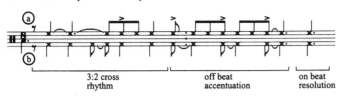

3:2 cross rhythm	off beat accentuation	on beat resolution

(a) rhythm of ex. 3-26B "Makala" Theme

(b) analyis showing patterns of cross rhythm and off beat accentuation

transcribed in example 3–26B highlights the prevalence of 3:2 and off-beat accentuation (see Ex. 3–27).

Polyphony

The polyphonic texture of this choral music is complex (ex. 3–28). Like a well-made multitrack rock 'n' roll recording, the layered parts in "Makala" sound new and fresh with each listening. Forest People use many different qualities of

Ex. 3–28.   Polyphony in "Makala."

Ex. 3–28. (*Continued*)

multipart song. I hear musical processes that can be labeled as heterophony, drone/ostinato, layering, counterpoint, and accompaniment. Happily, reality confounds neat analysis; there are no absolute distinctions among these polyphonic devices.

• **heterophony:** many simultaneous versions of a tune (ex. 3–28A–C).

• **drone/ostinato:** reiteration of a rhythmic pattern on very few pitches (ex. 3–28D–F).

• **layering:** parts with distinct polyphonic functions arranged according to pitch range (tessitura): (1) low-pitched parts outline the tonal movement of the theme (ex. 3–28G–J); (2) middle-pitched melodies introduce two new tonalities and other contrapuntal rhythmic features (ex. 3–28K–M, N–O); (3) the main tune is

Ex. 3–28. *(Continued)*

stated toward the higher range; (4) high-pitched yodeling (*diyenge* singular, *mayenge* plural) adds new counterthemes and more heterophony (ex. 3–28P–S).

• **counterpoint:** distinctive countermelodies, often in the yodel parts (ex. 3–28T).

• **accompaniment:** two drum parts and hand clapping (ex. 3–28U, adapted from Kisliuk 1991:219).

Tonality and Rhythm

As if this polyphonic sophistication were not enough, the BaAka do interesting things with pitch and rhythm as well. I hear three different scales in the melodies of "Makala." A six-pitch scale—E, D, C, B flat, G—predominates in the parts closely related to the theme (ex. 3–28A–J). Two other scales appear in melodies that seem auxiliary to the main action: a four-pitch scale—F sharp, E, D, B natural—allows for melodic parallelism (ex. 3–28K–M); melodies in another four-pitch scale—A, G, E, D—not only emphasize E and A but often have a distinctive rhythmic character as well (ex. 3–28N–O).

Ex. 3–28.   (*Continued*)

MUSIC-CULTURE AS AN ADAPTIVE RESOURCE

Restoring Balance

The active force of music-making contributes to the Forest People's enduring yet ever-changing way of life. The BaMbuti encode the practical, moral effect of song in their words for conflict and peace: *akami,* noise, and *ekimi,* silence or ordered sound (Turnbull 1983:50–51). Troubles arise when synergy among people and symbiosis with the forest is disrupted. Communal singing "wakes the forest," whose benevolent presence silences the *akami* forces (Turnbull 1962:92). With yodels echoing off the trees, the forest physically becomes one of the musicians.

Enacting Values and Creating Self

Improvised, open-ended polyphony enacts such egalitarian cultural values as co-operation, negotiation, argument, and personal autonomy. By making social relations tangible, performance helps individuals develop identity within a group. Kisliuk gives a firsthand report of her participation:

My senses tingled; I was finally inside the singing and dancing circle. The song was "Makala," and singing it came more easily to me while I danced. As I moved around the circle, the voices of different people stood out at moments, affecting my own singing and my choices of variations. I could feel fully the intermeshing of sound and motion, and move with it as it transformed, folding in upon itself. This was different from listening or singing on the sidelines because, while moving with the circle, I became an active part of the aural kaleidoscope. I was part of the changing design inside the scope, instead of looking at it and projecting in. (Kisliuk 1991:195)

Autonomy within Community

Most members of a BaAka community acquire music-making skills as they grow up (enculturation). During times of crisis, the group needs the musical participation of every member. We realize this in a memorable scene in Colin Turnbull's book *The Forest People:* even when others in the hunting group insult and ostracize a man for setting his hunting net in front of the others', he joins the all-night singing and is forgiven (Turnbull 1962:94–108).

Although collective participation in performance is highly valued, individuals may stand out. Kisliuk says that the community knows the composers of individual songs and originators of whole repertories like *mabo.* Explicit teacher-student transmission does take place between the old and young of one group and among members of groups from different regions. Turnbull writes of an acclaimed singer/dancer who seems particularly emotional and prone to time/space transformation during performances: "He was no longer Amabosu; he had some other personality totally different, and distant" (Turnbull 1962:89). BaAka repertory has a varied history and a dynamic future. Music connects the people to their past, while helping them negotiate their present.

CONCLUSION AS DISCUSSION

Contrary to the images of chaos and despair conveyed by international mass media, we have encountered African music-cultures of stability, resourcefulness, and self-respect. Abubakari Lunna's life story reveals the rigor of an African musician's education. The erudition, commitment, suffering, and love are profound. Although he says good drumming is "sweet," clearly it is not frivolous or just fun. Like the music of Frank Mitchell and Ramachandra Iyer, we could call it "deep" (see chapters 2 and 6). We have seen that many Africans value the achievements of their ancestors. The Ewe rigorously study *Agbekor* and recreate it with passionate respect in performance. Innovative *chimurenga* music draws its inspiration from classics of Shona repertory. Mande songs link wisdom of the elders to problems of today.

African music-cultures are strongly humanistic. The human body inspires the construction and playing technique of musical instruments like the *mbira* and *kora.* The spontaneous performances of postal workers and the ritual ceremonies of Forest People point out an important feature of many African music-cultures:

music serves society. As we have experienced, many kinds of African music foster group participation.

Although I encourage African-style musicking, musicians who cross cultural borders need sensitivity to limits and contradictions. To me, nothing approaches the power of time-honored repertory performed in context by born-in-the-tradition culture-bearers. The history of an African musical heritage like Mande *jaliya* casts a humbling light onto recent idioms. When non-Africans play African music, especially those of us with white skin, the legacy of slavery and colonialism affects how an audience receives the performance. Thomas Mapfumo, who as a young rock 'n' roller faced discrimination, now competes in the commercial marketplace with international bands that cover African pop songs. How many enthusiasts for African music love its aesthetic surface but regard spirit possession as superstition?

Music is a joyful yet rigorous discipline. I contend that the hard work of musical analysis yields important benefits. By making clear the sophistication of African musical traditions, analysis promotes an attitude of respect. Analysis helps us understand the inner structure of music; it provides an ear map for appreciative listening and informed performance. In this chapter I have emphasized musical examples with rhythms based on 3:2. As we have seen, this profound and elemental timing ratio animates many African traditions.

Analysis of musical structure raises big questions that resist simple answers: Can thought be nonverbal? What approach to music yields relevant data and significant explanation? By treating music as an object, does analysis wrongly alienate music from its authentic cultural setting? How can people know each other? Each chapter in this book benefits from this type of questioning. We seek to know how people understand themselves, but we must acknowledge the impact of our own perspective. Not only does an active involvement in expressive culture provide a wonderful way to learn about other people, but musicking can change a person's own life as well. From this perspective, ethnomusicology helps create new and original music-cultures.

Inquiry into music-culture need not be a passive act of cultural tourism. On the contrary, a cross-cultural encounter can be an active process of self development. When we seek knowledge of African music-cultures, we can also reevaluate our own. As we try our hands at African music, we encounter fresh sonic styles and experience alternative models of social action. Just as African cultures are not static, each student's personal world of music is a work in progress.

REFERENCES CITED

Amoaku, W. Komla
> 1985.   "Toward a Definition of Traditional African Music: A Look at the Ewe of Ghana." In Irene Jackson, ed., *More Than Drumming*, 31–40. Westport, Conn.: Greenwood Press.

Appiah, Anthony
> 1992.   *In My Father's House.* Cambridge, Mass.: Harvard Univ. Press.

Arom, Simha

  1987.   *Centrafrique: Anthologie de la Musique des Pygmees Aka.* Ocora CD559012 13.

———.

  1991.   *African Polyphony and Polyrhythm.* Cambridge: Cambridge Univ. Press.

Asante, Molefi

  1987.   *The Afrocentric Idea.* Philadelphia: Temple Univ. Press.

Bebey, Francis

  1975.   *African Music: A People's Art.* Trans. Josephine Bennet. New York: Lawrence Hill.

Behague, Gerard, ed.

  1984.   *Performance Practice: Ethnomusicological Perspectives.* Westport, Conn.: Greenwood Press.

Bender, Wolfgang

  1991.   *Sweet Mother: Modern African Music.* Chicago: Univ. of Chicago Press.

Berliner, Paul

  1993.   *The Soul of Mbira.* (Rev. ed.) Berkeley: Univ. of California Press.

Bohannan, Paul, and Phillip Curtin

  1995.   *Africa and Africans,* 4th ed. Prospect Heights, Ill.: Waveland Press.

Breasted, J. H.

  1906.   *Ancient Records of Egypt.* Chicago: Univ. of Chicago Press.

Chapman, D. A.

  1946.   *The Ewe Newsletter.* Achimota, Ghana: Achimota Press.

Charry, Eric

  1992.   "Music Thought, History, and Practice among the Mande of West Africa." Ph.D. diss., Princeton Univ.

———.

  1994.   "West African Harps." *Journal of the American Musical Instrument Society* 20:5–53.

Chernoff, John

  1979.   *African Rhythm and African Sensibility.* Chicago: Univ. of Chicago Press.

Davis, Art

  1994.   "Midawo Gideon Foli Alorwoyie: The Life and Music of a West African Drummer." M.A. thesis, Univ. of Illinois at Urbana Champaign.

DeVale, Sue Carole

  1989.   "African Harps: Construction, Decoration, and Sound." In Marie-Therese Brincard, ed., *Sounding Forms: African Musical Instruments,* 53–61. New York: American Federation of Arts.

Dieterlen, Germaine

  1957.   "The Mande Creation Myth." In Eliot Skinner, ed., *Peoples and Cultures of Africa.* Garden City, N.Y.: Doubleday.

Djedje, Jacqueline

  1978.   "The One-String Fiddle in West Africa." Ph.D. diss., Univ. of California at Los Angeles.

Eyre, Banning

  1988.   "New Sounds from Africa." *Guitar Player,* October, 80–88.

──────.
1991.　"On the Road with Thomas Mapfumo." *The Beat* 10(6): 48–53, 78.

Fiawo, D. K.
1959.　"The Influence of the Contemporary Social Changes on the Magico-Religious Concepts and Organization of the Southern Ewe-Speaking People of Ghana." Ph.D. diss., Univ. of Edinburgh.

Frye, Peter
1976.　*Spirits of Protest.* Cambridge: Cambridge Univ. Press.

Gates, Henry Louis
1988.　*Signifying Monkey: A Theory of African American Literary Criticism.* New York: Oxford Univ. Press.

Innes, Gordon
1976.　*Kaabu and Fuladu: Historical Narratives of the Gambian Mandinka.* London: School of Oriental and African Studies, Univ. of London.

Jackson, Bruce
1972.　*Wake Up Dead Man: Afro-American Worksongs from Texas Prisons.* Cambridge, Mass.: Harvard Univ. Press.

Jackson, Irene, ed.
1985.　*More Than Drumming.* Westport, Conn.: Greenwood Press.

Jones, A.M.
1959.　*Studies in African Music.* London: Oxford Univ. Press.

Kisliuk, Michelle
1991.　"Confronting the Quintessential: Singing, Dancing, and Everyday Life Among the Biaka Pygmies (Central African Republic)." Ph.D. diss., New York Univ.

──────.
In preparation.　*"Seize the Dance!": Performance and the Negotiation of Modernity among BaAka Pygmies.*

Knight, Roderic
1971.　"Towards a Notation and Tablature for the Kora." *African Music* 5(1):23–36.

──────.
1972.　"Kora Manding: Mandinka Music of the Gambia." Sound recording and booklet. Ethnodisc er 12102. Tucson, Ariz.: Pachart.

──────.
1984.　"Music in Africa: The Manding Contexts." In Gerard Behague, ed., *Performance Practice.* Westport, Conn.: Greenwood Press.

──────.
1991.　"Music Out of Africa: Mande Jaliya in Paris." *The World of Music* 33(1):52–69.

Koetting, James
1992.　"Africa/Ghana." In *Worlds of Music.* 2nd ed. New York: Schirmer Books.

Kubik, Gerhard.
1962.　"The Phenomenon of Inherent Rhythms in East and Central African Instrumental Music." *African Music* 3(1):33–42.

Ladzekpo, Kobla
1971.　"The Social Mechanics of Good Music: A Description of Dance Clubs among the Anlo Ewe-Speaking People of Ghana." *African Music* 3(1):33–42.

Lan, David
    1985.   *Guns and Rain*. Berkeley: Univ. of California Press.

Laye, Camara
    1983.   *The Guardian of the Word*. Trans. James Kirby. New York: Vintage Books.

Locke, David
    1978.   "The Music of Atsiagbekor." Ph.D. diss., Wesleyan Univ.

————.

    1982.   "Principles of Offbeat Timing and Cross-Rhythm in Southern Eve Dance Drumming." *Ethnomusicology* 26(2):217–46.

————.

    1983.   "Atsiagbekor: The Polyrhythmic Texture." *Sonus* 4(1):16–38.

————.

    1988.   *Drum Gahu*. Tempe, Ariz.: White Cliffs Media.

————.

    1990.   *Drum Damba*. Tempe, Ariz.: White Cliffs Media.

————.

    1992.   *Kpegisu: A War Drum of the Ewe*. Tempe, Ariz.: White Cliffs Media.

Mallows, A. J.
    1967.   *An Introduction to the History of Central Africa*. London: Oxford Univ. Press.

Manuel, Peter
    1988.   *Popular Musics of the Non-Western World*. London: Oxford Univ. Press.

Maraire, Dumisani
    1971.   *The Mbira Music of Rhodesia*. Booklet and record. Seattle: Univ. of Washington Press.

Miller, Christopher
    1990.   *Theories of Africans*. Chicago: Univ. of Chicago Press.

Mphahlele, Ezekiel
    1962.   *The African Image*. London: Faber and Faber.

Nketia, J. H. Kwabena
    1964.   *Continuity of Traditional Instruction*. Legon, Ghana: Institute of African Studies.

Nukunya, G. K.
    1969.   *Kinship and Marriage among the Anlo Ewe*. London: Athlone Press.

Quinn, Charlotte
    1972.   *Mandingo Kingdoms of the Senegambia*. Evanston, Ill.: Northwestern Univ. Press.

Saad, Elias
    1983.   *Social History of Timbuktu: The Role of Muslim Scholars and Notables*. Cambridge: Cambridge Univ. Press.

Senghor, Leopold Sedar
    1967.   *The Foundations of "Africanite" or "Negritude" and "Arabite."* Trans. Mercer Cook. Paris: Presence Africaine.

Skinner, Eliot, ed.
    1973.   *Peoples and Cultures of Africa*. Garden City, N.Y.: Doubleday.

Thompson, Robert F.
  1973. "An Aesthetic of the Cool." *African Arts* 7(1):40–43, 64–67, 89.

Tracey, Andrew
  1970. *How to Play the Mbira (Dza Vadzimu).* Roodepoort, Transvaal: International Library of African Music.

Turnbull, Colin
  1961. *The Forest People.* New York: Simon and Schuster.

———.
  1983. *The Mbuti Pygmies: Change and Adaptation.* New York: Holt, Rinehart, and Winston.

Waterman, Christopher.
  1990. "Our Tradition Is a Modern Tradition." *Ethnomusicology* 34(3):367–80.

Zantziger, Gei
  n.d. "Mbira: Mbira dza Vadzimu: Religion at the Family Level." Film. Available from Univ. Museum, Univ. of Pennsylvania.

ADDITIONAL READING

Brincard, Marie-Therese, ed.
  1989. *Sounding Forms: African Musical Instruments.* New York: American Federation of Arts.

Nketia, J. H. Kwabena
  1974. *The Music of Africa.* New York: Norton.

ADDITIONAL LISTENING

Berliner, Paul
  1995. *Zimbabwe: The Soul of Mbira.* Nonesuch Explorer Series 9 72054-2.

Chernoff, John
  1990. *Master Drummers of Dagbon, Vol. 2.* Rounder CD 5406.

Knight, Roderic
  1972. *Mandinka Kora.* Ocora 70.

Locke, David
  n.d. *Drum Gahu: Good-time Drumming from the Ewe People of Ghana and Togo.* White Cliffs Media WCM 9494.

Lunna, Abubakari.
  1996. Drum Damba featuring Abubakari Lunna, a Master Drummer of Dagbon. White Cliffs Media WCM 9508.

Mapfumo, Thomas
  1989. *Thomas Mapfumo: The Chimurenga Singles, 1976–1980.* Shanachie SH 43066.

CHAPTER FOUR

North America/Black America

JEFF TODD TITON

Music of work, music of worship, music of play: the traditional music of African-American people in the United States has a rich and glorious heritage, embracing generations of the black experience. Neither African nor European, it is fully a black American music, changing through the centuries to give voice to changes in black people's ideas of themselves. Yet despite the changes, it retains its black American identity, with a stylistic core of ecstasy and improvisation that transforms the regularity of everyday life into the freedom of expressive artistry. Spirituals, the blues, jazz—to Europeans, these unusual sounds are considered America's greatest (some would say her only) contribution to the international musical world. Of course, modern black music does not sound unusual to Americans, and that is because in this century the black style transformed popular music in America—the music of the theater, movies, radio, and television. Today, country music, rock, pop, and, tellingly, advertising jingles owe a great debt to the black sound. Locate some old 78 rpm records from around the turn of the century; perhaps someone in the neighborhood has a few in the attic, or you may find some in your college or local public library. The music on these old records will sound stilted, square, extravagantly dramatic, unnatural, jerky—not because of the recording process, but because of the influence of grand opera singing and marching band instrumental styles of the period. But in the 1920s, aptly called the Jazz Age, Bessie Smith and other African-American jazz and blues singers revolutionized the craft of singing popular music. Their approach was close to the rhythm and tone of ordinary talk, and this natural way of singing caught on. American popular music was never the same again.

MUSIC OF WORSHIP

The easiest way to get acquainted with a music-culture in the United States is to survey its popular music on the radio. Most American cities have one or two radio

144

stations programming black music. Listen for a couple of weeks and you will hear mostly contemporary music: rhythm and blues, soul, funk, reggae, hip-hop, with occasional side trips into older blues and jazz. But on Sundays the standard fare is recorded religious music, along with remote broadcasts of worship services from black churches in the city and surrounding suburbs. These live church broadcasts showcase a broad spectrum of black religious music: modern gospel quartets, powerful massed choirs, and soloists whose vocal acrobatics far exceed those of their pop music counterparts. Congregational singing is also heard on these broadcasts: camp-meeting choruses, particularly among Pentecostals, and hymns, particularly among Baptists. Listen now to a hymn (recorded selection 20) sung by a black Baptist congregation in Detroit. It is the first verse of the familiar Christian hymn "Amazing Grace," but the performance style is unfamiliar to most people outside the black church. A deacon leads the hymn. Because the microphone was placed next to him during the recording, his voice is heard above the rest. He opens the hymn by singing the first line by himself: "Amazing grace how sweet it sound." The congregation then joins him, and very slowly they repeat the words, sliding the melody around each syllable of the text: "Amazing grace how sweet it sound." Next, the deacon sings the second line by himself: "That saved a wretch like me"; then the congregation joins him to repeat it, slowly and melismatically (that is, with three or more notes per syllable of text): "That saved a wretch like me." The same procedure finishes the verse.

That one verse is all there is to the performance. The singers do not use hymn-books; they have memorized the basic tune and the words. Notice that the congregation, singing with the deacon, do not all come in at the same time; some lag behind the others a fraction, singing as they feel it. It is a beautiful and quite intricate performance; try singing along. The transcription of the first two lines (ex. 4–1) may be helpful, but after listening a few times you may be able to sing it, even without reading the transcription; after all, the people in the congregation learned it by ear.°

Next, look at the lyrics to "Amazing Grace" (fig. 4–1). This way of organizing the singing in church, in which a leader sings a line and then repeats it with the congregation, is called *lining out*. Lining out psalms and, later, hymns was a standard practice in colonial America. Black slaves and freedmen worshipped with whites and picked up the practice from their example. Today lining out survives in a great many black Baptist churches, whereas it remains in only a few white churches.

°Notation in this chapter employs an arrow above a notehead to indicate a pitch slightly higher (or lower, depending on the direction of the arrow) than notated but insufficiently high or low to be notated by the neighboring chromatic step. A solid line between successive noteheads indicates a vocal glide. Time value of grace notes should be subtracted from the previous note. An *x* on a staff space or line indicates the approximate pitch of an unstable, half-spoken syllable. A fermata above a notehead indicates a pitch held slightly longer than notated; an inverted fermata indicates a pitch held slightly shorter than notated. This additional notation is an attempt to make the Western staff-scale notation system more responsive to world music styles.

Ex. 4–1. Transcription, "Amazing Grace," as sung at the New Bethel Baptist Church, Detroit, Michigan, June, 1978. Recorded and transcribed by Jeff Titon.

Deacon (solo):

Amazing grace how sweet the sound

That saved a wretch like me

I once was lost but now am found

Was blind but now I see.

DEACON AND CONGREGATION (CHORUS):

AMAZING GRACE HOW SWEET THE SOUND

THAT SAVED A WRETCH LIKE ME

I ONCE WAS LOST BUT NOW AM FOUND

WAS BLIND BUT NOW I SEE.

Fig. 4–1. Lyrics to verse 1, "Amazing Grace," as lining-out hymn.

This version of "Amazing Grace" has many typical characteristics of African-American music in the United States. The words are sung in English, and they fall into stanzas as most English folk songs do. But the style of the performance is black African. The singers sway freely to the music, dancing it with their bodies. As we saw in chapter 3, the leader-chorus call-and-response is the predominant African group vocal organization. The singing tone quality alternates between buttery smooth and raspy coarse. Intonation is slurry around the third, fifth, and seventh degrees of the scales. The tune is playful, ebbing and eddying like the ocean tide.

These attributes of traditional African-American music can be understood more clearly if this version of "Amazing Grace" is contrasted with a British-American version of the same hymn from the southern Appalachian mountains (recorded selection 21). The white song leader stands erect like the soldier of the cross he is, chest out, eyes front, unmoving save for his hand, which marks the regular and clearly audible beat. Leader and congregation sing together instead of in call-and-response alternation. The choral texture is polyphonic instead of heterophonic. The song leader's tone quality is unvaryingly coarse, giving an impression of energetic seriousness rather than playful ecstasy. His tune is stately, measured, and decorated. The transcription (ex. 4–2) of the first two lines compares his singing to the tune as it is printed in the church hymnbook (ex. 4–3). His variations are deliberate, and they differ slightly from one another in each of the four verses that make up the performance. But they are restrained in comparison to the

Ex. 4–2. **Transcription, "Amazing Grace," as sung at the Fellowship Independent Baptist Church, Stanley, Virginia, August, 1977. Recorded and transcribed by Jeff Titon. The transcription follows the melody as sung by the songleader. Printed in the lower staff for comparison is the melody as written in the church hymnal. (See also ex. 4–3.)**

Ex. 4–3.   "Amazing Grace." SOURCE: Church Hymnal (Cleveland, Tenn.: Tennessee Music and Printing Co., 1951).

Amazing Grace

John Newton   Wm. Walker

melodic decoration sung by the black deacon. A few more hearings of this British-American example reveal subtleties such as the upward catch on the release of certain tones, as, for instance, at the end of the word "grace" in the very first line. Try imitating each version of this well-known song; both are much-admired examples of their kind. Your efforts to sing will increase your understanding of the musical styles—and your pleasure in the musical experience.

Our radio survey of black music reveals a vital church music culture. Suppose we enter the black church and observe it firsthand (see ill. 4–1). It is a Baptist church with a large sanctuary, seating perhaps fifteen hundred on this warm Sun-

Jeff Todd Titon

**Ill. 4–1. A young deacon chants an improvised prayer. The microphone
connects with the church's public address system. Detroit, Michigan, 1978.**

day morning. The men are dressed in blue or black vested suits, with black socks
and shoes. A few of the younger men are conspicuous in tan, baby-blue, or bur-
gundy colored suits with matching shoes. The women wear dark suits or dresses,
and many have on fashionable hats; all of them wear stockings and dress shoes.
Choir members have green robes over their formal attire. To keep a breeze, they
swish fans supplied by the funeral homes that have printed their advertisements
on them.

When we hear "Amazing Grace," we have come in on the deacons' devotional,
an early part of the worship service consisting of old-time congregational hymn
singing, scripture reading, and a chanted prayer (fig. 4–2; ex. 4–4) offered by a
deacon while the rest hum and moan a wordless hymn in the background. The
praying deacon improvises his chanted prayer—the words and tune—which begins as speech and then gradually turns to a chant with a definite tonal center,
moving at the close in a regular meter; the congregation punctuates the deacon's
phrases with shouts of "Yes," "Now," and so forth, which are intoned on the tonal
center (C in the musical example).

The deacons lead the devotional from the altar area, and after the devotional is
through, the activity shifts to the pulpit, where announcements are made, offerings are taken up, and responsive reading is led. Interspersed are modern gospel
songs, sung by soloists and the high-spirited youth choir, accompanied by piano
and organ. The preacher begins his sermon in a speaking voice, but after about
fifteen minutes he shifts into a hoarse musical chant (fig. 4–3; ex. 4–5), all the
while improvising and carrying on his message (ill. 4–2). As they did for the praying deacon, the congregation punctuates the preacher's phrases with shouts of

> O Lord. [Congregation: Yes!]
> Have mercy today, Father. [Yes!]
> You know where we at. [Yes!]
> You know our hearts. [Yes!]
> 5 You know our hearts' desire. [Yes!]
> Please Jesus! [Yes!]
> Please Jesus! [Yes!]
> Go with us today. [Yes!]
> I know you know me. [Yes!]
> 10 You know all about me. [Yes!]
> Now Lord. [Now Lord!]
> Now Jesus. [Now!]
> When we can't pray no more [Yes!]
> over here [Yes!]
> (Spoken): give us a home somewhere in thy kingdom.

Fig. 4–2.   Text, closing section of prayer.

"Well," "Yes," and so forth, on the tonal center. Sometimes the preacher fits his chant into a regular meter for brief periods, lasting from perhaps ten seconds to a minute. But more often the chanted phrases are irregular. Still, compared to phrases in ordinary conversation, they are relatively uniform and, when punctuated by the congregation, they give the impression of regularity. Speaking to me

Ex. 4–4.   Closing section of chanted prayer, by deacon and congregation of Little Rock Baptist Church, Detroit, Michigan, October, 1977. Recorded and transcribed by Jeff Titon. The congregation's response [Yes!] is in brackets; the transcription follows the melody (lines 3–10) as chanted by the deacon, who improvises the words and tunes as the spirit moves him.

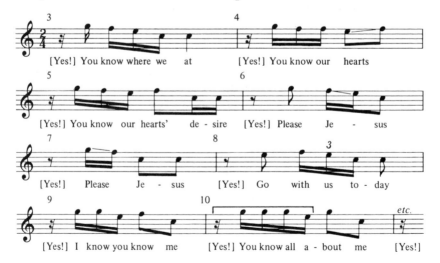

Nicodemus was a ruler.
He was a
rich man.
You know everybody loves money.
5 *Everybody loves to look, be looked upon.*
Everybody loves to be called somebody.
Ah I imagine Nicodemus was ah in that category.
And ah he heard about God.
I don't know where he heard about him back but he heard of
10 *something about God*
What he was doing.
And ah
he
made it up in his
15 *mind*
that he was going to see God.
And ahh he made
an appointment with him.
And ahh the Scripture says that it was at night.
20 *It's all right*
in the midnight
to make appointment with him.
It's all right
to make appointment with him
25 *if it is at noon day.*
You should make appointment with him.
I made appointment with him one day
and ahh
I told him my situation.
30 *Oh Lord.*
And everything went all right.
Mmm
hallelujah.
And Nicodemus said,
35 *he said, "I know*
that no man can do these things
except God be with him."
You know God says
in the
40 *Scripture here,*
he say you can do all things.
"You can do all things in my name
if you'll vow in me
and I'll abide in you."
45 *You should get in Christ.*
You should get in touch with God.
Learn a little more about him.
And when you've found Christ
just wrap around him and
50 *and everything will be all right.*

Fig. 4–3.   Text excerpt from chanted sermon.

**Ex. 4–5.   Excerpt from chanted portion of sermon, St. Mark's Baptist
Church, Minneapolis, Minnesota, August, 1968. Recorded and
transcribed by Jeff Titon. In reading the words, pause about 1/2 second
at the end of each measured line. This tune transcription of lines 20–25
follows the melody as chanted by the preacher who improvises the words
and tune as the Spirit moves him.**

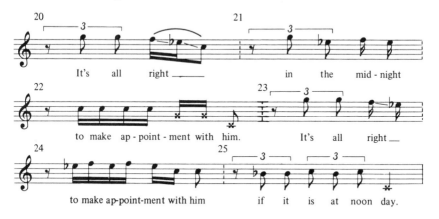

of the rhythm of his chanted preaching, Reverend C. L. Franklin of Detroit told
me, "It's not something I can beat my foot to. But I can *feel* it. It's in me." It is
also in the members of the congregation who sway back and forth with each
phrase.

Eventually the sermon closes and an invitational song follows, led by a soloist
from the choir (ill. 4–3). Three or four people heed the invitation and come for-

Jeff Todd Titon

**Ill. 4–2.   Reverend C. L. Franklin, pastor, New Bethel Baptist Church,
Detroit, Michigan, chanting ("whooping") as he delivers the sermon's
climax, 1978.**

Jeff Todd Titon

Ill. 4–3.   Temple of Faith Choir, Detroit, Michigan, 1978.

ward to join the church. A final offering is taken up, the preacher gives the bene-
diction, and the choir comes down from the choir stand, locks arms in the altar
area facing the pulpit, and joins the congregation in singing "Amen."

Altogether, song and chant have taken up at least half the running time of the
worship service: the old-style singing of the deacons' devotional, the traditional
chant of the prayer and sermon, and the modern gospel songs. The music is literally moving; it activates the Holy Spirit, which sends some people into shouts of
ecstasy, swoons, shakes, holy dance, and trance (ill. 4–4). If they get so carried
away that they are in danger of fainting or injuring themselves, they are restrained
by their neighbors until members of the nurses' guild can reach them and admin-
ister aid. In this setting, music is a very powerful activity—and the church is prepared for its effects.

Much of the music of black Christian worship in the United States is traditional. We have seen that the lining-out tradition dates from colonial America,
and many of the hymns sung are the same vintage. The black spiritual was a later
development, born of the integrated camp-meeting revivals in the late eighteenth
and early nineteenth centuries. Today they can be heard in their most traditional

Jeff Todd Titon

Ill. 4–4.   Religious music quickens the Holy Spirit and sends a woman into trance. Detroit, Michigan, 1977.

form as the "choruses"—one verse repeated several times—in Pentecostal services, while in Baptist and Methodist services they are featured in carefully arranged, multi-versed versions sung by trained choirs in a tradition that hearkens back to the Fisk Jubilee Singers of the late nineteenth century (ex. 4–6). The style of these chanted prayers and sermons is at least as old as the early nineteenth century, and probably older, though of course the deacons and preachers improvise the content. A great deal of scholarship has been devoted to the origins and meaning of the black spiritual (see, for example, Lovell 1972), but much research on the older hymns, modern gospel songs, chanted prayers, and sermons remains to be done.

MUSIC OF WORK

A work song, as the name suggests, is a song workers sing to help them carry on. The song helps by taking their minds off the monotonous and tiring bending, swinging, hauling, driving, carrying, chopping, poling, loading, digging, pulling, cutting, breaking, and lifting (ill. 4–5). A work song also paces the work. If the job requires teamwork, work song rhythms coordinate the movements of the workers (ill. 4–6).

Work songs were widely reported among black slaves in the West Indies in the eighteenth century and in the United States in the nineteenth. Most scholars believe black work songs must have been present in the American colonies, even though the documentary evidence is thin. While it is conceivable that African-American work songs were influenced by British work songs (sea chanteys and the like), the widespread, ancient, and continuing African work song tradition is the most probable source.

Ex. 4–6. "Swing Low, Sweet Chariot." Source: G. D. Pike, The [Fisk] Jubilee Singers (Boston: Lee and Shephard, 1873), p. 166.

Walker Evans, Courtesy of the Library of Congress

Ill. 4–5.   Farmer plowing field, Tupelo, Mississippi, 1936.

Work music is hard to find in the United States today. Where people once sang, machines now whine; the jackhammer has replaced the pickax. The once-vital black American work song tradition is dying.

But in an earlier period, African-Americans sang work songs as they farmed and as they built the canals, railroads, and highways that became the transporta-

Frederic Ramsey, Jr.

Ill. 4–6.   Workers lining track, Alabama, 1956.

tion networks of the growing nation. In his autobiography *My Bondage and My Freedom* (1855), ex-slave Frederick Douglass wrote: "Slaves are generally expected to sing as well as to work. A silent slave is not liked by masters or overseers. 'Make a noise,' 'make a noise' and *'bear a hand,'* are the words constantly addressed to the slaves when there is silence amongst them. This may account for the almost constant singing heard in the southern states." After Emancipation, the singing continued whenever black people were engaged in heavy work: clearing and grading the land; laying railroad track; loading barges and poling them along the rivers; building levees against river flooding; felling trees. And the inevitable farm work: digging ditches, cutting timber, building fences, plowing, planting, chopping out weeds, and reaping and loading the harvest.

The words and tunes of these work songs fit the nature of the work. People working by themselves or at their own pace in a group sang songs that were slow and without a pronounced beat; tunes were hummed or words were fit in as the singer wished, passing the time. As a farm boy, Leonard "Baby Doo" Caston learned to sing field hollers by copying the practice of older farmhands (ex. 4–7; recorded selection 22). Not surprisingly, the words of these songs show that the singers wanted to be elsewhere, away from work. In group labor that required teamwork and a steady pace, people sang songs with a pronounced beat, which coordinated their movements. About thirty-five years ago a rowing work song,

Ex. 4–7. **Transcription, field holler, sung by Leonard "Baby Doo" Caston, Minneapolis, Minnesota, May, 1971. Recorded and transcribed by Jeff Titon. Source: Titon 1974a.**

[Other stanzas:] *I'm going up the country baby and I can't take you.*
There's nothing up the country that a monkey woman can do.

Hey—captain don't you know my name?
I'm the same old fellow who stole your watch and chain.

I'm going away baby to wear you off my mind.
You keep me worried and bothered all the time.

"Michael, Row the Boat Ashore," was recorded by a group of white singers who had probably never come any closer to the work than crewing on the Connecticut River; but their version became a best-selling record on the popular music charts. The song was first reported in the 1867 collection *Slave Songs in the United States* (ex. 4–8). The words to work songs are open ended; that is, the song leader can improvise new lines ("Michael, row the boat ashore," or "O you mind your boastin' talk,") and repeat old ones until his stock is exhausted and his voice gives out, while the rest of the workers merely sing the responsoria burden ("Hallelu-jah!") after each line, in a call-and-response pattern.

Ex. 4–8.   Worksong, "Michael Row the Boat Ashore." Source: Slave Songs of the United States, compiled by William Francis Allen, Charles Pickard Ware, and Lucy McKim Garrison (New York: A. Simpson & Co., 1867), pp. 23–24.

Michael Row the Boat Ashore

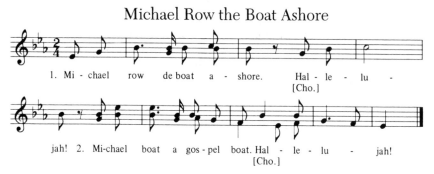

3. *I wonder where my mudder deh (there).*
4. *See my mudder on de rock gwine home.*
5. *On de rock gwine home in Jesus' name.*
6. *Michael boat a music boat*
7. *Gabriel blow de trumpet horn.*
8. *O you mind your boastin' talk.*
9. *Boastin' talk will sink your soul.*
10. *Brudder, lend a helpin' hand.*
11. *Sister, help for trim dat boat.*
12. *Jordan stream is wide and deep.*
13. *Jesus stand on t' oder side.*
14. *I wonder if my maussa deh.*
15. *My fader gone to unknown land.*
16. *O de Lord he plant his garden deh.*
17. *He raise de fruit for you to eat.*
18. *He dat eat shall neber die.*
19. *When de riber overflow*
20. *O poor sinner, how you land?*
21. *Riber run and darkness comin'.*
22. *Sinner row to save your soul.*

What makes a good song leader? What is the purpose of work songs? Collecting work songs in 1947 inside the Mississippi State Penitentiary at Parchman, Alan Lomax asked these questions of the African-American inmates whose singing he recorded:

LOMAX: Do you think it makes work easier when you sing?

INMATE: Yessir.

LOMAX: Do you think you can do more or do you think you can slack off when you sing?

INMATE: Nosir, what makes it go so better—when you're singing, you forget, you see, and the time just pass on 'way; but if you get your mind devoted on one something, it look like it will be hard for you to make it, see—make a day—the day be longer, look like. . . . So to keep his mind from being devoted on just one thing, why, he'll just practically take up singing, see. . . .

LOMAX: What's the most important thing about a good leader . . . does he have a real good voice or a strong voice or what?

INMATE: Well . . . now it wouldn't just exactly make any difference about the dependability of his voice or nothing like that, boss; but it would, it take the man with the most experience to my understanding to make the best leader in anything. You see, if you'd bring a brand new man here, if he had a voice where he would sing just like Peter could preach, and he didn't know what to sing about, well, he wouldn't do no good, see, but here's a fellow, he, maybe he ain't got no voice for singing, but he's been cooperating with the peoples so long and been on the job so long till he know just exactly how it should go, and if he can just mostly talk it, why, and you understand how to work, well it would go good with you—it don't make any difference about the voice. . . .

LOMAX: You mean he has to know the timing?

INMATE: Yessir . . . that's what it takes, the time, that's all it is. You can just whistle and, if you know the time and can stay in time with the axes, you can whistle and do, cut just as good as you can if you were singing . . . but you have to be done experienced. [Lomax 1976].°

The aesthetic standards of the African-American work song call for a good sense of the beat and the ability to time it to the work at hand. A sweet-sounding voice that is always in tune may be desirable in other situations, but it is not important in the work song tradition.

°© Alan Lomax. Used by permission.

Ex. 4–9. **Worksong, "Rosie." Sung by inmates of Mississippi State Penitentiary, Parchman, Mississippi, 1947. Collected by Alan Lomax; transcribed by Mieczyslaw Kolinski. Source: Courlander 1963. Reprinted courtesy of Columbia University Press.**

Rosie

Weren't gon - na mar - ry till ____ a ____ | Chorus | I go free,

I go free, Lor - dy, _____ | Chorus | I go free,

weren't gon - na mar - ry till __ a __ | Chorus | I go free.

Well _____ Ro - sie | Chorus | O Lord, gal.

ah _____ Ro - sie _____ | Chorus | O Lord, gal.

In some southern prisons black inmates sang work songs (recorded selection 23; ex. 4–9). This song, "Rosie," is used to regulate the axe-blows when felling large trees. Sometimes as many as ten men circle the tree and chop, five pulling their axes out just before the other five all strike at once. Axes are swinging through the air at all times, back and forth; the work is dangerous and the timing is crucial. Without work songs, the white and Latino inmates chopped two to a tree. With work songs, the black inmates chopped four, six, eight, or ten to a tree. The work goes faster and better, and the singing group feels pride and solidarity in its accomplishment. In the words of Bruce Jackson, an experienced collector of prison work songs, "The songs [may] change the nature of the work by putting the work into the worker's framework rather than the guards'. By incorporating the work with their song, by, in effect, coopting something they are forced to do anyway, they make it *theirs* in a way it otherwise is not" (Jackson 1972:30).

MUSIC OF PLAY

Having begun our acquaintance with African-American music through brief examinations of the music of work and worship, it is time now to turn to the music of entertainment, or play. True, there is an element of play in the performance of religious songs and work songs in the black tradition. Churchgoers admire the beautiful performance of a verbally adept preacher as he plays with the resources of language and gesture, and they clap their approval as a solo singer sustains a climactic pitch or goes through intricately improvised melodic variations with great feeling; work songs introduce a playful, distancing attitude toward the labor at hand. But although religious songs and work songs contain elements of play, their purpose is worship and work. In contrast, music of play plays for its own sake, for entertainment, for pleasure, even when its effect is educational, cathartic, or ecstatic.

We have heard the music of play in our radio survey, which led us to observe the music of worship in the church. If we walk through the black neighborhood outside the church after the service is over, we find ourselves surrounded by the music of play. Teenagers walk down the street carrying boom box radios with cassette and CD players that throb with the latest R&B and hip-hop hits. Young children skip rope on the side streets, chanting jump-rope rhymes and taunts at one another. Jukeboxes can be heard in the bars and barbecue joints that line both sides of the main street. When night falls, some of the bars have live entertainment—a local band that plays the blues, and in a fancy nightspot a nationally known jazz combo. Downtown in the city auditorium a nationally known artist is scheduled, while in the public gardens a concert of classical music offers the premiere performance of an atonal composition by a black composer who teaches at the city university.

BLUES

The local band that plays the blues will provide us with a detailed case study of blues music, which will be our subject for the rest of this chapter. The blues is a familiar music, but its very familiarity presents problems. Chief among them is the misconception that blues is a subset of jazz, that it was a historical phenomenon, a contributing stream that flowed, some time after Bessie Smith died, into the river of jazz. Nothing could be farther from the truth. Blues is best understood as a feeling—"the blues"—and as a specific musical form, whereas jazz is best thought of as a technique, as a *way* of forming. Jazz musicians applied their technique to the blues form, but blues did not lose its identity. Muddy Waters (ill. 4–7). B. B. King, Albert Collins, John Lee Hooker, and Buddy Guy, who rose to national prominence as blues singers, came from a vital tradition. Until the 1950s, when desegregation and the Civil Rights Movement changed African-American social and economic conditions, the blues music-culture, with its singers, country juke joints, barrelhouses, city rent parties, street singing, bar scenes, nightclubs, lounges, recordings, and record industry, was a significant part of the black music-culture in the United States. Nowadays the blues music-culture incorporates white as well as black musicians, and its audience is worldwide.

Blues and the Truth

The best entry into the blues is through the words of the songs. It is hard to talk at length about words in songs, and harder still to talk about music. As Charles Seeger, one of the founders of the Society of Ethnomusicology, reminds us, it would be more logical to "music" about music than to talk about it (Seeger 1977:16). And in the blues music-culture, when the setting is informal, that is just

Ill. 4–7. Muddy Waters (McKinley Morganfield), studio photo, Chicago, Illinois, early 1950s.

what happens when one singer responds to another by singing verses of his own. Another common response to blues is dancing. Dancers and listeners as a rule have no interest in an articulate body of blues criticism. Speaking of oral literature as a whole, Dennis Tedlock points up the paradox with gentle irony: "Members of primary oral cultures generally limit themselves to brief remarks about performances when they say anything at all, and such remarks are quickly forgotten. There is no such thing as an oral performance of the great critical discourse of the past" (Tedlock 1977:516).

The most common response to blues music is a feeling in the gut, dancing to the beat, nodding assent, a vocalized "that's right, you got it, that's the truth"—not unlike the black Christian's response to a sermon or a gospel song. A good, "deep" blues song leaves you feeling that you have heard the truth, and there is not much more that needs saying. But the words to blues songs are tough. They can stand up to inquiry, to analysis. Because the words pass from one singer to another as a coin goes from hand to hand, they become finely honed and proverbial in their expression: economical, truthful. Response to the words of the songs can be talked about in words. Moreover, blues lyrics have a legitimate claim as serious literature. As literary critics Cleanth Brooks, R. W. B. Lewis, and Robert Penn

Jeff Todd Titon

Ill. 4–8.   Lazy Bill Lucas, Minneapolis, Minnesota, 1968.

Poor Boy Blues

1. *I'm just a poor boy; people, I can't even write my name.*
   I'm just a poor boy; people, I can't even write my name.
   Every letter in the alphabet to me they look the same.

2. *Mother died when I was a baby; father I never seen.*
   Mother died when I was a baby; father I never seen.
   When I think how dumb I am, you know it makes me want to scream.

3. *Ever since I was the age around eleven or twelve,*
   Ever since I was the age around eleven or twelve,
   I just been a poor boy; ain't caught nothing but hell.

4. *When I was a child Santa Claus never left one toy.*
   When I was a child Santa Claus never left one toy.
   If you have any mercy, please have mercy on poor boy.

Fig. 4–4.   Text, "Poor Boy Blues."

Warren have written, "In the world of music the recognition of blues as art is well established. But waiving their value as musical art, we may assert that they represent a body of poetic art unique and powerful. . . . No body of folk poetry in America—except, perhaps, the black spirituals—can touch it, and much of the poetry recognized as 'literature,' white or black, seems tepid beside it" (Brooks, Lewis, and Warren 1973:II, 2759).

We begin by taking an extended look at a single blues performance (recorded selection 24), "Poor Boy Blues," by the Lazy Bill Lucas Blues Band (ill. 4–8). Bill Lucas is the vocalist; he accompanies himself on electric guitar, and he is joined by two other accompanists, one on acoustic guitar and the other on drums. The recording was made in Minneapolis, Minnesota, in 1970. Listen to it now, paying particular attention to the lyrics (fig. 4–4).

Response to the Lyrics of "Poor Boy Blues"

I did not choose "Poor Boy Blues" because the words were outstanding; they are typical. For me, some of it is good, some not; some of it works, some does not. "I'm just a poor boy; people, I can't even write my name" produces an automatic response of sympathy for the poor boy, but it is not a very deep response. I am sorry for the poor boy's illiteracy, but, heck, everyone has problems. When the line repeats I am anxious to hear how the stanza will close. "Every letter in the alphabet to me they look the same" brings to my mind's eye a picture of a strange alphabet in which all letters look alike or, rather, in which the differences in their shape have no meaning. The image is clear, it works, and it involves me. This poor boy may be illiterate, but he is perceptive. And not only does the image itself succeed, but the delay of the most important word in the line, *same,* until the end, and the impact of its rhyme with *name,* convinces me I am hearing the truth. Blues singer Eddie "Son" House told me this about how he put his blues stanzas together: "I had enough sense to try to make 'em, rhyme 'em so they'd have have *hits* to 'em with a meaning, some sense to 'em, you know" (Titon 1977:52) (ill. 4–9). The inevitable rightness of the rhyme—you expect it and it rewards you— hits harder than an unrhymed close, particularly because the end rhyme always falls, in blues, on an accented syllable.

I do not respond to "Mother died when I was a baby"; I resist a statement that sounds sentimental. This is not because I think of myself as some kind of tough guy, but because I want the sentiment to be earned. I much prefer the statement at the close of the line: "father I never seen." The effect is in the contrast between the mother who died and the father who might as well be dead. In the image of

Jeff Todd Titon

Ill. 4–9.   Eddie "Son" House, Minneapolis, Minnesota, 1971.

the father who has never been seen is the mystery of not knowing one's parents. It is not just missing love; for all we know the poor boy was raised by loving relatives. But a child takes after parents, inherits the biology, so to speak; without knowing your parents you do not fully know yourself. That is the real terror of the poor boy's life. "When I think how dumb I am, you know it makes me want to scream" is a cliché; the rhyme is forced. Okay, scream. Nor do I respond to the third stanza when I hear it; but when I think about it, it seems curious that the poor boy says he began to catch hell from age eleven or twelve. I guess he was catching it all along, but did not fully realize it until then. That is a nice point, but a little too subtle to register during a performance. I would have to sing it several times myself to appreciate that aspect of it.

The final stanza takes great risk with sentimentality, calling up Christmas memories, but it succeeds by a matter-of-fact tone—"When I was a child Santa Claus never left one toy"—that dispels the scene's stickiness. Santa Claus never left a toy for anyone, but a child who believes in Santa can enjoy an innocent world where presents reward good little boys and girls. If he could not believe in Santa, I wonder if he ever had any part of the innocent happiness people seem to need early, and in large doses, if they are going to live creative lives. Or it could have been the other way around: he believed in Santa, but Santa, never bringing him a toy, simply did not believe in him.

The song now leads up to it final line, a plea for mercy. "You" are addressed directly: if you have any mercy, show it to the poor boy. Will you? If you heard this from a blind street singer would you put some coins in his cup? Would you be more likely to show mercy to the poor boy than to someone down on his luck who just walks up and asks for spare change? The song will strike some people as sentimental, calling up an easy emotion that is just as quickly forgotten as it is evoked. T. S. Eliot, in a widely influential argument, said that in a work of literature any powerful emotion must have an "objective correlative"; that is, it must be demonstrated by the work itself that there is good reason for the emotion (Eliot 1920). Has "Poor Boy Blues" given you good reason for mercy? Have you been told the truth or were you played for a sucker?

Autobiography and the Blues

The effect of "Poor Boy Blues" on a generalized listener can take us only so far, because we have been considering the words in a broad, English-speaking context. What do the words mean to someone in the blues music-culture? What do they mean to Lazy Bill Lucas? As "Poor Boy Blues" is sung in the first person, does the "I" speak for Lucas? What, in short, is the relation of the song and the singer?

More than any other subject, the correspondence between the words to blues songs and the lives of the singers has fascinated people who write about the blues. The blues singer's image as wandering minstrel, blind bard, and untutored genius is idealized, but, according to Samuel Charters, "There is no more romantic figure in popular music than the bluesman, with everything the term involves. And it isn't a false romanticism" (Charters 1977:112). The result is that most books on blues are organized biographically. Some writers have gone so far as to derive the facts of an otherwise obscure blues singer's life and personality from the lyrics of his recorded songs. Published life stories of blues singers in their own words, on the other hand, are few (see, for example, Brunoghe 1964;Titon 1974a). If these first-person life stories are read properly, they can be understood as far more reliable expressions of the blues singer's own personality than his song lyrics are, because the lyrics often are borrowed from tradition. But whatever the impulse, most people assume that the lyrics of a blues song do speak for the singer; Paul Oliver wrote, for example, "One of the characteristics of the blues is that it is highly personalized—blues singers nearly always sing about themselves" (Oliver 1974:30). If that is true, then "Poor Boy Blues" should be a reflection of the life and thoughts of Lazy Bill Lucas.

I was a close friend of Bill Lucas's for six years, playing guitar in his blues band for two of them. During the course of our friendship I tape-recorded his recollections of his life for publication first in *Blues Unlimited* (Titon 1969), a British blues research journal, and later in the accompanying notes to his first American LP (Titon 1974b). Let us look, then, at parts of Lucas's life history and see if "Poor Boy Blues" speaks for him.

The Life History of Bill Lucas, Blues Singer°

I was born in Wynne, Arkansas, on May 29, 1918. I never heard my mother say the exact *time* I was born: she was so upset at the time I guess she wouldn't remember. I have two sisters and three brothers; I was third from my baby sister, the third youngest.

Ever since I can remember, I had trouble with my eyesight. Doctors tell me it's the nerves. I can see shapes, I can tell colors, and I know light and dark, but it's hard to focus, and no glasses can help me. An operation might cure it, but there's a chance it could leave me completely blind, and I don't want to take that gamble.

My father was a farmer out in the country from Wynne. He was a sharecropper, farming on the halvers.[†] In 1922 we moved to Short Bend, Arkansas, but my father wanted to get where there were better living conditions. A lot of his neighbors and friends had come up to Missouri and told him how good it was up there.

About every two or three years we moved from one farm to another. Some places you had good crops, according to the kind of land you had. Some places we had real sandy land, and that wasn't good; but in the places that were swampy, that black land, that was good. You know when you're sharecropping cotton and corn you look for the best location and the best living conditions. And you could move; you didn't have a lease on the place.

So my family moved to Advance, Missouri, in 1924. We moved by night but that doesn't mean we had to slip away. They loaded all our stuff in a wagon and we caught the ten o'clock train. That was my first train ride; I loved the train then. Advance was about twenty-five miles west of the river; it wasn't on the highway, just on the railroad. It was a little town of five hundred; it consisted of two grocery stores and a post office which doubled over into a saloon. We never did go to town much except on Saturdays.

°©1974 by William Lucas and Jeff Titon. A fuller version accompanies Titon 1974b.
†A sharecropping arrangement in which the landlord supplied the tenant with a shack, tools, seed, work animals, feed, fuel wood, and half the fertilizer in exchange for half the tenant's crop and labor.

In the summertime we'd go in about every week to carry our vegetables to sell in a wagon: watermelons and cabbage and stuff.

My father wanted to own his own farm, but that was impossible. That was a dream. He didn't have enough money to buy it and there weren't any loans like there are nowadays. We owned cattle, we owned pigs. We had about thirteen milk cows, and we had leghorn chickens that gave us bushels of eggs. We were better off than our neighbors because we would sometimes swap our eggs for something we didn't have. We were blessed with eggs and chickens and milk. We were blessed. I tried to, but I never did learn how to milk. I wasn't too much use on the farm. I did a lot of babysitting but not too much else.

There weren't many guitars around, but in 1930 my daddy got me a guitar. I remember so well, just like it was yesterday, he traded a pig for it. Money was scarce down there; we didn't have any money. The boy wanted $7 for it. We didn't have money but we had plenty of pigs. Our neighbors had some boys that played guitar, but they never did take pains and show me how to do it. I would just watch 'em and listen. I learned from sounds. And after they were gone, then I would try to make the guitar sound like I heard them make it sound. It was easier to play single notes than chords. Right now till today I don't use but two fingers to play guitar; I don't play guitar like other people. I wanted the guitar because I liked the noise and it sounded pretty.

After I got it and come progressing on it, a tune or two here or there, my dad and mama both decided that would be a good way for me to make my living. I knew all the time I wanted to make a career out of it, but after I came progressing on it, well they wanted me to make a career out of it too. But they said I had to be old enough and big enough to take care of it, not to be breaking strings and busting it all up.

My father got me a piano in 1932 for a Christmas present. That was the happiest Christmas I ever had. He didn't trade pigs for that; he paid money for it. Got it at our neighborhood drugstore. It was an upright. It had been a player piano but all the guts had been taken out of it. Well, at the time I knew how to play organ, one of those pump organs, I had played a pump organ we had at home that came about the same time as the guitar. A woman, she was moving, she was breaking up housekeeping, and she gave us the organ. It had two pedals on it and you'd do like riding a bicycle. So it didn't take me long to learn how to bang out a few tunes on the piano.

I didn't know what chords I was making. We got a little scale book that would go behind the keyboard of the piano and tell you all the chords. It was a beginner's book, in big letters. I could see that. You know, a beginner's book *is* in big letters. And I wanted to learn music, but after I got that far, well, the rest of the music books were so small that I couldn't see the print. And that's why I didn't learn to read music.

I did learn to read the alphabet at home. My parents taught me, and so did the other kids. I used to go to school, but it was just to be with the other kids, and sometimes the kids would teach me. I was just apt; I could pick things up. I had a lot of mother-wit.

So I bumped around on the piano until 1936, when we left the country and came to Cape Girardeau, Missouri. I had to leave my piano; we didn't have room for it. I almost cried. That was when I started playing the guitar on street corners. My dad had day work; that was the idea of him moving to the city, trying to better his living conditions. I forget what he went to work as: I think he worked in a coal yard. We stayed at my sister's house; one of my oldest sisters was married. But we had to go back to Commerce, Missouri. My dad couldn't make it in Cape Girardeau so we went to Commerce. I don't know what he thought he was going to do there because that was a little hick town, wasn't but about three hundred in population there. He didn't farm there; I vaguely can remember what we did now.

At that time I didn't know too much about blues. We had a radio station down there but they all played big band stuff and country and western music. But we didn't call it country and western music back then; we called it hillbilly music. Well, hillbilly music was popular there and so I played hillbilly music on the guitar and sang songs like "She'll be Coming 'round the Mountain" and "It Ain't Gonna Rain No More" and "Wabash Cannonball." The only time I heard any blues was when we'd go to restaurants where a jukebox was and they'd have blues records. And my daddy had a windup phonograph, and we had a few blues records at home by Peetie Wheatstraw and Scrapper Blackwell and Curtis Jones—the old pieces, you know. So I learned a little bit about blues pieces off the records I'd hear around home. I heard Bessie Smith and Daddy Stovepipe and Blind Lemon Jefferson.

At that time I didn't have any knowledge of music. I liked any of it. I even liked those hillbilly songs. And when I heard the blues I liked the blues, but I just liked the music, period. And when I played out on street corners, I'd be playing for white folks mostly, and that was the music they seemed to like better, the hillbilly music. So I played it because I'd been listening to it all the time on the radio and so it wasn't very hard for me to play. The blues didn't *strike* me until I heard Big Bill Broonzy; that's when I wanted to play blues guitar like him.

We lost our mother in 1939. We buried her in Commerce, and we left Commerce after she died. My dad, he went to St. Louis in 1940, still trying to find better living conditions. Later that year he brought me to St. Louis, and that's where I met Big Joe Williams. At that time he wasn't playing in bars or taverns; he was just playing on the street. So he let me join him, and I counted it an honor to be playing with Big Joe Williams because I had heard his blues records while I was still down South. And so we played blues in the street.

But I didn't stay in St. Louis long. My dad and I came to Chicago the day after New Year's in 1941. Sonny Boy Williamson° was the first musician I met with up there. I met him over on Maxwell Street, where they had all their merchandise out on the street, and you could buy anything you wanted on a Sunday, just like you could on a Monday. They had groceries, clothes, hardware, appliances, right out on the street, where people could come to look for bargains. That was a good place to play until the cops made us cut it out. I played a lot with Sonny Boy. Little suburban places around Chicago like Battle Creek, and South Bend. We were playing one-nighters in taverns and parties. Sonny Boy would book himself, and I went around with him. There wasn't much money in it; Sonny Boy paid my expenses and a place to stay with his friends. He was known all up around there. He played with me when he couldn't get nobody else. I didn't have a name at the time.† But I had sense enough to play in time and change chords when he changed; it wasn't but three changes anyhow. We didn't play nothing but the funky blues. He just needed somebody to keep time, back him up on guitar.

Big Bill Broonzy was my idol for guitar, and I'd go sit in on his shows. He'd let me play on the stand between times; I'd play his same songs. Bill knew I couldn't do it as well as he did, so he wasn't mad. In fact he appreciated me for liking his style. I also

°Harmonica player John Lee Williamson (d. 1948).
†He means the name Bill Lucas was unknown to the blues audiences.

liked T-Bone Walker, but he made so many chord changes! I was unfortunate to learn changes; I never did know but three changes on the guitar.

I used to play with Little Walter° on the street, too, in the black section, where they wanted the blues. I quit playing that hillbilly music when I left St. Louis. In St. Louis I was getting on the blues right smart after I met up with Big Joe Williams. But white folks in Chicago or here in Minneapolis don't like hillbilly music. They tell you right away. "What you think I am? A hillbilly?"

I started in my professional career in 1946 when I joined the union. We all joined the union together, me and Willie Mabon and Earl Dranes, two guitars and a piano. We took our first job in 1946 on December 20, in the Tuxedo Lounge, 3119 Indiana, in Chicago. The paid union scale, but scale wasn't much then. The leader didn't get but twelve dollars a night, the sidemen ten dollars. We worked from 9 P.M. until 4 A.M. It was a real nice club. These after-hours clubs always had good crowds because after two o'clock everybody would come in. We had a two-week engagement there, and I thought it was real good money. But then we were kicked back out on the street.

Little Walter and I used to play along with Johnny Young at a place called the Purple Cat—1947. That's where he gave me the name "lazy" at. We'd been there so long Little Walter thought I should go up and turn on the amps, but I never did go up and do that thing, so that's why he started calling me "lazy" Bill, and the name stuck.

In 1948 I started in playing with Homesick James, and sometimes also with Little Hudson. I started out Little Hudson on playing. When I first met him in Chicago around 1945 or 1946 he wasn't playing. Of course he had a guitar, but he wasn't *doing* nothing. I started him and encouraged him and so he'd come and sit in with me and Sonny Boy or me and Willie Mabon or whoever I'd be playing with. He just started like that. And when he got good he was respected. He had a right smart amount of prestige about him, Hudson did. I switched to playing piano in 1950 because they had more guitar players than piano players. But of course I'd been playing piano all along—just not professionally, that's all. Little Hudson needed a piano player for his Red Devils trio. Our first job was at a place called the Plantation, on Thirty-first Street, on the south side of Chicago.

I don't know where he got the idea of the name from, but the drummer had a red devil with pitchforks on the head of his bass drum. And he played in church, too! Would you believe they had to cover up the head of the drum with newspapers? He'd cover the devil up when he'd go to church.

I had a trio, Lazy Bill and the Blue Rhythm, for about three or four months in 1954 (ill. 4–10). We were supposed to do four records a year for Chance, but Art Sheridan went out of business and we never heard about it again. We did one record. Well, I didn't keep my group together long. You know it's kind of hard on a small musician to keep a group together in Chicago very long because they run out of work, and when they don't get work to do, they get with other guys. And there were so many musicians in Chicago that some of 'em were underbidding one another. They'd take a job what I was getting twelve dollars for, they'd take it for eight dollars.

I was doing anything, working with anybody, just so I could make a dime. On a record session, any engagement at all. For a while I was working with a disc jockey on a radio station. He was broadcasting from a dry cleaners and he wanted live music on his broadcast. I did it for the publicity; I didn't get any money for that. Work got so far

---

°Walter Jacobs, generally acknowledged as the finest blues harmonica player after World War II.

Courtesy of Jo Jo Williams

Ill. 4–10.   Lazy Bill and the Blue Rhythm, studio photo, Chicago, Illinois, 1954. L-R: Lazy Bill Lucas, James Bannister, "Miss Hi-Fi," Jo Jo Williams.

apart. Every time I'd run out of an engagement, it would be a long time before another one came through. And so Mojo and Jo Jo,° they had come up here to Minneapolis. They had been working at the Key Club, and they decided they needed a piano player. I wasn't doing anything in Chicago; I was glad to come up here. I had no idea I was doing to stay up here, but I ended up here with a houseful of furniture.

Lazy Bill Lucas and "Poor Boy Blues"

Bill Lucas's account of his life ends in Minneapolis in 1964. The following year I began my graduate studies at the University of Minnesota and met him at a university concert. By that time he had two audiences: the black people on the North Side of the city who still liked the blues, and the white people in the university community. The 1960s was the period of the first so-called blues revival (Groom 1971), during which thousands of blues records from the past four decades were reissued on LPs, dozens of older singers believed dead were "rediscovered" and recorded, and hundreds of younger singers, Bill Lucas among them, found new audiences at university concerts and coffeehouses and festivals. The revival,

°George "Mojo" Buford, harmonica player, and Joseph "Jo Jo" Williams, bass player.

which attracted a predominantly young, white audience, peaked in the great 1969 and 1970 Ann Arbor (Michigan) Blues Festivals, where the best of three generations of blues singers and blues bands performed for people who had traveled thousands of miles to pitch their tents and attend these three-day events. Bill Lucas was one of the featured performers at the 1970 festival. For his performance he received four hundred dollars plus expenses, the most money he ever made for a single job in his musical career.

In the 1960s and 1970s Bill Lucas could not support himself from his musical earnings. A monthly check (roughly a hundred times the minimum hourly wage) from government welfare for the blind supplemented his income. Blues music was in low demand; most of Minneapolis's black community preferred the current black popular music, while others liked jazz or classical music. Some even made a point of disliking blues, either because they were fundamentalist Christians who associate blues with sin, or because they viewed blues as the expression of a resignation that is out of touch with modern attitudes toward human rights. Nor was there sufficient work in the university community for Bill. He sang in clubs, bars, and at concerts, but the work was unsteady. When I was in his band (1969–71), our most dependable job was a six-month engagement for two nights each week in the "Grotto Room" of a pizza restaurant. Classified by the musicians' union as a low-level operation, it paid the minimum union scale for an evening's work from nine to one: $23 for Bill, $18 for sidemen (about $60 and $50, respectively in today's money). On December 11, 1982 Bill Lucas died. A benefit concert to pay his funeral expenses raised nearly two thousand dollars.

His life history not only gives facts about his life but expresses an attitude toward it, and both may be compared with the words of "Poor Boy Blues" to see whether the song speaks personally for Bill Lucas. Some of the facts of the poor boy's life correspond but others do not. I asked him whether the line about all the letters in the alphabet looking the same held any special meaning for him, and he said it did. Unless letters or numbers were printed very large and thick, he could not make them out. On the other hand, unlike the poor boy in the song who never saw his father, Lucas and his father were very close. Moreover, his experiences of Christmas were happy, and one year he received a piano. What about the attitudes expressed in the song and in the life history? Neither show self-pity. Bill did not have an illustrious career as a blues singer; he scuffled with hard times and took almost any job that was available. Yet he was proud of his accomplishments. "I just sing the funky blues," he said, "and people either like it or they don't."

"Poor Boy Blues" cannot therefore be understood to speak directly for Bill Lucas's personal experience, but it does speak generally for it, as it speaks for tens of thousands of people who have been forced by circumstances into hard times. Thus, in their broad culture reach, the words of blues songs tell the truth.

Learning the Blues

One question that bears on the relation between Lazy Bill Lucas and "Poor Boy Blues" is the authorship of the song. In fact, Lucas did not compose it; it was put together by St. Louis Jimmy Oden and recorded by him in 1942. Lucas learned the song from the record. Learning someone else's song does not, of course, rule out the possibility that the song speaks for the new singer, for he may be attracted to it precisely because the lyrics suit his experiences and feelings.

In the African-American music-culture almost all blues singers learn songs by imitation, whether in person or from records. There is no such thing as formal lessons. In his life history, Lucas tells how he listened to neighbors play guitar and how he tried to make it sound like they did. After he developed a rudimentary playing technique, he was able to fit accompaniments behind new songs which he learned from others or made up himself. Unquestionably the best way to come to know a song is to make it your own by performing it. Listen once again to "Poor Boy Blues" (recorded selection 24), and concentrate first on the instrumental accompaniment. The guitarists and drummer keep a triple rhythm behind Lucas's

singing. When Lucas pauses, the guitar responds with a sequence of single-note triplets (ex. 4–10). This triplet rhythm is a common way of dividing the beat in slow blues songs. When accented monotonously, as in many rock 'n' roll tunes from the 1950s, it becomes a cliché. Music students familiar with dotted rhythms (from marches and the like) should resist the temptation to hear this as a dotted rhythm. Recordings of white musicians before World War II attempting to play blues and jazz very often do not flow or "swing" because the musicians are locked into dotted rhythms.

Now listen to the rhythm of Lucas's vocal, and try to feel both rhythms, vocal and accompaniment, at the same time. You might find this attempt difficult. The reason is that Lucas very seldom sings squarely on the beat. The transcription of his melody (ex. 4–11) is an oversimplification for the sake of readability, but even here we see a great deal of syncopation, in seemingly delayed entrances or anticipations of the beat. Lucas is not having a hard time *finding* the beat; on the contrary, he deliberately avoids it.

The musical brilliance of "Poor Boy Blues" rests on the difference between vocal and instrumental rhythms. Accents contrast; at times each part has its own meter. The reason is this: while the accompanying instruments stay in triple

Ex. 4–10.   Rhythmic outline, "Poor Boy Blues."

Ex. 4–11. **"Poor Boy Blues," stanza 3, sung by Lazy Bill Lucas, Minneapolis, Minnesota, May, 1970. Recorded and transcribed by Jeff Titon.**

Poor Boy Blues

Lazy Bill Lucas

meter, Lucas sings in alternating duple and triple. In other words, passages of two-against-three polymeter (especially apparent at the outset of measures 1, 5, and 9 in ex. 4–11) alternate with passages of three-against-three single meter. I have written example 4–11 in $\frac{4}{4}$ to bring out the contrast. One feels that Lucas initiates each vocal phrase in triple meter, then quickly shifts to duple, hurrying his phrasing in imitation of speech rhythm.

In chapter 3 we saw that two-against-three polymeter characterizes black African music. Here we see a deep connection between African and African-American music: rhythmic complexity and polymeter. But our example from the blues is not just an instance of continuous polymeter, as in Africa. Rather, blues music (and jazz, and reggae) *shifts* into and out of polymeter, playfully teasing the boundary. When these shifts occur rapidly, the boundary between single meter and polymeter breaks down. The result is a new sense of time: the graceful forward propulsion we hear as "swing" that makes us feel like moving our whole body in response.

To sing "Poor Boy Blues" as Lucas does, begin by simply *saying* the words to get a feel for the speech rhythms. If you read music, use the transcription (ex. 4–11) as a guide, but always follow the recording. Listen to the way he slides up to the high G in measures 2, 6, and 10, indicated on the transcription by a solid line just before the note heads. Then hear how he releases "poor" (measure 9) and

Ex. 4–12.   The blues scale (key of G for convenience).

slides directly afterwards into "boy." This sliding and gliding is another type of musical "play," this time with the pitch, not the beat. Finally, listen to him attack the word "twelve" (measures 3 and 7) just ahead of the bar-line rather than as written.

Lucas sings "Poor Boy Blues" in a musical scale I have called the blues scale (Titon 1971). This scale (ex. 4–12) is uniquely African-American, though about fifty years ago it penetrated white American pop music. It typifies blues, jazz, spirituals, gospel tunes, and other black American music. It differs significantly from the usual Western diatonic major and minor scales, and it does not correspond to any of the medieval European church modes. The blues scale's special features are the flatted seventh and the presence of *both* the major and minor third. (Another special feature, seemingly a later development, is the flatted fifth.) A typical use of this double third, sometimes termed the "blue note" by the jazz writers, is shown in measure 8 of example 4–11: Lucas enters on the minor third and proceeds directly to the major third. This is yet another example of "playing" with the pitch in black American music.

If you are a guitarist, it will be easy to chord along with the record, reading the chord diagrams in figure 4–5. The transcription shows where the chords begin. Lucas plays "Poor Boy Blues" in the key of G. With the exception of his G and G^7 chords, he employs standard first-position fingering. He prefers the dominant to the dominant seventh (here D instead of D^7) on guitar, but the opposite when he plays piano.° Most of his single-note runs are made in the first position, but sometimes he moves up the guitar neck on the first two strings to play the highest notes. If you learn to pick out the accompaniment from the record by ear, you will be learning blues guitar in one of the traditional, time-honored ways.

Composing the Blues

Besides learning blues songs from other singers and from records, blues singers make up their own songs. Sometimes they think a song out in advance; sometimes they improvise it during performance. Often a performance is a combination of planning and improvisation. The blues song's first composition unit is the line. If you sing the blues most of your life, blues lines will run through your mind like proverbs, which many indeed are: for instance, "You never miss your water till your well runs dry." A male singer might rhyme it with a line like, "Never miss your woman till she say good-bye." (A female singer's rhyme: "Never miss your good man till he say good-bye.") The singer has just composed his stanza:

°Lucas accompanies himself on piano in another version of "Poor Boy Blues" on *Lazy Bill Lucas*, Philo LP 1007.

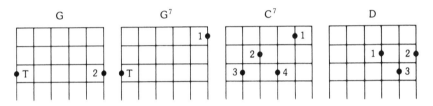

Fig. 4–5.   Guitar chord positions, "Poor Boy Blues."

You never miss your water till you well runs dry,
No, you never miss your water till your well runs dry,
I never missed my baby till she said good-bye.

It is unusual for a blues singer to "compose" self-consciously. Instead, lines and stanzas seem to "just come," sometimes in a rush but more often one at a time and widely spaced. Blues singer Booker White called the songs he made up "sky songs"; "I have an imaginary mind to do things like that. Didn't have nary a word written down. I just reached up and got 'em" (Evans 1971:253). Another blues singer, Robert Pete Williams, described how his songs came to him: "The atmosphere, the wind blowing carries music along. I don't know if it affects you or not, but it's a sounding that's in the air, you see? And I don't know where it comes from—it could come from the airplanes, or the moaning of automobiles, but anyhow it leaves an air current in the air, you see? That gets in the wind, makes a sounding, you know? And that sounding works up to be a blues" (Wilson 1966:21). Statements like these show the universal aspect of the blues and the singer as an interpreter of the natural world. The sounding airplane, the moaning automobile trace a human pattern in the surrounding atmosphere that "affects" only the gifted interpreter, the translator, the blues singer. When the singer turns it into a song for all to hear, the universal truth is apparent.

If the blues singer plans his stanzas in advance, he memorizes them, sometimes writing them down. As we have seen, the stanzas may or may not speak directly for the personal experience of the singer. St. Louis Jimmy, author of "Poor Boy Blues," said this about another of his songs, "Goin' Down Slow": "My blues came mostly from women. . . . 'Goin' Down Slow' started from a girl, in St. Louis—it wasn't me—I've never been sick a day in my life, but I seen her in the condition she was in—pregnant, tryin' to lose a kid, see. And she looked like she was goin' down slow. And I made that remark to my sister and it came in my mind and I started to writin' it. . . . I looked at other people's troubles and I writes from that, and I writes from my own troubles" (Oliver 1965: 101–2).

Songs that blues singers memorize usually stick to one idea or event. A memorized song, Lucas's "Poor Boy Blues" has four stanzas on the circumstances leading to the poor boy's cry for mercy. But the words in an improvised song seldom show the unity of time, circumstances, or feeling evident in a memorized song. After all, unless you have had lots of practice, it is hard enough to improvise rhymed stanzas, let alone keep to a single subject (compare McLeod and Herndon 1981:59 on improvised Maltese song duels). So an improvising singer usually throws in some memorized, traditional stanzas along with stanzas he puts together on the spot.

A Blues Song in the Making

Today a few blues songs are improvised in performance, but most are memorized beforehand. This memorization is a later trend in the history of the blues and results from the impact of commercial blues records (they began in the 1920s) on singers born after about 1910. Singers who wanted to make records studied them and got the idea that a song ought to last about three minutes (the length of a 78 rpm record) and stick to one theme—as most recorded blues songs did. So they composed and memorized their songs, and they memorized other singers' songs. Of course, they could not avoid learning traditional stanzas and building a mental storehouse of them, but more and more they sang from memory instead of improvising. Today the influence of records is overpowering, so singers seldom change lyrics when learning other people's songs and, like rock bands trying to "cover" hit records, they copy the instruments too. In short, most blues singers today think a blues song should have a fixed, not variable, text.

But a few older blues singers continue making up their own songs, improvising in performance and seldom singing a song the same way twice. Improvisation is of great interest because it helps us understand how the mind works. In improvisation the creative mind is on display. One older singer who improvised was Big Joe Williams, the man Lazy Bill Lucas sang the blues with on the streets of St. Louis in 1940 (ill. 4–11). In his songs we will take a closer look at improvisation, but first let us review his fascinating musical career.

Big Joe Williams was born on October 16, 1903, on a farm near Knoxford Swamp, just outside of the town of Crawford, Mississippi.° He made his first musical instrument when he was a young teenager. It was a one-stringed instrument called a "diddly-bow." "I made it from [hay] baling wire," he said. "Like I'd go to your house and take two spools, and I'd put one spool down at the bottom of the wall, one at the top, and when I want to make different tones . . . I'd take a bottleneck, or even a whole bottle." The diddly-bow was a common instrument among African-Americans in Mississippi, and it has been reported elsewhere (Evans 1970). The string is played by plucking one end and stopping the other end by sliding a bottle (or another smooth object) along its length. The distance of the string from the plucked end to where the object rests determines the pitch. It is easy to make and play the diddly-bow, and directions for doing it are given on pp. 185–88 of this chapter.

Still in his early teens, Big Joe Williams left his home and family and began a life on the road that continued for more than sixty-five years. Traveling through Alabama, he worked in the turpentine camps; in Mississippi, he worked on the

---

°Biographical information on Big Joe Williams comes from Leo W. Bruin, "Malvina My Sweet Woman: The Life Story of Big Joe Williams," booklet accompanying *Big Joe Williams,* Oldie Blues LP OL 2804 (Holland).

Jeff Todd Titon

Ill. 4–11.   Big Joe Williams at the Smithsonian Festival of American Folklife, Washington, D.C., 1976.

levee camps; but soon he had acquired enough skill to pursue a full-time musi-cian's career, traveling throughout the South and singing at house-rent parties in the cities, open-air or juke-joint Saturday night bootleg whiskey dances out in the country, in the lumber camps, barrelhouses, and wherever else people wanted good music and good times. Mississippi was his home base in the latter part of the 1920s, where he sang with the outstanding bluesmen of the period, including Charley Patton, father of the Mississippi Delta blues; his partner, Eddie "Son" House; and later, House's pupil, the legendary Robert Johnson. Songs, stanzas, and instrumental techniques passed from one singer to another in the folk tradi-tion of the downhome blues, a tradition and a style quite different from the blues of the same period sung by women like Ida Cox, Ma Rainey, Clara Smith, Ethel Waters, and Bessie Smith. These blues queens were stage show actresses, pop singers who took pride in their ability to sing the latest songs penned by a New York–based black Tin Pan Alley. Backed by jazz bands, their blues was quite sophisticated compared to the rough insistence of the down home vocal and guitar or barrelhouse piano sound.

From 1930 until 1949 Big Joe Williams lived and worked in St. Louis, making frequent trips south to Memphis and the Mississippi Delta, and north to Chicago. During this period he recorded several dozen commercial 78s, which RCA Victor sold on its Bluebird label. But musical styles and musical taste were changing, and the people came to prefer the smoother sounds of B. B. King and T-Bone Walker. He found it harder to support himself in the 1950s, while his record output dwindled and the jobs in clubs were fewer and farther between. He traveled more often, finding work in country juke joints where they still liked the old-fashioned sound. In the 1960s he became a central part of the blues revival in Chicago, singing and playing the blues at folk music clubs on Chicago's North Side, and recording several LPs for the Chicago-based Delmark label. But despite his new association with the promoters of the blues revival, he took to the road from time to time, traveling south to his old audiences. Fiercely independent, he never stayed long in one place. His fame spread to white audiences through the recordings he made for Delmark and Folkways, numerous appearances at colleges and folk festivals, and three European tours with the American Folk Blues Festival, in 1963, 1968, and 1972. As age overtook him, he moved back to his hometown of Crawford, Mississippi, but he had an active musical career at home and abroad until he died in 1982.

Throughout his more than sixty-year blues career, Big Joe Willams was a prolific blues composer. His best-known song is "Baby Please Don't Go," which dates from 1921 (fig. 4–6). Even in his seventies Williams continued to compose songs. At the 1976 Smithsonian Institution Festival of American Folklife, he was proud to perform his latest composition, "Watergate Blues," a topical song on some of the events surrounding the break-in at the Democratic national headquarters that led to the resignation of President Nixon. I recorded him singing it three times on three successive days, and I was not surprised to find that each version was different from the others.

If you look at the differences in these three versions (figs. 4–7a,b,c) you will begin to understand how the improvising blues singer composes at the moment of

Baby please don't go,
Baby please don't go,
Baby please don't go back to New Orleans 'cause I love you so.

Turn your lamp down low,
Turn your lamp down low,
Turn your lamp down low, crying all night long, baby please don't go.

Fig. 4–6.   Lyrics, "Baby Please Don't Go."

1. *Yes I went to the gas station this morning,*
   trying to get my gas ticket straight.
   He said, "No, Big Joe, you can't get but three gallons of gas
   because of this Watergate."
   Every time I'm telling you, I can't see a thing but Watergate.
   Well I'll be so glad, so glad, when President Ford gets everything straight.

2. *Well the rooster told the hen,*
   "I want all the hens to go out and lay."
   She said, "No: Watergate is in my house, boy,
   and I ain't gonna do what you say."
   Every time I reach for the newspaper I can't see a thing but Watergate.
   Well I'll be so glad, so glad, when President Ford gets everything straight.

3. *I want everybody*
   to leave President Nixon alone.
   Let him leave the hospital in California
   go back to his old home.
   Well oh, can't hear a thing but Watergate.
   I'll be so glad, so glad, when President Ford gets everything straight.

4. *I got a handful of nickels,*
   a pocketful of dimes,
   potful of water, good children,
   all the time.
   Oh yeah, can't hear a thing but Watergate.
   Be so glad when President Ford get everything straight.

Fig. 4–7a.   "Watergate Blues," version 1. July 3, 1976.

performance. Read them now (and pay particular attention to the stanzas that begin with the rooster addressing the hen). The first thing you notice is the stanza form. It differs from the typical three-line blue stanza of "Poor Boy Blues." In "Poor Boy Blues" Bill Lucas sang a line, then more or less repeated it, and closed the stanza with a rhyming punch line. Most blues stanzas fall into this three-line pattern, particularly traditional stanzas. But some, like "Watergate Blues," fall into a different line pattern consisting of a quatrain (four lines rhymed abcb) and a rhymed two-line refrain that follows to close out each stanza. The contrast between the three-line stanza and the quatrain-refrain stanza can easily be shown in a diagram, for the quatrain fits into the first four measures (bars) of the twelve-bar blues strophe, while the refrain fits into the last eight bars of the twelve-bar blues strophe (fig. 4–8). The quatrain-refrain pattern became popular after World War II. It usually offers story vignettes in the quatrain to prove the truth of the repeated refrain. In "Watergate Blues" the quatrains show why the "I" of the song thinks the Watergate affair is such a nuisance.

The stanza form, whether three-line or quatrain-refrain, is of course preset, and so it acts as a mold into which the improvising singer pours his words. Just *any* words will not do, because the refrain has to repeat, lines must rhyme, and

1. *Yes I went out to the gas station this morning,*
    tried to get my gas ticket straight.
    Said, "No, I can't guarantee but three gallons of gas
    Remember the Watergate."
    Oh, every time I look at my tv, can't hear a thing but Watergate.
    Well I'll be so glad, so glad, when President Ford get every doggone
    thing straight.

2. *Well the rooster told the hen,*
    "I want you to go and lay."
    Say, "Watergate my home and I
    don't play still."
    Every time I look at my tv, can't hear a thing but Watergate.
    Well, I'll be so glad when President Ford, lord, gets everything straight.

3. *I got a handful of nickels boys and*
    pocketful of dimes,
    houseful of children all
    all are mine.
    They was a-crying, Can't hear a thing but Watergate."
    I'll be so glad when President Ford gets every doggone thing straight.

Fig. 4–7b. "Watergate Blues," version 2. July 4, 1976.

the whole thing has to make sense. The quatrain-refrain form is a little more diffi-cult to improvise in because the quatrain lines are so short and come so fast. Now let us look at Big Joe Williams's improvisations in the three versions of "Water-gate Blues." You might think it would be easiest just to improvise in the quatrain and memorize the refrain; but if we compare the refrains Williams sings, we find differences, so it seems he has not memorized them. The general idea is the same—that is, the idea that everywhere the singer looks he cannot avoid news of Watergate. But the exact expression of that idea varies, as Williams substitutes the radio, television, and newspaper one for the other.

Now behind this apparently simple technique of substitution lies part of the explanation of the blues singer's ability to improvise. Let us remember how hard this is, compared, say, to a kind of improvisation we are familiar with because we do it all the time: namely, conversation. In conversation we can stop and think, but a blues singer has to keep going, and he or she also has to rhyme. So to help himself, the blues singer relies *partly* on memory. What is memorized are words that go together and the patterns of their togetherness. By combining and manip-ulating and substituting these word groups the singer puts together lines and stan-zas spontaneously. It is important to realize that this improvisation does not proceed word by word—that would be too hard—but word group by word group.

Suppose we call each of these word groups a *preform* (Titon 1978). A preform is something roughly presized and shaped that is brought back from storage and given its final form just before use. These blues word groups are preforms stored in the memory, then retrieved and given a final shape—verb tense, for instance,

1. *Yes I went out to the bus station this morning,*
    trying to get my ticket straight.
    Said, "You can't get but three gallons of gas boy you
    'cause you know this Watergate."
    And every time I pick up my paper I can't hear a thing but Watergate.
    Yes I'll be so glad when President Ford get every doggone thing straight.

2. *Well the rooster told the hen now,*
    "Want the hens all go lay."
    Said, "No; I'm not home, I can't lay no more,
    'cause I got nothing but Watergate."
    Whoa whoa lord I can't see a thing, yes nothing but Watergate.
    Yes I'll be so glad, so glad when President Ford gets every doggone thing straight.

3. *Well I want everybody*
    to leave President Nixon alone.
    Let him out the hospital in California
    and go back to his next home.
    Well, I say I can't hear a thing but Watergate.
    Every time I pick up my paper I read about nothing but Watergate.

4. *Well the rooster told the hen now,*
    "I'll be like a old crow.
    See, I got Watergate in my house and I can't
    live there no more."
    Every time I listen at the television can't see a thing but Watergate.

Fig. 4–7c.   "Watergate Blues," version 3. July 5, 1976.

or gender—just before singing. We need an illustration, and the stanzas in which Big Joe Williams begins, "I got a handful of nickels" will do (fig. 4–9). In each version, lines 1 plus 2 make up a preform, roughly stored and then sung almost identically. They end in "dimes," which has the long *i* plus the nasal near the close to set up the rhyme. Now in each version lines 3 plus 4 also make up preforms, but they are different preforms. So Williams found two different preforms, one in each version, for lines 3 plus 4, each ending the stanza sensibly and with a different but proper long *i* plus nasal rhyme. This is how the improvising blues singer builds up his lines and stanzas from preforms at the moment of singing.

If preforms always worked perfectly we would never know for sure that they (rather than straight memorization, or word-by-word improvising) were the key to improvisation in blues. But because they sometimes fail we can see them in process. In other words, we need to look at failed improvisations as well as successful ones to confirm that improvisation proceeds by preforms.

Consider the four quatrains in the three versions of "Watergate Blues" that begin, "Well the rooster told the hen." In three of them Williams follows this line with "I want the hens to go out and lay" or some rough variant. Each is sensible and effective, and together they suggest preforms. But the failure in stanza 2, version 2, confirms it. "Watergate my home and I don't play still" neither rhymes nor

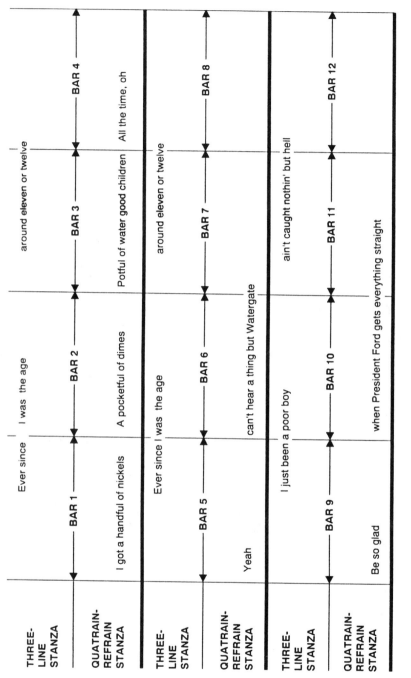

Fig. 4-8.   Two twelve-bar blues stanza forms compared.

Version 1 [Preforms 1 & 2]		Line	Version 2 [Preforms 1 & 3]	
Preform 1	*I got a handful of nickels,*	**(1)**	*I got a handful of nickels, boys,*	**Preform 1**
	A pocketful of dimes,	**(2)**	*Pocketful of dimes,*	
Preform 2	*Potful of water, good children*	**(3)**	*Houseful of children all*	**Preform 3**
	All the time.	**(4)**	*All are mine.*	

Fig. 4–9. **Two stanzas built from preforms compared.**

make sense. What happened? Williams sang "play," showing he had a good rhyme; he just failed to recall a good preform, like "'Ain't gonna do what you say." Probably his mind got stuck on a preform involving "play."

Is it possible that Williams memorized several slightly different quatrains? This tactic would have been terribly inefficient. If he wanted to sing from memory, he would memorize a single quatrain. No, I think the preform theory best fits the evidence. The idea is the same at the root of these rooster-hen quatrains: the hen cannot or will not lay because Watergate upsets her. Now, if Williams had memorized, the same idea would come out in the same quatrain every time, or at least many times. On the other hand, if Williams's memory failed he would pause— come to a dead halt, or garble. But—and this is crucial—Williams expresses the same idea wonderfully well in a variety of ways. He even varies his rhymes ("say" and "Water*gate*" rhymed with "lay"). Williams improvises, and the preform theory shows us how.

"Watergate Blues" is an unusual topical song, blending the winter 1973–74 gasoline shortage with the Watergate burglary. But the idea that the media spent too much time on Watergate was shared by many Americans who simply wanted to be done with it; and it appealed, also, to the audience at the Festival of American Folklike when Williams sang it not far from the Watergate building itself. The creative artist who continues to create in old age, whether a Big Joe Williams or a Pablo Casals, is always awe-inspiring. Perhaps the lesson is that creative artistry does not depend so much on youth and strength as on vision, and that vision may be sustained, and sustaining, into old age.

How to Make and Play a One-Stringed Diddly-Bow

The musical bow, a single string stretched on a frame of some kind, like a hunting bow, is a widespread tribal musical instrument. Related to it is the one-stringed diddly-bow, a traditional African-American instrument. Many blues singers who grew up on Southern farms—such as Big Joe Williams—recall it as their first musical instrument. One-String Sam accompanied himself on a small, portable diddly-bow as he sang "I Need $100" in Detroit in the early 1950s (recorded selection 25; fig. 4–10). I cannot make out the lyrics of stanza 2 with much confidence.

Despite its simple construction and playing technique, the diddly-bow produces a very satisfactory blues sound. It will be easy to build and learn to play it

1. *You know I talked with mother this morning,*
   mother talked with the judge.
   I could hear her, eavesdropping, you know I
   understood their words.
   > *She said, "I need $100.*
   > *You know I—.*
   > *You know I need $100*
   > *just to go my baby's bond."*

2. *You know me and my little girl got up this morning.*
   She said she wanted to freeze to death.
   Told her in the icebox to look in, baby I
   freeze my ice myself.
   > *I just need $100.*
   > *I say I need—.*
   > *You know I need $100*
   > *just to go my baby's bond.*

3. *You know I left your mother standing, baby,*
   In her doorway crying.
   Come begging and pleading don't
   mistreat your little girl of mine.
   > *I said, "Mother-in-law I need $100.*
   > *All I need's—.*
   > *All I need $100*
   > *just to go my baby's bond."*

4. *You know my houselady come telling about*
   want to talk for an hour,
   want to go to the Red Cross people you know
   want a sack of Red Cross flour.
   > *I told her all I need's $100.*
   > *All I need's—.*
   > *Baby if I had $100*
   > *I could go and go my baby's bond.*

Fig. 4–10.   Lyrics, "I Need $100."

even if you have never built an instrument before. Follow illustration 4–12, showing Compton Jones, or make the variant shown in fig 4–11. A list of building materials and a construction diagram for a portable diddly-bow are shown in this figure. The wood can be obtained free from the scrap pile of a sawmill or lumberyard. For a few dollars, any musical instrument store should be able to supply you with a single guitar machine head, some hard plastic bridge and nut material, and a steel string. Try to get a banjo string with a "loop end" that will fit easily over the wood screw at the bridge end of the instrument (see fig. 4–11).

Saw a notch for the nut near one end of the piece of wood, then cut the wood back to the end. Glue a piece of scrap wood to the bottom of the cutaway. Drill a hole for the string anchor pole and attach the machine head to the scrap wood

Cheryl T. Evans

Ill. 4–12.   Compton Jones plays the diddly-bow, near Sentatobia, Mississippi, 1971.

bottom. Make sure that the top of the string anchor pole is lower than the top of the nut (fig. 4–12).

Glue the nut flush against the notch so that the top of the nut is about ⅛ inch higher than the stringboard. Saw a notch for the bridge near the other end of the stringboard, and glue in the bridge so that it is about ¼ inch higher than the

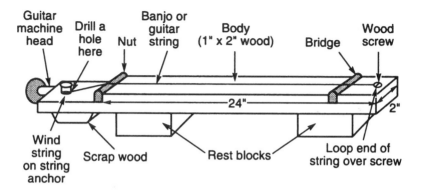

Fig. 4–11.   How to make a portable, one-stringed diddly-bow.

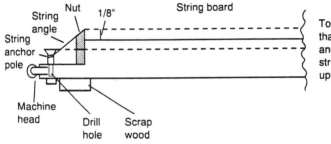

Fig. 4–12.   Close-up, nut end of diddly-bow.

stringboard. Insert a small wood screw between the bridge and the short end of the stringboard, leaving about ¹⁄₁₆ inch clearance between the board and the head of the screw to fit the string loop on. Glue two pieces of scrap wood underneath the stringboard to serve as a table rest. Attach the loop end of the banjo string over the wood screw, then push the other end through the machine head anchor pole, taking up most of the slack. Knot the string around the anchor pole and turn the machine head knob, tightening the string until when you pluck it, it produces the same pitch as the tonic (here, the lowest and most frequently played tone) on One-String Sam's accompaniment for "I Need $100." Check the pitch against the record.

Play your diddly-bow by plucking the string near the bridge with the thumb of one hand while sliding a smooth device such as a bottleneck, lipstick case, piece of copper tubing, pipe tool, or pocket knife atop the string with the other hand. For the moment, ignore the sliding aspect and concentrate on the hand that does the plucking. Leave the other hand out of it entirely. Now hold the diddly-bow with the heel of your plucking hand falling just between the wood screw and the bridge; slight pressure will prevent the instrument from moving on the table. Turn your hand counterclockwise and make a half-fist with your fingers loosely tucked so that your thumb is parallel to the string and can pluck the string comfortably in a motion away from your body.

The rhythm that One-String Sam uses in "I Need $100" is the same triplet rhythm that Bill Lucas used in "Poor Boy Blues": CHUNG, k'CHUNG, k'CHUNG, k'CHUNG, and so on. In musical notation:

The simplicity of the instrument allows us to invent a diddly-bow notation that shows how to play "I Need $100" or any other song. In the diddly-bow notation each triplet beat will be marked with a box:

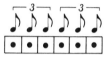

The basic rhythm for "I Need $100" comes out like this:

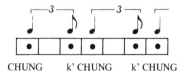

CHUNG k' CHUNG k' CHUNG

With your thumb plucking away from your body, play the diddly-bow in that rhythm for a while until it is comfortable. If your hand gets cramped, stop and shake it out. Keep it loose; move the whole thumb as a unit, not just the upper part above the knuckle. Come back to it every so often, and by the end of a day it will have become second nature.

That is about all there is to the right-hand part (or left-hand part, if you are left-handed) of "I Need $100." The other hand's part is even simpler; in fact, most of the time it does nothing at all while you pluck the tonic as you have just been practicing. At other times it slides a bottleneck or other smooth device along the top of the string to make the whining, zinging sounds you hear on the record.

Traditionally, the diddly-bow is played with a bottleneck slide. Any hard object that can be held easily in your hand will serve, but glass makes the best sound. Find a bottle with a cylindrical neck (fig. 4–13). Glass cutters are available at hardware stores and specialty shops, and they give a sure, neat cut. Another way to part the neck from the bottle uses simpler materials but it is not foolproof. You will need a bowl of ice water, a candle, and a piece of string about 4 inches long. Light the candle and wait until some molten wax forms around the wick well. Dip the string through the molten wax, covering it thoroughly. Before the wax on the string hardens, tie the string around the bottleneck where you want the break to occur. Then hold the bottleneck over the candle, lighting the waxed string so it burns evenly all around. While it is still burning, plunge the bottle, neck first, into

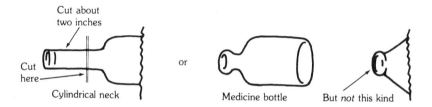

Fig. 4–13. Choosing the right bottle.

the ice water. Most of the time the neck will break off. Carefully file any jagged edges smooth. Alternately, use a glass medicine bottle whole, without cutting off the neck. Finally, bottlenecks have become so popular in the past few years that it is now possible to buy them in stores that sell guitars.

Hold the medicine bottle or bottleneck comfortably in your hand so you can rest it and slide it gently but firmly up and down the string of the diddly-bow from the nut to the area where your other hand plucks the string. If you press too hard, the string will touch the fingerboard and the sound of the plucked string will be muffled. If you don't press at all, the bottle will jiggle and rattle when the string is plucked. Gentle pressure gives a clear, ringing tone.

Practice sliding the glass on the diddly-bow. Make certain you have a good grip on the bottleneck so you can take it off the string when playing the tonic and can put it on the string at various locations. Pluck the string as you slide. Now, find the various simple pitch intervals with the slide on the string (fig. 4–14). The octave will be sounded when the slide is about halfway between the nut and bridge. With a pen or pencil, mark this point on the stringboard with the number 2 (for one-half the distance to the bridge). The perfect fifth will be sounded when the slide is one-third of the distance between the nut and bridge. Mark this point on the stringboard with a 3. The perfect fourth will be sounded when the slide is one-fourth the distance between the nut and bridge. Mark this point on the stringboard with a 4. The major third will be sounded when the slide is one-fifth the distance between the nut and bridge. Mark this point with a 5. These will be your reference points for the intervals used in "I Need $100," and of course they will come in handy as well when you want to play other songs.

The marks you have just made on your stringboard will easily be incorporated in our diddly-bow notation to indicate where to place the slide. A dot inside the notation box indicates that the slide is off the string; this is the tonic. Now each of the numbers on the stringboard can be put inside notation boxes to tell you where to place the slide as you pluck the string with the other hand. Try this:

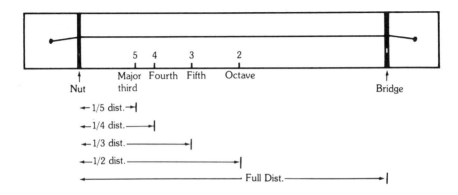

Fig 4–14. Marking intervals on the diddly-bow.

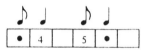

This four-tone sequence is one of Sam's typical moves in "I Need $100." He plucks the tonic for a count of one triplet, then puts on the slide at 4, plucks the string, and holds the tone for a count of two triplets. Next he moves the slide on the string back to 5—actually, slightly to the nut side of 5, because he uses a neutral rather than a major interval of a third—and plucks the string for a count of one triplet. Finally, he takes the slide off and plucks the tonic for a count of two triplets. Listen to the record and pick out the spots where he plays this sequence.

When you have mastered this four-tone sequence, you are well on your way to Sam's accompaniment for "I Need $100." The accompaniment Sam uses in the first stanza is written out in box notation in example 4–13. The jagged lines after 3 and 2 indicate a vibrato, which Sam makes by wiggling the slide back and forth quickly on the string in the general area of the stringboard mark. Put the record on and play along with One-String Sam.

Social Context and the Meaning of the Blues

The blues songs we have taken a close look at, "Poor Boy Blues," "Watergate Blues," and "I Need $100," are typical and can bring us toward a structural definition of blues as a song form. Textually, blues songs consist of a series of rhymed three-line or quatrain-refrain stanzas, each sung to more or less the same tune. Blues tunes usually consist of twelve-measure (bar) strophes, and they employ a special scale, the blues scale (ex. 4–12). They are rhythmically complex, employing syncopation and, at times, differing rhythms between singing and instruments. Many other attributes of blues songs—melodic shape, for instance, or the typical raspy timbre—are beyond the scope of an introduction but may be followed up elsewhere (see Titon 1977). But in one respect "Poor Boy Blues" and "Watergate Blues" are *not* typical: the subject of their lyrics. Most blues lyrics are about lovers, and they fall into a pattern arising from black American life.

The blues grew and developed when most African-Americans lived as sharecroppers on Southern cotton farms, from late in the nineteenth century until just before World War II, when farm mechanization began to displace the black workers and factory work at high wages in the northern cities attracted them. Down home, young men and women did not marry early; they were needed on the farm. If a young woman became pregnant, she had her baby and brought the child into the household with her parents. She did not lose status in the community, and later she often married the father of her child. When a woman did marry young, her partner usually was middle-aged and needed a woman to work and care for his children from a prior marriage. It was good to have plenty of children; when they came of age to work, more hands could go into the cotton and corn fields. Adoption was common; when families broke up, children were farmed out among relatives.

Ex. 4–13.   **Diddly-bow accompaniment for "I Need $100," as played by One-String Sam (recorded selection 25). Transcribed by Jeff Titon.**

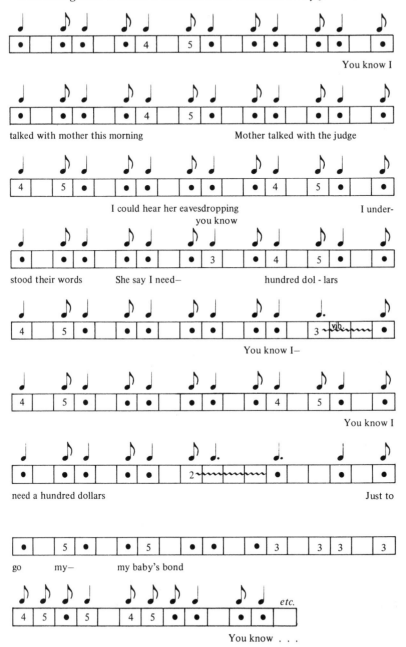

Sociologists and anthropologists, some of them (like Charles Johnson) black, studied this sharecropping culture in the 1920s and 1930s. Interested in patterns of love, marriage, and divorce, the fieldworkers found that partners separated because one could not live with the other's laziness, violence, or adultery. These reasons added up to "mistreatment," the very word they used. A woman was reported as saying her current lover was "nice all right, but I ain't thinking about marrying. Soon as you marry a man he starts mistreating you, and I ain't going to be mistreated no more" (Johnson 1966:83). Blue songs reflected these attitudes; mistreatment was the most common subject. Once the subject was established, people began to expect mistreatment as the appropriate subject for blues songs, and although many blues were composed about other subjects, the majority have to do with lovers and mistreatment. After World War II the sharecropping culture was less important; the action now took place in the cities where most had gone: Atlanta, New York, Washington, Detroit, Memphis, St. Louis, Chicago, Dallas, Houston, Los Angeles, Oakland. But black family patterns persisted among the lower classes in the urban ghettos, and so did the blues.

Blues lyrics about mistreatment fall into a pattern. The singer casts himself or herself in the role of mistreated victim, introduces an antagonist (usually a mistreating lover), provides incidents that detail the circumstances of the mistreatment, and draws up a bill of indictment. Then, with the listener's tacit approval, the victim becomes the judge, and the drama turns on the verdict: will he or she accept the mistreatment, try to reform the mistreater, or leave? Resigned acceptance and attempted reform resolve a minority of blues songs. Most often the victim, declaring independence, steps out of the victim's role with an ironic parting shot and leaves. "Dog Me Around," as sung by Howlin' Wolf, is typical in this regard (fig. 4–15; ill. 4–13).

In stanza 1 the singer complains of mistreatment, saying his lover treats him like a dog. "Dog me around" is black American slang for "treat me like a dog." We

Dog Me Around

1. *How many more years have I got to let you dog me around?*
   How many more years have I got to let you dog me around?
   I'd just as soon rather be dead, sleeping way down in the ground.

2. *If I treat you right you wouldn't believe what I've said.*
   If I treat you right you wouldn't believe what I've said.
   You think I'm halfway crazy; you think I ought to let you have your way.

3. *I'm going upstairs, I'm going to bring back down my clothes.*
   I'm going upstairs, I'm going to bring back down my clothes.
   If anybody asks about me, just tell 'em I walked outdoors.

Fig 4–15.   Lyrics, "Dog Me Around," by Howlin' Wolf (Chester Burnett). Copyright © 1974, Modern Music Publishing Co., Inc. Used by permission.

Jeff Todd Titon

Ill. 4–13.   Howlin' Wolf (Chester Burnett), Ann Arbor Blues Festival, Ann Arbor, Michigan, 1969.

learn in stanza 2 that the singer may also be guilty; "If I treat you right" implies mistreatment on both sides of the relationship. (Stanza 2 could be interpreted as dialogue spoken by the singer's mistreating lover; but without an obvious clue, like, "She said," point of view seldom shifts in blues lyrics.) The singer resolves the drama in stanza 3 when he declares that he will leave his lover. "Just tell 'em I walked outdoors" is an understatement that shows how little the affair means to him.

Blues music in African-American culture helps lovers understand each other and, since the themes are traditional and community-shared, blues songs give listeners community approval for separation in response to mistreatment. The listener who recognizes his or her situation in the lyrics of a blues song is given a nice definition of that situation and shown just what might be done in response. At a Saturday night party, or at home alone, a mistreated lover finds consolation in the blues (ill. 4–14).

The Blues Yesterday

In this chapter we have approached blues as an African-American music. And that is historically true: African-Americans invented blues music. But many non-African-American readers of this book already know something about blues because blues today extends well beyond the boundaries of the African-American music-culture. Today more people recognize the name of the British blues singer-guitarist Eric Clapton than Muddy Waters and Howlin' Wolf. About thirty-five years ago blues entered mainstream American culture, and in our mass-mediated global village today blues is an attractive commodity. You can hear blues played in Prague, Dar es Salaam, and Tokyo by citizens of Czechoslovakia, Tanzania, and Japan. Nowadays blues is regarded as a universal phenomenon, accessible to all. Yet it is well to remember its history within the African-American communities that nurtured it. The folklorist Alan Lomax believes that blacks were the first Americans to feel the alienation characteristic of the twentieth century, and that blues is the quintessential expression of that alienation.

It is true that African-Americans invented blues, and it is also true that early on people outside the black communities were attracted to it. The white folklorist Howard Odum, for example, collected blues songs in the South prior to 1910. The African-American composer W. C. Handy popularized blues in the 1910s

Frederic Ramsey, Jr.

Ill. 4–14.   Dancing at a juke joint, Alabama, 1957.

with songs such as "St. Louis Blues," but white singers such as Sophie Tucker recorded blues songs before African-American singers were permitted to do so. African-American blues queens like Bessie Smith made blues the most popular African-American music in the 1920s, and it attracted a small white audience as well as a large black one. The 1920s was also the decade in which downhome blues was first recorded: Blind Blake, the greatest ragtime guitarist; Charley Patton, a songster regarded as the father of Mississippi Delta blues; and a host of others who brought the music out of the local juke joints and house parties and onto recordings that were circulated back into the black communities. Jimmie Rodgers, the first star of country music, whose brief career lasted from 1927 through 1933, sang many blues songs, particularly his "blue yodels." Rodgers, a white Mississippian, learned many of his songs and much of his relaxed singing style from black railroad men. Blues has been an important component within country music ever since. African-American rhythms, jazz instrumental breaks, and the blues scale were critical in the formation of bluegrass, which ironically is usually regarded as one of the purest British-American musical traditions (see Cantwell 1984). And the banjo—the quintessential bluegrass instrument—is an African-American invention.

Blues always was a popular form within jazz and remains so today, often regarded there as a "roots" music. Bridging the line between blues and jazz in the 1930s and 1940s were the blues "shouters" such as Jimmy Rushing with Count Basie's orchestra. African-American rhythm and blues of the 1940s followed in the tradition of these blues shouters, such as Wynonie Harris, Tiny Bradshaw, and Joe Turner, along with crooners such as Charles Brown. In the meantime an urban blues sound arose featuring singers with small bands led by electric guitar. Aaron "T-Bone" Walker invented it in the 1940s, Riley "B. B." (Blues Boy) King made it immensely popular in the 1950s, and a host of imitators, black and later white, followed. Rock 'n roll in the 1950s began as a white cover of black rhythm and blues, but by the early 1960s black Americans were able to compete well in that arena, and singers like Ray Charles and Motown groups like Diana Ross and the Supremes were immensely popular among all young Americans. Ray Charles's biggest hit, "What'd I Say," was a blues song; blues like "Maybelline" were among Chuck Berry's best-selling recordings; and it even became possible for downhome singers like Jimmy Reed, whose "Big Boss Man" climbed high on the pop charts, to cross over.

Blues was crucial in the British rock of the 1960s. Groups such as the Rolling Stones (whose name came from one of Muddy Waters' songs, and whose early albums featured covers of Chicago blues) were part of the British blues revival. Dozens of British blues bands could be found in such cities as London and Liverpool, and talented instrumentalists such as John Mayall and Eric Clapton arose from this ferment in the 1960s. An American blues revival in the same decade gave white musicians Paul Butterfield and Charlie Musselwhite a start, and a new phenomenon appeared: bands whose personnel included a mixture of black and white musicians. Muddy Waters, for example, featured the white harmonica player Paul Oscher and in the 1970s had a white guitarist, Bob Margolin, in his

band. Lazy Bill Lucas, leader of the band I played in during the 1960s, led an integrated band.

By the early 1960s blues had become old-fashioned within African-American
communities. Outside of strongholds in the Mississippi Delta and Chicago, blues
was a marginal music, accounting for a small proportion of jukebox records and
receiving little radio airplay. Black intellectuals dismissed blues as a music of resignation, unfit for the contemporary climate of civil rights and black power. Soul
music was much more attractive. Yet during this same decade many blues singers
revived their careers, finding a new audience. The blues revival of the 1960s
brought commercially recorded blues music and black musicians before a largely
white public in North America and Europe. Magic Sam, B. B. King, Muddy Waters, and Howlin' Wolf represented the modern electric blues sound, while
singers who had made recordings before World War II performed acoustically on
the folk music circuit, sounding much as they had decades ago: Roosevelt Sykes,
Mississippi John Hurt, Son House, Skip James, John Lee Hooker, Lightnin' Hopkins, Big Joe Williams, and Booker White, to name a few. Buddy Guy and John
Lee Hooker, immensely popular today, were active but overshadowed in the
1960s revival.

Blues is a music steeped in tradition. It can alter its appearance to suit changing conditions of the blues music-culture. But despite varied techniques and instrumentation modern blues has not changed: the blues scale, the twelve-measure
form with its characteristic tonic–subdominant–dominant seventh harmonic support, the three-line or quatrain-refrain stanza, and the rhythm crossing between
vocal and accompaniment remain. Recorded sound quality aside, some blues
recordings made twenty or more years ago sound as if they might have been made
today. To hear an example of such a recording, listen to "Sweet Home Chicago"
by the Fieldstones, a Memphis-based blues band (recorded selection 26; ill.
4–15).

The Fieldstones consist of Wordie Perkins and Willie Roy Sanders, electric
guitars; Lois Brown, electric bass; Bobby Carnes, electric organ; and Joe Hicks,
vocal and drums. David Evans, who produced their album (*The Fieldstones:
Memphis Blues Today:* High Water LP 1001) and wrote the jacket notes, describes their music as sounding "as low down and funky as the most primitive cotton patch blues and at the same time as polished and contemporary as the latest
hit on the radio." Much of this polish results from the band's aesthetic preference
for a clean, crisp sound: they keep the drumheads very tight and the electric guitars amplified with only a minimum of distortion. And at the same time, the band
is based in tradition. Their repertoire includes blues songs like "Saddle Up My
Pony" and "Dirt Road" that are more than sixty years old, and the guitarists play
with their fingers instead of a pick, favoring the key of E like so many traditional
Mississippi Delta blues guitarists.

"Sweet Home Chicago" is a blues classic (fig. 4–16). First recorded by the legendary Delta bluesman Robert Johnson in 1936, it is a staple in the blues repertory and it has been recorded by several prominent rock bands. Robert Johnson
probably did not compose the song; most likely he drew on versions by Roosevelt

© Memphis State University; used by permission. (Photo: Tom Wofford and Art Grider)

Ill. 4–15.   The Fieldstones.

Sykes and James "Kokomo" Arnold current in oral tradition at the time of his recording. But he did originate its most distinctive feature: the walking bass line.

To be sure, "walking the basses" was a definitive characteristic of the boogie-woogie, barrelhouse piano style favored by blues pianists in the 1920's and 1930s. But Johnson took the idea of the walking bass and adapted a new version of it on the guitar, emphasizing the seventh chord (ex. 4–14); and this small but signifi-cant innovation was copied by a host of guitarists and, later, bass players. In the 1950s it became a familiar sound in rhythm and blues and rock 'n' roll. Johnson is also interesting to the blues historian because of his rhythmic innovations and the magnificent poetry of his lyrics. (His original recordings may be heard on the Co-lumbia CD C2K 46222, *Robert Johnson: The Complete Recordings.*)

This walking bass figures prominently in the instrumental introduction to the Fieldstones' version of "Sweet Home Chicago," where it may be heard in the electric bass and second guitar. The bass, guitars, and drums establish a strong triplet rhythm (see the discussion of "Poor Boy Blues" and ex. 4–10 above). And, like Lazy Bill Lucas in "Poor Boy Blues," Joe Hicks sings in a duple meter, play-fully lagging behind the beat, setting up some intriguing two-against-three polyrhythms in contrast to the instrumental accompaniment. It is almost as if he floats the lyrics atop the pulsating music. To really feel the syncopation, try singing along.

Sweet Home Chicago

1. *Come on, baby don't you want to go;*
Oh come on, baby don't you want to go
Back to the same old place, sweet home Chicago.

2. *Come on, baby don't you want to go;*
Oh come on, baby don't you want to go
Back to the same old place, sweet home Chicago.

3.   *One and one is two,*
     Two and two is four,
     Way you love me little girl, you'll
     Never know, crying "Hey,
         baby don't you want to go
Back to the same old place, sweet home Chicago."
[Spoken:] All right, let's go to the windy city, you all.

4. *Come on, baby don't you want to go;*
Oh come on, baby don't you want to go
Back to the same old place, sweet home Chicago.

5.   *Two and two is four,*
     Four and two is six,
     Way you left me little girl you left me in a
     Heck of a fix, crying "Hey,
         baby don't you want to go
Back to the same old place, sweet home Chicago;
Back to the same old place, sweet home Chicago;
Back to the same old place, sweet home Chicago."

Fig. 4–16.   Lyrics, "Sweet Home Chicago." Transcribed by Jeff Titon.

Ex. 4–14.   Outline of "walking bass" on guitar, after Robert Johnson, in key of C for convenience (Johnson usually played it in E).

Blues has its share of heroes and heroines who died too young. John Lee (Sonny Boy) Williamson, stabbed to death in Chicago in 1947, was an outstanding singer and blues harmonica player. Robert Johnson, poisoned in his twenties by his girlfriend's jealous husband, would have changed the course of blues history had he lived. As it was, although he had only two recording sessions, his impact upon post–World War II Chicago blues was immense. We turn now to the music of another Mississippi-born, blues singer-guitarist who died before his time: Magic Sam (Sam Maghett, 1937–1969). His first instrument was the diddly-bow. As a young teenager he moved to Chicago with his family. His club and record career began in the 1950s when he was still a teenager. After a stint in the armed services, he returned to the clubs on the west side of Chicago, where his generation of musicians was moving Chicago blues in the direction of soul: the music of James Brown, Otis Redding, Aretha Franklin—the most popular African-American music of the 1960s. Magic Sam recorded three albums for Delmark in Chicago, where he had made a considerable reputation for his soaring vocals and flashy guitar playing. But those who had heard him in the clubs said these studio albums failed to capture the brilliance of his live performances.

Things changed for Magic Sam abruptly at the 1969 Ann Arbor (Michigan) Blues Festival. B. B. King, Howlin' Wolf, Muddy Waters, Albert King, John Lee Hooker, Freddy King, James Cotton, Big Mama Thornton, Otis Rush, T-Bone Walker, Lightnin' Hopkins—virtually all the major contemporary blues artists performed at this three-day affair. Roosevelt Sykes, Big Joe Williams, Sleepy John Estes, and Son House represented an older generation whose careers had begun before World War II. And Luther Allison, Jimmy Dawkins, and Magic Sam were among those representing the future. It was a huge cutting contest, as each artist tried to outdo the others. When the dust settled, in blues writer John Fishel's words, "if one set [stood] out as surpassing all others in excitement and virtuosity, it [was] Magic Sam's" (1981).

It was Sunday afternoon, August 3, the last day of the festival, about 3 o'clock—not prime time. Casual in the extreme, Sam arrived a half hour late. He had to borrow a drummer from another band. Yet somehow in the performance they came together at the highest heat. It was all the more remarkable because of the sparse instrumentation: guitar, bass, and drums. Yet Magic Sam was no ordinary guitarist. On recorded selection 27, "You Don't Love Me," recorded at the festival from the audience, Sam played his guitar as both a lead and rhythm instrument, catching a riff that both hearkened back to the deepest blues of the Mississippi Delta and pointed forward to the grooves of the future. Above it all Sam's voice carried effortlessly to the ten thousand in the audience who picked up the groove and as if lifted to their feet by some unseen force danced for the remaining twenty minutes of his set.

Writing about Magic Sam's genius, Dick Shurman viewed him as a postmodern master: "His music had roots in the boogie he loved and in the tension and challenge created by the distraction of a noisy, bustling bar. He was able, *par excellence,* to turn the response of the audience into a foil and a force in the music. Partly because of his reliance on whatever equipment was available (like amps without reverb units and borrowed guitars) and partly because of the loose circumstances and the long nights (usually playing until 4 a.m.), Magic Sam was a world apart from the studio's time limits, structures, and formulas" (1981). Sam's career took off immediately after Ann Arbor. In the next month he toured the European blues clubs, a sure sign that he had arrived. On December 1, 1969, he died of a heart attack. He was 32 years old.

The Blues Today

Today a young blues singer with a very large following is Robert Cray. Born in Columbus, Georgia, in 1953, Cray grew up listening to soul music—the Stax/Volt sound of the 1960s, as well as to Ray Charles, Sam Cooke, and, perhaps the most important influence on his singing, Bobby Bland. In 1969 he heard the blues guitarist Albert Collins and modeled his guitar playing after him. Forming a band in 1974, he recorded his first album in 1978, *Who's Been Talkin'*, released in 1980. Several albums followed in which Cray fused a new sound, a mixture of blues, funk, and soul, that was very much his own. Most of his songs do not follow the twelve-bar blues form, but a few do, and we consider one of them now, "The Score." It may be heard on *Who's Been Talkin'*, Charly CRB 1140.

Cray begins "The Score" playing his electric guitar, then he sings a verse, responding on guitar in the silences after he signs each line (ex. 4–15). The rest of the band (piano, electric bass, drums) joins Cray in the second verse. A walking bass line is present like that in "Sweet Home Chicago" (recorded selection 26). Cray's guitar breaks after the verse become more adventurous. The lyrics draw up a familiar blues indictment: the singer's lover is cheating on him, and he says she must leave for good. The first verse is in AB form, the second is quatrain-refrain, and the third doubles the quatrain before the refrain. Even here, in a song that

Ex. 4–15. "The Score." Written by D. Amy. Administered by BUG. All rights reserved. Used by permission. (Transcription by Jeff Todd Titon.)

follows standard blues patterns rather closely, Cray chooses to extend the boundaries of the blues verse form.

For our last example of modern blues we turn to a contemporary masterpiece by an older singer, Otis Rush. "Ain't Enough Comin' In" (recorded selection 28) was voted the outstanding blues recording of the year 1994 by the readers of *Living Blues* magazine. The song starts with an authoritative drumbeat, and immediately the electric bass sets a heavy rhythmic riff that repeats till the end of the song, changing pitch when the chords change. In its rhythmic constancy the bass provides something like the bell pattern in *agbekor* (see chapter 3) that anchors the entire performance. The drummer plays simply but forcefully and unerringly, marking the beat 1–2–**3**–4, with the accent on 3. A rock drummer would be busier than this, and a lot less relentless. The electric bass is louder than the drums, characteristic of black popular music since the 1970s.

Listeners who can recognize the difference between major and minor chords will realize that this is a minor blues, built on the minor i–iv–v chords instead of the major ones. The first chorus is instrumental. Rush plays electric guitar lead above a riffing rhythm section that includes a trumpet and saxophone as well as an organ. The direct, spare playing here sets a somber mood for his powerful vocals that follow. The song features a bridge section ("Now when it's all over . . .") that departs from the usual twelve-bar blues pattern, but you will recognize that otherwise (except for the minor key) the song has a typical blues structure. After the vocals Rush takes the tune twice through with a guitar solo, and this is followed by two choruses in which a saxophone leads, taking some of Rush's ideas and developing them. The bridge returns, followed by two more verses, and Rush takes it out with one more instrumental chorus. Hear how the sound of the guitar vibrates at the beginning of the last chorus. This is a tremolo, and Rush is known for getting this effect by pushing his fingers from side to side on the strings (a hand tremolo) rather than using the tremolo bar attached to the electric guitar.

Rush's vocal style is striking. Like many blues singers he hoarsens his voice at times to show great emotion, but he also makes his voice tremble at times, an effect that mirrors his guitar tremolo (and vice versa). Blues writers have called Rush's voice "tortured" with a "frightening intensity" and a "harrowing poetic terror" (Rowe 1979:176); and "tense and oppressive" (Herzhaft 1992:300). There is no denying Rush has a full, powerful voice. Its vehemence and falling melodic curve may remind you of the Navajo Yeibechai singers (chapter 2). The lyrics (fig. 4–17) are clever and subtle. Rush wrote them. In the beginning of his career he relied on the professional songwriter Willie Dixon, but after his first hit songs he decided that he could "write one better than that" (Forte 1991:159). When I hear the first line, I think "ain't enough comin' in" refers to money; but in the second line Rush lets me know that I should think of the parallel between love and money: the singer feels that he's giving too much and not getting enough of either in return.

Who is Otis Rush? Is he the latest singer-guitarist to capitalize on the blues revival of the 1990s? Not at all: Otis Rush has been a blues legend since the 1950s, well known to musicians and serious blues aficionados if not to the general listening public. Stevie Ray Vaughn named his band Double Trouble in honor of

Oh, I ain't got enough comin' in to take care of what's got to go out.
It ain't enough love or money comin' in, baby, to take care of what's got to go out.
Like a bird I got my wing clipped, my friends; I've got to start all over again.

If the sun ever shine on me again,
Oh lord if the sun ever shine on me again.
Like a bird I got my wing clipped, my friends; I've got to start all over again.

Now when it's all over and said and done, money talks and the fool gets none;
The tough get tough and the tough get goin'; come on baby let me hold you in my
    arms.

It ain't enough comin' in to take care of what's got to go out.
Ain't enough love or money comin' in, baby, to take care of what's got to go out.
My friends, I got my wing clipped; I've got to start all over again.

When it's all over and said and done, money talks and the fool gets none;
The tough get tough and the tough get goin'; come on baby let me hold you in my
    arms.

Ain't enough comin' in to take care of what's got to go out.
It ain't enough love or money comin' in to take care of what's got to go out.
Like a bird I got my wing clipped, my friends; I've got to start all over again.

If you don't put nothin' in you can't get nothin' out;
You don't put nothin' in, baby, you can't get nothin' out;
Like a bird I got my wing clipped, my friends; I've got to start all over again.

**Fig. 4–17. Lyrics, "Ain't Enough Comin' In." Redorded selection 28.
Written by Otis Rush. © 1994 OTIS RUSH PUBLISHING (BMI)/
Administered by BUG. All rights reserved. Used by permission.**

Rush's finest song from that decade. Led Zeppelin covered Rush's "I Can't Quit
You Baby," with guitarist Jimmy Page lifting Rush's instrumental break note-for-
note (ibid.:156). Rush's guitar playing turned Eric Clapton into a disciple. When
Rush met Clapton in England in 1986 he called Clapton a "great guitar player"
and modestly went on, "Everybody plays like somebody. It's good to know that
somebody's listening. To me, I'm just a guitar player. I'm not trying to influence
nobody, I'm just trying to play, and play well. And hopefully I can sell some
records" (ibid.:161).

Otis Rush was born in Philadelphia, Mississippi, in 1934, and began playing at
age ten. Left-handed, he plays the guitar upside-down, which accounts for some
of his uniqueness (see ill. 4–16). Like Bill Lucas, he first sang country music, not
blues. It was not until he came to Chicago in the late 1940s and began visiting the
blues clubs that he decided to sing and play the blues. Among the musicians who
influenced him most strongly were B. B. King, T-Bone Walker, and Magic Sam;
but Rush has his own version of modern blues guitar. His style is subtle, spare,
cool, the instrumental equivalent of caressing a lover. There is nothing egotistical
about it, no showing off. His use of silence is brilliant. Like a fine aged wine at its
peak, at its best his music has great presence, neither understated nor flashy: substantial, direct, powerful, and commanding respect.

Jeff Todd Titon

Ill. 4–16.   Otis Rush performing at the 1969 Ann Arbor Blues Festival. Note that he plays left-handed.

Rush takes risks onstage and in recordings. Often he would rather try something new than stick with the same old thing, and as a result his performances are uneven. "I know I'm gonna mess up in places, but sometimes I get away with it," he said. "To me, I'm trying to learn how to play. I'm not ashamed to let people know I'm trying to learn. I'm scuffling, trying to find something new, trying to make it off the ground. I'll be reaching for sounds—right on-stage. I know I'm going to get caught; that's why you hear a lot of bad notes. I can't just play straight. If I hear something, I go after it. Sometimes it works out; then again, you get some bad collisions, so I try to cover it up. Just like a boxer: you get hit, you got to try to recuperate" (ibid.:159). Blues audiences came to feel that Rush never quite reached his potential. Indeed, there are a couple of places in "Ain't Enough Comin' In" where, if you listen closely, you'll hear a "bad collision." But in my view the risks are very much worth it, and the new album from which this song is taken represents a long overdue turning point in Rush's career. We can hope that in his sixties he can sustain it.

The Blues Music-Culture Today

In this book we have taken an approach in which we seek out music-cultures that correspond more or less to social groups and geographic regions: peoples who form a community and make music together. But this is not the only kind of music-culture. Mass-mediated popular music, presented outside community settings in concerts, recordings, radio, and television, forms communities of listeners and would-be performers that may otherwise have little in common with each other. Until the 1960s the blues music-culture was based in African-American communities; today it embraces people from all over the world. And blues is but one of many local and regional musics that have become immensely popular outside their area of origin: reggae is an obvious example of another. And today world music is presented from the concert stage in many cities in North America and Europe. (What kind of music-culture do the connoisseurs of world music represent?)

We return to the blues to seek answers. Robert Cray has told interviewers that he grew up in an integrated suburb and never experienced the hard times that his predecessors did. He never chopped cotton or plowed and smelled the back end of a mule all day long. He learned to play blues mainly by listening to recordings, not by imitating elder musicians in a local community. Yet there is no doubt that he is a fine blues singer and guitarist, although most of his songs do not follow standard blues forms. He thinks of himself as a blues singer, and he is being promoted as one. Is he? (And who is granted authority to say?) We pause to reflect on what happens once a musical genre has been popularized by the mass media, written about, studied, defined: some of that interpretive activity is carried back to performers, and now people expect the music to conform to those definitions. Record producers, promoters, writers, and lately scholars, few of them raised in African-American communities, are partly responsible for codifying the rules of the genre. How, once standardized, can blues music change and grow, yet still remain blues? Must singers stay with the old forms, changing only their contents— new wine in old bottles, new lyrics, new instrumentation, in old settings? Must festival promoters choose blues singers on the basis of how well they conform to the genre? Should a folklore police enforce the rules?

In the 1960s, blues, a music that had lost its great popularity among black Americans, captured the hearts of a new audience, young white Americans and Europeans, particularly those who saw in the blues a revolt against stifling middle-class values. In the 1970s the blues revival ebbed as many grew tired of the same old sound. Now, in the mid-1990s, we are in the midst of a new blues revival as a new generation of African-Americans honors blues as roots music and others discover the music for the first time.

In the house parties and juke joints of the rural South, especially in Texas, Arkansas, and Mississippi, solo singer-guitarists, sometimes with a friend sitting in on guitar or harmonica, continue to sing and play the blues for friends and neighbors. Outside this professional and semiprofessional blues music-culture are countless black blues singers and musicians who no longer perform regularly but who, without a great deal of persuasion, sing on occasion for family and friends. Today's most active blues music-culture is located in Chicago, a city with a history of great hospitality to the blues (see ill. 4–16). Dozens of blues clubs may also be found in such cities as Houston; St. Louis; Memphis; Clarksdale, Mississippi; Oakland–San Francisco; and Detroit. Well-known blues singers like B. B. King and Buddy Guy tour nationally and, sponsored by the U.S. Department of State, as goodwill ambassadors abroad.

A FEW FINAL WORDS

Just a few years ago I was in Chicago and heard a woman blues singer with a very powerful voice singing in a club, backed by a four-piece band. It turned out she had studied voice in preparation for the opera, then decided she would have a

Jeff Todd Titon

Ill. 4–16.   Cicero Blake, vocalist, performing with Mighty Joe Young's Blues Band at Eddie Shaw's Club, Chicago, Illinois, 1977.

better career singing blues. Do these historical, economic, and audience changes mean we should abandon our music-culture model (chapter 1) in the face of real-world complications? No, but we need to keep in mind that it *is* a model, an ideal. Music-cultures respond to economic, artistic, and interpretive pressures from without as well as within; music-cultures are not isolated entities. Music-cultures have histories that reveal that response to these pressures, and "catching" or defining a music at any given time comes at the expense of the long view. Finally, students of world music face the same problem that confronts other observers: the need to account for their own effects on what they observe.

Music of work, music of worship, and music of play: in this chapter, two brief examinations of work songs and religious music and an in-depth case study of the blues have introduced black music in the United States, its historical background, the part it plays in people's lives, and a perspective from which it can be approached. Instead of blues, many other contemporary black musics—jazz, for example, or rap or soul music—could have served equally for our case study. I have appended a short list of further reading, listening, and viewing, but the next logical step is fieldwork (chapter 10).

REFERENCES CITED

Brooks, Cleanth, R. W. B. Lewis, and Robert Penn Warren
    1973   *American Literature: The Makers and the Making.* 2 vols. New York: St. Martin's Press.

Brunoghe, Yannick, ed.
    1964   *Big Bill Blues.* New York: Oak.

Cantwell, Robert
    1984   *Bluegrass Breakdown.* Urbana: Univ. of Illinois Press.

Charters, Samuel
    1977   *The Legacy of the Blues.* New York: De Capo Press.

Courlander, Harold
    1963   *Negro Folk Music U.S.A.* New York: Columbia Univ. Press.

Eliot, T. S.
    [1920] 1964   "Hamlet and His Problems." In *The Sacred Wood.* Reprint. New York: Barnes & Noble.

Evans, David
    1970   "Afro-American One-Stringed Instruments." *Western Folklore* 29:229–45.

———.
    1971   "Booker White." In *Nothing But the Blues,* edited by Mike Leadbitter. London: Hanover Books.

Fishel, John
    1981   "Magic Sam and the Ann Arbor Blues Festival." Liner notes to Delmark DL-645/646, *Magic Sam Live.*

Forte, Dan
    1991   "Otis Rush." In *Blues Guitar,* ed. Jas Obrecht, 156–62. San Francisco: GPI Books.

Groom, Bob
    1971   *The Blues Revival.* London: Studio Vista.

Herzhaft, Gerard
    1992   *Encyclopedia of the Blues.* Fayetteville: Univ. of Arkansas Press.

Jackson, Bruce
    1972   *Wake Up Dead Man: Afro-American Worksongs from Texas State Prisons.* Cambridge, Mass.: Harvard Univ. Press.

Johnson, Charles S.
    [1934] 1966   *Shadow of the Plantation.* Reprint. Chicago: Univ. of Chicago Press.

Lomax, Alan
    1976   Brochure notes to *Negro Prison Songs from the Mississippi State Penitentiary.* Reissue of Tradition LP 1020 (see "Additional Listening"). Vogue Records (U.K.) VJD 515.

Lovell, John, Jr.
    1972   *Black Song: The Forge and the Flame.* New York: Macmillan, 1972.

Lucas, William ("Lazy Bill")
    1974   *Lazy Bill Lucas.* Philo LP 1007 (North Ferrisburg, Vt.).

McLeod, Norma, and Marcia Herndon
    1981   *Music as Culture.* 2nd ed. Darby, Pa.: Norwood Editions.

Oliver, Paul
    1965   *Conversation with the Blues.* London: Cassell.

————.
    [1972] 1974   *The Story of the Blues.* Reprint. Radnor, Pa.: Chilton Books.

Rowe, Mike
    1979   *Chicago Breakdown.* New York: Da Capo.

Seeger, Charles
    1977   *Studies in Musicology, 1935–1975.* Berkeley: Univ. of California Press.

Shurman, Dick
    1981   "Magic Sam: An Overview." Liner notes to Delmark DL-645/646, *Magic Sam Live.*

Tedlock, Dennis
    1977   "Toward an Oral Poetics." *New Literary History* 8.

Titon, Jeff Todd
    1969   "Calling All Cows." *Blues Unlimited,* nos. 60–63.

————.
    1971   "Ethnomusicology of Downhome Blues Phonograph Records, 1926–1930." Ph.D. diss., Univ. of Minnesota.

————, ed.
    1974a   *From Blues to Pop: The Autobiography of Leonard "Baby Doo" Caston.* Los Angeles: John Edwards Memorial Foundation.

————.
    1974b   *Early Downhome Blues: A Musical and Cultural Analysis.* Urbana: Univ. of Illinois Press.

———.
  1978 "Every Day I Have the Blues: Improvisation and Daily Life." *Southern Folklore Quarterly* 42.

Wilson, Al
  1966 "Robert Pete Williams: His Life and Music." *Little Sandy Review* 2 (no. 1).

ADDITIONAL READING

Albertson, Chris
  1972 *Bessie.* New York: Stein and Day. [Biography of Bessie Smith.]

Baldwin, James
  1965 *Go Tell It on the Mountain.* New York: Dell [Novel centering on black religious experience.]

Barlow, William
  1989 *Looking Up at Down.* Philadelphia: Temple Univ. Press.

Evans, David
  1982 *Big Road Blues.* Berkeley: Univ. of California Press.

Fahey, John
  1970 *Charley Patton.* London: Studio Vista [Life and music of important Mississippi blues singer.]

Ferris, William
  1978 *Blues from the Delta.* New York: Doubleday.

Franz, Steve
  1996 "The Life and Music of Magic Sam." *Living Blues,* no. 125, pp. 33–44.

George, Nelson
  1988 *The Death of Rhythm & Blues.* New York: Dutton.

Grissom, Mary Allen
  [1930] 1969 *The Negro Sings a New Heaven.* Reprint. New York: Dover Books.

Jones, LeRoi
  1963 *Blues People.* New York: Morrow.

Keil, Charles
  1966 *Urban Blues.* Chicago: Univ. of Chicago Press.

Leib, Sandra
  1981 *Mother of the Blues.* Amherst: Univ. of Massachusetts Press. [About Ma Rainey.]

Oster, Harry
  1969 *Living Country Blues.* Hatboro, Pa.: Folklore Associates.

Palmer, Robert
  1981 *Deep Blues.* New York: Viking Press.

Ramsey, Frederic, Jr.
  1960 *Been Here and Gone.* New Brunswick, N.J.: Rutgers Univ. Press. [Folk music.]

Shaw, Arnold
 1978   *Honkers and Shouters.* New York: Collier Books. [Rhythm 'n' blues.]
Titon, Jeff Todd
 1990   *Downhome Blues Lyrics.* 2nd ed. Urbana: Univ. of Illinois Press. [Anthology of post-WWII lyrics.]
Williams, Melvin D
 1974   *Community in a Black Pentecostal Church.* Pittsburgh: Univ. of Pittsburgh Press.

ADDITIONAL LISTENING

B. B. King Live at the Regal. ABCS509.

Bessie Smith: The World's Greatest Blues Singer. Columbia GP33.

Blues in the Mississippi Night. Rykodisc RCD 90155.

The Essential Gospel Sampler. Columbia CK 51763.

Let's Get Loose: Folk and Popular Blues Styles. New World NW 290.

Negro Blues and Hollers. Library of Congress AFS L59.

Negro Church Music. Atlantic SD-1351.

Negro Prison Songs. Tradition 1920.

Negro Religious Songs and Services. Library of Congress AFS L10.

One-String Blues. Takoma B 1023. [Diddly-bow.]

Religious Music: Congregational and Ceremonial. Library of Congress LBC 1.

Robert Johnson: The Complete Recordings. Columbia C2K 46222.

Roots 'n' Blues: The Retrospective. Columbia C4K 47911.

Roots of the Blues. New World NW 252.

ADDITIONAL VIEWING

The Blues Accordin' to Lightnin' Hopkins.
 VHS videotape, 31 min. Color. Directed by Les Blank. El Cerrito, CA: Flower Films, 1979.

Bukka White and Son House.
 VHS videotape, 60 min. Black and white. Yazoo Video, 1991. [Riveting performances of Mississippi Delta blues.]

Wild Women Don't Have the Blues.
 VHS videotape, 58 min. Color. Dir. Christine Dall. San Francisco: California Newsreel, 1989. [A documentary on women blues singers.]

A Singing Stream.
 VHS videotape, 57 min. Color. Dir. Tom Davenport. Delaplane, Va.: Davenport Films, 1987. [African-American religious music.]

CHAPTER FIVE

Bosnia and Central/Southeast Europe: Musics and Musicians in Transition

MARK SLOBIN

In this chapter we will concentrate on how change has come to local musical styles, using as a case study a corner of Southeast Europe—Bosnia—and the nearby countries of Hungary and Bulgaria (see map, fig. 5–1).

We start with the period just after World War II—around 1950—a time when great change was the order of the day in eastern Europe: communist rule began, lasting through about 1990, replacing a group of slowly industrializing, still heavily rural, capitalist societies with ambitious, managerial, totalitarian governments. Yet old ways continued into new times, as we hear in a song recorded in the early 1950s, about the rain, a universal theme for song-making. "Paparuda" (recorded selection 29, fig. 5–2) is sung here by Gypsy children in the countryside of Romania. As American students listen to "Paparuda" and look at the words, they might remember the traditional American song shown in Fig. 5–3; songs about nature can be found around the world.

The two rain songs share similarities: the type of singer (children) and the subject (a force of nature), but many sharp differences place them in contrast. The American song is a straightforward command chanted by a child who cannot go out and play. It has no special metaphors or figures of speech, just as no special costume or equipment is necessary to perform the song. In addition, the text is sung solo and even includes the child's name. Though addressed to the rain, it is meant for the singer. There is no social context for the tune: it does not speak for a group. Notice also that no special meaning attaches to the rain other than that it gets in the way of fun.

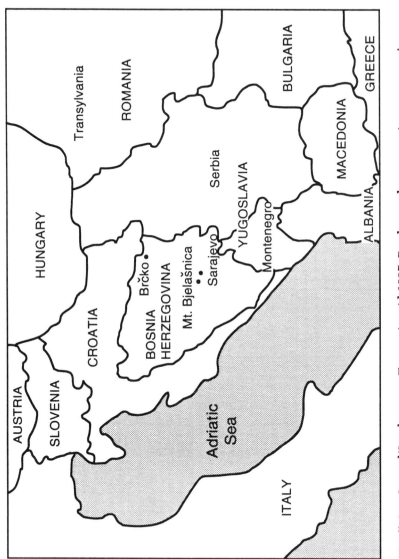

Fig. 5–1.   Central/Southeastern Europe in mid-1995. Borders and even country names are in dispute in some cases.

Paparuda, ruda (come, little rain, come!), come out and water us with
your full buckets over the whole crowd. When you come with the hose,
let it flow like water; when you come with the plow, let it run like
butter; when you come with the sieve, let it be a barnfull. Give me the
keys, old woman, that I may open the doors and let the rain come down.
Come, little rain, come!

Fig. 5–2. Romanian Drought Song, "Paparuda."

The words to the Romanian song differ drastically. They seek the rain's bounty
instead of better weather for playtime. From rain, the text shifts to the image of
the plow and butter, calling upon the fertility of the earth and the beasts. Instead
of denying the course of the seasons, the song impatiently begs nature to continue
the cycle of the seasons, from winter to spring—it seeks to continue, rather than
stop, action. The song rings with particular urgency because it is sung during
times of drought, when the villagers' subsistence is threatened through danger to
their crops. In short, the group performance emphasizes a real social context for
the song.

In the whole performance environment for the Romanian song, no detail
seems accidental. The children wear skirts made from flowers that are symbols of
spring, and they carry sieves, survival of a rain symbol of the ancient Greek gods.
The children themselves, and even the villagers, are probably unaware of the remarkable durability of these symbols over the centuries. The very presence of
children might stand for the rising generation, associated with the forces of
growth (versus decline and death). Growth seems invoked when the adults sprin-
kle the singing, dancing children with water. The "old woman" mentioned who
controls the keys to the rain is probably related to the effigy of a hag carried and
burned by children in other parts of the region as part of a spring ritual: she
stands for winter and must die. Thus a local village musical performance is connected to a network of regional beliefs and musical performances.

This social-regional nexus also determines the identity of the children: they are
Gypsies, members of an ethnic group that is often treated as outcasts from mainstream society yet respected for its music-making talents. The song thus taps into
a subtle sense of status, human values, and assigned roles at the same time that
the entire performance of "Paparuda" also belongs to the realm of magic and ritual, with the children acting as ambassadors to the forces of nature.

So what seems to be a "simple" song can be seen for what it really is—a complicated cultural package involving props, social organization, deeply held beliefs,
and a specific melodic-textual structure crafted for a particular social moment:
the time of drought.

Rain, rain, go away, little (name of singer) wants to play.
Rain, rain, go away! Come again some other day.

Fig. 5–3. American Children's Song, "Rain, Rain, Go Away."

What about the musical differences between the two rain songs? The American song needs no special rehearsing, since there is just one melody line and only two notes. Now try singing the Romanian song. First, you must divide your group into two parts: one chants the unchanging *hai ploitsa, hai!* line while the others have text (do it on a syllable like "la"). The singers with text also have different notes to think about: six here, as opposed to only two in the American song. As should be clear from this entire book, just because music comes from a technologically simpler environment, it doesn't mean that it must be musically less complicated—in fact, just the opposite is often true.

The rain song and its evocation of community come from a world of traditional music. That world was always turbulent; peasants in eastern Europe, as everywhere in agriculturally-based societies, were subject to tyrants and greedy landlords who controlled their economic fate, epidemics, natural disasters, and invasions. It was not a timeless, culturally unified zone of unchanging tales and songs. Most people knew at least two languages or dialects, and many were not only multilingual but also highly mobile, traveling from place to place or continent to continent for work and trade. Music traveled freely along mountain paths and highways, and in the twentieth century the slow spread of electrical and electronic media—record player, radio, then cassette and television—meant that people anywhere could be swayed by the seductive rhythms of the tango, the hot sound of jazz, or the hard beat of rock. Yet family, local, and national pride and memory ensured continuity. Along with every new layer of music-making, older material such as the rain song was being handed down as well, creating a multilayered musical world. You have already noticed that in most other world areas covered in this book, older musical styles tied to the past coexist with such recently invented styles as film music and local rock.

Since the first edition of this textbook appeared in 1984, the stability of most communities in parts of eastern Europe has been rocked by more drastic than usual political, social, and even violent military change. In the area that once was the country of Yugoslavia, in a divisive conflict that started in 1990, whole regions have forcibly exchanged or expelled populations, and warfare has left thousands dead and millions homeless.

So along with a wide selection of traditional and contemporary musics, this chapter will introduce you to three kinds of musical change in the region under discussion: dramatic and destructive transformation due to political upheaval, aesthetic and commercial shifts of style tied to a change in social direction, and personal reshaping by musicians who have moved from their homeland to the United States.

BOSNIA: FROM TRADITION TO DESTRUCTION

Our starting point is high in the mountains near the city of Sarajevo, in Bosnia (see ill. 5–1). From 1945 until 1991 Bosnia (and its adjacent area, Herzegovina) formed one of six republics that constituted a federated country called Yugoslavia ("land of the south Slavs"). Sarajevo had grown dramatically after World War II into a city of about a half million as peasants from mountain and lowland villages, as well as from smaller towns and cities, flocked to the newly emerging industries

Ill. 5–1.   Hay meadows above the village of Planinica, Bosnia. The village is visible in upper left corner. Credit: William G. Lockwood.

of that ancient town. The city's hosting of the 1984 Olympic Games was a high-point in its development as a world-class metropolis. Sadly, the regional war that followed the dissolution of Yugoslavia into new nation-states caused great loss of life and culture in the Sarajevo area, beginning in 1992. The highland villages near the Olympic site, focus of our first section (see ill. 5–2), had enjoyed longheld traditions of folk music and adjusted to newer styles coming in from nearby cities up to that point; but in 1992 the villages were totally destroyed and the population resettled, and so we will be looking at material that suddenly be-came historic. The fighting has changed not only political and ethnic boundaries but music as well. It is too soon to take up the implications of this violence-induced shift in sensibilities, so our musical survey will stop in 1991.°

°I am extremely grateful to Ankica Petrovic for first acquainting me with the riches of Bosnian music (and permission for ex.—) and to two graduate students from Sarajevo for their materials and exper-tise (background, translations) in compiling this chapter. Mirjana Laušević granted the use of her field materials in the following description of the Mt. Bjelašnica plateau (exx. 30–32 and pho-tographs). Ljerka Vidić Rassmussen contributed her extensive knowledge of the development of Yugoslav popular musics and helped with the difficulties of permissions for recordings (exx. 34 and 35) which have changed not only owners but countries since their publication. Note: I regret the nec-essary abridgement of some examples due to the time constraints of the accompanying tape/CD package. Deep thanks go to Bill Lockwood for offering his splendid photographs of rural Bosnia.

    This chapter is dedicated to all the musicians and musical traditions that, along with their commu-nities, have suffered destruction and displacement in the war that accompanied the collapse of feder-ated Yugoslavia in 1990.

Ill. 5–2.   The village of Planinica. Note the mosque on the right. Credit: William G. Lockwood.

First, we will get to know the villagers, and then we will listen to the urban music. Our concentration is on the Muslim population, people who have always spoken the same Slavic language (Serbo-Croatian) as their neighbors but who were converted to Islam during the 425-year occupation of the area by the Turkish-led Ottoman Empire (1463–1878).

MUSIC IN A MUSLIM HIGHLANDER VILLAGE

Mount Bjelašnica (pronounced "Bee-el-*osh*-nitsa"), "the White Mountain," stands as a snow-covered island in the Dinaric mountain range in an area where the mild Mediterranean climate confronts the cold continental weather to the east. Winters are long and harsh, and the soil is not very good for farming. Much of the local highlanders' traditional work involves keeping large flocks of sheep. Women do a lot of the livestock herding and milking, and have started to take cheese, milk, and butter to market. In recent years men have supplemented family income by working in industrial jobs in nearby towns and cities. As is common in such isolated environments, a small group of villages shares a common cultural core, and people give themselves a local name, here *planinstaci/planinke* (masculine/ feminine), from the word *planina*, mountain. As a local woman puts it, "Everything is almost the same in all fourteen villages." The villagers have a variety of names for other people, groups near and far that they find unlike themselves. Electricity reached this far-off plateau only in 1976, and its main musical impact was to make a much greater variety of music available. This import from the outside world was matched in recent years by an outflow of male villagers to work not just in nearby towns but as far away as Austria and Germany as part of a huge labor migration from the southern to the more prosperous northern regions of Europe. Many returning emigrants built modern houses with all the electronic conveniences, creating a new local social group: urbanized villagers.

As a result, highlander music-making offers a good example of musical layering. The older village song styles, which we will survey first, are extremely localized. The secular songs do not even contain much Islamic content, which was traditionally more fully developed in cities. The main local song genres differ only somewhat from those of neighboring ethnic and religious groups, implying a strong shared regional taste that is at the heart of what we usually call "folk music." The three types of local song everyone knows are all polyphonic; that is, they consist of different parts simultaneously sung by a small group of singers, rather than by one person singing alone or by everybody singing the same tune (unison). There are few musical instruments up on Mt. Bjelašnica, voices doing the work of communication in the fields and in the village square. The outflow of workers to the cities and the fact that boys no longer do the herding has meant that people have largely forgotten their old hand-made instruments, such as shepherd's flutes. For special occasions—fairs, festivals—songs and some electric instruments are joined with voices as accompaniment to dance. Despite all the change and the forgetting of many earlier forms of folklore, such as epic singing about local heroes, for Bosnian Muslims "folksong is perhaps the most viable verbal form of folklore . . . today" (Lockwood 1983:28).

One of the best times to catch a lively song and dance scene is a *mevlud* festival. Such a *mevlud* is a local version of a widespread ceremony based partly on reading a sacred text that centers on the birth of the Prophet Muhammad. These celebrations can happen at many different times in private to mark personal occasions, but they also are held as large public occasions every weekend in August, when urban workers are on vacation and can come home from as far away as Germany to have a good time in their native village. The event is in three parts: a religious ceremony, a fair, and an evening gathering, all collectively called *mevlud.* Village girls put on elaborate outfits (see Ill. 5–3), while young women who have moved to the city dress in a more urban style. Trucks arriving at the scene of the host village are covered with singing celebrants, with one truck trying to outdo another in song.

During the fair, hundreds of people gather on a meadow, with various groups of singers and musicians competing for space and attention. This is a moment of courtship, when young men and women size each other up, sing about each other, and present themselves the way they want to be understood: rural or urban, available or unavailable, bashful or bold. Girls stick with the singing group they've grown up with, but men move around from group to group. Intergroup competition lends an edge to the singing, and everyone evaluates one another's performances. Body posture, song texts, and attitude differ considerably, as we shall hear. Women tend to sing in a well-rehearsed, tight manner meant to show

Ill. 5–3.   The singers of Ex.—, near the village of Umoljani: Šecira Kadrić, Aiša Kadrić. Enisa Trešnjo. Credit: Mirjana Laušević.

that they have thought things through, are organized, and work hard, characteristics valued in a wife. The songs are complicated, multipart creations that depend on thorough knowledge and long experience, with a leader setting the pace. Only unmarried women sing, so they use the opportunity to enjoy their art during their peak singing years as well as to affirm sisterhood and to display themselves to the whole community, including parents, potential in-laws, and prospective husbands. Songs may praise women's solidarity as well as tease men or comment on the beauties and virtues of highlander life.

Throughout Bosnia and Herzegovina, a popular form of song among several ethnic groups is called *ganga*. *Ganga* singers meet at an early age (see ill. 5–3) and continue singing together for decades, fine-tuning their sensitivity to each other's sound and skills. Should a woman from a nearby village marry into another village, it might be hard for her to find singing partners even if her style is quite close to the local way of singing. Her new fellow singers will immediately notice even the slightest shade of difference in the nuances of local *ganga*. This highly valued form of singing sounds strange to outsiders, even to others in nearby regions, let alone western European or American listeners, mostly due to the insistence on very close intervals, which "grate" on the unaccustomed ear, and the uncompromising intensity of the delivery. The social organization of the group is reflected in the musical structure: a respected leader sets the tone, literally, and the fellow singers, usually two, chip in an accompanying pattern called "cutting,"

Ex. 5–1a. **Women's ganga song**

"chopping," or "sobbing" that is vocally and emotionally powerful, as you'll hear. Example 5–1 gives a schematic version of the two *ganga* songs (recorded selections 30 and 31). The pauses in the men's *ganga* are quite long; if you watch them, you might think they're not even about to sing, as they puff on cigarettes and look nonchalant. Just then, they break into coordinated song. A solo voice dominates in the first phrase (A); for the second and third (B, C), the group splits into parts that get extremely close and then break into an exuberant rise at the end. As the two lines get closer, the intensity of the effect of blended voices increases as the resonance produces "beats," sharp patterns of acoustic interaction, that are increased by the vocal techniques of the singers. Example 5–2 shows the acoustic complexity of *ganga* as measured by sophisticated software.

Of course, to experience *ganga* properly, you should be singing it or listening to friends' songs. Singers are very aware of the acoustic quality they are producing. They perceive their powerful voice production not just physically but sensually. They look forward to the extra resonance that emerges from singing pitches very closely together, enjoying the "cutting edge" of the vibrations. This means that *ganga* is difficult to record well. When the Bosnian ethnomusicologist Ankica Petrović took a group of women into the recording studio, the sound engineers tried to put a microphone on each singer separately to "clarify" the sound as individual tracks, but the women refused. They were used to performing their songs in a tight semicircle, touching shoulders, so they could listen properly to each other and create the right mood. This technique confused the engineers, but not the women. They were able to tell the technicians exactly where to place the microphone for the best sound quality.

Ankica Petrović has delved deeply into many sides of the singers' aesthetic, their feelings about their music. She finds a direct correlation between musical features and this aesthetic: "The melodic range and intervals in this polyphonic singing reflect mutual human relationships within the framework of small interacting communities, while the importance of individual personality is emphasized by individual improvisation. At the end of the *ganga*, when songs finish on two different tones a major second apart, it is as if different individuals are given the same rights in the community" (Petrović 1977:335). When *ganga* is sung right, it

Ex. 5–1b. **Men's ganga song**

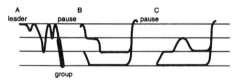

Ex. 5–2a.   Sonogram of women's *ganga* song. Horizontal axis is time, vertical is frequency. The same voices appear horizontally at different levels corresponding to the harmonic structure of the sound. Vocal lines appear darkest at pitch level where voice intensity is strongest. The boxed section shows "cutting" style of two voices intersecting sonically, shown by overlapping black peaks.

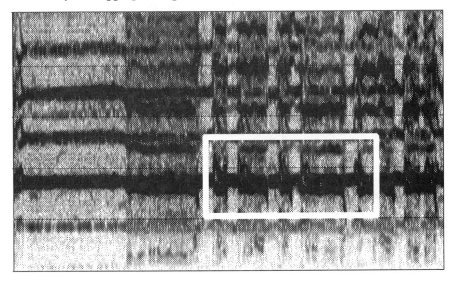

Ex. 5–2b.   Sonogram of men's *ganga*, also showing "cutting" technique in boxed section, similar to women's practice as in Fig. 5–2a.

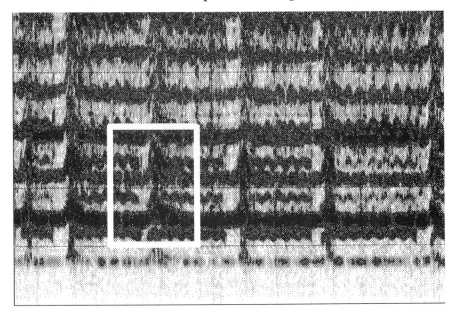

Ex. 5–2c. **Section of men's *ganga* near end of phrase. The sudden tapering-off of the sound at the right represents the spot here the men all make the "whoop" gesture at phrase-end. The boxed sections demonstrate the differing character of two voices. The one above, in zigzag pattern, is using a wide vibrato that registers here as a very regular pitch fluctuation. The lower voice, with dark circular markings, is pulsing in terms of amplitude, rather than pitch. Credit: Thanks to Fredric Lieberman for producing the sonograms using MacSpeech Lab and helping interpret them. Images enhanced with Adobe PhotoShop.**

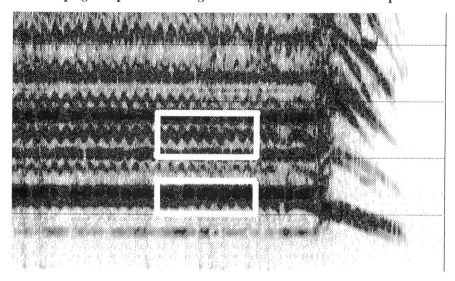

has a powerful effect on its performers and listeners: "Good performances can move them to tears and "shudders," but with a sense of happiness; and they arouse feelings of love and sexual passion among younger people, as well as strong feelings of regional identity among both young and old alike." (ibid.:331).

Let us look at the text of the women's song (fig. 5–4). In this lyric, a "tear" is something precious you do not easily let fall. "Take" here means marry. So the song is a warning to girls: don't let yourself be seduced by kisses, since an aggressive young man is probably not the reliable suitor you are looking for.

A typical male song takes a very different angle on boy-girl relations (fig. 5–5). Young men use the word *baraba* in most songs to describe themselves, which can be translated as rascal, rogue, hellraiser, someone dedicated to "living large" in a

> Sisters, hold on to your chastity like a tear;
> The one who kisses you will not take you.

Fig. 5–4. **Lyrics to highlander women's *ganga* song, sung by Šecira Kadrić, Aiša Kadrić. Enisa Trešnjo of Umoljani village.**

What lifts the heart of a rascal?
A liter of wine and a fine girl.

Fig. 5–5.   Lyrics to highlander men's *ganga* song.

macho way. Their way of singing is relaxed, self-confident, and boastful, and manhood is the main topic of songs. However, both men and women also sing songs praising singing itself as a foremost means of expression (fig. 5–6).

One can compare men's and women's texts to get a sense of the different takes on similar themes (fig. 5–7). This relationship between singing and gender, both performed and closely watched by everyone, can be found around the whole region. For nearby Albanians, Jane Sugarman proposes that "Singing, rather than merely reflecting notions of gender, also shapes those notions in return. Singing provides Prespare [the villagers she lived with] with a means of tangibly living out their strongly contrasting notions of femininity and masculinity. Through singing they are temporarily able to model their individual selves into the form of a cultural ideal . . . or they may use their singing to suggest its revision . . . [young adults] will experiment increasingly with ways of conveying through song new views of themselves as women and men" (Sugarman 1989:209).

Common to both sexes is a strong sense of place, embodied in many song texts that praise one's own village and ridicule others. But men and women convey differing senses of self in songs and dances. By and large, the highlander male repertoire is outwardly oriented and frank, the women's more intimate, poetic, and metaphoric. But in dance and clothing, women can also choose among ways of self-presentation. Mobility and the impact of outside musical styles have had their impact on how the sexes regard each other, or at least what ideal of femininity women might choose, urban or rural. Young women express this choice visibly in selecting a dance style.

The village girls want to express their strength and energy through dancing. They lift their legs high and stamp their feet. Those who want to display their urban manners dance closer to the ground, with smaller steps. Those who have lived in the town and cities away from the highlands can choose to identify them-

Men's text:
Since we have not sung, brother
The village is unhappy.
Women's texts:
I will sing out of spite for my sorrow
So it won't conquer me when it tortures me.

Oh god, what would happen if there were no singing?
What would my heart do with all its burden?

Fig. 5–6.   *Ganga* texts on the topic of singing.

Men's:	Enjoy your girlhood, girl, while you are at your mother's
	Once you're with me, you won't enjoy it.
Women's:	I didn't know, I didn't believe
	That the fawn (= boyfriend) is dearer than Mom.

Men's: Come, come, you dark one, it won't be in vain.
Let a rascal kiss you just once.
Women's: If I knew, dear, that I'd be yours
You wouldn't be able to count my kisses.

Men's: Little one, I love your bowlegs
More than a crate of Sarajevo beer.
Women's: My dear, your buddy got the better of you:
Instead of you, I love him.

Men's: Love me or love me not, little one,
My hand has caressed you.
Women's: You can love whomever you want now,
You loved me once as well.

Fig. 5–7. *Ganga* **texts on gender relations**

selves as more sophisticated, with less stress on their wood-carrying, sheep-herding, and cow-milking skills, underscoring the urban-rural divide that has run through the local scene ever since increased mobility allowed for more lifestyle choices. As one *ganga* text says, "All honor to the mountain, but I want to go to the valley/Let everyone go where she wants," or, as a girl from the village of Potoci sings: "I wouldn't get married in Potoci; I would rather poison myself," referring to her strong wish to move to the lowlands, to the larger towns and cities of Bosnia. It is to these lowlands urban settings that we now turn.

MUSIC OF RURAL AND URBAN LOWLANDS MUSLIMS

In the lowlands there are many other forms of singing (see ills. 5–4, 5–5, and 5–6), as well as more instrumental music than in the highlands. The most typical instrument of the region is the *šargija* (shar-ghee-ya), which came originally from the east, from what were Turkish-controlled regions in the old days, and which has become part of Bosnian life, played by Muslims and neighboring Serbs and Croats alike. The *šargija* is a plucked, stringed instrument; over the years the number of strings has been slowly increasing. As happens in many folk music settings, people in recent decades have wanted their instruments to produce more sound, projecting more loudness and richness; eventually, instrument types became electrified and amplified as radio, recordings, and outside influences offered people new ideals of what music "should" sound like.

In recorded example 32, the *šargija*, which once had four strings, now has six (some even have seven), and more frets, to allow for more notes to be played; the tuning is g′-g′-g′-c-f′-g″, where the bass string—c—is surrounded by three drones on g′ and two melody strings, one lower and one higher. The text praises the instrument itself (fig. 5–8).

Ill. 5–4.   Older styles: a song to attract bees into their hive, Planinica, 1967.
Credit: William G. Lockwood.

Ill. 5–5.   Older styles: a lullaby, Planinica, 1967. Credit: William G. Lockwood.

This song combines several musical threads that weave in and out of other examples. Two men sing together, but not mechanically: there is a lot of give-and-take in the way they jointly produce the words and in each man's voice quality and approach to the rhythm and phrasing of the words. They are doing the "same" thing, but in an individual way, an approach noted above for both men and women's *ganga* singing.

Another aspect of local musical thinking lies in the sense of rhythm. Notice that you can tap your foot or snap your fingers to some sections of the song, but not to others. This fluidity, this elastic sense of time is common to many musical styles of southeastern Europe and nearby areas of the eastern Mediterranean. Yet another interesting quality of this song is the way the *šargija* part is not just one line but projects multiple voices, closely positioned, that might remind one of *ganga* singing, even including the very close intervals. And each instrumental section is different—again, a flexible approach to detail pervades performance.

All of these sides of the song add up to an aesthetic: a perspective on how musical units should be put together, one that is the basis of a local and regional

O *šargija* made of poplar wood
May the one who builds you never get sick.

Fig. 5–8.   Lyrics, lowlands Bosnian Muslim song with *šargija* accompaniment, performed by Škiba and friends.

Ill. 5–6. Older styles: playing the *truba*, a shepherd boy's instrument, now little used. Credit: William G. Lockwood.

sound. There is a way of thinking, not just performing, that lies behind traditional music-making. As the folk singer Todora Varamezov of Bulgaria told the ethnomusicologist Timothy Rice, "Folk songs you can ornament and change as you want. If you change it, then you sing from the heart. It's not like you have learned it lifelessly, as if it's an obligation. Different people sing it different ways" (Rice 1994:110). At the same time, there is a limit to variation: "If singers altered the melody too much, they could count on hearing about it from the 'aunts' and 'grannies' who were watching and listening" (ibid.). "Tradition," then, means that both individual variation and collective responsibility coexist in each performance in this type of music-making, where people stand face to face and ear to ear and pay close attention. In music coming from pop recording studios or government-sponsored composers' desks, as we shall see below, the social contract about music is written very differently.

One of the important types of song associated with the Bosnian Muslim population is the *sevdalinka*. The root word, *sevda*, comes from Turkish and implies love in terms of passion, and also sadness. Originally, *sevdalinkas* were adaptations of tunes of *ilahija*, sacred songs. *Sevdalinkas* can have many different singing and accompaniment styles and topics. Hearing *sevdalinkas* on the radio and trying to sing them yourself was an early shift away from rural forms like *ganga* for village girls before more modern forms, like the pop and rock styles cited below, became available (Lockwood 1983:35). Our example (recorded se-

Ill. 5–7.   Dancing at a village wedding, Planinica, 1967. Credit: William G. Lockwood.

Ill. 5–8. The accordionist Murat Muratspahic plays for the young women,
Planinica, 1967. Like our featured musician, Mensur Hatić, this
accordionist has also emigrated. He lives in Canada, where he works
as a lumberjack near Vancouver. Credit: William G. Lockwood.

lection 32), sung by an older man, Hinzo Polovina, is about a wedding rather than the more common *sevdalinka* theme of romantic love. As in all *sevdalinkas,* symbols and metaphors, rather than straightforward commentary, make the point. To refer to the wedding is to touch upon a key memory of village life. As a researcher from nearby Hungary puts it, "Weddings rank foremost among popular customs: they are a veritable accumulation of ceremonies continuing mythical, religious-ritual, legal, economic, musical, and mimic elements. In some places they became almost festive plays with their chief and supporting characters, supernumeraries, fixed scene, time, music, dances, and audience" (CMPH 1956:689).

Among Bosnian Muslims, weddings can go on for an entire week. They include a great deal of music, which, as for festivals, is gender- and generation-marked, as the folklorist Yvonne Lockwood observed at a 1967 wedding:

> During the day, people came to welcome and see the bride, who sat shyly in the corner. Every night the older men of the village came to the house of the groom's parents where they sat in one room talking and drinking coffee. The maidens, lads, children, and young married men, including the groom, sang and danced in a second room. Behind the closed door of a third room, the women, bride, and young children congregated. Here, secluded from male observation, were some of the best singers and dancers in the village who now only perform at times like this. (Lockwood 1983:20)

The wedding song recorded in an urban radio studio differs dramatically from this traditional village scene. It comes through a radio speaker, not from the lively, charged space of a rural wedding, and is sung and played by professionals, not amateur village musicians. The accompaniment is a *tamburitza* orchestra. This type of ensemble dates back to about the 1840s, at a time when people in various European countries (notably Italy and Russia) were organizing orchestral ensembles out of older folk stringed instruments. Then, as now, folk music had a romantic aura connected to a preindustrial past imagined to be gentler than the modern world. At the same time, organizers of such groups have always insisted on precise, almost mechanized performance, an aesthetic deeply opposed to the more informal village way of music-making. It is not accidental that this new aesthetic arose with urbanization and the onset of a regimented work force in urban industrial contexts. As time went on, these folk orchestras also became connected to national pride and local identity. In the period of cultural control by the Communist Party, national identity and artistic expression were both tightly organized by the state. This approach was tried out first in what was the Soviet Union, the world's largest multiethnic country for nearly seventy-five years (1917–91) and the first nation-state to have a system completely based on socialist principles. Culture was under the control of a complex bureaucracy made of many organizations, and all the media—print and electronic, news and entertainment—were run by the government with no private enterprise allowed.

This state-managed cultural system spread to several eastern European countries in the period from 1945 until around 1990, when they were under direct influence of Soviet power as implemented by local regimes. This "east bloc" included Poland, Czechoslovakia (now the Czech Republic and Slovakia), Hungary, Rumania, and Bulgaria. Bosnia was part of Yugoslavia, whose leader, Tito, had broken away from Soviet control in 1948, but who maintained a comparable system of communist party-led government. The state acted as the main patron and policemen of all artistic—including musical—activity, deciding what could or could not be published, listened to, or supported. As we shall see below, the Yugoslav system was freer than that of its neighbors, producing some maverick musical results, but in the case of a radio orchestra such as the one that accompanies this *sevdalinka,* the goal is an official, not an informal or folk sound. Recorded selection 33 is very tightly arranged for voice and folk orchestra. This type of arrangement is a good example of managed traditionalism. You can hear the careful professionalism of "official culture" in the precisely orchestrated instruments and the somewhat reined-in voice of the singer. In fact, the directors of this ensemble prided themselves on working out the "sloppiness" of folk musicians (Lauševic 1994). This attitude combines the precommunist, bourgeois love for "updating" folk music with the socialist approach to "disciplining" national culture.

In the lyrics of the *sevdalinka* song (fig. 5–9), the figure of the golden thread from heaven that enwraps the bride, groom, and wedding party is an old image, a stock figure that appears in many songs.

The idea of folk ensembles like the *tamburitza* orchestra traveled well to places to which eastern Europeans emigrated, such as the United States. There, a Pittsburgh-based folksong and dance ensemble called the Tamburitzans has been in existence since 1936 (see Forry 1978) and continues to charm audiences not only in America but elsewhere on tour. Their publicity characterizes the group as "a spirited troupe" that has "captivated audiences throughout the Americas, the former Soviet Union and Europe with its joyful performances. . . . Wearing colorful native folk costumes, the Tammies offer a trip into some of the most fascinating parts of the Balkans and other lands with their lively village dances and vibrant songs" (World Music Institute brochure, 1994). Words like "colorful," "native," "folk," and "vibrant," coupled with "village," "fascinating," and "Balkans," evoke a concert experience that will be comfortably exotic, historic, ethnographic, yet also familiar (note the Americanized nickname, the "Tammies") and, above all, highly professional.

> That which trembles is full of pearls.
> These white castles [=homes] of ours are full of joy
> All the kinfolk are in the castle.
> The mother is celebrating the wedding of the son.
> Everybody is happy, but the mother most of all.
> They brought her the [flower name]-smelling maiden
> The golden thread stretched from the clear sky
> And wrapped around the groom's fez
> From the fez, it stretched around the bride's veil.

Fig. 5–9.   Lyrics lowlands Bosnian Muslim wedding *sevdalinka* song.

The same World Music Institute that described the Tammies in 1994 also featured the first American tour of an old folk-based troupe from Slovakia, a country in eastern Europe, that promised "dazzling folkdances, music and songs of a country which lies in the heart of Europe . . . highlighted by breathtaking acrobatic dances expressing the poetry, lyricism and passion of the Slovak people, their history and culture." Note the connection between the adjectives stressing showmanship—"dazzling, acrobatic"—and those underscoring soulfulness: "poetry," "lyricism," "passion." This approach to marketing goes back to the original purposes of professional "folk" ensembles: the projection of a local sensibility and history culled from peasant sources into an arena of modern theatrical performance by nonpeasants who "clean up" and "perfect" the expressive culture of ordinary villagers. This impulse began in intellectual circles over a hundred years ago, flourished under the state patronage of communist regimes, and continues in emigration and in postcommunist life as an expression of identity and as a vehicle for cross-cultural presentation and arts marketing. The idea has spread around the world, from the national dance troupes of African countries to the recently created folk ensemble of aboriginal peoples of Taiwan.

At the same time, the particular styles of music presented in this chapter have had a significant, long-term impact on less formal amateur song and dance activity in the United States (as well as western Europe), where for about fifty years informal "Balkan" groups have been a feature of the cultural landscape in college towns and cities across America. There is something about the infectious dance rhythms and soulful singing of the region that cuts across many social and geographic boundaries.

POPULAR MUSIC STYLES: "NEWLY COMPOSED FOLK MUSIC" AND ROCK

One of the bureaucratically defined styles of music that emerged in Yugoslavia's last decades (1960s–1980s) was called "newly composed folk music." Ordinarily we think of folk music as something handed down from generation to generation. Yet for the millions of Yugoslav villagers moving to big cities, their whole lifestyle was "newly composed" in the period beginning in the 1950s (see ills. 5–9, 5–10, 5–11). Similar seismic shifts of populations and musical styles happened in many countries of the world in this period, including (just a little earlier, in the 1930s and 1940s) the United States, where masses of black and white southerners moved to the big cities of the north, creating the urban blues (chapter 4) and parallel styles such as "honky-tonk" country music. In Peru, Mexico, India, and elsewhere, musics based loosely on elements drawn from earlier rural styles but "juiced up" in the city became the norm for a majority of the world's peoples. Yugoslavia was no exception.

The difference in eastern Europe was that the state, rather than a group of local entrepreneurs, monitored this development. Allowing some star performers to develop, the government nevertheless held on to control of record pressing plants, the airwaves, and the types of taxation placed on different kinds of music for a long time. In Yugoslavia, musics considered "useful" to social engineering

Ill. 5–9.   Villagers from Planinica going to the town of Bugojno, 1967.
Credit: William G. Lockwood.

Ill. 5–10.   The Muslim *kafana*, or coffeehouse, in the town of Bugojno, an
urban setting where current popular music is played, 1967.
Credit: William G. Lockwood.

Ill. 5–11.   A house museum in Sarajevo of the lifestyle of the urban Muslim upper class. Credit: Mirjana Lauševieć.

were not taxed, while those considered distracting or "vulgar" were taxed to show disapproval and to help subsidize the "right" kinds of music. Nevertheless, "newly composed folk music" took over the consciousness of most Yugoslavs, who identified with the combination of roots sounds and big-city topics, voices, and instrumentation.

Our example of "newly composed folk music" (recorded selection 34) comes from the work of Lepa Brena, the stage name of a young Bosnian Muslim woman from the city of Brčko. This fiery young blonde singer hit the top of the pop charts early in Yugoslavia, also starring in music video–like films. A very distinctive feature of the Yugoslav music-culture was the fact that the bureaucracy and Communist Party were perfectly willing to allow such stardom, even with its money-making potential, to flourish within a socialist state.

The musical makeup of the song seems to come mostly from the nearby region of Macedonia, part of which was once a republic of Yugoslavia and is now a separate nation. The rhythm can be beaten out as 2 + 2 + 2 + 3, or an overall pattern of 9, and is partly played on the Macedonian *darabuka* drum. This type of rhythm is common to the southeastern corner of Europe and adjacent Turkey. Locally, it is called a *cocek* ("chaw-check") dance. In the local sensibility, it is felt as "eastern," or "oriental," as are aspects of the voice quality and text delivery Lepa Brena offers here. In a sense, this sort of sound signaled "exotic" to the mainstream listener, providing a kind of local color that, although not exactly Bosnian, works in this song as part of the Bosnian boosterism the text declares (fig. 5–10).

Here the highlands we started our survey with stand unmistakably for the heart of Bosnian life. This is very like the nostalgic appeal in American country music to "the old mountain home." The pairing of sexual love with love of homeland is common enough in many world pop musics, the erotic often being a metaphor (in literature, music, or film) for nationalism, but also a way of selling songs.

Though newly composed folk music emerged from the experience of massive, sudden urbanization, it was not the only new sound in the cities. Rock, first a direct imitation of British and American groups, genres, and styles, slowly became domesticated in Yugoslavia as it did everywhere in Europe, finding its niche in the welter of local musics. In Bosnia, as elsewhere, it was largely educated, middle-class youth that took up this world style. In the socialist system, the children of bureaucrats, managers, and arts professionals tended to have a favored status and a different outlook than the children of former peasants. Many rock songs spoke to the concerns of rock worldwide—urban alienation, the generation gap, problems of love—but these had a more political edge in a controlling system like communism.

As our example of rock-oriented music, we'll listen to a folk-based song in tune with our topic, rather than the more philosophical, literary rock of singer-songwriters. "Da zna zora" (recorded selection 35), released in 1989, quotes a *varoška*, or small-town, song that has roots in the earlier twentieth century. It is by Zelijko Bebek, also the leader of the most famous Sarajevo band, Bijelo Dugma ("White Button"). Their leader, Bregović, used to say that "all of us are peasants three times removed" (in Glavan and Vrdolijak 1981). That distance is reflected in the very attenuated folk presence in this song; references to the folk tradition would probably be understood somewhat ironically by a hip, young, urban rock fan. The guest singer on "Da zna zora" is a popular singer of the style Lepa Brena represents, so this song is a fusion of urban subcultures: the more in-

1. I've been in eternal Rome, I've seen the Greek sea,
     But there's no better place than my Brčko
Chorus: Don't bother with a country that doesn't have Bosnia
     Or with a man who dozes when next to a woman.
2. There, where those highlands are, where the world is   brighter,
I've seen a lot of the world, but Bosnia's the dearest to me.
     [Chorus]
3. Whoever wants to understand Bosnia has to be born there;
     We Bosnians really know how to live life.
     [Chorus]

Fig. 5–10.   **Lyrics (translated), newly composed folk song by Lepa Brena, from the album *Lepa Bren & Sltaki Greh*, 1984, used by permission of PGP RTV.**

tellectual, British and American-influenced rock, and the more pop, folk-based "newly composed" style.

This mixture is apparent in the song's elements. It takes from tradition an old folk-style melody, a slow introduction to an up-tempo danceable tune, and some country sounds. From the rock world it takes the simple chord changes, the beat, the electric guitars with their tentative heavy metal licks, and the weary vocal style. The lyrics (fig. 5–11) are pretty straightforward.

As of the spring of 1992, neither the erotic localism of Lepa Brena nor the rock romanticism of Bebek and Beslić could speak to what befell Bosnia. As part of the dissolution of the country of Yugoslavia and the declaring of new nation-states, Bosnia became a battleground as soon as it declared itself a sovereign state in 1992. Not only did neighbors—Serbia and Croatia—engage their forces, but the multiethnic Bosnian population of Serbs, Croats, and Muslims split into warring camps and coalitions. Through 1996, thousands were killed, millions became refugees, and vast stretches of town and countryside were devastated by fierce fighting. The villages on Mt. Bjelašnica described above were destroyed by Bosnian Serbs, as was 85% of Lepa Brena's and Mensur Hatić's (see below) town, Brčko. Sarajevo, the capital of Bosnia, remained under Bosnian Serb siege for over three years—a particularly bitter turn of fate, since in that multiethnic city, ethnic and religious distinctions had seemed to dissolve into a congenial cosmopolitan culture between 1945 and 1990, most people's memory span. Music has also become a battleground, as pop and rock stars have emigrated or have taken sides in the conflict, causing reorientation of their audience. Lepa Brena, for example, sang for the Serbian cause. Songs, genres, and bands that were once national became identified with the various warring factions, who all turned to music videos to promote their cause.

Such scenes have occurred elsewhere in the world, causing severe dislocation and disjuncture. The musical life of such war-torn countries as Afghanistan or of the former Soviet lands Armenia, Georgia, and Tajikistan have been changed irrevocably. Even in more peaceful places, economic need and incentives have caused a huge world labor force to move from home, a phenomenon for which the bureaucratic-sounding term *deterritorialization* has been coined. Uprooted from familiar surroundings, often traumatized by memory, these world wanderers always find music to be an important lifeline connecting them to their past and to

> If the dawn knew how strongly I love
> Oh, the dawn wouldn't break for a year.
>
> Day and night, night and day, I drink a deep red wine;
> Oh, just before dawn I go home drunk.
>
> If the dawn knew which sweetheart I love
> The rosy dawn would never break.

Fig. 5–11.   Lyrics, "Da zna zora," Sarajevo folk-rock song. From the album *Bebek: Niko više ne sanja,* **1989, used by permission of Croatia Records.**

their loved ones far away. So it seems fitting to include in our short survey two musicians who are not living in Bosnia, but come from it, in this case carrying Bosnian traditions to the United States, but in very different circumstances: Mensur Hatić and Flory Jagoda.

MENSUR HATIĆ: VERSATILE MUSICAL TRAVELER

Mensur Hatić (pronounced "*Ha*-titch") was born in Bijelijna, halfway between the Bosnian towns of Brčko and Tuzla, in 1961 and grew up in Brčko, the predominantly Muslim city celebrated in the song by Lepa Brena, his compatriot (recorded selection 34). He now lives in Detroit, where he makes his living repairing accordions (see ill. 5–12). In 1994 I interviewed him there. Quite musical

Ill. 5–12.   Mensur Hatić (accordion) and Youri Younakov (clarinet) of Ivo Papazov's band Trakiya, playing at Ramblewood, a Balkan summer music camp at Darlington, Maryland, 1994. The Balkan music scholar Carol Silverman is at center. Credit: Mirjana Laušević.

from an early age, he was exposed to a variety of musics, taking advantage of both a network of public classical music school opportunities, particularly stressed in socialist countries, and the local ethnic and popular styles.

M.H. In the third grade, I was playing guitar on a vacuum cleaner, and I took the test for music school, and I passed. My father, he bought me a small accordion, and I started to play it. Back in Europe, in any music school, you have to play classical music. After that, I passed the test for music high school. About three hundred people were trying to get in, and thirty-two got in. I finished high school in 1980, majoring in both accordion and music theory.

M.S. What kind of music did you hear besides classical?

M.H. *Sevdalinka* was really popular. My father, he's a really good singer. He started playing accordion a long time; he pushed me for the accordion. He's the one who gave me a lot of *sevdalinka.* He knows thousands and thousands of songs.

In sixth grade I started playing for a folk dance club, and we traveled around all of Europe. That folk dance group used to dance Serbian, Macedonian, Croatian, Romanian, Bulgarian, all Balkan, not just Yugoslavian stuff. Something like folk dance club here in the United States. Difference is there, the government helped the organization, to take people from the street, give them something to do. We used to play not only in Germany, in Switzerland, wherever there are people from Yugoslavia. Italy, Austria, Denmark, Holland. Every Yugoslav national holiday we played in Germany or wherever. Everybody came, not just Yugoslavs, everybody who cares. We played also in France—everybody who likes music: "Yugoslav show tonight."

M.S. What did you do after high school?

M.H. After high school, you have to go into the army—nobody asks you. I stayed in the army twelve months and took examinations for college. In second year college, I started to play professionally. The town I used to live in, Brčko, about 35,000, not too many musicians. This guy I know, his sister is Lepa Brena, the most famous singer in Yugoslavia, so every summer we went out from Brčko for three months. On the weekend I can drive anywhere. Friday morning, Friday night we're in Germany, Monday afternoon, I'm back in my town. I used to make records and tapes. I sang second voice, keyboards, accordion. The guy who had a studio, he used to play rock music, but he didn't make any money on rock music, so he switched to folk music.

M.S. What did you do after college?

M.H. I went to Italy about two years, in the Ancona area, worked in the instrument factories, and after that I went to Germany, worked for Hohner [the major accordion and harmonica manufacturer]. I traveled back and forth, back and forth, from Germany to Italy to Brčko. I learned how to fix accordions, how to fix pianos, how to build everything. Between that, I used to play a lot, around the whole of Europe.

This account of Mensur's life through 1990 is richly layered in musical experience and travel. As a versatile musician, he quickly adapted himself to a continentwide network of Yugoslav touring groups and audiences, catering to the hundreds of thousands of expatriates scattered around western Europe. He enhanced his earning power by apprencticing in instrument building and repairing in major factories in two countries and by certifying himself as a music teacher in his hometown. With a secure base in Brčko, where he built himself a house complete with an elaborate stereo system, Mensur was both tradionalist and postmodernist, deeply Bosnian but internationalist in outlook, looking for the chance to use his skills, as musicians always have, to gain a foothold in a dynamic, insecure local economy and intercultural atmosphere. While other musicians in exile have failed to find a foothold, lost outside the environment of their particular audience, Mensur's flexibility has served him well.

Just before the onset of war in then-Yugoslavia, Mensur left for the United States, apparently anticipating and thus avoiding the conflagration that would engulf his town and country. Now he lives in Detroit in a neighborhood of older, reasonably priced housing with a large eastern European immigrant population set in a sea of ethnic diversity. Not surprisingly, he has found that his musical skills fit right in, and he plays for parties of former Yugoslavs and in local multiethnic clubs.

M.H.   The Yugoslav community doesn't have anything different from Yugoslavia. Sometimes I play for a wedding, a christening party, a shower, birthday party, everything. People are fighting in Yugoslavia, but we have the same music, no difference. I am Muslim, and I play with Macedonian, Serbian—I don't care. In New York I played Pakistan music for a Pakistani lady.

M.S.   What's the club like that you play in?

M.H.   It's the International Folk Dance Club. We have people from Turkey, Greece, Ireland, England, Middle East, Iraqi, Irani, also Albanian. We have Iraqi band, Yugoslav, Bulgarian, Romanian—depends how much money we have.

I use any chance, even today, to pick up anything from anybody. I'm not scared to ask any guy, Hey, can you teach me this? Musicians are always friendly people. I know myself, if somebody asks me to teach them, I say why not, five minutes. Music is music. I don't make any difference between Turkish music, American music. Music is the universal language.

We'll listen to a piece Mensur wrote himself, inspired by living near a train station (recorded selection 36). He takes the sound of the train and improvises on it in a very original fashion. This sort of piece is, as Mensur says, a kind of universal language; wherever trains have played an important part in people's lives, musicians have written train pieces. It is a particularly well-developed genre in rural black and white American music. Houston Baker cites the importance of train imagery in the African-American aesthetic, locating the crux of black experience "at the junctures, the intersections of experience where roads cross and diverge" (Baker 1984:8), surely an apt description of Mensur Hatić's on-the-road experience of life in Europe and America.

The piece has four distinct components: (1) a slowly accelerating theme at the beginning (A); (2) train whistle sounds; (3) a short, insistent repeated melody (B); and (4) a one-time improvised tune over steady bass (C). These combine in the pattern ABCBA, with the train whistle interjections providing an overall framework. The speeding-up of A at the beginning is matched by a slowing-down reprise of A at the end to make the whole piece cyclical.

In terms of style, two of Mensur's approaches are worth noting. One is the melodic structure of A. It is actually made up of two segments (see fig. 5–12) we can call a and b. Mensur plays ab, but then b itself repeats in its own extended form, b'. This freely expanding sense of melody is part of the improvisational aesthetic of folk music. The second place this can be heard is in the accompaniment to the B and C sections, played on the accordion buttons (the melody is played on the keys). Using the basic interval of a fourth (transcribed here as e-a), Mensur creates a steady bass line that moves against the melody, again in a free, shifting pattern of small melodic units.

FLORY JAGODA: KEEPER OF THE SEPHARDIC JEWISH TRADITION OF BOSNIA

Before World War II, the twelve thousand Jews of Sarajevo made up about 10 percent of the city's population and acted as lively, long-term contributors to the local culture and music. Tunes were shared by Jews, Muslims, Croats, and Serbs, each community adapting melodies to their own ritual or social needs. The Bos-

Fig. 5–12

nian Jews were mostly of Sephardic background. This means their ancestors were part of a wave of immigration from Spain after 1492, when the Christian rulers who reconquered Spain from the Muslims forcibly exiled the Jews and Muslims. The Jews, who had developed a long, collaborative cultural relationship with the Muslims, fled to Muslim-controlled areas of southeastern Europe, the eastern Mediterranean, and north Africa. These Spanish Jews, or Sephardim, had strong traditions of poetry and song dating back to the Middle Ages that they took with them to their new homes. Learning local languages, they also kept on speaking their own vernacular, a Spanish-based language called Ladino, or Judeo-Spanish.

During World War II the Bosnian Jews suffered the fate of their coreligionists across Europe, being deported to death camps by Nazi occupiers. Less than a thousand survived, now a vanishingly small percentage of the nearly half-million strong population of the newly swollen Sarajevo. This small postwar remnant kept up its culture, and during the early stages of the Yugoslav war of the 1990s, the Jews, onlookers to the conflict, helped as mediators. But by the mid-1990s very few Jews were left in Bosnia to carry on their centuries-old traditions, most having emigrated to Israel, the United States, or elsewhere.

Flory Jagoda (see ill. 5–13) was born in Sarajevo in 1923 to a Sephardic family—Altarac—known for its singers and musicians. She escaped from the region during World War II and emigrated to the United States, becoming the sole survivor of her family. By managing to escape her community's destruction, she is able to preserve the heritage of her childhood. She also enhances her tradition by making her own arrangements of folk materials, performing with other family members in an ensemble that has recorded and toured widely. Here is what Flory Jagoda says about her childhood and what she learned from her *nona,* her grandmother:

> In my Nona's kitchen there was a drawer that was magic to us children. It contained sheets upon sheets of paper written in Hebrew script which we could not decipher, but those words, when sung by my Nona, we understood. These Ladino songs had been learned from her mother, and her mother before her, and so on for generations. . . . I am trying . . . to again open my Nona's drawer and pass on a taste of the talent and way of life which produced the Altarac family, that it might live on, both in the songs I remember and in my own musical memories of that now-disappeared time.
> (Jagoda 1989)

For Flory Jagoda, then, it is the music that provides a sense of cultural continuity. When she escaped from the German occupation, she took her accordion with her, though she had to leave her grandmother's book of songs behind. Now she says, "Those songs my Nona sang and the accordion that saved my life were the only things I brought with me to America, the only things that were left from my childhood" (interview with M. Laušević, 1992).

Sephardic music has always been a "traveling" music. Although traditionally transmitted, it is amazingly diverse and lively, reflecting the various places and times that this resilient community (like similar Jewish groups elsewhere) has traversed. As Edwin Seroussi puts it,

Ill. 5–13.   Flory Jagoda, a Bosnian Sephardic Jewish singer who lives in the United States. Credit: Flory Jagoda.

The musical legacy of the Sephardim can be defined as a musical culture in flux. . . . Residues of melodies of medieval Spanish romances may be sung in a single breath by the same informant followed by a Judaeo-Spanish translation of a Turkish *sharki* [a type of classical song] or an Argentinian tango. A cantor, in the same service in the synagogue, may combine venerable old melodies which might carry vestiges from a pre-Expulsion [1492] repertory with tunes adopted from the dervish or Orthodox church rites in Turkey, or from the Andalusian secular repertory in Morocco. (Seroussi 1991:204)

Individual musicians, such as Mensur Hatić, can be strongly interested in keeping their ears open for new sounds, which they enjoy assimilating both for the sheer pleasure of learning and for economic viability. Whole communities, like the Sephardic Jews of Sarajevo, can also be musically adaptable and selective out of a survival sense of accommodation, because they have a variegated history of environments in which they have lived, or also just for the sheer aesthetic satisfaction of singing and playing across the full range of surrounding musical resources.

The song selected here from Flory Jagoda's ample storehouse (recorded selection 37, fig. 5–13) is about Sarajevo, about the men of the family, who can hardly wait for the end of the Sabbath so they can go out and party. She sings with her family group, who provide guitar and vocal backup, their contribution to the further transmission of their great-grandmother's songbook. To round out the complexity of such traveling transmission, in the late 1980s Flory Jagoda returned to Sarajevo to give a concert, and later some of her songs were played on the local television station, probably the first time Jewish songs were publicly aired. These songs were greeted enthusiastically by the remaining Jewish community, which had lost its tradition through the radical disjuncture of war and postwar cultural assimilation. So through the American channel of Jagoda's visit, this Sephardic music went back into circulation after a fifty-year absence.

> The roosters are starting to crow;
> It's time to get up,
> Let's not wait; the sun and the day
> Start up the happy crowd.
> From Havdalah to the Šadrvan°
> When the girls dance and sing.
> Until tomorrow, at dawn,
> The crowd disperses.

Fig. 5–13.   Lyrics (translated), Sephardic Jewish song "Klaro del Dija" from Sarajevo, sung by Flory Jagoda. Source: Global Village Music C139, used with permission.

°Havdalah is the Jewish ceremony that marks the transition from the Sabbath to the weekday world, on Saturday at sunset. The Šadrvan was a well-known Sarajevo café in the old days, located near the Jewish neighborhood.

Between them, Mensur Hatić and Flory Jagoda represent two common but contrasting versions of musical diaspora, or music of a population that feels distanced from its home and both have felt disjuncture and cultural loss through warfare. For the Sephardic Jews, the loss is total, as Sarajevo is unlikely to have a significant Jewish population in any foreseeable future. Flory Jagoda's adaptation to these conditions has been to embark on a personal quest for preservation and arrangement as a monument to a bygone culture and for her own sense of continuity. For the much younger Hatić, feeling the effect of a current war, flexibility and resourcefulness are the key to economic survival in the music business while he keeps a watchful eye on events back home to determine where his future lies. Both musicians use music as a lifeline in turbulent cultural waters, an impulse shared by countless millions of deterritorialized and migrant peoples at the end of the twentieth century.

BULGARIA AND HUNGARY: OTHER APPROACHES TO MUSICAL CHANGE

Yugoslavia's path to dissolution and destruction is one kind of story to tell about the change in eastern European music since 1990. From other nearby countries, those that have not suffered from violent transition, we can see some of the same trends, but in the light of a more peaceful cultural evolution. Examples from Bulgaria and Hungary will amplify the Bosnian situation outlined above and extend it geographically.

BULGARIA

In Bulgaria,[*] the state-ensemble approach to creating official culture that we heard in recorded selection 33 had an extraordinary history. Throughout the 1960s and 1970s classically trained composers working for the government transformed village songs into elaborate arrangements featuring careful harmony and a "clean" sound. In the late 1980s groups representing this kind of official music, sung and played by state radio troupes, toured western Europe and the United States and were acclaimed by western pop stars, selling many recordings under a heading invented by French promoters: "the mysteries of Bulgarian voices." Meanwhile, that particular form of official music was rapidly losing its validity and popularity back home in Bulgaria as part of the slow social, political, and cultural transition from the isolated communist era into an age of democratization and individual enterprise. Musically, in the vanguard of change was the clarinetist Ivo Papazov and his band Trakiya, who transformed what was called *svatbarska muzika,* "wedding music," into a technologically and musically sophisticated blend of local and global styles.

---

[*]I am grateful to Donna Buchanan, Timothy Rice, and Carol Silverman for their careful analysis of the social context of recent Bulgarian music (see Bibliography for references), and to Jane Sugarman for her reading of this chapter in manuscript.

Papazov, born in 1952, founded his band in 1974. He is of mixed ethnic background, Turkish and Rom ("Gypsy"), and so represents a minority voice in his local culture that has been an important factor in music-making for generations. In fact, his name was originally Ibrahim Hapazov, much less Bulgarian than it is now. At the beginning of this chapter, writing of the children's rain song from nearby Rumania, I mentioned that "Gypsies" (who prefer their own ethnic name, Rom or Roma) played a special part as musicians in traditional eastern European culture. The Turkish side of Papazov's background is also socially significant, since under the Ottoman Empire, Bulgaria, like Bosnia, was ruled by Turks for over four hundred years, until the late nineteenth century. This background made Papazov a problematic figure for the then-communist Bulgarian government, which made a point of trying to assert a standardized "Bulgarian" ethnicity and viewed any recognition of ethnic difference as a possibly punishable offense. Music is hardly an "innocent" fact of culture and, as in the case of Ivo Papazov, can often be the leading edge of identity conflicts and attempts at administrative control, as is apparent across most of the world at the end of the twentieth century.

Papazov's approach was to take traditional sounds from wedding and other celebrations and "juice them up" through electronic amplification and backup instruments (such as electric bass), as well as by adding blues, jazz, and rock riffs as part of long, exuberant sets performed for huge crowds. He already had a strong background in improvisation from the Turkish and Rom traditions. Often in direct opposition to official music-making, Papazov and other *svatbarska muzika* bandleaders became so popular that the government had to take account of them, finally offering some grudging approval just around the time that the old system fell, leaving the political and economic field open to those who, like Papazov, were ready for new openings.

He began to make recordings for sale in the West and to tour in Europe and America, articulating a philosophy of musical blending based on tradition that found a very receptive market as "world music" began to filter into the local bins at music stores in the Western world. As the ethnomusicologist Donna Buchanan, who has interviewed Papazov, says, "He views his folk jazz fusion style as a medium through which to improvise freely—a technique he learned by listening to recordings of Charlie Parker and Benny Goodman. Perhaps most telling is his comment that, 'I can eat the same dish twenty times, but I can't play one and the same thing twice,' which captures clearly the essentiality of improvisation to wedding music" (Buchanan in press). Another *svatbarska muzika* star, Teodosi Spasov, says that "improvisation is the means through which [the musician] achieves the free flight of his artistic fantasy. Improvisation is that which separates the free artistic souls from the whole terrestrial globe" (ibid.).

Papazov goes so far as to call his music *balkanski dzhaz,* "Balkan jazz," ("the Balkans" is the general term for southeastern Europe), but his sights are really set even beyond his region, as Buchanan points out: "He is struggling to create a musical style that supersedes his local senses of identity as a member of the ethnic Turkish and Rom subculture within Bulgaria, as a citizen of the Bulgarian nation, and as a representative of the Balkans. His stylistic aspirations bridge these affiliations with western musical idioms, creating an emblematic musical pastiche positioned squarely in the political economy of transnational popular culture" (Buchanan 1995:28).

The accompanying recording has one piece from Ivo Papazov and his band Trakiya from 1991 (recorded selection 38). It is called "Hristianova kopanitsa" and is based on a local dance-tune style of western Bulgaria. In her notes to this piece, Carol Silverman writes that "fast, asymmetric rhythms are characteristic of Bulgarian music; this example is, however, almost too fast to dance to!" (Silverman 1991). The rhythm here is a rather complicated pattern familiar to Bulgarian listeners and dancers: short-short-long-short-long (2 + 2 + 3 + 2 + 3). The piece consists of both solo and group playing with plenty of lively bass and drum rhythm backup; all of this is reminiscent of the classic jazz Papazov was listening to. Jazz is another style of modern music that took standard tunes meant for dancing and kept increasing the level of virtuosity until it became hard to dance to and transformed into a concert format. Indeed, some of Papazov's fans have complained that Trakiya's music is not "old-timey" enough for them. Another point of comparison to the Bulgarian band's approach might be to bluegrass, a post-World War II genre from the mountainous regions of the southern United States that drew attention with its alternation of dazzlingly rippling star solos by fiddles, banjos, and mandolins.

"Hristianova kopanista" starts with the basic folk tune, sparklingly played two times through. Notice that the melodic material is similar to Mensur Hatić's train piece, both emphasizing the big distance (an augmented second) between the second and third notes of the scale (fig. 5–12). This is tonal material common to a large area of southeastern Europe among many ethnic groups, but not much found as you go north and west. After the opening statements of the tune, a series of freely improvised solos follows, on saxophone, accordion, and clarinet, before the band comes back together to reprise the tune to end the piece. Notice how the drum set, imported from an American tradition, and the electric bass, a newcomer replacing older folk instruments, get freer and freer in their backup play as the piece progresses. Overall, this performance draws on notions of form familiar to local listeners, but also reminds one of the basic outline of a bebop jazz piece: statement of theme (the "head"), solos, return at end to theme.

But the bedrock beneath the solos is a traditional rhythmic framework, just as the basic melodic patterning—scale, style of ornamentation of a basic tune—is familiar from older village sounds. Adding electric bass and jazz drum set to a clarinet-and-accordion sound is a more recent trend: the Papazov style is an eloquent, sometimes witty, and always brilliant fusion of the traditional and the current, the Bulgarian and the imported.

The word *prestidigitation,* which usually refers to the "hand-is-quicker-than-the-eye" principle magicians use, literally means "fast fingers." Despite the novelty of Papazov's approach to modern musical magic, the concepts of patterned ornamentation and quickness of hand and mind are basic to more traditional Bulgarian styles as well. In marveling at the older bagpipe *(gaida)* styles that are part of the sonic memory inherent in Papazov's work, Timothy Rice writes about "the mystery of ornamentation." Describing his attempts to learn the *gaida,* the Bulgarian bagpipe, Rice notes "If the structural principles of gaida music are relatively straightforward, its rich ornamentation—and musicians' ability to play at enormous speeds—still seemed magical. . . . My preexisting Western concepts handled the rudiments of Bulgarian melody and rhythm adequately, but the manner of playing remained a mystery" (Rice 1994:77). Rice goes on to describe at length his conquest of digital subtleties through immersion in experience: "Perhaps the most profound discovery was that I learned to fuse my concepts of melody and ornamentation into a single concept expressed most vividly in the hands, not in musical notation—precisely the kind of integration I imagine young Bulgarian boys achieved when they learned this tradition." (ibid.)

Other pieces of Papazov's are even more pronounced in their borrowings from rock, blues, and jazz, adapted to basically local southeastern European/Turkish materials and approaches. Papazov's eclectic music has already become "classic," and there are doubtless new waves of tradition-based musical change on the way in Bulgaria now that the lid is off, from the governmental point of view, and the musical free market is open for business and competition.

Hungary: Learning from Traditional Music

Hungary is another nearby country that went through a communist period from the late 1940s to the late 1980s, with all the apparatus of state management suggested above. As in the case of Ivo Papazov, musical change started during this period and continued after the fall of communism. But the terms of change were different in Hungary, so to round out this short survey of a large region, let us add another influential approach to tradition: the collecting and performance of folk music not by government-sponsored researchers but by young amateurs searching for inspiration and spiritual guidance from village musicians.

In Hungary, as elsewhere (notably her huge eastern neighbor, Russia), some of the sons and daughters of the urban educated elite were drawn not only to rock music but also to the surviving folk music as another exit ramp from the official music highway. Forming small ensembles, they fanned out into the countryside as students and enthusiasts of old-time music. In part, the American "folk revival" movement since the 1940s helped set the stage for this eastern European move. Just as research-oriented musicians like Pete and Mike Seeger and Joan Baez searched out and learned from older folk musicians, recreating their music in coffeehouses and colleges, so city sophisticates in Budapest or Moscow felt the urge to discover, reevaluate, and translate downhome songs and dance tunes into neo-folk playing styles. Eastern Europeans were not alone here: in the 1970s all across western Europe as well, local folk-based bands reconfigured old songs and dance tunes, and these European ensembles themselves became highly influential in this fast-growing world of nonpop music-making.

This meant that for eastern Europe in the communist period, a "language" of modernized folk styles that was not invented by government bureaucrats became available through international youth festivals and recordings. This coincided with the expeditions of young collectors to the villages in search of "new" tunes and playing styles. In Hungary this movement became something of a major musical trend in the 1970s, spawning the growth of *tanchaz,* or folk dance-hall gathering places, workshops, and summer camps. Action ranged from intimate dance clubs to soccer-stadium arena concerts. The word itself came from the peasants, who used it as a term for a local dance place for young people rented from the landowner. Peasants hired Gypsy musicians for occasions that, like the Bosnian highlander festival, brought youth together to see and be seen. The difference is that the Hungarian villagers hired designated musicians from outside their ranks, instead of singing for each other as we saw on Mt. Bjelašnica.

What the young activists of the 1970s noticed was that the villagers within Hungary had mostly given up on downhome music-making. For source material, the urban intellectual musicians went, often secretly, to Transylvania, a largely Hungarian-populated province of neighboring Romania, where villagers, cut off from the mainstream of Hungarian music-making and culturally repressed by the Romanian government, had maintained a rich storehouse of traditional music. Back in the Hungarian cities, the industrialized masses were being spoonfed a diet of officially dispensed, obligatory "folk music" in school, municipal organizations, and the media under communism. Reclaiming the peasant heritage for city folk, the *tanchaz,* or Dance House, movement found a new way to tap into tradition, and as Béla Halmos told me in 1990, by the 1980s it used folk song texts "that could be politically understood" (that is, they introduced old songs that took on new meanings). As he said, "The Dance House movement aimed to learn, not only the music and dance, but a whole way of life on which to build a better Hungary. These are big words, but they happen to be true" (interview in Ronay 1991). The turn toward the peasantry (particularly the isolated Hungarian population of nearby Transylvania) is not new; romantics and nationalists of the nineteenth century also viewed the peasants as the wellsprings of tradition that had to be tapped for the national future. But as with the music of Ivo Papazov and his colleagues, the Hungarian government of the 1980s had a highly ambivalent attitude toward such initiatives from below, preferring to control all music-making through the elaborate state patronage system. Unlike in Bulgaria, the Hungarian "troublemakers" were not from "suspicious" ethnic groups and were not from professional musical families, but, perhaps even more threateningly, represented a broad slice of a general, amateur youth market not covered by available styles. Another problematic aspect for the pre-1990 socialist state was that since movements like *tanchaz* were not just local but widespread across all of western Europe, they implicitly linked Hungary to the threatening West in ways the establishment might find hard to accept.

As with young folksingers everywhere, the Hungarian activists were singing not just for social improvement but also for their own aesthetic and emotional satisfaction, as Marta Sebestyen, a leading singer in the Dance House movement, has said: "When they [the villagers] were singing, besides the collective pain, they were singing about their own pain, so it's very personal, which comes through the music. When I sing, I can also tell about my own problems in the song, and that's wonderful, and that's what makes these songs very up to date at the end of the twentieth century" (Interview in Ronay 1991).

Marta Sebestyen's band Muzsikás was preeminent in bringing this music to the attention of non-Hungarians, through a series of recordings released in the West. She speaks eloquently about the way she learned so well to sing songs in a style she did not grow up with:

> Everybody's asking me," Where the hell did you learn this style?" I was born with a sensibility, the ability of catching sounds and melodies. At the same time, with many visits and trips to Transylvania we added more, in experience, to learn the style. My maestros, my masters, were the old ladies and old men of the village. I was singing with these people, just sitting with them, eating with them, just holding their hands and going to church together, and that means a lot. If you try to learn these songs from notebooks, you'll never learn it. Something is missing—that is the real emotion, which you can only experience when you are there. (Ibid.)

Our example (recorded selection 39) shows Marta Sebestyen and the musicians of Muzsikás sensitively adapting a very old folk song for a modern audience. The song itself takes up a topic common across eastern Europe, the figure of the outlaw, often seen as a somewhat romantic figure battling an oppressive regime or invaders (fig. 5–14). The topic of exile, of being far from home and one's native language, is all too common as well. For at least 150 years, a substantial number of eastern Europeans have left home as emigrants, exiles, prisoners, and refugees.

In singing this old folk song, Marta Sebestyen stays very close to a village style of a rhythmically flexible performance that is at once carefully measured yet elastic, standing out against the very steady, slightly offbeat bass backup and the elab-

> Turn toward the sunset, my noble horse,
> For we are never coming back again.
> I'm going into exile to a faraway land.
> Never again will I see my beautiful motherland.
> Blow away, good wind, blow the dust on the long road
> and the footprints of my good horse.
> It was a good horse; God bless the person who trained it.
> In a foreign town, foreign people.
> I walk the streets, I don't know anyone.
> I would speak to them, but they don't understand me.
> This saddens my heart.

Fig. 5–14.   Lyrics, Hungarian Dance House–style piece, *Bujdosodal*, performed by Muzsikás, from the album *Soldier's Song*, used by permission of Rykodisc Records.

oration of the melody by the violins. The verses themselves are in a 6 + 6–syllable structure, one of the oldest poetic styles for folk song, related to the epic tradition. Muzsikás adds instrumental sections to the song: an introduction, interludes between sets of verses, and a postlude. The interludes are called *lassu,* a generic term for dance tunes, and are quite close to folk practice. Through these extensions, Muzsikás turns a song into a concert item or a CD track, but even in a village setting, a band might play a *lassu* with a song, and the audience might all chime in with a familiar song text.°

SUMMARY

Although musical traditions are in constant change everywhere, eastern Europe offers a striking recent example of major transition. This chapter centered on the example of Bosnia, part of the country of Bosnia and Herzegovina that was once part of a country called Yugoslavia, which collapsed violently around 1990, causing widespread destruction.

In Bosnia we started with a seemingly isolated mountain village with a Muslim population where old song styles accompanied a herding economy, but where the music culture had been already augmented by the men and women who traveled to nearby cities to work and brought back new sounds, with some men going to other parts of Europe for jobs and returning for hometown festivals where a variety of musics were displayed. Europe is an area where the ultramodern and the traditional have long coexisted, though this pattern has extended worldwide, as areas covered by other chapters in this book demonstrate. Because sound recording technologies, radio and television broadcasting, and the idea of a music "industry" were invented in Europe and the United States, these global trends started there first before spreading widely.

We followed Bosnian music through its contribution to a national commercialized popular music style, "newly composed folk music," and also noted its appearance in government-sponsored "official culture" ensembles. Since the time of the musical examples you have heard here, Bosnian music has undergone significant change owing to the destructive interethnic war that began in 1992. For example, war songs connected to music videos, some influenced by rap, became very popular, while local folk traditions like those of the Mt. Bjelašnica highlanders we surveyed have been largely curtailed because of the fighting.

To round out the discussion, we briefly visited nearby Bulgaria and Hungary, whose societies shifted from a communist to a capitalist-based democratic system without bloodshed. There, issues of how to present older traditions for a youth audience and how to market one's local sounds to the world take precedence. These are also globally relevant issues, but particularly pointed in the case of the dramatic shift of social, economic, and political orientation in our target area here, Central and Southeast Europe.

°I am indebted to Judit Frigyesi for the choice and analysis of this example.

REFERENCES CITED

Buchanan, Donna
    1996   "Wedding Music, Social Identity, and the Bulgarian Political Transition." In M. Slobin, ed., *Retuning Culture: Music and Change in Eastern Europe*. Durham N.C.: Duke Univ. Press.

CMPH (Corpus Musicae Popularis Hungaricae)
    1956   Vol. III/B *Lakodalom*, ed. L. Kiss. Hungarian Academy of Sciences.

Forry, Mark
    1978   "Becar Music in the Serbian Community of Los Angeles: Evolution and Transformation." In *Selected Reports in Ethnomusicology* 3/1, ed. J. Porter.

Glavan, Darko, and Drazen Vrdoljak
    1981   *Nista mudro*. Zagreb: Polet Rock.

Jagoda, Flory
    1991   Liner notes to *Kantikas di mi nona*. Global Village C139.

Lauševič,, Mirjana
    1993   "Rascals and Shepherdesses: Music and Gender on a Bosnian Mountain." M.A. thesis, Wesleyan Univ.

Lockwood, Yvonne
    1983   *Text and Context: Folksong in a Bosnian Muslim Village*. Columbus, Ohio: Slavica.

Petrović, Ankica
    1977   "Ganga, a Form of Traditional Rural Singing in Yugoslavia." Ph.D. diss., Queen's Univ., Belfast.

Rice, Timothy
    1994   *May It Fill Your Soul: Experiencing Bulgarian Music*. Chicago: Univ. of Chicago Press.

Ronay, Esther
    1991   *Transylvania: Land beyond the Forest*. Documentary film produced by Channel 4 Productions, London.

Seroussi, Edwin
    1991   "Between the Eastern and Western Mediterranean: Sephardic Music after the Expulsion from Spain and Portugal." *Mediterranean Historical Review* 6(2):198–206.

Sugarman, Jane
    1989   "The Nightingale and the Partridge: Singing and Gender among Prespa Albanians." *Ethnomusicology* 33(2):191–215.

ADDITIONAL READING

In addition to other works cited above, the best single introduction to the region and many of the issues addressed in this chapter is Rice 1994, which includes an ample CD of musical examples. A reader edited by Mark Slobin provides a survey of questions raised here by numerous authors, some cited in this chapter: *Retuning Culture: Music and Change in Eastern Europe* (Durham, N.C.: Duke Univ.

Press, forthcoming). For the genre of *ganga,* see Petrović 1977. For the ethnography of Bosnian Muslims, see William G. Lockwood, *European Moslems: Economy and Ethnicity in Western Bosnia* (New York: Academic Press, 1975). For Eastern Europe in general, the literature in English remains scanty. Separate country/topic articles in *The New Grove Dictionary of Music* offer good regional summaries. For Hungary, classic works are Béla Bartók, *Hungarian Folk Music,* 1931, reprinted twice in English; Zoltán Kodály, *Folk Music of Hungary* (Budapest: Corvina, 1960); Balint Sarosi, *Folk Music: Hungarian Musical Idiom* (Budapest: Corvina, 1986) and his *Gypsy Music* (Budapest: Corvina, 1978). For good examples of work on southeastern European peasant ritual, see Gail Kligman's books *Caluş: Symbolic Transformation in Rumanian Ritual* (Chicago: Univ. of Chicago Press, 1981) and *The Wedding of the Dead* (Berkeley: Univ. of California Press, 1988). For a general history of rock music through 1990, see T. Ryback, *Rock around the Bloc* (London: Oxford Univ. Press, 1990) and S. Ramet, ed., *Rocking the State: Rock Music and Politics in Eastern Europe and Russia* (Boulder, Colo.: Westview Press, 1994).

ADDITIONAL LISTENING

For Bosnia, there is the splendid CD *Bosnia: Echoes from an Endangered World,* Smithsonian Folkways CD SF 40407. Since the onset of war in the 1990s, it is difficult to keep track of shifting ownership of record labels and availability of locally produced albums for most of former Yugoslavia. Of the featured performers of this chapter, Flory Jagoda has three albums on the Global Village label, Muzsikás of Hungary has several albums distributed by Rykodsic, and Ivo Papazov has two albums, also on Rykodisc. For more general coverage of Central and Eastern Europe, the most easily available albums tend to be popularized versions or "official"-style ensembles aiming at an international market; many older documentary albums of more traditional sounds are hard to find, so are not listed here. Currently available on a record-store computer base are the following: Bulgaria: *Two Girls Started to Sing,* Rounder 1055; *Bulgaria Compilation,* Elektra/Nonesuch 79195; *Macedonia: Songs and Dances,* Elektra/Nonesuch 72038; Hungary: *Folk Music from Szatmari Region,* Hungaroton 18192; *Marta Sebestyen: Apocrypha,* a more experimental folk-based album, Rykodisc 1368; Albania: *Vocal and Instrumental Polyphony,* Chant du Monde LDY 274897.

CHAPTER SIX

India/South India

DAVID B. RECK

THE ENVIRONMENT—THE MUSICIAN

THE SETTING

Imagine in your mind's eye being dropped into the thriving city of Madras in South India. Under the burning tropical sun framed by large white clouds in a brilliant blue sky, beneath rising dust that hangs mistlike over the asphalt streets, palm trees, and whitewashed concrete buildings, you would be faced with a bewildering confusion of elements: the traffic, seemingly chaotic, pits colorful trucks, buses, taxis, and automobiles against a kaleidoscopic array of bicycles, mopeds, handcarts, motorcycles, and three-wheeled motor rickshaws (see ills. 6–1, 6–2). Streams of people, a human river, pour out from the sidewalks and onto the streets. The pungent odor of curries drifts through the air from restaurants and food stalls. Sidewalk vendors sit by their symmetrical arrangements of wristwatches, cutlery, and plastic toys. Others carry bananas, flowers, or rolls of brilliantly colored cloth in baskets on their heads. A roadside astrologer sits under a tree. A few feet down the street (under the next tree) might be a cobbler or a bicycle repairman.

Modern skyscrapers and high-rise apartments abut mud-and-thatch village style huts. Spacious air-conditioned movie theaters and showrooms for silks, motorcycles, refrigerators, and television sets border crowded bazaars with tiny shops selling jewelry, perfumes, rugs, and spices. Massive mills and factories producing everything from computers to automobiles contrast with the humble establishments of traditional craftsmen working with the tools and methods of generations past.

There are other jarring juxtapositions. A bullock cart with massive wheels creaks under the weight of its load, an electrical transformer. A loinclothed laborer, a turban protecting his head from the sun, stands momentarily next to a businessman holding a briefcase and dressed in fashionable Madison Avenue suit

252

Ill. 6–1.   Mount Road, one of the busiest commercial streets in Madras.

and tie. Hindu religious rites thousands of years old dedicate a nuclear power generator. The old and the new, the indigenous and the transplanted, coexist. It is almost as if the layers of four thousand years of history have been frozen—in people, objects, beliefs, lifestyles, buildings—to exist simultaneously in an inexplicable present.

Ill. 6–2.   Bunder Street in Georgetown, a section of Madras which grew up around the offices, warehouses, and fort of the British East India Company.

The facts about India are staggering. Its population of over 700 million (one-fifth of the world's population) exists in an area less than half the size of the United States. There are fifteen major languages (most with different alphabets) and dozens of dialects. India's history is a continuous thread going back to the great cities of the Indus Valley civilization (3000–1500 B.C.E.).

Owing perhaps to its geography—a peninsula cut off from neighboring lands by jungles, deserts, and the towering Himalaya mountains—India has developed forms of culture and lifeways that are distinctly its own. Yet because of its size and its variety of terrain there are also great regional differences.

The largest such division is between the Hindi-related language groups of the North and the Dravidian-speaking peoples of the South, a division that is paralleled in the two styles of "classical" music: the northern *hindusthani* style and the southern *karnataka* tradition.

Numerous influences have come into India, the earliest being the immigration of Aryan people from central Asia (beginning in the second millenium B.C.E.), whose Indo-European language was related to the languages of Europe. Perhaps the most important later influences came from the Islamic conquests (beginning in the twelfth century C.E.) and the British, who made India "the jewel of their colonies" (seventeenth to twentieth centuries). Cultural ideas, along with technology, came with each group, but a characteristic pattern has emerged each time: the new ideas (and people) were absorbed, assimilated, and digested, emerging finally in a new and undeniably Indian synthesis.

In music this synthesis and transformation can be seen in the relationship between the *ragas* (music/expressive modes)° and forms of India and those of Iran and the Middle East (the Islamic influence), or in the adaptation of the European violin, clarinet, and harmonium—all played in a distinctly Indian manner—from the English.

The arts, along with the sciences and philosophical and religious thought, have flourished in India from the earliest times. Great kings and great dynasties built thousands of magnificent palaces, temples, forts, towers, tombs, and cities. Indian sculpture in stone, wood, or bronze and Indian painting (notably the book-size miniatures) rank among the greatest masterpieces of world art. Traditional literature is dominated by the two major epics—the *Ramayana* and the *Mahabharata* (written down between 400 B.C.E. and 400 C.E., but believed to exist in oral traditions much earlier). There have been dozens of major authors, poets, and playwrights, however; the most famous was Kalidasa, who lived in the fourth and fifth centuries; and there are numerous collections of stories and fables.

Indian soil has also been the locus of great religious development. The four *Vedas* (believed to have crystalized as early as 1200 B.C.E.) and the later *Upanishads* contain religious and abstract philosophical thought of such logic and beauty that they have fascinated Western thinkers such as Thoreau and scientists such as Robert Oppenheimer. The *Puranas* (first century C.E. to the present) are filled with the myths of the gods and goddesses of popular Hinduism. Thinkers such as Shankara (?788–829) rank among the great philosophers of the world.

°An English equivalent follows the italicized word here and, where appropriate, throughout this chapter.

The ancient physical and mental disciplines of yoga are now practiced by millions of Americans and Europeans and taught in universities and meditation centers, and even on television. In recent times, activist saints such as Mahatma Gandhi (1869–1948) have preached nonviolence combined with radical social action to a passive world.

Excellence in the arts continues today in many areas. Musicians such as Ali Akbar Khan or Ravi Shankar are as well known in the West as rock and pop stars. Satyajit Ray was one of the acknowledged masters of contemporary cinema; R. K. Narayan's novels, written in English, have won widespread critical acclaim. And there are hundreds of poets, musicians, painters, authors, filmmakers, and thinkers of great depth and skill whose work is not known abroad. Finally, there are the many humble craftsmen, carrying out centuries-old traditions in weaving, fabric painting, embroidery, metalwork, wood carving, jewelry, basketry, and other crafts, who support an export trade of fine handmade goods admired throughout the world.

The problems of modern India are immense. Successive governments have attacked but not completely solved serious problems of overpopulation, terrorism, social order, and an agriculture dependent on monsoon rains, which may either bring famine if they fail or devastating floods and hurricanes if they are too heavy.

The political system, based on British parliamentary rule, is democratic, though it can appear chaotic to an outsider. And change is occurring in the face of

Ill. 6–3.   The traditional wedding of a young couple is laced with ancient ritual and music. Note the garlanded images of Hindu deities on the wall.

the apparent immovable inertia of age-old traditions. There are, therefore, steel mills and locomotive factories and nuclear power plants; there are soft drinks, modern airline and railway systems, computers everywhere, well-equipped armed forces, and a growing and prosperous middle class with world-class competence and brilliance particularly in the sciences, technology, and business. There are subways, skyscrapers, discos, and jazz bars. At the same time there is the juxtaposition of the new with the archaic—in customs, lifeways, ways of seeing, and ways of doing. The old, traditional ways survive through all the changes of time and history (see ill. 6–3). This coexistence is part of the amazement and fascination of India—and perhaps also part of its strength.

MANY MUSICS

If we were to stroll through one of the more traditional neighborhoods of Madras, like the section of Mylapore, we might come into contact with many forms of music. The music that we hear would reflect many levels of folk or popular or classical art, many layers of society. It may be built on ancient traditions passed down by generations, or new ones; it may have sprouted and grown on Indian soil, or it may be an exotic transplant, undergoing a process that, unless stopped by outright rejection, will ultimately metamorphose it into an Indian synthesis (see ill. 6–4).

The predominant music here and elsewhere in South India, blasting out of house radios or loudspeakers mounted at the front doors of shops and tea-stalls, is the sound of "cine music." Listen to the recording of "Engal kalyanam" ("Our Wedding"; recorded selection 40; fig. 6–1). Indian pop music is called "cine

Ill. 6–4.   A poster advertises *Thillana Mohanambal*, **a popular Tamil movie adapted from a famous novel about the romance and marriage of a dancer and a musician.**

Our marriage is a confusion/commotion marriage!
  Sons-in-law spend for the marriage
    and the father-in-law puts up the *pandal*[1]
      to receive gifts.

Morning is the wedding, and evening is the wedding night.
  Enliven! Love marriage.[2]
Tomorrow won't the marriage altar give the garlands?[3]
  Won't the drums drum with the pipes?

The lovers' story is performed in the eyes.
  How much struggle: to perform in the eyes!
A colorful chariot is running beside me;
  Heaven is coming to us!

Mother-in-law is putting on eye makeup
  And the sons-in-law are staring at the mirror;
Processions wind along the streets with firecrackers,
  And all are giving their blessings.

Shall we have ten to sixteen children?
  Shall the trimness of the body be lost?
You hated men,
  (Yet) you gave desire!
    I am the God of Love!
      You are the reason!

Your cheeks are inviting me;
  The thoughts are asking for one.
Eyes are like bright lightning;
  What are the pleasures we haven't experienced?

He [father-in-law] had prayed to the God of Tirupati[4]
  To perform the marriage in Tirupati
    So that they [the bride and groom] might live
      prosperous lives.

Sons-in-law should come home
  and give a send-off to the father-in-law
    so that he can take up *sanyasin*![5]

—translation from the Tamil
by S. B. Rajeswari

1. *Pandal:* a temporary wedding canopy of bamboo and palm leaves.
2. A "love marriage" is contrasted with a marriage arranged by parents, often with pragmatic objectives.
3. The bride and groom exchange garlands at an important part of the ceremony.
4. Tirupati is the site of the great temple to Lord Venkateswara, the most popular shrine in South India.
5. That is, the new son-in-law should take over the responsibilities of his wife's father, who can then retire and take up a religious life (*sanyasin*).

Fig. 6–1. Lyrics to "Our Wedding."

music" or "film music" because almost all the songs come from hit movies in Hindi, Tamil, or other regional languages. Virtually all movies are musicals. Cine music is a curious and sometimes bizarre blend of East and West: choppy and hyperactive melodies, often in "oriental" scales, are belted out by nasal singers over Latin rhythms and an eclectic accompaniment that may include trap set, electric organs and guitars, violins, xylophones, celeste, bongos, *sitar, tabla,* or bamboo flute. More recently some genres of Indian pop music have been crafted to sound exactly like their Western pop counterparts, with only their lyrics in Indian languages making them distinguishable from the latest hit tune. The lyrics of cine songs tend to focus on the eternal trivia and complications of love and romance. "Engal kalyanam" takes a light-hearted look at the commotion and excitement of an Indian wedding, with the ever-present relatives and the joyful feelings of the happy couple.

The same musical characteristics hold for many of the forms of folk music and street entertainments: for snake charmers piping on their *punjis* (a kind of gourd-and-reed bagpipe), for mendicants playing small gongs or the conchshell *shanku,* for musicians accompanying acrobats and dancers or street theater (see ill. 6–5).

Often forms of music are connected with forms of worship. Each large temple has its musicians: singers of ritual songs, performers of *harikatha bhagavatham* (a kind of storytelling and sermon interspersed with classical and religious song), or the religious ensemble of double-reed *nagaswaram* and drums, which provide music for temple and household ceremonies, processions, and weddings. Part of the ritual to Ayyappan—a god whose temple is located deep in the jungles of the

Ill. 6–5.   C. P. Saraswathi, a wandering minstrel, accompanies herself on the kudam. A member of a household offers her rice in exchange for her song.

southern mountains—is the sound of the *panchavadyam,* a ten- to twenty-man percussion orchestra. Listen to the recording of this ensemble, turning the volume up to the loudest level possible without distortion (recorded selection 42). This is only a fragment of a performance that you must imagine as lasting all night long. Try to get a feeling for the numbing power of the sound through its complexity, loudness, and continuousness over a long period of time. *Panchavadyam* percussion music is based on long rhythmic cycles marked by ostinato patterns played by the group over which individual soloists alone, or in rapid alteration, improvise. Rhythm and drumming in India are among the most complex in the world.

There may also be unmodified transplants. Student rock bands play hits from England and America; Westernized clubs may have a dance combo or jazz band; Christian churches sing hymns or mount a Christmas production of Handel's *Messiah.* And there is the curious hybrid from the British military bands of the colonial era: the street bands, which—sometimes elaborately uniformed—play Western band instruments (bass and snare drums, cymbals, trumpets, trombones, clarinets, saxophones, and so on). These groups blast mostly unison melodies from the pop music repertoire to claphammer percussion as they march in wedding, temple, and political processions.

We might also hear more traditional types of music. Minstrels carrying simple instruments like the one-stringed gourd and bamboo *ektara* or the washtub bass–like *kudam* (literally "clay pot") sing from door to door hoping for a few *paisa* (pennies) or a gift of rice. Listen now to "Nagapattu" ("Song to the Snake Deities") sung by C. P. Saraswathi, a minstrel from the Kerala region of South India, as she accompanies herself on the *kudam* (recorded selection 41; fig. 6–2). Musical elements such as an "oriental" scale, melodic ornamentation, drone, assymetrical phrasing, and a strongly accented rhythmic accompaniment mark this (quite sophisticated) folk song as distinctly "Indian" and connect it to "classical" traditions found in the same culture.

Finally, echoing from concert halls, from temples, from *nagaswaram* piping ensembles, and from radios we would hear *karnataka sangeeta* (both words are accented on the second syllable), the classical music of South India. We call it classical not because it is necessarily more complicated or polished or difficult to perform than many of the folk traditions, but because it has a status as a cultivated high art form in India similar to that of "classical," or "art," or "serious" music in the West. This status is today shared by the classical dance traditions such as *bharata natyam, kathak,* or *odissi.*

Listen to the example of *karnataka* music on the cassette (recorded selection 43), or to any of the recordings recommended in the discography. Try to become familiar with the sound and style of *karnataka sangeeta* so that you can form a background for the explorations and analysis that follow later in this chapter. Make a list of some of the characteristics of the music. Try humming or singing along with the slower passages. Best of all, try listening to *karnataka* music intensively over a period of several days (or even a week), even while you read, talk, daydream, or do chores. Try to absorb as much of the music as you can.

Then, when the dark ages had passed,
It happened thus to Garudan.[1]

A dance and flowers of great beauty were offered,
As salutation to God in those ways [paths].

Garudan's desire to elevate himself to nobility
Had been apparent earlier in the clouds.

The orphans[2] went to the Mother,
Bowing down in obesiance to Her.

Whereupon that Mother
Kissed them with great joy.

All the wickedness that had come to pass
Was whispered into Her ear.

"Wickedness has befallen me in this, my child!
The wretch that I am!" Kadru[3] fearfully declared.

"Let what is my due
Be fulfilled unto me."

Hearing this, Garudan was alarmed;
"O Mother, what can I do about this?

This web of deceit (iniquity) is spun.
What must I do that it may end?" . . .

> Partial and free translation—
> P. George Mathew

1. Garudan: the great mythical bird, the mount of the god Vishnu.
2. The orphans: that is, the cobras, snakes.
3. Kadru: mythical mother of the snakes.
   The allusions of the song text are to epic legends concerning the origins of the snakes before time began.

Fig. 6–2. Song to the Snake Deities.

A DAY IN THE LIFE OF RAMACHANDRA, A MUSICIAN OF MADRAS

Mylapore, one of the older neighborhoods of Madras, like many sections of the great city, was originally a town in itself. Built around the great Shiva temple of Kapaleeswara, Mylapore is made up of back-to-back one-, two-, and three-story houses with flat or red-tiled roofs. Its streets are lined with the tiny shops of craftsmen and businesses, and with open-air markets. Here we might notice some of the problems of Madras and other large Indian cities: overcrowding, inadequate sanitation, insufficient water (clusters of women with pots around public faucets), fickle supplies of electricity. We might also notice that everyday life—far from being shut up boxlike in individual houses—spills out into the communal spaces of courtyards, onto the sidewalks and the street. Life is too crowded in individual homes and in the city to be anything but gregarious (see ills. 6–6, 6–7).

Ill. 6–6.   A Mylapore street band whose members adapt Western musical instruments to Indian folk and popular music.

Ill. 6–7.   Children play on the small lane in front of Ramachandra's house. Most homes in Madras are similarly built with stucco and brick or concrete. The windows are laced with metal bars, since glass would make the houses too hot in the tropical climate.

In the maze of Mylapore, on a tiny lane approachable only by footpath, is the modest house of Sri Veena Thirugokarnam N. Ramachandra Iyer. As in the case of many South Indians, we can tell much about him by his name: *Sri* (pronounced "shree") means "sir" or "mister"; *Veena* refers to the fact that he is a musician, a master of the seven-stringed plucked *veena; Thirugokarnam* is the name of his ancestral village, the place of his birth; *N.* is the initial of his father's given name; *Ramachandra* is his own given name; and *Iyer* is a caste-name signifying that he is a member of the Brahmin caste, that his ancestral ties are to the region of the Tamils (now the state of Tamilnad), and that his religious sect regards Shiva as the supreme deity.

To place oneself by name is very important to South Indians. Everyone is born into a caste that (while things are changing gradually) can predetermine many things: social status, how you speak, whom you can eat with, whom you can marry, and what jobs or profession you may or may not pursue, as well as certain social and religious practices and obligations. Ramachandra's caste, Brahmin, is socially high (though a Brahmin may be poor) and is traditionally associated with the Hindu priesthood, with scholarship and teaching, and (in the South) with music.

Ramachandra is a frail, shy man in his sixties, whose traditional clothes and hairstyle (shoulder-length hair tied in a knot) and religious markings signify that he is conservative and traditional. His movements are often birdlike, and neighbors regard him as a little eccentric (an excusable fault for an artist). His shyness disappears, however, when he picks up his *veena* and plays or teaches; in fact, he has a ready wit and a good sense of humor. He tries to be "a good man," living according to his *dharma*—that is, holding to high ethical standards; but he is confused by the dog-eat-dog mentality, the imperfections, and the instability both of the modern world and of the music scene in Madras.

When Ramachandra was a boy living in a small village in the tiny kingdom of Puddukottai, near Tanjore, his father decided that he was to become a *veena* player and sent him to study with his uncle, Karaikudi Sambasiva Iyer, one of the greatest virtuosi of modern times. The decision was not a rash one, since his family had included seven generations of *veena* players before him. Many of his ancestors had served as musicians attached to the courts of the *rajas*—the kings and princes—of the area.

After his apprenticeship and marriage, Ramachandra was encouraged by a wealthy patron to move to Madras, then as now the center of the *karnataka* music world. He quickly became established as a teacher and has supported himself and his family (a wife and three sons) in a manner that has not changed substantially in the past twenty years. Although it was not Ramachandra's fate to become a famous concert musician like his *guru*, he plays occasional weddings and temple concerts and is highly regarded by his colleagues.

A typical day in Ramachandra's household begins around 5:30 in the morning. The women get up first and begin work in the kitchen. The men rise next, washing their faces and brushing their teeth. The children are last.

Ramachandra's household is a "joint" or "extended" family. Besides him and his wife (who make most of the decisions, since they are senior members of the family group), there are the eldest and youngest of his three sons, their wives, and four grandchildren (see ill. 6–8). In all, ten people live in the five tiny rooms of the house; and those who have jobs pool their income to help maintain the household.

The house is like thousands of others in Madras. Thick brick and concrete walls, glassless steel-barred windows, and a red tile roof enclose a cavelike space of tiny rooms. Tables, cabinets, chairs, trunks, and a couch encroach upon the limited floor space, since most rooms (except for kitchen and pantry) serve multiple functions throughout the day. The main living room, for example, serves as a bedroom at night, music room during lessons, dining room during meals, and a living space at other times. In the back is a small open-air courtyard adjoined by sheds containing a washroom and a toilet. A single hand pump brings water up from the city water pipes, but when water pressure drops (a daily occurrence) water must be carried from a nearby well.

Ramachandra and his family, though they are middle class, have few possessions, especially when compared with habitually acquisitive Americans. A few faded and framed photographs and calendar prints of the Hindu gods hang from nails on the bare concrete. Besides pots and pans, clothes, and other items needed for day-to-day living, only a table radio, a thermos bottle, an electric wall clock, a rotating electric fan, and a television set—some presented to Ramachandra by his students—stand out as "luxury" items. A large cabinet dominating the

Ill. 6–8.   Musical tradition is adsorbed by younger generations through daily contact: Ramachandra and his daughter-in-law Saraswati encourage his grandchild to try his hand at strumming the _veena_. The family shrine can be seen in the background.

main living hall contains Ramachandra's most valuable possessions: two magnificent *veenas* of jackwood and brass with ivory inlay. With these instruments in the
cabinet are old music books, pictures of Ramachandra's parents and *guru,* and the
miscellaneous paraphernalia of a musician. At night Ramachandra removes his
prized foreign-made wristwatch (an Italian Timex), bought on his only trip
abroad, and locks it with other valuables in the cabinet.

The early morning hours in Madras are among the most pleasant of the day.
Usually a breeze blows in from the Bay of Bengal, rustling the leaves of palm
trees and awakening a noisy population of crows. It is relatively cool—in the 70s.
Ramachandra's family moves through its regular morning ritual of hot coffee or
milk, baths, shaving, getting dressed in fresh clothes, reading the Tamil newspaper (Tamil is the language of Madras), listening to the news or *karnataka* music
on the radio, taking care of the children, marketing, and preparing and eating
breakfast. Considerable logistics are required with so many people moving
around in such a small space.

The milkman arrives on his rounds, driving his sleepy herd of buffalo before
him and milking at every doorstep. Ramachandra's daughter-in-law or niece
sprinkles water outside the front door and paints a beautiful symmetrical design
on the ground in front of the house by sifting flour between her fingers. These
designs, done every day by South Indian women, are called *kolams* or *rangoli* and
are considered to bring good luck.

Meanwhile, at around 7:00 A.M., the first of Ramachandra's students arrives.
The two *veenas* are lifted out of the cabinet and placed on straw mats on the floor.
Ramachandra sits facing his student and the lesson begins. Every note, every ornament, every phrase is taught in the traditional way: Ramachandra plays, the student watches his hands, listens, and then imitates. Bit by bit the phrases of a *raga*
or a composition are built up, perfected, and memorized. There is no musical notation. "This is the 'thousand-times' method," Ramachandra has said. "Once you
learn something in this way you can never forget it . . . the 'book' is in your head
and in your hands."

Ramachandra's lessons have an air of relaxed formality. It was different in the
old days, the days of Ramachandra's apprenticeship. Then, he remembers, students moved into the household of the *guru,* to live as part of his extended family.
As many as five or ten students might be living with a well-known *guru* at any
given time. In exchange for lessons, students, helped out in the household, and
occasional gifts were given by their parents to the teacher. Much of the learning
was simply by "osmosis," by living in an environment filled with music "twenty-
five hours a day."

Discipline was strict, and the *guru* demanded the utmost in respect and obedi-
ence. Students became familiar with the whack of a teacher's hand on the top of
the head or a slap on the hands with a stick. Fear, it was thought, makes you try
harder!

The *guru,* one's principal teacher, is remembered and venerated for a musician's entire lifetime. The reason for this respect is that—unlike the West, where
most of our knowledge exists in books and computers—in India, the *guru* is the

ultimate source of all the student's musical knowledge. He holds within him a whole musical tradition stretching into the past, as well as compositions, improvisatory skills, and vocal or instrumental techniques. He is like a living, human library. And what he gives to his students, despite his apparent cruelty or harshness, must ultimately be regarded as a priceless gift.

A music lesson lasts an hour, more or less. And as the morning wears on, other students (mostly children, girls in their teens, or adult women) appear, to wait quietly in a front room until they are called for their lesson. Each pays Ramachandra a monthly stipend, according to his or her family's means. It is not much.

During the lessons, life in the household goes on. The grandchildren are fed and the eldest is sent off to school. The sons and niece and nephew go off to work. Vendors come to the door selling flowers, vegetables, pots and pans, plastic toys, and other items with characteristic and almost musical calls. At midmorning, around ten o'clock, Ramachandra takes a break from his lessons. It is time for his morning bath, his *puja* (or household worship), and his morning meal.

Ramachandra, cleansed by his bath, goes to a mirror, combs and oils his long, graying hair (tying it into the traditional bun), and applies scented sandalwood paste to his arms, chest, and forehead. He applies a dime-sized circular red spot of *kumkum* to his forehead. Seated on a small wooden pallet and surrounded by ritual objects, he performs his daily *puja*. Before him is a small cabinet, the family shrine, containing framed prints, gold-plated reliefs, and small statues of some of the gods of the Hindu pantheon. Represented among them are Shiva, the main deity of Ramachandra's sect; Saraswati, the goddess of music and learning; and a photograph of Ramachandra's musical *guru*, whom he venerates along with the gods. There are also pictures of the famous composers of the *karnataka* tradition.

After the *puja*, Ramachandra eats his morning meal. Since this is usually the principal meal of the day, it includes generous servings of rice, various vegetarian curries, lentil sauce, and hot pepper soup, with spicy pickles and chutney and yogurt. His wife or daughter-in-law serves, bringing the food out hot from the kitchen.

Dressed in the traditional *veshti* (ankle-length white cloth draped around the waist), loose-fitting *juba* (or *kurta,* the sometimes embroidered shirts now sold in Indian clothing shops all over the United States), and sandals, Ramachandra walks under the shade of a large black umbrella or boards a cycle-rickshaw or a bus to give lessons in the homes of his wealthier students. On some days he returns home for a midafternoon rest. He may then chat with his wife, play with his grandchildren (swinging them in a hammock suspended from the ceiling), help with a little housecleaning, or spread a mat on the floor under the ceiling fan and take a nap. Three days a week he must leave again, after the afternoon *tiffin* (snack) around four o'clock, and travel to a small music school to give group *veena* lessons. On these days he will not get home again until eight or nine o'clock in the evening.

Meanwhile, during the day the women of the household may find moments to rest. They listen to the radio, gossip with their neighbors, or, in late afternoons when the markets are open again, go out to shop. Most women in South India are expected to fill the traditional role of mother and housewife. However, many—if they belong to the middle or upper classes—have had musical training, and they make up much of the audience at concerts. Today many of the most famous performers (voice, *veena*, violin, and flute, but only rarely the drum) in the *karnataka* tradition are women.

Like the early morning, late afternoon is also a nice part of the day in Madras. Shadows lengthen, a sea breeze blows off the heat of the day, and people pour out onto the streets to conduct business, visit friends, shop, worship, or simply take a stroll. The sounds of bells, the double-reed *nagaswaram,* and drums float out of the crowded Hindu temples to compete with a cacophony of radios, loudspeakers, vendors' calls, taxi and bus horns, and bicycle bells. The cooling twilight hangs as if it will never end.

It is at this time of day—around five or six o'clock—that concerts usually begin. Programs are sponsored by *sabhas,* cultural clubs that bring to their members and the general public a series that includes music, dance, Tamil plays, and sometimes even movies. The large and prestigious *sabhas* have their own buildings, often large shedlike structures with open sides to catch the evening breeze. The smaller *sabhás* may meet in the assembly hall of a high school or some other meeting place. The audience sits either in chairs or, more traditionally, on large striped rugs or mats spread on the floor in close proximity to the musicians, who cluster on a slightly raised platform. The musicians' cronies or fellow musicians tend to sit at the front where they can offer reactions and encouragement through stylized motions like head-shaking or a throwing out of the hands, tongue-clicking, or verbal comments like "Yes, yes!," "Beautiful!," or "Good!"

Concerts are relaxed and (compared to classical concerts in the West) informal. Members of the audience may count time with their hands, periodically converse with friends, or occasionally get up and take a stroll or buy betel nuts or a soft drink at the refreshment stand. There are no printed programs; mature musicians are not likely to plan their entire program in advance, and a knowledgeable audience is familiar with the repertoire of songs, *ragas,* and *talas* (time cycles). A program may last as long as three and a half or four hours without an intermission. The music (which we shall examine later) is a mixture of precomposed songs and improvisation; the musician is both an interpretive artist and a creator.

Most concerts feature vocal music, and the singer may be accompanied by a second voice, violin, and drums—sometimes with additional percussion. Solo instrumental concerts might feature the violin, the bamboo flute, or the *veena.* When a concert ends there is usually little or no applause; the audience, many of whom might have arrived late and left early, simply files out and heads for home, humming, perhaps, a tune or two, while a few well-wishers congratulate the musicians and chat with each other.

Returning to the daily life of a musician, the working members of Ramachandra's household come back home around 6:00 P.M. Evenings—unless everyone goes out visiting or to a movie—are spent together playing with the children, doing chores, receiving guests, or listening to a favorite radio quiz show or watching a television drama. Often one of Ramachandra's friends drops by, and they may chat for hours about music, religion, or acquaintances in Madras or in the country. Here Ramachandra is most at his ease, laughing, punning, chewing betel nuts and *pan* leaves, confident, through the warmth and admiration of his friends, all of them traditional men like himself and most of them musicians, of the worth of his life as a musician.

On Fridays, a holy day for Hindus, and on festival days, Ramachandra takes his *veena* in the evening and, sitting alone before the family shrine, plays for himself, for practice, and as a meditation, an offering to the gods. Music for him, as for other traditional Indian musicians, is far more than a beautiful art form. Intimately connected with religion, it is a form of yoga, a path and a spiritual discipline that can lead to a deep inner experience of reality, the truth behind all existence. Musicians, it is believed, through devotion to music and the discipline of their art, can touch the mysteries of *Nada-Brahma,* "God-as-Sound."

Ramachandra and his family, like other traditional South Indians, eat a light evening meal rather late, around 8:00 or 9:00 P.M. After dinner it is time for sleep. The family bedding is brought down from overhead storage and spread on the floor. The lights go out, muffled voices can be heard in the darkness; then, one by one, everyone drops off to sleep.

Perhaps in the stillness before he, too, falls asleep, Ramachandra thinks of his life, of his role as one musician who both connects through his *guru* to a chain of musicians stretching back in Indian history for thousands of years, and also projects himself through his students to the future. Through thousands of musicians like himself *karnataka* music has lived and continues to live. A break in the chain would end it forever. Perhaps in his mind's ear Ramachandra thinks of the hundreds of *ragas* and beautiful compositions stored in his memory. Or perhaps he thinks of the insecurities and mundane worries of day-to-day existence as a musician in Madras. But eventually for him, too, sleep must come. A day in the life of a South Indian musician, Sri Veena Thirugokarnam N. Ramachandra Iyer, has come to an end. Tomorrow will be much the same.

KARNATAKA SANGEETA, THE CLASSICAL MUSIC OF SOUTH INDIA

Ramachandra's tradition—and that of the flutist T. Viswanathan and drummer Ramnad V. Raghavan, who play the classical music example, recorded selection 43—is called *karnataka sangita,* music of the Carnatic, the southern plateau. Its roots lie in the distant past. The earliest extant theoretical work is the *Natya shastra* by Bharata, a treatise on theater, dance, and music dating from between the second century B.C.E. to the fifth century C.E. Through the centuries many more important scholarly books on music have been written, perhaps the most noteworthy of which is the medieval *Sangeeta ratnakara* (c. 1210–47) by Sarangadeva.

Stone sculpture on the ancient temples and palaces as well as miniature paintings give us a visual record of ensembles, instruments, and the where and how of performance through several thousand years. In addition, there are many references to music in the epics, the *Mahabharata* and *Ramayana,* as well as in stories and religious writings. But the actual sound and practice of Indian classical music, as it grew and developed through generation after generation of musicians working in the courts of kings or in the immense temple complexes, has been lost. One of the characteristics of an oral tradition such as that of Indian music is that it lives day to day in performance, in human beings, the musicians. It cannot be frozen in time, either by being written down (as words can), or by being preserved as a visual entity (such as a photograph or painting), though today sound recordings and videotape can preserve a particular performance.

From about the thirteenth century scholars began to notice a difference in India between the classical style of the North (today called *hindusthani* music) and of the South (*karnataka sangeeta,* or Carnatic music). While both styles use *ragas* (melodic modes) and *talas* (metric cycles) and have many similarities, the systems also differ considerably. We might say (simplifying tremendously) that the northern style and its instruments (like the *sitar, sarod,* and *tabla*) have been more greatly influenced by Persian and other elements of Islamic culture. In *hindusthani* music seemingly timeless broad improvisations eventually evolve into sections of brilliant virtuosity. By contrast the *karnataka* style of the more orthodox Hindu South is built around an immense repertoire of precomposed songs. The musical texture tends to sound more busy and active, more consistently ornamented.

Try comparing examples of *hindusthani* and *karnataka* music from some of the recordings listed in the discography. Juxtapose vocal selections or instrumental selections in both styles. Try to make a list of similarities and differences.

Karnataka sangeeta began to stabilize into its present shape in the sixteenth century. Purandara Dasa (1484–1564), sometimes called the "Father of *karnataka* music," composed not only many songs but the standard lessons and exercises that are still memorized by every music student today. A "golden age" occurred between about 1750 and 1850 when the forms and performance style that have continued to the present day were set. Thousands of new *kritis* (compositions) were composed, new *ragas* were invented, and the conceptual forms of older *ragas* expanded. Three great saint-composers dominate this period and the *karnataka sangeeta* tradition as a whole: Syama Sastri (1762–1827), Tyagaraja (1767–1847), and Muttuswamy Dikshitar (1776–1836) (ill. 6–9). A clever South Indian proverb compares the music of the *trimurthy,* the "three deities." Dikshitar is said to have written music that is like a coconut: the "hard shell" of his brilliantly intellectual musical structures and complex, scholarly, and sometimes esoteric texts "must be broken to taste the sweet nut and milk inside." By contrast, Syama Sastri's music is said to be like a banana: "the fruit is not so difficult to get to, but still one must peel off the bitter skin"—Sastri's complicated rhythms and *talas* (cycles) of five and seven beats—"before enjoying its flavor." But Tyagaraja's songs are said to be like fresh, ripe grapes; both poetry and melody are immediately accessible: "to enjoy it one needs merely to bite into it. Even the skin is soft and sweet." It is no wonder, then, that Tyagaraja's extraordinarily beautiful

Ill. 6–9.   Three great saint-composers (left to right): Muttuswamy Dikshitar, Tyagaraja, and Syama Sastri, as seen in contemporary prints.

songs dominate the repertoire, loved and held like precious gems in the hearts and memory of musicians and music lovers alike.

A PERFORMANCE SEGMENT: THE SOUND WORLD

Now that we have become familiar with the sound and style—and some of the background—of *karnataka* music, we can begin to explore the music itself, how it is put together and shaped in performance. What we might call a "performance segment" is a unit in a concert that is built by the musician around the central core of a precomposed piece, a song. This unit may include various types of im- provisation in the same *raga* and *tala* as the core piece. A concert is made up of a series of such performance segments (as many as twelve or fourteen), each in a different *raga* and based upon a different composition.

The individual South Indian musician can exercise great flexibility in his shap- ing of each performance segment. That is, he can select from a number of differ- ent options and procedures. We shall look into some of these possibilities later. But first, listen to the performance built upon "Ivaraku jucinadi," a short but beautiful song by the great poet and composer Tyagaraja (recorded selection 43). The performers are T. Viswanathan, who plays the bamboo flute, and Ramnad V. Raghavan, who accompanies on the *mridangam* (pronounced "mm-ree-*dan*-gam") drum (ill. 6–10). Both musicians come from celebrated musical families and have concertized extensively in India and throughout the world. Viswanathan—who is the brother of India's greatest dancer within living memory, Balasaraswati—has received the highest honors possible for a musician in India, and in the United States has been awarded the coveted National Heritage Fellowship Award by the National Endowment for the Arts. Both musicians have taught for many years at Wesleyan University in Connecticut.

Ill. 6–10.   T. Viswanathan, flute; Ramnad V. Raghavan, *mridangam*.

As you listen to the performance, make a list of the characteristics of *karnataka* music style and of the instruments. Then try to chart out the overall structure of the piece. What seems to be composed? And what seems to be improvised? Compare what you have discovered with the analysis that follows.

INSTRUMENTS

Viswanathan's instrument is a side-blown flute made of hollowed-out bamboo, a little less than a foot and a half in length. Flutes for classical music are usually tuned to a tonic on E flat, though Viswanathan's is tuned to C. The mouth hole and seven (sometimes eight) finger holes are burned into the bamboo with a hot metal rod. Since only a single *raga* scale of seven tones to the octave naturally occurs with the placement of the holes (*raga harikambhoji*, equivalent in Western music to a major scale with a flat seventh), the musician must achieve the tuning of the other seventy-one *melakarta* scales—as well as the subtle intonation and ornaments of each of hundreds of *ragas*—with intricate variances of fingering (partially covering some holes) and embouchure (changing the angle of the breath in the mouth hole to flatten or sharpen the pitch). Thus, while the South India bamboo flute itself is perhaps one of the world's simplest instruments, its playing technique is extraordinarily complex.

Raghavan's instrument, the barrel-shaped double-headed *mridangam,* is the principal drum of South Indian classical music. Its body is made from a hollowed-out log of jackwood. The leather skins of the two drumheads are held by leather strapping buttressed by movable pegs jammed beneath to aid in tuning. Both heads are made from multiple layers of leather, the outer layers cut with circular holes in the middle. The lower (untuned) left-hand head has a blob of wet wheat paste applied in the center to give it a booming sound. The center of the right-hand head (which is tuned to the tonic note, the *sruti*, of the soloist, in this case the flute) has a hard, metallic black spot made from many finely polished layers of rice paste and other ingredients. The sophistication of these drumheads, combined with the hand and finger techniques of the drummer, makes possible up to fifteen or more distinct sounds (many at different pitches). The use of the fingers as miniature drumsticks allows the drummer to play passages of incredible speed and complexity. The *mridangam* is propped horizontally in front of the player, resting between knee and ankle, as he sits on a mat on the floor.

Scholars in ancient India classified instruments (*vadyas*) by their acoustical properties. The modern classification of musical instruments devised by Eric M. von Hornbostel and Curt Sachs in the twentieth century is based on the ancient Indian system. The divisions are as follows:

1. *Tata vadyas:* the sound is produced by stretched strings that are plucked, bowed, or hit (e.g., lutes, fiddles, and zithers).

2. *Sushira vadyas:* the sound is produced by breath or wind (e.g., flutes, oboes, clarinets, and trumpets).

3. *Avanaddha vadyas:* the sound is produced by stretched skin (e.g., drums).

4. *Ghana vadyas:* the sound is produced by striking solid objects (e.g., cymbals or gongs).

In the *karnataka* music tradition, *tata vadyas* (or chordophones, i.e., strings), are the seven-stringed plucked *veena* with an ornate body, inlaid with deer horn or ivory and carved out of jackwood (see Illustration 6–8); the *gottuvadyam*, like the *veena* but played with a slide, much in the manner of a Hawaiian, or steel, guitar; the *tambura*, a plucked four-string drone lute; and the violin, adapted from the West but played with a distinctly Indian manner and sound. *Sushira vadyas* (or aerophones, i.e., winds) include the bamboo open-holed flute; the *nagaswaram*, a large double-reed pipe with a sound something like a saxophone; the clarinet, adapted from the West; and the *sruti*-box, a tuned-reed drone harmonium. *Avanaddha vadyas* (or membranophones, i.e., drums), include, besides the double-headed *mridangam*, the *kanjira*, a tambourine made of lizard skin, and (occasionally) the North Indian double drum, the *tabla*. *Ghana vadyas* (idiophones, i.e., solid—nondrum—percussion) are the *ghatam*, a large clay pot held in the lap of the bare-chested player; and the *morsang*, a metal jew's harp. Both of these instruments can play all the rhythmic patterns of the *mridangam*. In dance and temple ensembles the *talam*, or finger cymbals, are also used to keep time.

Many more instruments in all categories may be found in the folk and religious traditions of South India.

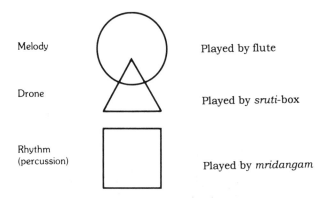

Melody	Played by flute
Drone	Played by *sruti*-box
Rhythm (percussion)	Played by *mridangam*

Fig. 6–3.   The three layers of the musical texture.

THE ENSEMBLE

One way of looking at the music of India is to divide the musical texture (and the instruments) into functional layers. On the recording, you may have noticed that the *veena* plays drone notes (to be discussed next) and melody notes. There is no harmony, that is, not in the way that we in the West are used to. When the *mridangam* enters, a new functional layer appears: the rhythmic. Thus we might draw a picture using symbols for each functional layer (fig. 6–3).

In our recording, two musicians on only two instruments, the bamboo flute and *mridangam*, with the background drone provided by an electronic *sruti*-box,

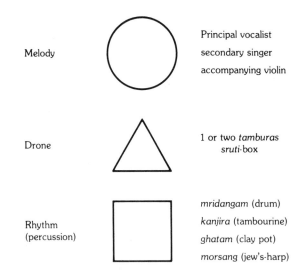

Melody	Principal vocalist secondary singer accompanying violin
Drone	1 or two *tamburas* *sruti*-box
Rhythm (percussion)	*mridangam* (drum) *kanjira* (tambourine) *ghatam* (clay pot) *morsang* (jew's-harp)

Fig. 6–4.   Layers of the musical texture with added instruments.

can take care of all the functions necessary in the texture of *karnataka* music. But one of the marvels of the tradition is that instruments and musicians can be added to each functional layer. For example, the flute is frequently joined by an accompanying violin, or more rarely by a second flute in duet. Or if a vocalist is the principal soloist, he or she may be joined by a backup singer and an accompanying violinist, who echoes and shadows what the vocalist does. The melody layer would then have three musicians. The drone layer could include several special instruments: one or two *tamburas* and/or the reed organ *sruti*-box. On the percussion layer, the *mridangam* player could be joined by performers on the clay pot *ghatam,* the *kanjira* tambourine, or the jew's harp *morsang.* One could thus in a large ensemble have as many as ten musicians working within the three functional layers (see fig. 6–4). Because each layer is strictly defined by function and because within each layer there are traditionally accepted ways of doing things, ways for the musicians to relate to each other, there is never any confusion. There is not even (among professionals) a need for rehearsals. Musicians simply appear for a concert, sit down, and play (see ill. 6–11).

Try listening to some of the suggested recordings in the discography. Map out what the instruments are and how they fit into each of the three functional layers, melody, drone, or rhythm.

SRUTI (THE DRONE)

Central to the texture of much of India's music, folk and classical, is the idea of the drone, an unchanging tone or group of tones against which the melody moves. (We in the West are familiar with drone notes in bagpiping, five-string banjo play-

Ill. 6–11.   A vocal music ensemble. The singer is B. Rajam Iyer, the violinist is M. S. Gopalakrishnan. The string *tambura* provides a drone, as does a *sruti*-box, which is partially obscured behind the singer. M. A. Easwaran plays the *mridangam*.

ing, fiddling, and the mountain dulcimer.) The drone, or *sruti* (pronounced "*shroo*-ti), marks the tonal center—the center of gravity—for the melody and its *raga*. Unobtrusive, calm, quiet, static, the drone is like the earth from which the melodies of the musicians fly, from which they start and to which they return. It is like a blank movie screen on which images, actions, and colors are projected; the screen in essence does nothing, but without it the movie would be lost, projecting into nothingness.

In our recording you may have noticed that the sound of the *sruti*-box is the first thing heard, before the entrance of the flute, providing a constant background for the performance. In other performances—such as those by Ravi Shankar, or the Beatles' songs influenced by Indian music—one may hear a reed organ–like drone or the nasal, buzzing sound of the plucked *tambura*.

In *karnataka* music the notes used for the drone are the tonal center and the perfect fifth above it. Indian musicians may choose whatever tonal center is convenient for their instrument or their vocal range. For simplicity we have written our notation in concert C, although the *sruti*, the tonic or tonal center, is not fixed, but can be transposed to any pitch (ex. 6–1).

Each note of a *raga* relates to drone notes in varying degrees of consonance and dissonance. The dissonant notes tend to "pull" (almost as if in a gravitational field) toward tones that blend with the drone. Try singing the *raga* scales (ascending and descending) in example 6–2 against a drone (played or sung). Hold each tone for a full breath, giving yourself time to see how it blends with or pulls against the drone. The first *raga* scale in example 6–2, *mayamalavagaula*, is the first *raga* learned by students in the *karnataka* music tradition.

RAGA (THE EXPRESSIVE MODE)

Listen again to the first three minutes of the performance by T. Viswanathan (recorded selection 43). Use a stopwatch or a wristwatch (with hour, minute, and second hands starting at twelve o'clock) to help identify sections in our analysis.

The flute begins alone (without the drum) in a kind of free-flowing melodic improvisation called *alapana*. The melody evolves gradually, without a sense of beat

Ex. 6–1.   The tonal center and perfect fifth as drone notes.

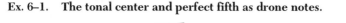

tonal center "*sa*"   perfect fifth "*pa*"

drone notes (strings) on the *veena*   drone notes (strings) on the South Indian *tambura*

Ex. 6–2. Singing exercises, raga scales against drones.

*Pronounced "sah," "ree," "gah," "mah," "pah," "dah," "nee," "sah."

or time cycles. Pauses between musical phrases are filled in with drone notes. There are slides and tremolos, trills, bends, barely heard grace notes, and vibratos—a whole range of *gamaka* (ornamentation). In many *ragas* the tones are sharper or flatter than those we are used to in Western classical musical, particularly on the fixed-pitch tuning of the piano. And the intervals of the scale might be quite different. But in this case—*raga sankarabharanam* (pronounced "*shan*-ka-ra-*bha*-ra-nam")—the basic unornamented scale (if we were to hear it) is the same as the Western major scale. Try to observe the many ways in which the *raga sankarabharanam* in performance is made to sound different from the major scale.

The ancient texts define a *raga* as being "that which colors the mind." In fact, in Sanskrit the primary meaning of the word *raga* is "coloring, dyeing, tingeing." This connection with generating feelings and emotions in human beings, "coloring the mind," is important because a *raga* is much more than what we in the West might call a "scale." A *raga* is in some ways a kind of mystical expressive force with a musical personality all its own. This "musical personality" is, in part, technical—a collection of notes, scale, intonations, ornaments, characteristic melodic phrases, and so on. Each *raga* has its rules and moves, something like the game of chess. While some of the facts about *ragas* can be verbalized and written down, a musician does not memorize a *raga* or learn it from a book. (*Ragas* are too elusive for that!) Rather, one gets to know a *raga* gradually—by contact with it, hearing it performed by others, performing it oneself—almost as one gets to know a friend by his or her face, clothes style, voice, and personality.

Traditionally *ragas* are said to have "musical-psychological resemblances." A particular *raga* may be associated with certain human emotions, (actual) colors, various Hindu deities, a season of the year, a time of day, or with certain magical properties. Contemporary South Indian musicians are not overly concerned with these associations, but they are aware of the expressive force of *ragas*, their power, and their capability to create deep feelings in the human heart.

T. Viswanathan's *alapana* uses the scale, melodic phrases, intonation, and ornaments that mark the *raga* as *sankarabharanam*, the *raga* set by the composed song that forms the core of the performance segment. Sankara (lit. "auspicious") is one of the names of the great god Shiva, and *bharanam* means "upholding, supporting, preserving." This ancient and powerful *raga* is considered to be exceedingly complex, a major *raga* whose many facets may be explored by a musician in lengthy *alapanas* or other forms of improvisation. It may, in fact, be the centerpiece of a concert. Though serious in tone, it also has a sweetness to it; and it is perhaps this pleasing quality that makes it one of the most popular *ragas* in the *karnataka* tradition.

SCALE, *RAGA SANKARABHARANAM*

The *sankarabharanam* scale is shown in example 6–3 both in plain notation and ornamented as it might be sung by a South Indian musician. It has the same seven notes in both the ascending and descending scales. Almost all the notes may be decorated with appropriate oscillations, slides, bends, flickering turns, and sliding glissandos: a network of *gamakas* that also give *sankarabharanam* its personality. The subtlety of these ornaments cannot be shown precisely in our staff notation, but they may be heard if you listen closely.

Try singing or humming along with the opening passages of the *alpana* (recorded selection 43). You can notice two things from this example (and from the recording). First, a "note" in *karnataka* music is not necessarily a single tone (as in one piano key); rather, it can be a whole constellation of tones, a miniature universe of sound. Second, movement between tones tends not to be in discrete steps like a staircase (as in a piano keyboard), but rather continuous, with portamentos and glissandos (fig. 6–5).

Certain notes in *raga sankarabharanam* seem to be stable places of rest. Melodic phrases may come to closure on these tones, center on them, emphasize them, and extend them into notes of longer duration. We might call these centering notes "pillar tones" (ex. 6–4).

Finally, there are special note groups, melody bits, and musical phrases that are typical of *raga sankarabharanam*. These are like the face and physical features of a person; to a musician they are the most obvious features of the *raga*.

Ex. 6–3. *Raga sankarabharanam*, **scale plain and with** *gamaka* **(ornamentation).**

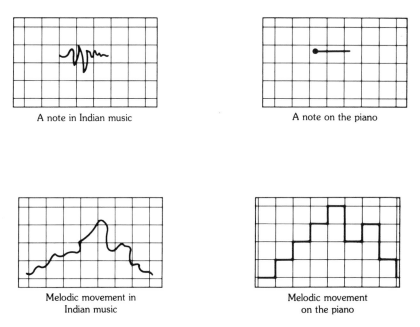

Fig. 6–5.   Notes and melodic movement, compared with piano.

Viswanathan's *alapana* exposition of *raga sankarabharanam* is relatively brief, about three minutes in length (recorded selection 43), and shows careful planning of its proportions. Using a stopwatch or wristwatch you can trace the commentary that follows. Beginning on the phrase *ga, ri, sa, sa* (E, D, C, C), he begins his exploration of the lower octave, centering on *sa* (middle C). At about :15 he moves down to a centering on lower *pa* (G), playing beautiful phrases in the lower register of the flute. At 1:00 he plays a long note on *sa* (middle C) and begins the next stage of the *alapana*: the ascent through the middle range to the upper octave. After a brief centering on *ga* (E), he moves up to *pa* (G) as his pillar tone, and the phrases gain more speed and energy. At 2:00 he reaches high *sa* (c′) and the third stage of the *alapana*—exploration of the highest octave and virtuosic sweeps through the full range of the instrument. Reaching up to high *ri* and *ga* (d′ and e′) he breaks into *brikkas*, lightning-fast phrases of passagework that bring the improvisation to a climax. Finally at about 2:45 he begins (as he likes to put it) his "return home," the final descent to a coming-to-rest on *sa* (middle C) at 3:00. Viswanathan's improvisation, though brief, is in fact an encapsulated form of *alapanas* that may be up to twenty minutes in length. As he notes in his classic

Ex. 6–4.   "Pillar tones" in *raga sankarabharanam.*

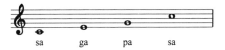

sa   ga   pa   sa

Adi tala: 4 + 2 + 2 = 8 beats

1   2   3   4   /5   6   /7   8 //

Clap   ‿‿‿‿ Clap   Clap

    Finger Count*   Wave   Wave

*2nd beat = little finger and thumb.
3rd beat = ring finger and thumb.
4th beat = middle finger and thumb.

Fig. 6–6. Counting in *adi tala.*

scholarly work on the form (Viswanathan 1975), the basic plan, with minor variants, remains the same.

TALA (THE TIME CYCLE)

Immediately after the *alapana* comes the rendition of the *kriti* ("composition"). The *kriti* "Ivaraku jucinadi" is of course in the same *raga* as the *alapana*, since the core piece sets the *raga* for the entire performance segment. But a new element has been added along with the drum: a *tala*, or time cycle.

The *tala* in this case is *Adi*, a time cycle of eight beats subdivided 4 + 2 + 2. *Adi tala* may also be counted with the hands, as shown in figure 6–6. The *tala* cycle, once it has entered along with the *mridangam* drum, will continue now until the end of the performance segment. Try counting the *tala* along with the recording.

Karnataka music theorists have listed dozens of possible *talas*. However, only a few are commonly in use today. Practice counting the *talas* listed in figures 6–7 and 6–8. See if you can count along as you listen to some of the recordings in the discography (usually the *tala* of a performance segment will be identified).

Ata tala: 5 + 5 + 2 + 2 = 14 beats

1 2 3 4 5 /6 7 8 9 10/11 12 /13 14 //

Clap ‿‿‿‿ Clap ‿‿‿‿ Clap   Clap

  Finger count*   Finger count* Wave Wave

2nd beat = little finger and thumb.
3rd beat = ring finger and thumb.
4th beat = middle finger and thumb.
5th beat = index finger and thumb.
(same fingers for beats 7 through 10)

Fig. 6–7. Counting in *ata tala.*

Rupaka tala: 1 + 2 = 3 beats

    1   /2   3   //

Clap Clap

          Wave

(Khanda) Chapu Tala: 2 + 3 = 5 beats

    1   2   /3   4   5   //

Clap * Clap Clap *

*space (i.e., nothing)

Misra Chapu tala: 3 + 2 + 2 = 7 beats

    1   2   3   /4   5   /6   7   //

Clap Clap * Clap * Clap *

Triputa tala: 3 + 2 + 2 = 7 beats

    1   2   3   /4   5   /6   7   //

Clap ⌣ Clap   Clap

    Finger count* Wave   Wave

2nd beat = little finger and thumb.
3rd beat = ring finger and thumb.

Fig. 6–8. Counting in some additional *talas*.

Many *tala* cycles also occur in slow tempo. In this case one would add an extra pulse, an "and" between each beat, as in figure 6–9.

You may have noticed that the *tala* cycles of *karnataka* music differ from the meters of Western music (time signatures of 4/4, 3/4, 2/4, 6/8, and so on) in a significant way. *Talas* may be built from uneven groupings of beats (4 + 2 + 2, 1 + 2,

Adi tala (slow tempo)

  1 . 2 . 3 . 4 . /5 . 6 . /7 . 8 . //

   (&) (&) (&) (&)   (&) (&)   (&) (&)

Clap ————————Clap   Clap

    Finger count   Wave   Wave

Fig. 6–9. Counting in slow tempo with added pulses (compare with fig. 6–6).

and so on). These groupings are marked by hand claps (fig. 6–8). Even *talas* with the same total number of beats—such as the last two examples in figure 6–9, *Misra Chapu tala* and *Triputa tala*—may sound different because of the different accents created by the beat groupings and by the hand claps. (Try performing these two *talas* and comparing their sound.)

MUSICAL STRUCTURE: IMPROVISATION

The classical music of India—North and South—has two facets: *kalpita sangeeta*, or precomposed music, and *manodharma sangeeta*, improvised music. We have seen that in a typical concert there is a balance between the tasteful and beautiful rendering of the composition of the great masters and the contemporary musician's exploration of his own creative imagination and skill. These balances work through an intricate framework of procedures and possibilities, and the musician's improvisation itself works within the limits of a kind of "musical tool kit" handed to him by his tradition.

There are four major types of improvisation found in *karnataka* music:

1. *Alapana* is a free-flowing gradual exposition and exploration of the *raga*, its facets, characteristic *gamaka*, and moods—cycles—and its phrases evolve in proselike "breath rhythms." It is improvised before a composition and introduces the *raga* of the composition.

The *alapana* follows a general plan set both by the tradition as a whole and by the individual improvisational habits of the musician. Both combine to make the musician's tool kit. *Alapanas*, as we have seen, are often shaped by a centering on "pillar tones" that are progressively higher and by a gradual climb to the highest range of the instrument or voice. There is then a quick descent back down to the middle register, with an ending on the tonal center. The slower phrases are occasionally broken by quick virtuoso bursts of fast notes called *brikkas*.

2. *Tanam* is a more rhythmic exposition of the *raga*, a lively and strongly articulated working through permutations and combinations of note groups. Although *tanam* is not restricted by the cycles of any *tala*, it does have a strong "beat sense." Its highly rhythmic phrases tend to fall within constantly changing patterns of twos and threes (♫'s and ♫♫'s), setting up melodic and rhythmic units of asymmetrical length. *Tanam* is shaped like an *alapana*, moving from low phrases to a high peak, followed by a descent. *Tanam* occurs after the *alapana* and before the composition. Viswanathan chooses not to use this form in his performance (recorded example 43).

3. *Niraval* is an improvised variation on one melody line, or phrase, of the song. It takes the words and their rhythmic setting as a basis, spinning out gradually more and more elaborate and virtuosic melodic variations. (In an instrumental performance, the words are thought of by the performer, though they are not, of course, "heard" by the audience.) Since the same words appear over and over again in different melodic settings, an almost mystical transformation occurs: new meanings take shape and disappear, hidden associations emerge, and subtle nuances come into focus.

Niraval occurs within the composition—following the melody line upon which it is based. It fits within the *tala* cycle of the piece (as well as the *raga* mode). Viswanathan also opts to skip this form in his performance.

4. *Svara kalpana* ("imagined notes") occurs after *niraval*—that is, in the middle of a composition—or after a complete run-through of the song. It fits into both the *raga* and the *tala* of the composition. *Svara kalpana* is without a text; instead, it is sung to the names of the notes: *sa, ri, ga, ma,* and so on. The improvised sections return again and again to the "island" of a theme taken from the composition. *Svara kalpana* improvisations increase in length gradually from a few notes (before the theme) to extended passages many cycles in length and full of complicated rhythmic and melodic invention and clever calculation. In some respects *svara kalpana,* especially when sung, is similar in sound to the "scat singing" of jazz.

MUSICAL STRUCTURE: THE *KRITI*

All compositions in *karnataka* music are songs, melodies with words. The composer is also a poet (although his poetry may be free verse), and his text—even when it deals with love—is usually of a religious nature. The thousands of songs of the tradition have been passed down from generation to generation like jewels on a string. But because they are not precisely notated, rather taught and learned orally, there is no definitive version of a song (in the sense that a symphony or sonata by Beethoven or Mozart exists in an "original," which has been written and can be printed on paper). As it passes through different lines of teachers and disciplines, *gurus* and *sishyas,* on its journey from the composer to the present, the same composition may take different shapes. Yet a composition, a song, remains itself—different versions coexist—just as a jazz tune remains itself despite the many interpretations of different singers and musicians over the years.

The *kriti* (composition), is the major form of South Indian concert performance.° It is amazingly flexible, almost liquid in its structure and expressive potential; some *kritis* are tiny, others are massive pieces extending ten or fifteen minutes in length. Most of the major composers—such as the "big three" of Tyagaraja, Dikshitar, and Syama Sastri—have concentrated on *kritis* for the expression of their musical and poetic thought. Each treats the form in his own way, with his own touch. The *kriti* may be performed alone on a concert program, for its own intrinsic beauty, or it may serve as the core piece for improvisations that are woven before, in the middle of, or after it.

The *kriti* has three sections:

1. *Pallavi* ("the sprouting," "blossoming"): the opening section. The name of the *kriti* comes from the first several words of the *pallavi*—*Ivaraku jucinadi* in the

---

°Other forms are the *varnam,* a kind of "concert etude"; the slow and stately *padam* and the lively *tillana* and *javali* (all three adapted from the dance tradition); the *bhajana,* a devotional song; and the *pallavi,* a single melodic phrase expanded through manipulation and improvisation. See the recordings in the discography for examples of all these forms.

kriti of Viswanathan's performance. The *pallavi*—both melody and words—is extremely important because part of it recurs rondolike after the next two sections. Its size is often expanded through *sangati* (variations) on its melody lines.

2. *Anupallavi* ("after the sprouting, blossoming"): a secondary, contrasting section, often pushing to a kind of climax before a return to the *pallavi* theme. It also may be expanded through composed *sangati* on its melody lines. In some *kritis* there is a recapitulation of the tune of the *anupallavi* (but not its words) to form the last part of the next section, the *charanam.*

3. *Charanam* ("verse" or "foot"): usually a more relaxed, tranquil section. Occasionally it is a series of energetic "verses" that alternate with the *pallavi* theme. As noted above, the latter half of the *charanam* may incorporate all or part of the melody of the *anupallavi,* giving the impression of a kind of recapitulation. There is a rondolike return to the *pallavi* theme at the end.

An additional section, lively and highly rhythmic, called a *chitta svaram* if it has no words or a *svara sahityam* if it has a text, may be interposed after the *anu-*

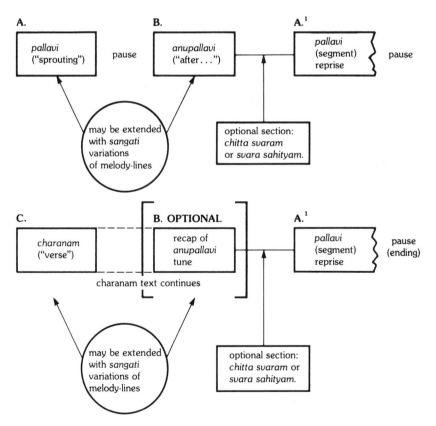

Fig. 6–10. Structure of the *kriti.*

pallavi, the *charanam,* or both, before the reprise of the *pallavi* theme. Often this section will be added by a later composer or musician.

We can map out the form of the *kriti* as shown in figure 6–10. There are, of course, any number of diversions from this scheme. But many of the *kritis* of the *karnataka* music tradition can fit into or otherwise relate to our map. The three major sections are set off in performance by a pause, during which the drummer comes to the forefront with cadential rhythmic patterns.

Ex. 6–5. Kriti "Ivaraku jucinadi" in notation.

Ex. 6–5. (*Continued*)

All in all, the *kriti* as a composition is a magnificent form, balancing repetition, reprises, and melodic recapitulation of larger units with variation and new and unexpected material. Its poetic text gives it an extra dimension, as does the *raga*, the "mysical expressive force" from which its melodies are spun.

A transcription of Viswanathan's notation of his version of "Ivaraku jucinadi" is given above (ex. 6–5). Notice that the notation is in effect the skeletal form of the melody, without the many twists and turns of the *gamaka* ornamentation or the subtle flexibility of the rhythmic interpretation. All melodic lines in this *kriti* begin 1½ beats after the first pulse of the *tala* cycle (their ending overlapping into the first 1½ beats of the next *tala* cycle).

The *pallavi* section consists of the opening melody line (1), which is repeated, and its *sangati* (2), which is repeated in alternation with a new melody line (3). A repetition of the first phrase of melody line 1 closes out the section. In performance the drummer marks this closure with a thrice-repeated *mora* pattern occurring in the extra *tala* cycle.

The first *anupallavi* melody contrasts sharply with the ascent/descent contour of the *pallavi* tunes, centering on high sa (c'), descending, and then climbing up again. Both melody lines, (5) and (6), are repeated. A return to the opening melodic phrase of the *kriti* (1) and a second drum *mora* closes out the section.

The *charana*, with its centering on *pa* (G), is more static and relaxed. Typical of the composer Tyagaraja, the last part of the *charana* comprises a recapitulation of the melodies of the *anupallavi*. A final return to melody line (1), which by now is heard as a kind of refrain, and a third drum *mora* close out the rendition of the *kriti* (at about 5:15 on the stopwatch). The song is finished, but in Viswanathan's performance (recorded selection 43) it is time for further improvisation.

THE SONG TEXT

Tyagaraja's "Ivaraku jucinadi," the core piece of the performance segment, is like most *kritis* a devotional song whose text is addressed to one of the deities of Hinduism. In this case the god is Vishnu, the Preserver of the Universe, with several subtle references to his earthly incarnations as the handsome and heroic godkings Krishna and Rama. The language of the song text is Telugu. Figure 6–11 gives a literal translation by T. Viswathanan and a free translation by C. Ramanujachari (1966).

Of course, in an instrumental performance the words are not audible as they would be in a vocal performance. Yet both the musicians and the more sophisticated members of the audience will know the song text (much as we may reflect upon the lyrics of a Beatles or Tin Pan Alley tune performed in an instrumental arrangement). In fact, some traditional *veena* players may sing at times as they play, and in concerts T. Viswanathan often puts aside his flute to sing certain passages.

SVARA KALPANA IN THE PERFORMANCE

After the performance of the complete *kriti* (about 5:15 on the stopwatch), Viswanathan begins playing *svara kalpana* improvisations. (If there were a violin accompanist or another melodic soloist, the musicians would alternate, "trade" solos.) The improvised *svaras* always return to a phrase from the song, which forms a kind of fixed island in the ever-changing sea of improvisation. This island is called the *idam* (lit. "place"), and it has two aspects: (1) the *raga* note on which the phrase starts, and (2) the place in the *tala* cycle where it begins.

In Viswanathan's performance "the place" is the opening phrase from the song (melody line 1), which begins on the note *ga* (E) 1½ beats after the beginning of the *tala* cycle (ex. 6–6). The musician must shape his improvisation so that the *svaras* lead smoothly back to the *idam*.

Svara kalpana may occur in two degrees of speed. In the first speed the predominant movement is two articulated notes per beat (there may also be some

Pallavi:	*ivaruku*	Thus far
	jucinadi	(lit. seeing) witnessed, waited
	inkanaritiya?	still, should it be so?
Anupallavi:	*pavananu seyu*	(You) who have the power to purify everything
	saktikanagani	which cannot be controlled (destroyed)
	papamugalada?	is there any sin?
	ksrivarada	dark boon-giver (Rama, Krishna, Vishnu)
	nan.	mine.
Caranam 3:	*nagasana*	O rider of Garuda!
	sadagamna	(I who am) always pleading,
	ghruna sagara	Compassion-Ocean,
	ninnuvina	other than yourself
	evaru?	who is there?
	nive	(believing) you alone (are my)
	gatiyani	savior,
	vevega	urgently (lit, fast)
	moralanidu	(who is) beseeching,
	tyagarajuni	Tyagaraja,
	ragarahita	O one without attachment,
	nan.	me.

Is not what You have so long witnessed enough?
Should You continue to be so?
Is there any sin which cannot be destroyed by Your all-purifying power?
Without worshipping Your lotus feet, through greed I have become more and more tan-
  gled in the bondage of *samsara* (the eternal cycle of birth and death),
And I have been unable to bear the consequent distress.

Who is there for me except You?
Taking You to be my only savior,
I have been submitting my plaintive prayers to You.

Fig. 6–11.   Lyrics, "Ivaraku jucinadi."

notes held longer). In the second speed, the predominant movement shifts to a double-time of four articulated notes per beat (fig. 6–12).

Viswanathan's *svara kalpana* improvisations begin in slow speed, first *kala* (at about 5:15 on the stopwatch), immediately after the drum *mora*. After several short improvisations, each leading to the "place," he builds a longer passage beginning with an exploration of the low register and working up to a climax in the

Ex. 6–6.   Opening phrase (*idam*) of "Ivaraku jucinadi."

i _ va-ra-ku - ju   . . .

The svara kalpana begins in the first *kala*, or, the first degree of speed. This means that the predominant movement is in eighth notes (two to a beat):

beat:

predominant movement:

Notice how the improvisations keep returning to the "island" of the theme taken from the charanam ("verse"):

improvised notes — theme —   improvised notes —   theme — etc.

The *svara kalpana* improvisations shift gears and move into double-time. In this "second *kala*," or second degree of speed, the predominant movement as in sixteenth notes (four to a beat):

beat:

predominant movement:

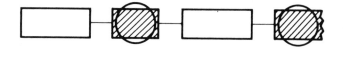

Fig. 6–12.   The Svara kalpana.

upper octave (at 6:00). There is a sudden shift to double-time—second *kala*—at 6:15. Again the improvisations begin with short passages (each resolving on the *idam*) and a buildup to improvisations of greater and greater length. The final passage culminates with a shift of the "place" to the first beat of the *tala* cycle and the note *pa* (G).

At this point (about 7:15) a process called *koraippu* (lit. "shortening") begins. The musician first fills two cycles of the *tala* with increasingly complex and rhythmically inventive passages. A relatively fixed group of five notes leads to the resolution. Then the improvised passages are progressively compressed to one *tala* cycle (8 beats), ½ cycle (4 beats), ¼ cycle (2 beats), and finally one beat or less. Notice how Raghavan supports the process with his drum rhythms.

The *svara kalpana* section ends with final passagework leading up to a rhythmic and melodic *mora*, a precomposed, thrice-repeated closing pattern (at about 8:35). Viswanathan in this performance plays notes in the *raga* to the rhythmic structure in example 6–7.

This *mora* has several interesting features in its arithmetic. First, each of the

Ex. 6–7. Rhythmic outline of T. Viswanathan's *mora* that brings his *svara kalpana* to a close.

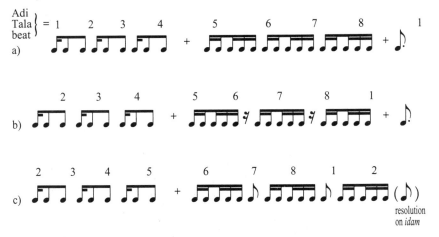

three larger "repetitions," (a), (b), and (c), are slightly different: they grow in length, creating a pleasing asymetry. Second, the primary rhythmic motives (♩♩♩ and ♩♩♩♩) are based on units of 5 ♪'s, whose accents pull against the regular 4s and 8s of the *tala* cycle. Finally, the total duration of the *mora* is equal to three *tala* cycles plus 1½ beats. This means that the musician can begin his pattern on the first beat of the *tala* and that that extra 1½ beats are exactly what he needs to lead back to the *idam* of the first melody of "Ikaru jucinadi."

Try performing the rhythm of the *mora* in the abstract (without a beat). Then try performing it as you count *tala*. Notice how the accents of the pattern of the *mora* build up rhythmic tension against the beat and the *tala* cycle until the final resolution.

South Indian musicians take great pleasure in such complicated calculations in *svara kalpana*. It is part and parcel of the performer's tool kit. In a sense, the cerebral nature of this aspect of musical thinking balances another highly prized quality: *bhava*, or pure emotional expression.

THE DRUMMER'S ART

Until now we have concentrated on the melodic aspect of *karnataka* music. But drumming in India is not only important in the texture of performance but fascinating, complicated, and exciting in itself as well. The *mridangam* drummer and other percussionists play in an improvisatory style based on hundreds or thousands of rhythmic patterns that they have memorized, absorbed, and stored in the memory of their brains and hands. In the heat of a performance the percussionist may use precomposed patterns, arranging them like a master of collage in predictable or unpredictable groupings. Or he may create entirely new groupings or patterns, spontaneous, yet within the limits and grammar of his rhythmic language (see ill. 6–12).

At the basis of the *mridangam* drummer's art are between fifteen and seventeen drug strokes—distinctive individual tones produced on different parts of the

Ill. 6–12.   Drummers in a religious procession in Madras. Even folk musicians such as these play rhythmic patterns of great complexity.

drumheads by different finger combinations or parts of the hands. These strokes, individually and when put together into rhythmic patterns, can be expressed in *solkattu*, spoken syllables that imitate the sound of the drum stroke and precisely duplicate each rhythmic pattern. Normally, spoken *solkattus* are used only in learning and practice, but there is also a tradition in South India to recite *solkattu* as part of a concert performance.

Simplifying greatly, we might map out the various levels of the South Indian drummer's art, beginning with the microcosm of the individual drum strokes and ending with the macrocosm of an entire performance-segment accompaniment or a percussion solo (called a *tani avartanam*); see example 6–8.

Ex. 6–8.   Map of South Indian drummer's art.

LEVEL I:

Basic drumstrokes and sound on the *mridangam*—2 or 3 for the left hand, about 14 for the right hand and fingers.

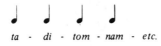

ta - di - tom - nam - etc.

LEVEL 2:

Tiny cell-like rhythmic patterns, such as:

connected with various stroke arrangements:

ta - ki-ta	*ta - ka- di-mi*	*ta -lan - gu*
di - ki-ta	*ki- ta - ta-ka*	
tom - ki-ta	*na -ka-tan-gu*	
nam - ki-ta		
	etc.	

LEVEL 3:

Brief rhythmic patterns of several (or more) beats built from combinations of rhythmic cells, like:

na-ka-tan-gu ki - ta - ta-ka

or:

din - ta-din - ta - ta-din - ta - ta-din - ta - ki -ta

LEVEL 4:

Longer strings of rhythmic pattern combinations, and *moras* (3-times-repeated ending formula) like:

di - tan - ki-ta   na-ka-tan-gu   ki -ta-ta-ka   tom- -

tan-gu   ki -ta-ta-ka   tom- -

tan-gu   ki -ta-ta-ka   tom- (x 3)

(The above *mora* pattern repeated three times fits 16 beats, 2 cycles of *adi tala* (4 + 2 + 2 = 8 x 2). If done right, the final *"tom"* should come on the downbeat of the 17th beat.)

Ex. 6–8. *(Continued)*

LEVEL 5:

Large sections improvised/composed/arranged on the spot, or pre-planned/pre-composed/memorized. One such larger pre-composed section in *Adi tala (4 + 2 + 2 =)* is given below:

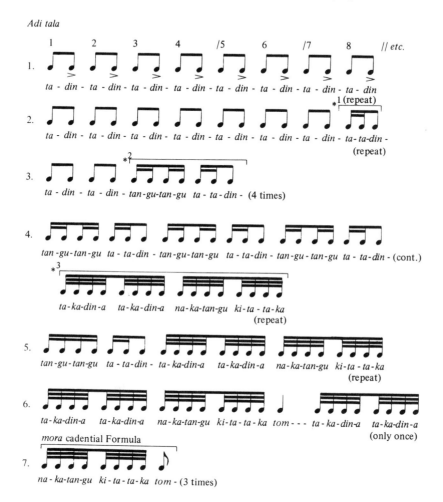

Adi tala

We can learn a number of things about South Indian drumming from the above exercise complicated though it seems, taken from the elementary lessons for drum students. First, changes or variations are added gradually to repetitions of familiar materials. Notice how the new elements (marked *1, *2, and *3) are tacked on to the ends of the repeating rhythmic patterns.

Second, different speeds of patterns are used structurally. Notice in our example how the ♩'s are replaced by patterns of ♫♫'s and then ♬♬'s. Often the same rhythmic pattern will be played at double-time or triple-time (or it will be slowed down to half-time) giving it in essence "a new face."

Ex. 6–8. (*Continued*)

Third, try fitting the exercise into *Adi tala* (4 + 2 + 2 = 8) time cycles (with the beat = ♩). You will find that as the patterns progress they begin to shift and pull against the clockwork regularity of the *tala* cycles. This pull is called "counter-rhythm" or "cross-rhythm" and it is one of the essentials of Indian drumming. There is a constant working away from, a contradicting of, the beat and/or the *tala* cycle.

Finally, you will notice that the exercise—like all larger sections—ends with a *mora,* a cadential formula repeated three times. If you have counted correctly the last *"tom"* of the *mora* (on the third repetition) will come on a downbeat of a *tala* cycle.

LEVEL 6:

Accompaniment of a *kriti* or of an entire performance segment. Improvisation of a *tani avartanam* (percussion solo.)

Now listen one more time to the performance segment (recorded selection 43). This time focus on Ramnad V. Raghavan's drumming. Like the melodic soloist, the South Indian drummer (and his accompanying percussionists, if any) follows a kind of "map" of procedures. At times he may simply keep time, keep *tala.* Or he may "shadow" or reflect the subtle rhythms and phrases of the melodic soloist. A good drummer knows the repertoire of songs in the *karnataka* tradition, he knows their flow and feeling, and he shapes his accompaniment to what we might call "the rhythmic essence" of each song.

The drummer emerges from the background during pauses or long-held notes in the melody; he also emerges at cadential points, marking the endings and "joints" of sections (as we have seen) with his formulaic *mora* (ending) or cadential patterns with their threefold repetitions. And if an improvising melodic soloist pops into a formulaic pattern, an alert drummer is quick to recognize the pattern, duplicate it with an ornamental drum version, and carry it to the end.

It is important to remember that the South Indian percussionist (like the melodic soloist) is not merely "playing off the top of his head." Through years of training and study and listening, his brain is, in a sense, programmed with hundreds of building blocks, formulas, and possibilities of larger combinations. He is also calculating constantly, like a master mathematician, how his formulas and patterns of asymmetrical lengths will fit into or against the *tala* cycles, how they will come out right at the end (on the downbeat of the *tala* cycle or the beginning of a song melody line).

But the drummer is much, much more than a manipulator, merely shifting around and arranging pieces of an invisible rhythmic jigsaw puzzle. Rather, he is creating within a system. And in the process he may compose variations, superimpose sometimes startling juxtapositions, flow from easy time keeping to mind-boggling complicated patterns or sections, stop for meaningful pauses and start again, support a melodic soloist or work cleverly against him, or stamp out the identity of cadences—the "joints" and endings of sections of compositions.

Though we have only touched the surface of the drummer's art, we can begin to appreciate what must be a rhythmic system as complicated as any in the world, a system that balances beautifully with the complexities of melody seen in the *ragas*. As an old Sanskrit verse says:

श्रुतिर्मतिा लय: पिता

Sruti marta layah pita
"Melody is the mother, rhythm is the father."
(after P. Sambamoorthy)

The final section of the performance (at about 8:50 on recorded selection 43) is a drum solo, a *tani avartanam*. Though brief, barely two minutes in length, it contains many of the features of an extended drum solo (ten to fifteen minutes in length) that one might hear in a concert. At times, as the scholar David Nelson has observed, the drummer may merely be marking time. Then he will proceed into a complex rhythmic composition—composed not on paper but in the drummer's head. These compositions usually involve permutations of rhythmic ideas, or repetitions of a lengthy pattern in different degrees of speed (while the beat of the *tala* remains constant). At about 9:20 on the stopwatch Raghavan, for instance, moves into a section in *tisram;* that is, instead of the rhythmic flow moving in beat divisions of 2s, 4s, or 8s, each beat is now divided into triplets—3s and 6s. Thirty seconds later the pulse shifts back to duple and a cascade of drum timbres and lightning-fast drum strokes build to the climactic thrice-repeated final *korvai* (beginning at 10:20). A transcription of Raghavan's *korvai* is given in Ex. 6–9.

One can observe that the *korvai* (its totality played three times) comprises three parts. Each part, labeled (a), (b), or (c), also comprises three sections; each part is illustrative of one of the types of shorter cadential *mora* which might be used by melodic musicians to close off their improvisations. In the first, (a), the rhythmic unit gets progressively shorter in a proportional relationship of 8 to 6 to 4 (♪♩ ♫♫♫ + ♪ ♫♫♫ + ♫♫♫). In the second, (b), the rhythmic unit (♫♩ ♫♫♫) remains unchanged, but its three repetitions are separated by a space (𝄽) until a resolution (♪.). In the third, (c), the rhythm (now ♫♩ ♫♫♫) is simply repeated three times. Each repetition of the *korvai* is 16 beats in length, fitting two cycles of *adi tala* perfectly. (The total duration of the thrice-repeated korvai is 48 beats, 6 cycles of *adi tala*.) Since the resolution must occur after 1½ beats to fit the beginning of the song and its *idam*, the entire pattern is shifted by the drummer to begin 1½ beats into the *tala* cycle.

On the resolution of the *korvai* the flute reenters with the opening phrase of the song and the performance segment is concluded.

AN EAR MAP

In their brief performance (recorded example 43; fig. 6–13) T. Viswanathan and Ramnad V. Raghavan have encapsulated many of the elements that in a concert

Ex. 6–9.

Plan of Ramnad V. Raghavan's Final *Korvai*

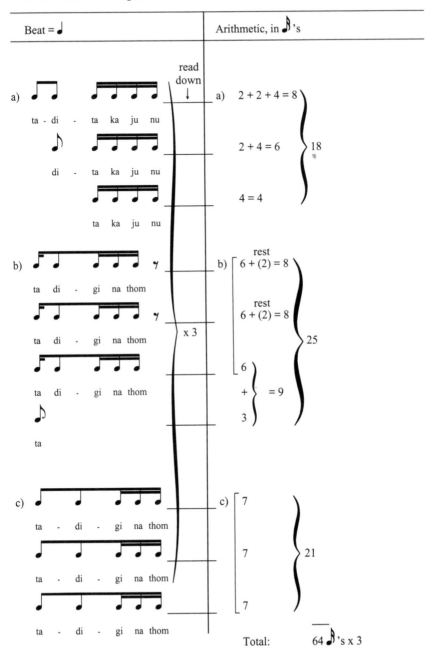

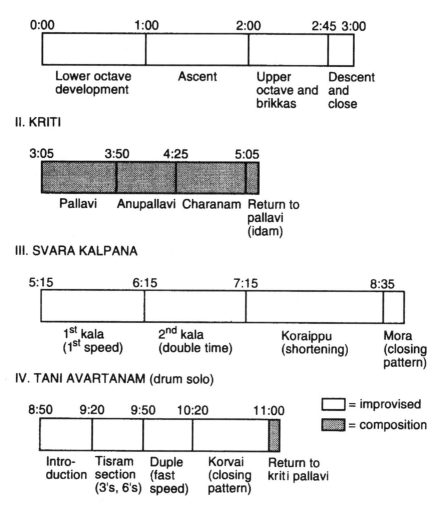

Fig. 6–13. Ear Map of *Ivaraku jucinadi* (recorded example 43).

performance segment might be stretched to last as much as forty-five minutes. The relative proportions of the improvisations and song would remain much the same, though the musical development would occur at a much more leisurely pace.

On another occasion, at another performance, the musicians might decide—using the same *kriti* as a core piece—to choose another set of balances. Because the soloist draws from his musical tool kit—the procedures and ideas and performance habits stored in his memory, as well as his conceptual image of the *raga*—much in his successive performances might be the same. But much, sparked by the creative instinct, would be new or different. That is one of the wonders of the *karnataka* music tradition.

INDIAN MUSIC AND THE WEST

India's has long been a culture able to absorb outside influences and make them her own. Common classical instruments such as the *sitar* and *tabla* have musical lineages that can be traced through Iran and central Asia as far east as north Africa. Three and a half centuries of British colonial rule also left its mark, as have an increasing awareness in the late twentieth century of European and American pop and classical music brought by radio and cable television, CDs, and cassettes. As early as the nineteenth century Indian composers wrote "exotic" pieces (in a genre known as "English notes") that parodied the choppy, unornamented tunes and four-square rhythms of British waltzes and military marches. The great composer and poet Dikshitar even set Sanskrit lyrics to such well-known tunes as "God Save the Queen."

The syncretic nature of Indian "cine music" (sometimes described as a musical *masala,* a spicey soup that can include almost anything) has contributed to a culture in which the Western violin, clarinet, mandolin, guitar, saxophone, synthesizer, and banjo have been used and accepted in Indian classical performance. And since the 1970s Indian musicians have been quick to recognize that the improvisational nature of jazz might relate well to *raga* improvisation in Indian music, and the genre known in India as "fusion" continues to attract a younger generation.

In addition, more than ever before Indians are studying, working, and living abroad. Cohesive communities of Indian immigrants, many trained in music, are now found in almost every major city or university town on earth. The children of first-generation immigrants especially often find themselves in a bicultural world where the "Indianness" of their home and family must be balanced with the pervasive dominance of the mainstream cultural environment. The result has been a development of various Indo-pop styles such as "bhangra" in England or "tassabeat soca" in Trinidad, which combine drones, scales, and sometimes the instruments of Indian folk and classical traditions with the beat and electric sound of mainstream rock and pop styles.

Indian music has also infiltrated the West through the interest of European and American musicians. Beginning in the 1950s the *sitar* virtuoso Ravi Shankar was and continues to be a seminal figure. Having spent years in Paris as a boy with the dance troupe of his brother, Uday Shankar, he was able to move with sophisticated ease in the elite worlds of Western classical and pop music. By the 1960s his *sitar* performances with the *tabla* master Alla Rakha at venues as varied as the Edinburgh Music Festival and the Monterey Pop Festival eventually gave him superstar status. At the same time his activities varied from writing film scores (Satyajit Ray's *Apu* trilogy) to more experimental work.

Shankar has over the years released a number of collaborative recordings—all of them "west meets east" musical dialogues—with famous Western musicians, among them the concert violinst Yehudi Menuhin, the French flute virtuoso Pierre Rampal, the jazz musician Paul Horn, and the minimalist composer Philip Glass. (See the discography at the end of this chapter.) In the album *East Greets East* he performs with traditional Japanese musicians, and his *Ravi Shankar and*

Friends, a late 1960s album made in San Francisco with several dozen Western and Indian musicians (including one listed enigmatically as "Harris Georgeson"), includes Indo-pop instrumentals and a ballet score. In addition Shankar has composed two concertos for *sitar* and symphony orchestra.

In the mid-1960s Shankar acquired the most famous of his students, George Harrison of the Beatles. Harrison's interest in Indian classical music and religious philosophy (the Beatles, along with other celebrities, were for a time under the sway of the guru Maharishi Mahesh Yogi) resulted in a finely crafted series of Indian-based songs ranging from "Love Me Too" to the philosophical "The Inner Light," the latter recorded in Bombay. Many of John Lennon's compositions in this period also had an Indian influence, though the synthesis was more opaque. For example, in "Tomorrow Never Knows" drones, exotic riffs, and Indian instruments float in a complex hallucinogenic texture of backward tapes and sound effects (described by one writer as "a stampeding herd of elephants gone mad") to evoke the otherworldly dream state of the lyrics, themselves inspired by the *Tibetan Book of the Dead* as interpreted by the LSD guru Timothy Leary.

Listen to "Love Me Too" from the 1966 album *Revolver.* The *sitar* begins with a brief introduction of the notes of the *raga*-like scale in unmeasured time, a hint of *alapana.* A background drone of *tambura* and bass guitar continues throughout. The *tabla* drumbeat enters, establishing a driving metrical pulse of the *tala*-like cycles. Harrison's vocal line is sung in flat tones and ends with a descending melisma of distinct Indian vocal sound. In the chorus the repetitive riffs alternating between *sitar* and voice are reminiscent of the "question and answer" interplay among Indian musicians in performance. An improvisatory *sitar* and *tabla* interlude with *tala*-like metrical cycles of seven beats, later changing to five- and three-beat cycles, leads to the final rendition of chorus and verse. The instrumental postlude in faster tempo corresponds to the ending climactic sections of *hindusthani* music performance. All of this in a three-minute song!

Collaborations between Western pop and Indian musicians have continued to the present. The English jazz guitarist John McLaughlin in his groups the Mahavishnu Orchestra and Shakti turned to South Indian musicians such as L. Shankar, violin, Ramnad V. Raghavan, *mridangam,* and Vinayakram, *ghatam,* to create a *raga*-based improvisatory fusion music. And groups such as the Canadian percussion ensemble Nexus regularly use Indian instruments and such musicians as the Toronto-based *mridangam* virtuoso Trichy Sankaran.

Indo-pop music has flourished especially in England, where large immigrant communities from former colonies continue to generate new forms and sounds. The singer and composer Sheila Chandra, born to Indian parents in 1965, has treated diverse musical influences East and West with intelligence, wit, and sensitivity. A former child television star, in the 1980s she joined with Steve Coe and Martin Smith to form an innovative band, Monsoon, dedicated to the creation of a new popular music based on an English/Indian fusion. In her more recent work Chandra has focused on the unique qualities of her voice—often set simply against electronic and acoustic drones—and explored the synthesis of world vocal music traditions from the British Isles, Spain, India, and North Africa. An old English ballad with its bittersweet lyrics, modality, and traditional ornaments may turn smoothly into the liquid shapes of a North Indian *raga* improvisation, and back again. An Andulusian melody in Spanish may shift to an Arabic call to prayer; or a Gregorian chant may metamorphose into secular—but aurally related—musical worlds.

Listen to the exquisite love song "Ever So Lonely/Eyes/Ocean" from the 1993 album *Weaving My Ancestor's Voices* (Real World/CAROL 2322-2) by Chandra and Steve Coe. Set simply against synthesizer and drone with no percussion, the evocative English lyrics and *raga*-based melody shift in the central section from folk ballad style to the sound and ornaments of an Indian *alapana,* only to return chameleonlike at the end to the style of the opening. In her "Speaking in Tongues" I and II from the same album Chandra adopts the lightning-fast language of spoken Indian drum patterns (*bols,* or *sollkattu*) to create rhythmic compositions of great ingenuity and playfulness, moving from set traditional patterns familiar to every Indian drummer to whispers, clicks, and at times whimsical gibberish. Of her vocal art, Chandra has written: "Some people seem to be interested in analysing the *differences* between different cultures and traditions. I'm interested in comparing the *similarities* and weaving them together—to take threads of thought that come from different techniques and singers and weave them into my own pattern." (1992 CD album Notes to *Weaving My Ancestor's Voices* CAROL CD 2322-2)

In South India the composer and songwriter Ilaiyaraja is a superstar, a musical genius with a celebrity compared to that reserved in the United States for a Michael Jordan, a Madonna, or a Harrison Ford. Born in a small village in 1943 to a family in the lowest stratum of the Indian caste system (*harijan,* or untouchable), Ilaiyaraja left high school to join an itinerant family band formed by his stepbrother to provide entertainment at political rallies and village festivals. Seeking his musical fortune in Madras, he apprenticed himself to "Master" Dhanaraj, a film and pop song composer for one of the big film studios. The eccentric "Master" proved to be the catalyst for the development of his young student's talent, teaching him not only the techniques of scoring Indian films but also the *karnataka* classical tradition, Western music notation, and the music of Mozart, Bach, and Beethoven. Ilaiyaraja supported himself by playing guitar in various studio orchestras. In his spare time he arranged Western pop songs by Paul Simon, the Beatles, and others.

Ilaiyaraja's big break came in 1976 when he was hired to provide the songs and background music for the hit film *Annakkili.* In contrast to the glitzy, shallow, urban Indian pop songs of that day, Ilaiyaraja echoed the earthy rural theme of the film by drawing upon South India's folk song tradition. His vibrant folklike melodies, backed by driving rhythms and an orchestra of folk instruments, took the country by storm, blaring from radios and marketplace loudspeakers, sung by housewives, children, taxi drivers, and minstrels alike. In the ensuing years Ilaiyaraja was to write songs and the background music for nearly seven hundred films. Much of his music has drawn upon his knowledge of the traditional *karnataka raga* system, as well as his skill at adapting Western concepts of harmony, counterpoint, and orchestration into the Indian context. He has become so famous that his name precedes those of the movie stars in posters and titles. Today he heads a large music production company, with a state-of-the-art recording studio and a large staff of musicians, producers, and technicians. A highly disciplined artist, each day he disappears into his studio in the early morning hours to compose, emerging in the afternoon for recording sessions that may last well into the night.

Listen to Ilaiyaraja's composition "I Met Bach in My House" from his album *How to Name It?* (Oriental Records ORI/AAMS CD-115). The piece illustrates the facility with which the composer can handle Western and Indian musical elements. A brief *alapana* by the violin soloist serves as an introduction. With the entrance of the string orchestra we suddenly find ourselves in the Baroque musical world of J. S. Bach. The music is, in fact, based on the Prelude from Bach's Third Partita for violin. The solo violin enters again, flitting through the contrapuntal texture like a soloist in a concerto, but this violin's sound, style of playing, intonation, and ornaments are pure South Indian. The synthesis works because the major scale of the Bach prelude, despite its harmonic and contrapuntal usage, is similar to the scale of the solo violin's *raga sankarabharanam.* (This is the same *raga* used in recorded selection 43.) Ilaiyaraja has been quick to recognize the similarities between the two styles, East and West, and their adaptability to creative synthesis.

INSTRUMENT BUILDING AND PERFORMANCE

We are by now familiar with much of the sound world of *karnataka* music. We have taken a brief glance into its environment and history, we have traced a musician's day in the city of Madras, we have listened to snippets of various types of nonclassical music, and we have explored one performance in the classical tradition in all its intricacies. But listening, observing, rationalizing about, untangling concepts expressed in words on a page, looking at them from the outside, can carry us only so far. To begin really to understand a musical culture we must bring the music into ourselves, into our own imaginations, into our voices, and into our hands.

What music really is (we all know) is something of a mystery. It transcends the metaphors of words and analysis. It moves in the beautiful but invisible world of feeling and human expressivity. In India this expression, this magical transference of sound into feeling, into human emotion, is called *bhava.* Without it, music—no matter how proficient technically—is considered to lack life, to lack warmth, to lack "a heart."

The instruments that we shall make or adapt cannot, of course, compare with the exquisitely crafted instruments of an Indian artisan using the skills passed down for generations and a lifetime of experience. We should not expect them to. Rather, our instruments, like the many folk instruments of India, will be functional: they can make the music we want to make on them. And they can teach us.

Similarly, our performances cannot compare with those of *karnataka* musicians who have undergone years of exacting training and apprenticeship and who have grown up in the tradition. Still, our own involvement will help us gain some insight into the way a performance in South Indian classical music works; it will give us firsthand contact with some of the techniques and skills contained in the musician's tool kit, with *ragas,* with improvisational and compositional forms, in short, *with the music itself,* how it flows and how it feels.

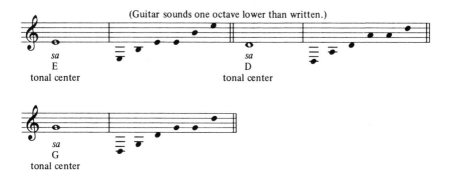

(Guitar sounds one octave lower than written.)

Instrument Building

For the accompaniment of singing you will need an instrument to provide a background of *sruti* (drone). For instrumental performance you will need an instrument capable of providing both a single-line melody and a *sruti*.

For either purpose a guitar (or banjo, or other stringed instrument)° may be adapted. Simply retune the guitar so that all the strings are either on the tonal center (*sa*) or on the perfect fifth (*pa*) (ex. 6–10). Most music shops carry an adapter (costing a few dollars), which raises the strings of an ordinary guitar, making it more suitable for slide or "bottleneck" guitar. You can also buy (or make— see Fig. 6–14) a slide to use with a guitar or with the instrument you make.

Making a Slide Veena (fig. 6–14)

Materials needed:

a piece of wood 2½ to 3 feet in length (1 × 2 or 1 × 4)

a piece of wood (1 × 1 or 1 × 2) the same length

2 plastic gallon apple cider or milk jugs (or other, similar resonators)

about 1 foot of corner molding

4 to 6 guitar or banjo machine heads

4 to 6 guitar strings (D, G, B, and several E strings)

4 to 6 beads or washers

Tools needed:

hammer and a variety of small nails

drill (hand or electric) with a variety of bits, one at least as large as the rod of the machine heads

Elmer's, Weldwood, or Hyde glue

C-clamps

(a chisel and a rat-tail file, if necessary, for the fitting of the machine heads)

°A violin or other fretless bowed or plucked instrument may also be used.

STEP 1

In the center of either end of what will be the underside of the neck/fingerboard (the 1 x 3, or 1 x 4):

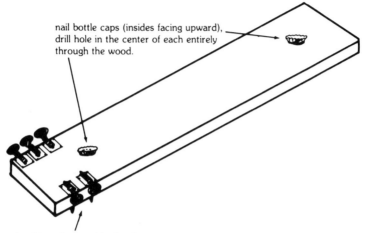

nail bottle caps (insides facing upward), drill hole in the center of each entirely through the wood.

Drill holes for and nail in guitar machine-heads. You may need to enlarge the holes with a rat-tail file, and do some chiseling to make insertion of the playing strings possible.

STEP 2

On the underside of the neck/fingerboard:

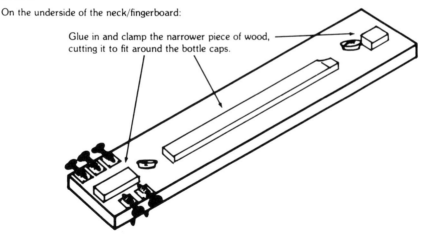

Glue in and clamp the narrower piece of wood, cutting it to fit around the bottle caps.

This is for added strength.

Fig. 6–14.   Steps in making a slide veena.

STEP 3

Cut 2 bridges from the corner molding.
Make them the width of your neck/fingerboard.
Add a tiny notch to hold each string.

STEP 4

Install the strings.

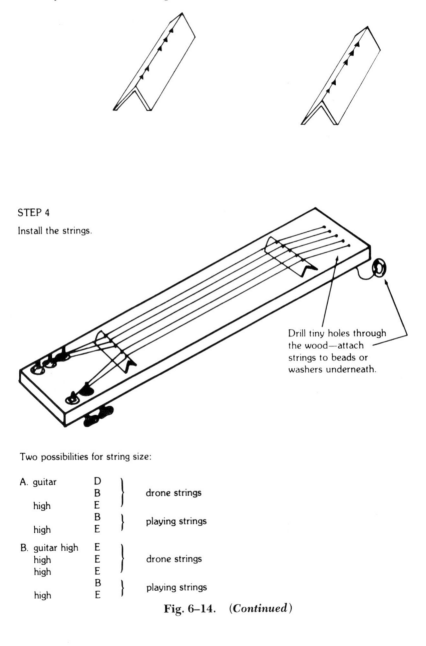

Drill tiny holes through
the wood—attach
strings to beads or
washers underneath.

Two possibilities for string size:

A. guitar   D }
                B } drone strings
   high   E }
                B } playing strings
   high   E }

B. guitar high E }
   high   E } drone strings
   high   E }
                B } playing strings
   high   E }

Fig. 6–14.   (*Continued*)

In the case of possibility B, attach 2 screws long (high) enough to hold the tension of the 2nd & 3rd drone strings in the following way:

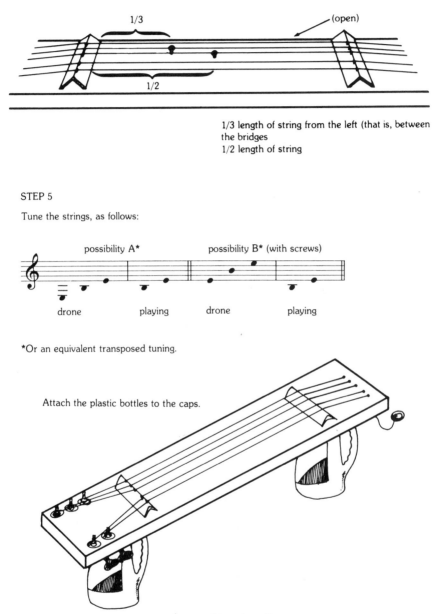

1/3 length of string from the left (that is, between the bridges
1/2 length of string

STEP 5

Tune the strings, as follows:

possibility A*   possibility B* (with screws)

drone   playing   drone   playing

*Or an equivalent transposed tuning.

Attach the plastic bottles to the caps.

Fig. 6–14. (*Continued*)

STEP 6

Mark the chromatic scale with a colored felt-tipped pen on the wood underneath the playing strings, left to right.

You will want to make additional markings (in a different color or removable) to show where the notes of your *raga* lie on the fingerboard.

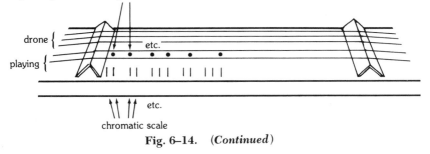

Fig. 6–14. (*Continued*)

PLAYING TECHNIQUE

Place your *veena* in front of you on the floor or on a table (fig. 6–15). Pluck or strum with the fingers of the right hand. In the left hand slide a bought slide, a small cylindrical glass bottle, a piece of metal tubing, or the back of a knife blade or handle to achieve different notes. Be sure to damp the nonsounding part of the string with the side of your hand holding the slide to prevent unwanted sounds.

The drone strings will always be played as open strings. You will touch the slide only to one or the other of the two playing strings.

Practice playing notes on your instrument, alternating them with occasional strums of the drone strings. Try playing various *gamakas* (ornaments): sliding from one tone to another, oscillating between two tones, or putting a heavy vibrato on a tone. After you have developed some mastery of the playing technique of your instrument, you are ready to apply yourself to the lessons that follow.

Fig. 6–15.   Veena, playing position.

INVENTING A *RAGA*

Each *raga* (expressive mode)—"that which colors the mind"—is built from a complex combination of elements that combine to produce a unique musical personality. In this section we shall look at some general characteristics of *ragas* in the South Indian tradition.

SCALES

The Melakarta *System*

The *melakarta* system sets up seventy-two basic "parent" or "generative" scales. Each of these scales (or *melas*) has seven tones. The system is based on a gradual permutation of the tones of the chromatic scale, each parent scale arranged (and numbered) in a logical order. We can simplify the system as shown in figure 6–15 (as before, all examples are shown with a tonal center of C; the tonal center may be transposed to any pitch).

Try discovering some of the seventy-two possible parent scales of the *melakarta* system. Simply read figure 6–15 from left to right following the grid of possible channels. Once you find several scales that you like, try improvising in them; get familiar with their sound and explore their possibilities.

Janya *(Derived)* Ragas

The *melakarta* scales are still only scales; they do not have the fully developed musical personality that would make them into *ragas*.

A *melakarta raga* is a seven-note *raga* whose ascending and descending scales (in regular order) are the same as the parent *melakarta*. The addition of ornaments, special intonation, and characteristic melodic turns and phrases gives it a complete musical personality.

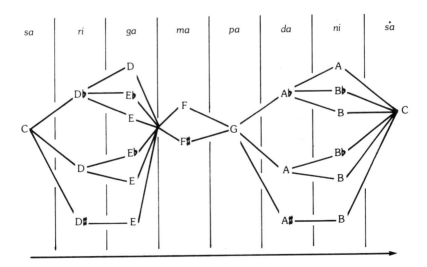

Fig. 6–16. *Melakarta* **system showing** *raga* **scales.**

Ex. 6–11.   Some *varja ragas*, with parent scales.

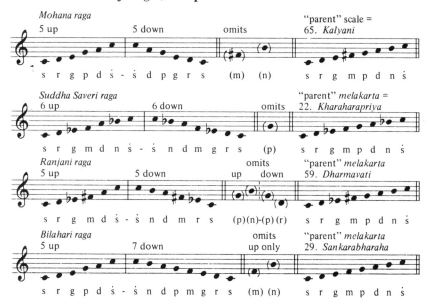

By contrast, *janya* (derived) *ragas*, though descended from parent *melakarta* scales, differ from them in one of the following ways:

1. *Varja ragas* omit some notes in ascent or descent (the scales of *ragas* may be the same going up and coming down, or they may differ). One may have any combination of seven-, six-, or five-note scales (see ex. 6–11).

Try inventing some *varja raga* scales, omitting notes from the parent *melakarta* in ascent or descent (or both).

2. *Vakra ragas* take a zigzag melodic movement either in ascent or descent, or both (see ex. 6–12).

Try your hand at inventing several *vakra* (zigzag) *raga* scales.

Ex. 6–12.   Some *vakra ragas*, with parent scales.

3. *Bhashanga ragas* can have a "visiting note," an accidental note belonging to the parent scale from which it is derived. The visiting note usually does not occur often, but appears in special places or within special musical phrases (see ex. 6–13).

Again, try inventing a *raga* scale with a visting note.

Finally, a *raga* scale may combine all of the above possibilities: a single *raga* could be *varja* (omitted notes), *vakra* (zigzag), and *bhashanga* (visiting notes) at the same time.

TONES

One of the popular myths about Indian music is that it is based on scales of micro-tones, "intervals in the cracks of a piano keyboard." We have just seen that *raga* scales usually have a maximum of seven notes, and often have fewer. The micro-tones in Indian music, then, have less to do with the scale itself than with the fine tuning of individual tones in the scale.

We have also noted earlier how each tone may be performed with all kinds of little things happening in it: subtle twists and turns, slides, oscillations, and touches of other notes. This *gamaka* is essential to the "musical personality" of the *raga*. As an ancient sage and theorist, Bharata, has written:

> Music without gamaka
> Is like a moonless night,
> A river without water,
> A vine without flowers,
> And a lady without jewelry.
>
> [After P. Sambamoorthy]

Within a given *raga* the *gamaka* is not rigid. Each tone may be ornamented in a variety of ways depending on the musical context or the mood or invention of the performer (staying within, of course, a range of possibilities proper for a specific *raga*).

Ex. 6–13. Some *bhashanga ragas*, with parent scales.

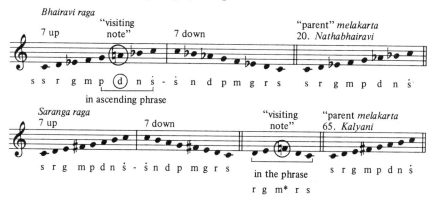

Contrasting with *gamaka* are tones (often *sa* [the tonal center] or *pa* [the fifth]) that are sung or played plainly, without any vibrato or oscillation whatsoever.

Finally, the tones in a *raga* may exist in a kind of hierarchy. There are important tones that seem to exert a "gravitational pull" on other notes, which rotate around them almost like the sun, planets, moons, and asteroids of a solar system. Earlier we called these important tones "pillar tones." Indian theory classifies tones in the following way:

jiva svara: the mystical "life note" of a *raga.*

amsa svara: the predominant note, resting note.

raga chhaya svara: the "shadow note" that reveals the individuality of a *raga.*

dirgha svara: a note that can be held for a long time, emphasized.

alpatva svara: a very unimportant note that must be only lightly touched, or passed over.

Many of the above categories are interchangeable, and the same tone in a *raga* could fall into several categories.

Try adding more subtle characteristics to certain tones in your *raga* scale: intonation, *gamaka,* and a hierarchy of pillar tones and lesser notes. Search especially for a *jiva svara,* a "life note," which in its uniqueness captures the essence of your *raga.*

Phrases

A large part of the musical personality of a *raga* (its *svarupa,* "own image") is made up of a collection of characteristic phrases, as recognizable as the face or particular way of walking (or talking) of a human being. Just as in people, there are *ragas* that are powerful, deep, and complicated (with many phrase possibilities) and there are *ragas* that are simple and straightforward (with fewer phrase possibilities). And there are also *ragas* that are highly eccentric "oddballs."

Especially characteristic phrases are classified as

ranjaka: "sweet," the musical equivalent of a dish of ice cream.

chaya: "shadowing" the inner essence of the *raga.*

rakti: "charming," "especially pleasing."

visesha: "unusual," used only a few times in a performance.

Besides the special phrases, there are the workaday phrases that move up and down through the scale and ornamented notes of the *raga,* that is, through the rules and the labyrinth of possibilities set by our musical game.

In general, the phrases of Indian music tend to work within limited pitch areas and to rotate around the *raga's* pillar tones. They tend not to have the neatly balanced boxlike phrase shapes of Western classical and folk music. Rather, the melodic phrases in Indian classical music can be angular and asymmetrical, or spin out seemingly endlessly like the thread on a weaver's loom. They can rest and balance on a single tone, or explore the infinite possibilities of two or three tones subtly varied. Or they can dart like insects or butterflies, or explode into sudden fireworks. But here we are talking as much about style as about *raga*.

Explore your own *raga*(s). Try to discover what seem to be "sweet" or important musical phrases. Make a catalog of them.

PSYCHOACOUSTICS

On the one hand (I am sure we will all agree by now), *ragas* are a complex technical musical machinery with many "rules" and "moves." But on the other hand, in our original definition, "a *raga* is that which colors the mind." A *raga* then—beyond its technical characteristics, like a human being beyond his or her appearance and anatomy—is a mystical expressive force, a "something beautiful" creating emotional response.

There are many stories about the power of *ragas*. It is said that *raga deepak* ("lamp"), performed by exceptional musicians, can light the wicks of lamps or cause heat and fire; *raga megha* ("cloud") can bring rain; *raga vasanta* ("spring") can bring a cooling breeze; or *raga nagavarali* ("most excellent snake") can charm cobras (see ills. 6–13, 6–14).

Theoretical works of the Middle Ages consistently assign *ragas* to times of the day when it is most appropriate to perform them. The eight watches of the day were

1. Early morning (before light and dawn)
2. Sunrise
3. Morning
4. Noontide (midday)
5. Afternoon
6. Sunset
7. Early evening
8. Nocturnal (late night)

Example 6–14 shows the scales of two *karnataka ragas* associated with a time of day. Try performing them during their "proper hour."

The old texts also assigned *ragas* to the six seasons of the Indian climate: winter, spring, summer, rainy season, autumn, and early winter. Especially important (musically, and in poetry and painting) is spring, with its festivals of renewal and the blossoming of flowering trees, the return of tropical birds, and the erotic buzzing of bees. Summer, the hot season, comes in April and May. Intolerable heat (up to 120 degrees Fahrenheit) scorches trees and fields and brings human activity to a standstill. But the coming of the monsoon in June with its billowing clouds and torrential rains changes everything almost overnight. The temperature drops 20 or 30 degrees, the earth turns green again, crops are planted, and human activity begins anew. The rainy season is connected with the "storms" of human passion and love and thus finds echoes in poetry, painting, and *ragas*.

॥वसंतरागिनी॥ सिखिंडिबृहीबयबहुरूतुमुखबिकंनूतलतांकुरे॥बुबुतुता
॥बासमनेगमर्हिं मनोहरयेवबसंतरागः॥२१॥

Ill. 6–13.   A *raga* painting depicting *raga vasanta* (spring). Here the god Krishna, renowned for his flute playing, and his female accompanists celebrate the joys of spring.

Try performing within the scales of the two *ragas* given in example 6–15, associating them in your mind with the appropriate seasons.

Many of the beautiful *ragamalas*—miniature paintings of *ragas*—take advantage of the imagery offered by seasonal connections: the lush, blooming foliage of spring surrounding beautiful women in colorful *saris*, for example, or lovers re-

Ill. 6–14.   An itinerant snake charmer, R. Vedan, plays the *punji,* **an instrument traditionally associated with the charming of snakes, in this case a python.**

clining in a palace chamber while outside the rain pours from billowing black clouds cut by jagged bursts of lightning.

Finally, *ragas* have been attached to specific emotions—the nine *rasas,* or "sentiments." The word *rasa* literally means extract or juice, flavor; in fact, one can go into a South Indian restaurant and order *rasam,* a hot, spicy soup. The most important modes associated with music are:

love (in all its aspects)

sadness, loneliness

Ex. 6–14.   Scales, *ragas bauli* and *nilambari*.

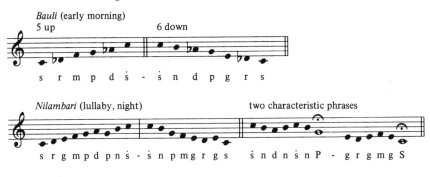

strength, heroism

peace, tranquility

The other *rasas* are wonder, horror, the comic, disgust, and anger. Two additional moods often believed to be expressed in music are *bhakti* (pure, religious devotion) and *gana rasa* (abstract aesthetic enjoyment).

Now see if the *ragas* you have been building seem to express a time of day, a season, or an emotion or mood. Choose a name for your *raga*(s).

By now you will have nearly concluded inventing a *raga*. Here again are the factors you must take into consideration:

1. *melakarta:* "parent" scales

2. *janya:* "derived" scale

    a. *varja:* five, six, or seven notes up

                five, six, or seven notes down

    b. *vakra:* zigzag scale up and/or down

    c. *bhashanga:* "visiting note(s)" not belonging to the parent *melakarta*

3. tones: intonation, *gamakas* (slides, vibratos, oscillations, turns, mordents, grace notes, and so forth), pillar tones, the *jiva svara* ("life note")

4. phrases: characteristic, sweet, or rare phrases

Ex. 6–15.   Scales, *ragas vasanta* and *megha*.

5. psychoacoustic properties: mood, time of day, season, magical qualities, and so on

6. name of *raga*

Spend some time with your *raga,* singing or playing it, exploring its characteristics, working within its rules and moves until they become almost second nature. Get to know its "mystical expressive personality," its idiosyncrasies. Then you will be ready to try to shape a brief *alapana.*

REFERENCES CITED

Isaac, L.
    1967   *Theory of Indian Music.* Madras: L. Isaac.

Mathew, P. George
    1989   Personal communication, song translation.

Mohan, Anuradha.
    1994   "Ilaiyaraja: Composer as Phenomenon in Tamil Film Culture." M.A. thesis, Wesleyan Univ.

Raghavan, Ramnad V.
    1971   Personal communication, drumming lessons.

Rajeswari, S. B.
    1989   Personal communication, song translation.

Ramanujachari, C.
    1966   *The Spiritual Heritage of Tyagaraja* (Translations of song text by Tyagaraja.) Madras, India. Sri Ramakrishna Math.

Reck, David
    1985   "Beatles Orientalis: Influences from Asia in a Popular Song Tradition." *Asian Music* 16(1):83–149.

———.
    1983   "A Musician's Toolkit: A Study of Five Performances by Thirugokarnam Ramachandra Iyer." Ph.D. diss., Wesleyan Univ.

Sambamoorthy, P.
    1963   *South Indian Music,* book 4. Madras: Indian Music Publishing House.

———.
    1964   *South Indian Music,* book 3. Madras: Indian Music Publishing House.

Viswanathan, T.
    1975   "Raga Alapana in South Indian Music." Ph.D. diss., Wesleyan Univ.

COMMERCIAL RECORDINGS CITED

The Beatles
    1966 *Revolver.* Parlophone CD. CDP 7 464412.

Sheila Chandra
    1971 *Silk.* Shanachie CD. 64035.

———.
    1992 *Weaving My Ancestor's Voices.* Caroline CD. CAROL 2322-2.

———.

  1994 *The Zen Kiss.* Caroline CD. CAROL 23422.

Ilaiyaraja

  n.d. *How to Name It.* Oriental Records CD. ORI/AAMS CD-115.

John McLaughlin

  n.d. *Best of Mahavishnu.* Columbia PCT-36394.

———.

  n.d. *Shakti.* Columbia Jazz Contemporary Masters CD. CK-46868.

Ravi Shankar

  1978 *East Greets East.* Deutsche Grammophone 2531-381.

———.

  1971 Concerto for Sitar and Orchestra. Angel SPD 36806.

———.

  n.d. *Ragamala: Concerto for Sitar and Orchestra No. 2.* Angel DS 37935.

———.

  n.d. *West Meets East* (with Yehudi Menuhin) I–III. Angel S-36418, S-36026, SQ-37200.

CLASSROOM RESOURCES

Kumar, Kanthimathi, and Jean Stackhouse

  1988 *Classical Music of South India: Karnatic Tradition in Western Notation.* Stuyvesant, N.Y.: Pendragon Press. (Beginning lessons and simple songs with free translations of song texts.)

Nelson, David

  1989 *Madras Music Videos.* (Videotapes of concert performances of South Indian music.) Available from D. Nelson, 340 Westhampton Road, Northampton, Mass. 01060.

ADDITIONAL READING

Basham, A. L.

  1959 *The Wonder That Was India.* New York: Grove Press.

Brown, Robert E.

  1971 "India's Music." In *Readings in Ethnomusicology,* ed. David P. McAllester, 192–329. New York: Johnson Reprint.

Edwardes, Michael

  1970 *A History of India.* New York: Universal Library.

Lanmoy, Richard

  1971 *The Speaking Tree: A Study of Indian Culture and Society.* New York: Oxford Univ. Press.

Shankar, Ravi

  1968 *My Music, My Life.* New York: Simon and Schuster.

Wade, Bonnie

  1988 *Music of India: The Classical Traditions.* Riverdale, Md.: Riverdale.

ADDITIONAL LISTENING

Write to the sources listed below for catalogues.

The World Music Institute, Inc., 109 West 27th Street, Room 9C, New York, N.Y. 10001, has an extensive catalogue of Indian (and world) music, including most of the recordings listed below.

Another resource is Earth Music, P.O. Box 2103, Norwalk, Conn. 06852.

Nonesuch (Explorer Series) CD and phonograph recordings: performances by T. Viswanathan (flute), K. V. Narayanaswamy (vocal), Ramnad Krishnan (vocal), Ram Naryan (*sarangi*) and others with excellent notes.

Folkways (ethnic series) field recordings of folk music.

The French labels CBS and Ocora (available from the above sources) offer excellent recordings of Indian folk and classical music.

Oriental Records, Inc., P.O. Box 387, Williston Park, N.Y. 11596. Ph. 1-800-336-6969. Compact discs, phonograph recordings, and cassettes. Besides many CDs by Ilaiyaraja, recommended performances include those by Alathur Srinivasa Iyer (vocal), T. N. Krishnan (violin), Namagiripettai Krishnan (*nadhaswaram*) and *karnataka* music performed on saxophone, mandolin, *jalatharangam* (porcelain bowls), and guitar. North Indian music by Ravi Shankar (*sitar*), Ali Akbar Khan (*sarod*), Hariprasad Chaurasia (flute), Nikhil Bannerjee (*sitar*), Shivkumar Sharma (*santoor*), Parween Sultana (vocal), and others.

Ravi Shankar Music Circle, 7911 Willoughby Avenue, Los Angeles, Calif. 90046. CDs, LPs, and cassettes by many of the top performers of Indian classical music. Besides those noted above are Lakshmi Shankar (vocal), Imrat Khan (*surbahar* [bass *sitar*]), L. Subramanian (violin), U. Srinivas (mandolin), T. Viswanathan (flute), S. Balachander (*veena*), and an anthology of South Indian music. Many are reprints of out-of-print recordings from the 1960s. Also available are some innovative experiments using synthesizers, jazz, and unusual instrumental combinations.

Indian grocery stores often carry cassettes of Hindi or regional pop music; many also offer video rental of Indian movies, some with subtitles. Ask the clerk for recommendations.

CHAPTER SEVEN

Asia/Indonesia

R. ANDERSON SUTTON

Indonesia is a country justly proud of its great cultural diversity. Nowhere is this diversity more evident than in the stunning variety of musical and related performing arts found throughout its several thousand populated islands. Known formerly as the Dutch East Indies, Indonesia is one of many modern nations whose boundaries were formed during the centuries of European colonial domination, placing peoples with contrasting languages, arts, systems of belief, and conceptions of the world under a single rule. The adoption of a national language in the early twentieth century was a crucial step in building the unity necessary to win a revolution against the Dutch (1945–49). More recently, a pan-Indonesian popular culture is contributing to an increased sense of national unity, particularly among the younger generation. Nevertheless, though we can identify some general cultural traits, including musical ones, shared by many peoples of Indonesia, it is problematic to speak of an "Indonesian" culture, or an "Indonesian" style of music. Regional diversity is still very much in evidence.

Most Indonesians' first language is not the national language (Indonesian), but instead one of the more than two hundred separate languages found throughout this vast archipelago. And though many Indonesians are familiar with the sounds of Indonesian pop music and such Western stars as Whitney Houston and Bruce Springsteen, they also know, to a greater or lesser extent, their own regional musical traditions. Many kinds of music exist side by side in Indonesia, in a complex pluralism that reflects both the diversity of the native population and the receptiveness of that population to centuries of outside influence. Indonesia is, then, a country that can truly be said to be home to worlds of music.

What sort of impressions might you first have of this country? You would probably arrive in the nation's capital, Jakarta, a teeming metropolis of about nine million people—some very wealthy, most rather poor. Jakarta is near the western end of the north coast of Java, Indonesia's most heavily populated (but not largest) island (see fig. 7–1). The mix of Indonesia's many cultures is nowhere more fully realized than in this special city. Many kinds of music are heard here.

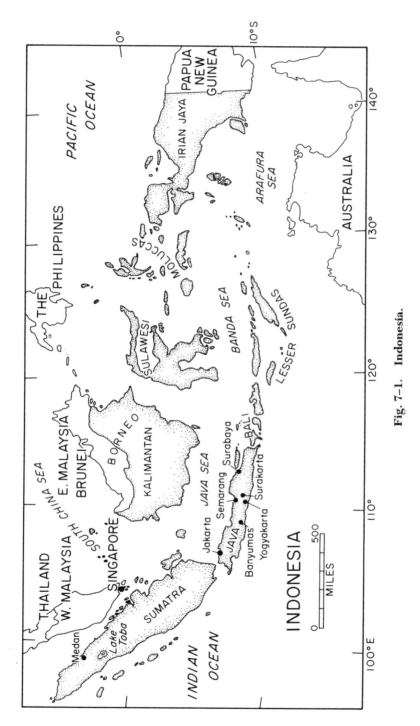

Fig. 7-1. Indonesia.

Western-style night clubs and discos do a lively business until the early hours of the morning. Javanese *gamelan* (percussion ensemble) music accompanies nightly performances of *wayang orang* theatre (an elaborate type of dance-drama from central Java). You might also run across Jakarta's own *gambang-kromong* (small percussion ensemble), and perhaps a troupe from Bali, Sumatra, or any of the many other islands performing traditional music and dance at the Jakarta arts center Taman Ismael Marzuki. Once you get your bearings, learn to bargain for taxis or motorized pedicabs, and develop a taste for highly seasoned food, you can get a sense of Indonesia's many cultures by roaming this complex city. But much of what you encounter here has stronger roots in the various regions from which it has been derived.

CENTRAL JAVA

Java is an island of just less than 50,000 square miles—very nearly the size of New York State and slightly smaller than Nepal. With close to 100 million people, it is one of the most densely populated regions in the world. (Indonesia's total population is about 180 million.) Most of the central and eastern two thirds of the island is inhabited by Indonesia's largest ethnic group, the Javanese, 70 million people who share a common language and other cultural traits, including music, though some local differences persist. In the western third of the island live the Sundanese, whose language and arts are distinct from those of the Javanese. Despite its dense population, Java remains mostly a farming society, with wet-rice agriculture as the predominant source of livelihood. While most Javanese profess to be Muslim, only a small percentage follow orthodox practice. More adhere to a syncretic blend of Islam with Hinduism and Buddhism (introduced in Java over one thousand years ago), and with what most scholars believe to be a still earlier layer of belief in benevolent and mischievous spirits and in ancestor veneration. The worldview that embraces these many layers of belief is often referred to as *kejawèn*—literally, *Javanese,* or *Javaneseness,* a term that indicates its importance in Javanese self-conception.

From Jakarta a twelve-hour ride on bus or train through shimmering wet-rice fields, set in the plains between gracefully sloping volcanic mountains, leads to Yogyakarta (often abbreviated to "Yogya" and pronounced "Jogja"), one of two court cities in the cultural heartland of central Java. The other, less than fifty miles to the northeast, is Surakarta (usually known as "Solo"). Most Javanese point to these two cities as the cultural centers where traditional *gamelan* music and related performing arts have flourished in their most elaborate and refined forms. These courtly developments are contrasted with the rougher styles associated with the villages and outlying districts.

Yogya is a sprawling city with a population of close to 400,000. It has few buildings taller than four stories. Away from the several major streets lined with stores flashing neon signs and blaring loudly amplified popular music, Yogya is in many ways like a dense collection of villages. Yet at its center is one of Java's two major royal courts (*kraton*), official home of the tenth sultan (His Highness Hamengku

Buwana X). Unlike any Western palace or court, the *kraton* is a complex of small buildings and open pavilions, appropriate for the warm, tropical climate. Its design is not merely for comfort, however. The *kraton* is endowed with mystical significance as an earthly symbol of the macrocosmos, the ordered universe, with orientation to the cardinal directions. And the ruler, whose residence is located at the very center of the *kraton,* is, like the Hindu-Javanese kings of many centuries ago, imbued with divine powers.

In many of these pavilions are kept the court *gamelan* ensembles. Some date back many centuries and are used only for rare ritual occasions; others were built or augmented more recently and are used more frequently. Most of these, like other treasured heirlooms belonging to the court, are believed to contain special powers and are shown respect and given offerings. Also kept in the palace are numerous sets of finely carved and painted *wayang kulit* (shadow puppets made of water buffalo hide) used in all-night performances of highly sophisticated and entertaining shadow plays. Classical Javanese dance, with *gamelan* accompaniment, is rehearsed regularly and performed for special palace functions.

Though the *kraton* is still regarded as a cultural center, it is far less active now than it was prior to World War II (during which the Japanese occupied Indonesia). Much activity in the traditional Javanese arts is to be found outside the court, sponsored by private individuals and also by such modern institutions as the national radio station and public schools and colleges. In the rural villages, which long served as a source and inspiration for the more refined courtly arts, a variety of musical and related performing arts continue to play a vital role in Javanese life.

GAMELAN

The word *gamelan* refers to a set of instruments unified by their tuning and often by their decorative carving and painting (see ill. 7–1). Most *gamelans* consist of several kinds of metal slab instruments (similar in some ways to the Western vibraphone) and tuned knobbed gongs. The word "gong" itself is one of the very few English words derived from Indonesian languages. (Two others are "ketchup" and "amok.") In English, gong may refer to any variety of percussion instrument whose sound-producing vibrations are concentrated in the center of the instrument, rather than the edge, like a bell. In Javanese it refers specifically to the larger hanging knobbed gongs in *gamelan* ensembles and is part of a family of words relating to largeness, greatness, and grandeur—*agung* (great, kingly), *ageng* (large), and *gunung* (mountain). In addition to gongs and other metal instruments, a *gamelan* ensemble normally has at least one drum and may have other kinds of instruments: winds, strings, and wooden percussion instruments (xylophones).

Some ancient ceremonial *gamelans* have only a few knobbed gongs and one or two drums. The kind of *gamelan* most often used in central Java today is a large set, comprising instruments ranging from deep booming gongs three feet in diameter to sets of high-pitched tuned gongs (gong-chimes) and slab instruments, with three drums, several bamboo flutes, zithers, xylophones, and a two-stringed fiddle.

Ill. 7–1. The *gamelan* **Kyai Kanyut Mèsem ("Tempted to Smile") in the Mangkunegaran palace, Surakarta, Central Java. In foreground:** *gong ageng* **and** *gong siyem.* **(Photo courtesy of Arthur Durkee, Earth Visions Photographics.)**

Instruments in the present-day *gamelan* are tuned to one of two scale systems: *sléndro,* a five-tone system made up of nearly equidistant intervals, normally notated with the numerals 1, 2, 3, 5, and 6 (no 4); and *pélog,* a seven-tone system made up of large and small intervals, normally notated 1, 2, 3, 4, 5, 6, and 7. Some *gamelans* are entirely *sléndro,* others entirely *pélog,* but many are actually double ensembles, combining a full set of instruments for each system. The scale systems are incompatible and only in a few rare cases are they played simultaneously. The tones of neither of these scale systems can be replicated on a Western piano. Example 7–1 shows the Western major scale, consisting of "whole-tone" and "half-tone" intervals (e.g., eight adjacent white keys on the piano, starting with C as "do") in comparison with sample intervals for one instance of *sléndro* and one of *pélog* (these are not entirely standardized, as I shall explain below).

The instrumentation of a full *sléndro-pélog gamelan* varies slightly but usually includes all or most of the instruments given in the list below. Most of these are illustrated in figure 7–2.

Knobbed Gong Instruments

GONG AGENG: largest of the hanging gongs, suspended vertically from a wooden frame; one or two in each *gamelan;* often simply called *gong;* played with a round, padded beater.

Ex. 7–1. **Western scale and representative *pélog* and *sléndro* scales. Based on measurements of *gamelan* Mardiswara, Wasisto Surjodiningrat et. al., 1972:51–53.**

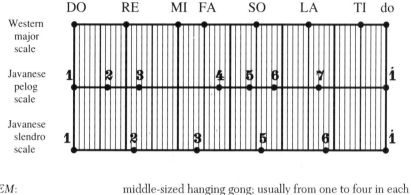

SIYEM: middle-sized hanging gong; usually from one to four in each *gamelan;* also called *gong suwukan;* played with a round, padded beater.

KEMPUL: smallest hanging gong; from two to ten per *gamelan;* played with a round, padded beater.

KENONG: largest of the kettle gongs, resting horizontally in a wooden

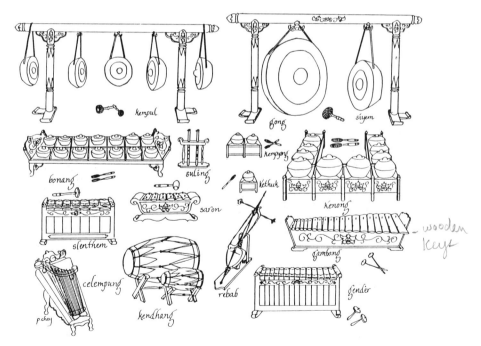

Fig. 7–2. **Central Javanese *gamelan* instruments. (Illustration by Peggy Choy.)**

	frame; from two to twelve per *gamelan;* played with a padded stick beater.
KETHUK:	small kettle gong; one for each scale system; played with a padded stick beater.
KEMPYANG:	set of two kettle gongs, smaller than *kethuk;* used only for *pélog;* played with two padded stick beaters.
BONANG BARUNG:	set of ten, twelve, or fourteen kettle gongs resting horizontally in two parallel rows in a wooden frame; one set for each scale system; often simply called *bonang;* played with two padded stick beaters.
BONANG PANERUS:	smaller member of the *bonang* family; same as *bonang barung* but tuned an octave higher; one for each scale system.

Metal Keyed Instruments

SARON DEMUNG:	largest member of the *saron* (single-octave metallophone) family; six or seven thick metal keys resting over a trough resonator; usually one or two for each scale system; often simply called *demung;* played with a wooden mallet.
SARON BARUNG:	like *saron demung,* but an octave higher; usually from two to four for each scale system; often simply called *saron.*
SARON PEKING:	like *saron barung,* but an octave higher; often simply called *peking.*
GENDÈR SLENTHEM:	six or seven thin metal keys suspended by strings over cylindrical resonators made of bamboo or metal; one for each scale system; often simply called *slenthem;* played with a padded disc beater.
GENDÈR BARUNG:	thirteen or fourteen thin metal keys, suspended over cylindrical resonators; one for *sléndro,* two for *pélog: bem* (with tones 1, 2, 3, 5, and 6 in each octave) and *barang* (with tones 2, 3, 5, 6, and 7 in each octave); often simply called *gendèr;* played with two padded disc beaters.
GENDÈR PANERUS:	like *gendèr barung,* but an octave higher.

Other Melodic Instruments

GAMBANG:	seventeen to twenty-three wooden keys resting over a trough resonator; one for *sléndro;* one or two for *pélog* (if two, like *gendèr barung* and *gendèr panerus;* if only one, exchange keys enable player to arrange instrument for *bem*—with 1s—or for *barang*—with 7s); played with two padded disc beaters.
CELEMPUNG:	zither, usually supported at about a thirty-degree angle by four legs, with twenty to twenty-six strings arranged in ten to thirteen "double courses" (as on a twelve-string guitar); one for *sléndro,* one or two for *pélog* (cf. *gambang*); plucked with thumbnails.

SITER:	smaller zither, resting on floor or in horizontal frame, with from ten to twenty-six strings in single or double courses, one for *sléndro*, one or two for *pélog* (cf. *gambang* and *celempung*); plucked with thumbnails.
SULING:	end-blown bamboo flute; one for *sléndro*, one or two for *pélog*.
REBAB:	two-stringed fiddle; one or two per *gamelan*.

Drums

KENDHANG GENDHING:	largest of the hand drums; two leather heads, laced onto a barrel-shaped shell; one per *gamelan*.
KENDHANG CIBLON:	middle-sized hand drum, like *kendhang gendhing*; often simply called *ciblon*.
KENDHANG KETIPUNG:	smallest hand drum, often simply called *ketipung*.
BEDHUG:	large stick-beaten drum; two leather heads, tacked onto a cylindrical shell; one per *gamelan*.

There is no standard arrangement of these instruments in the performance space, though almost without exception they are placed at right angles to one another, reflecting the Javanese concern with the cardinal directions (see ill. 7–2). Generally the larger gong instruments are in the back, with the *saron* family immediately in front of them, *bonang* family and *bedhug* drum to the sides, other melodic instruments in front, and the *kendhang* drums in the center. The place-

Ill. 7–2.   **Gamelan musicians in the Kraton Kasunanan (royal palace) in Surakarta, Central Java. In foreground: *bonang* (left) *gendèr* (right). (Photo courtesy of Arthur Durkee, Earth Visions Photographics.)**

ment of the instruments reflects their relative loudness and their function in the performance of pieces, which I will discuss shortly.

The *gamelan* instruments are normally complemented by singers: a small male chorus (*gérong*) and female soloists (*pesindhèn*). Java also supports a highly developed tradition of unaccompanied vocal music (*tembang*), which serves as a major vehicle for Javanese poetry. In fact, the word *tembang* is best translated into English as "sung poetry." Although Javanese have recorded their *tembang* in several writing systems for over one thousand years, these are normally neither read silently nor read aloud in a speaking voice, but sung. Even important letters between members of the nobility were, until this century, composed as *tembang* and delivered as song. Though the postal system has eliminated this practice, vocal music, whether with *gamelan* or unaccompanied, enjoys great popularity in Java today.

The relation between vocal and instrumental orientations in *gamelan* music is reflected in the two major groupings of instruments in the present-day Javanese *gamelan*: "loud-playing" and "soft-playing." Historical evidence suggests that these two grouping were once separate ensembles and were combined as recently as the sixteenth or early seventeenth centuries. Loud-playing ensembles were associated with festivals, processions, and other noisy outdoor events, and were strictly instrumental. Soft-playing ensembles were intended for more intimate gatherings, often indoors, and involved singing. Even today, performance style distinguishes these two groupings. In loud-playing style, only the drums and louder metal instruments are used, as listed below in the column on the left. In soft-playing style, these instruments, or most of them, are played softly, and the voices and instruments listed below in the column on the right are featured.

Loud-Playing Instruments	*Soft-Playing Instruments*
gong ageng	*gendèr barung*
siyem	*gendèr panerus*
kempul	*gambang*
kenong	*celempung*
kethuk	*siter*
kempyang	*suling*
bonang family	*rebab*
saron family	
slenthem	
kendhang family	
bedhug	

GAMELAN CONSTRUCTION

Bronze is the preferred metal for *gamelan* manufacture, owing both to its durability and to its rich, sweet sound quality. Brass and iron are also used, especially in rural areas. They are considerably cheaper than bronze, easier to tune, but less sonorous. Bronze *gamelan* instruments are forged (some cast in their basic shapes and then forged) in a long and difficult process. Though the metal worker in many societies occupies a low status, in Java he has traditionally been held in very high regard. The act of forging bronze instruments not only requires great skill but is also imbued with mystical significance. Working with metals, transforming molten copper and tin (the metals that make bronze alloy) into sound-producing instruments, is believed to make one especially vulnerable to dangerous forces in the spirit world. It is for this reason that the smiths make ritual preparation and may actually assume mythical identities during the forging process. The chief smith is ritually transformed into Panji, a powerful Javanese mythical hero, and the smith's assistants become Panji's family and servants (see Kunst 1973:138; Becker 1988).

The largest gongs may require a full month of labor and a truckload of coal for the forge that heats the metal. Only after appropriate meditation, prayer, fasting, and preparation of offerings does a smith undertake to make a large gong. The molten bronze is pounded, reheated, pounded, reheated, and gradually shaped into a large knobbed gong that may measure three feet or more in diameter. A false hit at any stage can crack the gong and the process must begin all over.

GAMELAN IDENTITY

A *gamelan,* particularly a bronze set with one or two fine large gongs, is often held in great respect, given a proper name, and given offerings on Thursday evenings (the beginning of the Muslim holy day). Though *gamelan* makers have recently begun to duplicate precise tuning and decorative designs, generally each *gamelan* is a unique set, whose instruments would both look and sound out of place in another ensemble. Formerly, attempting even to copy the tuning and design of palace *gamelan* instruments was forbidden, as these were reserved for the ruler and were directly associated with his power.

The variability in tuning from one *gamelan* to another is certainly not the result of a casual sense of pitch among Javanese musicians and *gamelan* makers. On the contrary, great care is taken in the making and in the occasional retuning of *gamelan* sets to arrive at a pleasing tuning—one that is seen to fit the particular physical condition of the instruments and the tastes of the individual owner. I spent one month with a tuner, his two assistants, and an expert musician as they gradually reached consensus on an agreeable tuning and then altered the tuning of the many bronze gong and metal slab instruments through a long process of hammering and filing—all by hand. Bronze has the curious property of changing tuning—rather markedly during the first few years after forging, and more subtly over a period of twenty to thirty years, until it is finally "settled." It might seem that the lack of a standard tuning would be cause for musical chaos, but the actual latitude is rather small.

GAMELAN PERFORMANCE CONTEXTS

Despite the changes wrought by modern institutions (formal musical instruction in schools and dissemination through the mass media) in the contexts of music-making and the ways music is understood, Javanese music is more closely interrelated with other performing arts and more intimately bound to other aspects of life than are the arts in the West. "Concerts" of *gamelan* music simply do not occur, at least not in anything like the circumstances of a concert of Western classical music. The closest thing to a *gamelan* "concert" in Java is *uyon-uyon* (or *klenèngan*), but these are better understood as social events that involve *gamelan* music. They are usually held to commemorate a day of ritual importance, such as a birth, circumcision, or wedding. Normally a family sponsors such an event and invites neighbors and relatives, while others are welcome to look on and listen. The invited guests are served food and are expected to socialize freely through the duration of the event. No one expects the guests to be quiet during the performance of pieces or to pay rapt attention to them the way an audience does at a Western concert. Rather, the music, carefully played though it may be, is seen to contribute to the festiveness of the larger social event, helping to make it *ramé* (lively, busy in a positive way). Connoisseurs among the guests will ask for a favorite piece and may pay close attention to the way the ensemble or a particular singer or instrumentalist performs, but not to the exclusion of friendly interaction with the hosts and other guests. While the music is intended to entertain those present (without dance or drama), it also serves a ritual function, helping to maintain balance at important transitional points in the life of a person or community.

More often, *gamelan* music is performed as accompaniment for dance or theater—a refined female ensemble dance (*srimpi* or *bedhaya*; see ills. 7–4, 7–5);

Ill. 7–3.   Musicians playing the *gamelan* Kyai Kanyut Mèsem.
Mangkunegaran palace, Surakarta, Central Java. In foreground: *Sarons,*
kempul, and *gongs* on left: *saron peking* and *bonangs* on right. (Photo
courtesy of Arthur Durkee, Earth Visions Photographics.)

Ill. 7–4.   Dancers at Pujokusuman in Yogyarkarta perform a *srimpi*, female court dance. (Photo by Peggy Choy.)

Ill. 7–5.   Dancers at the Pakualaman palace in Yogyakarta perform a *bedhaya,* **female court dance (here with innovative costumes). (Photo courtesy of Arthur Durkee, Earth Vision Photographics.)**

a flirtatious female solo dance; a vigorous, martial lance dance; or an evening of drama based on Javanese legendary history, for example. A list of traditional genres currently performed in central Java with *gamelan* accompaniment would be long. Some are presented primarily in commercial settings, with an audience buying tickets. Others are more often part of a ritual ceremony.

The genre held in the highest esteem by most Javanese, and nearly always reserved for ritual ceremony, is the shadow puppet theatre (*wayang kulit*), which dates back no less than one thousand years (see ill. 7–6). Beginning with an overture played on the *gamelan* during the early evening, shadow puppet performances normally last until dawn. With a screen stretched before him, lamp overhead, and puppets to both sides, one master puppeteer (*dhalang*) operates all the puppets, performs all the narration and dialogue, sings mood songs, and directs the musicians for a period of about eight hours, with no intermission.

The musicians do not play constantly throughout the evening, but must be ever-ready to respond to a signal from the puppeteer. He leads the musicians and accents the action of the drama through a variety of percussion patterns that he plays by hitting against the wooden puppet chest to his left and by clanging metal plates suspended from the rim of the chest. If he is holding puppets in both hands, he uses his foot to sound these signals. He must be highly skilled as a manipulator, director, singer, and storyteller.

Ill. 7–6. Puppeteer Ki Gondo Darman performing *wayang kulit* **at the ASKI Performing arts academy in Surakarta. (Photo courtesy of Arthur Durkee, Earth vision Photographics.)**

What the puppeteer delivers is not a fixed play written by a known playwright, but rather his own rendition of a basic story—usually closely related to versions performed by other puppeteers, but never exactly the same. It might be a well-known episode from the *Ramayana* or *Mahabharata*, epics of Indian origin that have been adapted and transformed in many parts of Southeast Asia and have been known in Java for one thousand years. The music is drawn from a large repertory of pieces, none specific to a single play and many of which are played in other contexts as well.

A good musician knows many hundreds of pieces, but the pieces, like the shadow plays, are generally not totally fixed. Many regional and individual variants exist for some pieces. More important, the very conception of what constitutes a *"gamelan* piece" or *"gamelan* composition" (in Javanese: *gendhing*) is different from the Western notion of musical pieces, particularly as that notion has developed in the Western art music or "classical" tradition.

GAMELAN MUSIC: A JAVANESE GENDHING IN PERFORMANCE

We can best begin to understand what a Javanese *gendhing* is by considering one in some detail—how it is conceived and how it is realized in performance. Listen to "Bubaran Kembang Pacar" (recorded selection 44). This is from a tape I made in a recording session in Yogya with some of the most highly regarded senior musicians associated with the court. It was played on a bronze *gamelan* at the house of one of Yogya's best known dancers and choreographers, Dr. Soedarsono, who founded the National Dance Academy (ASTI) in Yogya and now is rector of the Indonesian Arts Institute there. You will note that it is an example of loud-playing style throughout. And you might have guessed that it is in the *pélog* scale system, with small and large intervals. It uses the *pélog bem* scale—tones 1, 2, 3, 5, and 6, with an occasional 4, but no 7. But what about its structure: How are the sounds organized in this piece—or, more precisely, this performance of this piece?

Unless they are connected directly to a previous piece in a medley sequence, Javanese *gendhings* begin with a solo introduction, played on one instrument or sung by a solo singer. Here a short introduction is played on the *bonang barung* by Pak Sastrapustaka, a well-known teacher and musician (1913–91). During the latter portion, this *bonang* is joined by the two drums *kendhang gendhing* and *ketipung*, played (as is customary) by one drummer—in this case, the court musician Pak Kawindro. The drummer in the Javanese *gamelan* acts as a conductor, controlling the tempo and the dynamics (the relative levels of loudness and softness). He need not be visible to other musicians, since his "conducting" is accomplished purely through aural signals. He does not stand in front of the ensemble but sits unobtrusively in the midst of it.

Although we discussed the choice of "Bubaran Kembang Pacar" at this recording session, experienced musicians recognize the identity of the *gendhing* from the introduction and do not need to be told what piece is about to be performed. The *bonang* player (or other musician providing an introduction) may simply play the introduction to an appropriate piece and expect the other musicians to follow. At the end of the introduction, most of the rest of the ensemble joins in, the large gong sounds, and the main body of the *gendhing* begins.

The structure of this main body is based on principles of balanced, binary (duple) subdivision and of cyclic repetition. The basic time and melodic unit in *gendhing* is the *gongan*, a phrase marked off by the sound of either the largest gong (*gong ageng*) or the slightly smaller gong *siyem*. For most *gendhings*, these phrases are of regular length as measured in beats of the *balungan*, the melodic part usually played on the *slenthem* and the *saron* family—almost always some factor of two: 8 beats, 16 beats, 32 beats, 64 beats, 128 beats, 256 beats. (In the genre of pieces that serve as the staple for accompanying dramatic action, as we shall see below, *gongans* are of irregular length and the regular unit is marked instead by the smaller gong *kempul*.) A *gongan* is subdivided into two or four shorter phrases by the *kenong*, and these further subdivided by *kempul, kethuk,* and in some lengthier pieces by *kempyang*.

The result is a pattern of interlocking percussion that repeats until an aural signal from the drummer or one of the lead melodic instruments (*bonang* in loud-playing style, *rebab* in soft-playing) directs the performers to end or to proceed to a different piece. Whereas in Western music composers must provide explicit directions for performers to repeat a section (usually by means of notated repeat signs), in Javanese *gamelan* performance repetition is assumed.

As we speak of "phrases" in describing music, borrowing the term from the realm of language, Javanese also liken the *gongan* to a sentence and conceive of the subdividing parts as "punctuation." For "Bubaran Kembang Pacar," after the gong stroke at the end of the introduction, the pattern of gong punctuation shown in example 7–2 is repeated throughout. The time distribution of these punctuating beats is even, but the degree of stress or weight is not (even though no beat is played louder than any other on any single instrument). Javanese listeners feel the progression of stress levels indicated in example 7–3, based on the levels of subdivision.

The strongest beat is the one coinciding with the largest and deepest sounding phrase marker, the *gong* (G), and with the *kenong* (N)—at the end of the phrase. Javanese would count this as one, *two*, three, **four**, etc., with the strongest beat being the sixteenth. This is the only beat where two punctuating gong instruments coincide. It is this "coincidence" that gives a sense of repose, a release of the rhythmic tension that builds through the course of the *gongan*.

Although in the West one may dismiss events as "mere coincidence," in Java the simultaneous occurrence of several events, the alignment of days of the week and dates (like our Friday the 13th), can be profoundly meaningful. It is not uncommon to determine a suitable day for a wedding, or for moving house, based on the coincidence of a certain day in the seven-day week with a certain day in the Javanese five-day market week, and this in turn within a certain Javanese month (in the lunar calendar rather than the solar calendar used in the West). And the simultaneous occurrence of what to Westerners would seem to be unrelated (and therefore meaningless) events—such as the sounding of a certain bird while in the course of carrying out a particular activity—can be interpreted in Java as an important omen.

This deep-seated view of the workings of the natural world is reflected in the structure of *gamelan* music, where coincidence is central to the coherence of the music. The sounding of the *gong* with the *kenong* marks the musical instant of greatest weight and is the only point at which a *gendhing* may end. Yet other lesser points of coincidence also carry weight. If we consider the piece from the perspective of the *balungan* melody, it is at the coincidence of the *balungan* with the *kenong* strokes that the next strongest stress is felt. And in pieces with longer *gongans* (e.g., 32, 64, or 128 beats), where there are many more *saron* beats and therefore many of them do not coincide with any punctuating gong, each *kenong* stroke and even each *kethuk* stroke may be an instance of emphasis and temporary repose.

Ex. 7–2.   Interlocking punctuation pattern in "Bubaran Kembang Pacar."

```
t = kethuk                 .   .   .   .   .   .   .   .   .   .   .   .   .   .   .   .
N = kenong             t   w   t   N   t   P   t   N   t   P   t   N   t   P   t   N
P = kempul                                                                         G
G = gong or siyem
w = rest
. = one beat in balungan melody
```

Ex. 7–3.   **Stress levels in punctuation pattern of "Bubaran Kembang Pacar."**

```
SUBDIVISIONS
full gongan:                                                              G
1st level:            N              N              N              N
2nd level:    w           P              P              P
3rd level: t     t     t     t     t     t     t     t

           ----------------------------------------------------------------

           wk  md  wk  str wk  md  wk  str wk  md  wk  str wk  md  wk  xstr

beat no.   1   2   3   4   5   6   7   8   9  10  11  12  13  14  15  16
```

(wk = weak; md = medium; str = strong; xstr = very strong)

The ethnomusicologist Judith Becker and her former student Stanley Hoffman have found it useful to represent the cyclic structure of *gendhings* by mapping patterns onto a circle, relating the flow of musical time to the recurring course traced by the hands on a clock. The pattern used in "Bubaran Kembang Pacar," then, can be notated as shown in example 7–4. Becker has argued convincingly that the cyclic structure of Javanese *gendhings* reflects the persistence of Hindu-Buddhist conceptions of time introduced to Java during the first millennium C.E. and not wholly eliminated by the subsequent adoption of Islam. (For an elaboration of this theory, see Hoffman 1978, Becker 1979, and especially Becker 1981.)

Today, the players of most of the punctuating instruments have a choice of pitch in performance of many pieces. Their choice is normally determined by the

Ex. 7–4.   **Punctuation pattern of "Bubaran Kembang Pacar" represented as a circle.**

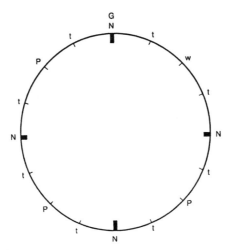

balungan melody tone played simultaneously, or the one about to be emphasized in the following phrase. However, when performing pieces in loud-playing style it is not unusual to use a single pitch throughout, reflecting earlier practice, when only one *kempul* and one or two *kenongs* were made for each *gamelan*. Here the musicians opt for this older practice; they use *kempul* tone 6 throughout, and a special *kenong* tuned to tone 5 in the octave below the other *kenong*. The *kethuk*, as is customary in Yogya, is tuned to tone 2. The *gong* player chooses to sound the *gong ageng* only for the first and last *gong* strokes; otherwise he plays the smaller *gong siyem*, tuned to tone 2.

The punctuation pattern and its relation to the *balungan* melody is indicated in the first word of the full nomenclature of a *gendhing*. In fact, the way Javanese refer to *gendhings* normally includes their formal structure (in this case *bubaran*—sixteen beats per *gongan*, four *kenong* beats per *gongan*), the name of a particular melody (in this case "Kembang Pacar"—a kind of red flower), the scale system (*pélog*), and the modal category (*pathet nem*).

Let us now consider the *balungan* melody of this piece, notated as performed on the *saron demung, saron barung,* and *slenthem* (ex. 7–5). The system used here and elsewhere in this chapter is the cipher notation system now widely used throughout central and eastern Java. Dots in place of numerals indicate a rest— or, more correctly, the sustaining of the previous tone. Dots below numerals indicate the lower octave, and dots above indicate the higher octave. An extra space or two is often given after groups of four beats as a means of demarcating a "measure"—though in Java the stress is on the *last* beat, not the first. Nowadays many Javanese musicians refer to notation to learn or to recall particular pieces, but they do not generally read from notation in performance. And what is notated is usually only the *balungan* melody and introduction; the parts played on other instruments are recreated in relation to the *balungan* melody and are open to some degree of personal interpretation.

The piece consists of four *gongans* (each, of course, with the same *bubaran* structure), played one after the other. Each of the first three begins with a measure that is played three times in succession and ends on the same tone as the

Ex. 7–5. Introduction and *balungan* melody for "Bubaran Kembang Pacar."

						G
						N
Introduction	(on bonang):	5 3 5 .	2 3 5 6	2 4 5 4	2 15555

Main Body					G
punctuation (same each gongan):	t w t N	t P t N	t P t N	t P t N
1st gongan:	3 6 3 5	3 6 3 5	3 6 3 5	6 5 3 2
2nd gongan:	6 5 3 2	6 5 3 2	6 5 3 2	5 3 5 6
3rd gongan:	2 1 2 6	2 1 2 6	2 1 2 6	3 5 3 2
4th gongan:	5 3 5 .	2 3 5 6	2 4 5 4	2 1 6 5

previous gong tone. This kind of regularity enhances the balanced symmetry provided by the punctuation structure. The fourth *gongan,* which stands out with its one rest (fourth beat) and lack of internal repetition, is melodically very similar to the introduction and leads right back into the first.

The whole main body can be repeated as many times as the drummer desires, or as is appropriate to the context in which it is performed. Pieces in *bubaran* form usually are played at the end of performances—*bubar* means "to disperse." The guests or audience are expected to leave during the playing of the piece; thus the number of repetitions may depend on the length of time it takes those in attendance to get up to leave.

Already we have a fairly good understanding of the structure of this piece as performed. Let us focus our attention now on the part played by the drummer, using the smallest and largest drums in combination. Throughout the piece he plays a pattern specific not to this particular piece, but, like the punctuating pattern, generic to the *bubaran* form. That is, the drumming for any of the forty or so other pieces in this form would be the same: a particular introductory pattern, several variant patterns for the main body, and a special contrasting pattern reserved only for the playing of the final *gongan* and which, together with the slowing of tempo, acts to signal the ending. The patterns are made up of a vocabulary of drum strokes, each with a name that imitates onomatopoetically the actual drum sound (ex. 7–6). It is the drummer who first begins to play faster, thereby signaling the ensemble to speed up at the end of the second time through the large cycle of four *gongans.* As warning that he intends to end, he alters the last

Ex. 7–6. Drum patterns for "Bubaran Kembang Pacar."

```
Introduction:                                             ‾‾‾‾‾‾ N/G
   5    3    5    .    2    3    5    6    2    4    5    4    2  1 5 5 5 5
                                          T    T    d    D    T  d   d   .

Main Body:
              t    w    t    N    t    P    t    N    t    P    t    N    t    P    t   N/G
   (e.g.)     3    6    3    5    3    6    3    5    3    6    3    5    6    5    3    2
   A:         d    d    d D  .    d    d    d D  .    d    d    d D  .  d D d D    d D  .
                                                    (played in 1st, 2nd, & 4th gongan)

              2    1    2    6    2    1    2    6    2    1    2    6    3    5    3    2
   B:       T d D  . T d D  .  T d D  . T d D  .  T d D  . T d D  .  d D d D    d D  .
                                                    (played in 3rd gongan)

              5    3    5    .    2    3    5    6    2    4    5    4    2    1    6    5
   Ending:  T d d    d    D    T d d D T d D    d D T d T d T    D d    D    d d  .
                                                    (played in 4th gongan, last time)
```

d =   dung (a high, resonant sound produced by one or two fingers striking
       the larger head of the ketipung)
T =   Tak (a short, crisp sound produced by slapping the smaller head of the
       of the ketipung with the palm)
D =   Dang (a deep sound, produced by hitting the larger head of the
       kendhang gendhing, often in combination with Tak on the ketipung)

few strokes in the penultimate *gongan* (from dDdD .dD. to dDdD .TdD). This way the other musicians all know they are to slacken the tempo, though the precise rate is determined by the drummer. The playing of the ending pattern through the last *gongan* confirms his intentions.

We have seen how the punctuating gong parts and the drumming fit with the *balungan* in "Bubaran Kembang Pacar." We can now turn to the elaborating melodic instruments—here the *bonang barung* and *bonang panerus*—which normally play at a faster rate, subdividing the *balungan* part and providing variations based on the *balungan* melody. In pieces with *balungan* played at slower tempos, the *saron peking* also provides a limited degree of melodic elaboration, but in Yogyanese court style the instrument is sometimes omitted (as it is here).

It was mentioned earlier that the only part normally notated is the *balungan*. Other melodic parts are derived through processes generally understood by practicing musicians. Ideally all musicians can play all the parts. In reality, this is true only in the best professional groups; but most musicians have at least a passive knowledge of the workings of all the instruments and know how to respond to various signals and subtler nuances.

The two *bonangs* here perform in a style called "walking," usually alternating left and right hands in sounding combinations of tones derived from the *balungan*. The *bonang barung* part played the first time through the four *gongans* is notated in example 7–7. The arrangement of kettle gongs on the instrument is given in the upper portion of the figure, and the notation below (with the same cipher system used to notate the *balungan*).

Ex. 7–7. *Bonang barung* **part played in "Bubaran Kembang Pacar."**

In subsequent repetitions the *bonang barung* part remains similar, but not identical. The variations reflect the sensibilities of the player, who both adjusts to tempo changes and alters his patterns purely for the aesthetic enjoyment of variation. He has not learned a particular *bonang* part or set of variations, note for note, for this one piece. Rather, he has thoroughly internalized a vocabulary of patterns which he knows by tradition to fit with certain phrases of *balungan*. What he usually will have learned about the particular piece, other than its *balungan*, is the octave register in which to play his variations (e.g., 3 6 3 6 rather than 3̇ 6̇ 3̇ 6̇).

The *bonang panerus* plays similar sorts of variations of the *balungan* melody, but at twice the rate of the *bonang barung*. Example 7–8 gives *balungan, bonang barung*, and *panang panerus* for the first *gongan*. The arrangement of kettles is identical to that of *bonang barung*, though each is tuned an octave higher than the corresponding *bonang barung* kettle. You can see in this figure how the two *bonangs* vary by repetition: 3 6 in the *balungan* becomes 3 6 3 6 in the *bonang barung* part and 363.3636 in the *bonang panerus* part—all heard simultaneously. Yet it is not simply a matter of mechanical replication throughout, for alternate tones can be substituted (e.g., 6 5 3 5 instead of 6 5 6 5) and other choices can be made. Still, we can understand why the Javanese refer to the *saron* and *slenthem* melody as *balungan*: the term literally means "outline" or "skeleton." And it provides just that for the elaborating instruments and, in soft-playing style, for the voices as well. The degree to which the *saron* and *slenthem* part actually sounds like an outline depends on its tempo and the resulting levels at which it is subdivided by the elaborating instruments.

IRAMA LEVEL

In this performance of "Bubaran Kembang Pacar," the *bonang barung* plays at twice the density of the *balungan*, subdividing it by two. This ratio defines one of five possible levels of *balungan* subdivision, known as the *irama* level. If the tempo had slowed sufficiently (as we shall see in the next piece), the *bonang barung* would double its ratio with the *balungan*, subdividing each beat by four. Ward Keeler aptly likens the process to a car shifting gears, in this case downshifting as it goes up a steep grade (Keeler 1987:225). And the *bonang panerus*, in order to maintain its relationship with the *bonanb barung*, would double as well, resulting in an eight-to-one ratio with the *balungan*. At the slowest *balungan*

Ex. 7–8. *Bonang barung* **and** *panerus* **parts for "Bubaran Kembang Pacar," first** *gongan*.

```
balungan:    3  6  3  5    3  6  3  5    3  6  3  5    6  5  3  2

bon. bar.:  3 6 3 6 3 5 3 5  3 6 3 6 3 5 3 5  3 6 3 6 3 5 3 5  6 5 3 5 6 . 6 .
                                                                        2   2

bon. pnr.: 363.3636353.3535 363.3636353.3535 363.3636353.3535 656.6535626.626.
```

tempo, the *bonang barung* would have a ratio of sixteen beats to one *balungan* beat, and the *bonang panerus*, along with several of the soft instruments, would play a full thirty-two beats for each *balungan* beat!

PERFORMING YOUR OWN *GAMELAN* MUSIC

All you need is a group of seven or eight people in order to get the feeling of *gamelan* ensemble performance. They can use any percussion instruments available, such as Orff instruments, or simply use their voices. Start by assigning each punctuating instrument to one person. The gong player can simply say "gong" (in a low, booming voice), the *kempul* player "pul" (middle voice) the *kenong* player "nong" (long and high) and the *kethuk* player "tuk" (short and low). Another can be assigned to play the drum pattern (saying the syllables given in the patterns in example 7–6 above). Then the remaining performers can divide among themselves the *balungan* melody and, if they are inclined, some *bonang* elaboration. With a larger group, people can double up on all instruments, except the drum.

First try the piece we have listened to, since the tune is familiar. The "drummer" should control the tempo and play the ending pattern, slowing down to end. Try different versions with different numbers of repetitions. You can end at any gong tone; it does not have to be at the end of he fourth *gongan*. Then try the piece given in example 7–9, called "Bubaran Udan Mas" (literally, "Golden Rain"). You can hear it on the recording *Javanese Court Gamelan from the Pura Paku Alaman* (Nonesuch H–72044). The gong punctuation is the same as in "Bubaran Kembang Pacar," but the melody is different. The sequence is as follows: introduction, first *gongan* twice, second *gongan* twice, and so on—until your drummer signals an ending. Try to learn it well enough that you are not reading notation but, like a Javanese musician, using your ears rather than your eyes.

Ex. 7–9. "Bubaran Udan Mas," *pélog pathet barang*—for performance.

```
Introduction:                                .    .                    N/G
                  7   7   7   5   6   7   2   2   7   6   5   6   7   6   5
                                             T   T   d   D   T   d   d

Main Body:
              t   w   t   N   t   P   t   N   t   P   t   N   t   P   t  N/G
(balungan:)   6   5   3   2   6   5   3   2   3   3   2   3   6   5   3   2

(bonang:)  6 5 6 5 2 . 2 .  6 5 6 5 2 . 2 .  3 3 3 . 3 3 . .  6 5 6 5 2 . 2 .

(balungan:)  7   5   6   7   5   6   7   2   2   7   6   5   6   7   6   5

(bonang:)  7 5 7 5 6 7 6 7  5 6 5 6 7 2 7 2  2 7 2 7 6 5 6 5  6 7 6 7 5 5 5 .
```

Approximate equivalents in Western pitches for **pélog** scale:

(1 = D), 2 = E, 3 = F, (4 = Ab), 5 = A, 6 = Bb, 7 = C   (1 and 4 not used here)

A JAVANESE *GENDHING* IN SOFT-PLAYING STYLE

Listen to the next recorded selection "Landrang Wilujeng," *pélog pathet barang* (selection 45). The title word, *wilujeng,* translates literally as "safe," "secure." This piece is often performed at the beginning of ceremonies or rituals to ensure the safety not only of the community involved but also of the ceremony or the performance itself. The recording was made at the house of my teacher Pak Suhardi, who lives just outside of Yogya and directs the professional *gamelan* musicians at the Yogya branch of the national radio station (Radio Republik Indonesia, or R.R.I.). Some of the performers are professional musicians (at R.R.I. and elsewhere); others are Suhardi's neighbors who gather at his house for regular weekly rehearsals on his *gamelan.*

The instruments, which fill much of his modest house when they are spread out for playing, are mostly iron and brass. Perhaps you noticed the contrast in sound quality as the metal percussion instruments first enter. But for soft-playing style, the quality of singing and of the various soft-sounding instruments is what matters most, rendering the contrast between bronze and other metals far less significant than in loud-playing. It is for this reason that some Javanese say the soft-playing music is more a music of the common people (who cannot afford large bronze ensembles) and the loud-playing music more a music of the court and nobility.

This example contrasts with the previous recorded selection in many ways. It is in soft-playing style, with voices and the various soft-sounding instruments featured. The introduction is played on the *rebab* (fiddle), with the subtle slides and nuances one could not produce on a fixed-pitch instrument such as the *bonang*. The pattern of punctuation (*ladrang*) is nearly the same as in the previous piece, but expanded to fit with *gongan* phrases thirty-two beats in duration, rather than sixteen. The players of the *kempul* and *kenong* do not limit themselves to one tone but instead use a variety of tones, matching or anticipating important tones in the melody (see notation in example 7–10).

Ex. 7–10.   "Landrang Wilujeng," *pélog pathet barang.*

```
                                                          ___N/G
Introduction:             7 3 2  6 7̄2̄. 3  7 7 3 2  7 67276
                                                           . .  . .

A: (umpak section)

     t    w    t  N3    t   P6    t   N5    t   P3    t   N6    t   P3*   t   N6/G
    2 7 2 3  2 7 5 6  3 3 . .  6 5 3 2  5 6 5 3  2 7 5 6  2 7 2 3  2 7 5 6
                                                 *(if going to ngelik, P6)

B: (ngelik section)
     t    w    t  N6    t   P7    t   N6    t   P6    t   N7    t   P6    t   N6/G
    . . 6 .  7 5 7 6  3 5 6 7  6 5 3 2  6 6 . .  7 5 7 6  . 7 3 2  . 7 5 6
```

PATHET

This piece uses the *pélog* scale system, as did "Bubaran Kembang Pacar," but is classified as *pathet barang*. Javanese generally identify three *pathet* in each of the two scale systems, ordered in relation to the progression in which they are featured in the all-night shadow puppet performances:

	sléndro pathet	*pélog pathet*
ca. 9:00 P.M.–midnight	*nem*	*lima*
ca. midnight–3:00 A.M.	*sanga*	*nem*
ca. 3:00 A.M.—6:00A.M.	*manyura*	*barang*

In actual shadow puppetry today the first phase may start before 9:00 and last until well after midnight. The second begins as late as 2:00 A.M. and the third as late as 4:30. Several schemes are given for music performed outside the shadow puppet context, but current practice indicates little relation between time of day and *pathet*. Instead, pieces in *sléndro pathet nem* or *pélog pathet lima,* which are usually calm and subdued in mood, tend to be played relatively early in a performance, regardless of the time of day.

Much effort has been spent in defining *pathet* with reference to the melodies of *gamelan* pieces, particularly the *balungan*. The famous Dutch ethnomusicologist Jaap Kunst noted that certain phrase finals were more common in one *pathet* than another, especially for pieces played primarily in *sléndro* (Kunst 1973). Mantle Hood, one of Kunst's students and a major figure in establishing ethnomusicology in the United States, devoted an entire book to the subject, concluding that *pathet* can be distinguished by different cadential patterns in the *balungan* part and by the avoidance of certain tones (Hood 1954).

With a larger body of data than was available to Hood, Judith Becker found *pathet* to be "based upon three interlocking factors: (1) melodic pattern, formula, or contour, (2) the pitch level of that pattern, and (3) the position of the pattern within the formal structure of a piece" (Becker 1980:81). In *sléndro,* for instance, a measure with the contour of three conjunct steps downward can occur in any *pathet*. Measures beginning on tone 5 and descending to 1 (5 3 2 1) are relatively common in both *sléndro pathet manyura* and *sléndro pathet sanga,* but in *manyura* they normally do not end in a strong position (e.g., with a *gong* stroke), whereas in *sanga* they often do. Measures with the same descending contour but beginning on tone 6 and descending to 2 (6 5 3 2) are common in both *pathet manyura* and *pathet nem,* but those ending in gong position are more likely to be *pathet nem.*

Javanese often speak of register or pitch level in relation to *pathet,* likening it in some ways to Western concepts of key. Indeed many *gendhing* are played in several *pathet,* just as Western popular tunes are often transposed from one key to another. The relationship to "key" is most apparent not in the single-octave *balungan* melody but in the parts played on instruments with wider ranges and in the singing. Instrumentalists and singers learn a vocabulary of melodic patterns, which they can readily transpose up or down—and even between scale systems. For example, the pattern one uses to arrive at tone 6 in *sléndro pathet manyura* can be realized one tone lower, with the same physical processes (i.e., the same hand movements of the player) to end on 5 in *sléndro pathet sanga*. In fact, most Javanese say that *pathet sanga* is simply *pathet manyura* down one tone. But *sléndro pathet nem,* said to be the lowest of the three *sléndro pathet,* is often described by musicians as consisting of an ambigious mix of phrases from the other two *sléndro pathet,* as is the case in our third example (discussed later).

Pélog *pathets* are understood slightly differently. *Pathet barang* is easily distinguished by the presence of tone 7 and the avoidance of tone 1. Differentiating *pathet lima* from *pathet nem* presents greater problems, since both avoid tone 7, employ the other six *pélog* tones, and do not seem to be simply one or more tones above or below one another. Javanese musicians often disagree over which of these two is the correct *pathet* category for a given piece. Perception of a piece's mood, which is determined by other factors beside melodic contour and register, may also contribute. The calmer pieces would be classified as *pathet lima* and livelier ones as *nem.*

These few preceding paragraphs have not been sufficient even to present a thorough survey of the many ideas about the concept of *pathet.* But at least you realize that, though it is usually translated as "mode" in English, *pathet* is somewhat more complicated than its Western counterpart. The word *pathet* literally means "limit" and is related to other Javanese words for stopping or delimiting. In many ways it indicates something about the limitations of the piece in question— the tones that will be played or emphasized in the *balungan* melody, the pitch level of the other parts, the mood, and (especially for shadow puppetry accompaniment) the time of day or night at which it is appropriately played. Though the association with mood and time of day suggests comparison with Indian *raga* (see chapter 6), *pathet* is actually a very different concept. *Ragas* are differentiated from one another by details of interval structure and ornament, as well as contour, and not by register. Hundreds of *ragas* are known, thousands theoretically possible. Indian musicians do not, to my knowledge, transpose pieces from one *raga* to another, since the *raga* is so essential to the aesthetic impact of the piece. *Pathet* is a far more general concept. Only a few *pathet* are identified for each of the two scale systems, and transposition from one *pathet* to another occurs with some frequency.

INSTRUMENTAL PLAYING IN "LADRANG WILUJENG"

Now we can return to the example "Ladrang Wilujeng" (selection 45)—a piece that is often performed in *sléndro pathet manyura* as well as *pélog pathet barang* simply by transferring the melodic patterns from one system to the other. Notation is given in example 7–10, above, for the introduction, the *balungan,* and the *gong* punctuation (with pitch choices for *kempul* and *kenong*).

This piece is considerably more challenging to follow than the previous one. It slows and changes *irama* level in the third measure (3 3 . .), settling by the end of the first *gongan* to a tempo of about thirty-six *balungan* beats per minute. The *umpak* is played twice, then the *ngelik* once, then *umpak* twice again, *ngelik* again, and so on, ending in the *umpak:* A A B A A B A A B A. For the final two *gongans,* the tempo first speeds up (but with no change in *irama* level) to about forty-two beats per minute, and then slows gradually to the final *gong.* A solo female vocalist (*pesindhèn*) sings for most of the first two *gongans.* At the beginning of the first *ngelik* and from then on, all the singers join to sing in unison. And the *balungan* part is no longer played explicitly! Instead, the *balungan* instruments play simple variations based on the *balungan.*

It will be helpful in following the flow of the piece to use a stop watch, starting with the introduction. Elapsed time is given for the end of each *gongan* and for other significant events:

	(minutes:seconds)
Beginning of introduction, on *rebab*	0:00
Gong at end of introduction, ensemble enters	0:07
Change of *irama* level	0:19
Gong at end of first *umpak*	0:50
Singers enter in unison	1:43
Gong at end of second *umpak*	1:44
Gong at end of first *ngelik*	2:37
Gong at end of third *umpak*	3:32
Gong at end of fourth *umpak*	4:27
Gong at end of second *ngelik*	5:20
Gong at end of fifth *umpak*	6:14
Drummer signals acceleration in tempo	6:48
Gong at end of sixth *umpak*	7:04
Gong at end of third *ngelik*	7:49
Drummer signals gradual slackening in tempo	8:17
Final *gong* at end of seventh *umpak*	8:45

The drummer, with the same two drums used in the previous example (*kendhang gendhing* and *ketipung*), plays standardized patterns specific to *ladrang* formal structure: a *ladrang* introduction, a *ladrang* slowing-down pattern (in the first *gongan*), standard *irama dadi* (literally "settled" *irama* level—i.e., four *bonang barung* beats per *balungan* beat) patterns for most of the rest of the performance (with a standard *ngelik* variation each time the *ngelik* is played), and finally an ending pattern during the final *gongan.* In accord with the soft-playing style, the drumming is softer and sparser than in loud-playing. Example 7–11 gives the standard pattern used, with minimal variation, throughout all the *umpak gongans* but the first and final ones.

Other instrumentalists play variations of the *balungan* melody, producing such a complex heterophony that some scholars prefer to identify *gamelan* music as "polyphonic," noting the stratification of layers: parts moving at a wide variety of tempi—some at a much faster rate or higher density than others. Generally it is

Ex. 7–11.   **Drum pattern for Landrang Wilujeng," *irama dadi.***

```
2   7   2   3     2   7   5   6     3   3   .   .     6   5   3   2
. . . . . . d   d . d D . . . .     . d . d .dDd.Dd   . . .d D . d D

5   6   5   3     2   7   5   6     2   7   2   3     2   7   5   6G
d D . d .dD . T   d d d D d .dD d   .dD dD.dD.dD.dD   . . .d .dD d D
```

the smaller, higher-pitched instruments that play at the faster rates and the larger, deeper ones at the slower rates. You can get a sense of this stratification by considering the frequency with which the gong is struck, comparing it to *kenong* (here four times per gong), then *balungan* (here eight beats per *kenong*), and then the subdividing parts (*bonang barung* and *saron peking* four times per *balungan* beat, *bonang panerus* and many of the soft-playing instruments eight times per *balungan* beat). Thus, the instruments playing at the fastest rate, mostly those of higher pitch, actually play 256 beats for every one beat of the gong!

Above I indicated that in this example the *balungan* is varied even on the instruments that usually sound it explicitly. After the first two *gongan*, where the balungan is played normally, the *saron barung* usually plays the second *balungan* tone on the first and second beats, and the fourth *balungan* tone on the third and fourth. The *saron demung* sounds these tones of the *saron barung*, but inserts "neighbor" tones (the next highest or next lowest tone) between the beats. And the *slenthem* plays the *saron demung* part, but delayed by a quarter of a *balungan* beat to interlock with the *demung* (ex. 7–12). Variations occur, particularly when the *balungan* is "hanging"—that is sustaining one tone (e.g., 3 3 . . ; or . . 6 .).

The combination resulting from the interlocking of *slenthem* and *saron demung* here is identical to what the much higher-pitched *saron peking* plays, duplicating and anticipating the *balungan* tones in a manner that also resembles closely the walking style of *bonang* playing. This means of varying the *balungan* characterizes *peking* playing generally and is not limited to the few cases where the *balungan* is only implied (ex. 7–13).

Throughout "Ladrang Wilujeng" the *bonangs* play in "walking" style, mixed with occasional reiteration of single tones or octave combinations, as we found in the first example. The lengthier time interval between *balungan* beats here, however, provides opportunity for greater melodic and rhythmic independence from the *balungan* melody. The phrase shown in example 7–14 is played (with occasional variation) on the *bonang barung* with the *balungan* 2 7 5 6.

The various soft-playing instruments provide more elaborate variations, more independent of the *balungan* part and often inspired by phrases in the vocal parts.

Ex. 7–12.   **Variations by *balungan* instruments in "Ladrang Wilujeng."**

```
(balungan:      3   5   6   7P   6   5   3   2N -- not played)

saron barung:   5   5   7   7    5   5   2   2
saron demung:   3 5 3 5 6 7 6 7  6 5 6 5 3 2 3 2
   slenthem:     3 5 3 5 6 7 6 7  6 5 6 5 3 2 3 2
```

Ex. 7–13. *Saron peking* **part for passage in "Ladrang Wilujeng."**

(balungan: 3   5   6   7P   6   5   3   2N)

saron peking: 3355335566776677 6655665533223322

It is difficult to hear clearly all the soft instruments, since they blend together in the thick texture of soft-playing style. As an example, let us consider the *gambang* (xylophone), which plays mostly "in octaves"—the right hand usually sounding the same tone as the left, but one octave higher. The excerpt is from the middle of the *umpack* section, fourth statement (4:00 to 4:15 on the stop watch) (ex. 7–15). In other statements of this passage, the *gambang* part is similar, but not identical. Good players draw from a rather large vocabulary of patterns and vary the repeated passages in performance with a degree of individual flexibility, though not with the range of spontaneity we associate with improvisation in jazz or Indian music. The *gambang* player, like the other *gamelan* musicians whose part is not completely fixed, operates with a system of constraints (not quite "rules" or "laws"). At the end of a measure, the *gambang* and *balungan* tones almost always coincide; at the midpoint (second beat), they usually do; on other beats they often do not, even though the *gambang* sounds eight (or some cases as many as thirty-two) times as many tones as the *balungan*.

Singing in "Ladrang Wilujeng"

Solo singing with *gamelan* is also based on notions of flexibility and constraint. During the first two *gongan* one of the female vocalists sings florid vocal phrases that weave in and out of the *balungan* part. Although her part employs a much freer rhythm than the steady pulsation of most of the instruments (e.g., the *gambang* discussed above), her melody is also constructed from phrases that usually end on the same tone as the *balungan* phrase, even though in current practice she often reaches that tone a beat or two later than most of the other instruments. Her phrases resemble those of other singers, but in at least some small way they are her individual patterns. The vocal text used by the solo singer (difficult to determine in this recording) is not specific to the piece, but one of many in a well-known verse form fitted to the structure of this *ladrang* and to many pieces in this and other forms.

In contrast to the soloist, the chorus sings a precomposed melody. The text, although agreed upon before performance, is again a generic one, used in many *gamelan* pieces and having no connection with the meaning of the title of this piece. To a great degree, Javanese melody and Javanese texts lead independent lives. A single melody, for example, may be sung with a variety of texts; and a

Ex. 7–14. *Bonang barung* **part for passage in "Ladrang Wilujeng."**

balungan: 2   7   5   6N

bonang barung: 2̇ 7 7̄5̄5̄ 5 7 . . 5 7 7̄5̄. 6 7 . 6

Ex. 7–15. *Gambang* playing in "Ladrang Wilujeng."

balungan:	5	6	5	3P
r.h.	2 3 2 3 5 5 3 5 5 3 5 3 5 3 5 6	2 7 6 5 3 5 2 7	6 6 6 2 2 7	2 3
l.h.	2 3 2 3 5 2 3 5 2 3 5 3 2 3 5 6	2 7 6 5 3 5 2 7	6 7 6 2 6 7	2 3

balungan:	2	7	5	6
r.h.	3 5 6 7 6 2 7 6 5 6 3 2 7 3 2 7	7 2 7 2 7 6 5 3	3 5 3 5 6 6	5 6
l.h.	3 5 6 7 6 2 7 6 5 6 3 2 7 3 2 7	3 2 7 2 7 6 5 3	3 5 3 5 6 3	5 6

single text may be heard in a variety of *gamelan* pieces—depending on the wishes of the performers or sometimes (but rarely) the requirements of a particular dramatic scene.

The choral text is one of many *wangsalan*, in which the meaning of seemingly unrelated phrases in the first part suggests the meaning or sound of words or phrases in the second part. This kind of literary indirection is greatly loved in Java and can be seen as an aesthetic expression of the high value placed on subtlety and indirection in daily life. To "get" the connections, one must know traditional Javanese culture rather well: history, legends, nature, foods, place names (in both the real and the mythological worlds), and the Javanese shadow puppet tradition with its many hundred characters. Javanese poetry is difficult to render in English. The Javanese is given first, with word-by-word translation second (with some double meanings), followed by a freer translation underneath (fig. 7–3). Some of the *wangsalan* riddles here are obscure even to most Javanese. An explanation of two of them should suffice to give you an idea of how they work. In the first line of verse I, the words "satriya ing Lésanpura" ("a knight in the kingdom of Lésanpura") suggest the sound of the first word of the second line "setyanana," as the shadow puppet character named Setyaki is a well-known knight who came from Lésanpura. "Kala reta," in the first line of verse III, suggests not the sound but one meaning of the root particle in the compound "Mbang-embang" in the second line. Though the two-word expression "kala reta" can mean "centipede," the two words translate individually as "time" (kala) and "red" (reta). "Bang," the root of "mbang-embang," is another word for red, and "bang-bang wétan" (literally "red-red east") is a Javanese expression for dawn.

In this example, as is common in pieces where male and female singers join to sing in unison, the text is interspersed with extra words and syllables whose meaning may be obscure (underlined in example 7–16), and portions of the text may be repeated. These characteristics strongly suggest the relatively greater importance of what we would call the "musical" elements (pitch and rhythm) over the words, with the word meaning often obscured and the words serving primarily as vehicles for beautiful melody. The notation in example 7–16 shows the scheme for the first verse (with *balungan* and *gong* punctuation given above the vocal line). The

I. *Manis rengga,*   *satriya ing Lésanpura*
    sweet decoration (colorful sweet snack), knight of/in Lésanpura
    Beautifully adorned, the knight from Lésanpura [a kingdom in the *Mahabharata]*

    Setyanana yén laliya marang sira
    Be loyal   if   forget to   you.
    You should be loyal, even if you forget yourself.

II. *Tirta maya, supaya anyar kinarya*
    Water pure, so that quickly be made
    Beautiful clear water, let it be done quickly

    Ning   *ing   driya, tan na   ngalih amung sira*
    purity/emptiness of/in heart, not exist move   only you
    With the purifying of my heart, there is nothing that moves, only you.

III. *Kala reta,*   *satriya ngungkuli jaya*
    Time red (centipede), knight surpass   glory/victory
    At dawn, the knight proves exceptional in his glory

    Sun mbang-embang hamiséa   jroning pura
    I hope/yearn for   have power within domain/palace
    I yearn to exercise power here in this domain.

Fig. 7–3.   Choral text in Javanese and English.

second verse operates the same way, with repetition of the last four syllables at the end of one *umpak* and repetition of the first four syllables of the second line in the next *umpak.* Only the final verse (here the third, but this could have gone on for many more verses) ends after one *ngelik* and one *umpak* and thus does not reach the "Adèn, adèn" interjections and the repetition of the first four syllables we would expect in the next *umpak* if the performance did not end where it does.

BIOGRAPHY OF KI NARTOSABDHO, A *GAMELAN* MUSICIAN, COMPOSER, AND PUPPETEER

To this point we have focused mostly on musical sound and its structure. But what of the people who are most drawn to this music—the musicians themselves? Javanese and foreign scholars alike have often mentioned the close interrelationship among the arts in Java. In fact, the status of "musician" does not preclude one from dancing or performing puppetry. Many of the better performers in one art are quite competent in several others. In the following several pages I am going to let a consummate artist, one famous as a *gamelan* musician, composer of new pieces, and shadow puppeteer, speak for himself. The biography I provide is based on an interview my wife and I conducted in 1979 with Ki Nartosabdho (1925–85). (His music is discussed at length in Becker 1980.)

We began by asking him how he became a shadow puppeteer, and he proceeded to tell us the story of his life from early childhood memories with very little interruption from us. I have chosen to omit my wife's and my occasional

Ex. 7–16. **Choral vocal part for "Ladrang Wilujeng," first verse.**

Chorus enters at end of second <u>umpak</u> (1:45 on stopwatch):   6 6N/G
                                                                          <u>Andhé</u>

<u>ngelik</u>:
```
      .    .    6    .    7    5    7    6N    3    5    6    7P    6    5    3    2N
      --------------7----2---    2-376--------    2-327------675----6532
                    é           ba-  bo          Ma- nis      reng-  ga


      6    6    .   .P    7    5    7    6N    .    7    3    2P    .    7    5    6N/G
      ---------    6-535----6-722----3276----- 567-   5-632----- 723--223276
                   sa- tri-    ya    ing               Lé- san         pu- ra,
```

<u>umpak</u>:
```
      2    7    2    3    2    7    5    6N    3    3    .   .P    6    5    3    2N
      ---------         2--3232--76--53-----       3-566-----5675----6532
                        Ba-bo ba- bo                Se- tya-   na-    na


      5    6    5    3P    2    7    5    6N    2    7    2    3P    2    7    5    6N/G
      --------    6-753--2-2-2---232-376-------      2--33------722----3276
                  yèn  laliya marang si-ra           ma- rang    si-    ra
```

<u>umpak</u>:
```
      2    7    2    3    2    7    5    6N    3    3    .   .P    6    5    3    2N
      ---------         2--3232--76--53-----       3-566-----5675----6532
                        A- dèn a- dèn                Se- tya-   na-    na


      5    6    5    3P    2    7    5    6N    2    7    2    3P    2    7    5    6N/G
      (no vocal, until end of line, where next verse begins):            6  6
                                                                         <u>An-dhé</u>
```

questions, some of which merely sought clarification of vocabulary. Only toward the end did our questions seek to fill in some details concerning his musical experiences. I have also chosen to omit Ki Nartosabdho's occasional questions about our background and about the English words for various Indonesian and Javanese words and concepts.

KI NARTOSABDHO: Since I sat at my school desk in second grade, I had a knack for the arts. Which ones? Painting. A child's paintings, but even so, with cubist style, realism, expressionism, and my own creations: for instance, a lamb being chased by a tiger, things like that. Now, they really did not give lessons in those kinds of painting for children my age, but I made every effort to see duplications of pictures made by other painters at that time. After beginning to learn to paint, I began to learn classical-style dance. I'd dance the role of a monkey, an ogre, and so forth. We actually learned a lot about classical dance—not everything, but a good deal. At that time I lived in my small village, in the Klatèn area [between Yogya and Solo]—called Wedhi. I was born in Wedhi on August 25, 1925. There, when I was twelve years old and in third grade, we had a teacher who gave dance lessons. He was from Solo. We studied so hard that we were able to put on quite an impressive show. It was really rare for village children to have the opportunity to study with a "classical" dance teacher from Solo.

After dance, I began to learn Western music—violin, guitar, cello, and *keroncong.* [*Author's note:* The *keroncong* is a small chordophone, like an ukulele, played in the Western-influenced Indonesian genre of the same name. The violin, guitar, and cello he studied were for this same genre, and not for "classical" Western music.] By village standards I did just fine, but not by city standards. After that, I studied *gamelan* music. All these interests took their toll—requiring one to spend time, emotions, and especially money. Especially for musical instruments, what was I to use to purchase one? A guitar in 1937 cost six gulden—Dutch money—or we would say six rupiah [Indonesian currency]. I was the eighth of my brothers and sisters, I was the youngest. And I was born into a family that was poor, lacking in possessions, in work, and especially in education. So it is clear that, no matter how much I wanted something, I could not continue my education without any income. My father died just after I began second grade, and my mother, a widow, was already old. So I earned money by making masks—yes, masks—in order to be able to continue school. And I managed to finish fifth grade. And I used to have Dutch language classes after school, but they cost 1.25 gulden each month, so I only took Dutch for two months. They threw me out—because I couldn't pay!

Now, rather than hang aimlessly about the house, when I was a teenager I took off without even asking my mother's permission. Where in the world would I go, I didn't know. Like a bird in flight, not knowing where I might perch. It was as if I needed some time to suffer—Excuse me, I don't usually come out with all this about myself, but today I am—Anyway, like a bird in flight, no idea where I should perch. I might even be called a *gelandangan* (homeless street person). If not a *gelandangan,* then an outcast, or a forgotten soul.

I felt that the perch I should take was only to join and follow performing groups: both *kethoprak* [musical drama, with stories from Javanese legendary history] and *wayang orang* [musical dance-drama, based on the same Indian epics as shadow puppetry]. First I joined a *kethoprak* group, working as an actor and as a *gamelan* musician. But what I got for it was very minimal—both artistically and financially. And what was more, the coming of the Japanese reinforced my feeling that I had to keep drifting. A life of wandering about, and in tattered clothing. There were lots of clothes then that no human being should have to wear [burlap bags, etc., as the Japanese took much of the cloth during their occupation], but like it or not, circumstances required it. In Javanese there is a saying: *nuting jaman kalakoné* ["following the times is the way to act"—i.e., "go with the flow"]. There are lots of sayings and stories that still have mystical content in Indonesia, still plenty. And you should know, even though in your country there is so much great technology, in Indonesia traditional and mystical matters still persist and are even gaining in strength.

So, I played with about ten *kethoprak* groups, only one month, then move, three months and move, at the longest, only four or five months, then move. It is called *lècèkan*—not taking care of oneself. Then one day I was playing *kendhang* for a *kethoprak* group named Sri Wandowo, playing in Klatèn. This was in 1945, just before the Proclamation of Independence [August 17]. There was a manager, the manager of the Ngesthi Pandhawa *wayang orang* troupe, who happened to be eating at a little eating stall (*warung*) behind the *kethoprak* stage where I was playing. As he ate, he heard my drumming and it made an impression. After going home—from eating frogs' legs—he called three of his troupe members and asked them to find out who it was playing *kendhang* for the *kethoprak*. After that, in brief, I left Sri Wandowo and joined Ngesthi Pandhawa. And what startled the other members was that I was the only member who was nervy enough to play *kendhang* at his first appearance. I had lots of experience drumming, but what I knew needed "upgrading."

Now, this guy named Narto [i.e., Nartosabdho] was a man without upgrading. Three-quarters of the Ngesthi Pandhawa members scorned me, ridiculed me, and seemed disgusted by my behavior. A new member already nervy enough to direct and play *kendhang?* Now, in the old days, Ngesthi Pandhawa was just an ordinary *wayang orang* troupe, with lots of free time in its schedule. Well, I took steps for "evolution"— not "revolution," but "evolution." Where was our "evolution"? On the stage of Ngesthi Pandhawa, both in the *gamelan* music and in the dance, and in the new pieces I composed—I should say "we" composed. These were very popular with the public, with the audience. From village tunes to new tunes unknown in Java, such as waltz-time. [Several other composers have also experimented with *gamelan* music in triple meter, including the Yogyanese Hardjosoebroto. It is not clear who can rightfully claim to have done it first.] The piece was "Sang Lelana" ("The Wanderer"). Also there was "Aku Ngimpi" ("I Dream") and "Sampur Ijo" ("The Green Scarf"), even for dance!

And [the vocal parts] for these waltz pieces could be duet or trio: one, two, or three voices [singing different melodies]. When we tried these out at Ngesthi Pandhawa, there were people who predicted that I would go crazy. My response was that we are all human. God gives us cattle, not beefsteak. Once we are given cattle by God, we have the right to transform it into something that is appropriate and useful, in accordance with our taste. All the better if we can bring in rhythms (meters) from outside Indonesia, as long as we don't change or destroy the original and authentic Indonesian rhythms. For example [he taps—on the "x"s—and hums (ex. 7–17)], yes, three-four. Now in the old days this didn't exist. And even now, when it does, it causes hassles for all the instruments played with two hands—*kendhang, gendèr, gambang*—hassles, but it turns out it is possible. At first [they played] only the simplest of patterns; now it is enjoyed by many listeners: experts [players] and those who only wish to listen. Now obviously I faced some defiance, lots of criticism that I was destroying [tradition]. I was called "destroyer." But I didn't take it just as criticism, but rather as a whip—to push me to find a way. Indeed the criticism was justified. So maybe not only in my country, but in yours too, if there is something startling and seemingly irrational suddenly applied [e.g., in the arts], it gives rise to much protest and criticism, right? So maybe the life of mankind everywhere is the same. What differs is just their appearance, their language, their traditions, but life is the same, right?

As it turned out I did okay. My manager gave me something: not money, but a name. Before, I had been Sunarto, now Nartosabdho [from *sabda*—see below]. I gratefully accepted this honor, though not without careful consideration of its justification. In Indonesia often a name is taken from one's profession. For example, Pak Harja Swara [*swara* = voice, sound] was a vocalist, *gérong*. Then Harjana Pawaka. *Harjana* means "safe" [cf. *wilujeng*], and *pawaka* means "fire"; he was on the fire brigade [he

Ex. 7–17.   Excerpt of Nartosabdho piece in triple meter.

```
 x     x     x     x     x     x     x     x     x

Gong . . 3 5 7 6 6 . 5 3 6 5 5 . 3 2 7 2 . . 5 6 5 3N

      . . 7 2 6 7 7 . 3 2 7 2P
```

uses the Dutch *brandweer*], someone who puts out fires. Wignya Pangrawit: *wignya* means "skilled," and *pangrawit* "a *gamelan* player"; so he was someone skilled at playing *gamelan*. Then Nyata Carita: *nyata* is "clear," "evident," and *carita* is "story"; he was a puppeteer who was accomplished, skilled in storytelling. And I was given the addition *sabda. Sabda* is "the speech of a holy man." But here I was a composer and drummer at Ngesthi Pandhawa, specializing in *gamelan* music. It did not seem possible that I would utter such speech. I taught singing and *gamelan*. So I wondered how my profession might fit with this name *sabda*.

[*Author's note:* In *wayang orang*, one person sits with the musicians and acts as a "*dhalang*"—not operating puppets, but providing narration and singing the mood songs known as *sulukan*. We learned from interviewing other members of the Ngesthi Pandhawa troupe that one night when the usual *dhalang* was unable to perform, Nartosabdho took over and, to the amazement of the audience, showed himself to have a fine voice, facility with the somewhat archaic *dhalang*'s language, and a thorough knowledge of the story. This preceded his debut as a *wayang kulit dhalang*.]

Well, on April 28, 1958, I earned the title "*dhalang*" [here, puppeteer for *wayang kulit* (ill. 7–7), not *wayang orang*] in Jakarta, at R.R.I. People heard that I was learning to do shadow puppetry, and in January 1958 I was called by the broadcast director, Pak Atmaka—he's still alive. Would I do a broadcast? [Javanese shadow puppetry, though it uses beautifully carved and painted puppets, is often broadcast over the radio. The audience follows the story by recognizing the particular vocal quality given to each character by the puppeteer, and can also enjoy the music.] I replied that I would not be willing right away. The broadcast would be heard all over Indonesia, maybe even outside the country. This was before all the private radio stations, so broadcasts from the central studio could be heard clearly [at great distances]. I agreed to perform in a few

Ill. 7–7.   Ki Nartosabdho as puppeteer (*dhalang*), performing *wayang kulit*. (Photo courtesy of Judith Becker.)

months, in April. What shape should my puppetry performance take, how classical, how innovative? Could I match the quality of my accomplishments in *gamelan* music? How to proceed, it is always a puzzle. There was a woman, a singer (*pesindhèn*) who made a promise: if I could perform shadow puppetry all night, she would give me a kiss. A kiss of respect, right, not an erotic kiss, not a "porno" kiss!

Sometime after coming home to Semarang from performing in Jakarta, I had a guest. His name was Sri Handaya Kusuma, and he came on behalf of the Medical Faculty in Yogya. He wanted a performance around Christmas time. [*Author's note:* Though few Javanese are Christian, Christmas is a holiday, and schools are normally on a short break beginning shortly before Christmas and lasting until after the New Year.] I was asked to perform a "classic" story. Now requests began to come in one after the other: Jakarta, Yogya, Surabaya, Solo. Yes, I was earning money, but more important, I was also earning my name. Nowadays I perform once or twice a week, but have more requests than that. I have even played at the presidential palace in Jakarta for Pak Harto [President Suharto] four times.

How did I learn? I am what you would call an "autodidact" ["*otodidak*"]. I read and so forth, but it also took looking at a lot of shadow puppetry performances. I would watch all the puppeteers I could, not only the older ones, but also the younger. And each performance, by whatever puppeteer, offered something new that I could and should incorporate in my own performance.

What about musicians? When I first played in Jakarta, it was the R.R.I. musicians who accompanied me. Elsewhere, I would take a few of those closest to me, my *gendèr* player, Pak Slamet, who came from Yogya and still plays at R.R.I. Semarang. And my drummer was the late Pak Wirya. Since 1969 I have had my own group, Condhong Raos, mostly younger musicians, under thirty-five years of age.

In the early 1970s I began to make cassettes, first of my new *gamelan* pieces, then of full-length shadow puppet performances. There were some discs produced by Lokananta [the National Recording Company] in the 1960s, too. My first set of *wayang* cassettes was the story "Gatutkaca sungging," recorded in 1974, if I remember correctly. Not so long ago. I don't really have a favorite story—how can you say one is better than another? If someone wants to hire a puppeteer and asks for "Parta krama" [Parta, i.e., Arjuna, gets married], for example, no puppeteer should say he doesn't like that story. That wouldn't be very good!

What changes do I foresee in the next five or ten years? It may be possible to predict changes in technology, but not in culture, not in the arts. Some people think *wayang kulit* should be given in the Indonesian language. To me, if a change adds to the beauty of the art, then it can be accepted. If not, then it cannot be. In Javanese there are many ways to say "eat," or "sleep." [He goes on to give examples. Different honorific levels of vocabulary permeate Javanese but are almost entirely absent from Indonesian. Nartosabdho implies, without stating explicitly, that he finds *wayang* more beautiful in Javanese and would like to keep it that way.] I have taken *gamelan* music from various areas of Java, even Sunda and Bali, and used them in the *gara-gara* [a comic interlude occurring at the beginning of the *pathet sanga* section, ca. 1:00 A.M.]. Not only have I studied these different songs, but I have even taken liberties with them. But other aspects of my puppetry have not been influenced by other regional styles. My style is basically Solonese. Who can predict if it will change, or how it will change?

The preceding few pages have presented my English translation of much of what Ki Nartosabdho told my wife and me when we visited him in his modest home (certainly modest for a performer of his status and popularity) in Semarang.

Though he was still giving one or two strenuous all-night *wayang* performances per week, he was already suffering from a kidney disease. In late 1985 Ki Nartosabdho died and left a legacy of hundreds of new *gamelan* vocal pieces, hundreds of musical recordings, and close to one hundred recordings of all-night *wayang* performances. His group Condhong Raos still performs music, but at present no one stands out as such a clear "superstar" within the world of traditional Javanese performing arts—a world that, until the era of mass media, really knew no "star system" at all.

GAMELAN MUSIC AND SHADOW PUPPETRY

Now that we have had a glimpse of a man deeply involved in both *gamelan* music and shadow puppetry, it is fitting to consider some of the music most closely associated with shadow puppet performance. Both of the pieces we have studied so far are seldom played for dance or dramatic accompaniment. The musical staples of the shadow puppet repertory are pieces with dense *kenong* and *kempul* playing, and *gongans* of varying length—pieces that generate a level of excitement, partly because of the dense gong punctuation. For each *pathet* there are at least three of these staple pieces: relatively calm (*ayak-ayakan*), somewhat excited (*srepegan, playon*) and very excited (*sampak*). The *gong* punctuation is densest in the very excited pieces and less so in the calm pieces. Which piece is to be played is determined by the puppeteer, who must be just as thoroughly at home with the *gamelan* music as he is with the many hundreds of characters and stories that make up this tradition.

We are going to listen to two versions of one of these pieces, the Yogyanese "Playon Lasem" *sléndro pathet nem* (selections 46 and 47). Depending on the mood the puppeteer wishes to establish, the piece can be played in loud-playing style or in soft-playing, or switched at any point. (*Ayak-ayakan*, the calmest of the three, is usually in soft-playing style; and *sampak*, the most excited, is always performed in loud-playing style). Also, the length of the piece can be radically tailored to suit the needs of the dramatic moment. Sometimes it may go on, through repetition of a central section, for five or ten minutes. The first instance we will hear takes a little over a minute, only beginning to repeat when the puppeteer signals the playing of a special ending phrase. All the musicians must know one or two of these ending phrases for each *gong* tone and be ready to tag the appropriate one onto any *gongan* if the signal comes.

Example 7–18 gives *balungan* notation for the entire piece. The *gong ageng* or *siyem* sound at the end of each line, as written. The *kenong* plays on every *balungan* beat, the *kempul* every second beat (except where the *gong* sounds), and the *kethuk* between the beats. Notice that here the frequency of "coincidence" between *gong* punctuators is very high: every second beat! To Javanese, this makes for exciting music, appropriate for scenes charged with emotion, even for fights. Quick rapping on the puppet chest signals the musicians to play. The drummer, playing the middle-sized drum (*ciblon*), and sometimes the *kenong* player as well, enter just before the rest of the ensemble.

During the course of the all-night performance at which I recorded these examples, the puppeteer (Ki Suparman) signaled this piece to be played eighteen

Ex. 7–18. *"Playon Lasem," sléndro pathet nem.*

```
Introductory portion:        (signal....)  5        Length of Gongan
                    6 5   6 5 6 5   2 3 5 6            10 beats
                 1 6 5 6   2 3 5 3   2 1 2 1           12 beats
                 2 1 2 1   6 5 3 5   2 3 5 6           12 beats
                 1 6 5 6   5 3 2 3   1 2 3 2**         12 beats

Repeated portion:
        [: 5 6 5 3  5 6 5 3   6 5 2 6   5 2 3 5*       16 beats
                               3 2 3 2   6 5 2 3        8 beats
           5 3 5 3  5 2 3 5   1 6 5 3   2 1 3 2        16 beats
                               6 6 1 2   3 5 6 5        8 beats
                    2 1 2 1   2 1 3 2   5 6 1 6        12 beats
                               3 2 5 3   6 5 3 2 :]     8 beats
```

Endings:
*   * from gong tone 5 (first rendition):   2 1   3 2 1 6
*   ** from gong tone 2 (second rendition): 5 3   2 1 2 6

- -

Punctuation Pattern for playon/srepegan form:

```
kempul & gong:    P   (repeat x ?)   G     e.g.:  P   P   P   P   G
kenong & kethuk:  tNtN (repeat x ?) tNtN         tNtNtNtNtNtNtNtNtN
balungan:         . .  (etc.)        . .          6 5 6 5 6 5 2 3 5 6
```

times—all, of course, within the *pathet nem* section of the night, which lasted from about 9:00 A.M. until about 1:30 A.M. The first rendition you hear (selection 46) begins in soft style, but speeds and gets loud by the end of the first *gongan*, then proceeds through the entire melody, begins to repeat the main section, and ends, on signal, after the first *gongan*. In the second rendition (selection 47), entirely in loud-playing style, the musicians never even reach the "main" section. To add variety to this rendition, played quite late during the *pathet nem* section (ca. 12:30 A.M.), the *saron* players play variant phrases for some of the passages notated above, though the *slenthem* player holds to the previous version.

Even without such change, we can see that this one piece has the potential for a great variety of renditions, through changes in tempo, instrumentation, and ending points. This is the essence of shadow puppet music—a very well known piece, played over and over, but uniquely tailored each time to fit precisely with the dramatic intentions of the puppeteer, and kept fresh by the inventiveness of the instrumentalists and singers, who constantly add subtle variations.

BALI

Lying just east of Java, separated by a narrow strait, is the island of Bali, whose unique culture and spectacular natural beauty have fascinated scholars, artists, and tourists from around the world. It is also a place where almost everyone takes part in some activity we would call artistic: music, dance, carving, painting. And while the Balinese demonstrate abilities that often strike the Westerner as spectacular, they maintain that such activities are a normal part of life. The exquisite masked dancer by night may well be a rice farmer by day, and the player of lightning-fast interlocking musical passages accompanying him may manage a small eating stall.

Most of the several million people inhabiting this small island adhere not to Islam, Indonesia's majority religion, but to a blend of Hinduism and Buddhism resembling that which flourished in Java prior to the spread of Islam (ca. 15th-16th centuries C.E.). Though it would be a mistake to believe that what exists in Bali today represents a living museum of Javanese Hindu-Buddhist culture, the Balinese and Javanese share elements of a common cultural heritage. As in Java, we find percussion ensembles known as *gamelan* (or *gambelan*), with metal slab instruments and knobbed gong instruments that look and sound very similar to those of the Javanese *gamelan*. Some of the names are the same (*gendèr, gong, gambang, saron, suling, rebab*) or similar (*kempur, kemong*). Most ensembles employ some version of the *pélog* scale system (some with all seven tones, others with five or six). The accompaniment for Balinese shadow puppetry (as in Java, called *wayang kulit*) employs the *sléndro* scale system, although the instruments used consist only of a quartet of *gendèrs* (augmented by a few other instruments for *Ramayana* stories). Many Balinese pieces employ gong punctuating patterns similar in principle to those of Java. The Balinese play *gamelan* for ritual observances, as in Java, though usually at temple festivals, or in procession to or from them, rather than at someone's residence.

Nevertheless, certain characteristics clearly distinguish the music of these two neighboring cultures. One fundamental difference is that the Balinese maintain a variety of ensembles, each with its distinct instrumentation and associated with certain occasions and functions. There is no single large ensemble that one can simply call "the Balinese *gamelan*." Still, the style of music one hears performed on most ensembles in Bali is (1) strictly instrumental, (2) characterized by changes in tempo and loudness (often abrupt), and (3) requires a dazzling technical mastery by many of the musicians, who play fast interlocking rhythms, often consisting of asymmetrical groupings of two or three very fast beats. People often comment that Balinese music is exciting and dynamic in comparison to other Indonesian musics, exploiting contrasts in the manner of Western art music.

They may also comment on the shimmery quality of the many varieties of bronze ensembles. This quality is obtained by tuning instruments in pairs, with one instrument intentionally tuned slightly higher in pitch than its partner. When sounded together, they produce very fast vibrations. In the West, piano tuners rely on these same vibrations, called "beats," to "temper" the tuning, though on a piano it is intervals that are made intentionally "out of tune," rather than identical strings sounding the same tone. Of course, the intentionally "out-of-tune" pairs of metallophones are perceived to be "in tune" (i.e., "culturally correct") in Bali, just as the piano is in our culture.

The most popular ensemble in Bali today is the *gamelan gong kebyar*, which developed only during the early twentieth century, along with the virtuosic dance it often accompanies (also called *kebyar*—literally "flash," "dazzle"). *Kebyar* music is indeed "flashy," requiring not only great virtuosity of the players but also a consummate sense of "ensemble"—the ability of many to play as one. This music can be heard on any of a number of commercially available recordings (see the discography at the end of this chapter).

Rarer today, though making something of a comeback in modified form after its near extinction seventy years ago with the decline of the Balinese courts, is the *gamelan semar pegulingan* (ill. 7–8). The name has been rendered in English as "gamelan of the love god." It was formerly played for the king's pleasure within the court during the late afternoon and evening, and with slight modification became the favored ensemble to accompany the famous *lègong* (an intricate dance performed by three young girls). It is a rather delicate sounding ensemble, yet unmistakably Balinese. It is this ensemble that the late composer and scholar of Balinese music Colin McPhee heard by chance on early recordings and that enticed him to travel in 1931 to Bali, where he stayed to study Balinese music for nearly ten years.

Listen to "Tabuh Gari" (selection 48), which serves in Bali as a closing piece, a counterpart to the *bubaran* pieces in Java. "Tabuh Gari" begins with an introduction (*pengawit*) in two sections. The first starts in free rhythm (without steady pulse) on the *trompong*, a set of fourteen kettle gongs, like the Javanese *bonang*, but in a single row. The second section (*penyumu*) begins as other instruments join and establish a pulse: at the first sound of the *kempur*, the largest gong in the ensemble, similar to the Javanese *siyem*.

Ill. 7–8. **The *gamelan semar pegulingan* of Teges, Kanyinan, Pliatan, Bali. (Photo courtesy of Richard Wallis.)**

At the next sound of the *kempur* (32 beats after the first), the full ensemble plays the main section (*pengawak*). The main body, which resembles the Javanese *balungan* in its regular, even rhythm, is played on single-octave *gendèr*-type instruments known as *jublags* (or *calungs*). Every fourth tone is stressed by the *jegogans*, which are like the *jublags*, but an octave lower. Delicate and skillful interlocking is performed on higher-pitched instruments of the *gendèr* family (*kantilans* and *gangsas*). Four bamboo flutes (*sulings*) double the faster instrumental parts. Other percussion instruments provide secondary punctuation and emphasis. The *pengawak* stops momentarily at the next *kempur* stroke, only to start up again and repeat. A second pause leads on to the final, livelier section, the *pengecèt*, which is played over and over. The tempo is controlled throughout all sections but the first by the interlocking patterns of two drummers, each playing a double-headed cylindrical drum (*kendang*).

The Balinese have long used a system of notation for recording the melodies of their most sacred pieces, though they do not use notation in performance. The system is based on contrasting vowel sounds, naming tones *dong, déng, dung, dang,* and *ding* (with variants for six- and seven-tone melodies). Since you have already had to learn one new notation system in this chapter, and since it is readily applicable to Balinese as well as Javanese *pélog,* I have decided on notation in Javanese cipher for the main melody (*jublag* part) in the *penyumu, pengawak,* and *pengecèt* sections (ex. 7–19). This may not sound like the "main" melody at first hearing, since the faster-moving and more rhythmically varied elaborations of this melody are more audible throughout. The tempo is roughly forty-eight beats per minute in the *penyumu,* thirty-six beats per minute in the *pengawak,* and sixty-six beats per minute for most of the *pengecèt* (speeding toward the end).

Even in this piece, representing a style of considerable age and what might be called the quieter side of Balinese music, you can hear the shimmering metallic filigree, the asymmetrical rhythms, and the changes in tempo so important to Balinese music. I hope this one brief example has whetted your appetite to explore the incredible variety of Balinese music, which, more than any other Indonesian

Ex. 7–19. "**Tabub Gari,**" **played on** *gamelan Semar Pegulingan.*

```
Introduction (on trompong):                    . . . 5P      P = kempur

Penyemu:      1 3 6 3   1 3 1 5   2 5 2 6   5 6 3 6
              5 6 2 3   5 2 3 5   6 5 3 2   5 3 2 6P

Pengawak:     5 6 1 2̲ *3 2 5 6̲   5 6 1 2̲   3 5 3 5̲      _ = jegogan
              6 5 3 5̲   2 3 5 6̲   5 6 3 5̲   3 6 5 3̲
              1 2 3 2̲   5 6 5 3̲   5 3 1 2̲   1 6 5 3̲
              5 3 5 6̲   5 6 3 5̲   6 5 3 6̲   5 3 1 2̲
              6 1 5 3̲   2 6 1 2̲P  (1st time: . . . 2̲, return to *3, above)
                                  (2nd time: . 5 . 2̲P, move on to pengecèt)

Pengecèt:     3 5̲ 3 2̲P 3 5̲ 3 2̲P  1 6̲ 3 2̲P 1 6̲ 3 2̲P  (repeat many times)
```

tradition, is well represented on records commercially available in Europe and North America.

NORTH SUMATRA

From Bali or Java to North Sumatra is a considerable distance, both culturally and geographically. Though influenced to some degree by Indian culture during the first millennium C.E., the Batak people, the main inhabitants of the province of North Sumatra, now have largely converted to Protestant Christianity or to Islam. The Christian Bataks sing hymns at their Sunday church services with an exuberance and an accuracy of pitch that would put most Western congregations—and even many choirs—to shame. Be that as it may, a variety of indigenous musical genres still thrive among the Batak, and many of these are central to rituals that are only marginally related to Christianity or Islam, if at all. Just as the majority of Javanese Muslims partake in rituals involving *gamelan* music and Hindu-based shadow puppetry, so the Batak Christians adhere in varying degrees to beliefs and ritual practices that were prevalent prior to the coming of Christianity.

Most celebrated of the Batak ensembles are the varieties of percussion and wind ensembles known as *gondang* or *gordang,* which usually include a set of tuned drums that, from a Southeast Asian perspective, can be seen as counterparts to the kettle-gong chimes (*bonang* or *trompong*). These can be heard on several fine recordings available commercially (see Additional Listening). Our brief encounter with music in North Sumatra is from a ritual observance I attended among the Karo Batak, living in the highlands west of Medan and north of the large and beautiful Lake Toba.

A woman in the town of Kabanjahe was planning to open a beauty parlor in part of her house and wished to have the space purified and to secure blessing for her new business by seeking harmony with the spirit world. This she hoped to accomplish by sponsoring and participating in a ceremony involving music and dance and during which she contacted her immediate ancestors through the help of a spirit medium (*datu*). Members of her family gathered, along with sympathetic neighbors (some more orthodox Christians were not so sympathetic) and even a few foreign visitors, including myself. To my surprise I was urged to take photographs and record the event, and with what little equipment I had brought with me, I did so.

The ceremony lasted for nearly five hours, with several long sections of continuous music. Family members and some neighbors joined the woman in a traditional line dance. The *datu* sang incantations, sometimes while dancing. He spoke gently to the woman and sometimes loudly to the spirits. With some difficulty the woman was eventually able to go into trance and the evening was deemed a success.

The musical group engaged for the evening was a small ensemble performing *gendang keteng-keteng,* a form of traditional Batak music employing a small two-stringed, boat-shaped lute (*kulcapi*), two bamboo tube zithers (*keteng-keteng*) and a porcelain bowl (*mangkuk*). On each of the tube zithers, thin strips had been cut and stretched, forming taut filaments. To one filament on each was attached a small bamboo disc. These remarkable instruments sound a kind of interlocking percussive filigree. But in addition, when the filaments with the discs are struck, they vibrate over a hole cut in the bamboo and produce a deep, vibrato sound remarkably like a small gong. The ensemble played continually for many hours, with the *datu* singing part of the time. Melody, filling in, gong punctuation—here were the essential elements, it seemed, for music-making not only throughout much of Indonesia but also much of Southeast Asia.

The few excerpts I provide in recorded selection 49 cannot give a real sense of the long ritual, but at least they offer an introduction to musical sounds that contrast with the *gamelan* ensembles we have heard and yet bear a certain distant likeness to them. The first excerpt is from the early part of the ceremony. The *kulcapi* player, Tukang Ginting, provides what is basically a repeating, cyclic melody that he varies (see ill. 7–9). The "clickety" sounds are the two percussionists playing the bamboo *keteng-keteng* instruments, filling in the texture to give a constant "busy" sound, which seems to characterize much music throughout Indonesia (see ill. 7–10). What is especially remarkable, in light of the other music we have heard, is the way in which the porcelain bowl and the gong sound relate. The gong sound occurs at regular time intervals, as one so often finds in Java and in Bali. It is subdivided by the porcelain bowl sound, which we hear coinciding with the gong sound and at the midpoint between them—like a *kenong* subdividing and coinciding with a gong in Java.

The second excerpt is taken from a climactic moment in the evening when the woman first thought she was going into trance. (She did not succeed at this point, but did an hour or so later.) The musical intensity has increased by compressing the time interval between gong beats; the tempo speeds and then doubles during this excerpt. The porcelain bowl consistently subdivides the time between gong beats, even in the very fast portion, resembling structurally the *wayang kulit* music of Java (like the "Playon" we studied earlier).

With its gong punctuation, coincidence, cyclic melody, binary rhythms, and fast-moving and dense percussion playing, this music seems clearly a relative of the *gamelan* music we heard earlier. I have intentionally stressed the similarities, but it is important to realize that these are *structural* similarities, easy to identify from a theoretical perspective. However, the differences are profound enough that the Batak and Javanese care little for each other's music. To the Javanese, clacking bamboo is no substitute for the varied drum strokes of the *kendhang,* the interlocking melodies of the *bonang,* or the heterophonic wanderings of the various soft-ensemble instruments in the Javanese *gamelan.* To the Batak, the thick-textured and often mighty sound of the full Javanese *gamelan* cannot afford the personal intimacy of the small *kulcapi* ensemble, nor the spontaneity of the *kulcapi* player that we hear in these excerpts.

Perhaps with these few examples of traditional music from several regions of Indonesia you begin to gain an understanding of the national motto *Bhinneka Tunggal Ika*—a phrase in Old Javanese meaning "Unity in Diversity." In the arts we indeed find great variety, but underlying elements shared by these arts attest

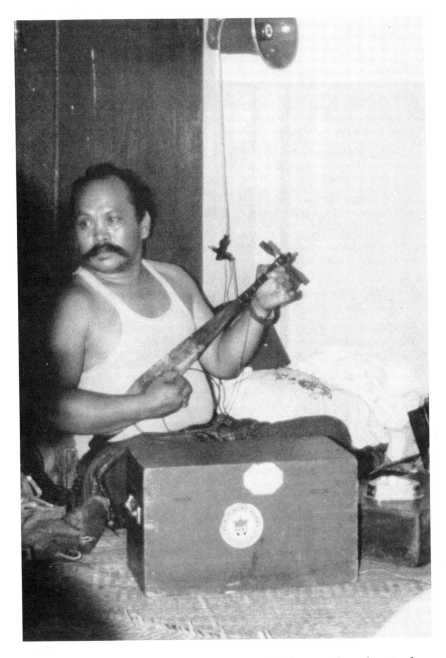

Ill. 7–9.   Tukang Ginting plays the Karo Batak *kulcapi*, Kabanjabe, North Sumatra. (Photo by R. Anderson Sutton.)

Ill. 7–10.   Members of Tukang Ginting's *gendang keteng-keteng* **group, playing the bamboo tube zither** *(keteng-keteng)*, **Kabanjabe, North Sumatra. (Photo by R. Anderson Sutton.)**

to the appropriateness of the motto. As we turn to examples of recent popular music, we find another layer of Indonesia's musical diversity—one to which many Indonesians are exposed and one that is especially meaningful to younger Indonesians from many regions.

INDONESIAN POPULAR MUSIC

Most of the music Indonesians would identify as "popular" is, like most popular music anywhere in the world, characterized by the use of at least some Western instruments and Western harmony (see Hatch 1989). It is disseminated through the mass media, performed by recognized stars, and is essentially a "commercial" genre. Without going into the interesting history of Western-influenced music in Indonesia, which has primarily been in the popular vein, I would like to introduce two varieties of contemporary popular music that represent contrasting orientations within the "pop" music world in Indonesia. We will consider one key representative superstar from each.

The first variety is called *dangdut*, in imitation of the sound formerly made on hand drums and more recently on trap set and electric guitar. The musician known during the 1970s and 1980s as the "king of *dangdut*" is Rhoma Irama. Born in 1947 in West Java, he learned to play electric guitar and showed greater interest in music than in the formal schooling his mother was struggling to pay for. In his late teens he dropped out of school and joined the underground music movement, heavily influenced by Western rock (and banned by then-president Sukarno).

Rhoma soon became disenchanted with rock. By his own account, he then consciously set out to create a sound that would satisfy the craving of Indonesian youth for a "modern" musical style, but that would at the same time sound clearly Indonesian (or at least "Eastern") in contrast to Western rock (Frederick 1982:109). He turned to a Western-influenced genre, *orkès melayu* music, whose origins are traced to the urban areas of North and West Sumatra and which incorporated influences from the soundtracks of the many Indian films that have long enjoyed wide popularity in Indonesia (compare "Engal kalyanam" from chapter 6 [recorded selection 40]). Even with its quasi-Western harmonic basis, this music was clearly "Eastern," characterized by highly ornamented singing and flute playing.

Rhoma Irama set out to make a commercial mark, and he succeeded spectacularly. Like most pop stars, he has sung about love, but he has also presented forthrightly his own ideas about his country and, perhaps most persistently, about his religion. He was one of the first Indonesian popular artists to make the pilgrimage to Mecca, and has used both his music and his films to spread his Islamic message. One of his first hits (1977) was a piece about greed, entitled "Rupiah" (the national currency). It was banned by government officials, who thought it "debased the national currency" (Frederick 1982:117). Another early song, also banned, was "Hak Azasi" ("Basic Rights"), which described human rights—including freedom of religion and freedom of speech.

Listen to "Begadang II" (recorded selection 50; fig. 7–4), which was the most popular song of 1978 and established Rhoma as a star. The song bears the same title as the hit film for which it served as the theme song. *Begadang* is a Jakarta term for staying up all or most of the night, usually to socialize with friends. Not only does this serve as a typical example of the *dangdut* musical sound as Rhoma Irama developed it, but the text shows his clear orientation toward lower-class youth. Like most of his music, it appeals to the youthful urge to dance and is often used to accompany popular social dancing akin to rock or disco dancing in the West.

Eighteen years after this big hit, Rhoma Irama is still producing top-selling cassettes and has starred in a number of films in which—to the chagrin of more conservative Indonesian Muslims—he proselytizes for Islam through his loud, electric *dangdut* music. Unlikely as it may seem, then, Rhoma Irama is an Islamic rock star, and an enormous commercial success. His passion for communicating his vision of a more perfect society, holding closely to the teaching of Islam, has led him into the realm of politics. In 1982 he endorsed the Islamic opposition party and played at a rally in Jakarta that erupted in violence shortly before the elections took place. Yet recently he has, most likely with some reluctance, joined the incumbent party and even played at functions of the very body that has represented the clearest threat to Islamic political power in Indonesia: the army.

Apa artinya malam minggu	What good is Saturday night
Bagi orang yang tidak mampu?	For those who are not well-to-do?
Mau ke pesta tak beruang;	Want to go to a party, but have no money;
Akhirnya nongkrong di pinggir jalan.	Wind up squatting by the side of the road.
Begadang, marilah kita begadang,	Stay up, let's stay up,
Begadang sambil berdendang;	Stay up and sing;
Walaupun kita tidak punya uang	Even though we don't have money
Kita juga bisa senang.	We can still have fun.
Bagi mereka yang punya uang	Those who have money
Berdansa-dansi di nite club;	Dance at night clubs;
Bagi kita yang tak punya uang	Those of us who have no money
Cukup berjoget disini.	Just dance here [by the road].
Bagi mereka yang punya uang	Those who have money
Makan-makan di restoran;	Always eat in nice restaurants;
Bagi kita yang tak punya uang	Those of us who have no money
Makannya di warung kopi.	Just eat at makeshift roadside stalls.

Fig. 7–4.   Lyrics to "Begadang II."

From Rhoma's *dangdut,* we now turn to a genre sometimes known as *pop berat* (literally "heavy pop"; see Hatch 1989) or sometimes as *pop kreatif* ("creative pop"), represented by Guruh Sukarnoputra. Contrasting in many ways with Rhoma Irama and the many other *dangdut* singers, Guruh is of the elite. He is the youngest living son of the founding father of the Republic of Indonesia, President Sukarno. Born in 1953, Guruh was raised in the presidential palace in Jakarta, college educated, and formally trained not only in piano but in traditional Javanese and Balinese *gamelan.* Like his father, Guruh feels an intense patriotism that at times seems to blind him to the glaring inequities in contemporary Indonesian society. And, again like his father, Guruh is far from orthodox Islam and sees Indonesia's culture as pluralistic and inescapably mixed with influences from the West. But where President Sukarno wielded power like a latter-day god-king with a matchless gift of oratory, Guruh does so through his music.

It was after his father's death in 1970 that Guruh began his musical career, playing first with a pop music group in Jakarta. After several years of architectural study in Holland, he formed his innovative and highly acclaimed Guruh Gipsy group. In early 1977 he released the *Guruh Gipsy* cassette, which one critic later called the most important Indonesian cassette of the 1970s. Here Guruh demonstrates musically his penchant for unusual juxtapositions and superimpositions of Western and Indonesian elements. And he also demonstrates a worldly musical sophistication, with arrangements drawing on a full spectrum of American popular styles from circus music to Motown soul music, 1930s crooning to 1980s heavy metal. Where Rhoma Irama's music is consistently *dangdut,* with little variety in instrumentation or conception, the music of Guruh Gipsy sounds radically different from one cut to the next and often even within one single piece. It is a music for listening, not for casual social dancing.

Listen to the several excerpts from a lengthy (sixteen-minute) piece entitled "Indonesia Maharddhika," which translates as "Indonesia [is] Free," using an intentionally archaic word for "free": the Sanskrit-sounding *maharddhika*, rather than the modern Indonesian *merdeka* (recorded selection 51; fig. 7–5). The first excerpt combines acid rock, a gapped scale closely resembling *pélog*, and Old Javanese poetry. The second presents a combination of interlocking Balinese metallophones (*gangsas*) with electric guitar and synthesizer, and the third an optimistic, patriotic text with episodic breaks. Traditional Javanese court poets often incorporated their names within their poems by means of a device known as *sandhi asma* (literally "hidden name"), whereby the first syllable of each line was part of the author's name. Guruh uses the device, constructing the lines of poetry so that the first syllables or first letters conceal the first names of members of Guruh Gipsy: Oding, Roni, Chris, and Guruh.

Since the release of this important cassette, Guruh's music has become increasingly less experimental, but remains both sophisticated and eclectic. More recent cassettes show influences from driving disco music, sassy Broadway musicals, soft Brazilian sambas, stirring Sousa marches, late Romantic opera, and even the dissonant orchestral sonorities of twentieth-century Western concert music. He has mounted a number of spectacular performances, which combine such blatant signs of patriotism as red and white costumes (the national colors) and incessant flag-waving on stage, with music performed by a variety of popular stars. These shows have been fantastically expensive by Indonesian standards, some costing over $100,000, with tickets priced far beyond the reach of any but the most wealthy. Guruh's musical expressions of patriotism have drawn considerable criticism from the press, who have labeled it both "elitist" and "naive."

Guruh and Rhoma Irama are but two of several hundred pop stars in Indonesia today. The contrasts between them and between their musical sounds can begin to give you an idea of the complexity of Indonesia's popular music—still

A: (In Old Javanese language)
Om awighnam astu
*DING*aryan ring sasi karo
*RO*hinikanta padem
*NI*citha redite prathama . . .

B: Instrumental (Balinese *gamelan* with electric guitars and synthesizer)

C: (In Indonesian language)
*C*erah gilang gemilang	Clear and bright
*H*arapan masa datang	The hope for the coming era
*R*ukun damai mulia	Harmonious, peaceful, glorious
*I*ndonesia tercinta	Beloved Indonesia
*S*elamat sejahtera	Safe and prosperous
*GU*nung langit samudra	Mountain, sky, ocean
RUH semesta memuja.	The whole spirit worships.

Fig. 7–5.   Excerpts from "Indonesia Maharddhika."

mostly unexplored by research scholars. Despite his recent political shift, Rhoma is a strong Muslim. His roots are humble, and he speaks to the disenfranchised masses. Guruh's public persona is enigmatic, even meek, his religions beliefs more syncretic. His tastes in songwriting and stage production, combined with his direct descent from a leader of mythical stature (the father of the country) make him a very different sort of pop figure altogether. Rhoma's songs are more straightforward than Guruh's. The texts are clearly audible, like the throbbing beat of his *dangdut* music, and their meaning obvious. Guruh's are more complex; he often chooses obscure words and unusual musical elements. Where Rhoma's music has consistently and consciously been molded by mass taste and has been popular throughout the entire nation, Guruh's has had to build its own following, mostly among urban elite youth on Java.

Yet both of these stars have drawn on Indonesia's regional traditions, and they have aspired to use their music to do more than entertain. Both offer spiritual guidance to their listeners and followers. Rhoma sees himself as a powerful spokesman for Islam, Guruh for the past glory and future hopes of the nation. Both have expressed some dissatisfaction with things as they are. Ultimately they both acknowledge their social identities in the styles of music they make. Each "knows his social place"—and maintains a separate artistic style as a result. Yet Indonesia prides itself on the ability to tolerate diversity and to achieve coexistence. Through even these two pop music stars we glimpse that diversity and find that it applies not only to traditional regional culture but also to popular music disseminated nationally.

REFERENCES CITED

Becker, Judith
    1979 "Time and Tune in Java." In *The Imagination of Reality: Essays in Southeast Asian Coherence Systems,* ed. A. L. Becker and Aram A. Yengoyan, 197–210. Norwood, N.J.: Ablex.

    ———.
    1980 *Traditional Music in Modern Java: Gamelan in a Changing Society.* Honolulu: Univ. Press of Hawaii.

    ———.
    1981 "Hindu-Buddhist Time in Javanese Gamelan Music." In *The Study of Time,* vol. 4, ed. J. F. Fraser. New York: Springer-Verlag.

    ———.
    1988 "Earth, Fire, *Sakti,* and the Javanese Gamelan." *Ethnomusicology* 32(3):385–91.
Frederick, William
    1982 "Rhoma Irama and the Dangdut Style: Aspects of Contemporary Indonesian Popular Culture." *Indonesia* 34:103–30.
Hatch, Martin
    1989 "Popular Music in Indonesia (1983)." In *World Music, Politics and Social Change,* ed. Simon Frith, 47–67. Manchester: Univ. Press.

Hoffman, Stanley B.
   1978   "Epistemology and Music: A Javanese Example." *Ethnomusicology* 22(1):69–88.

Hood, Mantle
   1954   *The Nuclear Theme as a Determinant of Paṭet in Javanese Music.* Groningen, Netherlands: J. B. Wolters.

Kunst, Jaap
   1973   *Music in Java: Its History, Its Theory, and Its Technique.* 2 vols. 3rd rev. ed. by Ernst Heins. The Hague: Martinus Nijhoff.

Surjodiningrat, Wasisto, P. J. Sudarjana, and Adhi Susanto
   1972   *Tone Measurements of Outstanding Javanese Gamelans in Jogjakarta and Surakarta.* Yogyakarta: Gadjah Mada Univ. Press.

ADDITIONAL READING

ON MUSIC:

Becker, Judith, and Alan Feinstein, eds.
   1984, 1987, & 1988   *Karawitan: Source Readings in Javanese Gamelan and Vocal Music.* 3 vols. Ann Arbor: Univ. of Michigan Center for South & Southeast Asian Studies.

Hood, Mantle, and Hardja Susilo
   1967   *Music of the Venerable Dark Cloud: Introduction, Commentary, and Analysis.* Los Angeles: Univ. of California Press.

Kartomi, Margaret
   1980   "Musical Strata in Java, Bali, and Sumatra." In *Musics of Many Cultures,* ed. Elizabeth May, 111–33. Berkeley: Univ. of California Press.

Lindsay, Jennifer
   1992   *Javanese Gamelan: Traditional Orchestra of Indonesia.* 2nd ed. New York: Oxford Univ. Press.

Manuel, Peter
   1988   *Popular Musics of the Non-Western World: An Introductory Survey.* New York: Oxford Univ. Press (esp. pp. 205–20).

McPhee, Colin
   1966   *Music in Bali.* New Haven, Conn.: Yale Univ. Press.

Simon, Artur
   1984   "Functional Changes in Batak Traditional Music and Its Role in Modern Indonesian Society." *Asian Music* 15(2):58–66.

Sumarsam
   1995   *Gamelan: Cultural Interaction and Musical Development in Central Java.* Chicago: Univ. of Chicago Press.

Sutton, R. Anderson
   1987   "Identity and Individuality in an Ensemble Tradition: the Female Vocalist in Java." In *Women and Music in Cross-Cultural Perspective,* ed. Ellen Koskoff,

111–30. Westport, Conn.: Greenwood Press. Reprint. Urbana: Univ. of Illinois Press, 1989.

———.
    1991   *Traditions of Gamelan Music in Java: Musical Pluralism and Regional Identity.* Cambridge: Cambridge Univ. Press.

Tenzer, Michael
    1991   *Balinese Music.* Berkeley, Calif., and Singapore: Periplus.

Vetter, Roger
    1981   "Flexibility in the Performance Practice of Central Javanese Music." *Ethnomusicology* 25(2):199–214.

ON INDONESIA:

Anderson, Benedict R. O'G.
    1965   *Mythology and the Tolerance of the Javanese.* Ithaca, N.Y.: Cornell Modern Indonesia Project.

Becker, A. L.
    1979   "Text Building, Epistemology, and Aesthetics in Javanese Shadow Theater." In *The Imagination of Reality: Essays in Southeast Asian Coherence Systems,* ed. A. L. Becker and Aram A. Yengoyan, 211–43. Norwood, N.J.: Ablex.

Geertz, Clifford
    1960   *The Religion of Java.* New York: Free Press.

Holt, Claire
    1967   *Art in Indonesia: Continuities and Change.* Ithaca, N.Y.: Cornell Univ. Press.

Keeler, Ward
    1987   *Javanese Shadow Plays, Javanese Selves.* Princeton, N.J.: Princeton Univ. Press.

Ricklefs, M. C.
    1993   *A History of Modern Indonesia since c. 1300.* 2nd ed. Stanford, Calif.: Stanford Univ. Press.

ADDITIONAL LISTENING

JAVA:

Court Music of Kraton Surakarta. World Music Library KICC 5151.

The Gamelan of Cirebon. World Music Library KICC 5130.

Gamelan Garland: Music from the Mangkunegaran at Surakarta. Performed on Gamelan Kjai Kanjut Mesem. Fontana 858 614 FPY.

Gamelan Music from Java. Recorded in the Kraton, Surakarta. Philips 831 209 PY.

Indonesian Popular Music: Kroncong, Dangdut, and Langgam Jawa. Smithsonian Folkways SF 40056.

Java: Gamelans from the Sultan's Palace in Jogjakarta. Musical Traditions in Asia. Archiv 2723 017.

Java: Historic Gamelans, Unesco Collection, Musical Sources, Art Music from Southeast Asia Series, IX-2. Philips 6586 004.

Java: "Langen Mandra Wanara," Opéra de Danuredjo VII. Musiques traditionelles vivantes III. Ocora 558 507/9.

Javanese Court Gamelan from the Pura Paku Alaman, Jogyakarta. Nonesuch Explorer Series H–72044.

Javanese Court Gamelan, Vol. II. Recorded at the Istana Mangkunegaran, Surakarta. Nonesuch Explorer Series H–72074.

Javanese Court Gamelan, Vol. III, recorded at the Kraton, Yogyakarta. Nonesuch Explorer Series H–72083.

The Music of K. R. T. Wasitodiningrat. CMP Records CD 3007.

Music from the Outskirts of Jakarta: Gambang Kromong. Smithsonian Folkways SF 40057.

Music of the Venerable Dark Cloud: The Javanese Gamelan Khjai Mendung. Institute of Ethnomusicology, UCLA. IER–7501. (Performed by UCLA study group, mostly Americans; recorded in Los Angeles.)

Musiques popularies d'Indonésie: Folk Music from West-Java. Anthologie de la musique populaire. Ocora OCR 46. (Various Sundanese genres.)

Sangkala. Icon 5501 (Distributed by Elektra/Asylum).

Songs before Dawn: Gandrung Banyuwangi. Smithsonian Folkways SF 40055.

The Sultan's Pleasure: Javanese Gamelan & Vocal Music. Music of the World T-116.

Street Music of Central Java, recorded in Yogyakarta. Lyrichord LLST-7310.

BALI:

Bali: Court and Banjar Music. UNESCO Collection, Musical Sources, Art Music from South-East Asia, IX–1. Philips 6586 008.

Balinese Theatre and Dance Music. UNESCO Collection, Musical Sources, Art Music from South-East Asia, X–1. Philips 6586 013.

Gamelan Music of Bali. Lyrichord LLST–7179.

Gamelan Semar Pegulingan: Gamelan of the Love God. Recorded in Teges Kanyinan, Pliatan, Bali. Nonesuch Explorer Series H–72046.

Kecak from Bali. Kecak Ganda Sari. Bridge BCD 9019.

Music for the Balinese Shadow Play: Gendèr Wayang from Teges Kanyinan, Pliatan, Bali. Nonesuch Explorer Series H–72037.

Golden Rain. Nonesuch Explorer Series H–72028.

Music from the Morning of the World. Nonesuch Explorer Series H–72015.

OTHER INDONESIAN ISLANDS:

The Angkola People of Sumatra. An Anthology of South-East Asian Music. Institute for Musicology, University of Basle. Bärenreiter–Musicaphon BM 30 L 22568 LC 0522.

Batak of North Sumatra. New Albion Records NA 046 CD.

Gendang Karo, Nord Sumatra/Indonesia. Museum Collection Berlin (West) MC 13; 66.28321 01/2.

Gondang Toba, Nord Sumatra/Indonesia. Museum Collection Berlin (West) MC 12; 66.28287 01/2.

Music of Madura. Ode Record Company CD ODE 1381.

Music of Nias and North Sumatra: Hoho, Gendang Karo, Gondang Toba. Smithsonian Folkways SF 40429.

Les Musiques de Célèbes Indonésie: Musique Toraja et Bugis. Anthologie de la musique des peuples. Société Française de Productions Phonographiques, Paris. AMP 7 2906.

Cassette recordings of most popular and traditional musical genres from Indonesia are widely available in Indonesia, where they are sold commercially. The Modern Indonesian Cultures Collection at the University of Wisconsin-Madison includes a collection of nearly 1,000 such cassettes, representing a broad cross-section of what is available, particularly in Java and Sumatra.

ADDITIONAL VIEWING

Karya: Video Portraits of Four Indonesian Composers (videorecording), 1992. Directed and produced by Jody Diamond. Distributed by American Gamelan Institute, Box 5036, Hanover, NH 03755. Balinese, Javanese, and Batak composers talk about their recent work.

The JVC Video Anthology of World Music and Dance (videorecording), 1990. Edited by Fujii Tomoaki, with assistant editors Omori Yasuhiro and Sakurai Tetsuo; in collaboration with the National Museum of Ethnology (Osaka); produced by Ichikawa Katsumori, directed by Nakagawa Kunihiko and Ichihashi Yuji. Victor Company of Japan, Ltd., in collaboration with Smithsonian Folkways Recordings. Distributed by Rounder Records, Cambridge, MA 02140. 30 videocassettes + guide.

Volume 9 contains footage of Javanese shadow puppetry (poor quality), along with studio footage of Balinese *kecak* ("monkey chant") and Sundanese music (recorded in Japan).

Volume 10 contains a variety of Balinese examples, recorded in Bali, mostly employing a *gamelan semar pegulingan* (even for contexts in which this ensemble is not appropriate).

BALI:

Bali Beyond the Postcard (16mm film and VHS videorecording), 1991. Produced and directed by Nancy Dine, Peggy Stern, and David Dawkins. Distributed by Filmakers Library, New York, NY; and by 'Outside in July', 59 Barrow Street, New York, NY 10014. *Gamelan* and dance in four generations of a Balinese family.

Compressed Version of a "Gambuh" (Dance Drama) in Batuan (16mm film), 1981. Produced by T. Seebass and G. van der Weijden. Distributed by Institut für den Wissenschaftlichen Film, Göttingen, Germany. Performance of *gambuh,* 'classical' Balinese dance-drama.

Releasing the Spirits: A Village Cremation in Bali (VHS videorecording), 1991 [1981]. Directed by Patsy Asch, Linda Connor, *et al.* Distributed by Documentary Educational Resources, Watertown, MA. Cremation rituals in a central Balinese village.

Shadowmaster (16mm film, and VHS videorecording), 1980. Directed by Larry Reed, distributed by Larry Reed Productions, 18 Chattanooga Street, San Francisco, CA 94114. A fiction film about the social and artistic life of a Balinese shadow puppeteer in contemporary Bali.

JAVA:

Bird of Passage (16mm film), 1986. Directed by Fons Grasveld. Distributed by Netherlands Film Institute, Postbus 515, 1200 AM Hilversum, The Netherlands. Javanese traditions in Java, Suriname, and the Netherlands.

The Dancer and the Dance (16mm film and videorecording), [1990?]. Produced by Felicia Hughes-Freeland. Distributed by Film Officer, Royal Anthropological Institute, 50 Fitzroy Street, London, England W1P 5HS. Javanese court dance in its current social context.

Traditional Dances of Indonesia, Dances of Jogjakarta, Central Java: Langen Mandra Wanara (videorecording), 1990 [from 16mm film made in 1975]. Directed and produced by William Heick. Distributed by University of California Extension Media Center, 2176 Shattuck Ave., Berkeley, CA 94704. Dance-opera presenting episode from the *Ramayana.*

Traditional Dances of Indonesia, Dances of Surakarta, Central Java: Srimpi Anglir Mendung (videorecording), 1990 [from 16mm film made in 1976]. Directed and produced by William Heick. Distributed by University of California Extension Media Center, 2176 Shattuck Ave., Berkeley, CA 94704. Refined female court dance.

(Ten additional videorecordings from the same distributor present additional dances from Java, as well as dances from Bali and West Sumatra.)

NORTH SUMATRA:

Karo-Batak (Indonesien, Nordsumatra)—Gendang—Musik "mari-mari" und "patam-patam." (16mm film), 1994. Directed by Artur Simon. Distributed by Institut für den Wissenschaftlichen Film, Göttingen, Germany. Ceremonial music performed by *gendang keteng-keteng* ensemble.

Karo-Batak (Indonesien, Nordsumatra)—Tänze anlässlich einer Haarwaschzeremonie in Kuta Mbelin (16mm film), 1994. Directed by Franz Simon and Artur Simon. Distributed by Institut für den Wissenschaftlichen Film, Göttingen, Germany. Dances associated with the hair-washing ceremony of Kuta Mbelin, North Sumatra.

(Fourteen additional films from the same distributor cover performing arts of Karo and other Batak groups in North Sumatra and of Kayan-Dayak groups in West Kalimantan [Borneo].)

CHAPTER EIGHT

East Asia/Japan

LINDA FUJIE

Present-day Japan impresses the first-time visitor as an intense, fascinating, and sometimes confusing combination of old and new, of Eastern and Western and things beyond categorization (see fig. 8–1). Strolling through the Ginza area of Tokyo, for example, you find many colorful remnants of an earlier age sprinkled among the gigantic department stores and elegant boutiques; and always there is the ubiquitous McDonald's (pronounced *Makudonarudosu*). Tiny noodle shops and old stores selling kimono material or fine china carry the atmosphere of a past era. Looming over a central boulevard, in the midst of modern office buildings, is the Kabuki-za, a large, impressive theater built in the traditional style.

As the visitor begins to sense from the streets of Japan's capital, many aspects of Japanese life today—from architecture to social attitudes to music—are an intriguing mix of the traditional and the foreign. Japan has absorbed cultural influences from outside her borders for centuries, many of which originate in other parts of Asia. The writing system comes from China, and one of the major religions, Buddhism, is from India, through Korea and China. Connections with Chinese and Korean music and musical instruments are a fundamental part of the history of traditional music in Japan.° In the late nineteenth and twentieth centuries, European and American ideas and objects have also had a major impact on Japanese culture.

Although cultural borrowing has clearly been important in Japanese history, the worn-out stereotype of the Japanese as "mere imitators" must also be laid aside. The Japanese have developed a unique culture, both through their own creativity and by imaginatively adapting foreign elements into their own culture. During much of her history, geographical and political circumstances have isolated Japan to the extent that such independent creativity and adaptation were necessary. A group of islands separated from the Asian continent by an often

°In this chapter, "traditional music" in relation to Japan will refer to those musical genres developed mainly in pre-Meiji Japan—that is, before 1868 and the beginning of a period of strong Western influence on Japanese music.

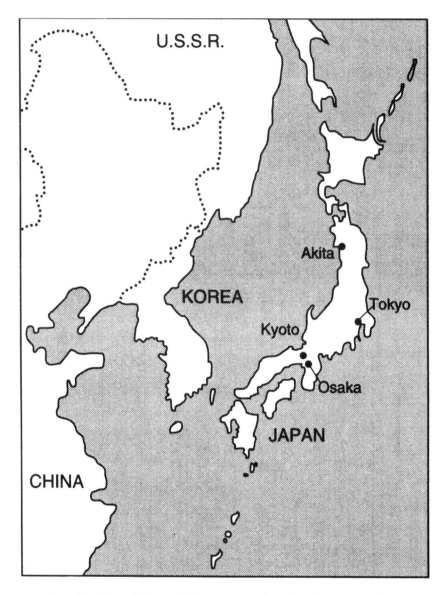

Fig. 8–1.   Map of Japan. Cities mentioned in this chapter are shown.

treacherous sea, Japan set herself apart for several centuries. This isolation reached its height in the Tokugawa, or Edo, period (1600–1867), when Japan's borders were mostly closed to the outside world. Many customs and ideas that we consider "traditionally Japanese" were developed during this period. Most traditional music presented in this chapter, for instance, dates from the Tokugawa period, though its roots may go back farther.

On the whole, Japan's culture combines a deep respect for tradition with creativity and flexibility. Many layers of culture, musical and otherwise, exist side by side, different yet harmonious. One sign of this diversity lies in the music the Japanese listen to today.

LISTENING HABITS
OF CONTEMPORARY JAPANESE

In concert halls, theaters, clubs, and bars, Japanese looking for entertainment find all kinds of live musical performances: Japanese traditional music, Western classical music, rock, jazz, punk, country and western, and music from around the world. In addition, television, radio, tapes, and compact discs provide recorded music of every imaginable type.

The kinds of music Japanese most enjoy listening to and performing usually vary by the age of the listener.° Japanese children learn to play the recorder and sing European, American, and Japanese folk songs in their schools; many also take private lessons on a Western musical instrument. Children learn and sing theme songs from television shows and commercials, and these sometimes become hit records. As teenagers, many Japanese listen to the latest hits from the West as well as to Japanese popular music. Teenagers know a great deal about the latest developments in sound technology and spend more on music—recordings and equipment—than any other segment of the population. Among young adults, tastes tend toward the more mellow popular music genres, such as contemporary folk and so-called golden oldies, or Western classical music or traditional folk songs. At this stage in life, singing with the *karaoke* machine can become an important form of musical entertainment. Middle-aged adults like to listen to older Japanese and Western popular songs, Western classical music, and Japanese folk songs. Along with older people, the middle-aged are most likely to enjoy traditional Japanese music, which they hear on television and at live performances.

Given the high quality of audio and video equipment available in contemporary Japan, it is not surprising that people use the mass media for most of their music listening. About one in four Japanese listens to music solely through television sets (NHK 1982:38). Each week, Japanese public and private television stations broadcast a dozen or more music-variety shows. Many of these feature popular music, but some offer performances of *kabuki* theater, Western opera, or symphonies. Young people in particular listen to music on cassette tape players, compact discs, and the radio (NHK 1982:47). Japanese also listen to many live performances featuring both Japanese and foreign performers. On the whole, however, Japanese listening is similar to that in many other highly industrialized countries: the people listen more to recorded music than to live performances, and they are not always fully attentive to it. Music is heard in the background of

---

°The following statements are based on the results of a comprehensive survey of Japanese musical tastes made in 1981 (NHK 1982:68–77).

everyday life, whether it is Muzak in a coffee shop or music coming from a radio or television set kept on while people go about their normal activities.

In the last hundred years, the Japanese have become more involved with new music, devoting less time to traditional music. Since the Meiji period (1868–1911) Western music has been influential, and its spread has been officially encouraged through the education system. Despite the overwhelming influence of music from outside Japan, however, traditional music remains viable. The *kabuki* and *bunraku* theaters in the larger cities are still well attended, as are concerts of traditional instrumental and vocal music. Teachers of instruments such as the *shakuhachi* and the *shamisen* still find many interested pupils of all ages, and televised instruction for such instruments in recent years has helped bolster their popularity. Perhaps the large amount of Western influence has made young people more appreciative of the different beauty of Japanese music and its special relationship to Japanese history and culture.

GENERAL CHARACTERISTICS OF JAPANESE TRADITIONAL MUSIC

To begin to understand traditional Japanese music it is helpful to examine its general characteristics. There are exceptions to these generalizations, but they should be used as a point of reference for the musical examples that follow.

PITCH/SCALES

Like Western music, Japanese music divides the octave into twelve tones. The Japanese tonal system is based on the Chinese system, which in turn developed in a similar way to the Pythagorian system of the West. These notes, when put in pitch sequence, represent an untempered chromatic scale of 12 semitones. While equal temperament has strongly influenced contemporary performers, the exact intervals between notes still differ in traditional music according to genre, school, the piece performed, and the individual performer (Koizumi 1974:73). No single set of pitches is used by all musicians. For example, the mode system used in *gagaku* (orchestra music derived from T'ang China) differs from that used in music for the *koto* (a thirteen-stringed zither). The *gagaku* modal system is linked to Chinese systems, while the *koto* system developed several centuries later in Japan.

Considering this diversity in scale systems, it is not surprising that music historians have developed a wide range of theories to describe them. According to one of the traditional theories, much Japanese music (excluding older genres like *gagaku* and Buddhist chanting) is based on two pentatonic scales, either with or without semitones. The scale used frequently in music for the *koto* and the *shamisen* (a three-stringed lute) is called the *in* scale and contains semitones (e.g., D, E♭, G, A, B♭). The *yo* scale, without semitones (D, E, G, A, B), is often heard in folk songs and early popular songs such as "Nonki-bushi" (recorded selection 56). These scales are shown in example 8–1 with their auxiliary notes in parentheses.

Ex. 8–1. *In* **and** *yo* **scales**

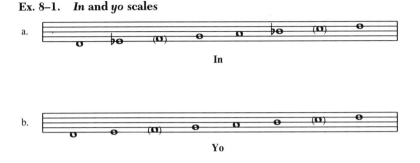

In

Yo

A more recent theory holds that the traditional concept of the pentatonic scale (such as the *in* and *yo* scales) does not adequately explain what is found in the music itself. Instead, it is more useful to interpret Japanese music on the basis of "nuclear tones," located a fourth part, and the main notes that appear between them (Koizumi 1974:76). Actually, the pitches thus produced are the same in the genres of music mentioned above: the *miyako-bushi* scale applies to *koto* and *shamisen* music and the *minyō* scale is found in folk song (ex. 8–2). What is new in this theory is the emphasis on fourths. In fact, much melodic movement tends to emphasize this interval (e.g., the use of *miyako-bushi* nuclear tones in "Hakusen no," recorded selection 53).

TIMBRE

The Japanese aesthetic sense favors the use of a broad range of sounds and tone qualities in their music. In particular, "unpitched" sounds are commonly heard in the middle of instrumental melodies. When we hear a sound wave with a stable frequency, it is easy for us to distinguish pitch. But if the frequency varies too quickly, we do not hear a pitch. A cymbal, for example, is unpitched compared to an oboe. In Japanese music, examples of unpitched sound include the very breathy sound made on the *shakuhachi* bamboo flute, or the hard twang produced when the plectrum strikes the *shamisen* lute. Just as Japanese poetry is full

Ex. 8–2. *Miyako-bushi* **and** *minyō* **scales**

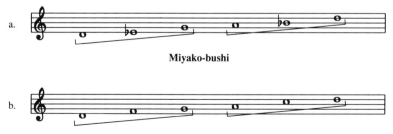

Miyako-bushi

Minyō

of appreciation for unpitched sounds of nature such as water flowing or trees whispering in the wind, Japanese music recreates such sounds for the enjoyment of their listeners. (An example of this characteristic can be heard in recorded selection 52, "Tsuru no sugomori.")

MELODY/HARMONY

The diversity of Japanese melodies makes generalization difficult—the melodies of folk songs differ greatly in rhythm, pitch, and structure from those of *shakuhachi* music, for example. Japanese melodies often contain short motifs that are repeated, in part or in their entirety, throughout a piece. (See, for example, recorded selection 53, "Hakusen no," in which segments of phrases are repeated and varied.) In the theater, quoting melodic patterns from other contexts is a favorite device to inform the audience of the thoughts of a character or to foreshadow an upcoming event. Complete repetition of phrases sometimes occurs at the beginning and end of a piece, such as in the *shamisen* accompaniment to "Hakusen no," thereby lending an air of finality to the conclusion.

In the *shakuhachi* piece (recorded selection 52) the pitch movement in the melody strikes the non-Japanese listener as extremely slow; in fact, the dynamic and timbre changes give the melody its life, rather than rapid changes in pitch. In contrast to this, much vocal music contains elaborate vocal ornamentation, as heard in recorded selections 53 and 54.

The interval of the fourth often appears in the melodic material of Buddhist chanting and in instrumental music such as *koto* and *shamisen* music—even larger leaps occur often in the latter case. In vocal music, both syllabic and melismatic treatment of text can be found, but narrative styles like the music of the puppet theater described later tend toward syllabic text setting, which emphasizes the words.

Only Western-influenced Japanese music uses Western harmony; traditional music is dominated by a monophonic or heterophonic sound. Most common when two or more instruments (or voice and instrument) play together is a heterophonic texture, in which both or all parts play basically the same melody but in slightly different versions.

RHYTHM

One distinctive characteristic of Japanese music lies in the flexibility of pulse in many pieces. We sense a pulse in music when we hear notes that are dynamically accented. In Western music, pulses almost always occur at regular time intervals (forming "beats"), and are arranged most commonly in groups of two, three, four, or six (creating a "meter"). Music can also have irregular intervals between the pulses, however, and this is sometimes called "beatless" or "flexible" or "free" rhythm. Those accustomed to Western music may have difficulty at first listening to music that lacks a steady beat because it seems "hard to follow" without the firm rhythmic structure they expect. But this music conveys a powerful expression of feeling because of its freedom and flexibility. Such beatless rhythm is found in many kinds of Japanese music, from folk song to music of the *shakuhachi* (recorded selections 52, 53, and 54). Even when a steady beat is present, there can be a sense of flexibility to it, as in the festival music example presented later.

When there is a sense of beat in Japanese music, those beats usually occur in groups of two, four, or eight. Triple meter is rare, though it can be found in some folk and children's songs.

Japanese music uses a wide variety of tempos, from very slow to very fast. Often, in music associated with the theater, the tempo accelerates as excitement and drama build in the play. A typical musical form called *jo-ha-kyū*, described below, is outlined through changes in tempo.

Tempos are not determined by metronome but are learned through imitation and trial and error. As in a Western classical music ensemble, when a Japanese ensemble sits down together to rehearse, it is not uncommon for one member to say, "That was a bit too fast last time, don't you think?" or "Why did we slow down at that point?" Through negotiation and trial and error, they settle into a tempo and changes in that tempo that are acceptable to most members. Experienced solo performers tend to play the same piece at almost the same tempo each time, though performances of the same work by different performers sometimes show a surprising tempo variance. This variation can be linked to difference in stylistic school or to personal interpretation.

MUSICAL FORM

The most common musical form in Japanese music is called *jo-ha-kyū* and is based mainly on rhythmic rather than melodic changes. Found in music for the *gagaku* orchestra, this form profoundly affected *nō* theater as well as other instrumental and vocal genres.

Jo means "introduction" and is the slow beginning section: *ha* is literally "breaking apart," and here the tempo builds; finally, *kyū*, or "rushing," finds the tempo reaching its peak, only to slow before the piece ends. As a loose form, this tripartite structure applies in some cases to entire pieces as well as to sections of those pieces and individual phrases, as in the "Rokudan" piece described later.

To summarize, the three characteristics of traditional Japanese music that most exemplify its uniqueness and beauty are (1) variety of timbres, including unpitched sounds; (2) heterophonic treatment of voices in an ensemble; and (3) flexibility of pulse found in both solo and ensemble music. These elements occur in most of the traditional music described in this chapter.

In the following sections, several different kinds of Japanese music will be explained, illustrating some of the colorful diversity of musical life in that country today. The first four of these types developed largely during the Tokugawa period. The history of each instrument or musical genre provides a fascinating look into the rich, vibrant life of traditional Japanese cities and villages during the times of the *samurai*, wandering Buddhist priests, and *geisha*.

The *shakuhachi* flute is linked to the social turbulence of early Tokugawa times, as well as to Zen philosophy and aesthetics. A *shakuhachi* piece provides an example of free rhythm, one of the most important characteristics of Japanese music. Also during the Tokugawa period, merchants took up the *koto* zither and made it one of the most commonly played instruments. The example of *koto* music displays the *dan* form of musical structure as well as the *jo-ha-kyū* principle. The *geisha* and a female composer of the late Tokugawa period were important in the development of the short *kouta* songs. These songs, sung to the accompaniment of the *shamisen,* exemplify heterophonic texture in Japanese music. A description of the *bunraku* puppet theater and its music, *gidayū-bushi,* illustrates the strong connection of music with the theater and describes teaching methods old and new.

These kinds of music are generally labeled "art" or "classical" music. In comparison to "folk" music, art music has stricter guild systems, more regulation over skill level, and more professionalism. The terms "art" and "folk" are imported from the West, however, and the dividing line between the two categories has become blurred today as folk musicians become more professionalized and form their own guild systems.

Next, two kinds of music termed "folk" are described: folk song from northern Japan and instrumental festival music from Tokyo. While both of these date from the Tokugawa period or earlier, they will be described in their contemporary contexts to show the reader how traditional music is faring in modern-day Japan. Musically, the folk song example shows the intricate ornamentation and the use of "microtones" that are characteristic of folk music from the northern region; the festival music example illustrates ensemble practice. Finally, we will explore present-day Japanese popular music, which shows musical features of both East and West, and the world of *karaoke* singing, in which live singing and technology are mixed in a unique way.

SHAKUHACHI

Considering its range of tones from soft and ethereal to rough and violent, the *shakuhachi* appears surprisingly simple in construction. This flute is made of a length of bamboo from the bottom part of a bamboo stalk, including part of the root. The name *shakuhachi* derives from the length of the standard instrument. *Shaku* signifies a traditional unit of measure (equivalent to about 30 cm) and *hachi* stands for 8, together meaning 1.8 *shaku,* or about 54 cm. (Players also use different lengths, sometimes to match the range of the other ensemble instruments.) The standard *shakuhachi* has four holes in the front of the instrument and one in the back for the thumb of the left hand.

The *shakuhachi's* versatility in pitch and tone production is, in fact, due to its construction. Held vertically, the flute has a mouthpiece at the top which is cut obliquely on the side away from the player. By partially covering the fingerholes and changing the angle of the lips to the mouthpiece, a player can produce a wide variety of pitches and tone qualities. Not only does the *shakuhachi* easily produce microtones, but it also generates tones ranging from "pure" (with few overtones) to very breathy, sounding almost like white noise. Many Western-influenced contemporary compositions have been written for the *shakuhachi* because of its versatility in pitch and tone quality.

Solo *shakuhachi* performance flourished during the Tokugawa period (1600-1867). This was a golden age in Japanese cultural life. It was a time of peace, during which the *shōgun* living in Tokyo ruled over a united country, while the Kyoto emperor held only nominal power. After centuries of violent struggles between different factions of aristocrats and military leaders, Japan welcomed peace and prospered under it.

But long-lasting peace meant trouble for members of the *samurai* class. *Samurai* warriors enjoyed high status during the years of fighting, but afterward many *samurai* of lower rank were released from their duties, becoming *rōnin*, or "masterless *samurai*."° The Tokugawa regime found it expedient to uphold the social class system established in earlier times: at the top were *samurai*, followed by farmers, craftsmen, and finally merchants. By issuing edicts designed to set up boundaries between these classes, the government tried to prevent movement between them. For this reason, even though they were without a means of support, *rōnin* were not allowed to change their class status as *samurai*, though some managed to do so. A number became teachers or writers, others became farmers, and still others became hired bodyguards for rich merchants. The image of the proud, swaggering, brave *samurai*, as projected in *samurai* movies, is largely based on the *rōnin* of the Tokugawa period, who were actually unemployed *samurai*.

Another option for the *rōnin* was to take religious orders and beg on the streets and highways of Japan. In fact, in Tokugawa society, it was considered more honorable to beg than to "lower" oneself by becoming a merchant or farmer. One group of *rōnin* who took religious orders were called *komusō*. *Komusō* (literally, "emptiness monks") were Buddhist priests who wandered the countryside, playing the *shakuhachi* and begging. The standard *komusō* costume included a large, basket-shaped hat made of cane, through which the wearer could see but not be seen. It was rumored that the *komusō* were government spies, taking advantage of their right to travel throughout the country wearing a costume that shielded their identity (Blasdel 1988:103–7).

These *samurai*-turned-priests made their mark on the *shakuhachi* repertoire. The *honkyoku*, or main solo repertoire for the instrument, derives from the pieces played by the *komusō*. All of these pieces, the most spiritual and meditative of the present-day *shakuhachi* repertoire, have a free rhythm; that is, they lack a regular beat.

Komusō were organized into the Fuke sect of Buddhism, which propagated a Zen basis for *shakuhachi* playing. Zen Buddhism, a philosophy that has spread throughout much of Asia and the world in various forms, is based on the idea that intellect is not needed in the pursuit of truth. We can search to know *about* things, but we do not really *know* them. To know them, we must throw away our notions of scientific investigation and logical reasoning and instead rely upon a heightened awareness and intuition about life.

°The term *rōnin* has been given a new meaning by the Japanese. High school graduates who fail college entrance examinations and must wait until the following year (or years) to pass the exams are also called *rōnin*.

Various means for reaching that state of heightened awareness of enlightenment (*satori* in Japanese) have been proposed. These include pondering *kōan,* or paradoxical riddles (the most famous is "What is the sound of one hand clapping?") and the practice of *zazen,* sitting in silent meditation. In the Fuke sect, playing the *shakuhachi* also was regarded as a means for reaching enlightenment. For this reason, the *shakuhachi* was not called a musical instrument by its performers but a *hōki,* or "spiritual tool." The spiritual approach to the playing of the instrument is called *suizen,* or "blowing Zen."

According to *suizen,* the goal of *shakuhachi* coincides with the goal of Zen: to reach enlightenment, proceeding into unlimited "knowing." How this is done is not formulated precisely (as it cannot be, from the Zen perspective), but one common notion is called *ichōon jōbutsu,* or "enlightenment in a single note." According to this theory, one could reach enlightenment suddenly when blowing a single tone.

Breathing is crucial in *shakuhachi* playing and its connection with Zen. The exhaling of breath is heard in the dynamic level and tone quality of a pitch; at the same time, it carries with it the possibility of instant spiritual enlightenment. Thus, each moment of "performance," whether the intake of breath or its slow release, whether the subtle, delicate shading of a tone or the explosion of air through the instrument, can be interpreted in the context of a larger spiritual life.

The breathing pattern is important in learning to play the *shakuhachi.* Each phrase takes one full breath, with dramatic shifts in dynamic level according to how quickly the air is expelled. The typical phrase in *shakuhachi honkyoku* music follows the natural breathing pattern, the sound growing fainter toward the end of the phrase as the air in the lungs runs out. When this dynamic pattern is broken by a gradual or sudden increase in volume, it makes a pronounced impression on the listener.

The performer of the *shakuhachi* piece in recorded selection 52, Kawase Junsuke, is one of the best-known *shakuhachi* musicians in Japan and the head of a stylistic school of playing (see ill. 8–1). Here he is playing with his sister, Kawase Hakuse,° on the *shamisen;* she is also an active performer, particularly in the *kabuki* theater.

This piece, a part of the *honkyoku* (solo) repertory of the Kinko style of performance, is called "Tsuru no sugomori," or "Nesting Cranes." (The version recorded here is performed in the *kabuki* theater and therefore is accompanied by *shamisen;* this part is not notated in the following transcription.) The music describes a winter scene during which cranes make their nests. The fast trills in the *shakuhachi* imitate the bird's fluttering wings. "Tsuru no sugomori" is performed in one of the most famous *kabuki* plays, *Kanadehon chushingura,* or Treasury of Local Retainers, during a scene when parting lovers suddenly notice the scene outdoors.

The first time one listens to this piece, it is best just to sit back and relax, appreciating the overall mood. For later listening, the transcription in example 8–3 shows in Western notation the general outline of the piece. Western notation is

°Japanese names are given in the Japanese order: family name followed by given name.

Ill. 8–1.   Kawase Junsuke playing the *shakubachi*.

limiting in conveying uneven rhythms, and so the transcription here is only approximate in time values. Phrases—defined by points at which a breath is taken by the musician—are numbered for reference.

After listening to this piece a few times, one may sense that certain phrases are repeated; in fact, this short piece has many repetitions of melodic material. For example, phrase 1 is heard again (with some modifications) in phrases 6, 9, 17, and 24. The group of phrases numbered 1 to 5 are repeated in phrases 9 to 13, and most of the other phrases are variations on previous melodic material. There is also a clear climax to the piece, created by changes in pitch and dynamics.

Ex. 8–3. **Transcription, "Tsuru no sugomori."**

Ex. 8–3.   *(Continued)*

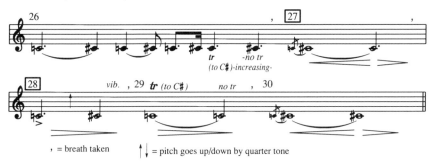

‚ = breath taken   ↑↓ = pitch goes up/down by quarter tone

One of the most obvious characteristics of this piece is the constant change in dynamics within one phrase. Almost every phrase increases or decreases in volume; in many cases the musician increases the volume on one long note and decreases it on the next one. This careful breath control must be learned and practiced over years to prevent running out of breath too soon and to maintain constant control over tone quality.

A knowledge of some of the techniques used to play *shakuhachi* will help explain how some of the tones in this performance are produced. Sometimes the player flattens or sharpens a pitch by changing the angle of the lips to the mouthpiece. This is called *meri* when the pitch is lowered, producing a soft tone, and *kari* when the pitch is raised. (Occasionally the pitch is lowered and again raised, as at the end of phrase 22.)

The musician changes pitch also through finger techniques, depending on the effect desired. A finger can slowly open or close a hole, it can quickly tap a hole (creating an accent), or cover only a portion of a hole. These techniques are necessary because tonguing is not used to separate notes in *shakuhachi* playing.

Different techniques of breath release into the flute also create interesting effects such as *muraiki*, an explosion of breath into the instrument. In addition, *shakuhachi* players use flutter tonguing, finger tremolos, and vibrato—all of which can be heard in the first few phrases of "Tsuru no sugomori." One common technique of producing vibrato is to shake the head while blowing into the instrument, either from side to side or up and down.

This piece shows at least two of the three basic characteristics of Japanese music listed above: a variety of timbres within one piece and a flexibility of pulse. Some notes have a thin sound, while others have rich, full tone. Some notes sound "purer" to our ears, and others are breathier. The *shakuhachi* player expresses the music through such changes in timbre. With the exception perhaps of contemporary music, this variety of tone quality is rarely found within a single piece written for a Western wind instrument. In terms of Japanese musical aesthetics, however, this contrast of timbres is important to the texture and expression of the piece.

The lack of a regular pulse means that learning a piece requires a good ear and an excellent sense of timing on the part of the student. Most forms of musical notation convey the time durations of notes easily if the music has a steady pulse. But without such a pulse, the original time values are difficult to communicate in a written score. Perhaps this is one reason that musical notation never developed into an important teaching tool in most forms of traditional Japanese music. Because Japanese musicians could not rely on scores to teach them the rhythm of a piece, they used them more as a device to help them remember how the piece should sound. First, of course, performers must acquire this memory by listening to their teacher (and perhaps other students) many times.

The idea of *ma* (literally "space" or "interval") is linked to both rhythm and to the Zen background of *shakuhachi* playing. *Ma* refers to the overall timing of a piece—not just the pauses and rests, but also the relationship between sound and silence upon which all music is fundamentally based. It embraces the idea that sound enhances silence and silence enhances sound. This emphasis on silence conforms with Zen ideas concerning the importance of emptiness and space. The player who is aware of *ma* begins his notes with an instinctive care for the length and quality of the silences before and after. This concept applies particularly to music with a beatless rhythm, since the sounds and silences fall at irregular points and the player is more active in creating those moments.

Performers often link the concept of *ma* to the quality of a musical performance. Musicians speak of "good *ma*" or "bad *ma*," referring to the quality of the sounds and silences and their proportion to one another. When this proportion is deemed appropriate—a subjective judgment that is learned only from years of experience—then the performance has been successful.

Though the Fuke sect priests have long disappeared from the roads of Japan, many players keep the *shakuhachi* tradition alive today, both in Japan and abroad. Because of the instrument's versatility of pitch and timbre, composers and performers like to use it in various contemporary genres, such as jazz, fusion, and New Age music. At the same time, the meditative, spiritual nature of the *honkyoku* is continually reaffirmed through performances given by several active *shakuhachi* masters, such as Yamaguchi Gorō, Aoki Reibo, and others.

KOTO

The graceful music of the *koto* is familiar to many foreigners, since it has become well known outside Japan through concerts, records, and tapes. Whether played as a solo instrument or in an ensemble, with a vocal part or without one, the *koto* has for several centuries been one of the most popular traditional instruments of Japan.

The contemporary *koto* is a long (about 1.8 meters), wooden instrument with thirteen stings, traditionally silk but now also nylon. Bridges (called *ji*) hold the strings above the surface of the instrument, one for each string. These bridges are movable, so the player can set them at different places along the string, depending on the desired tuning.

Like the prototype of the *shakuhachi,* the ancestor of the *koto* came to Japan from China during the early centuries of cultural exchange, after which the instrument was gradually adapted to its present form. After several centuries of use by an elite few, during the Tokugawa period the *koto* gradually spread in popularity to different segments of Japanese society. At this time changes in teaching and in the *koto* repertoire stimulated many men and women to learn it (Malm 1959:169). Growing numbers were merchants, the class that officially held the lowest status but was gaining rapidly in wealth and influence. By the beginning of the Meiji period in 1868, the *koto* could be found in many private homes as well as in teahouses and theaters, and skilled *koto* performance had become a sign of good breeding for young women. Most of the *sōkyoku* (or *koto* music) pieces performed today were written during the Tokugawa period, when new schools and styles of playing arose. At this time the *koto* was used in ensembles with the *shamisen* and later the *kokyū* or *shakuhachi*, combinations that brought an important form of chamber music into Japanese life.

One of the most famous *koto* pieces is entitled "Rokudan," or "Six Sections." It is typical of the *danmono* type of instrumental pieces, consisting of several "steps," or sections, known as *dan*. Each *dan* contains 104 beats and is repeated several times, with great variation. A short introduction of four to eight beats (four beats in the case of "Rokudan") begins the piece, and each *dan* follows the last without a break. The first four beats are followed by six *dan,* each 104 beats long.[*] Hearing the piece one time, however, can indicate that the *danmono* is anything but a simple theme-and-variation form, since the sections are difficult to tell apart. Even after listening to the piece several times, one might not be able to tell where a new *dan* begins because the melody of each *dan* is made up of short figures that are generally difficult to distinguish. The second and third *dan* are perhaps recognizable as related to the first, for they are closer to the melodic content of the first *dan;* after that the similarity in thematic material becomes less clear. Some basic melodic figures are heard again, but in a different part of the *dan,* or in a different range or rhythmic pattern.

Therefore, rather than trying to distinguish each section, it makes more sense to listen for the repetition of the short melodic figures as well as larger overall patterns. Some of the brief melodic-rhythmic patterns that recur include a descending dotted figure and octave leaps. As for larger patterns, the *jo-ha-kyū* structure mentioned in the beginning of this chapter may be applied to the piece as a whole. The first two *dan* make up the *jo,* or introductory section; the second two *dan* find the tempo increasing, as in a *ha* section; and the tempo reaches its height in the final two *dan,* or the *kyū* section. The tempo slows down only toward the end, in the last twenty-two beats or so, ending in a long glissando. This form is also followed in individual *dan,* in which one can also sense a gradual building of tension.

In listening to this stately piece, we hear in the beginning four beats of "introduction" a long note of two beats followed by a descending note a fourth away,

---

[*]Several recordings of "Rokudan" are available on CDs and tapes. One performance can be found on the CD *Sô,* vol. 6 of the series "Japanese Traditional Music," which is listed under "Additional Listening" at the end of this chapter. A transcription of this piece appears in Adriaansz 1973:66–93.

Ex. 8–4.   "Rokudan," introductory figure.

and then an interval of a fifth (ex. 8–4). This figure is easy to hear throughout the piece. The following beat of silence represents the first beat of the material repeated in each *dan*.

A careful listener can hear a variety of timbres and interesting tonal effects. Sometimes the pick of one finger sliding down the string creates a pitchless sound; sometimes glissandos brush the strings. There may be changes in pitch that sound like a sliding from one note to the next and back again. This is a result of changing the pressure exerted in the left hand on the string as the right hand plucks it. Such delicate shifting of pitch and tone color give *koto* music a special beauty.

KOUTA

Another of the well-loved Japanese traditional instruments is the *shamisen*, a three-stringed long-necked lute (see ill. 8–2). In contrast to the *shakuhachi*, which has associations with austere spirituality and meditation, the *shamisen* is

Ill. 8–2.   *Geisha* performing at a party. The woman on the right holds a *shamisen*.

often used to convey an outpouring of emotion and drama. For this reason it is considered an excellent instrument for the theater, expressing highly dramatic situations in the *bunraku* puppet theater to great effect. It is also used in another major theatrical form, *kabuki,* and sometimes to accompany folk song, as in recorded selection 54. In a more intimate setting, the *shamisen* also accompanies short, evocative songs called *kouta* (literally, "short song").

The present-day *shamisen* is a descendent of a long line of related instruments stretching back to the *sanshin* of Okinawa, the *san-hsien* of China, and perhaps further back to the Middle East or Central Asia.° While the Okinawan *sanshin* is covered with snakeskin, on the Japanese mainland the instrument is traditionally covered with cat skin, or sometimes dog skin. (As these are now expensive, however, plastic is commonly found on *shamisen* used for practice.) There are different kinds of *shamisen,* varying in shape, weight, material, and overall size; the type used depends on the musical genre played. The instrument that accompanies *kouta* songs, for example, is smaller and lighter than the one used in *bunraku* puppet theater.

The body of the *shamisen* is made of a wooden box roughly square in shape, covered on both sides with skin or plastic. A long piece of wood, forming the unfretted neck, is inserted into this box. Pegs at the top of the neck hold the three strings, each string of a different thickness. In some kinds of music, a large plectrum is used for striking and plucking the instrument. Sometimes in *kouta,* however, the bare fingers or fingernails pluck the strings, producing a lighter, less percussive, sound.

A rather unusual sound in the *shamisen* confirms the importance of unpitched sounds in Japanese music. This is a special buzz or hum called *sawari* (literally, "touch"), which is purposefully added to the instrument when it is made. The lowest string does not rest on the upper bridge but resonates against a special cavity made near the top of the instrument's neck. This string sets a noise in motion, to which the other strings can contribute in sympathetic vibration. The result is a pitchless buzzing sound that is essential to the tonal flavor of the *shamisen.* Whereas such buzzing noises are avoided in instruments used in Western classical music, Japanese instrument makers intentionally build these timbres into their instruments. Buzzing is also deliberately built into many African instruments (see chapter 3).

The *kouta* is a song form that evokes many images and allusions in a short (generally, one- to three-minute) time. *Kouta* as we know it today dates from the mid-nineteenth century, though the same name was used to describe another kind of song in earlier centuries (Kurada 1982:894–95).

The development of the present-day *kouta* is closely linked to the participation of women in Japanese traditional music. One of the earliest composers of *kouta* was O-Yo (1840–1901). The daughter of the head master of *kiyomoto* (a style of *shamisen* music used in *kabuki*), O-Yo was an excellent musician. As a woman,

°Theories that the Chinese *san-hsien* derived from Egyptian or Persian sources are summarized in Kikkawa 1981:157–58.

she was not allowed to take over her father's position after his death; instead she married a man who then inherited his title. But O-Yo took up most of his duties.

O-Yo was not allowed to play the *shamisen* on the *kabuki* stage, since only males appeared there. She was nevertheless an active performer at private parties in teahouses and restaurants. For such private gatherings she probably composed *kouta* such as "Saru wa uki" thought to be the first *kouta* ever composed (Kikkawa 1981:350). Although women were banned from participating in many of the elite forms of music performance in Japan, they played a key role in teaching that music to generations of male performers. O-Yo herself was an important transmitter of the *kiyomoto* tradition of her father, teaching it to many people from all parts of Japan.

O-Yo's musical world and her involvement with both an older form of music (*kiyomoto*) and a new form (*kouta*) can best be understood in the context of the *iemoto* guild system. This system, active also in O-Yo's time, is a powerful influence on the traditional arts—music, dance, flower arranging, the tea ceremony, and many other artistic areas. The guild is the transmitter of knowledge and the legitimizer of teachers and performers in each art form.

In music, several different guilds may be involved with one type of music (for example, music for the *shakuhachi* or for the *nō* theater), but each guild will have its own slightly different performance style and repertoire. By illustration, one who wishes to become a *shakuhachi* performer must decide which style he or she wants to learn, then become affiliated with the guild that follows that style. Often this affiliation lasts as long as the individual performs on the *shakuhachi*.

Guilds not only transmit knowledge; they also control quality. Each guild sets the standards for teachers and pupils. If an individual works diligently, he or she may be given a license to teach and an artistic name from the guild. The *iemoto* system thus provides a structure through which the arts have been taught, performed, and preserved for hundreds of years in Japan.

The hierarchy of this *iemoto* system is rigid, bearing some similarity to the familial-paternalistic social structures found throughout Japanese society. Traditionally, the leader of each school inherits that position and strictly regulates rights to perform or teach. In theory, this system controls the "correct" transmission of musical information, but it also allows some leaders to exploit their helpless students. A greedy leader, for instance, might demand large amounts of money for the licenses required to be recognized as a qualified performer and teacher of his school, and the student would have no choice but to pay.

On the other hand, the number of scrupulous *iemoto* leaders and teachers far outweighs the number of exploitative ones; most teachers provide a great deal of support and encouragement to their students. Overall, the *iemoto* system has contributed positively to maintaining the artistic level in traditional Japanese music. Its strict regulation of performance standards has preserved musical traditions that could otherwise have changed drastically or even died out through the years.

According to the rules of this system, new composition in many genres of music was discouraged or even forbidden. This conservatism is linked to a reverence for tradition in the arts that is still prevalent among Japanese musicians today. Many believe that the "classic" body of music has been handed down with painstaking precision for decades or centuries through the toil of countless musicians. The composition of a new piece of music by an individual was for years considered "arrogant self-expression." If a new piece were composed and proved to have merit, it had to be ascribed to the leader of the guild, who in turn might attribute it to an earlier *iemoto* leader. This reluctance to accept new compositions meant that if they were written, they often had no official recognition. For this reason, when someone like O-Yo composed new music, it was in a new genre such as *kouta*. Because there was no *iemoto* associated yet with that kind of music, the restrictions that would otherwise apply toward composition did not exist.

Today, among the forms of traditional music we can still see this restriction on new composition to some degree. New pieces are now written for traditional instruments in Japan, but they are often created outside of the traditional genres, such as in a mixture of *kabuki* music and rock known as *"kabuki* rock." Otherwise, as a rule, only high-ranking members of an *iemoto* create new compositions in a traditional mode.

By the end of the Tokugawa period, the *kouta* was linked to the *geisha* of the city of Edo (which became known as Tokyo in 1868) and the life of the teahouses. For many people today, the lively, intense world of Edo during the Tokugawa period epitomizes the Japanese spirit. Though the official Japanese capital was Kyoto, where the emperor resided, Edo was the actual seat of government where the *shōgun* held state in his castle. It was also the most populous city in Japan as well as one of the largest in the world. The influx of people from all over the country, crowded into tenements and wildly pursuing wealth, pleasure, or both, spurred the coining of the phrase "Edo wa tenka no hakidamari" (Edo is the nation's rubbish heap).

The streets teemed with *chōnin*, townspeople who were members of either the merchant or the artisan classes. With the expansion of the economy during the peaceful Tokugawa period, some *chōnin* became wealthy and powerful. They patronized the theaters, teahouses, and brothels, making their increasingly sophisticated mark on the aesthetics of the drama, music, and dance of the period: a sense of style that combines wit, sensuousness, and restraint. The Edo pursuit of momentary pleasure represents the epitome of the *ukiyo*, or "floating world."

The *kouta*, as sung by the *geisha* of such licensed quarters as the Yoshiwara area of Edo, reflects their world of beauty and style. The songs' lyrics often convey romantic or erotic themes, but such references are subtle. Puns, double-entendres and poetic devices appear frequently in *kouta* lyrics, and sometimes even a Japanese will miss their suggestive undertones.

In the *kouta* example found in recorded selection 53, entitled "Hakusen no" ("A White Fan"), both the image of a white fan and the beauty of nature are used as metaphors for romantic commitment. This particular song shows little of the whimsical side of *kouta;* it is considered suitable for performance at wedding banquets or private parties. At the wedding banquet, this song would be sung to the honored couple.

Though declining in numbers, *geisha* are still trained in Japan to entertain at such occasions. The traditional musical instrument of the *geisha* is the *shamisen,* which is used often to accompany vocal music such as the *kouta*. This recording was made by a *geisha* in the 1960s who lived near the former Yoshiwara quarter of Tokyo.

Figure 8–2 shows the lyrics of the *kouta* and an English translation. (The letters on the left-hand side refer to melodic material and will be explained below.)

Traditional Japanese poetry arranges lines according to their syllabic content, favoring lines with five and seven syllables. The lyrics of "Hakusen no" contains alternating lines of five and seven syllables. (Extended vowels and the letter *n* at the end of a syllable count as separate syllables.) A poetic device known as *kakekotoba*, or "pivot word," is found on the sixth line: the word *kagayaku* ("shimmering") can be interpreted as both referring to the silver node of the fan (the pin holding the fan together at the bottom) and to the pine tree boughs, "shimmering" in the shadows. Such pivot words are often found in Japanese poetry and are made possible by the flexibility of Japanese grammar.

Several auspicious symbols appear in the text. The pine tree has a special symbolism for the Japanese as a tree of special beauty and longevity. A clear pond, "undisturbed by waves or wind," also presents a peaceful, auspicious image of the future life of a couple. The words *sue hirogari* literally refer to the unfolding of a fan, but can also mean to enjoy increasing prosperity as time goes on.

Example 8–5 is a transcription of "Hakusen no" and, as in the *shakuhachi* example, the difficulties of conveying uneven time values in Western notation are apparent. The vocal part has been inserted rhythmically in relation to the steady beat of the *shamisen*, which is the easiest part to follow.

This transcription shows only the vocal and *shamisen* parts; in the recording, we also hear an accompanying ensemble made up of the *ko-tsuzumi* and *otsuzumi* drums and the *nōkan* flute. These instruments, typical of the *nō* theater,

A	Hakusen no	A white fan
B	sue hirogari no	spreading out
C	sue kakete	lasting forever
B	kataki chigiri no	the firm pledges
(A)	gin kaname	like the silver node of the fan
(B)	kagayaku kage ni	shimmering in shadows
D	matsu ga e no	the boughs of pine trees
E	ha-iro mo masaru	the splendid leafy color of
(B)	fukamidori	a deep green
E	tachiyoru niwa no	the clearness of the pond
(E)	ike sumite	in the garden approached
(B)	nami kaze tatanu	undisturbed by waves of wind,
C	mizu no omo	the surface of the water
B	urayamashii de	What an enviable life,
(B)	wa nai ka na.	don't you think?

Fig. 8–2. "Hakusen no."

were added to the commercial recording of this song; *geisha* also sing "Hakusen no" with the *shamisen* alone. Another sound not transcribed above are the calls known as *kakegoe*, which help to cue the ensemble as well as add to the atmosphere of the song.

Earlier in this chapter a heterophonic relationship between two or more parts was defined as typical of Japanese ensemble music. In recorded selection 53, such a heterophony characterizes the voice and *shamisen*. Rather than sounding simultaneously on the same beat, the two parts tend to weave in and out; sometimes

Ex. 8–5.   Transcription of "Hakusen no."

Ex. 8–5. (*Continued*)

the voice precedes the *shamisen* in presenting the melody and sometimes the *shamisen* plays the notes first. The result of this constant staggering and shifting is a duet in which the melody is shared and enhanced by both voice and instrument. An example of this heterophony can be found in the third line, as the *shamisen* anticipates several of the sung notes. Listening carefully to the entire song, try to find other such examples. Are there also times when the voice anticipates what the *shamisen* will play?

One of the most interesting aspects of the vocal part is the flexibility of beat, which contrasts to the even beat of the *shamisen*. See, for example, how the

Ex. 8–6.   Motif in *shamisen* part, "Hakusen no."

rhythm of the vocal and *shamisen* parts fit together in the line beginning "tachi-yoru . . ."; just as the listener thinks a predictable pattern has been established, the rhythm shifts. The sophistication of this kind of rhythmic contrast has appealed for centuries to the Japanese ear. Together, melodic and rhythmic variety in Japanese ensemble music create a complex, often exciting musical texture.

The vocal melody contains several thematic phrases that repeat in slightly varied forms. The letters next to the text in figure 8–2 show one way of interpreting these phrases. Repeating letters indicate phrases that are repeated exactly or nearly exactly, while letters in parentheses signify more modified repetitions. For example, the seven different phrases marked "B" have in common long, repeated notes followed by a descending interval, highly ornamented, of a third to a sixth, or some part of this combination.

The *shamisen* part opens and closes the song with the same rhythmically emphasized theme, and it occasionally plays a short solo phrase between lines of text. Sometimes, small motifs are repeated; one that occurs several times is shown in example 8–6.

This and other similar motifs in the *shamisen* part stress the notes D and G. The scale used in "Hakusen no" is the *in* scale (shown in ex. 8–1), based on D. However, there are constant shifts to the same scale based on G, which is closely related to the D scale. A prominent difference between the two scales lies in the A flat found in the G scale, whereas the D scale contains an A natural. Another scale shift takes place in the line "kagayaku . . . ," which stresses the notes G, D♭, C, denoting a temporary change to the C-based *in* scale. Such rapid changes from one scale to another are common in Japanese music even in short songs like *kouta*.

Hearing this song, the listener is drawn into the refined yet playful atmosphere of the Tokugawa teahouses. Now we shall turn to a more dramatic atmosphere, the highly charged puppet theater.

GIDAYŪ-BUSHI:
MUSIC OF THE PUPPET THEATER

During the Tokugawa period, theater was one of the most popular forms of entertainment among the townspeople. While *nō* was a favored pastime of the elite, attendance at *kabuki* and *bunraku* (puppet theater) was restricted to members of the artisan and merchant classes (Ernst 1956:10). This restriction did not prevent members of the higher *samurai* class from sneaking into the theaters, sometimes wearing large hats or scarves over their heads to hide their identity.

Music is important in *kabuki* and *bunraku* theater, both as a background to the actions onstage and as an essential element of the play itself. In *bunraku*, for ex-

Ill. 8–3.   *Bunraku* stage. From this high view, we can see the sunken stage, not normally seen by the audience. The doll on the left plays the *shamisen*.

ample, two musicians—a narrator-singer and a *shamisen* player—tell the story, speak and sing for the puppets, and provide scenes with background music (see ill. 8–3).

Japanese puppet theater uses elaborately costumed, large-sized dolls that are brought almost to life by skilled puppeteers and musicians. The *bunraku* plays include some of the most beautifully written works of Japanese drama, expressing intense emotions that appealed to the tastes of the Tokugawa townspeople. The skillfully manipulated dolls, realistic scenery, and emotion-packed music, all part of a passionately dramatic scene, often reduce audiences to tears (ill. 8–4).

Important puppets require three manipulators: one for the head and right hand, one for the left hand, and one for the feet. Apprentice manipulators normally require several years of training on the feet, and then several more years on the left hand before they become chief manipulators, who are allowed to manipulate the head and right hand. These manipulators wear black, with hoods over their heads, so as to "disappear" in the background.°

To the right of the main stage is a smaller stage on which the narrator-singer (*tayū*) and *shamisen* player sit. At the beginning of the performance, or in the

---

°Well-known manipulators can appear with their faces exposed, and even in festive costumes, but the emotional content of the scene ultimately dictates the costumes of manipulators. In solemn scenes, for example, all manipulators will normally appear hooded and in black.

金時 時代物の豪放な武将

孔明 思慮深く優美な相で、一抹
の愁いを含んでいる四十歳
から五十歳前後の武将

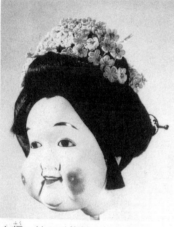

お福 娘の三枚目

傾城 最も華麗なかしら
太夫職としての教養をそな
え、色気のあるうちに張り
と意気地をもつ

Ill. 8–4. *Bunraku* doll heads. On the upper left is a tough *samurai*, on the
upper right is a more refined *samurai*, on the lower left is a plain young
girl of the merchant class, and on the lower right, the elegant head of a
young beauty.

middle of a play when a change in musical personnel is needed, the wall of the smaller stage rotates to reveal the musicians on the other side. (For some scenes, more than one *tayū* or *shamisen* player may be needed, and these make their entrance from the wings of the stage in a less dramatic way.) Before beginning the play, the *tayū*, who is sitting on the floor, lifts the text from the lacquered lectern on which it rests and bows with it—a sign of respect and a prayer for a good performance (see ill. 8–5).

Together, the narrator and the *shamisen* player try to fill the puppets with life, expressing emotion that is sometimes blatant and exaggerated, sometimes subtle and subdued. As one *tayū* states: "The whole point of *bunraku* is to portray human emotions and situations in life so that people's hearts are moved, so that they feel something special about the particular aspect of life the play deals with, whether loyalty, sacrifice, one of the many forms of love, or a dilemma one encounters in life" (Adachi 1985:65).

Working toward this goal, neither *tayū* nor *shamisen* player is regarded as more important than the other; instead, they form a closely cooperating team. Sensing each other's feelings (as well as those of the audience), the two make

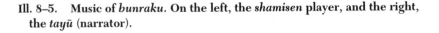

Ill. 8–5. Music of *bunraku*. On the left, the *shamisen* player, and the right, the *tayū* (narrator).

subtle adjustments in their singing and playing in order to convey emotion through the dolls as effectively as possible. One narrator working in Osaka (the traditional capital of *bunraku*) told me: "When I play with a *shamisen* player that I've known and performed with for many years, we are so accustomed to sensing each other's moods and feelings from performing onstage that I can tell as soon as we sit down together whether or not he's had a fight with his wife that morning!"

To a listener unfamiliar with *bunraku,* the energetic narration of the *tayū* can sound startlingly exaggerated. Indeed, it seems amazing that one man can have the stamina to shout, growl, and sing out for such a long time, filling the hall with his large voice.° Developing this kind of stamina takes years of training, and sore throats are not uncommon among those in this profession. One narrator describes his training this way:

> No matter how big the theater, we never use a microphone; all is produced from our bodies alone. You must practice producing the voice from your lower abdomen. When we become narrators, we're told, "Make your voice come from your *hara* (lower abdomen)!" And we wonder how that is possible. We learn abdominal breathing, a breathing movement in your stomach. You take in big breaths and let out just enough. You must feel in every part of your body that the voice accompanying the breath is there. But before you understand how the voice can come out of the abdomen, you really have to suffer a lot.†

Some *tayū* even use a small bag of sand, inserted inside the kimono near the stomach, which they use as a kind of "leverage" for their hands and stomach muscles to obtain the air they need.

Traditional training of the *tayū* and *shamisen* player was more strict than at present. Until the early part of this century, the apprentice narrator or *shamisen* player normally moved into his teacher's home at the age of six or seven. After years of helping with household chores, he was permitted to help his master prepare for performances and then, finally, to receive lessons himself. In the meantime, before beginning his own lessons, the apprentice had already listened to thousands of hours of lessons and performances of those around him, absorbing much about the music. In actual lessons, it was important for him to learn to imitate what he heard quickly, since new material might be presented only once or twice before he was expected to have memorized it. The *shamisen* player Tsuruzawa Juzō, born in 1899, describes his training in the following way:

> Nowadays people ask about the hardships of my early training. At the time I didn't think a thing about it. Life was that way then and young people were used to discipline, punishment, and grueling training. . . . My teacher would play a passage, maybe fifteen minutes long, just once. I was expected to play along with him. Next I was made to play the passage solo. My teacher would sit there scowling at me, scolding, sometimes hit-

---

°The *tayū* is referred to as a male here, but there have been female narrators as well, particularly from the mid-nineteenth to the early twentieth century. Today, female amateur *tayū* perform in some small theaters throughout the country (Motegi 1988:206–20).
†Personal communication with Toyotake Sakitayu, April 26, 1986.

ting me in the face. Knowing the punishment that lay in store, I learned quickly to listen very, very carefully, straining every fiber in my body to absorb everything I possibly could with eyes, ears and mind.

In those days, our whole life was Bunraku. We had no movies, no coffee shops, no radios, no popular music to distract us. . . . Our heads were full of Bunraku and only Bunraku. (Adachi 1985:79)

After World War II, however, this teaching process changed dramatically. The *bunraku* theater itself went through difficult times after 1945, partly because of a decline in the wealth of its former sponsors, and partly from an overall decrease of interest in the traditional arts. As professional *bunraku* performers found it more difficult to make a living, new trainees declined in number. Furthermore, even those who were willing to study for a career with such an uncertain future were often discouraged by the rigorous training involved. To counter these trends, new teaching methods were developed to ensure that *bunraku* music, *gidayū-bushi*, would be passed on to future generations. These methods rely on relatively short training hours; one can finish the *tayū* training course of the National Theater in two years, for example.° New features of this training course include the use of standardized instructional methods, scores, and tape recorders to record lessons and performances. While these methods do produce an adequate narrator or *shamisen* player in a short amount of time, the resulting uniformity of performance and interpretation is deplored by older musicians:

They [the performers trained by the new methods] make no distinction in their playing between scenes with different settings. Even the same melody should have different emotional tones, depending on the context. It all comes from practicing with tapes, without giving any thought to the meaning of the text. They master the form but cannot express the content. With tapes you can practice in your sleep. (Motegi 1984:105)

The modern methods used to transmit *bunraku* music allow students to learn faster and with less pain. But the new training produces a different quality of performer.

All of the musical genres described in this chapter so far are closely tied to the social life of the Tokugawa period, from which several common threads emerge. For one, we see how the four-tiered class system shaped and defined various aspects of musical life. Many musical and art forms were limited, even by official decree, to a specific class: the *shakuhachi* to the *rōnin* priests, or the *kabuki* and *bunraku* to the merchant class. Social change during the Tokugawa period also reflected changes in music and class, as formerly elite instruments such as the *koto* were spread to the lower merchant class.

The next two kinds of music that we will examine, folk song and festival music, traditionally have belonged to the farming class or the poorer merchants in the cities. But people from many levels of society, in Tokugawa times as now, know these musics. Folk and festival music are still found in many everyday locations: in the streets, in the fields, and at social occasions of both the city and countryside.

°The National Theater of Japan is a government-sponsored institution that contains facilities for the presentation of traditional theater, dance, and music, as well as for the training of future artists.

FOLK SONG

In traditional Japan, people sang folk songs, or *minyō*, while they planted the rice in spring, threw their fishnets into the sea, wove cloth, and pounded grain. Folk songs accompanied many daily activities—to relieve boredom, to provide a steady beat for some activity, as encouragement for a group working at some task, as individual expression, or as a combination of these.

While the everyday uses of folk song have not entirely disappeared from Japan, fewer contemporary Japanese are finding them relevant to their lives. Seventy-six percent of the Japanese population lives in cities, where everyday activities involve riding crowded trains and sitting at desks all day rather than planting rice and weaving cloth (Sōri-fu 1982:22). Still, based on a 1982 survey of musical preferences, folk song, or *minyō*, is one of the most popular forms of music in Japan today (NHK Hōsō 1982:68).

The continuing popularity of folk songs is tied to their identification with the countryside and a sometimes romanticized vision of rural life on the part of city dwellers. Folk songs evoke a past thought to be simpler and more natural, and this appeals to many Japanese today.

In addition to an association with rural life, many Japanese folk songs connect to a specific region of the country. This is the case in "Nikata-bushi," in recorded selection 54, from the region of Akita, in northwestern Japan. With the growth of industry in the years after World War II, many Japanese left the rural areas to find work in the cities, and today people from a particular region—or their descendants—gather in many of these urban areas and sing folk songs as reminders of the villagers from which they came.

> Despite increasing geographic mobility and cultural homogenization, the Japanese identification of people and songs with their original home areas is still very strong: a Tokyo laborer whose family roots are in the northern prefecture of Akita will be expected to enliven a festive gathering with an Akita folk song. (Hughes 1981:30)

Furusato, or the concept of a home community, maintains a strong emotional grip on today's urban dwellers—even if they left home several decades earlier. The folk song, with its associations and allusions to a particular region, expresses their nostalgia for a faraway place. Thus, nostalgia not only for a different time, but for a different place as well underlies their popularity.

Finally, perhaps because *minyō* were traditionally sung by ordinary people, not trained professionals, the Japanese still find them easy to learn and appreciate—for the Japanese not only listen to folk songs but usually learn to sing a few as well, either from family and friends or in elementary school. Often they sing them at parties, when they are called on to sing a favorite song. Real enthusiasts take lessons with a good singer and attend folk song clubs or other gatherings where they can perform in front of other enthusiasts. Amateur folk song contests have become a regular feature on Japanese television, presenting folk singers from around the country. In these contests, singers give their renditions of folk songs, which are then evaluated by a board of "experts," who might tell the singer that his or her vibrato is too broad or hand gestures too dramatic for that particular song.

Folk song preservation societies have sprung up around the country (Groemer 1994). These societies are formed by amateurs who aim to "preserve" a particular local song and a style of performing that song. The activities of these clubs help foster pride and a sense of identity among the dwellers of a village or a neighborhood within a city (Hughes 1981; 1990–91).

Folk song performance has become more professional and standardized in recent years due to televised *minyō* and the changing tastes of the public. For example, *kobushi*, the sometimes complex vocal ornamentation of a melodic line, is frequently used to separate the good performers from the bad. One critic of this trend claims: "There is a tendency to think that the most excellent kind of folk song is that sung by a person with a good voice who can produce interesting kinds of vocal ornamentation. But if folk song is valued only for interesting ornamentation, it becomes nothing more than a 'popular song'" (Asano 1966:211). The critic noted, however, that national tastes and way of thinking have changed so much since 1945 that perhaps there is no way of avoiding change in folk singing.

Training to sing folk song at a professional level demands years of study. In recent years, folk song has developed its own *iemoto*-like system, modeled after that found in traditional art music. Asano Sanae, the singer on recorded selection 54, for example, has been a pupil of the *shamisen* player Asano Umewaka for several years (see ill. 8–6). In the manner of the *iemoto* system, she received her artistic

Ill. 8–6.   Folk singer of Akita. The woman on the right is Asano Sanae, who sings recorded selection 54. A fellow apprentice, Asano Yoshie, stands in the middle. This picture was taken in 1986 at the Folklife Festival of the Smithsonian Institution, Washington, D.C.

Ill. 8–7.   Asano Umewaka before singing Akita folk songs at the Folklife
Festival of the Smithsonian Institution, Washington, D.C.

name from him, including her teacher's last name. As a teenager, she moved from Osaka to Akita to become his apprentice, and she now participates regularly in concerts and competitions. Her teacher, in his seventies at the time of this recording, grew up in the Akita area and spent most of his life as a farmer, while slowly gaining a local and then a national reputation as a fine player of the Tsugaru *shamisen,* a type of *shamisen* used for virtuoso accompaniment of folk song. His former students live throughout Japan and teach his style of *shamisen* playing and singing.

According to Sanae, Asano himself can be hard taskmaster, but he teaches his pupils with great care. She underwent a kind of apprenticeship, helping with household chores and her teacher's performances while receiving lessons. Therefore, she experienced the everyday exposure and learning from repetition that the *gidayū-bushi* apprentices of earlier times had (see ill. 8–7).

Listening to recorded selection 54, a song called "Nikata-bushi," we hear first the sound of the *shamisen* but with a stronger tone than we heard in the *kouta* example. This *shamisen* is indeed different in construction, with a larger body, longer neck, and thicker skin. The first notes sound on the open strings, allowing the player to tune his instrument before beginning the piece. (You can hear the pitch change slightly as the player adjusts the strings.) The same "tuning" occurs later, in the instrumental interlude between verses.

The song text is composed of two verses, each set in the syllabic pattern typical of folk song: 7–7–7–5 (fig. 8–3).

The text of each verse is set to almost identical music, even down to the ornamentation used. Similarly, the patterns heard in the *shamisen* part between the two verses almost repeat the patterns played in the introduction.

As in the *kouta* example, the instrument plays a more or less steady pulse while the voice has a flexible rhythm. Look, for example, at the long notes and ornamentation in the vocal part, as seen in this transcription of the beginning of the second verse (ex. 8–7). In the transcription a time line underneath follows the regular beats of the *shamisen* part, so that the vocal part can be seen in relation to a steady unit of time.

This transcription was made at half speed, in order to catch the different pitches that normally hit our ears at a rapid pace. Pitches that are discernible at

Nikata tera-machi	The temple town Nikata
no hana baasama	a woman selling flowers
hana mo urazu ni	she doesn't sell them
abura uru.	but enjoys herself instead.
Takai o-yama no	On a high mountain
goten no sakura	a cherry blossom tree at a mansion
eda wa nana eda	has seven branches
yae ni saku.	and blossoms abundantly.

Fig. 8–3.   "Nikata-bushi" (folk song).

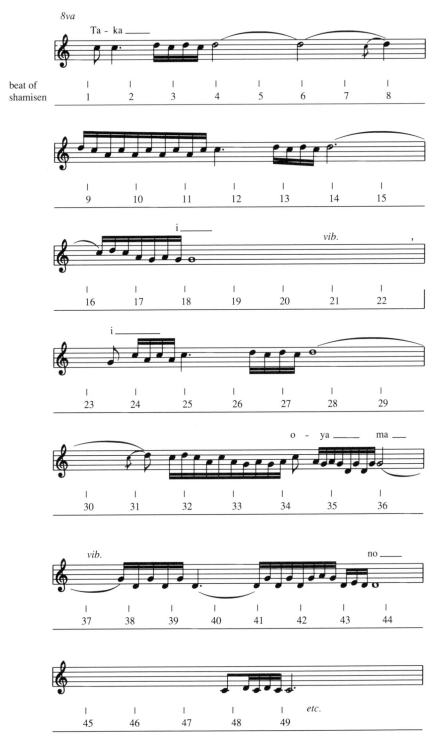

that speed are notated; vibrato within a range of less than a semitone is simply marked "vib." Looking at the different methods of ornamenting notes, we find many instances of rapid fluctuations between the note just voiced and a new note, before the new note is sounded and held. We also find several instances (for example, during the word *o-yama*) when a trill is performed between two notes that are as far apart as a perfect fourth. This technique of ornamenting the line requires great vocal control.

The perfect fourth and perfect fifth are important intervals in many Japanese folk songs. In the transcribed section, for example, the longest notes are D", G' and D', and these tones are the pivotal notes throughout the song. Both the *yo* scale and *minyō* tetrachords can be discerned here. Just before the voice enters with each verse, the *shamisen* player makes an exclamation that sounds like "huh!" This is another example of *kakegoe*, as first heard in the *kouta* selection.

Sanae's elderly teacher might be considered a "true," old-fashioned folk singer and *shamisen* player in this Tsugaru style, having learned it from childhood in his own native area. On the other hand, Sanae has studied purposefully to become a professional folk singer. This training is reflected in many ways in her performance, such as her ornamentation, precision, clarity of voice, and general presentation. Her singing of *minyō* interests us, however, because Japanese increasingly value these qualities today in a *minyō* singer.

FESTIVAL MUSIC: *MATSURI-BAYASHI*

Strolling down the street, visitors to Japan may be lucky enough to run into a boisterous crowd celebrating a *matsuri*, or Shinto festival. As people spill over from the sidewalks into the streets, a parade marches by with people dressed up in *kimonos*, some riding in floats or carrying huge portable shrines. In the heart of all the activity is a Shinto shrine, with the distinctive red *torii* gate, where scores of vendors are selling steaming noodles and old-fashioned toys, or offering chances to win a goldfish. In the background, the music of the festival, *matsuri-bayashi*, adds life and gaiety to the scene as the sounds of a graceful bamboo flute and booming drums fill the air (ill. 8–8).

Even in Tokyo, the capital and largest city of Japan, Shinto festivals are still held within the business districts and small neighborhoods scattered across the city. In every corner of the city—even in the most expensive commercial districts—a Shinto shrine can be found that serves as the tutelary or guardian shrine for that area. By offering prayers and festivities to the god-spirit, or *kami*, housed in the shrine, the residents receive the spirit's blessings for the year.

Although there is no legal or official relationship between a Shinto shrine and its neighborhood, many residents still feel it is important to help sponsor and participate in the traditional festival each year. They form committees and raise money to buy costumes, repair the parade floats, and so on. The festival is usually maintained in older neighborhoods with a stable population because of tradition—the residents have enjoyed their neighborhood *matsuri* for several generations. In Japanese cities, the neighborhood has been traditionally an important

Ill. 8–8. A Tokyo festival. The grounds of the Shinto shrine are covered with the booths of food and game vendors.

social unit—neighbors all knew one another and helped each other when needed, through both formal neighborhood associations and informal ties.

Since the end of World War II, however, there has been a dramatic rise in the mobility of the population as well as an increase in the white-collar sector of the population. As a result, urban neighborhood social ties have become more fragile because of shallower acquaintances with neighbors and fewer professional ties between them. Thus, some neighborhoods with a high turnover of population are also finding the traditional *matsuri* a good way to encourage a feeling of neighborhood friendliness.

With the high cost of living in Tokyo, families with roots in that city are moving in greater numbers to the suburbs. But there still remain some people like the Ueno family, who have lived in Tokyo for several generations. Teachers and performers of festival music, they live in the heart of *shitamachi,* or the "downtown" area. This is the older commercial area, long since passed up in large-scale development projects, where narrow streets are still lined with small, two-story wooden houses. Tokyo has some of the highest land prices in the world, and most houses seem to take up an unbelievably small amount of land. They are built so that their sliding front door comes right up to the sidewalk, leaving no land left unused. To provide some greenery in their surroundings, many residents put out pots of flowers and small trees on the sidewalk. Because the walls of the house are so thin, one can often hear, just walking by, all that goes on within—the television blaring, arguments between children, dishes being washed, and so on. Some of the buildings have small shops on the first floor, above which the shopkeepers and their families live. The women go shopping for groceries at the neighborhood stores, though they also sometimes shop at the big department stores outside their neighborhood. If there are no bath facilities in the house, the whole family bathes in the neighborhood public bathhouse. Bringing soap and plastic bucket with them, they spend time there each day chatting with friends. This close proximity and everyday contact with neighbors brings about a spirit of cooperation and solidarity within the community rarely seen in the suburbs of Tokyo.

When it is time to hold a festival at the small neighborhood shrine, much of the neighborhood becomes involved. The festival is usually held over two or three days. On a stage on the shrine grounds, a musical group—the *matsuri-bayashi*—plays throughout the day as a musical offering to the *kami* spirit. At some shrines, mimed skits and dances are performed as well to musical accompaniment.

The main event of the festival is a parade that winds through the neighborhood streets. Its principal element is the *mikoshi*, a portable shrine in which the *kami* of the shrine has been temporarily installed. The *kami's* ride through the neighborhood blesses it for the coming year. The shrine is elaborately decorated in gold and black lacquer and sometimes weighs as much as two tons (making it less "portable" than the translation of the term suggests). From fifty to more than one hundred men (and, lately, women too) hoist it on their shoulders and, tossing it up and down, carry it through the streets for several hours. Shouting repeatedly *"was-shoi,"* or some such exclamation to coordinate their movements, the *mikoshi* bearers make a colorful sight, dressed in traditional cotton jackets and pants. Along the parade route, spectators cheer them on. During this often rowdy parade, several festival music groups play at different locations: some remain at the permanent shrine, some perform on platforms along the parade route, and others play in floats in the parade (ill. 8–9).

Five musicians play the music of the *matsuri-bayashi* of Tokyo: two play the shallow double-headed drums called *shimedaiko* (or, more commonly in Tokyo, *shirabe*); one plays the *ōdaiko,* a deep-barreled drum; one the *shinobue,* a transverse bamboo flute; and one the *yosuke,* a hand-held gong. In other parts of Japan, different instruments are used for festival music, but these almost always include flutes and drums (see ill. 8–10).

A close musical relationship is crucial to the performance of *matsuri-bayashi.* Each of the musicians, while specializing on one instrument, must learn them all to become proficient. Only then can each one listen to the others' parts and know exactly where every player is in the piece. This degree of familiarity is important because the different instruments often "bend" the rhythm slightly by either holding back or speeding up their tempi. The gong player must keep an absolutely steady beat, though not sounding all the possible beats. After treating the constant beat so flexibly throughout most of the piece, all the instruments should meet exactly together at the end of each phrase. When well done, this simultaneous finish is regarded as the sign of a truly skillful ensemble. But if a member of the ensemble gets "lost" while playing with the beat in this way, the result can be

Ill. 8–9.   *Matsuri-bayashi* ensemble in the festival parade.

Ill. 8–10. *Matsuri-bayashi* of Tokyo. The two *shimedaiko* drums are on the right, the *ōdaiko* on the left. This was a performance at Columbia University, New York.

disastrous. Only the best ensembles, with years of experience performing together, can carry off this rhythmic game properly.

The example of *matsuri-bayashi* heard in recorded selection 55 is called "Yatai" and is the opening and closing section of a longer piece called "Kiribayashi" by the Ueno group. (The *yatai* is the wagon used to carry the *matsuri-bayashi* musicians in the festival parade.) The highly ornamented flute melody leads in and out of each section, while the vigorous drum patterns resound at increasing tempi. The main part of this section, after a short introduction, consists of seven repeated phrases (sometimes with variations thrown in), which accelerate with each repetition. At the end of one of these cycles the flute signals for the group to enter a final "coda" section.

In "Yatai," the first drum that enters is a *shirabe*; it sets the tempo for the entire piece. The flute enters with its introductory phrase, joined soon after by the two *shirabe* drums; finishing this section is a two-beat stroke by the large *ōdaiko* drum.

Even in this piece, with a heavy regular beat provided by the *shirabe* drums, the flute part and the deeper *ōdaiko* can vary the tempo just a little in order to make the rhythm more interesting. The flute's heavy ornamentation masks some of this rushing and holding back, but still the player is expected to meet the others at the end of each phrase.

This is the first piece taught to a new pupil in *matsuri-bayashi* by the Ueno family of downtown Tokyo: rapid repetition occurs, student copies teacher. Comparing their typical *matsuri-bayashi* lessons to the lessons in *gidayū-bushi,* we see some similarities to the past but without the pressure of the old days. A lesson with Ueno Mitsuyuki and his son Mitsumasa might proceed as follows.° The student slides open the front door and calls out, "Good evening." Upon being invited to enter, the student immediately removes his shoes and takes a big step up to the level of the first floor of the house. There, on the *tatami* mats, the student bows to Ueno-*sensei* (*sensei* means teacher) and his family, who are all seated in an inner room. The lesson takes place in the room entered by the front door, and since musical instruments and household items are stacked along the walls, the sitting space is only about two meters by two meters. The family is still eating dinner and talking loudly to each other over the sound from the television set.

The teacher likes to chat with students before beginning a lesson. He might talk about his experiences in Tokyo during the war, or the latest *kabuki* performance he attended, or a recent argument with a neighbor. Then, after more students have arrived, either he or his son begins the lesson. In place of a real drum they use an old tire because of the neighbor's complaints about late-night practice sessions. This tire is placed in the middle of the tiny front room. Students and teacher sit on their knees around it, sticks in hand. The teacher begins to teach a new phrase of a piece by hitting the tire in mirror image to the way the performer normally plays, so that the students looking at him can easily learn the correct hand movements.

While striking the "drum" (the *shirabe,* or small drum, part is normally taught first), the teacher also calls out syllables to help the students remember the rhythm of the phrase they are playing. When there is no drum part, he hums or sings the flute melody and inserts some of the *ōdaiko* beats as well by hitting the side of the tire with one of his sticks. All parts are taught through a type of solmization (the syllables that stand for pitch or rhythm). Most genres of traditional Japanese music have their own solmization systems.

In *matsuri-bayashi,* the solmization of the *shirabe* part in the main section of the recorded selection is shown in figure 8–4.

It is not difficult to reproduce this rhythmic pattern by tapping a flat surface with the fingers. Begin each phrase with the right hand and do not use the same hand for two consecutive beats, except at the beginning of a new phrase (which should start with the right hand again). Comparing this solmization (which is sometimes called *shōka* in Japanese) to the Western notation shown, we can see that "ten" equals two half-beats, "tsu" equals a half-beat rest, and "ke" equals a half-beat following a half-beat rest. (No syllables are spoken on the last beat of the phrase, though a rest of one beat occurs there.)

Students write down these syllables to help them remember the rhythmic patterns of the drums, and a similar system helps them to memorize the flute melody. However, merely hearing the syllables, without hearing them performed, gives only a vague notion of how they are to be played. The "score" that results is at best a memory device to help the student recall what was taught. As a conse-

°The elder Ueno passed away in 1983, but the present tense is used here to refer to his life and work.

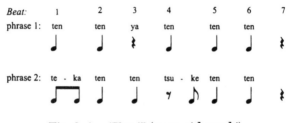

Fig. 8–4. "Yatai" (*matsuri-bayashi*).

quence, Japanese music characteristically lacks a detailed notation system. The teacher is critical to a student's mastering any musical form. Without teachers who are willing to convey a great deal of their musical knowledge, students would be helpless, for scores do not give them access to real musical knowledge.

A good relationship with a knowledgeable teacher is also essential if a student wants to learn any *hikyoku,* or secret pieces. Found in many genres of traditional music, including *matsuri-bayashi,* the secret repertoire consists of rarely performed pieces handed down only to the most trusted of pupils. In the style of festival music taught by the Ueno family, the secret pieces were described by the son as not technically difficult but valued mainly because of their exclusivity. In the past, this knowledge was so guarded that some *hikyoku* have disappeared because teachers have died before finding pupils worthy of learning their secrets.

The lives of Ueno Mitsuyuki and his son vividly exemplify the traditional and contemporary backgrounds of those who love Tokyo festivals and festival music. *Matsuri-bayashi* is traditionally performed by amateurs such as the Uenos, while *kagura,* the mimed plays based on Shinto themes, is carried out by professional actors and musicians (ill. 8–11). According to the father, performing *matsuri-bayashi* strictly as an amateur is important because it is really a pious act of offering entertainment to the gods, not a "performance" or "show." Therefore, he performs only at the festivals themselves. The son, however, while preferring to play at festivals, also plays occasionally with some of the professional *kagura* musicians who have learned how to play *matsuri-bayashi.* These musicians are frequently hired to provide a musically festive atmosphere at secular occasions such as wedding receptions and department store openings.

For both father and son, however, *matsuri-bayashi* remains secondary to their main profession, which is *chōkin,* or metal carving. This intricate art uses silver and gold to create jewelry (such as pins and ornaments for the *kimono*), sword guards, Japanese pipe holders, and small, elegant statues of Buddha. The technique, a combination of engraving and inlay, required years of training and great patience.

The life of Ueno Mitsuyuki epitomizes the spirit of the Edo *matsuri-bayashi.* Born in 1900 in the old downtown area of Tokyo, Ueno proudly tells of his family's long history in Edo. They came to Edo at the beginning of the Tokugawa era (in the early seventeenth century) from Aichi Prefecture. His grandfather was of

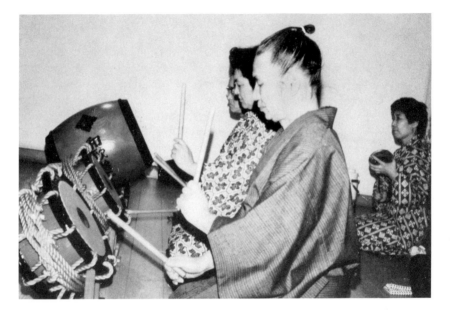

Ill. 8–11.   **Ueno Mitsuyuki playing** *matsuri-bayashi.*

the *samurai* class, which was dissolved with the class system during the Meiji period. In the 1880s, Ueno's father learned metal carving and *matsuri-bayashi.*
Ueno's mother, as the daughter of the priest of an important shrine in the area,
was active throughout her life in their own neighborhood festival.

At the age of fourteen, Ueno began to study metal carving seriously, dropping
for a time all other hobbies and interests. After he had finished his metal carving
training with his father, Ueno studied *matsuri-bayashi* with his uncle, a talented
musician. Ueno says: "In the old days, the teacher told the students they were stu-
pid and played poorly and maybe even hit them, but without explaining exactly
what was wrong. In this way, I learned both *matsuri-bayashi* and metal carving—
the technique became a part of my bones. But these days, people want to be told
exactly what is wrong so that they can learn the art quickly and start making
money from it." He learned *matsuri-bayashi* easily and soon became well known
for his flute-playing style.

Ueno was too old to be accepted in the military during World War II, and he became active in the neighborhood association, which organized drills and fought fires
in his area. He recalls the many times American planes dropped bombs on Tokyo,
which quickly set afire the closely packed wooden houses, leaving thousands homeless within minutes. But he also blames the military leaders of Japan for dragging
their country into such a bloody war, and laments the loss of life on all sides.

When he was thirty-six, relatively late in life, Ueno married a woman from his
own neighborhood in Tokyo. His son Mitsumasa was born in 1953, when Ueno
was already in his fifties, and he was therefore determined to teach the boy the

skills he knew as early as possible. Knowing how long it would take to learn the intricate arts of metal carving and *matsuri-bayashi*, Ueno was afraid there would not be enough time for him to teach everything he knew to his son. He began teaching Mitsumasa the drum part of *matsuri-bayashi* when the boy was three, and metal carving when he was seven. Lessons were conducted every day for one hour after school. By the time he was fifteen, Mitsumasa had become proficient enough in both arts to satisfy his father that his skills had been faithfully transmitted to the next generation.

Ueno told me that he was never bored. Every day he rises after only four or five hours of sleep and, no matter what the weather, strolls to the various shrines in his neighborhood at 4 A.M. to offer prayers. He then begins his work day upstairs in his workshop, together with his son. Sitting side by side, they work almost every day of the week. Father and son stop for a meal at midday; in the early evening, with the disappearance of daylight, they finish their day's work. (Because the work is so intricate, working by daylight is much easier than by artificial light.) Around 7 P.M. three days a week, the first pupils arrive and the music lessons begin. As there is a great deal of chatting and serving of tea, the lessons sometimes go on until 10 or 11 P.M.

The father exhibits a characteristic typical of the *Edokko*, or "child of Edo"—a nonchalant attitude toward money. For instance, he refuses to sell pieces of his metal carving of which he is especially fond. Also, he readily turns down commissions for work, even when in need of it, if making the requested object does not appeal to him. As Ueno put it: "If you had the choice between gold and silver or paper (money), which would you prefer? And we're not talking about just plain gold and silver, but something you've created out of them which is unique in the world." Then he gave a self-deprecatory laugh and said, "Do you believe there are such innocent people left in the world as myself?" By the same token, the Uenos accept only a small amount of money for the music lessons they give. The father once confided that they would rather give the lessons free, but found that people did not take them seriously if they did not pay something for them.

In spite of their relative poverty and busy lives, the Uenos still find the materials and the time to create with their own hands many of the items needed for the annual neighborhood festival. These include masks and costumes for the mimed plays in which they participate, as well as the drawing of designs to be dyed in to the material of the musicians' *kimonos*.

Ueno feels that his profession of metal carving and his hobby of *matsuri-bayashi* have one important quality in common. This is the feeling, as a practitioner, that one is never "finished," or has reached a point of perfection. "This is what makes life interesting: that which you want to do is never in a state of perfection, so you always have to strive to do better. That's why I enjoy metal carving and why I enjoy *matsuri-bayashi*."

As for the son, Mitsumasa, from the earliest moment he can remember, his father reiterated the importance of his learning both metal carving and *matsuri-bayashi* as soon as possible. In the beginning, Mitsumasa says, he was actually not very interested in carving; but his father said, "Just give it a try." And so, he says, "I've been giving it a try for over twenty-five years now!"

Now the son is proud of carrying on the work of his father, both the metal carving and the festival music. Mitsumasa is one of the few young practitioners of metal carving, and he already has won many prizes for his work. As for *matsuri-bayashi,* he says, "I've got that music in my blood now, so as long as I'm around, I want to be playing it." As was the case with his father, the son's flute playing has become well admired, and professional musical troupes seek his services.

Today, both folk song and festival music are becoming professionalized and standardized. Folk song in particular seems to be adopting the standards of the "art" genres like *shakuhachi* and *koto* music, with their *iemoto* systems, rankings, and artistic names. As for *matsuri-bayashi,* not only the younger Ueno, but many other Tokyo *matsuri-bayashi* players feel the lure of professional troupes, aware of the income and prestige they could attain as a member of such a company. As musicians join *iemoto* and professional organizations, the pressure to conform to certain performance standards increases.

POPULAR MUSIC

The traditional music genres described up to now had been conveyed from performer to audience without electronic media for many centuries. At a single performance the audience of these traditional genres was relatively small, and establishing rapport with that audience was crucial to success. Today, music performances are regularly presented on radio, television, and other media. A single recorded performance may be heard by millions of people who are unseen to the musicians.

In addition to changing the ways traditional music is played and perceived, mass media and technology have also stimulated the growth of a new kind of music in Japan, which we shall call here "popular music."° Since 1907, when the first commercial music recording was released in Japan, the composition, performance, and appreciation of music has changed dramatically. Music recorded specifically for commercial release in Japan, with the aim of appealing to the mass audience, exhibits several characteristics:

1. Performance within a set time limit (generally three to five minutes);

2. A focus on themes that appeal to a broad public (though regional or specialty audiences are also sometimes targeted);

3. Stanza form and a steady beat, making the music more accessible to the Japanese who have become more accustomed to Western music;

4. In live performance, performers aim to reproduce the recorded version of the music so as to fulfill audience expectations;

5. Music rises and falls dramatically in popularity over time.

°Popular music is defined here as music primarily created for and transmitted by the various mass media. While some genres of so-called popular song that flourished among the masses in pre-Meiji Japan also have exerted an impact on the popular music of today, only those genres particularly linked to contemporary popular genres are discussed here.

This "Top 40" mentality was novel to the Japanese; in their previous experience it was common for many kinds of music dating from different eras in Japanese history to survive side by side as vital elements of the country's musical life. Now, through the association of songs with a specific point in time, generations have begun to identify with "their" songs, with the result that music can be used as an age marker.

Through the mass media, music performed by "others" (particularly professionals) became more available to more people than ever before. Today, there is scarcely a home in Japan without a radio, television set, or stereo, and many have all three. As people listen to the same recordings and to the same performance of a song, they are united by a common musical experience; they also develop certain expectations as to what music should sound like.

Of course, a similar process has occurred worldwide as popular music has penetrated all corners of the globe. In Japan, the spread of music through records, tapes, and compact discs has advanced very rapidly. In fact, since the mid-1970s, their combined sales have exceeded "those of all other capitalist nations, except the USA" (Mitsui 1984:107). Furthermore, the Japanese have far more opportunities to hear American and European popular music than Western listeners generally have to hear non-Western popular music. One industry survey shows that since 1970, about two-fifths of all popular music recordings produced in Japan were recorded by foreign musicians, most of whom were American or European (Mitsui 1984:107).

HISTORICAL BACKGROUND

The types of popular music found in today's Japan developed as the modern Japanese state emerged. It is interesting that the present-day music scene has evolved into an exceedingly diverse one in a country known in the past for its high degree of cultural homogeneity. The rise of this contemporary heterogeneous music-culture and specifically "Japanese" popular music can be traced to the latter half of the nineteenth century. At this time, wide-ranging reforms were introduced to Japanese society to enable the country to deal with Western powers. The traditional class system was abolished, and the authority of the Tokugawa regime was replaced by a government headed by the Emperor Meiji. He left Kyoto and set up a new capital in what was now called "Tokyo," or Eastern Capital. This government introduced a constitutional monarchy and made many structural changes in the society to allow a mercantile and industrial economy to flourish.

After their long era of isolation, the Japanese felt it necessary to "modernize" life around them, which for a while meant adopting Western models. Leaders rapidly installed a system of compulsory education and decided, from reading about the Dutch and French school systems, that Japan also needed compulsory singing in its schools. In the late 1870s Izawa Shuji, a Japanese school principal who had studied in Massachusetts, and Luther Whiting Mason, an American who was director of music for the Boston primary schools, developed a plan for music instruction in Japanese public schools.

In the following years *shōka* songs were introduced to meet a goal of teaching songs that blended Japanese and Western elements. The newly composed songs used melodies based on a traditional Japanese scale within the structure of a stanza form and a regular meter. Other songs introduced in the schools contained Western melodies such as "Auld Lang Syne" and "Swanee River" set with Japanese texts. Through songs like these, both *shōka* and Western songs, the Japanese masses were introduced to Western musical structure, scale, and rhythm.

In the last decades of the nineteenth century, different opinions emerged over Japan's future direction. According to one faction, Japan should aim toward a democracy similar to that of the United States. Others, however, supported a strong monarchy and political power for the small group of advisers around the emperor. These people believed that the emperor should stand as the symbol of the nation and its long history and spirit; he would lead the Japanese to a new era of world leadership.

In the end, those who supported the monarchy gained political supremacy, and their spiritual descendants eventually led Japan to political and military expansion and World War II. But during the Meiji period these arguments were still far from settled, and the public became highly involved in them. In the 1880s, when the People's Rights Movement urged further democratization through the establishment of a parliament, a new kind of song called *enka* evolved to express the goals of the movement. The words of one such song, "Oppekepe," written in 1887, show how political the early *enka* were:[*]

> I'd like to make those who dislike "rights and happiness" [for the people] drink the water of freedom. Those in their fancy Western hairdos and hats, who dress in stylish garb, their outward appearance may be fine but their political thinking is inadequate; they don't understand the truth of the land. We should sow the seeds of freedom in their hearts.[†]

The very title of another song, popular from 1886 to 1888, indicates its incendiary purpose: "Dynamite Song." Its first verse reads:

> Yamato [meaning "Japanese"] spirit is polished with rain
> From the tears of the advocates of People's Rights.
> Promote the national interest and the people's happiness
> Foster the National Resources
> Because if this is not done—
> Dynamite! Bang! (Malm 1971:278)

These deeply political *enka* songs were transformed through the decades to become sentimental songs full of nostalgia and longing; but their early influence on the development of Japanese popular song as a whole is unmistakable.

The *enka* song called "Nonki-bushi" ("Song of the Lazy Man") was composed in 1918, and was an early "hit" (recorded selection 56). Its composer was Soeda

[*]Actually, the words to this song are not so much "sung" to a melody as recited like a rhythmic chant.
[†]Author's translation.

Azembo, one of the most famous of the early Japanese popular music composers. Soeda began his career as an *enka* singer, but by the early twentieth century the *enka* had already changed in character dramatically, as you will realize from listening to this selection. The lyrics exemplify a typical "silly" song that was popular in the vaudeville halls of the day and reappeared many times over the years in Japan (fig. 8–5).

The singer of this original recording, Ishida Ichimatsu, also wrote the lyrics to this song. Ishida, born in 1902, was studying law in Tokyo when he met Soeda through a musical club. He then began his career in song writing and singing, producing many 78 rpm hit records. In the post–World War II years, Ishida entered politics and was reelected several times to the National Diet before his death in 1956.

Comparing this song to the earlier examples of Japanese vocal music found in this chapter, we find some astonishing differences: a steady beat in the melody, the repetition of stanzas, the quality of the voice, and the narration of small stories in each verse. The effects of Western popular music here are obvious. On the Japanese vaudeville stage, the repetitive structure was convenient because it allowed the performer to add new verses—perhaps pertaining to timely political issues, or making fun of someone in the audience—as he desired.

One aspect of Japanese vocal music that remains, however, is a vestige of the rich tradition of ornamentation. Listen for the quick ornaments placed over some notes in this verse and in following verses. Recreating these ornaments is to this day still considered essential in the performance of *enka,* even among amateurs.

In the transcription of the first verse (ex. 8–8), a short introduction is played by a violin based on the melody of the last phrase, "He he, nonki da ne" ("Ha ha, how lazy"). This same phrase appears briefly between each verse and at the conclusion of the song. Otherwise, the violin follows the vocal line with only slight embellishments. When "Nonki-bushi" was written, the practice of harmonizing *enka* with chords had not yet replaced the single string instrument—first *shamisen*, then the violin, in later years the guitar—in supporting and occasionally embellishing the melodic line.

In the 1990s the *enka* still has many fans, but it has undergone several transformations since the days of "Nonki-bushi." In the years after World War II, *enka* became a highly sentimental song genre that most commonly evoked images of *sake* bars, with the ubiquitous red lantern hanging outside, port towns (the site of many sad farewells), and foggy or rainy, lonely evenings.

One might imagine that the older generation would be most likely to appreciate such nostalgic expressions of sadness. Indeed, for many younger people who grew up with rock music, *enka* sounds too old-fashioned and sentimental for their taste. By the mid-1970s the audiences for *enka* were growing older, and the genre did not seem to hold much appeal for younger listeners. But then a new phenomenon called *karaoke* appeared on the scene, reinvigorating the *enka* and bringing it to a new, younger audience.

Karaoke means "empty orchestra" and designates the technological development that allowed anyone with the proper equipment to sing their favorite songs

Nonki no tōsan	The lazy man
o-uma no keiko	rides a horse
o-uma ga hashirihajimete	and it begins to run
tomaranai.	and won't stop.
Kodomo wa omoshirosō ni	A child enjoys this, asking,
Tōsan, doko e yuku.	"Hey, where are you going?"
Doko e yukun da ka	"If you want to know where I'm
o-uma ni kiito kure	going, better ask the horse!"
He he nonki da ne.	Ha, ha, how lazy!
Nonki na tōsan no	The lazy man—
bōya ga hadaka de	his son was naked
kaachan ga kimono o	and the mother scolded him
kiyo to shikattemo	to put on his kimono.
bōya wa iya da to itte	The boy said he wouldn't
kimono o kinai	put on his kimono.
. . . Choito Tōsan, bōya ga	"Hey, Father, our son is naked—
hada de komarimasu wa yo.	do something!"
Nanda nanda bōya kaze o hiitara	"What's this! Son, what will
doo surun da	you do if you catch a cold?"
dete kita tōsan ga maruhade	said the father, coming out
	stark naked.
He he nonki da ne.	Ha ha, how lazy!
Nonki na tōsan	The lazy man
O-mawari-san ni natta kedo	became a policeman but
Saaberu ga jama ni natte	his saber got in the way
arukenai	and he couldn't walk.
ichido koronde mata mata	He fell once, then again
korobi	and again.
Sakki okinakereba yokatta	"It would've been better if
mono ni to sa	I hadn't gotten up again!"
he he nonki da ne.	Ha ha, how lazy!"
Nonki na tōsan	The lazy man
teppo katsuide	carries his rifle
haruka kanata o naganureba	looking at a far-off tree
	branch
tsugai no hato poppo ga	a pair of pigeons are
narande tomatteru.	sitting together.
Aida o neratte uttara	"If I aim for the middle, I
dotchika ataru daro.	should hit one, I guess!
he he nonki da ne.	Ha, ha, how lazy!
Nonki na tōsan	The lazy man
koe hariagete	shouted to the others,
mina kite miro taihen da	"Everyone, come and see—
hayaku kite miro	come quickly and see
mattaku taihen da	it's incredible!
are miro suita densha ga	Look there—an empty train
tōtteiru	is going by!"
he he nonki da ne.	Ha, ha, how lazy!

Fig. 8–5. "Nonki-bushi."

Ex. 8–8. "Nonki-bushi," first verse.

to a full orchestral accompaniment. A typical set-up includes a cassette tape play-back machine on which is played a prerecorded tape of the musical accompaniment to a favorite song, and one or two microphones for amplifying the voice as the amateur sings the melodic line.

Enka were, and continue to be, the songs of choice for most *karaoke* users. Other kinds of music found on *karaoke* tapes include Japanese folk and contemporary "pop" songs, as well as Western popular songs; but the majority are some kind of *enka*. A *karaoke* singer may either sing the lyrics of these songs from memory or consult a book containing the lyrics to hundreds of songs.

A large variety of *karaoke* machines are produced in Japan, ranging in price from about $200 to $5,000, but averaging about $2,000. The difference in price is determined by the machine's features. The more expensive models are used in restaurants, bars, wedding halls, and banquet rooms. At these places, customers or guests sing songs of their choice from a wide selection available on tape, singing either alone or in couples. Models priced in the middle range are often installed in smaller bars as well as touring buses and trains so that Japanese traveling in groups can sing to each other on long trips. The inexpensive models are designed for home use, so that users can practice for these "public" performances. There are even battery-powered models for outdoor use.

Sales of *karaoke* machines indicate how widespread its popularity has become. In 1978, 100,000 sets were sold, but within five years, this figure had jumped to 1,100,000 sets, resulting in $625 million in sales. A report in *Time* magazine noted that this is more than was spent that year in the United States on gas ranges ("Closet Carusos" 1983:47).

The *karaoke* technology made available to the consumer was developed to support and enhance his or her voice as much as possible. One can adjust the volume of the vocal part in relation to the instrumental background, and even switch on an echo device when desired (to add a kind of "singing-in-the-shower" effect). Some equipment is digitized, permitting singers to change the key of the original accompaniment tape to one in their own register. Even the musical accompaniment is designed to be helpful to the singer; the orchestra stays in the background to avoid stealing the show from the singer, but one instrument reinforces the melodic line, in case the singer becomes lost.

This equipment has reinforced the traditional Japanese custom of group singing. Japanese feel that singing helps to establish a relaxed atmosphere and feeling of closeness with others. Social groups—based on professional, school, familial, or community relationships—are important in Japanese life, and the Japanese put much effort into harmonious relationships within these groups. For example, to improve relations among company employees, management organizes special activities such as group tours to spas and drinking parties. On these occasions, *karaoke* is used to break down the social barriers created by the company hierarchy. For this purpose, mere conversation, even when mixed with drinking, does not suffice because it is based on knowledge and wit. But *karaoke* is a different kind of socializing, and the most sentimental, nostalgic ideas can be expressed—and are even encouraged—when sung through the *karaoke* machine.

Karaoke singing also reinforces group harmony through the expectation that each member of a group will participate by singing in front of the group. Even if someone feels embarrassed and wants to refuse, he or she usually gives in and sings at least one song in order to maintain the spirit of group harmony. In recent years, *karaoke* has become popular around the world; one can find "*karaoke* bars" in South America, Europe, and the United States, for example. However, public *karaoke* singing in these continents does not influence and control group social dynamics to the same degree as in Japan and other Asian countries.

Karaoke technology works also as an outlet for stress. For instance, the echo feature gives singers a sense of removal from their everyday identity. One Japanese, living in America, stated: "It's great to hear your own voice, resounding throughout the room. You feel all your tension disappear." Some businessmen in Japan enjoy going to *karaoke* bars after work just for that purpose: to relieve the accumulated stress from a day of work by belting down a few drinks and belting out a few songs. One survey shows that *karaoke* is most popular among male, white-collar workers between the ages of twenty and forty-nine; the same survey also found that, within any age group, those who enjoyed *karaoke* the most were "those who like to sing" and "those who like to drink" (NHK Hōsō 1982:24–25).

Even Japanese businessmen living abroad find *karaoke* bars in which they can spend their afterhours. In New York City, for example, where a large population of Japanese businessmen work, some twenty or more *karaoke* bars had sprung up by the mid-1980s, and a fierce competition had broken out among them to install the latest technological developments in *karaoke*. One such development is the laser disc video machine, which shows a series of videotaped scenes to accompany each song. Besides the added visual stimulation, it is said that this apparatus also has the advantage that the singers need not have their heads buried in the lyric book but can look up at the screen and at their listeners.

While the content of the music is quite different, there is an interesting similarity in the way *enka* songs (as sung over *karaoke* machines) and traditional music are learned. Both involve aural skills—listening very carefully to an "original" version (of the recording in the case of *enka*, and of the teacher in traditional music) and imitating it as skillfully as possible. These days, some notation can also be involved. Real *karaoke* enthusiasts can even study with a teacher for pointers or technique but, for the most part, singers become familiar with the melody and interpretation of a song after listening to a recorded professional version many times.

At the top level of performance, though, *karaoke* performances are expected to produce more than exact imitations of another's performance. For example, more expensive models of *karaoke* machines can automatically score a performer on a scale of 1 to 100. One enthusiast told me that in his experience "exact" reproduction of a song in its original interpretation might bring you a score of 98 or 99, but not 100. For the highest score, an element of "personal expressiveness" is necessary, while at the same time one must show complete mastery of the original version. In the traditional music genres described earlier, we have seen this same standardization of music performance among the lower-ranking performers, with expectations for more personal creativity at the master level.

By the same token, master performers of *gidayū-bushi* music, festival music, and other kinds of music discussed here also should go beyond imitating their teachers. For most, however, simply meeting the criteria of imitation—as promoted at most levels of the *iemoto* system—is a lifelong task. Few performers reach the stage where personal interpretation is acceptable, and even then it can be controversial.

Karaoke's impact on the musical life of the typical Japanese should not be underestimated. The use of these machines by people of all ages has widened the average person's song repertoire. The musical generation gap, prompted by the growth of popular music, has narrowed somewhat as a result of *karaoke* activity. Within one social group, members of different generations hear and learn songs from one another's repertoires. Singing together encourages this intergenerational learning process.

The music industry has had good reason to be pleased with *karaoke's* popularity. This technology not only provides a new avenue for merchandizing recorded music (the *karaoke* tapes) but in some cases stimulates sales of the original version of a popular song—when people like a song sung by someone at a bar, they sometimes purchase the record themselves in order to learn it.

Enka's popularity has spread to younger age groups because of social *karaoke* singing. At the same time *enka* composers have adapted their songs to the tastes of the younger generation. Background accompaniment ranges from the earlier simple guitar accompaniment to sophisticated orchestral arrangements and heavier, rock-type beats. More "upbeat" *enka* have been issued, with faster tempos and more optimistic lyrics, though these are still in the minority. Finally, vocal ornamentation, so emphasized in earlier *enka,* is toned down in the newer versions because the youth are more accustomed to hearing Western-style vocalization.

The *enka* song found in recorded selection 57 ("Naite Nagasaki," or "Crying Nagasaki") is typical of the more old-fashioned variety of *enka* meant for a middle-aged audience. Recorded in 1988 by a *geisha,* the mournfully romantic theme of the song, its orchestral background, and its vocal style appeal to people who visit a bar with a *karaoke* machine after a long day at work and want to indulge in a little emotionalism. The text (fig. 8–6) describes a woman alone in her room as she contemplates the departure of her lover.

Several images brought out in the song are common to many *enka* songs. The setting of the port town of Nagasaki conjures up romantic associations and particularly the sadness of lovers parting. The scenes of drowning oneself in *sake,* crying in the windy night, and—on top of all that—rain are also found in hundreds of other *enka* songs. For such themes, the Japanese prefer to use a natural minor scale, sometimes with the sharped seventh added. At times, the melody too emphasizes the sad mood, for example in the setting of the words "Naite, naite . . . ," as though the singer were sobbing (ex. 8–9).

The form of the song is also typical of *enka,* as we have already seen in "Nonki-bushi"—a simple strophe with a refrain. It opens and closes with instrumental sections, which also recur between strophes. As soon as the voice enters, the background accompaniment becomes minimal, consisting mainly of a bass guitar playing a bass line and other orchestral and electronic instruments filling in the harmony. This accompaniment begins to expand towards the end of the stanza as the vocal part reaches the climax at "Naite, naite . . ."

Harmonically, *enka* tend to use a conservative progression of chords, like most Western popular music. There is a brief modulation to the relative major (on the last "Nagasaki"), but otherwise the main movement is between the tonic, subdominant, and dominant of A minor.

Compared to "Nonki-bushi," "Naite Nagasaki" contains far more complicated orchestration, the use of background singers, and other elements indicative of Western popular music. However, the occasional use of vocal ornamentation reflects Japanese taste in vocal quality. Examples can be found in the slight tremolo heard in the voice in the line "nobori no ressha," the occasional use of vi-

Saka no mukō ni	On the other side of the hill
yogisha ga mieru	I can see the night train.
Anata noseteku	Taking you away,
nobori no ressha	the northbound train.
Okuritai kedo	I want to send you off
okureba tsurai	but if I do it will be painful.
Heya no mado kara	From the window of my room
te o furu watashi	I wave good-bye to you.
Naite naite naite	Crying, crying, crying,
Nagasaki	Nagasaki,
Ame ni narisō, ne.	It looks like rain, doesn't it?
Wakarenakereba	That you were someone
naranaihito to	with whom I'd have to part—
shitte inagara	although I knew this,
moyashita inochi	a burning fate,
sugaritsukitai	wanting to cling to you,
Maruyamadōri	along the Maruyamadōri [street name]
jitto koraete	with steady endurance,
aruita watashi	I walked:
Naite naite naite	Crying, crying, crying
Nagasaki	Nagasaki.
Ame ni narisō, ne.	It looks like rain, doesn't it?
Minato yokaze	The night wind from the port
fukikomu kabe ni	blows against the wall
furete setsunai	making flutter
anata no heyagi	your robe hanging there.
nigai o-sake o	I drown myself
abiteru watashi	in bitter *sake*.
Naite naite naite	Crying, crying, crying
Nagasaki.	Nagasaki.
Ame ni narisō, ne.	It looks like rain, doesn't it?

Fig. 8–6.   "Naite Nagasaki" ("Crying Nagasaki").

brato before the end of a stanza, and the final ornamented fall from the B to the A at the end of the transcribed stanza.

The large Japanese music industry produces many other kinds of popular music in addition to *enka*. Some are strongly influenced by Western genres, and some show connections to Japanese musical traditions. The term *kayōkyoku* describes Japanese popular song as a whole, and particularly the songs, including *enka*, that mix Western and Japanese musical elements. This combination is usually a blend of Japanese melodies made from pentatonic scales with Western harmonic progressions and metrical organization. Since the mid-1970s, however, many of the contemporary songs have been written in Western scales, especially major modes, conforming to the imported music listened to by Japanese youth.

The labels identifying different kinds of Japanese popular music are very con-

Ex. 8–9. **Transcription of "Naite Nagasaki" (first verse).**

fusing (as they can be in Western popular music as well) because they are so often inconsistently applied; but the following labels are the most common.

GUNKA

Literally "military songs," *gunka* were first composed and gained popularity during the Russo-Japanese War of 1904–1905. More songs were composed in succeeding military engagements. People in their sixties and seventies now strongly associate such songs with their youth during World War II and therefore are still extremely fond of them. Influenced by military music of the West, these songs are written in stanza form, often with trumpet and other brass instruments in the instrumental accompaniment. Not all are enthusiastic about fighting and war. Some songs were written from the point of view of a lonely mother waiting for her soldier-son to come home, or of a soldier on the front who has just lost his best friend in battle.

FOLK SONG

Fōku songu can apply to either Western "new" folk songs, as sung by musicians such as Joan Baez and Bob Dylan, or to the Japanese songs written mainly in the 1960s and 1970s that were influenced by such music. Japanese folk singers of this period typically wrote the words and music of the songs they sang. This practice was different from the separation of songwriter, lyricist, and singer that had formerly predominated in Japanese popular music. Musically, these songs can scarcely be differentiated from their Western counterparts; the lyrics, however, sung in Japanese, often refer to social or political issues that are specifically Japanese.

NEW MUSIC

Also written phonetically to imitate the English words (*nyū myūshiku*), this term developed in the late 1970s to designate a music that had grown out of the "folk song" style. Represented at first by singer-songwriters such as Yoshida Tokurō and Minami Kōsetsu, "new music" songs generally convey an introverted, personal point of view that appeals to today's young people. In this type of song, the melody, usually written in the natural minor scale and in short phrases, is given more importance than the presence of a strong beat.

POPS

Appearing from the late 1970s and aimed at a teenage audience, music of this kind is ordinarily sung by teenagers themselves, some as young as fourteen. These singers, mostly female, are discovered by production companies that send talent scouts all over the country. Upon locating a promising candidate, the company decides on the appropriate image for the singer, trains her to sing in a certain way, and choreographs her performances. Television is an important medium for these teenage performers, as a new singer can gain instant fame with an appearance on one of the numerous musical variety shows. Performing in costumes that accentuate an image of youth and innocence, dozens of these singers rise and fall in the Japanese music business each year, while a few lucky ones manage to maintain long-term careers.

These songs are usually Western sounding in arrangement and melody and, to add a touch of sophistication and exoticism, often include a few words of English in the lyrics. Typically, English words or phrases are alternated with Japanese lines, but the English may not be strictly idiomatic. Figure 8–7 shows an example from one song, with the Japanese phrases translated in parentheses.

In addition to *gunka, fōku songu,* new music, and pops, there are easy listening, rock, punk, and many other kinds of popular music, mostly based on Western models but sometimes deviating from those models in interesting ways. In addition, popular music and musicians from other parts of Asia have gained popularity since the early 1990s. This trend can be linked to the rising number of Asian immigrant workers and to the increase in travel by Japanese to Taiwan and Southeast Asia.

We have reviewed a small sample of the wide variety of music heard in Japan today. This sample contains many examples of the mixture of native with foreign elements in the evolution of new musical forms. The *shakuhachi* was developed from an instrument of Chinese origin that entered Japan around the eighth century. The Zen philosophy that underlay the instrument's use in meditation also originated in China. The prototype of the *shamisen,* used to play *kouta* and music of the puppet theater and to accompany traditional folk song, can be traced to Okinawa, China, and beyond. Most of the instruments of the festival music ensemble also originated in China and underwent adaptation in Japan. Finally, popular music as a whole is based in form, rhythmic and harmonic structure, and instrumental accompaniment on Western music; only the melodic component and the lyric content in some cases reflect Japanese traditions.

Of course, one can question the concept itself of "tradition" or the "traditional culture" of a nation or people, especially in terms of "purity" of origin. What culture group in the world has not borrowed cultural elements from another, with the roots of that borrowing going so far back that few think of the idea or custom as "borrowed"?

We find, in examining the Japanese music-culture, the expression of some aspects of the varied Japanese character. For instance, popular nonsense songs like "Nonki-bushi" (recorded selection 56) find their roots in a certain outlandish

I had understood your heart
Ima made wa kotoba ga nakuta tie
(Up to now, without any words)
Oh, please tell me your heart
Ima sugu ni . . . ru, ru, ru, ru
(Right away, ru, ru, ru, ru)°

Fig. 8–7. "Himitsu no kata."

°From the song "Himitsu no kata," sung by Iijima Mari. Victor Records VDR–6, 1984.

sense of humor that the Japanese sometimes indulge in. (Anyone who has watched Japanese television for any length of time, particularly game shows, can attest to this.) On a more sober note, the idea of emptying one's soul and reaching a state of selflessness as preparation for the performance of both *shakuhachi* and the music of the *bunraku* theater reflects the strong underlying influence of Zen thought in Japanese culture. This influence touches many other areas of Japanese daily life, not only in mental preparation for a future task, but also with stress on self-control and self-discipline. Finally, the indulgence in pathos and extreme emotional anguish, as expressed in *enka* songs as well as in the music of the puppet theater, reveals another side of the Japanese character. Listening to Japanese music and learning about its connections to past and present society, we become aware of the richness of Japanese life.

REFERENCES CITED

Adachi, Barbara
    1985   *Backstage at Bunraku: A Behind-the-Scenes Look at Japan's Traditional Puppet Theater.* New York: Weatherhill.

Adriaansz, Willem
    1973   *The Kumiuta and Danmono Traditions of Japanese Koto Music.* Berkeley: Univ. of California Press.

Asano Kenji
    1966   "Nihon no minyō" (Folk Song of Japan). Tokyo: Iwanami Shinsho.

Blasdel, Christopher Yohmei
    1988   *The Shakuhachi: A Manual for Learning.* Tokyo: Ongaku no Tomo Sha.

"Closet Carusos: Japan Reinvents the Singalong."
    1983   *Time,* 28 February 1983, 47.

Crihfield, Liza
    1979   *Kouta: "Little Songs" of the Geisha World.* Rutland, Vt.: Charles E. Tuttle.

Dalby, Liza Crihfield
    1983   *Geisha.* Berkeley: Univ. of California Press.

Ernst, Earle
    1956   *The Kabuki Theatre.* Honolulu: Univ. Press of Hawaii.

Groemer, Gerald
    1994   "Fifteen Years of Folk Song Collection in Japan: Reports and Recordings of the 'Emergency Folk Song Survey.'" *Asian Folklore Studies* 53(2):199–225.

Herd, Judith Ann
    1984   "Play it again, Isamu!" *Mainichi Daily News,* 9 July 1984, 9.

Hughes, David
    1981   "Japanese Folk Song Preservation Societies: Their History and Nature." In *International Symposium on the Conservation and Restoration of Cultural Property,* ed. Organizing Committee of ISCRCP. Tokyo: Tokyo National Research Institute of Cultural Properties.

——————.
    1990–91   "Japanese 'New Folk Songs,' Old and New." *Asian Music* 22(1):1–49.

Kikkawa Eishi

    1981   *Nihon ongaku no rekishi* (The history of Japanese music). Osaka: Sōgensha.

Koizumi Fumio

    1974   *Nihon no ongaku* (Japanese music). Tokyo: National Theater of Japan.

Kurada Yoshihiro

    1982   "Kouta." In *Ongaku daijiten* (Encyclopedia musica), ed. Shitanaka Kunihiko. Tokyo: Heibonsha.

Malm, William

    1959   *Japanese Music and Musical Instruments.* Rutland, Vt.: Charles E. Tuttle.

—————.

    1971   *Modern Music of Meiji Japan.* In *Tradition and Modernization in Japanese Culture,* ed. Donald H. Shirley. Princeton, N.J.: Princeton Univ. Press.

Mitsui Toru

    1984   "Japan in Japan: Notes on an Aspect of the Popular Music Record Industry in Japan." *Popular Music* 3:107–20.

Motegi Kiyoko

    1984   "Aural Learning in *Gidayu-bushi:* Music of the Japanese Puppet Theatre." *Yearbook for Traditional Music* 16:97–107.

—————.

    1988   *Bunraku: Koe to oto to hibiki* (Bunraku: Voice and sound and reverberation). Tokyo: Ongaku no Tomo Sha.

NHK Hōsō Seron Chōsajo, eds.

    1982   *Gendaijin to ongaku* (Contemporary people and music). Tokyo: Nippon Hōsō Shuppan Kyōkai.

Sōri-fu (Prime Minister's Office)

    1982   *Population of Japan: 1980 Population Census of Japan.* Tokyo: Statistics Bureau.

ADDITIONAL READING

Brandon, J., W. Malm, and D. Shively

    1978   *Studies in Kabuki: Its Acting, Music and Historical Context.* Honolulu: Univ. Press of Hawaii.

Fujie, Linda

    1986   "The Process of Oral Transmission in Japanese Performing Arts: The Teaching of *Matsuri-bayashi* in Tokyo." In *The Oral and the Literate in Music,* ed. Yoshihiko Tokumaru and Osamu Yamaguti. Tokyo: Academia Music.

Gestle, C. Andrew, Kiyoshi Inobe, and William P. Malm

    1990   *Theater As Music: The Bunraku Play "Mt. Imo and Mt. Se": An Exemplary Tale of Womanly Virtue.* Michigan Monograph Series in Japanese Studies, 4. Ann Arbor: Center for Japanese Studies, University of Michigan. (With 2 sound cassettes.)

Gutzwiller, Andreas, and Gerald Bennett

    1991   "The World of a Single Sound: Basic Structure of the Music of the Japanese Flute Shakuhachi." *Musica Asiatica* 6:36–59

—————.

    1992   "Polyphony in Japanese Music: Rokudan for Example." *Chime* 5:50–57.

Hughes, David
    1990–91   "Japanese 'New Folk Songs,' Old and New." *Asian Music* 22(1):1–49.
Keene, Donald
    1990   *No and Bunraku: Two Forms of Japanese Theater.* New York: Columbia Univ. Press.
Kishibe Shigeo
    1984   *The Traditional Music of Japan.* Tokyo: Ongaku no Tomo Sha.
Okada Maki
    1991   "Musical Characteristics of *Enka*." *Popular Music* 10(3):283–303.

ADDITIONAL LISTENING:

CD series, "Nihon no dentô ongaku" (Japanese Traditional Music), published by King Record Co. (2-12-13 Ottowa, Bunkyo-ku, Tokyo 112), 1990.

Vol. 1. *Gagaku.* KICH 2001.

Vol. 2: *Nôgaku.* KICH 2002.

Vol. 3: *Kabuki.* KICH 2003.

Vol. 4: *Biwa.* KICH 2004.

Vol. 5: *Shakuhachi.* KICH 2005.

Vol. 6: *Sô.* KICH 2006.

Vol. 7: *Sankyoku.* KICH 2007.

Vol. 8: *Shamisen I.* KICH 2008.

Vol. 9: *Shamisen II.* KICH 2009.

Vol. 10: *Percussion.* KICH 2010.

CD Series, "Music of Japanese People," published by King Record Co. (same address as above), 1991.

Vol. 1: *Harmony of Japanese Music.* KICH 2021.

Vol. 2: *Japanese Dance Music:* KICH 2022.

Vol. 3: *Japanese Work Songs.* KICH 2023.

Vol. 4: *Jam Session of Tsugaru-Shamisen.* KICH 2024.

Vol. 5: *Music of Okinawa.* KICH 2025.

Vol. 6: *Music of Yaeyama and Miyako.* KICH 2026.

Vol. 7: *Music of Amami.* KICH 2027.

Vol. 8: *Music of Japanese Festivals.* KICH 2028.

Vol. 9: *Soundscape of Japan.* KICH 2029.

Vol. 10: *A Collection of Unique Musical Instruments.* KICH 2030.

OTHER RECORDINGS

Japan: Ainu Songs. Unesco Collection/Auvidis D8047. CD.

Japon: Kinshi Tsuruta. Satsuma Biwa. Ocora HM83. CD.

Japon: Musique du Nô. Shakkyo (Pont en pierres). Ocora HM65. CD.

Japon: Shômyô. Buddhist Liturgical Chant, Tendai Sect. Ocora HM80. CD.

Kagura. Japanese Shinto Ritual Music. Hungaroton HCD 18193. CD.

Music of the Bunraku Theatre. JVC World Sounds VICG-5356. CD.

The Music of Japan, IV—Buddhist Music. Unesco Collection/Musicaphon BM30-L2015. LP.

Yoshitsune: Songs of Medieval Hero Accompanied by the Biwa. BMG Victor CR10080-81. LP.

ADDITIONAL VIEWING

A Shamanic Medium of Tagaru. 1994. Directed by Yashuhiro Omori. Distributed by National Museum of Ethnology, Osaka, Japan. Video, color, 92 min.

Shinto Festival Music. 1994. Produced by Eugene Enrico and David Smeal. Distributed by Center for Music Television, Norman, OK. Video, color, 29.5 min.

Nagauta: The Heart of Kabuki Music. 1994. Produced by Eugene Enrico and David Smeal. Distributed by Center for Music Television, Norman, OK. Video, color, 30 min.

The following video series are devoted to various forms of Japanese music, dance and theater. Both series distributed by Multicultural Media, Ltd., Barre, VT. (tel. 802-223-1294). The distributor can provide specific information about the content:

A Video and Sound Anthology of Japanese Classical Performing Arts, vols. 1–25. Video cassettes with books. Produced by Victor Company of Japan, Ltd.

The Video and Sound Anthology of Japanese Traditional and Folk Arts, vols. 1–14. Video cassettes with books. Produced by Victor Company of Japan, Ltd. .

CHAPTER NINE

Latin America/Ecuador

JOHN M. SCHECHTER

Latin America is a region of many regions. It is a continent and a half with more than twenty different countries in which Spanish, Portuguese, French, and dozens of Native American languages in hundreds of dialects are spoken. It is, at once, the majestic, beautiful Andes mountains, the endless emptiness of the Peruvian-Chilean desert, and the lush rain forests of the huge Amazon basin. Latin American cultures are also enormously diverse, yet most share a common heritage of Spanish or Portuguese colonialism and American and European cultural influences. Several ports in Colombia and Brazil were major colonial centers for the importation of black slaves; Latin America remains a rich repository of African and African-American music-cultural traditions, including rituals, musical forms and practices, and types of musical instruments. Native American cultures that were not eradicated by European diseases have in many cases retained certain distinctive languages, dress, musical forms, and music rituals.

In Latin American culture, mixture is the norm, not the exception. When you walk through the countryside of Ecuador, for example, you hear a Spanish dialect borrowing many words from Quichua, the regional Native American language. The local Quichua dialect, conversely, uses many Spanish words. South of Ecuador, in the high mountain regions of Peru, the harp is considered an indigenous instrument, although European missionaries and others in fact brought it to Peru. In rural areas of Atlantic coastal Colombia, musicians sing songs in Spanish, using Spanish literary forms, but these are accompanied by African-style drums and rhythms and by Amerindian flutes and rattles. In northern highland Ecuador, African-Ecuadorians perform the *bomba,* a type of song that features African-American rhythms, Quichua Indian melodic and harmonic features, and Spanish language—with sometimes one or two Quichua words. Overall, it is hard to maintain strict cultural divisions because the intermingling of Iberian (Spanish and Portuguese), African, and Native American strains is so profound in the Latin American experience.

When you first think of Latin American music, you might hear in your mind's ear the vibrancy of the rhythms in salsa. There is an enormous variety of beaten

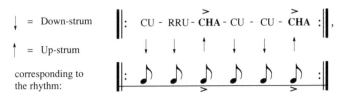

Fig. 9–1. *Cuatro* **strumming pattern.**

and shaken rhythm instruments, such as claves, bongos, congas, and maracas, both in salsa and throughout Latin America. In distinctive sizes and shapes, the guitar is prominent in Latin American folk music. In Peru and Bolivia, for example, a type of guitar called the *charango* may have as its body the shell of an armadillo. There are other types of Latin American music with which you might also be familiar, including bossa nova, the calypso, and the tango.

VENEZUELAN *JOROPO*

Listen to recorded selection 58, "Pajarillo," What is most impressive about it? Is it the very fast tempo, with the basic quarter-note beat going beyond the top marking (208) on the metronome? Or is it the way the guitarist (here playing a *cuatro*, in Venezuela a small, four-string guitar) strums his chords not only with remarkable speed and agility but also in an apparently fixed rhythmic pattern? The variety of percussion of the salsa band is now concentrated in a single instrument, the maracas, resounding with machinelike precision. The singer skillfully delivers his text ("Ah, fly, fly, little bird, Take wing, if you want to fly away . . .") in a free, declamatory style, yet uses mostly pitches that fall within the two principal chords in the piece, D minor (tonic) and A major (dominant).

This is an example of the *joropo*, the national dance of Venezuela, heard here in a 1968 recording. One standard *joropo* ensemble is the one we hear: *cuatro*, maracas, and harp. To understand the apparently fixed rhythm, we can use an onomatopoeic device taught to *cuatro* players in Venezuela to try to capture the character and rhythmic feel of *joropo*. The *cuatro* strumming pattern is vocalized as shown in figure 9–1.

Rolling your *r*'s on *rru* as best you can, say, "Cu-rru-*cha*-cu-cu-*cha*" about as fast as you can, along with the recorded selection, and you will find yourself in synch with the *cuatro*'s rhythmic strumming. You will find yourself chasing after—and with luck, beginning to catch—Venezuelan *joropo*.

The harp's function is related but somewhat different. Here outlining a three-quarter meter (shown in ex. 9–1), sometimes with closely related rhythmic forms,

Ex. 9–1.   **Rhythmic pattern played by harp.**

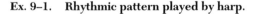

Ex. 9–2.   Harp patterns in the Venezuelan *joropo* **"Pajarillo."**

and

(i)   (iv)   (V)

the harp provides not only rhythmic but melodic and ultimately harmonic under-
pinning, with patterns such as those shown in example 9–2. After establishing
these basic patterns, however, the harpist improvises on their melodic contours
and syncopates their rhythms to contribute to the unique motoric sound of
joropo. The harp is vital in Venezuelan *joropo*; it has been essential in Latin
American music making for hundreds of years and it remains so today, as this
chapter will later reveal.

NUEVA CANCIÓN: "EL LAZO," BY VÍCTOR JARA

Although the guitar is played in ensembles, by itself it accompanies solo folk song
throughout Latin America. As in the Venezuelan *joropo,* the instrument typically
provides a characteristic regional rhythm. Moving from north to south on the
South American continent—from Venezuela to Chile—we listen to "El lazo," a
powerful folk song composed (ca. 1964) and performed on guitar by a great figure
in Chilean modern music, Víctor Jara (recorded selection 59).

The regional rhythm in example 9–3 is not the driving "Cu-rru-*cha*-cu-cu-*cha*"
of the Venezuelan *joropo* but a variant of the *cueca,* a Chilean folk dance. This
pattern can be felt in either ¾ or ⁶⁄₈ time. The text and music of "El lazo" are presented in example 9–4.

As a frame for the piece, there is a speechlike section, identical at the beginning and end of the song. The thought is somber: "When the sun bent low"; "on a
dark ranch"; "on a humble ranch"; and the picture stark: an old man (so we soon
find out) at sunset, on a poor ranch, in Lonquén, Víctor Jara's childhood village.
The melody is similarly stark and hesitant, in the minor key, chantlike; sing the
first three lines to get the feeling of the mood Jara is setting. Like the song itself,
the "spoken" section is framed, beginning and ending with the same text couplet,
set to the same melody.

Ex. 9–3.   Cueca rhythmic pattern in "El lazo."

Ex. 9–4.   Transcription of "El lazo," words and music by Víctor Jara.
Copyright © 1976 Mighty Oak Music Ltd., London, England. TRO-Essex
Music International, Inc. controls all publication rights for the U.S.A. and
Canada. Used by permission.

Ex. 9–4. (*Continued*)

(2) El lazo como serpiente
se enroscaba en el nogal
y en cada lazo la huella
de su vida y de su pan.

(3) Cuanto tiempo hay en sus manos
y en su apagado mirar
y nadie ha dicho—está bueno
ya no debes trabajar.

Las sombras etc . . .

(4) Sus lazos han recorrido
sur y norte, cerro y mar,
pero el viejo la distancia
nunca la supo explicar.

(5) Su vida deja en los lazos
aferrados al nogal.
Después llegará la muerte
y también lo laceará.

(6) Qué importa si el lazo es firme
y dura la eternidad,
laceando por algún campo
el viejo descansará.

Cuando el sol etc . . .

The Noose

When the sun was setting
I found him.
In a gloomy hut
in Lonquén.
In a poverty stricken hut
I found him.
When the sun was setting
in Lonquen.

His hands, although so old,
were strong in their plaiting.
They were rough and they were tender
with the animal skin.

The plaited noose, like a snake,
curled around the walnut tree
and in every mesh was woven
his life and his bread.

How much time is contained in his hands
and in his patient gaze
and nobody has said: "That's enough,
you should not work anymore."

The shadows fell interlacing
the last light of the day
The old man weaves some verses
to capture some gaiety.

His nooses have traveled
south and north, coast and mountain,
but the old man never learnt
what distance really means.

He leaves his life in plaited leather
knotted to the walnut tree
Soon death will come
and that too will be plaited in.

What does it matter if the noose is firm
and lasts for eternity.
Intertwined with some country place
the old man at last will rest.

When the sun setting
I found him. . . .

With the stage set, Jara spins the details, through strophes 1 through 6, and through the midsong "speech" section, which is halting in character, like the opening "spoken section," if different musically. The tale concerns an aged man, portrayed with hands old yet strong, rough yet tender, plaiting whips and lassos. In the Latin American countryside, one often comes upon older men and women plaiting animal hide for whips, or cactus or wool fiber for use as rope, sandal tops, bags, or blanket ends. A good example can be seen in the film *Juan Félix Sánchez* (1982), written and directed by Calogero Salvo, which focuses on the craft of a Venezuelan Andean weaver and his wife. This type of work requires great skill and enormous patience. Jara's admiration for the craftsperson's talent and patience is undisguised. The man of Lonquén is known far and wide for his whips, and their creation is his very life.

Listening to "El lazo," we become aware of the constant *musical* "plaiting" as well: Jara weaves a variety of arpeggiations into a cohesive musical fabric. We feel the musical shuttle moving nearly continuously, through both the strophes and the middle "spoken" section, or recitative. The music acts as a metaphor for the rope-plaiting activity—the musical gesture evoking the plaiting gesture.

Jara further interweaves the music with the metaphors and similes in the text. The plaited lasso, like a snake, is curled around the walnut tree, the shadows tie together the final daylight, and the old man himself braids verses to bind up joy. We also admire the man of Lonquén because his work is *firme*: it endures. Jara exalts the skill and dedication of the plaiter of Lonquén and, by association, of Chilean rural craftspersons in general. The musician-poet is given to humble admiration for rural artists in other songs, too, such as his "Angelita Huenumán," (1964), in which he sings the praises of a Mapuche Indian woman (Jara's mother, Amanda, was of Mapuche ancestry) who dedicates her life to making beautiful blankets. Once again, focus on the hands.

Why does Jara glorify the creative genius of rural Chileans? The answer lies partly with Jara himself, a man of Lonquén, in rural Chile; it lies partly with his place in the modern song movement of Chile, and—sometimes with different names—of all Latin America: *Nueva Canción,* or "New Song."

Nueva Canción is a song movement that stands up for one's own culture, for one's own people, in the face of oppression by a totalitarian government or in the face of cultural imperialism from abroad, notably the United States and Europe. It developed first in the southern cone of South America—Argentina, Chile, and Uruguay—during the 1950s and 1960s, and it has spread throughout Latin America. As we know from our own history, the 1960s in particular witnessed violent upheavals. Assassinations and urban violence in the United States were echoed in Latin America: nearly every country in South America, as well as Cuba and the Dominican Republic in the Caribbean, saw revolution, massacre, underground warfare, or other forms of violent social and political confrontation.

In Argentina, the Perón regime saw the country prosper, bringing rural dwellers, many of indigenous ancestry, to the city of Buenos Aires, with their own musical heritages. In addition, Argentinian radio stations were instructed to program substantial amounts of national music. Thus, where the tango had dominated popular music until the mid-1950s, a new Argentinian music began to be created in the late 1950s and early 1960s, by such groups as Los Chalchaleros, Los Fronterizos, and notably, by the guitarist-composer-singer Atahualpa Yupanqui. A careful researcher into Argentinian musical folklore, Atahualpa Yupanqui combined a remarkable guitar technique with evocative melody and poetry to create a truly new music. The metaphoric thrust of Jara's "El lazo" appears prominently in Yupanqui's poignant "Camino del indio," for example, in which the composer depicts a rural path as the window through which we see the sufferings of the Indian of the *campo*, or countryside. Yupanqui and his fellow Argentinian artist-pioneers sought to create songs with profound musical and textual meaning, songs rooted in their country's rural folklore, songs instilled with the goal of renewal, of reinvigoration (Carrasco Pirard 1982:605–6).

The breath of renewal spread to Uruguay and to Chile, where Violeta Parra was a fundamental moving force. A multifaceted artist—musician, poet, painter, tapestry embroiderer, sculptress, potter—Violeta Parra immersed herself in the folklore of Chile, initially in her home region of Chillán, southern Chile, then in Santiago Province, and ultimately throughout the length of the country. Her enormous collecting efforts helped significantly to make Chilean folksongs legitimate and known on the national level. In 1964 she set up a cultural center in La Reina, on the outskirts of Santiago, where she coached musicians. Both here and at the Peña de los Parra—a coffeehouse focusing on folklore, run by Isabel and Ángel, her two oldest children—the *Nueva Canción* movement took shape in the 1960s. Many of its pioneering artists had done their own fieldwork, traveling widely through the Chilean countryside to hear and document principally rural traditions in music and music-related customs. Thus, the *Nueva Canción* musicians sought to reproduce wherever possible authentic, traditional styles (like Jara's *cueca* variant, in "El lazo") and to use traditional instruments (Violeta Parra's preference for the *charango*), to express their views on contemporary events and issues. The 1969 Primer Festival de la Nueva Canción Chilena, sponsored by the Universidad Católica in Santiago, gave the now-recognizable movement a name (Morris 1986:119–20).

Like Jara's "El lazo," Violeta Parra's own songs may draw on natural contexts: "Rin [a Chilean rhythm] del angelito" (1964–65) depicts the joyous atmosphere of a Chilean wake for a dead child—a subject that also drew Víctor Jara to compose a song ("Despedimiento del angelito" ["Farewell of the Little Angel"]) and a subject we will look at more closely later in this chapter. On the other hand, Parra's music may be highly satirical, as in "¿Qué dirá el Santo Padre?" ("What will the pope say?" ca.1957, fig. 9–2).

The Chilean writer Fernando Alegría comments that Parra first cries out here against injustice, then appeals to the pope to make a statement on these conditions—yet he remains silent throughout the song. Like the majority of Latin Americans, most Chileans are Roman Catholics; the Catholic Church has frequently been in the forefront of the struggle for human rights in Latin America.

Miren cómo nos hablan de libertad	Look how they speak to us of liberty
Cuando de ella nos privan en realidad.	When really they deprive us of it.
Miren cómo pregonan tranquilidad	Look how they proclaim peace
Cuando nos atormenta la autoridad.	When the authorities torment us.
Chorus: *¿Qué dirá el Santo Padre que*	What will the pope, who lives
vive en Roma	in Rome, say
Que le están degollando sus palomas?	To the fact that they are beheading
	his doves?
Miren cómo nos hablan del paraíso	Look how they speak to us of Paradise
Cuando nos llueven penas como granizo.	When afflictions rain down on us
	like hail.

Fig. 9–2.   Some lyrics from "¿Qué dirá el Santo Padre?" by Violeta Parra.

Ultimately, though regrettably after her death in 1967, Violeta Parra's plea brought a response from the Vatican: in April 1987 Pope John Paul II visited Chile, spoke out against conditions of oppression, and met with indigenous peoples, encouraging them to sustain their cultural values (Levy 1988).

Finally, though by no means have we exhausted the full range of song types produced by this great artist, Violeta Parra has composed love poetry. In the highly moving "Gracias a la vida," ironically written just before her 1967 suicide, the artist thanks life for having given her the eyes, ears, words, feet, heart, laughter, and weeping through which she might perceive and approach the man she loves.

Nueva Canción artists seek to reinvoke and revalidate traditional lifeways of forgotten but valued persons and peoples. These musicians also express their social consciousness. They speak out in a clear voice against conditions of oppression, advocating social change. Víctor Jara's "Preguntas por Puerto Montt" (1969), notably *devoid* of metaphor and speaking in a direct and accusatory tone, is a stream-of-consciousness monologue decrying a March 6, 1969, government-sanctioned attack on unarmed peasant families in this Chilean port city. In the 1970 Chilean presidential campaign, Quilapayún, an important *Nueva Canción* ensemble formed in the mid-1960s, accompanied speakers for Salvador Allende's broad-based Popular Unity party, which had brought together workers, peasants, and students into a mass movement. A musical example of this remarkable spirit of unity is Jara's "Plegaria a un labrador" ("Public Prayer to a Worker"), which was composed for the 1969 first Festival of Chilean Song. Modeled on the Lord's Prayer, it is an impassioned call for worker solidarity (fig. 9–3). "Stand up and look at your hands."

In 1973 the elected Marxist government of President Allende was overthrown in a bloody coup; Allende and some 2,800 others lost their lives, hundreds disappeared, and thousands were jailed. On September 18, 1973, a young man ushered

Levántate y mírate las manos,	Stand up and look at your hands,
Para crecer, estréchala a tu hermano,	Take your brother's hand, so you can grow,
Juntos iremos unidos en la sangre,	We'll go together, united by blood,
Hoy es el tiempo que puede ser mañana.	The future can begin today.
Líbranos de aquel que nos domina en la miseria,	Deliver us from the master who keeps us in misery,
Tráenos tu reino de justicia e igualdad . . .	Thy kingdom of justice and equality, come . . .
Hágase por fin tu voluntad aquí en la tierra,	Thy will be done, at last, here on earth,
Danos tu fuerza y tu valor al combatir. . . .	Give us the strength and the courage to struggle. . . .

Fig. 9–3.   Some lyrics from "La plegaria a un labrador" by Víctor Jara.

Joan Jara into the Santiago city morgue, where she found the body of her husband, Víctor Jara, "his chest riddled with holes and a gaping wound in his abdomen. His hands seemed to be hanging from his arms at a strange angle as though his wrists were broken" (Jara 1984:243). The singer who had cried out in word and song on behalf of "him who died without knowing why his chest was riddled, fighting for the right to have a place to live" (lyrics to "Preguntas por Puerto Montt"), the singer whose songs had so often lauded eloquently the hands of his people (in "El lazo," "Angelita Huenumán," and "Plegaria a un labrador"), had met his fate—in a stroke of terrifying irony—with his own chest riddled with holes, his own hands made lifeless.

Numerous *Nueva Canción* musicians were imprisoned or remained in exile, but to gain support for human rights in Chile they continued to spread the message of *Nueva Canción* in performances abroad. Within Chile, the movement went underground and was transformed into *Canto Nuevo*.

After the overthrow of Allende, the music of *Nueva Canción* was prohibited on the airwaves and removed from stores and destroyed. Certain prominent folkloric instruments associated with *Nueva Canción*, such as the *charango,* were also prohibited (Morris (1986:123). In the repressive political and cultural atmosphere, the metaphoric character we have seen in the songs of Atahualpa Yupanqui, Víctor Jara, and Violeta Parra now became exaggerated and intensified, in order to express thoughts that would have been censored if stated directly. In "El joven titiritero" ("The Young Puppeteer"), by Eduardo Peralta, for example, a puppeteer's departure and hoped-for return served as a metaphor for exile and renewed hope.

The status of *Canto Nuevo* was precarious. The government issued permission to perform a concert, but the permission was abruptly revoked; radio programs featuring its music were established, then eliminated; Jara cassettes were at one moment confiscated, subsequently sold openly in stores. With changing political conditions, banished musicians have been permitted to return to Chile; the group Inti Illimani returned from Italy in 1988, after fifteen years in exile.

A February 1994 concert on the campus of the University of California at Berkeley saw Inti Illimani, created by a group of Santiago university students in 1967, now considerably evolved from its earlier heyday. In addition to the now-familiar *Nueva Canción* panpipes, *charango,* and *kena* (Andean vertical notched flute), the seven-member aggregate now incorporated instruments not native to Chile or to the Andes: hammered dulcimer, soprano saxophone. The ensemble's multi-instrumentalists now performed sophisticated, tailored arrangements, featuring contemporary, highly coloristic harmonizations of traditional Andean and Caribbean genres. To these points, Inti Illimani musicians have remarked that the ensemble's extended years in exile—one-half their total years of existence—have led them to more universal creative roots (González 1989:272–73). The group's repertoire in this highly polished performance was remarkably variegated, showcasing the breadth of Latin American (if elaborately disguised) forms: hocketing panpipes (see discussion of Bolivian *k'antu,* below), Peruvian *wayno,* Venezuelan *joropo,* Chilean *cueca,* Ecuadorian *sanjuán* (discussed later in this chapter), "traditional" *Nueva Canción* (Jara's "El aparecido" [1967], made famous in an Inti Illimani arrangement), Cuban *son,* and Mexican *ranchera.* Inti Illimani toured the U.S. in fall 1995, performing in Nebraska, Michigan, Wisconsin, Missouri, Illinois, and Washington D.C.

New Song is still a living international movement. It is traditional and regional in its roots, yet modern and socially conscious in its musical style and message. It reacts to penetration by foreign cultures, seeking instead to draw attention to the people—often the forgotten people—and to their struggles for human dignity.

BOLIVIAN *K'ANTU*

Certain *Nueva Canción* performers such as Inti Illimani chose the *zampoña,* or panpipes, among other traditional instruments, to symbolize their esteem for the native traditions of the Andes and neighboring regions. Although panpipes are widely known outside South America, the depth of the panpipe tradition in South America is remarkable. Today, we can find a huge number of named varieties of panpipes among native peoples from Panama down to Peru, Bolivia, and Chile. In Peru and Bolivia, cultures dating back some fifteen centuries knew and played panpipes of bamboo or clay.

Listen to recorded selection 60, "Kutirimunapaq," performed by Ruphay, a Bolivian ensemble. They are playing a type of ceremonial panpipe music from the altiplano, called *k'antu.* Using Western notation, we could notate what seems to be one melody line, at least, as shown in example 9–5.

The entire piece is played three times. Sing the melody to get a feel for the rhythm and flow of this *zampoña* music. Listening again, you'll note that the

Ex. 9–5.   **One melody line of the *k'antu* "Kutirimunapaq."**

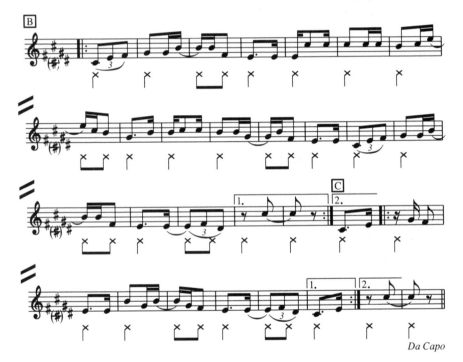

Da Capo

sound seems richer than on first hearing; you hear a panpipe ensemble playing what seems to be the same melody at various pitch levels, one at an octave below the original pitch level, another a perfect fourth above that lower octave, or a perfect fifth below the original octave (ex. 9–6).

"Kutirimunapaq," which means, roughly, in the Quechua language, "So that we can return," is music of the Kallawaya people, who live on the eastern slope of the Bolivian Andes, north of Lake Titicaca, close to the Peruvian border. (In Peru and Bolivia the language is called Quechua; in Ecuador the dialects are called

Quichua.) The Kallawaya *campesinos* (farmers, peasants) live at different altitudes in the Charazani Valley—from 9,000 to 16,000 feet above sea level. Those at the lower elevations speak Quechua and cultivate potatoes, barley, and beans; at the upper elevations they speak Aymara and keep llamas, alpacas, and sheep. Perhaps some 3,500 years ago, Quechua and Aymara were a single language. The Incas adopted Quechua as their official language, and spread it with them throughout their empire (ca. 1200–1533). Today, from 5.5 to 8 million Andeans in Bolivia, Peru, Argentina, and Ecuador speak Quechua (or Quichua), while a minority speak Aymara (Bastien 1978:xxi). "Kutirimunapaq" is a *k'antu* from the community of Niñokorin, at 11,000 feet.

The Kallawaya musicians term these bamboo panpipes (*zampoña* in Spanish) *phukuna,* from the Quechua verb *phukuy,* to blow. The *k'antu* ensembles, for which the Charazani region is famous, each comprise twenty to thirty *phukuna*-playing dancers, who move in a circular pattern. Some of them simultaneously beat a large, double-headed drum, called a *wankara*. The triangle (in Quechua, *ch'inisku*) we hear in recorded selection 60 is often present as well.

The Kallawaya play the *phukunas* in their dry season, which lasts roughly from June to September; they play transverse flutes (played horizontally, like the Western silver flute) or duct flutes (played vertically, and constructed like a recorder) during the rainy season, which lasts from November to at least late February. The preference on the altiplano for duct flutes, in particular, during the rainy season may be related to the belief that their clear sound attracts rain and prevents frost, necessary conditions for the growth of crops. Finally, the word *k'antu* might be related to a widely known flower of Bolivia, the *kantuta,* or it might be derived from the Spanish word for song, *canto.*

Our ensemble consists of *phukunas* of different sizes, yet all with the same basic construction, in terms of numbers of tubes. Each musical register is represented by one named pair of panpipes, consisting of an *ira* set of pipes (considered in the Bolivian altiplano to embody the male principle, and serving as the leader) and an *arca* set of pipes (considered to embody the female principle and serving as the follower). In our context, the *ira* set has six pipes, the *arca* set has seven; we may refer to this type as 6/7-tubed. The different-sized instruments play the same melody, which results in the rich musical fabric of parallel octaves, fifths, and fourths.

There are at least two especially interesting aspects of this music. One is the doubling of the melodic line; the other is the way a melody is produced. Doubling the melody at a fixed interval (parallel fifth, parallel fourth, parallel octave) was used in medieval plainsong. By the ninth century, plainsong (one-line Christian liturgical chant) was being accompanied either by one lower part at the octave below or by a lower part at the fourth or fifth below. Another alternative augmented the two-voice complex to three or four voices by doubling one or both lines at the octave. Thus, early medieval Europe had musical textures with parallel octaves, fourths, and fifths very similar in intervallic structure (if not in rhythm) to what we hear in twentieth-century Bolivian *k'antu.* In twentieth-century Africa, songs in parallel fourths and fifths are found among groups that have the tradition of pentatonic, or five-pitch, songs, such as the Gogo people of Tanzania; a good example of a Gogo song in parallel fourths and fifths appears in Nketia 1974:163.

Many peoples have used, and continue to use, the performance practice of hocketing. Performing music in hocket is a uniquely communal way of making music. Hocket music is social music, for you cannot play the entire melody your-self—you need one or more partners to do it with you. In Africa the hocket tech-nique appears in certain xylophone musics, among horns, flutes, and panpipes, and with voices among the Bushmen and Pygmy peoples (chapter 3). Certain music in several parts in thirteenth- and fourteenth-century Europe used notes and rests in a way that the melody line was effectively divided between two voice-parts: as one sounded the other was silent. A hiccup (*hoquetus* in Latin, the likely derivation of the term) effect was thus created. Hocketing with panpipes also ap-pears closer in time and space to our modern Bolivian music. In Panama, the Kuna Indians play six-tube *guli* panpipes. Each person holds one tube, with the melody distributed among all six players. The Kuna also play *gammu burui* pan-pipes. Each fourteen-tube set is bound into two groups, or rafts, of seven tubes (two rafts of four-tube and three-tube size, held side by side), the melody distrib-uted between the two seven-tube players in hocket technique (Smith 1984: 156–59, 167–72).

As among the Kuna, in Bolivian *k'antu* the hocket procedure is integral to the overall musical fabric. In fact, hocketing is actually required by the way the *phukunas* are constructed. Although there are types of altiplano panpipes with from three to seventeen tubes, a very widely used type is 6/7-tubed—that is, the "total" instrument has thirteen tubes, consisting of one line, or rank, of six tubes (the *ira*) and one rank of seven tubes (the *arca*). This *phukuna*, or *siku* (the name used by the Aymara Indians, who inhabit the upper elevations of this same alti-plano zone), may be tuned in E minor (or in another perspective, G major), as shown in figure 9–4.

The type of *phukuna* shown in this figure has made an accommodation to European-derived scales. Not all *zampoñas* of the altiplano are tuned in this dia-tonic manner; many have different scales. This basic tuning is nonetheless widely found among both Quechua-speaking and Aymara-speaking peoples.

When the full instrument is combined (six- and seven-tube ranks joined to-gether or played by two people) we have a thirteen-tube E-minor scale, over the space of an octave and a half with subtonic below (D), or a thirteen-tube G-major scale, going up to the tenth above and down to the perfect fourth below (D) (fig. 9–5).

The formal structure of "Kutirimunapaq" is ABC, each section being repeated, then the entire piece repeated twice, for a total of three times. This is a character-istic structure for the Bolivian *k'antu*, accommodating the continuous dancing that goes with the music-making. Counting the number of different notes that sound in this particular *k'antu* we find that, within the octave, five notes predomi-

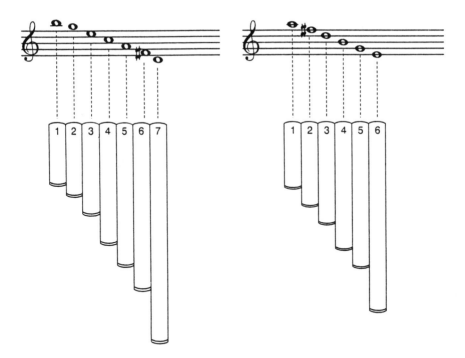

Fig. 9–4. Example of *phukuna* tuning. Left: seven-tube *arca* rank. Right: six-tube *ira* rank.

nate: C♯ E, F♯, G♯ and B. Then, the C♯ and E come back in the upper octave. Note that C♯ not E, serves as the tonic pitch in this case. There is one more note used: D♯; notice, though, that it comes in only at the end of sections A, B, and C—once each time. This *k'antu* is primarily five-pitch, or pentatonic. We will find later in the chapter that many traditional dance musics in the Andes region are similarly pentatonic, though certainly not all of them. "Kutirimunapaq" is strongly rhythmic, with the steady beat of the *wankara* supporting the beat. Andean dance music, from Bolivia up to Ecuador, has this powerful rhythmic cast, underscoring its dance function.

Hocketing panpipes, with rhythmic melodies played in parallel fifths and octaves and with strong, steady rhythm on a large drum, begin to distinguish this Bolivian altiplano stream of Latin American music. The evocation of Native American cultures such as this high-Andean one, through use of Andean instruments, begins to demarcate *Nueva Canción*. New Song is not only nostalgic, though. It is also politically committed and international. Above all, it speaks of and on behalf of the people—characteristically, the forgotten people.

North of Chile, Bolivia, and Peru is a nation of many other unsung (or less-sung) persons and peoples, a country itself frequently overlooked in discussions of Latin America: Ecuador.

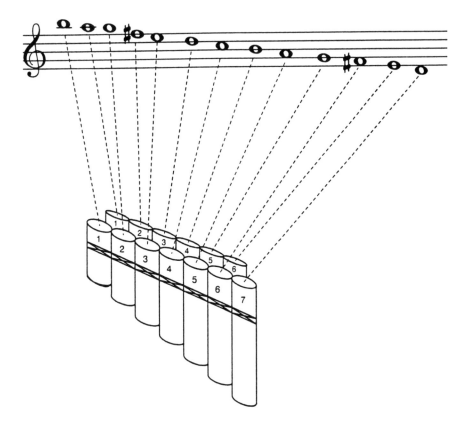

Fig. 9–5.   Tuning of full thirteen-tube *phukuna*.

THE QUICHUA OF THE NORTHERN ANDES OF ECUADOR

We can best appreciate the traditional nature of northern Ecuadorian Quichua music by knowing something of the traditional setting in which Quichua live. The musicians we will be listening to live in *comunas,* or small clusters of houses, on the slopes of Mt. Cotacachi, one of several volcanoes in the Ecuadorian Andes. These *comunas* lie outside the town of Cotacachi, in Imbabura Province (see fig. 9–6). The Quichua spoken in Cotacachi-area *comunas* was spoken there four hundred years ago. Today in Ecuador more than one million people speak the language.

In addition to the language, the agriculture and material culture of the Andes around Cotacachi are traditional. In this rich green countryside dotted with tall eucalyptus, at 8,300 to 9,700 feet above sea level, maize has been the principal cultivated crop for hundreds of years. You have already seen how Latin Americans braid natural fibers into useful objects; Cotacachi Quichua also use the thick

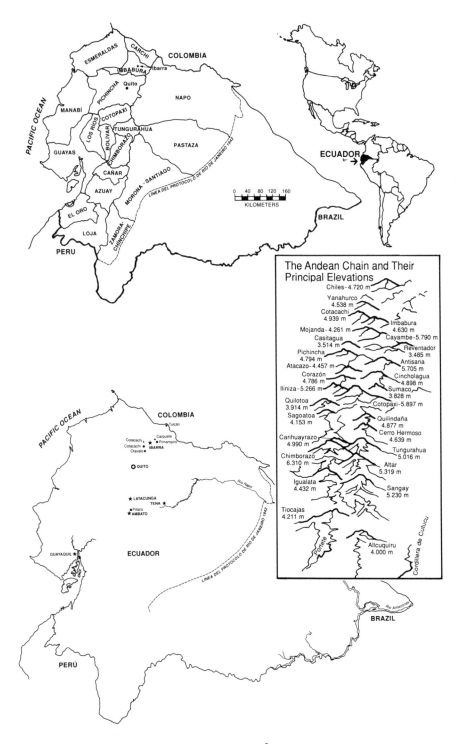

Fig. 9–6.   Ecuador.

trunks of the local cactus, *cabuya*, to make stools for the home. The harpist who plays all night in the home of a recently deceased Quichua infant sits on a *cabuya* stool.

Quichua homes typically have one room, often with a covered patio, both with dirt floor. Regional Quichua homes have been constructed this way for four hundred years. The home of twelve-year-old harpist, César, and his parents, Mama Ramona and Miguel Armando, in the *comuna* of Tikulla outside Cotacachi, is shown in illustration 9–1.

Styles of dress have also remained basically the same since the sixteenth century. Everyone covers his or her head to protect it from the intense heat and light of the near-vertical sun at midday. (Cotacachi is almost precisely on the Equator.) Women wear cloths, and men wear hats. Quichua women wear embroidered blouses, over which they drape shawls (in Quichua, *fachalina*). Their two skirts, one blue and one white, are secured by two woven belts: a wider, inner belt, called the *mama chumbi* (mother belt) and a narrower, outer belt, called the *wawa chumbi* (child belt). You will come across this word *wawa* later, when you accompany the harpist as he plays at a *wawa velorio*, or wake for a child. These belts are designed in this region usually with names of Imbabura towns, and they are traditionally woven on home back-strap looms by Quichua families in various *comunas*. Men and boys have traditionally worn a white or blue shirt, white pants, and dark poncho, though today in Imbabura you will see Quichua teenagers wear-

Ill. 9–1.   Home of Mama Ramona and Miguel Armando in the *comuna* of Tikulla, outside Cotacachi, May 1980. Photograph by John M. Schechter.

ing English-language sweatshirts and jeans. Any large gathering of Quichua, such as for Saturday market or Palm Sunday procession, is still largely a sea of blue and white.

In illustration 9–2 we see three generations of father-son relationships within the same family. Of the grandfather's traditional dress, his adult son retains the white sandals, white shirt, pants, and hat, while his grandson wears Western-influenced clothes.

There is a strong sense of community among Cotacachi Quichua, arising from a common Quichua language (and regional dialect), a common dress, and common aspects of material culture. Quichua eat the same diet of beans and potatoes they grow in their own plots. They gather together regularly for weekly markets, for periodic community work projects (*mingas*), and for fiestas—such as a child's wake.

In 1980 few Cotacachi Quichua owned vehicles; by 1990 a few community leaders possessed new pickup trucks. In any case, Quichua homes on Cotacachi's slopes are for the most part not located on roads but interspersed along a network of footpaths called *chaki ñanes*. Without telephones, families communicate only by foot, along *chaki ñanes*; recalling Atahualpa Yupanqui's "Camino del indio," these paths bear the weight of Quichua women carrying infants, brush, and food to and from market, and of Quichua men carrying potatoes, milled grain, or perhaps a harp (see ill. 9–3). For all Quichua, the way around the slopes on *chaki ñanes* is second nature; the harpist contracted to play at a *wawa velorio*, or child's wake, is able to reach the home of the deceased child, one and a half hours up

Ill. 9–2.   **Three generations of Quichua men, May 1980. Photograph by John M. Schechter.**

Ill. 9–3.   *Chaki ñan* (Ecuadorian footpath), May 1980. Photograph by John M. Schechter.

Mt. Cotacachi, from his own home, at night, with no illumination other than the moon. Walking (in Quichua, *purina*) is so vital in daily life that, as we will see, it finds its way into speech and song.

THE MUSICAL TRADITION: *SANJUÁN*

The common language, dress, material culture, daily labor, and importance of *purina* all find a musical echo in *sanjuán*. The term *sanjuán* may be found at least as early as 1860. At that time, it referred either to a type of song played at the festival of St. John (San Juan) the Baptist held in June or to a type of dance performed at that festival.

Today, the instrument Cotacachi Quichua often use to perform *sanjuán* is the harp without pedals, often referred to in English as the diatonic harp because it is usually tuned to one particular scale and is not capable of being quickly changed to another. Reflecting their other deep-rooted traditions, Quichua have been playing the harp in the Ecuadorian highlands for hundred of years; in the eighteenth century, it was the most common instrument in the region. The harp's popularity in the Andes is not limited to Ecuador; in the Peruvian highlands, it is so widespread among Quechua that it is considered a "native" instrument.

Of course, you have already heard the harp in Venezuelan *joropo*; in fact, you can hear different types of harp in various folk and indigenous musics from Mexico to Chile. Brought from Europe initially by several different groups of missionaries, especially the Jesuits, and even by the first Conquistadors, the harp has been in Latin America for more than four hundred years. In Chile the tradition of female harpists is strong; this is a heritage of sixteenth-century Spain, when women were virtuosos on the instrument. Elsewhere in rural South America, including Ecuador, harp performance by folk and indigenous musicians follows the gender principle of organization in instrumental music so that women have rarely been included. Most Latin American diatonic harpists have been and are today male. In other musical arenas, such as *Nueva Canción*, women such as Violeta Parra have been in the forefront.

The Imbabura harp is common only in Imbabura Province (ill. 9–4). It appears as an oddity among harpists in central highland Ecuador, where musicians play a larger instrument. The type of harp Raúl plays here is made of cedar and uses wooden nails. The sound emanates through three circular holes on the top of the soundbox; they are always found in the pattern shown in figure 9–7, on either side of the column, or pole, that connects the neck to the soundbox.

Looking at Raúl's harp, you may think that the instrument has an unusual shape, compared to Western harps with which you may be familiar. The Imbabura harp's column is straight but short, giving the instrument a low "head," or top. Its soundbox is distinctively arched, wide, and deep. On older harps in this region, bull's-hoof glue was used. The tuning pegs are made of iron or wood. The

Ill. 9–4. **Harpist Raúl, playing his Imbabura harp, March 1980. Photograph by John M. Schechter.**

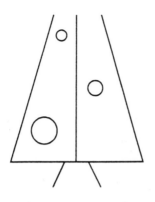

Fig. 9–7.   Schematic diagram showing position of soundholes in an Imbabura harp.

single line of strings is typically a combination of gut, possibly nylon, and steel. The gut strings—used for the bass and middle registers—used to be made by the Quichua themselves from the cut, washed, dried, and twisted intestinal fibers of sheep, dog, cat, or goat. Sometimes musicians use nylon strings for the middle register, or range, of notes. The steel strings, closest to the performer, play the treble register, or melody line. Once again relying on their environment for necessary materials, Quichua musicians may use the legbone of the sheep (in Quichua, *tullu*: bone) to tune the pegs on the harp neck.

This Imbabura harp is a descendant of sixteenth- and seventeenth-century Spanish harps, as shown by shared features of tuning, construction, configuration, and stringing. Based on what we know now, the Imbabura harp has remained essentially unchanged in appearance for one hundred to two hundred years, and possibly longer (Schechter 1992).

Recorded selection 61 is a *sanjuán* entitled "Cascarón," played in April 1980 by the Quichua master harpist Efraín in the patio of his home in the *comuna* of Saltamora, outside Cotacachi. Harpists play the higher, or treble strings (treble clef part, below) with their stronger hand, the lower, or bass, strings (bass clef part, below) with their weaker hand. Efraín, left-handed, plays treble with the left hand, bass with the right hand (ill. 9–5). The musical transcription of Efraín's "Cascarón" performance appears in example 9–7. Each transcription of Cotacachi Quichua music in this chapter begins with a small stemless pitch; this corresponds either to the pitch to which that harp was tuned by that harpist on that day, or to that singer's tonic on that occasion. For comparison, all transcriptions of Cotacachi Quichua music are given in the key of D minor.

In general, the form of "Cascarón" is typical of Cotacachi Quichua *sanjuanes*. It is fundamentally a repetitive form, in which one or two different phrases are perhaps irregularly inserted into an otherwise similar phrase pattern. In *sanjuán*, the primary motive (the A phrases in Efraín's "Cascarón") predominates. These are the melodies you identify with a particular *sanjuán*. The *sanjuán* phrase often lasts eight beats, and frequently the rhythm of the first half of the phrase is identical, or nearly identical, to the rhythm of the second half. Figure 9–8 diagrams

Ill. 9–5.   Harpist Efraín, playing his Imbabura harp, April 1980. Photograph by John M. Schechter.

Ex. 9–7.   Transcription of the *sanjuán* "*Cascarón,*" played by Efraín.

Ex. 9–7. (*Continued*)

Ex. 9–7.   (*Continued*)

Ex. 9–7.   *(Continued)*

```
T 1/2T B B
AAAAAAAATBB
AAAAAT1/2TBB
AAAAAT1/2TBB
AAAAATBB
AAAATT chord
```

Fig. 9–8. Phrase structure, Efraín's *sanjuán* "*Cascarón.*"

"Cascarón" in eight-beat phrases; we use *A* for primary motive, *B* for contrasting motive, and *T* for the triadic arpeggiation that usually constitutes either introductory or transitional materials.

The *A* motive predominates in this song. The consecutive *A* statements are varied by a rather fixed sequence of one, one and one-half, or two *T* statements followed by two *B* statements. Although not in quite as regular a fashion as Efraín's "Cascarón," most performances of *sanjuán* follow this general pattern, with *A* statements predominating, and sometimes without any *B* statements at all.

Look at A^1 (the first statement of the eight-beat *A* phrase) and sing the eight quarter-note beats. Then sing A^2 and A^3. You will begin to sense the feeling of *sanjuán*: eight-beat phrases, usually without rests, with the consecutive statements of the primary motive slightly varied. Note that in this case A^1 differs from A^2 only in the first sixteenth note of each statement. Nevertheless, the first two notes, A and D, respectively, fall within the tonic key of D minor. The A^3 version partakes of the *T* phrase, with the first beat now identical to the first beat of *T*. Typically in *sanjuán* varied numbers of consecutive *A* phrases will alternate with two *B* phrases, and often these stress the note a perfect fourth higher than the tonic (here, G, related to D). In October 1990 discussions, Efraín told me that these *B* phrases are called *esquina* (in Spanish, "corner") phrases: reflecting the pattern of the *sanjuán* dance, at these *B* moments, dancers turn and begin to move in the opposite direction.

Sanjuán also provides interesting details of interval structure and rhythm. In the *A* statements, the three notes D–C–A and their intervallic relationships (major second and minor third) are prominent. Compare this with the *B* statements, G–F–D, the same intervallic series, now a perfect fourth higher. Listen also to the rhythm of all the statements—*T*, *A*, and *B*—and note that in all cases the rhythm of the eight-beat phrase is the same (ex. 9–8). Also, the rhythm of the first four beats (the first half) of the phrase is echoed by the rhythm of the second half. Example 9–9 illustrates how regular these rhythmic features are. This collection, recorded in Cotacachi *comunas* in 1979–80, also gives you a dozen *sanjuanes*

Ex. 9–8. Rhythmic pattern of the *sanjuán* "*Cascarón.*"

Beat number: 1   2   3   4   5   6   7   8

Ex. 9–9.   Twelve Cotacachi Quichua *sanjuanes*.

1. Ilumán Tiyu
(all but Jorge
María , the oldest
harpist)

2. Ilumán Tiyu
(Jorge María)

3. "Cascarón"

4. Ñuka llama
di mi vida

5. Carabuela

6. Chayamuyari
warmiku

7. Llakishamari
nirkanki

8. Rusa María
Kituaña

9. Segundito
Muynala

10. "Llaki llakilla
purini"

11. NI.5

12. Ñ6"
(Jorge María)

to learn and practice singing. Note the eight-beat patterning and the equal rhythm halves; "Cascarón" is number three.

Certain *sanjuanes*, such as "Ilumán tiyu," are often sung, while others such as "Cascarón" and "Carabuela" are typically played instrumentally. You can find words for all the commonly sung *sanjuanes* in Schechter 1982:II:379–456. After singing or listening to all twelve of these *sanjuanes*, you will begin to sense that some combination of two (or all three) of the motives shown in example 9–10 is

Ex. 9–10.   Characteristic *sanjuán* rhythmic figures.

strongly characteristic of *sanjuanes.* Just as the major second–minor third pattern is distinctive for melody in *sanjuán,* so also are these patterns distinctive for *sanjuán* rhythm.

As for harmonic relationships, "Cascarón's" melody and Efraín's accompanying bass line illustrate the prominence of the minor tonic key and its relative major key: the arpeggios (*T*) stress the minor key (D minor), the *A* sections emphasize the relative major (F major). The high B flat of the *B* statements, together with the D and F in the bass, suggest a feeling of the key of B-flat major—the subdominant key, or IV, of the relative major, F. The musics of many Andean peoples reflect this close relationship of the minor to its relative major. We will call this relationship *bimodality.*

In Cotacachi Quichua *sanjuán* the music is basically repetitive, with a single predominating motive, often eight-beat phrases, nearly identical first-half and second-half rhythms, characteristic pitch and rhythmic motifs, and harmonic support that demonstrates the bimodal relationship of minor to relative major. These features give many of these twelve *sanjuanes* a similar sound and provide the grammar of the musical language of Cotacachi Quichua *sanjuán.* Or, as Bruno Nettl has put it, "in each . . . musical language, some style features dominate and coalesce into a mainstream," that is, a homogeneous core (1983:49).

SANJUÁN AND COTACACHI
QUICHUA LIFEWAYS

Do Quichua speakers throughout the Ecuadorian Andes know "Cascarón"? How is *sanjuán* performed on the Imbabura harp? On which occasions is it performed? What are the characteristic verse structures when *sanjuanes* are sung? How do these structures or the specific texts reflect aspects of daily Cotacachi Quichua lifeways?

For students of music-cultures, Imbabura Province and the region around Cotacachi in particular are special, even unique, sites. Writing sixty-five years ago, an Ecuadorian musicologist commented that the Quichua of Imbabura had "a special musical aptitude" (Moreno Andrade 1930:269); an Ecuadorian anthropologist once remarked to me that the region around Cotacachi as well known as a "music box." A lyre on the flag of Cotacachi County confirms the central role music occupies in the region, and an author of a recent book on Imbabura traditions even suggests that to speak of Ecuadorian music is to speak of the music of Cotacachi (Obando 1988:155).

This feeling came also from the Imbabureños themselves, both Quichua- and Spanish-speaking. They insisted on the uniqueness of their own music in relation to that of every other region. In response to questions about the spread of a particular *sanjuán*, for example, Cotacachi Quichua answered, *"Cada llajta."* *Cada* is Spanish for "every," and *llajta* is Quichua for "community." *Cada llajta* is the idea that every community has its own music, or its own mortuary customs, or its own dress, or its own dialect of Quichua. *Cada llajta* extends even to the way Quichua is to be written in Ecuador. In 1980 meetings, representatives of various Quichua communities decided to permit the "speakers of each dialect to determine their own form of writing the language." (Harrison 1989:19). *Cada llajta* seems to operate elsewhere in Ecuador as well. In April 1980 my wife and I moved from the northern to the central highlands; I sang and played on the Imbabura harp *sanjuanes* well known in Cotacachi to Quichua speakers in this new region. Although they had never heard these songs before, they came to learn and enjoy the pieces. When *sanjuanes* are imported into other regions, the *indígenas* often name them with reference to their origin. *"Sanjuán* from Cotacachi," or *"Sanjuán* from Otavalo" (a town near Cotacachi).

Cada llajta also dictates the performance media and the performance practices. *Sanjuanes* are sung and played by Cotacachi Quichua of all ages, by women and men, girls and boys. They are performed by unaccompanied voices, by vocal duos, by voice and harp—with a *golpeador* (one who beats rhythm on the harp), by solo harp and *golpeador,* by voice and guitar, by solo *kena,* by solo *bandolín* (a fretted mandolin), or by ensembles of various instruments. When you hear *sanjuán* played on the Imbabura harp, you will also see a person kneeling in front of or alongside the harp. This is the *golpeador* (in Spanish, *golpear*: to hit), who beats the lower part of the harp soundbox in rhythm to the *sanjuán.* Illustration 9–6 shows Miguel Armando, the regular *golpeador* for his two harpist sons, César and Sergio, assuming a *golpeador* posture for César. Ramona, the harpists' mother, is alongside.

All Cotacachi Quichua harpists remark that the *golpeador* and his dependable, metronomic rhythm are essential to proper *sanjuán* performance. The *golpe* is the bedrock upon which the harpist's concentration rests. Without it, he cannot work. Note, for example, the prominent *golpe* in Efraín's "Cascarón" performance, by his friend Martín Mateo. This rhythmic hitting of the harp soundbox is not unique to Cotacachi, Ecuador; it appears in diverse folk harp traditions in central highland Ecuador, Peru, Argentina, Chile, and Mexico.

The treble register of the Imbabura harp is tuned to a six-pitch, or hexatonic, scale in the natural minor key, omitting the second scale degree. For example, in our D-minor scale, the harpist will tune his treble register to the following pitches: D, F, G, A, B flat, C, and D (upper octave). This tuning permits him to play the full range of mostly pentatonic *sanjuanes* in his repertoire, as well as the occasional hexatonic one—for example, "Ilumán tiyu," normally played with G minor, not D minor, as tonic. The hexatonic pitches present on the D-minor-tuned harp permit the use of A, the second degree in the key of G minor. "Ilumán tiyu" requires that second scale degree. The middle register typically is likewise

Ill. 9–6.   Miguel Armando in *golpeador* posture, with César playing harp, May 1980. Photograph by John M. Schechter.

hexatonic. The bass register is tuned so that the harpist may play the minor tonic triad, with upper and lower octaves, in alternation with (i.e., one or sometimes two hand-positions away from) the relative major triad (ex. 9–11). He uses four fingers of the hand (excluding the little finger), skipping one string between each finger, often two strings between index finger and thumb.

In the *comunas* outside Cotacachi, the *arpero* (harpist) and *golpeador* perform *sanjuanes* in at least three festive contexts: *matrimonio* (wedding), *misai* (private Mass), and *wawa velorio* (child's wake). Quichua in this region celebrate a five-day wedding. Within the Saturday to Wednesday cycle, Sunday or Monday sees the *ñavi maillai*, a ritual washing of feet and face, at which harp music is present. A *misai* is a private Mass held to a saint: after the Mass in the cantonal church, the statue of the saint—the *santo*—is returned to its altar in its owner's home; a meal is prepared for the Mass offerer, and a musical fiesta is celebrated through the

Ex. 9–11.   Tuning of bass register of Imbabura harp.

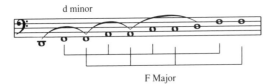

night. In *wawa velorio*, held all night at the deceased child's home, *sanjuán* music predominates.

Sanjuán at *wawa velorio*, as elsewhere, is dance music. You can do the *sanjuán* dance step as you practice from your list of twelve *sanjuanes*. Men and women hold their hands behind their backs and stomp to each quarter-note beat. Step forward with your left foot, joining with the right foot on the next beat. Then move your right foot back first, followed by your left foot. When dancing *sanjuán*, keep your upper torso stiff, your knees bent, and your lower body relaxed, with a good bounce and stomp. The signal to turn around while dancing is (shouted) "Tigrashpa!" or "Tigrapai!"

We can view the *sanjuán* dance step as an emphatic back-and-forth walking, a stomp, to the music. At the child's wake, this stomping is performed all night as the *arpero* plays *sanjuanes* at length, sometimes several strung together without interruption. As a forceful walk-ing to music, *sanjuán* emphatically asserts the action of walking. It serves as a kinetic endorsement for both the walking and the Quichua way of life that depends on it. Let us delve further into Cotacachi Quichua walking, which, as we have already observed, is vital to communication, to daily tasks—in short, to survival.

WALKING IN *SANJUÁN*:
THE VITAL-DOMAIN METAPHOR

Walking as the paramount daily activity of Cotacachi Quichua emerges in expressive culture not only in dance but in song text as well. This probably should come as no surprise, for any such distinctive facet of local ecology or behavior is bound to manifest itself in word and song. Among the Kwakiutl of Vancouver Island, for example, a person's wealth and guests were considered his "salmon" (Boas 1940[1929]:234). For the Kaluli people of the Papua New Guinea rain forest, waterway terms are a prominent source of metaphors, including metaphors related to Kaluli music theory. In Kaluli culture, kinds of water become kinds of sound; the term for "waterfall," in particular, is the point of departure for a series of metaphors relating to musical structure (Feld 1981:26). Other writers, too, have discussed how vital domains of experience, for particular cultures, have served as the fount for broad streams of localized metaphor. In Asturias, Spain, for example, agricultural metaphors remain strong in Asturian deepsong—among miners, who in most cases retain some ties to the land (Fernandez 1978).

Outside Cotacachi, in the *comunas*, walking is necessary for the survival of *comunas* as well as for individual sustenance. Quichua community leaders frequently say that their particular *comuna* will succeed or fail depending on whether it can obtain outside aid. Rousing *comuna* residents to support the *comuna* and searching for assistance from provincial authorities demands footwork. Their view is that *comunas* will flourish only with persistent *purishpa* (walking) on their behalf. Moreover, on the personal level *purina* becomes to "walk" for one's educational benefit and to enable oneself to carry out family obligations. *Purina*,

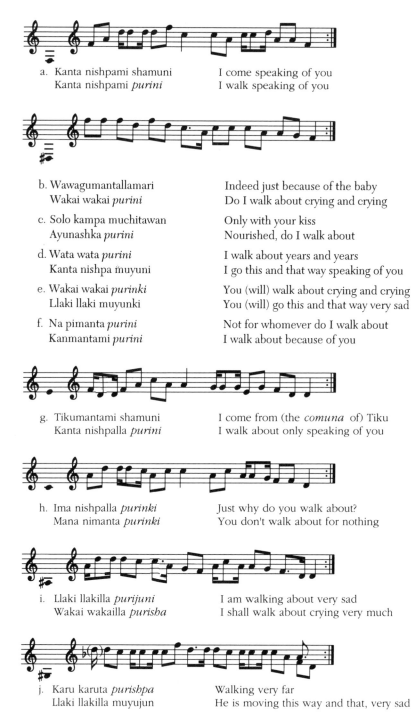

a. Kanta nishpami shamuni — I come speaking of you
   Kanta nishpami *purini* — I walk speaking of you

b. Wawagumantallamari — Indeed just because of the baby
   Wakai wakai *purini* — Do I walk about crying and crying

c. Solo kampa muchitawan — Only with your kiss
   Ayunashka *purini* — Nourished, do I walk about

d. Wata wata *purini* — I walk about years and years
   Kanta nishpa muyuni — I go this and that way speaking of you

e. Wakai wakai *purinki* — You (will) walk about crying and crying
   Llaki llaki muyunki — You (will) go this and that way very sad

f. Na pimanta *purini* — Not for whomever do I walk about
   Kanmantami *purini* — I walk about because of you

g. Tikumantami shamuni — I come from (the *comuna* of) Tiku
   Kanta nishpalla *purini* — I walk about only speaking of you

h. Ima nishpalla *purinki* — Just why do you walk about?
   Mana nimanta *purinki* — You don't walk about for nothing

i. Llaki llakilla *purijuni* — I am walking about very sad
   Wakai wakailla *purisha* — I shall walk about crying very much

j. Karu karuta *purishpa* — Walking very far
   Llaki llakilla muyujun — He is moving this way and that, very sad

Fig. 9–9. The Quichua verb *purina* in Cotacachi *sanjuán* couplets.

k. Juyaimantalla *purini*   I walk about just because of love
   Llakimantalla muyuni   I go this and that way just because of sadness

l. Kanmantallami *purini*   I walk about just because of you
   Tutai tutailla *purini*   Nights and nights I walk about

Fig. 9–9. (*Continued*)

the inescapable daily activity of walking, becomes a positive metaphor in speech: it is behavior worthy of others' esteem because it is done on behalf of others; it is behavior leading to one's own enhanced self-respect.

In the texts of sung *sanjuán* the *purina* metaphor is "extended." In the metaphoric mechanism of extension, one takes experience from a domain where it is easily understood and uses it as the basis for domains more abstract and ambiguous. In sung *sanjuanes*, *purina* appears prominently in texts, notably as a verb of action. Figure 9–9 shows *sanjuán* verse couplets, with their primary (A) motives.

Purina in these *sanjuán* texts extends to emotion. The verses express either emotional release through walking ("I walk about crying and crying") or emotional involvement through walking ("I walk about because of you"; "Nights and nights I walk about"). *Purina* may be traced through its various metaphoric courses—from walking along the *chaki ñan* (footpath), to walking for the benefit of the *comuna* or for one's own betterment, to wandering, going about, for love, sadness, or as an outlet for other emotions. We notice how walking becomes extended to encompass the abstract, from physical movement for survival, to movement for broadly social purposes, to movement for personal, emotional reasons.

You have looked at the musical character and the phrase structure of *sanjuán*, and you have seen how *purina* functions in *sanjuán* song text as a metaphor reflecting the vital domain of walking in Cotacachi Quichua daily life. Let us now learn two *sanjuanes* that, for different reasons, might be called "classics."

TWO "CLASSIC" *SANJUANES*

In chapter 2 David McAllester calls certain Navajo great ceremonial chants "classic." Two Imbabura Quichua *sanjuanes* qualify as classics in their highland region: "Rusa María wasi rupajmi" and "Ilumán tiyu." "Rusa María" (recorded selection 62; ex. 9–12; fig. 9–10) was in 1980 one of the most beloved *sanjuanes* of the Cotacachi Quichua *comuna*.

An important disc of Imbabura Quichua music, *Ñanda mañachi 1* (1977), begins side A with this *sanjuán*, and the record jacket back presents an essay, "Un país llamado Rosa María," ("A Land Called Rosa María") in which this particular *sanjuán* becomes a metaphor for the Quichua way of life in this entire

Ex. 9–12.   *Sanjuán*, "Rusa María wasi rupajmi."

region. In our field recording, Gerónimo on vocal, Sergio on harp, and his father, Miguel Armando, on *golpe*, perform this *sanjuán* at a *wawa velorio* in January 1980. You will hear noise as the microphone is passed back and forth from singer to harpist.

What is it about "Rusa María" that delivers such a strong message of life in Imbabura? "Rusa María" speaks of tragedy, drunkenness, and fright, as well as courting. The first double couplet suggests resignation in the face of a disastrous house fire. Quichua homes higher up Mt. Cotacachi have thatched roofs (see Schechter 1992:141 for a photograph), instead of tile, with wooden support beams. The family meal is cooked over an open hearth, and destruction by fire is an ever-present possibility. When I asked about this verse ten years later, in September 1990, Imbabura Quichua musicians told me that "Rusa María's" home might well be small and old; she might be expressing both anger and the confidence that her neighbors, feeling sympathy, might build her a new home, larger and better. Quichua families are accustomed to disaster, relating both to property and, as we shall see, infant death.

Alcoholic beverages can be another source of social tragedy. Much of the alcohol consumed in the Cotacachi countryside in 1980 was cane alcohol (*trago*), brought as contraband from another region of Ecuador. Frequently, the owners of the small stores in the *comunas* would mix this *trago* with water, berry juice, or other substances, and the effects could be unpredictable. Consumption of *trago* or other alcohol is vital in Cotacachi rituals (such as a child's wake) and in Andean rituals in general throughout Peru and Bolivia. Yet overconsumption of *trago* can

Rusa María wasi rupajmi	Rusa María's house burning
Mas ki rupachun nishkashi,	So let it burn, she seems to have said,
Rusa María wasi rupajmi	Rusa María's house burning
Mas ki rupachun nishkashi,	So let it burn, she seems to have said,
Taita Manuilpash machashkamari	And Manuel, a father, very drunk
Manllarishkami wakajun,	Frightened, is crying,
Taita Manuilpash machashkamari	And Manuel, a father, very drunk
Manllarishkami wakajun,	Frightened, is crying,
Wambrakunapash kwitsakunawan	And young men and young women
Sirinkapajmi rishka nin,	Went to lie down together, they say,
Wambrakunapash kwitsakunawan	And young men and young women
Sirinkapajmi rishka nin.	Went to lie down together, they say.

Fig. 9–10.   Lyrics to "Rusa María."

produce hallucinations, strongly emotional behavior, and in the case of adulterated *trago*, even blindness or death.

"Rusa María" refers also to courting. *Wambra* and *kwitsa* may mean either young man and young woman, or boy and girl. Courting begins in the schoolyard and elsewhere at age twelve or thirteen. Quichua often marry in their mid- or late teens.

"Rusa María" speaks of the inevitable in Cotacachi Quichua life: the natural environment, ritual practice in conflict with economic exploitation, and cultural expectation and human instinct. In the final analysis, "Rusa María" is a song, danced to on festive occasions; it is a source of joy and pride to all the *indígenas* of Cotacachi.

In the case of the highly popular (both in 1980 and still in 1990) *sanjuán* "Ilumán tiyu" ("Man of Ilumán"), we know the composer: Segundo Galo Maigua, a Quichua composer-guitarist-singer of the Imbabura village of Ilumán. Galo Maigua's *sanjuán* compositions are often motivated by autobiographical forces. His fame among Imbabura Quichua is attested to by wide acknowledgment of his being the composer of highly popular *sanjuanes* and by his ensemble Conjunto Ilumán's high level of demand, locally, and their having produced as of 1990 one commercial cassette.

My fieldwork in 1990 in Imbabura brought to light the fact that *sanjuán* may often take on the nature of a ballad, even in instances where that fact is not immediately obvious. The thoughts of a *sanjuán* text typically express the essence of a large story, making the *sanjuán* a highly distilled ballad form, the synoptic character of the text being in keeping with the elliptical character of Andean poetry dating back to Incaic times. With "Ilumán tiyu," the ballad nature—the story behind the *sanjuán*—is not at all obvious. Recorded selection 63 is of the composer, Galo Maigua, playing guitar and singing "Ilumán tiyu" (fig. 9–11), together with his Conjunto Ilumán, on October 27, 1990, in the village of Ilumán, in the home of a local policeman (ill. 9–7). One regular member of the ensemble, a noted harpist, was unable to be present on this occasion. As with *indígena* harpists, so too was there a proliferation of *indígena* violinists in eighteenth-century highland Ecuador (Schechter 1992:55). The tradition of Quichua violinists is particularly strong today in the Otavalo-Ilumán area of Imbabura.

What had never been comprehensible, since my 1980 research, when I recorded numerous versions of "Ilumán tiyu" in the environs of Cotacachi, was the nature of the lyrics. When I was informed that Segundo Galo Maigua was in fact the composer of this *sanjuán*, I tried, during a visit to his Ilumán home on September 30, 1990, to ascertain what might lie behind words that seem merely a statement that the man singing and speaking is an *indígena* from Ilumán.

Galo Maigua described the tale behind the text. He told me that before he composed "Ilumán tiyu," he had become extremely ill with tuberculosis; the condition of his lungs had deteriorated, and he believed he was about to die. Although during 1972–73 wanderings through the *comunas* around Cotacachi he had sung the melody to a variety of words (Galo says he composes by first hearing

Ilumán Tiyu cantanmi,	The man from Ilumán sings,
Ilumán Tiyu nijunmi.	The man from Ilumán is saying.
Ilumán Tiyu cantanmi,	The man from Ilumán sings,
Ilumán Tiyu nijunmi.	The man from Ilumán is saying.
Sultira kashpa paya kashpa,	Being a young (unmarried) woman, [or an] old woman,
Ñuka tunupi bailapai.	Dance to my song.
Sultira kashpa paya kashpa,	Being a young (unmarried) woman, [or an] old woman,
Ñuka tunupi bailapai.	Dance to my song.
Este es el indio de Ilumán	This is the *indígena* of Ilumán
Él que canta sanjuanito.	He who sings sanjuán.
Este es el indio de Ilumán	This is the *indígena* of Ilumán
Él que canta sanjuanito.	He who sings sanjuán.
Para que bailen toditos,	So that all [men] might dance,
Para que bailen toditas.	So that all [women] might dance.
Para que bailen toditos,	So that all [men] might dance,
Para que bailen toditas.	So that all [women] might dance.
Ilumán Tiyu cantanmi,	The man from Ilumán sings,
etc.	etc.
Sultira kashpa paya kashpa,	Being a young (unmarried) woman [or an] old woman,
etc.	etc.]

Fig. 9–11.   Lyrics to "Ilumán Tiyu."

a melody, later setting text), he now determined that he would like everyone—be they young woman or old woman, for example—to dance to this, his song, after his death. In effect, "Ilumán tiyu" was ultimately texted as Galo's final statement of his identity to posterity: "I"—the man singing, speaking—am a man from Ilumán; remember me by remembering my music: "dance to my song." In sum, what appeared to the uninformed listener to be innocuous words came, on greater understanding, to have profound import for a composer believing himself to be on his deathbed.

Spanish speakers will note that the intermingling of Spanish and Quichua words we spoke of early in this chapter appears prominently in this *sanjuán.* Moreover, the verse, "Este es el indio de Ilumán, él que canta sanjuanito," is a translation of the first, critically important, verse; Galo Maigua commented to me that a major area radio station had prompted him to produce the parallel text in Spanish. Other Galo Maigua–composed *sanjuanes,* such as "Antonio Mocho" and "Rusita Andranga," share the distilled-ballad character of "Ilumán tiyu." Both of these *sanjuanes,* along with "Ilumán tiyu," appear on the commercial cassette *Elenita Conde,* by Conjunto Ilumán; the cassette was mastered in Otavalo and mass-produced in Bogotá, Colombia, somewhat prior to 1990.

Ill. 9–7. "**Ilumán tiyu**" **composer, Segundo Galo Maigua (far right), with his ensemble, Conjunto Ilumán, October 1990. Photograph by John M. Schechter**

THE ANDEAN ENSEMBLE PHENOMENON

Conjunto Ilumán represents a now-broad phenomenon, both in the Andes and beyond: the Andean ensemble. Other Ecuadorian ensembles focusing on Quichua or *Nueva Canción* musics over the last twenty years have included Ñanda Mañachi (Quichua: "Lend me the way"); 1977, 1979, 1983); Conjunto Indígena "Peguche" (Spanish: *indígena* ensemble from the village of Peguche [near Otavalo]; 1977); and Jatari (Quichua: "Get up!"; 1978). The carefully and elaborately produced albums of Ñanda Mañachi, in particular, are notably evocative of the Quichua music-culture of Imbabura.

Today in the Otavalo Valley, teenagers and young men are actively engaged in music-making. In Imbabura, one radio station has had an annual festival of musical ensembles, in which any and all area village ensembles may participate, each playing perhaps two songs on the radio. In July 1990 this village ensemble marathon featured enough groups for the radio festival to last twelve hours. Music-making is an important means of socialization among Quichua youths who have long since ceased attending school and who find few community activities available to them, except for volleyball, which is pursued with a vengeance in the village plazas and *comunas* of Imbabura. You will hear Quichua teenagers rehearsing diligently, on weekends, at a member's home, performing a few traditional *sanjuanes* and, like their counterparts in the United States, often experimenting with their own compositions.

The Bolivian ethnomusicologist Gilka Wara Céspedes has recently remarked that "the Andean Sound is becoming a part of the sonic scene from Europe to Japan" (1993:53). In Quito, the capital of Ecuador, musically polished Quichua ensembles from Ecuador and Peru are featured regularly and prominently on the main tourist thoroughfares. Where Andean *indígena* textile manufacturers have for years traveled the international byways, selling their home-woven ponchos, blankets, and scarves, today the entrepreneurial instinct remains intact but the product has frequently changed: from bulky woolens to featherweight cassettes and CDs, delicate bamboo *zampoñas* and *kenas*. Beyond Ilumán and Quito, one can enjoy "the Andean Sound" in New York City subway stations, in San Francisco's Union Square, in front of Il Duomo in Florence, Italy, and even on Arbat Street in central Moscow. In September 1993 a Virginia-based Bolivian ensemble, Ollantay, was featured in the annual summer concert series produced by the American Folklife Center on the plaza in front of the Library of Congress's Jefferson Building, in Washington, D.C.

The United States is unquestionably a vital part of the international Andean sonic scene. Amauta, based in Seattle, comprises Chilean and Bolivian musicians, playing traditional Andean instruments; they appeared recently at the Seattle Northwest Regional Folklife Festival. (*Amauta* is from the Quechua *jamaut'a*, "wise;" the *amautas* were one of three types of specialists, in the Inca Empire, responsible for preserving the memory of past Inca leaders. They created brief historical stories that were passed on through oral tradition to succeeding generations; Schechter 1979:191–92). Condor, out of Corvallis, Oregon, is an ensemble of five professional, college-educated musicians from Argentina, Peru, and Mexico; the group focuses on traditional Andean musics. Andanzas (Spanish: "wanderings") performs music from a variety of Latin American and Caribbean traditions; this widely traveled, four-member ensemble includes musicians from Argentina, Bolivia, and Mexico, as well as a classically trained American harpist. Andesmanta, an ensemble of Ecuadorian musicians playing traditional highland Ecuadorian musics—including *sanjuanes*—as well as other South American folk musics, has performed at Carnegie Hall and the Metropolitan Museum of Art. Among the most well established of American-based Andean groups is Sukay (Quechua: "to work furrows in straight lines," or "to whistle musically"), formed originally in 1974, with some eight albums by 1994, along with performances at Lincoln Center and major folk music festivals. The California-based group Chaskinakuy (Quechua: "to give and receive, hand to hand, among many") is distinguished by its size—two musicians—and by the fact that both are non-Andeans: founder Edmond Badoux of Switzerland, and companion Francy Vidal of California. Now in their tenth year, Chaskinakuy is also unique in that Edmond, a careful student of Andean music-culture, performs several less common (for these American-based ensembles) but important and often distinctly traditional instruments: Peruvian harp, pelican-bone flute, long straight trumpet, condor-feather *zampoña,* and *pututu* (Quechua: "conch trumpet") (Ross 1994:19–24). Chaskinakuy tours California annually and has produced two recordings. A list of selected recordings by these and other Andean ensembles can be found in Ross 1994:27.

Finally, Andean ensembles are taking root in American universities. With the strong beginning of the *Nueva Canción* ensemble Toqui Amaru (Mapuche and Quechua: "chief serpent"), founded at the University of Texas at Austin in 1976 by Renato Espinoza of Chile, with Guillermo Delgado and Enrique Cuevas of Bolivia, Néstor Lugones of Argentina, and American Alejandro Cardona, UT/Austin has for some years maintained an Andean ensemble among their other Latin American groups. At the University of California at Santa Cruz, students perform in beginning- (Voces [Spanish: "voices"]) and advanced-level (Taki Ñan [Quichua: "song path"]) Andean ensembles; Taki Ñan, which recorded an in-house cassette in 1992, focuses on traditional Andean musics in Spanish and Qui(e)chua, as well as *Nueva Canción* musics.

Returning from Andean America to the Andes of Imbabura, the traditions of the Quichua of Cotacachi—the people, the language, the dress, the material culture, the character of *sanjuán* and the harp that plays it—have been preserved for hundreds of years. *Cada llajta* (individual character of the community) ensures the uniqueness of many aspects of their expressive culture. However, the Cotacachi Quichua share some traits with other regions and cultures of Latin America. One of these is the wake ritual for a dead child. Let us look at *wawa velorio* to see how it accommodates *cada llajta* with broader beliefs and practices that transcend cultural and political boundaries.

WAWA VELORIO

In Imbabura as elsewhere in Latin America, infants struggle to survive. In three consecutive months in 1979–80 I witnessed three *wawa velorio* rituals on Cotacachi's slopes. I observed a fourth child's wake there in August 1990. The infant mortality rate in Ecuador continues to be very high; deaths are caused in large part from intestinal and respiratory diseases. Our own history has seen high infant mortality rates: in the era of Puritan New England (1620s to 1720s), in Boston, as many as three in ten persons died in infancy. The death of young children in Ecuador and throughout Latin America is a daily tragedy, one that through its very frequency ironically serves to preserve dozens of unique regional traditions of genre, instrument, and dance.

We turn to our visits, with the harpist and his family, to *wawa velorios* on Mt. Cotacachi. After nightfall, Sergio, the harpist contracted to provide music for the wake (ill. 9–8), his younger brother and apprentice-harpist, César, and their family leave their Tikulla home for the home of the deceased. After more than an hour's uphill winding journey on *chaki ñanes*, their father and *golpeador* Miguel Armando bearing the family harp, they arrive. At about 9:30 Sergio sits down with his harp next to the platform bearing the deceased infant. A few candles illuminate the casket and the home. After tuning, Sergio plays a strongly percussive music called *vacación* (recorded selection 64; ex. 9–13). The all-night *wawa velorio*—the wake for the deceased Quichua child—has begun.

Ill. 9–8.   Harpist Sergio, March 1980. Photograph by John M. Schechter.

Vacación (the same term is used for both the genre and the title itself) differs audibly from *sanjuán.* First, *vacación* does not require a *golpeador* but is performed by the harpist alone. Second, it is not sung but is purely instrumental. Where *sanjuán* is in simple meter, *vacación* lacks the regular stresses that characterize a particular meter. *Vacación* is not built, like *sanjuán,* in eight-beat phrases but in long, descending cycles. *Sanjuán* is dance music; *vacación* is not.

   Sanjuán is performed throughout the night at *wawa velorio,* accompanying the dancing of family and guests. *Vacación* is tied to two special ritual moments: at the outset of the wake, and whenever behavior centers on the deceased child. Harpists informed me that they play *vacación* at the beginning of the ritual in order to drive out the *demonio,* or devil, from beneath the platform supporting the deceased child. The second ritual moments include late-evening adorning of the corpse, and dawn closing of the casket.

Ex. 9–13.   Partial transcription of *vacación*, played by harpist Sergio at child's wake, February 1980.

actual minor tonic: **a**
transposed to **d minor**

Before playing *vacación,* after playing it, and periodically throughout the night, the harpist and his family are offered food and drink—bananas, homemade bread, barley gruel, maize gruel, stewed corn, and *trago.* We have mentioned the central importance of *trago* consumption in ritual settings both in Cotacachi and throughout the Andes. In *wawa velorio,* most of those present consume the drink. The man (never a woman) with the *trago* bottle and plastic cup goes around the room, offering a *copa* (cup) of *trago* to each man and woman: "Ufyapai!" ("Drink!"), he says; the one being offered the *copa* usually first asks him to drink—which he does—then accepts the offer him- or herself.

Until approximately midnight, Sergio performs mostly *sanjuanes.* By 10:30 P.M. he has played some five to ten *sanjuanes,* including perhaps "Carabuela," "Llakishamari nirkanki," "Ilumán tiyu," and "Rusa María." Occasionally, to keep the dancing going, he changes from one *sanjuán* to another without stopping. There is a distinctly regular and nearly metronomic tempo sense about this father-son duo. Miguel Armando's *golpe* is solid and reliable, invariant, and Sergio's rhythm is strong and regular. Vocalists for the duo may be Sergio's companions, Roberto and Gerónimo. One sings with Sergio. The voice-harp duo performs typically texted *sanjuanes,* including "Rusa María" and "Ruku kuskungu." To enhance the *alegre,* or happy, character of the festive ritual, the harpist likes to have near-constant chatter together with his music and *golpe.*

Around 10:30 P.M., perhaps in the middle of playing a *sanjuán,* Sergio suddenly stops and shifts into *vacación.* Now the child, in its casket, is removed from the platform where it has been prominently displayed and placed on the floor for adorning and crowning. The infant is given usually to its mother, who mourns the loss of her baby with a lament. This sobbed music uses the principal notes of *vacación:* D–C–A (scale degrees 8–7–5 of D minor). A crown of flowers is put on the baby's head. Its waist and wrists are wrapped in ribbons, and bouquets of flowers are placed alongside the body in the casket. During this entire time, Sergio plays *vacación,* and he stops only when the infant and its casket are again placed on the platform.

Although dancing to *sanjuán* was slow to start, by 1:30 A.M. everyone is dancing: with the air growing colder, at nine thousand feet, the music and the festive night are warming up. The godmother and the father might begin to dance, prompting Sergio to shout a pleased: "Achi mamaka kallarinka ña!" ("The godmother will begin [to dance] now!") Gerónimo shouts: "Shinlli shinlli bailapankich' kumarigukuna!" ("Dance really strongly, dear *comadres!*"). Sergio now hardly stops for small talk, immediately replenishing the musical warmth with one, then another *sanjuán*—maybe several strung together.

He now begins to alternate *sanjuán* with *pareja,* a slightly faster music, also for dancing but usually without text.

Very late, at about 3 A.M., Sergio leaves the harp and asks his younger brother, César, to take over (ill. 9–9). With very few people still awake, César plays a string of short *sanjuanes.* There is no banter between César and his *golpeador*-father, as there had been more naturally between musicians of the same generation, such as

Ill. 9–9.   Harpist César, March 1980. Photograph by John M. Schechter.

Sergio and Gerónimo. This is *sanjuán* without reaction—functional dance music with little function, since no one is dancing.

At about 5 A.M. everyone is awake and shares a morning meal of boiled potatoes. Before sunrise (an hour later) Sergio again takes over the harp, tuning and perhaps playing a *pareja*. Suddenly, he shifts into *vacación* and the casket is taken outside onto the patio. Sergio stops quickly, picks up the harp, and heads outside. Recorded selection 65 begins with Sergio performing *vacación* as the casket is being taken outside. He then remarks, ". . . sacando para afuera" ("[They're] taking [it] outside"). He heads at once outside and there the mother begins to sing her lament.

The mother bids farewell to her child for the final time. She heard cycles of *vacación* for a few minutes just before the casket's removal outside. Now, as if on cue, and almost precisely at sunrise, she expresses her heartfelt grief in a lament that, as in the night before, uses almost exclusively the same three important pitches from *vacación:* D–C–A (in Sergio's actual tuning these pitches are G♯–F♯–D♯). Soon after she begins, Sergio, also near the casket, repeats *vacación* on the harp. Both musical expressions are *of* the child: the mother's *to* the infant, the harpist's *about* the infant, marking behavior directed toward it. Because the infant is open to view for only a few more minutes, the focus of everyone's attention is on her (referring here to a January 12–13, 1980, ritual for a two-year-old girl). Although *vacación* does not "accompany" the mother's lament (they are simultaneous but independent musical expressions), nevertheless they *are* together—in time, in object focus, in musical pitch, and in structure (like *vacación*, the lament is cyclical in form, always beginning with the G♯ and descending through the F♯ to the D♯).

The mother at this point will typically sing-sob alone. On this particularly January 1980 morning, her sobs make it difficult to render most of the words precisely. Clearly she is addressing her baby daughter, whom she calls *warmiku* ("little woman"). She sobs-sings in short phrases that ultimately descend to the lowest pitch. (Respecting the mother in this moment of profound personal grief, I omit the transcription of this lament.)

Lamenting at dawn, the mother caresses her child's face or entire wrapped body one last time. Then the *golpeador* hammers on the lid of the casket, and when the child is no longer visible Sergio stops playing *vacación*. Just after 6 A.M. the godfather hoists the casket to his shoulder and everyone walks down the mountain to the town of Cotacachi, where the child is buried in the cemetery. After the burial the party adjourns to a *cantina* (tavern), where Sergio continues to play *sanjuanes* on the harp for dancing throughout the day.

Dancing, all night, at a child's wake. On Cotacachi's slopes and throughout Latin America, *wawa velorio*—or *velorio de angelito*—is a celebration. We find this surprising, perhaps. We might feel some of the confusion of a French baron, Jean Charles Davillier, who came upon a festive child's wake while traveling in the Spanish Mediterranean in the 1870s (1874:409; see ill. 9–10). He could not understand the merrymaking—in this case, a couple dancing a *jota,* accompanying themselves with castanets. One of the relatives informed him: "Está con los

Ill. 9–10.   A festive child's wake in the Spanish Mediterranean, 1870s; illustration by Gustave Doré.

ángeles" ("She is with the angels"). The explanations are the same on this side of
the Atlantic. For example, when nineteenth- and twentieth-century French and
American visitors to Argentina and Chile unexpectedly come upon children's
wakes, they are consistently told that the gathering is a celebration in honor of the
little angel, who is in the breast of God, or that the little angel has died in innocence and has gone to heaven. Therefore, there is to be rejoicing, not weeping. In
our discussion of Violeta Parra, we mentioned that the great majority of Latin
Americans are Roman Catholic. In Roman Catholicism, baptism confers a vital
regeneration in Christ and thus an unconditional promise of salvation to a bap-
tized child dying in infancy. In Catholic Spain and Latin America, the deceased
infant is believed to dwell among the angels—to be an angel. This is cause for rejoicing.

The joyful rite is both broad and deep in Latin America. We read accounts of
children's wakes in this hemisphere going back to 1788 in Puerto Rico (Abbad y
Lasierra 1788:281–82). In the nineteenth or twentieth centuries, *velorio de angelito*, or *wawa velorio*, or *baquiné* (as the rite is known among African-Antillans
of Puerto Rico) was celebrated in Argentina, Brazil, Chile, Colombia, Cuba, the
Dominican Republic, Ecuador, Mexico, Nicaragua, Panama, Paraguay, Peru,
Puerto Rico, and Venezuela.

If we can understand something of the philosophy behind the joyful character
of the Latin American child's wake, celebrating the ascension of the sinless infant
into the realm of the angels, then how does *wawa velorio* fit into the category of
funeral rituals? A ritual is a formal practice or custom, and rural dwellers have
both calendric rituals, tied to cycles of agriculture, religion, or national celebration, and life cycle rituals, marking significant transitional moments in the life of
any individual. Funeral rites are life cycle rituals.

Within the formal practice or custom, you will see actions that are prescribed—obligatory, standardized, conventional. At *wawa velorio*, I was struck
by the precision with which certain prescribed actions were carried out: *vacación*
always began the wake; it always accompanied movement of the corpse, usually
in its open casket, from one place to another; at dawn, as the casket was brought
outside for closing, the mother began her lament, almost as if on cue. Interestingly, in Hungary, laments are to be performed quite strictly at specified
moments of the period after death, and at burial; one of the specific points is
when the casket is closed (Boilès 1978:130). During the period of immediate
mourning, when all are able to view the corpse, there is always a conventional-
ized, dramatized outburst of grief; the corpse is usually the center of attention.
There may be ritual forms of fondling the corpse—the body is sometimes
stroked and embraced (Malinowski 1954[1925]:49). Thus we saw and heard, in
the Cotacachi *comuna*, the child conspicuously displayed during the night, the
lament seemingly almost "cued," and the Quichua mother caressing her child on
the patio of their home.

Indeed, in keeping with our understanding of the prescriptive nature of ritual,
we find that most accounts of Latin American (and Spanish, as well) children's
wakes share certain prominent behaviors, regardless of cultural group or country.

The child is always conspicuous by its presence, in the same room in which family and friends dance to the favorite music (*sanjuán* in highland Ecuador, *jota* in Mediterranean Spain) of the region: thus, *cada llajta* in operation. The infant is not only present but raised: lying on the elevated platform, seated on the table, tied to a ladder placed atop the casket, suspended from the roof, or pushed back and forth between poles. Each of these types of ritual gestures symbolizes the transformation into an angel and entry into eternity. Similarly, the infant is washed and dressed in the finest clothing available and is bedecked in ribbons, flowers, and paper or cardboard wings. Upon the child's head is a crown of real or artificial flowers, and this wreath is essential: the crown is both ubiquitous (in Latin American and Spanish children's wakes) and ancient (the practice of crowning dead children dates back to the time of the ancient Greeks). The atmosphere of the wake is always festive, with dancing, food, and alcoholic beverage.

A number of Spanish and Latin American visual and literary artists have depicted the child's wake in paintings, novels, short stories, plays, and poems; many of these portrayals are critical of what the native artists view as an indefensible diminution of a life, in making its extinction the pretext for merrymaking. Nevertheless, the Latin American child's wake is a deep-rooted ritual and one that embodies local-cultural preferences in expressive culture—song types, dance types, instrument types. Whether or not local artists or outsiders approve of the *velorio de angelito,* the practice does serve as a reliable stamp—designed by the culture itself—of that local culture at that point in time (Schechter 1994b).

THE CAREER DILEMMA
OF DON CÉSAR MUQUINCHE

We have seen how vital the harpist is in Quichua children's wakes in northern highland Cotacachi. The harpist is also very visible in the central highlands, especially in Tungurahua Province (see map, fig. 9–6). One talented individual artist, Don César Muquinche, is a harpist of Illampu, a village outside Ambato, in Tungurahua (ill. 9–11). As you can see, Don César's harp is considerably larger than the Imbabura harps. It is modeled on the harps of Paraguay; these instruments are distinguished by their substantial size and by their neck shape—an inverted arch. The neck's tuning pegs are guitar-type mechanical tuning pegs, used also by the Paraguayans. The pattern of small, paired sound holes on either side of the column—holes that in fact come at the ends of (barely visible) painted S shapes—dates to Spanish harps of the seventeenth century.

An artist of national stature, Don César plays numerous musical genres, including *sanjuanito,* an adaptation of the Imbabura *sanjuán.* In recorded selection 66 we hear him playing an *albazo* called "Toro barroso" (Spanish: "Reddish Bull"). *Albazos* are well known among Spanish speakers throughout the highlands and even throughout the country. They are heard everywhere on the radio and at public and private celebrations.

Ill. 9–11.   Don César Muquinche, harpist of Illampu, Tungurahua Province, at his home, August 1980. Photograph by John M. Schechter.

Don César's decision to take up the harp was complicated. His father, Don Francisco, had been a professional harpist. Attending his father's performances as a child, the son witnessed the physical suffering that this career brought with it. César initially decided he would apprentice as a hatmaker. But Don Francisco advised his son that whatever César chose to do, he should select something that would make him content and leave him with good memories. Ultimately, these words led César back to music. His decision to be a musician was also a reflection of Don César's great admiration and respect for his father—specifically for his father's ability to resist the temptations inherent in the harpist's career—and for his father's concern for him and serious advice.

In fact, both father and son followed similar paths. Both had a strong business orientation. Don César speaks of Naranjo's harps, and the services of Camilo Borja, Don Francisco, and himself as harpists as being "in some demand." Don César saw himself as being upwardly mobile; he disdained his own *indígena* roots. Yet both he and his father performed for both *indígena* and *blanco* (white) society. They bridged this cultural gap as performers. Finally, both Don César and his father learned to play in ensemble as well as solo, and to adapt to changing performance arenas, such as radio and television.

We will see that both men appreciated playing as an art. They felt great pride in developing it both for their own self-esteem and for the satisfaction of their clients. Don César's highest compliment to artists or craftspersons was to call them "artists of quality."

In July 1980, after I had studied with him for several months, Don César Muquinche told me about the development of his artistic career. Let us look at the types of conflict he faced and how he finally resolved them, choosing harp music over hatmaking. Through his thoughts we can gain some insight into the reputation, the *fama,* of a harpist in Ecuador. I conducted the interview in Spanish and translated it into the English that follows:

DON CÉSAR MUQUINCHE: I was born in 1920, here in Illampu (Tungurahua). My father, Francisco, was planning to become a tailor—to make men's suits. Well, he heard Camilo Borja play—a man who lived just alongside us—and, on hearing him play the harp, my father paid attention. And he said, "I would like to learn harp from this man."

My father then proposed to Borja that he teach him the harp. The man said yes and told him, "Let's make a deal: you make me trousers and I will give you harp lessons." My father told me that he had these lessons every day; he was very interested in learning quickly, taking advantage of the goodwill of the maestro.

When Borja saw that my father was beginning to play the harp fairly well, the maestro, who was in great demand at that time, told him he needed to buy his own harp. . . . There was a man, Segundo Alejandro Naranjo, who made fine instruments—very special harps. They had a fantastic resonance. . . .

My father told me that the harps made by this man were instruments in some demand and of very fine quality; there was no danger that the glue might loosen from the pieces. Even when the harp was hit hard, the wood would not dent or come loose, as might happen today with harps made of rough wood. . . .

My father was in demand in various places—in fiestas, in *wawas muertos* [dead children, i.e., *velorio de angelito,* or *wawa velorio*]. . . . And with the rhythm of this beating upon the harp, they [the father and his *golpeador*] put on a fine show, without the need of other instruments.

[At children's wakes] the *golpeador* had to stay right there, by the harpist. Then, there were other events—*matrimonio,* patron saint fiestas. Among [*indígenas*], the *matrimonio* lasts three or four days. And the harpist has to be *there.* Day and night. . . . It is the same in the fiestas—of devotion to some saint, for example. In the *wawas muertos,* some better-off people had it lasting some three days, but without doubt, one night and one day, for sure. . . . In gratitude for their having been well entertained, the people had to treat the *golpeador* and the harpist to some gifts, like *medianos,* as they call them here: a whole chicken, a rabbit, or a *cui* [Quichua: "guinea pig"; these are native to the Andes, and groups of them are kept in the house by many rural residents of highland Ecuador; today they are raised, killed, and broiled and used as gifts for fiestas or, as here, for the harpist and *golpeador*]—a thing of great value.

Yes, they made a good ensemble. And ever since I could remember, my father was in great demand—as much among the *indígenas* as among the white people. He became an innovative, popular artist who liked to entertain. [He played for] the people of society—a governor, a subtreasurer, here or beyond—in Quito [the capital], in different places. My father was very much in demand, very important: an artist of quality. He traveled to Quito, through the entire country. He became a very well known artist . . . a very distinguished artist, for every class of society.

The musicians might go to their engagements in a cart pulled by a horse. At times, they went on horseback, to Quito—carrying the harp, cushioned and secured with a scarf, or something else soft. There was a person who led the horses. [My father] told me about this.

Sometimes, traveling in this way was very trying. Finally my father said, "No, I won't travel like that. If we could go in those carriages . . . then I would go. I think I have been treating myself badly." And the people [provided what he requested], as they seemed to want my father's services greatly. Many times he went to Riobamba [capital of Chimborazo Province, just south of Tungurahua Province], I recall.

When I began growing up, I sometimes accompanied him, to see how he was treated, or how he might have been suffering. I saw that my father, being responsible, did not get drunk at the fiestas; he was careful to fulfill his responsibilities honorably. And wherever he went, the people paid him well. . . . But it is sad that he had to suffer a lot [owing to the extremely long hours, the demands for continuous music, and the constant pressure to partake of alcohol with the guests] because the people never tired of enjoying themselves. So I felt bad for my father, and I said to him, "Now, father, when can I learn how to play, to help you?"

I lament the death of my father. But he left good memories, as an artist—very good memories. He died while still capable, surrounded by the profits of his labors. By contrast, [another] harpist of quality [whom I knew] died poor because he was quite a womanizer. They say he squandered all he had earned, drinking with women. He died, poor, leaving his children poor. By contrast, my father said, "I have to extract a good inheritance from this profession [of harpist]. If the upper-class people occupy me well, pay me well, if the *indígenas* also pay me well, why not plant crops? Why not use [the money] for land, in things that are to serve me for life?"

My father thought about this very conscientiously. He [bought land and] worked the fields two or three days each week; he did not attend to the fields any more than that because he was in great demand in this career of music. My mother worked the fields more.

Now that I was becoming a young man, I had to think about it. There were harpists who went around poorly dressed, barefoot, dirty; I looked, and realized that my father took very good care of himself. There were other harpists, but awful ones. They got drunk and walked around looking like a mess—not even the instruments were well treated. And that's worse.

And so I said no, I do not want to be a harpist because they get very drunk. Of course, my father is fine, he takes care of me; but I see that most people put pressure on the harpist—they say, "Drink, maestro," with great fervor. "Drink." They put it into your mouth. I said to myself, "Not me . . . I won't dedicate myself to the harp." My father, when they asked him to drink, said, "Don't force me to. I must carry out my responsibilities and earn my money. After I have completed my commitment for which you have hired me, then I shall be delighted to drink. But I have to be responsible for my musical colleagues; they come with me, to earn a living. And since I made the contract, I have to charge the *patrón* who has contracted me and, in turn, pay my *compañeros,* in order to assure their accompaniment in the future. If I get drunk, I can't discharge either my contract or my agreement to pay my *compañeros,* who came along expecting me to pay them. Thus you are hurting me [by insisting that I drink and get drunk.]" This retort worked very well.

Nevertheless, I still felt very suspect about being a harpist. I told my father that I did not wish to be a musician but rather a hatmaker. I liked seeing young women or men who appreciated a truly elegant hat. And there was a hatmaker of first quality, a man by the name of Segundo Villa Paredes, in Ambato [the provincial capital of Tungurahua]. I went there and learned all that the maestro had to teach—how to make hats. I was there some two years, while I was young. I think I was already hatmaking by the age of fifteen years. By the age of eighteen or twenty I was a [hatmaking] maestro.

I became independent and set up a workshop in Ambato. I worked for the "people of society," who liked my style of work. I had all the confidence of these people, and it went well for me. I had quite a nice workshop there in the city of Ambato.

When my father saw that I was a successful [hatmaking] maestro, he told me, "Son, I congratulate you. You have distinguished yourself, now, don't you see? Now, I am going to recommend to you that you take advantage, in your *youth,* of your profession. Of music, I have my fond memories. In the same way, I would recommend that you take advantage of, enjoy, your profession." I had to listen to my father, pay attention to him: he was making this recommendation for my own good.

Well, when I had become a very popular maestro, well esteemed and with plenty of work there in the city, guaranteeing me a good living, some people came to me on their own to ask that I teach them the craft of hatmaking. Others came so they might help me expedite my commitments to deliver the completed work. I accepted them as working assistants. I looked for those who already knew the craft. Others came and said, "Maestro, be so kind as to teach my son the profession." "Delighted," [I said,] and accepted them.

Soon I organized the work for those who had come to help and those who had come to learn, and I had some free time. Over there the people already knew—"You're the Muquinche—?" I said, "Yes." "Listen, and your father is a harpist of quality?" I said, "Yes." "And you don't know anything?" "I too know a little bit." "And why don't you let us hear it? Why don't you bring a harp here to your workshop and play for us? Let us hear what your style is like, or how you play."

I thought, "Perhaps, yes, I must have a harp—as recreation from work."

Since the people had requested me to play the harp for them, I had a harp made. I brought it to my workshop, and I began to play it. Every once in a while, as a rest, I would sit down and begin to play . . . some people came, curious. "It sounds nice, it sounds—" this or that. "Play, maestro, play," they exhorted me. "Play the harp, maestro." "Play the harp." And I had to listen to them: "Fine, I'm delighted to. Sit down." I had them sit down in one spot, and I would do a small performance.

Meanwhile, some of the people continued talking with me: "Why not better dedicate yourself to the harp?" At times, to my good friends, I paid attention to this. But of some people, I thought, "These [people] are going to do me harm," because they said [as many had done to my father], "Look, maestro, you play beautifully; accept just one [drink]." I said, "No, I have my business—I have my workshop. I have this—how can I abandon my workshop?" When I put it this way, some withdrew their invitation; others continued asking me to play: "Play the harp, maestro." I said to myself, "Listen, this is bad; I am going to get hooked on this."

Well, as I was getting popular with my music, there came this man, I remember, from Radio Ambato, a man by the name of Villa Lobos, the manager of Radio Ambato. Juan Villa Lobos. Well, he said, "Maestro, can you do programs for Radio Ambato?" . . . I said, "Fine."

Well, then, I had to put attention into improving my art. And he said to me, "Maestro, would you be able to play together with other instruments, to make a nice *conjunto* (ensemble), with violins, *bandolín,* guitar, and flute?" I said, "Yes, sir, but only with the agreement that it is to be you who is in charge of getting these people together; if it is to be left to me to do this, then, no. I am busy." The man [did it], of course, since he liked the idea of organizing a *conjunto típico* ["typical" ensemble], as we called it. . . . A very nice ensemble was thus created, now along with the harp . . . it was a great hit with the people—"Such-and-such *conjunto,* directed by . . ." They named me director of the ensemble.

We did the Radio Ambato programs Saturdays and Sundays—Saturdays in the afternoon and Sundays at midday. This was all the time, for some three years in a row. Every weekend.

This man Villa Lobos came to my hat workshop when I was about twenty-eight years old. . . . I was by then a harpist, no? By then, I had practiced my profession [of hatmaker] for some eight years. When I came into popularity [as a harpist], I was twenty-eight years old. . . .

My father visited me and said, "César, you came to like the harp?" I said yes. He answered, "Very well, between the music and the hats, I think that you are going to become a rich man—for you are accumulating money." I confided in him that I did the same as he. With the monies that I earned—as much from the music as from the hats—I bought some small pieces of land. . . .

Well, trying to maintain the workshop, trying to fulfill my commitments, I came home from work at any old hour—at dawn, practically exhausted, wasted. To get the work done, I had to dig in and work myself.

I became ill. A fever, a lung infection, or a typhoid fever. This illness was very strong . . . it was in 1949. It was serious. I had to be hospitalized. Thank God, my hour had not yet arrived. I recuperated, my health restored. My father procured doctors to attend to me. . . .

[One] doctor said, "You have to stop practicing one of your professions. If you continue at this rate, with the hats and the music, you won't do anything, neither the one nor the other. There is a danger that very easily you could drive yourself to complete exhaustion. Continue only with the music, or continue only with the hats." Of course I had to obey him. I said, "Very well. If I try to force it—the attention to the hats, and to the music, as well—I'll be treating myself very badly." I had to pay attention to the doctor.

And so I felt myself obliged to leave the profession of hatmaking.

[Don César continues, discussing how his harp career continued to develop, to a substantial degree through his performances on radio—in Ambato, Guayaquil, Quito— as well as on television. He, too, was occasionally taken to play on horseback, in areas around Illampu, Don César himself occasionally carrying the harp on his shoulder. More typically, now, a car is sent for him and then returns him to his home—or, for performances at distant locations, he is sent the travel fare.]

ELSEWHERE IN ECUADOR

We began with the comment that Latin America was a region of many regions, and we explored three of these. We went on to examine quite closely one region of Ecuador—northern highland Cotacachi, its Quichua culture, its *sanjuán,* and its *wawa velorio* music ritual. We met a harpist of the central highlands, Don César Muquinche, and became acquainted with his music and his career. Let us conclude with a look at two other cultures and regions of Ecuador: the lowland Quichua of the Napo region of the eastern Ecuadorian jungle, and African-Ecuadorians of the Chota River valley, who live approximately two hours north of the Quichua of Cotacachi.

Recorded selection 67 is a curing song of a Quichua-speaking shaman of the jungle lowlands of eastern Ecuador. Among South American Indians in general, song is intimately connected to shamanism. The shaman is believed to be capable of communicating with spirits, in ecstatic "flights" entered into to cure patients but occasionally to cause illness, as well (Olsen 1980:368). The principal means for reaching this ecstatic state is through song, though certain cultures—including the Quichua-speaking peoples of the Napo River region—also use hallucinogens to achieve the trance state believed essential to effect a cure. Many Native American shamans of Ecuador, Peru, and Venezuela are male, but the *machi*—the shaman of the Mapuche people of Chile—is female.

The history of shamans reaches back thousands of years. The word *shaman* comes from the Tungus language of Central Asia and Siberia; its root, *sam-,* has the notions of dance/leap, on the one hand, trouble/agitation, on the other (Rouget 1985:126). Chanting highly rhythmic music, accompanying himself or herself on a rattle, drum, or other beaten or shaken instrument (here a leaf bundle), the shaman travels back and forth between this world and a supernatural realm of souls and spirits. In this way, the shaman acquires the power needed to cure.

Jungle Quichua believe that the illness the shaman is requested to cure is created by "spirit projectiles" sent by another shaman. The curing shaman "sees" these darts, obtains the power to remove them from the patient, and sends them back to the shaman who induced the illness. In the recording, made in 1976, a sick woman was brought to the shaman's home. The Napo shaman has already entered the world of the spirits when he begins his chant. Now he is able to "travel" between the spirit world and the world of his patient.

In this song, the shaman sings of a male jungle spirit, who then arrives. The shaman becomes this spirit and prepares to summon more spirits to him. Next, he experiences the sensation of soaring about; with this vision, he must fend off danger from multiple flying darts and lances. He chants that he is being protected by the shield of Sungui, master spirit of the water domain. Indeed, he is chanting

Ex. 9–14. Transcription of part of curing song of Napo lowland Quichua shaman.

(CONTINUES)

while seated on a special stool, carved in the image of a water turtle to represent the seat of power of Sungui. Ultimately, the shaman acknowledges several other arriving spirits, in addition to Sungui—all of which provide him, he says, with power to cure his patient. The Napo shaman believes that his chants come from the spirits he seeks to contact and that he is the vehicle by which the spirits may communicate with the world of humans (Whitten et al. 1979:2–6). For a detailed account of lowland Ecuadorian Quichua shamanic curing sessions, see Whitten 1976:154–59.

Example 9–14 shows one rendition in Western notation of part of the Napo shaman's song. Notice first that the chanting is strongly rhythmic, dictated by the regular grouping of two eighth notes in the leaf-bundle rattle. Second, one pitch, G, is central, for the shaman always ends his musical phrases on this pitch. Selecting one, or perhaps two, pitches as an axis is characteristic of shamanic chanting in many Native American cultures of South America, among them the Napo Quichua, the nearby Shuar, and the Mapuche of Chile. Third, notice the pulsations of the shaman's voice. These are characteristic of this Native South American's singing, as they were for certain types of singing among Native North Americans, for example, the Iroquois and the Sioux (see chapter 2). Fourth, the chant also has segments made up of three notes (D–E–G), and of four notes (G–A–B–high D); considered as a whole it has five different notes (D–E–G–A–B, with the upper D replicating the lower D at the octave).

The music of a neighboring group, the Shuar, frequently uses only three different pitches (tritonic); and we know that the *sanjuanes* of highland Cotacachi Quichua are prevailingly five-pitched, or pentatonic. It is interesting that these lowland Quichua—who speak the same language (different dialect) as the highlanders but who share the jungle environment and shamanic curing belief system with the Shuar—use prominent elements of both musical systems.

Finally, although the recording does not provide a literal translation of the words of the shaman's song, its notes inform us that the shaman is relaying a tremendous amount of information in his chant. We alluded above to this wide range of "journey" experience. This probably accounts for the fact that this and other lowland Quichua and Shuar shamanic chants have one musical note to one syllable of text—a "syllabic" style of singing words. This is an efficient means by which to convey in music a great deal of information—either experience or belief. In the tradition of the Western Roman Catholic Church, for example, the Credo section of the Mass ("I believe in one God. . . . And in one Lord, Jesus Christ. . . . And I believe in the Holy Ghost . . .") also conveys an enormously lengthy text and is also syllabic.

The music of the shaman of lowland Ecuador—and of Native American shamans throughout the length and breadth of South and North America—is incantation: it is a magical music that aims for a period of time to transform the world, to modify the course of events toward a particular desired end (Rouget 1985:131).

AFRICAN-ECUADORIAN MUSIC OF THE CHOTA RIVER VALLEY

On October 27, 1979, I was fortunate to meet Germán Congo, the excellent lead guitarist of the ensemble Conjunto Rondador (the *rondador* is a single-rank panpipe of Ecuador) at one of their performances in Ibarra, the capital of Imbabura

Province. Germán invited me to visit him and his musician-brothers in the Chota Valley. Some months later, on March 1, 1980, my friend Don Valerio, my wife, Janis, and I journeyed to Chota. This was the first of several visits to Chota and Ibarra, in 1980 and again in 1990, my research focusing on the musical artistry of the Congo brothers, their colleague Milton Tadeo, and fellow Chota musicians (Schechter 1994a).

When we think of Latin American regions that have large populations of African-Americans, Ecuador does not usually come to mind. Yet as much as 25 percent of the country's population is African-Ecuadorian. They are heavily concentrated in coastal Esmeraldas Province, which neighbors Imbabura Province. The first Africans arrived in Ecuador in the sixteenth century, after which Jesuit missionaries brought in large numbers of African slaves to work on plantations both on the coast and in the central highlands: indigenous labor was hard to find in some areas and unwilling to serve as slaves in others. The relatively small pocket of approximately fifteen thousand African-Ecuadorians in the Chota Valley, comprising ten to fifteen small villages, has an uncertain origin. The most widely accepted view is that the African-Ecuadorians of the Chota Valley are descended from slaves held by the Jesuits on their plantations in the highlands (Lipski 1987:157–58).

The best-known musicians today in the Chota Valley are the guitarist-composer-singers Germán, Fabián, and Eleuterio Congo and their colleague, Milton Tadeo. Fifteen years ago they played mostly around their home village of Carpuela; today they are regional celebrities with regular weekend performances locally, on the coast, and in nearby Colombia. As of October 1990 they had recorded six long-playing records within seven years. The Congo brothers are the third generation of composer-performers in their family.

In recorded selection 68 Fabián and Eleuterio Congo perform "Vamos pa' Manabí" ("Let's go to Manabí" [a coastal province next to Esmeraldas]). Both men play guitar; the voice is Fabián's (ill. 9–12). The text is reproduced in figure 9–12.

Notice first that, in contrast to the straight tone of the Quichua singers two hours down the road, Fabián's tone has substantial vibrato. Chapter 4 contains a good deal about the character and importance of improvisation in African-American music. In this African-Ecuadorian song you can hear a distinctive freedom of expression in melody and rhythm—especially in the instrumental parts. Contributing to the feeling of rhythmic freedom is the fact that Fabián regularly syncopates his rhythm—that is, he seems to sing "between" the beats of the guitars' pulse instead of with those strong beats. The guitars, too, play syncopated rhythm, especially in the "instruments alone" sections. After listening a few more times, try singing along with Fabián; the text is not long or complicated. See if you can begin to feel the subtle rhythm of the syncopated song; the more you practice, the closer you will get to this relaxed feeling and the more you will enjoy singing "Manabí."

We have been discussing the African-American character of "Manabí." One Ecuadorian ethnomusicologist has expanded this idea, referring to the *bomba*

Ill. 9–12. **Fabián Congo, guitarist-singer-composer. Ibarra, Ecuador, August 1990.**

(the genre of which "Manabí" is an example) of Chota as an "*Indo*-Hispano-Afro-Ecuadorian" hybrid music (Coba Andrade 1980:185). Where, then, is the "Indo," the Native American character? Recall from our discussion of nearby Cotacachi *sanjuán* that the accompaniment is often in the minor paired with the relative major key. In Fabián's and Eleuterio's "Manabí," two chords prevail: F major and its relative minor, D minor. We are reminded of *sanjuán* not only by this key relationship but also by the minor-key arpeggiations of the guitar, as at the beginning of the song. Recall that this type of introductory arpeggiation is also characteristic of *sanjuán* when played on the Imbabura harp. The T motive of Efraín's "Cascarón" is an example of this.

Finally, the word *wambrita* occurs in the text of "Manabí." This word is Quichua, not Spanish. Depending on the region of the Ecuadorian highlands and

Para no sufrir hagamos así (repeated)	So as not to suffer, let's do this:
Vámonos de aquí para Manabí (rptd 3 ×)	Let's go from here to Manabí.
(Instruments alone)	
Por donde yo estoy, muy lejos de tí (rptd)	Where I am, very far from you,
Siento el corazón, wambrita, por tí (rptd 3 ×)	I feel you in my heart, dear young woman.
(Instruments alone)	
Cuando yo estoy muy lejos de tí (rptd)	When I am very far from you
Siento el corazón, wambrita, por tí (rptd 3 ×)	I feel you in my heart, dear young woman.

(This text has been published; see Coba Andrade, 1980:209.)

Fig. 9–12.   Lyrics for Chota Valley *bomba* "Vamos pa' Manabí."

on its context in a sentence, *wambra* (and its affectionate diminutive, *wambrita*) may mean either "young man" or "young woman." In "Rusa María" it meant "young man"; in "Manabí" it means "young woman."

"Vamos pa' Manabí" is a rich musical expression of a border region: African-Ecuadorians, close to a major Quichua cultural zone, within a Spanish-speaking nation. It is not surprising to discover in this piece musical and textual characteristics associated with all three of these cultures. In this case, though, probably the sum of the parts does not create the whole: This *bomba* from Chota is unique not merely because of its several individual features but also because of the distinctive artistry of its performers, Fabián and Eleuterio—a quality that cannot be captured on paper.

DESPEDIDA, OR FAREWELL

You have heard examples from many different music-cultures of Latin America: the unmistakable razor's edge tempo and tension of Venezuelan *joropo,* the eloquent metaphors and profound sentiment of Víctor Jara, and the depth and richness of hocketing altiplano panpipes in ensemble. You have learned of the lifeways, harp, and songs of the Quichua of highland Ecuador, and you have witnessed the poignant Quichua ritual of *wawa velorio*—dancing at the wake of a child. Where Jara pointed to the plaiter of Lonquén and to Angelita Huenumán, we have singled out for recognition a number of individual "artists of quality," in Muquinche's phrase—artists who are probably among the forgotten persons of Latin America, including the harpists Efraín, Sergio, and Don César himself, the Napo lowland Quichua shaman, and Eleuterio and Fabián Congo. In their own worlds of music, these artists are highly esteemed, for they practice music-cultural traditions—*sanjuán* and *bomba,* child's wake and shamanic healing, harp with *golpeador*—that their cultures prize highly and have preserved for hundreds of years.

Our sense of community is bound up with our identification with our own musics and music-rituals. In one realm or another, we all obey the dictate of *cada llajta:* each of us, ultimately, is musically, linguistically, and certainly in many other respects, of *a* place.

REFERENCES CITED

Abbad y Lasierra, Fray Iñigo
    1788   *Historia geográfica, civil y política de la Isla de S. Juan Bautista de Puerto Rico.*
           Madrid: Imprenta de Don Antonio de Espinosa.

Bastien, Joseph W.
    1978   *Mountain of the Condor: Metaphor and Ritual in an Andean Ayllu.* St. Paul,
           Minn.: West Publishing Co. American Ethnological Society Monograph 64.

Boas, Franz
    [1929] 1940   "Metaphorical Expression in the Language of the Kwakiutl Indians." In
           Race, Language, and Culture. New York: Free Press.

Boilès, Charles L.
    1978   *Man, Magic, and Musical Occasions.* Columbus, Ohio: Collegiate.

Carrasco Pirard, Eduardo
    1982   "The Nueva Canción in Latin America." *International Social Science Journal*
           94 (34:4):599–623.

Céspedes, Gilka Wara
    1993   "*Huayño, Saya,* and *Chuntunqui:* Bolivian Identity in the Music of 'Los
           Kjarkas.'" *Revista de Música Latinoamericana/Latin American Music Review*
           14(1):52–101.

Coba Andrade, Carlos Alberto
    1980   *Literatura Popular Afroecuatoriana.* Otavalo, Ecuador: Instituto Otavaleño de
           Antropología.

Conjunto Ilumán
    n.d.   *Elenita Conde.* Commercial cassette by this Ecuadorian Quichua ensemble. Pre-
           1990. Ensemble directed by Segundo Galo Maigua of Ilumán, Ecuador.

Conjunto Indígena "Peguche" [Ecuador]
    1977   *Folklore de mi tierra.* Orion 330-0063. Industria Fonográfica Ecuatoriana
           (IFESA). Guayaquil, Ecuador. Dist. by Emporio Musical S.A., Guayaquil and
           Psje. Amador, Quito.

Davillier, Le Baron [Jean] Ch[arles]
    1874   *L'Espagne.* Illus. G. Doré. Paris: Hachette.

Dicks, Ted, ed.
    1976   *Victor Jara: His Life and Songs.* London: Elm Tree Books.

Feld, Steven
    1981   "'Flow Like a Waterfall': The Metaphors of Kaluli Musical Theory." *1981 Year-*
           book for Traditional Music 13:22–47.

Fernandez, James W.
    1978   "Syllogisms of Association: Some Modern Extensions of Asturian Deepsong."
           In *Folklore in the Modern World,* ed. Richard M. Dorson, 183–206. Paris:
           Mouton.

González, Juan Pablo
    1989   "'Inti-Illimani' and the Artistic Treatment of Folklore." *Revista de Música Lati-noamericana/Latin American Music Review* 10(2):267–286.

Harrison, Regina
    1989   *Signs, Songs, and Memory in the Andes: Translating Quechua Language and Culture.* Austin: Univ. of Texas Press.

Jara, Joan
    1984   *An Unfinished Song: The Life of Víctor Jara.* New York: Ticknor and Fields.

Jatari!! 4
    1978   [*Fadisa.* Fábrica de Discos S.A.] Quito, Ecuador. 710129.

Levy, Lisa, producer and narrator
    1988   "Violeta Madre." 4-part series on the life and work of Violeta Parra. 2 cassettes. KAOS-FM, Evergreen State College, Olympia, Washington.

Lipski, John M.
    1987   "The Chota Valley: Afro-Hispanic Language in Highland Ecuador." *Latin American Research Review* 22(1):155–70.

Malinowski, Bronislaw.
    [1925] 1954   "Magic, Science, and Religion." In *Magic, Science, and Religion and Other Essays.* Garden City, N.Y.: Anchor Books.

Moreno Andrade, Segundo Luis
    1930   "La música en el Ecuador." In *El Ecuador en cien años de independencia, 1830–1930,* vol. 2, ed. J. Gonzalo Orellana. Quito: Imprenta de la Escuela de Artes y Oficios.

Morris, Nancy
    1986   "*Canto porque es necesario cantar:* The New Song Movement in Chile, 1973–1983." *Latin American Research Review* 21(2):117–36.

Muquinche, César
    1980   Interview. July 12. Illampu, Tungurahua Province, Ecuador.

Nettl, Bruno
    1983   *The Study of Ethnomusicology: Twenty-nine Issues and Concepts.* Urbana: Univ. of Illinois Press.

Nketia, J. H. Kwabena
    1974   *The Music of Africa.* New York: Norton.

Ñanda mañachi 1 (Préstame el camino).
    1977   Prod. Jean Chopin Thermes. Llaquiclla. IFESA. Industria Fonográfica Ecuatoriana S.A. Guayaquil, Ecuador. 339-0501. Recorded in Ibarra, Ecuador.

Ñanda mañachi 2 (Préstame el camino)
    1979   Prod. Jean Chopin Thermes. Llaquiclla. IFESA. Industria Fonográfica Ecuatoriana S.A. Guayaquil, Ecuador. 339-0502. Recorded in Ibarra, Ecuador.

Ñanda mañachi/Boliviamanta: Préstame el camino desde Bolivia. Música quichua del equinoccio Andino. Churay, Churay!
    1983   Llaquiclla. Fediscos. Guayaquil, Ecuador. Onix L.P. 59003.

Obando, Segundo
    1988   *Tradiciones de Imbabura,* 3rd ed. Quito: Abya-Yala.

Olsen, Dale A.
  1980 "Symbol and Function in South American Indian Music." In *Musics of Many Cultures: An Introduction,* ed. E. May, 363–85. Berkeley: Univ. of California Press.

Ross, Joe
  1994 "Music of the Andes." *Acoustic Musician Magazine,* June, 18–27.

Rouget, Gilbert
  1985 *Music and Trance: A Theory of the Relations between Music and Possession.* Trans. Brunhilde Biebuyck. Chicago: Univ. of Chicago Press.

Salvo, Calogero, writer/director
  1982 "Juan Félix Sánchez." Filmed in El Potrero, Mérida, Venezuela, November 1981 and February 1982.

Schechter, John M.
  1979 "The Inca *Cantar Histórico:* A Lexico-Historical Elaboration on Two Cultural Themes." *Ethnomusicology* 23(2):191–204.

———.
  1982 "Music in a Northern Ecuadorian Highland Locus: Diatonic Harp, Genres, Harpists, and their Ritual Junction in the Quechua Child's Wake." 3 vols. Ph.D. diss., Univ. of Texas.

———.
  1983 "*Corona y baile:* Music in the Child's Wake of Ecuador and Hispanic South America, Past and Present." *Revista de Música Latinoamericana/Latin American Music Review* 4(1):1–80.

———.
  1987 "Quechua *Sanjuán* in Northern Highland Ecuador: Harp Music as Structural Metaphor on *Purina*." *Journal of Latin American Lore* 13(1):27–46.

———.
  1992 *The Indispensable Harp: Historical Development, Modern Roles, Configurations, and Performance Practices in Ecuador and Latin America.* Kent, Ohio: Kent State Univ. Press.

———.
  1994a "Los Hermanos Congo y Milton Tadeo Ten Years Later: Evolution of an African-Ecuadorian Tradition of the Valle del Chota, Highland Ecuador." In *Music and Black Ethnicity: The Caribbean and South America,* ed. Gerard H. Béhague, 285–305, Coral Gables, Fla.: University of Miami North-South Center/Transaction.

———.
  1994b "Divergent Perspectives on the *velorio del angelito:* Ritual Imagery, Artistic Condemnation, and Ethnographic Value." *Journal of Ritual Studies* 8(2):43–84.

Smith, Sandra
  1984 "Panpipes for Power, Panpipes for Play: The Social Management of Cultural Expression in Kuna Society." Ph.D. diss., Univ. of California, Berkeley.

Whitten, Norman E., Jr.
  1976 *Sacha Runa: Ethnicity and Adaptation of Ecuadorian Jungle Quichua.* Urbana: Univ. of Illinois Press.

Whitten, Norman E., Jr., et al.
    1979   "Soul Vine Shaman." Urbana, IL.: Sacha Runa Research Foundation Occa-
            sional Paper no. 5.

ADDITIONAL READING

Aretz, Isabel
    1967   *Instrumentos musicales de Venezuela.* Cumaná, Venezuela: Editorial Universi-
            taria de Oriente.
——, relater
    1977   *América Latina en su música.* México, D.F.: Siglo Veintiuno Editores.

Aretz, Isabel, Gérard Béhague, and Robert Stevenson
    1980   "Latin America." In *The New Grove Dictionary of Music and Musicians,* ed. S.
            Sadie, 10:505–34.

Baumann, Max Peter
    1985   "The Kantu Ensemble of the Kallawaya at Charazani (Bolivia)." *Yearbook for
            Traditional Music* 17:146–66.

Béhague, Gérard
    1973   "Latin American Folk Music." In *Folk and Traditional Music of the Western
            Continents,* ed. Bruno Nettl, 179–206. Englewood Cliffs, N.J.: Prentice-Hall.
——.
    1979   *Music in Latin America: An Introduction.* Englewood Cliffs, N.J.: Prentice-Hall.
——.
    1984   "Patterns of *Candomblé* Music Performance: An Afro-Brazilian Religious
            Setting." In *Performance Practice: Ethnomusicological Perspectives,* ed. G.
            Béhague, 222–54. Westport, Conn.: Greenwood Press.
——, ed.
    1994   *Music and Black Ethnicity: The Caribbean and South America.* Coral Gables,
            Fla.: University of Miami North-South Center/Transaction.

Carvalho-Neto, Paulo de
    1964   *Diccionario del folklore ecuatoriano.* Tratado del Folklore Ecuatoriano
            1. Quito: Editorial Casa de la Cultura Ecuatoriana.

Cavour, Ernesto
    ca.1974   *La zampoña, aerófono boliviano: Método audiovisual.* La Paz(?): Ediciones
            Tatu.

Fairley, Jan
    1985   "Annotated Bibliography of Latin-American Popular Music with Particular
            Reference to Chile and to Nueva Canción." In *Popular Music, vol. 5, Continu-
            ity and Change,* 305–56. Cambridge: Cambridge Univ. Press.

Fuks, Victor
    1988   "Music, Dance, and Beer in an Amazonian Indian Community." *Revista de
            Música Latinoamericana/Latin American Music Review* 9(2):151–86.

Grebe, María Ester
    1973   "El Kultrun mapuche: un microcosmo simbólico." *Revista Musical Chilena*
            27(123–24):3–42.

List, George
  1983 *Music and Poetry in a Colombian Village: A Tri-Cultural Heritage.* Blooming-
        ton: Indiana Univ. Press.

Olsen, Dale A.
  1974 "The Function of Naming in the Curing Songs of the Warao Indians of
        Venezuela." *Anuario/Yearbook for Inter-American Musical Research* 10:88–122.

———.
  1975 "Music-Induced Altered States of Consciousness among Warao Shamans."
        Journal of Latin American Lore 1:19–33.

———.
  1980 "Folk Music of South America: A Musical Mosaic." In *Musics of Many Cultures:
        An Introduction,* ed. E. May, 386–425. Berkeley: Univ. of California Press.

———.
  1986–87 "The Peruvian Folk Harp Tradition: Determinants of Style." *Folk Harp
        Journal* 53:48–54; 54:41–58; 55:55–59; 56:57–60.

Parra, Isabel
  1985 *El libro mayor de Violeta Parra.* Madrid: Ediciones Michay.

Parra, Violeta
  1970 *Décimas: Autobiografía en versos chilenos.* Santiago de Chile: Ediciones Nueva
        Universidad, Universidad Católica de Chile, Editorial Pomaire.

Ramón y Rivera, Luis Felipe
  1969 *La música folklórica de Venezuela.* Caracas: Monte Avila Editores.

Robertson, Carol E.
  1979 "'Pulling the Ancestors': Performance Practice and Praxis in Mapuche Order-
        ing." *Ethnomusicology* 23(3):395–416.

Roel Pineda, Josafat
  1959 "El Wayno del Cuzco." *Folklore Americano* 6–7:129–246.

Rush, Alfred C.
  1941 *Death and Burial in Christian Antiquity.* Catholic University of America Stud-
        ies in Christian Antiquity, no. 1, ed. J. Quasten. Washington, D.C.: Catholic
        University of America Press.

Seeger, Anthony
  1979 "What Can We Learn When They Sing? Vocal Genres of the Suya Indians of
        Central Brazil." *Ethnomusicology* 23(3):373–94.

———.
  1987 *Why Suyá Sing: A Musical Anthropology of an Amazonian People.* Cambridge:
        Cambridge Univ. Press.

Slater, Peter Gregg
  1977 *Children in the New England Mind in Death and in Life.* Hamden, Conn.: Ar-
        chon Books/Shoe String Press.

Stevenson, Robert
  1968 *Music in Aztec and Inca Territory.* Berkeley: Univ. of California Press.

Turino, Thomas
  1983 "The Charango and the *Sirena:* Music, Magic, and the Power of Love." *Revista
        de Música Latinoamericana/Latin American Music Review* 4(1):81–119.

———.
1989 "The Coherence of Social Style and Musical Creation among the Aymara in Southern Peru." *Ethnomusicology* 33(1):1–30.

———.
1993 *Moving Away from Silence: Music of the Peruvian Altiplano and the Experience of Urban Migration.* Chicago: Univ. of Chicago Press.

Valencia Chacón, Américo
1981 "Los Chiriguanos de Huancané." *Boletín de Lima* 12–14:1–28.

ADDITIONAL LISTENING

Afro-Hispanic Music from Western Colombia and Ecuador
1967 Rec. and ed. Norman E. Whitten, Jr. Folkways FE 4376.

El cancionero noble de Colombia
1962 Rec. Joaquín Piñeros Corpas. Bogotá: Ministerio de Educación-Editorial Antares-Fontón. 3 discs, 36 pp. text.

Cantan Garzón y Collazos [Colombia]
n.d. (pre-1970) Industria Electro-Sonora, Medellín, Colombia. Sonolux LP 12-104/IES-1.

Clásicas de la canción paraguaya: Alfredo Rolando Ortiz, arpa
n.d. (pre-1980) Industrias Famoso, Quito, Ecuador. LDF-1015.

The Inca Harp: Laments and Dances of the Tawantinsuyu, the Inca Empire [Peru]
1982 Rec. Ronald Wright. Lyrichord LLST 7359.

Indian Music of Mexico
1952, 1962 Rec. Henrietta Yurchenko. Ethnic Folkways Library FE-4413. 4 pp. notes by Gordon F. Ekholm and Henrietta Yurchenko.

Mountain Music of Peru
1966 Rec. John Cohen. Folkways FE 4539.

Mushuc huaira huacamujun: Conjunto indígena "Peguche" [Ecuador]
1979 Industria Fonográfica Ecuatoriana S.A. (IFESA). Runa Causay. Guayaquil, Ecuador. 339-0651.

Music of the Jívaro of Ecuador
1972 Rec. and ed. Michael J. Harner. Ethnic Folkways Library FE 4386.

Música andina de Bolivia
1980 Rec. with com. by Max Peter Baumann. Lauro Records, LPLI/S-062. 36 pp. booklet.

Música folklórica de Venezuela
n.d. (post-1968) Rec. Isabel Aretz, Luis Felipe Ramón y Rivera, and Alvaro Fernaud. International Folk Music Council, Anthologie de la Musique Populaire. Ocora OCR 78.

Perou: Julio Benavente Diaz: "Le charango du Cuzco"
1985 Rec. Rafael Parejo et Regina Baldini. Ocora. Musiques traditionnelles vivantes. Sacem. 558 647.

Pre-Columbian Instruments: Aerophone [Mexico]
    1972   Prod. Lilian Mendelssohn, with Pablo Castellanos. Played by Jorge Daher, Ethnic Folkways Library FE 4177.

ADDITIONAL VIEWING

Ayala, Fernando and Héctor Olivera, dirs.
    1972   *Argentinísima I.* In Spanish, without subtitles. Featured performers: Atahualpa Yupanqui, Ariel Ramírez, Los Chalchaleros, Mercedes Sosa, Astor Piazzolla, others. MEDIA HOME ENTERTAINMENT, INC., 510 W. 6th St., Suite 1032, Los Angeles, CA 90014.

    ———.
    1976   *El Canto Cuenta su Historia.* In Spanish, without subtitles. Film/video. Featured performers: Cayetano Daglio, Ángel Villoldo, Francisco Canaro, Carlos Gardel, Rosita Quiroga, Ignacio Corsini, Ada Falcón, Agustín Magaldi and Pedro Noda, Marta de los Ríos, Margarita Palacios, Eduardo Falú, Los Cantores de Quilla Huasi, Jorge Oafrune, Amelita Baltar, Hermanos Abalos, others. CONDOR VIDEO (A Heron International Company), c/o Jason Films, 2825 Wilcrest, Suite 670, Houston, TX 77042. Aries Cinematográfica, Argentina.

Benson-Gyles, Anna, prod. [no director listed]
    1980   *The Incas.* ODYSSEY Series. Executive Producer: Michael Ambrosino; Narrator: Tony Kahn. For ODYSSEY: Producer: Marian White; Editor: David Berenson. Co-production of British Broadcasting Corporation (BBC) and Public Broadcasting Associates, Inc., Boston, MA. INCAS/ODYSSEY SERIES/Box 1000, Boston, MA 02118. PBS VIDEO, 1320 Braddock Pl., Alexandria, VA 22314.

Cohen, John, dir.
    1979   *Q'eros: The Shape of Survival.* 53 min. color. 16mm film/video. Berkeley: UNIVERSITY OF CALIFORNIA, EXTENSION CENTER FOR MEDIA & INDEPENDENT LEARNING, 2000 Center St., 4th floor, Berkeley, CA 94704.

    ———.
    1984   *Mountain Music of Peru.* 60 min. color. 16mm film/video. Berkeley: UNIVERSITY OF CALIFORNIA, EXTENSION CENTER FOR MEDIA & INDEPENDENT LEARNING, 2000 Center St., 4th floor, Berkeley, CA 94704.

Cross, Stephen, dir.
    1977   *Disappearing World: Umbanda: The Problem Solver.* In English, and, in Portuguese with English subtitles. Series Editor: Brian Moser; Anthropologist/Narrator: Peter Fry. PUBLIC MEDIA VIDEO, 5547 N. Ravenswood Ave., Chicago, IL 60640-1199; Granada Colour Production, Granada UK.

Dibb, Michael, dir.
    1985   *What's Cuba Playing At?* (*¿Qué se toca en Cuba?*) 72 min. In Spanish, with subtitles. BBC TV PRODUCTION, in association with Cuban Television. CENTER FOR CUBAN STUDIES, 124 W. 23rd St., New York, NY 10011.

Hernández, Amalia, dir.
1989   *Folklórico: Ballet Folklórico de México.* In Spanish, without subtitles. Featured performers: Ballet Folklórico de México. MADERA CINEVIDEO, 525 E. Yosemite Ave., Madera, CA 93638.

Rivera, Pedro A. and Susan Zeig, dirs.
1989   *Plena is Work, Plena is Song.* 16mm film/video. CINEMA GUILD, INC.: 1697 Broadway, Suite 506, New York, NY 10019-5904.

Schaeffer, Nancy
1995   "Directory of Latin American Films and Videos: Music, Dance, Mask, and Ritual." *Revista de Música Latinoamericana/Latin American Music Review* 16(2):221–41.

CHAPTER 10

Discovering
and Documenting
a World of Music

DAVID B. RECK, MARK SLOBIN,
AND JEFF TODD TITON

MUSIC IN OUR OWN BACKYARDS

All of us are familiar with the tale (or movie) of Dorothy and her adventures with
the Tin Man, the Lion, and the Scarecrow in the fantastic land of Oz. But most of
us have forgotten Dorothy's startling discovery once she got back to Kansas: home
was where her heart was, a fascinating world of people, family, neighbors, and
friends, and of things that before her adventures she had overlooked. This is a familiar theme in literature the world over. The hero or heroine (ourselves) travels
to faraway places, sees and does fabulous things, meets incredible people, or
searches for marvelous treasures. But invariably the rainbow leads home; the pot
of gold is buried in one's own backyard; the princess is none other than the girl
next door.

In our explorations of the world's musics we—both students and scholars—are
fascinated by cultures and peoples greatly separated from us in geography or
time, in sound and style, in ways of making and doing music. In a sense, for every
one of us there is an Oz. But there is also a music-culture surrounding us, one
that we see and hear only partially because it is too close to us, because we take it
for granted, as fish do water. Our musical environment is held both in us (in our
perceptions and memories) and by other members of our community, only a fraction of whom we may know. It expands out from us (and contracts into us) in a series of concentric circles that may include family, ethnic groups, regional styles,
our hemisphere, and cultural roots (Western Europe, Africa, and so on). It is
available to us live or mechanically reproduced. It comes to us out of history (the
classical masterworks, old-time fiddle tunes, or bebop jazz) or it is a product of

the here and now (the latest hit on the pop music charts or the avant-garde "new thing"). Our surrounding musical universe seems to us multifaceted and immensely complicated.

Gathering reliable information on contemporary music is what this chapter is all about. We want to encourage you to seek out a nearby musical world, to observe it in person, to talk with the people involved in it, to document it with tape recordings and photographs, and to present the information in a project that will make a contribution to the body of knowledge about contemporary musical activities. If this research project is part of a course, you should check with your instructor for specific directives. What follows is a general guide, based on the experience we and our students have had with similar projects at our colleges and universities.

Selecting a subject for your research is of course the first step in the project. Songs and instrumental music in North American culture serve a great many purposes and occur in a staggeringly wide variety of contexts, from singing in the shower to the Metropolitan Opera, from the high school marching band to the rock festival, and from the lullaby to the television commercial jingle. Some of it is trivial, some of it is profound. It is all meaningful. To help you select a subject, let us impose order on our surrounding music-culture by means of a few organizing principles: family, generation, avocation, religion, ethnicity, regionalism, nationalism, and commercialization. As you read through the following brief survey you may find some subjects that interest you. Here we focus on North American examples, but if you are using this book elsewhere you should apply these (and perhaps other) organizing principles to examples you think of from your own music-culture. Later we will give you some specific suggestions.

FAMILY

As is true of all cultures, North Americans first hear music in the context of family life (ill. 10–1). Much of that music comes from the records on the family stereo, radio, or television, and this "canned" music is especially important in developing children's musical taste. People often say they were very strongly influenced by the kind of music they heard before they were old enough to have their own records or choose the station on the family radio. Yet despite the parents' intentions, youngsters often rebel against parents' taste in music and choose to listen to what is favored by people their own age. There is usually some live music in the family as well. Many mothers and grandmothers sing lullabies, for example. These can be important, since in North America, as elsewhere, lullabies not only lull but promise, praise, and teach cultural values. Sometimes lullabies are the only songs in a foreign language that American children with strong ethnic backgrounds hear, since people (particularly grandparents) often fall back on old, familiar languages for intimate songs.

Another important family context is the automobile, where families learn songs and sing together on weekends and vacations. This is not as surprising as it appears, for the family car has become one of the basic centers of family experience, and it is one of the important places where the family gathers for an extended

Walker Evans. Courtesy of the Library of Congress

Ill. 10–1.   A sharecropper family sings hymns in front of their home, Hale County, Alabama, 1936.

(some might say forced) period of time without outside distractions. The family used to have to choose between making their own music in the car or being force-fed by the radio, but the recent invention of automobile cassette recorders and compact disc players allows a family to have more control over what they hear when they drive.

In short, most Americans have an early layer of songs learned in childhood in a family setting. Often they are just songs for entertaining children, with no deep cultural message to impart. What they do teach are the musical tastes and orientation of the particular social group, whether rural Quebecois, California suburban, Illinois heartland, Appalachian mountain, or New York inner-city. Children then work in harmony with (or against) this basic musical background as a part of growing up and finding their individual identity.

GENERATION

Much American music-making is organized along generational lines. Schools, church classes, scouting groups, sidewalk children's games, college singing groups, and many other musical situations include people of about the same age. Songs learned by these groups may stay with them as they grow older: imagine the twentieth or fiftieth college class reunion, where the aging ex-students keep singing the songs of their generation.

Yet the amount of generational mixing in American musical life has grown under the influence of television and recordings. In pop music much of the music thought to belong only to the young in the 1960s, such as the music of the Beatles, appealed to older generations as well. And today's youngsters like their parents' music better than their parents liked theirs. Other styles, such as country fiddling, which not long ago attracted mainly older musicians, have been picked up by young people, and now at a fiddle contest like the one held in Hartford, Connecticut, every year, the age spread of performers runs from eight to eighty. In ethnic musics too, young people have taken to learning traditional songs from their grandmothers instead of laughing at the old folks' songs as they might have one or two generations ago.

Generational blurring is part of the process of musical homogenization we will see at work in still other areas of our music-culture. There is not so much difference between the sexes musically as there used to be. Just as women now take up sports like race-car driving and become professional jockeys, so more females play instruments, such as the drums and saxophone, that used to be largely limited to males. A whole genre that used to be male—barbershop quartet singing—now has a parallel female style, exhibited by groups such as the Sweet Adelines. A women's bluegrass group call themselves the All Girl Boys. We will see the effect of regional and ethnic blurring below.

AVOCATION

Music as hobby is an important part of American life. A barbershop quartet program lists the wives of the singers as "Thursday Night Widows"—perhaps one reason for the formation of women's quartets. Many Americans feel the need for a strong group hobby, and of course some of this impulse is channeled into musical organizations. A local American Legion Post, or an ethnic group like the Polish Falcons, may have a band; here the music-making is part of the feeling of group solidarity. Being able to field a band for the local parade or festival brings the group visibility and pride. Individual members may find performing in a fife-and-drum corps or the Governor's Footguard Band (to use Connecticut examples) a satisfying way to spend leisure time. Black youngsters in high school and college form extracurricular, informal singing groups whose repertoire includes rhythm and blues or gospel music hits; sometimes these groups become semiprofessional or even fully professional, as they get older. Most high schools and colleges can boast a few rock bands and possibly even a jazz group, as well as cocktail pianists, folk-singing guitarists, and chamber music ensembles.

RELIGION

Religion is one of the better-documented areas of North American musical life. We know about music's role in many religious movements, ranging from the eighteenth-century Moravians through the revival movements of the nineteenth century and the founding of new sects such as the Mormons. Much has been written about the appropriateness of certain types of music-making in religious settings, such as organ playing in the Jewish synagogue or the introduction of folk and jazz elements to church services. The black spiritual is the object of scholarly study, while the tent revival preacher, the snake handler, and the ecstatic evangelistic churches receive attention from journalists (see ill. 10–2). But the musical activities of contemporary, mainline middle-class churches, synagogues, and mosques are little studied. Of interest also are the songs of new, unofficial religious movements, such as small meditation groups based on Christian or oriental religious thinking. These groups need to encourage solidarity and teach their

Ill. 10–2.   Music almost always accompanies formal rites of passage, such as this old-time river baptism. Slabtown, Virginia, 1930s.

message, but they have no traditional music. Often they change the words of well-known songs as a way of starting, just as Martin Luther changed the words of German drinking songs 450 years ago to create a body of sacred songs we know as Protestant chorales. The new unofficial groups may also work hard on developing an "inner music" of their members, through which the individual believer reaches the desired state of tranquility.

ETHNICITY

Ethnicity is the oldest consideration in the study of the American music-culture in the sense that America is usually regarded as a nation of immigrants. It is also one of the newest considerations because of the current interest in the public expression of ethnic identity, a trend that gathered force beginning in the 1960s.

Throughout American musical history, ethnicity has played a major role. Whether in the dialect and songs of the French Acadians in New Brunswick, the heroic *corrido* ballads sung along the Rio Grande by Mexican-Americans, the retelling of the story of hard-hearted Barbara Allen by British-American ballad singers, or the singing of a Yiddish lullaby in a Brooklyn tenement, Americans have maintained distinctive ethnic boundaries through music. Music's function as a sign of group solidarity and common ancestry is nowhere clearer than in the variety of songs, dances, and instrumental tunes that characterize the American ethnic mosaic. Students in the United States whose parents or grandparents stopped public singing of Old World songs on their way to becoming "one-hundred-percent Americans" now become enthusiastic about joining ethnic music groups or studying their group's heritage. Other parents and grandparents, of course, never stopped singing their native songs. American ethnic music has always involved transcontinental exchange. On the one hand, Greek-Americans are influenced by new developments in popular music in Athens, while on the other, Polish-American records find great favor among farmers in far-off mountain villages in Poland. American jazz and country music have spread around the world, from Holland to Russia and Japan. A very complicated interplay goes on between black music in the United States and the Caribbean (ill. 10–3). A single song may show layer upon layer of musical travel. Reggae developed in Jamaica, where it represented a blend of Afro-Caribbean and black U.S. soul music. This already complicated style came to America from England, where pop groups repackaged it and exported it, and the cycle continues: reggae is now popular in some parts of Africa.

Jeff Todd Titon

Ill. 10–3.   One of Boston's Caribbean steel-drum bands performs at a women's prison. 1979.

Much of the older ethnic music of North America has changed in ways described in chapter 5. For example, some twentieth-century fiddle contests encourage showing off in front of the crowd. Some New England contests include young fiddle players who have classical training, or who specialize in the "trick and fancy" category of virtuoso pieces instead of the standard old-time jigs, reels, and waltzes of the Northeast. Official events such as open contests push style in directions that may be unfamiliar to older country performers, for whom fiddling meant a way to pass the time or to earn a night's pay by playing for eight solid hours of dancing.

On the other hand, folk festivals in the U.S. such as the Smithsonian Institution's Festival of American Folklife and the National Folk Festival seek out traditional singers, musicians, and craftspeople, and to present them insofar as possible in traditional contexts. Not that they are necessarily against change and progress, however; at the Bicentennial Festival of American Folklife, for example, one of the staging areas was called Old Ways in the New World. Here traditional performers from various Old World countries were flown to America and presented alongside their New World ethnic counterparts: Polish-American musicians alternated with folk singing and dancing groups from Poland; Louisiana Cajuns and French-Canadian fiddlers alternated with their counterparts from France; and all learned from the musical interchange.

REGIONALISM

Regionalism in North America is thought to have declined with the spread of the interstate highway system, chains of fast-food restaurants, and the spread of television, all of which began in the 1950s. But just as the ethnic groups never really dissolved into the so-called melting pot, so regional homogenization never really took place in American life. Regionalism crops up in the names of styles, like the Chicago blues sound, the Detroit "Motown" soul sound, or even within ethnic styles, like the distinction between a Chicago and East Coast polka type. The crisp bowing, downbeat accents, and up-tempo performance of a fiddle tune in the Northeast bears little resemblance to the same tune's performance in the Southwest, with its smooth bowing and more relaxed beat. In country music today, the Nashville sound can be distinguished from the Texas sound, reflecting earlier differences between country and country-western styles. Likewise, the same hymn tune shows considerable variation even within the same denomination in different parts of the country. One Indiana Primitive Baptist was overheard to comment on the slow, highly decorated tunes of her Primitive Baptist neighbors to the Southeast: "They take ten minutes just to get through 'Amazing Grace'!" There are also local preferences for types of ensembles. The Governor's Footguard Band, formed in Connecticut before the American Revolution, is unlikely to have a counterpart in Kansas. Connecticut's fife-and-drum corps can be found in many good-sized Connecticut towns, whereas the Midwest is the heartland of the marching band.

Like ethnicity, regionalism is coming back into fashion. There are now so many local festivals that books of listings are published. In some locales, mock battles are fought again and again for tourist throngs, with appropriate live or recorded music. One very visible regional music performance is the singing of "My Old Kentucky Home" at the May running of the Kentucky Derby. In a recent year 150 thousand spectators joined in, and millions of television viewers were on hand to link the song and event to the region of its origin. The media scour America each year for feature stories; in the process they turn what were once regional events, like the annual celebration of a smelly and foul-tasting Appalachian vegetable called the ramp, into national news, thereby making regionalism a commercial product. However, musical boosterism is not always successful. In 1975 Los Angeles gave up looking for a city song to rival "I Left My Heart in San Francisco." The ten-year song search failed despite entries praising "sandy beaches free from leeches" and other unworkable solutions.

In summary, if only in terms of marketing advantage and a renewed desire for local color, regional diversity has not yet been replaced by a homogenized American music. The USA is still too large and diverse to turn all music into brand names or to have the entire population respond equally to all music, and the search for revival or for novelty continues.

NATIONALISM

A breakaway colony that declared its independence and fought a war to preserve it, the United States long ago began seeking ways to establish a national musical identity. We have already commented on its distinctive musical profile generated by ethnic and regional stylistic interactions. Popular national sentiment was also evoked by the frequent performance of patriotic songs, a tradition that has declined only in recent decades. Official music plays less of a part in American life now than when John Philip Sousa's band and its imitators played flag-waving tunes on the bandstand for Sunday promenaders, or when schoolchildren knew all the verses of the national anthem. When Gerald Ford was vice-president, he asked that the University of Michigan football fight song be played to greet him instead of a national ceremonial song—a sign of the decline of official music.

The change may also be seen by comparing the program for a large public concert in New York's Central Park in 1916 with one in 1976. For the earlier event, the composer Arthur Farwell produced a chorus of eight hundred and a full orchestra to accompany twenty-five thousand New Yorkers in classical music, people's hymns that Farwell wrote for the occasion ("March! March!" and "Joy! Brothers, Joy!"), well-known old-time favorites, such as "Old Black Joe," and patriotic songs. The event closed with the multitude singing "The Star-Spangled Banner." In the 1976 event, the city shared sponsorship with an FM rock station. Only young people's music was played; there was no public singing. The crowd mingled, listened, and some danced; others relaxed and smoked. Marijuana was sold openly.

Perhaps our most obvious repertoire of national music consists of Christmas songs such as "Jingle Bells," "Deck the Halls," "Rudolph the Red-Nosed Reindeer," and the like. During the holiday season it is almost impossible to escape them. The curmudgeon who shoos away carolers from his front yard is said to lack the Christmas spirit, and he soon gains a neighborhood reputation as a Scrooge.

COMMERCIAL MUSIC

Much of the music in our culture is supplied by paid professionals. It is remarkable that our complex culture continues to carry on the musical situations described earlier in non- or preindustrial societies. Though a genre like the funeral lament has largely dropped out of America, rituals like weddings and initiations (bar mitzvahs, debutante parties, senior proms) that mark a change of life still demand solemnization by music. A wedding may take place in a park with a Good Humor truck, balloons, and jeans instead of in a formal church setting, yet music remains indispensable even if it consists of pop tunes instead of an official wedding march. There are other carryovers from early ritual as well. Elegant yacht clubs tend to schedule dances during full-moon evenings, continuing a practice of certain ancient cultures.

A great deal of the commercial music Americans come into daily contact with may be described as "disembodied," by which we mean that the listener does not feel the physical presence of the performer and many times cannot even see the original musical situation (ill. 10–4). Some of this music can be partially controlled by the listener who selects recordings from his or her collection to fit a mood. Choices are made from an entirely private domain of recordings over which the person has complete control regarding the selection of the music and the length of the listening experience. Although it is possible to imagine the original musical situation—concert or recording studio—there is no possibility of interaction with the performers, and the sounding music is the same each time it is heard.

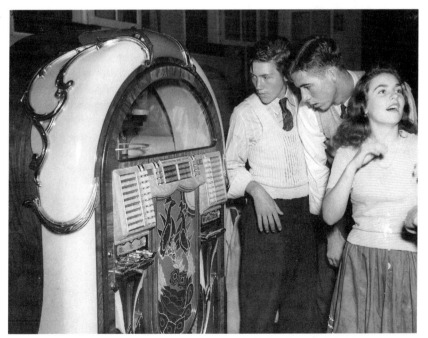

John Collier. Courtesy of the Library of Congress

Ill. 10–4.   Dancing to records on a juke-box, West Virginia, 1942.

At the opposite end of the spectrum of disembodied commercial music is public background music. There is no logical connection between event and music in a supermarket such as there is in one's own room listening to a stereo. In the case of background music of the type used in offices and factories, the employer has chosen the music, which is manufactured by the supplier to have the effect of increasing worker productivity. This of course represents a particularly powerful type of unrequested music, and there is a split among the captive audience as to whether listeners appreciate its existence.

DOING MUSICAL ETHNOGRAPHY

Your aim in discovering and documenting a world of music is a *musical ethnography,* a written representation and description of a music-culture, organized from the standpoint of a particular topic. (Your writing may be accompanied by photographs, tape recordings, and even videotapes that you make while documenting the music-culture.) The goal of musical ethnography is to understand a music-culture or some part of it from a native's or insider's point of view (see Spradley 1979:3). What does that point of view encompass? Recall how in chapter 1 we divided a music-culture into four components: ideas, social organization, repertories, and material culture. Approaching a music-culture for the first time, you may feel overwhelmed; but if you organize your thinking about what you see and hear under the outline in table 1–1, you will be well on your way to documenting the music-culture.

The music in the repertory can be recorded for later study and analysis. Much of social organization and material culture can be observed. By listening to musicians talk with each other, and by talking to them, you begin to understand their ideas about music, and through interviews you can learn more about those ideas, the repertory, social organization, and material culture. (After all, conversations and interviews formed the basis for the musicians' life histories in this book.) But discovering and documenting a world of music is not like examining an amoeba under a microscope. People will differ in how they behave, what they believe, and what they say to you. Different people will sing "the same tune" differently. Under these conditions, representing and describing a music-culture, even a single aspect of it, is a complex and subtle undertaking.

SELECTING A SUBJECT:
SOME PRACTICAL SUGGESTIONS

It goes almost without saying that your field project will involve you in collecting, understanding, and organizing information about music in order to present it. It differs from the usual undergraduate research paper in that its focus is on a musical situation that you seek out from people rather than from books in a library. In ethnomusicology, as in anthropology and folklore, this in-person witnessing, observing, questioning, tape recording, photographing, and in some cases performing is called *fieldwork:* work "in the field" rather than the laboratory or library.

This is not to say that library research is useless or should be avoided. It may be possible to find background information on your topic in the library, and you should not overlook the opportunity to do so. But the thrust of your project takes you into the field, where you will obtain your most valuable and original information. Collecting, understanding, and organizing information about music are, of course, interrelated. You will begin with certain insights about the information you collect. As you organize it, you will gain new insights as you move toward an understanding of the musical situation from the web of information you have gathered.

You can approach the choice of a research subject in different ways. First, you might try to chart out the music you hear daily:

1. Keep a log or journal of all the music heard through three or four days, or a week. Note the context, style, and purpose of the music. Calculate how much of your day is spent with music of some sort.

2. Record, videotape, or simply describe in words several television commercials that employ music. Note the style of the music and the image it attempts to project. How is the music integrated into the message of the advertisement? Is it successful? Offensive? Both?

3. Make a map of the uses of music in a motion picture or television drama as you watch it. For comparison, select a soap opera and a crime-fighting show, or a situation comedy and a popular dramatic series.

4. Survey the stores in your area and their uses of background music. Interview salespeople, managers, owners, customers (always obtaining their permission). See what they say about music and sales.

5. Survey the contents of jukeboxes in bars and restaurants. Interview the manager about the content of his jukebox and the preferences of his or her clientele.

A second approach is to examine the music in your own background. Explore your memory of songs and music. Note how your racial, religious, and ethnic heritage influenced the music you heard and your current musical interests. How has your musical taste changed as you have grown older? Survey the contents of your CD and tape collection or preferences in radio listening. The same questions can be asked of your brothers and sisters, your parents, or other members of your family.

A third approach is to explore music in your community—college or hometown. Here you can interview people, listen to musical performances, possibly take part in them yourself, and gather quite a lot of information. Listed below are several possible subject headings:

Ethnic groups

Piano teachers

Private instrumental instruction (music stores, private lessons in the home)

Choir directors

Church organists, pianists, and so on.

School music (elementary, junior high, high school)

Music stores

Musical instrument makers

Background music in public places

The club scene (bars, coffeehouses, restaurants, clubs)

Musical organizations (community choral groups, bands, barbershop quartets, etc.)

Part-time (weekend) musicians

Professional or semiprofessional bands (rock, pop, jazz, rhythm and blues, country, gospel, etc.)

Chamber music groups

Parades and music

Disc jockeys

Symphony orchestras

A fourth approach narrows the subject and concentrates on an individual musician's life, opinions, and music. Often we focus our attention on the musical superstars, but in the process we forget the many fine and sensitive musicians, many of them amateurs, who live in our communities. Senior citizens, teachers, owners of record or music stores, or tradespeople like the local barber, janitor, or factory worker have sometimes had rich musical experiences as professional or part-time musicians. To search out such people is not always easy. Try the musicians' union, ethnic organizations, word of mouth, school or college music teachers, radio station disc jockeys, the clergy, club owners, newspaper columnists and feature storywriters, or even local police stations and fire departments. Musicians can be approached directly at fairs, contests, festivals, concerts, and dances. Many colleges and universities have foreign student associations that include amateur musicians, and they can tell you about others in the area. Ethnic specialty restaurants and grocery stores are another resource.

The musical world that surrounds you is so diverse you may feel swamped, unable to focus your energy. But when it finally comes down to deciding on a subject for your project, two guiding principles will help you out: choose something you are interested in, and choose something you have access to. It will be hard to succeed if you are not curious about the music you examine, and you will have to be close to it to look at it carefully.

COLLECTING INFORMATION

Once you have chosen a subject, your next move is to immerse yourself in the musical situation, consider what aspects of it interest you, and select a topic. Then plan how you will collect information—what questions to ask when you talk to the musicians or others involved, what performances to tape record, and so forth. Almost always you will need time and the flexibility to revise your plans as you collect the information you need. Most people will be happy to tell you about their involvement with music so long as you show them you really are interested.

GAINING ENTRY

Musical activities usually have a public (performance) side and a private (rehearsal) side. The performance is the tip of the iceberg; you will want to understand what lies beneath, and that is best learned by talking to the people involved. If you must approach a stranger, it may be helpful to arrange an introduction, either by a mutual friend or by a person in authority. Protocol is important in some cases. If, for example, you will be talking with musicians in an ethnic organization, it is wise to approach the president of the organization and seek his or her advice. Not only is he or she in a position to give you good suggestions, but a president needs to know what is going on; it is expected. In other situations it is best to let the people in authority know what you intend to do, and why, but to avoid having them introduce you, particularly if their authority is legal only, and they do not belong to the same racial or ethnic group as the people whose music you will be studying.

The first contact is especially important because the way you present yourself establishes your identity and role. That is one reason why it is essential to take the time to be honest with yourself and others about your interest in their music and the purpose of your project. If you are a college student, you may find yourself being assigned the role of the expert. But this is a role to avoid. The people who give you information are the experts, and you are the student who wants to learn from them. Otherwise you would not seek their help. You hope they will be willing to let you talk with them, observe, and, if it is appropriate, participate in the music.

SELECTING A TOPIC

Usually your subject takes in several music situations, and you will find yourself having to choose among them so as not to undertake a larger project than you can accomplish. If, for example, you are interested in Irish-American music in your community, you may find that there is so much going on that a survey of it all will be superficial, and so you will decide to concentrate on one aspect of it, perhaps the musical tradition of one family, or the musical scene in a particular club. Remember once again to choose something you are interested in and have access to.

The next step is one of the most difficult: selecting a topic. A topic is more than just a subject. It is a subject viewed from a particular angle, from a certain perspective, and with a limited goal in mind. "The Jewish cantor" is an example of a subject, something to investigate. "Musical training of Jewish cantors in New York City" is a topic. The cantor is viewed from a special perspective: his training. You want to understand what the training is and what the results are. Another example of a subject is "the Outlaws, a local country music band." A topic that involves the band might be "gender and gender roles in the music of the Outlaws, a local country music band." Here the focus is on the band members' attitudes, interactions, lyrics, social scene, and so forth. By themselves, subjects cover too much ground. Topics focus your attention on specific questions that will help you organize the information you collect.

As you think about a topic, reread chapter 1 and see how the four-part model of the music-culture can help you select aspects of your subject that you are interested in. Do you want to focus on conceptions of music, social organization, repertories, or material culture? Of course, these aspects are interrelated, and it will be difficult to ignore any of them completely; nevertheless, concentrating most of your attention on one of them will help you select a topic you can manage, and it will give you some initial ideas to think about as you gather your information.

LIBRARY RESEARCH

Depending on the topic you have selected, it may be a good idea to visit the library at this point to see whether anyone has published research on your topic. The electronic card catalog can be helpful; look under such headings as "music," "folk music," "popular music," and whatever categories are closely related to your subject. It may be useful to spend a couple of hours in the music section of the library stacks, looking at books on the shelves and opening any that might be centered in your subject, for it is almost impossible to know where to look for everything in the card catalog alone.

After you have checked the card catalog and the stacks, look in the reference section for such bibliographies as *The Music Index* and *RILM,* as well as specialized bibliographies and references works. The reference librarian can help you find these. If your library subscribes to *Ethnomusicology,* the journal of the Society for Ethnomusicology, you will find in each of its three yearly issues an invaluable guide to published research in the "Current Bibliography and Discography" section. It will be worth seeking this journal in other libraries nearby if yours does not subscribe to it.

In addition to *Ethnomusicology,* you may find some of the following periodicals helpful: *Latin American Music Review; Journal of Popular Music and Society; Journal of American Folklore; The Black Perspective in Music; Journal of Jazz Studies; Living Blues; Stereo Review; Journal of Popular Culture; Yearbook of the International Council for Traditional Music; Foxfire; Southern Exposure; Southern Folklore Quarterly; Asian Music; Music Educators' Journal; Western Folklore; Journal of Country Music; American Music; World of Music; Popular Music; Frets; Black Music Research Journal; Bluegrass Unlimited; The Devil's Box; The Old-Time Herald.*

Another good reason for visiting the library early in your project is that you may find a reference to a promising article or book that you will need to request on interlibrary loan. But avoid the temptation to read everything that looks as if it might somehow be relevant. The thrust of your project is outward into the field. Library research merely provides background information, and sometimes it cannot even do that—your subject may not have had attention in print, or the little that has been written may not be very useful. But if research on your topic has been published, you will be able to undertake a better project if you are familiar with it; and the people whose music you are studying will often be able to suggest good books and articles for you to read, saving you time in your search.

PARTICIPATION AND OBSERVATION

Returning now to the field requires a basic plan of action. Which people should you talk with? What performances should you witness? Should you go to rehearsals? What about a visit to a recording studio? If you are studying a music teacher, should you watch a private lesson? Should the teacher teach you? Will you take photographs? Movies? Videotape? What kind of tape-recording equipment can you get? Who will pay for it? You probably have been thinking about these and many similar questions, but one more than you should pay attention to at this time is your personal relationship to the people whose music you will study. Should you act as an observer, as a detached, objective reporter? Or should you, in addition to observing, also participate in the musical activity if you can?

Participating as well as observing can be useful. (It can be quite enjoyable as well.) You hope to learn the music from the inside. You will come to know some of the musical belief system intuitively. You will not have to hang around the edges of the action all the time, depending on others to explain all the rules.

But participating has its drawbacks. The problem with being a participant-observer is that you sometimes know too much. It is like the forest and the trees: the closer you are to a situation, the less of an overall view you have, and in order to address your project to an outside reader, you will need to imagine yourself an outsider, too. We tend to filter out the regularities of our lives. If we had to remember every time we met a stranger whether our culture says we should shake hands, rub noses, or bow, we would be in constant panic, and if we had to think hard whether *red* means stop or go, driving would be impossible. This filtering process means that we take the most basic aspects of a situation for granted. So if you are participating as well as observing, you must make a special effort to be an outsider and take nothing for granted. This dual perspective, the view of the participant-observer, is not difficult to maintain while you are *learning* how to participate in the musical situation. In fact, when you are learning, the dual perspective is forced on you. The trouble is that after you have learned, you can forget what it was like to be an outside observer. Therefore it is very important to keep a record of your changing perspective as you move from outsider to participant, and this record should be written in your field notes or spoken into your tape recorder as your perspective changes.

What if you work as an observer only and forgo participation? There are some advantages to doing so. It saves time. You can put all your energy into watching and trying to understand how what people tell you is going on matches what you can actually see and hear going on. You can follow both sides of "what I say" and "what I do" more easily with someone besides yourself. On the other hand, you do not achieve objectivity by keeping yourself out of the action. Your very presence as an observer alters the musical situation, particularly if you are photographing or tape-recording. In many situations you will actually cause *less* interference if you participate rather than intrude as a neutral and unresponsive observer.

ETHICS

There is an important ethical dimension, a right-and-wrong aspect about doing fieldwork. Most colleges and universities have a policy on research with human subjects designed to prevent people from being harmed by the research. If your research project is part of a course, be sure to discuss the ethics of the project with your teacher before you begin and, if things change, as you proceed. In any case, think carefully about the impact of what you propose to do. *Always* ask permission. Understand that people have legal rights to privacy, and to how they look, what they say, and what they sing, even after it has gone onto your film or tape recorder. Be honest with yourself and the people you study about your interest in their music and the purposes of your project. Tell them right from the start that you are interested in researching and documenting their music. If you like their music, say so. If the project is something for you to learn from, say so. Explain what will happen to the project after you finish it. Is it all right with them if you keep the photographs and tapes you make? Would they like a copy of the project? (If so, make one at your expense.) Is it all right if the project is deposited in the college or university archive? Most archives have a form that the people (yourself included) will sign, indicating that you are donating the project to the archive and that it will be used only for research purposes. If this project is not merely a contribution to knowledge but also to your career (as a student or whatever), admit it and realize that you have a stake in its outcome. Ask the people whose music you are studying why they are cooperating with you and what they hope to achieve from the project, and bear that in mind throughout. And *never* observe, interview, make recordings, or take photographs without their knowledge and permission.

Today many ethnomusicologists believe that it is not enough simply to go into a musical situation and document it. The fieldworker must give back something to the people who have been generous with their thoughts, their music, and their time. In some cultures, people expect money and should be paid. It is possible for fieldworkers to act not simply as a reporter, or analyst, but also as cultural and musical advocates, doing whatever they can to help the music they are studying to flourish. Some excerpts from a brochure describing the Folk Arts Program of the National Endowment for the Arts illustrate the advocacy viewpoint:

> We define our responsibility as the encouragement of those community or family-based arts that have endured through several generations and that carry with them a sense of community aesthetic. . . . We attempt to help smooth the flow of cultural experience, so that all peoples can move confidently into their own futures, secure in the knowledge of the elegance and individuality of their own cultural pasts.

Some ethnomusicologists in the United States work for arts councils, humanities councils, and other government agencies in "public sector" jobs where they are expected to identify, document, and present authentic folk and ethnic musicians to the public. Many taxpayers believe that if government supports the fine arts, it should also support folk and ethnic arts. In fact, most European governments do more than the United States and Canada to preserve and promote their folk and ethnic music. Ethnomusicologists hear a similar kind of commercial popular music throughout the world, and many conclude that local musics—of which there are a great variety—are endangered. It is to humankind's advantage to have many different kinds of music, they believe. For that reason, they think advocacy and support are necessary in the face of all the forces that would make music sound alike the world over. This argument may at first seem remote to your project, but not when you think about your own involvement with the people and music you are studying.

FIELD EQUIPMENT: NOTEBOOK, TAPE RECORDER, CAMERA

The perfect fieldworker has all-seeing eyes, all-hearing ears, and total recall. But because none of us is so well equipped, we suggest you rely on written notes, tape recordings, and photographs that you yourself make in the field. These documents serve two purposes: they enable you to reexamine at leisure your field experiences when you write up your project, and, since they are accurate records of performances, interviews, and observations, they may be included in the final form your project takes. On the other hand, field equipment presents certain difficulties: it costs money, you need to know how to work it properly, and you may have to resist the temptation to spend much of your time fiddling with your equipment when you should be watching, thinking, and listening instead.

Fifty years ago, fieldworkers relied primarily upon notetaking, and today it is still indispensable. No matter how sophisticated your equipment is, you should carry a small pocket notebook. It will be useful for writing down names and addresses, directions, observations, and thoughts while in the field. In the days before sound recording, music was taken by dictation in notebooks. While this is still possible, it is not advisable except when performances are very brief and you have the required dictation skills. Dictating a song puts the performer in an unnatural context and changes the performance. However, notebooks are especially useful for preserving information learned in interviews, particularly if a tape recorder is unavailable or awkward in the interview situation. In addition, you should make an effort to write down your detailed impressions of the overall field situation: your plans, questions, any difficulties you meet with; as complete a description as possible of the musical situation itself, including the setting, the performers, the audience, and the musical event from start to finish; and your reactions and responses to the field experience as it takes place. Your field notebook becomes a journal or diary that you address *to yourself* for use when you write up your project.

Most university music departments and many university libraries now loan inexpensive portable cassette tape recorders to students for use in field collecting projects. Whether you use a tape recorder, and if so what type it is (microcassette, portable cassette, home stereo cassette deck, etc.) is largely a matter of the nature of your project and your and your instructor's expectations. The inexpensive portable cassette recorders are best suited to recording speech (interviews, for example). Although they come with built-in microphones, the sound quality can be improved dramatically if you use an inexpensive external microphone plugged into the recorder's microphone input jack. So equipped, a portable cassette tape recorder may be adequate for your needs. It should go without saying that you will want to be thoroughly familiar with its operation so that your recordings are accurate. But the portable cassette recorder is mechanically simple, and anyone can learn to operate it in just a few minutes. Most important, put the microphone in the right spot. If the sound is soft or moderate and it comes from a small area (a solo singer, a lesson on a musical instrument, or an interview, for example), place the microphone in close and equidistant from the sources of the sounds. If the sound is loud and widely spread out (a rock band or a symphony orchestra, for example), search out "the best seat in the house" and place or hold the microphone there. Make a practice recording for a few seconds and play it back immediately to check microphone placement and make certain the equipment is working properly. Take along spare batteries and blank tapes (see ill. 10–5).

If properly used, even the simplest cameras take adequate pictures of musical performances. A picture may not be worth a thousand words, but it goes a long way toward capturing the human impact of a musical event. An instant-picture camera is especially useful because you will be able to see the photograph immediately and correct mistakes (such as standing too far from the action) at once. A "portrait" or close-up lens placed in front of the regular lens will allow you to fill up the whole picture with a musical instrument. Instant pictures have another advantage: you can give them (well, not all of them) to the people you photograph.

Americans are in love with technology, even technology to get away from technology (backpacking equipment, for example). If you already know a lot about tape recording or photography, and you own or can borrow high-quality equipment, by all means use it. Some of the photographs in this book and the accompanying recordings were made by the authors using professional equipment; after all, fieldwork is a part of our profession. But the more sophisticated our equipment is, the more difficult it is to use it to its full potential. There is a story (and it is a true story) about a photographer who went to a rock music festival and brought only his pocket camera. In the photographer's pit in front of the stage, he had maneuvered himself into the best position and was standing there taking pictures when a professional nudged him, saying, "Get out of here with that little toy!" The pro stood there with cameras hanging from his neck and shoulders, covering his body like baby opossums on a mama opossum. "Well," said the amateur, yielding his position with a smile, "I guess if you need all of that equipment, you need to stand in the right spot, too!"

INTERVIEWING

Interviews with people (consultants) whose music you are studying are a useful means of obtaining basic information and getting feedback on your own ideas. But be careful not to put words in your consultants' mouths and impose your

James T. Koetting

**Ill. 10–5.   A chief checks the quality of a recording of his musicians.
Kasena-Nankani Traditional Area, Ghana.**

ideas. The first step in understanding a world of music is to understand it as much
as possible in your consultants' own terms. Later you can bring to bear on the musical situation your own perspective. Remember that much of their knowledge is
intuitive; you will have to draw it out by asking questions.

Come into the interview with a list of questions, but be prepared to let the talk
flow in the direction your consultant takes it. In his 1956 preface to *Primitive Man
As Philosopher* Paul Radin distinguishes between two procedures for obtaining

information: question-and-answer, and "letting the native philosopher expound his ideas with as few interruptions as possible." Your consultants may not be philosophers, but they should be given the chance to say what they mean. Some people are by nature talkative, and you will be thankful of it. Others need to be put at ease; let the person know in advance what sort of questions you will be asking, what sort of information you need, and why. Often you will get important information in casual conversations rather than formal interviews; be ready to write down the information in your field notebook. Some people are by nature silent and guarded; despite your best intentions, they will not really open up to you. If you encounter that sort of person, respect his or her wishes and make the interview brief.

Beginning fieldworkers commonly make two mistakes when doing interviews. First, they worry too much about the tape recorder, and their nervousness can carry over to the person they interview. But if you've already gotten the person's consent to be interviewed, it should not be hard to get permission to tape the interview. One fieldworker always carries her tape recorder and camera so they are visible from the moment she enters the door. Then she nonchalantly sets the tape recorder down in a prominent spot and ignores it, letting the person being interviewed understand that the tape recorder is a natural and normal part of the interview. Still ignoring the recorder, she starts off with the small talk that usually begins such a visit. Eventually the other person says something like, "Oh, I see you're going to tape-record this." "Sure," she says steadily. "I brought along this tape recorder just to make sure I get down everything you say. I can always edit out any mistakes, and you can always change your mind. This is just to help me understand you better the first time." She says once they have agreed to be interviewed, nobody has ever refused her tape recorder. But she adds that if anyone told her to keep the recorder shut off, she would certainly do so.

A second problem is that beginning fieldworkers often ask leading questions. A leading question is a question that suggests a particular answer. This makes the information they get unreliable. In other words, it is not clear whether the person being interviewed is expressing his or her own thoughts, or just being agreeable. In addition, leading questions usually result in short, uninteresting answers. Study this first dialogue to see how *not* to interview:

FIELDWORKER 1: Did you get your first flute when you were a girl?

CONSULTANT: Yeah.

FIELDWORKER 1: What was the name of your teacher?

CONSULTANT: Ah, I studied with Janice Sullivan.

FIELDWORKER 1: When was that?

CONSULTANT: In college.

FIELDWORKER 1: I'll bet you hated the flute when you first started. I can remember hating my first piano lessons.

CONSULTANT: Yeah.

The trouble here is that the consultant gives the kinds of answers she thinks are expected of her. She is not really telling the fieldworker what she thinks. She is not even giving the conversation much thought. The fieldworker has asked the wrong kind of questions. Now look what happens when another fieldworker questions the same person.

FIELDWORKER 2: Can you remember when you got your first flute?

CONSULTANT: Yeah.

FIELDWORKER 2: Could you tell me about it?

CONSULTANT: Sure. My first flute—well, I don't know if this counts, but I fell in love with the flute when I was in grade school, and I remember going down to a music store and trying one out while my father looked on, but I couldn't make a sound, you know!

FIELDWORKER 2: Sure.

CONSULTANT: So I was really disappointed, but then I remember learning to play the recorder in, I think it was third grade, and I really loved that, but I didn't stick with it. Then in college I said to myself, I'm going to take music lessons and I'm going to learn the flute.

FIELDWORKER 2: Tell me about that.

CONSULTANT: Well, I had this great teacher, Janice Sullivan, and first she taught me how to get a sound out of it. I was really frustrated at first, but after a while I got the hang of it, and she would always tell me to think of the beautiful sounds I knew a flute could make. I used to think a flute could make a sound like water, like the wind. Well, not exactly, but sort of. And then Mrs. Sullivan let me borrow a tape of *shakuhachi* music— you know, the Japanese flute?—and I *heard* different kinds of water, different kinds of wind! I knew then that I would play the flute for the rest of my life.

Compare the two fieldworkers' questions: "Did you get your first flute when you were a girl?" is a leading question because it leads to the answer, "Yes, I got my first flute when I was a girl." What is more, fieldworker 1 implies that most people get their first flutes when they are girls, so the consultant probably thinks she should answer yes. By contrast, the question of fieldworker 2—"Can you remember when you got your first flute?"—is open-ended and invites reflection, perhaps a story. When the consultant says "Yeah," fieldworker 2 asks for a story and gets a much better—and different—answer than fieldworker 1. Go over the rest of the first interview, see how fieldworker 1 injects her opinions into the dialogue ("I'll bet you hated the flute when you first started"), and fails to draw out the consultant's real feelings about her lessons, whereas fieldworker 2 establishes better rapport, is a better listener, asks nondirective questions, and gets much fuller and truer answers.

If your project concentrates on a single consultant, you may want to obtain his or her life story (Titon 1980). For this purpose a tape recorder is virtually a necessity. Since the way your consultants view their lives can be as important as the factual information they give, you should try to get the life story in their own words as much as possible. This means refraining from questions that direct the story as you think it should go. What is important is how your consultant wants it to go. Come back later, in another interview, to draw out specific facts and fill in gaps by direct questioning. In the initial interview, begin by explaining that you would like your informant to tell you about his or her life as a musician (or whatever is appropriate—composer, disc jockey, etc.) from the beginning until now. Once begun, allow plenty of time for silences to gather thoughts. If he or she looks up at you expectantly, nod your head in agreement and try repeating what has just been said to show that you understand it. Resist your impulses to ask direct questions; write them down instead, and say you'll come back to ask questions later; for now you want the story to continue.

Not everyone will be able to tell you his or her musical autobiography, but if you are fortunate enough to find someone who can, it may turn out to be the most important part of your project. On the other hand, if your consultant's life story is a necessary part of your project, but you cannot obtain it except by direct and frequent questioning, you should certainly ask the questions. If you get good answers, the result will be your consultant's life *history,* a collaborative biography rather than an autobiography.

Interviews, then, with the people whose music you are studying (and perhaps with their audience) are important for obtaining factual information and testing your ideas. They are also important because through them you can begin to comprehend the musical situation from their point of view: their beliefs, their intentions, their training, their feelings, their evaluations of musical performance, and their understanding of what they are doing—what it is all about. Ultimately, since this is your project, you combine their ideas with your own when you write the project up using the information you have collected.

OTHER MEANS OF COLLECTING INFORMATION

Another technique, often used in social science research, is the questionnaire. Its role in studying music is limited, but there are projects in which it can be helpful. Often this circumstance occurs when you wish to map out the general nature of a situation before moving into a specific sub-area to focus on. For example, to work on the meaning of pop songs in students' lives, it can be handy first to circulate a questionnaire to uncover the eventual sample you will study intensively. Questionnaires are most at home in studies of musical attitudes. To find out how shoppers react to supermarket background music, it would be hard to set up interviews but easy, if the store manager agrees, to arrange for distributing a questionnaire.

Aside from questionnaires, which seek out information, you might come upon information already gathered: autobiographical manuscripts, diaries, and tape recordings made by informants for themselves. Clubs, fraternities, schools, churches, and various organizations often store away old materials that shed light on musical activities. At concerts, the programs handed out can be rich in information, ranging from description of the music to the type of advertisers that support the concerts. Membership lists and patrons' lists may be included as well.

Newspapers are enormously helpful. Hardly a day passes without journalistic commentary on the musical environment, in news stories, reviews, and advertisements. Feature stories provide up-to-date information on current concerts, trends, and musical attitudes, both locally and nationally, while advertising can furnish insights into the ideals of the American musical world projected by the media, ideals that influence most of us one way or another. For example, an ad for an expensive home entertainment system designed to bring music into every home offers a direct connection between musical style and the rooms of the house: "101 Strings in the greenhouse, Bach in the bedroom, Frank Sinatra in the living room, Gershwin in the den, the Boston Pops on the patio, the Rolling Stones outside by the pool." What better brief description of middle-aged, middle-class musical taste could be found?

FINISHING THE PROJECT

After you have done all the hard work of organizing and collecting information, what do you do with it? Now is a good time to return to your original plan of action and list of questions you wanted to ask about the musical situation, particularly with reference to the four-part model that forms the basis of chapter 1. These questions and the information you have gathered offer a natural organization for your project. Remember that your purpose is documentation and understanding. Specific advice on how to write it up and what form to present it in will be available from your instructor.

Be sure to keep in mind that you are not the only one affected by your finished project. Other people's feelings and, on occasion, social position are reflected in your work. Be clear in what you say about the people you worked with. Confidentiality may be important; if people asked you not to use their names or repeat what they said to you, respect their wishes. It is possible—even customary in many anthropological works—to change names of people or places to make certain no one is identified who does not want to be. Imagine the problems created for the member of a band who criticizes the leader if the words get back to the group, or for a school music teacher if he criticizes the school board to you in private and you quote him.

Checking back with informants is very helpful to clear up research questions. As you interview, collect information, and think about the musical situation you study, new questions always will occur to you. It is no different when you write up your project; you will probably find that it will be helpful to get back in touch with your consultants and ask a few final questions so that you will be satisfied with your project when you have finished it.

In our preface we wrote of our intention that our readers "experience what it is like to be an ethnomusicologist puzzling out his or her way toward understanding an unfamiliar music." A good field project inevitably provides just that experience. Valuable and enjoyable in and of itself, discovery and documentation of a world of music takes on added significance because it illuminates, even in a small way, our understanding of music as human expression.

REFERENCES CITED

Spradley, James P.
   1979   *The Ethnographic Interview.* New York: Holt, Rinehart, and Winston.
Titon, Jeff Todd.
   1980   "The Life Story." *Journal of American Folklore* 93:276–92.

ADDITIONAL READING

Collier, John, Jr., and Malcolm Collier
   1986   *Visual Anthropology: Photography As a Research Method.* Albuquerque: Univ. of New Mexico Press.
Georges, Robert A., and Michael O. Jones
   1980   *People Studying People.* Berkeley: Univ. of California Press.
Golde, Peggy, ed.
   1986   *Women in the Field: Anthropological Experiences.* 2nd ed. Berkeley: Univ. of California Press.
Goldstein, Kenneth
   1964   *A Guide for Fieldworkers in Folklore.* Hatboro, Pa.: Folklore Associates.
Hattersley, Ralph
   1978   *Beginner's Guide to Photographing People.* Garden City, N.J.: Doubleday.
Herndon, Marcia, and Norma McLeod
   1983   *Field Manual for Ethnomusicology.* Norwood, Pa.: Norwood Editions.
Hood, Mantle
   1982   *The Ethnomusicologist,* chapters 4 and 5. 2nd edition. Kent, Ohio: Kent State Univ. Press.
Ives, Edward D.
   1980   *The Tape-Recorded Interview: A Manual for Fieldworkers in Folklore and Oral History.* Knoxville: Univ. of Tennessee Press.
Jackson, Bruce
   1987   *Fieldwork.* Urbana: Univ. of Illinois Press.
Karpeles, Maud
   1958   *The Collecting of Folk Music and Other Ethnological Material: A Manual for Field Workers.* London: International Folk Music Council and Royal Anthropological Institute.

Marcus, George E., and Michael M. J. Fischer
   1986   *Anthropology As Cultural Critique.* Chicago: Univ. of Chicago Press.

Rabinow, Paul
   1977   *Reflections on Fieldwork in Morocco.* Berkeley: Univ. of California Press.

Sanjek, Roger, ed.
   1990   *Fieldnotes: The Makings of Anthropology.* Ithaca, N.Y.: Cornell Univ. Press.

Spradley, James P., and David W. McCurdy.
   1972   *The Cultural Experience: Ethnography in Complex Society.* Chicago: Science
          Research Associates.

Wax, Rosalie.
   1971   *Doing Fieldwork: Warnings and Advice.* Chicago: Univ. of Chicago Press.

Wengle, John L.
   1988   *Ethnographers in the Field: The Psychology of Research.* Tuscaloosa: Univ. of
          Alabama Press.

See also *Ethnomusicology,* Vol 36, no. 2 (1992), a special issue on fieldwork in the public
interest.

Index